Swimming Dynamics

Winning Techniques and Strategies

Cecil M. Colwin

Ottawa, Canada.
23rd March 1999.

To Mark Sandilands —
With best regards and Thanks
for your kind interest —
Sincerely,
Cecil Colwin

MASTERS PRESS

NTC/Contemporary Publishing Group

Library of Congress Cataloging-in-Publication Data

Colwin, Cecil.
    Swimming dynamics / Cecil Colwin.
        p.   cm.
    Includes index.
    ISBN 1-57028-206-4
    1. Swimming—Coaching.   I. Title.
GV837.65.C66   1998
797.2'1—dc21   98-34051
                                                CIP

Cover design by Nick Panos
Cover photograph copyright © Art Brewer/Tony Stone Images

Published by Masters Press
A division of NTC/Contemporary Publishing Group, Inc.
4255 West Touhy Avenue, Lincolnwood (Chicago), Illinois 60646-1975 U.S.A.
Printed in the United States of America
International Standard Book Number: 1-57028-206-4

99 00 01 02 03 04 VL 20 19 18 17 16 15 14 13 12 11 10 9 8 7 6 5 4 3 2 1

CONTENTS

Chapter 9
INTO THE MILLENNIUM **339**

Epilogue

PREFACE

I am a part of all that I have met;
Yet all experience is an arch where-thro'
Gleams that untravell'd world, whose
*   margin fades*
For ever and for ever when I move.
                                    —Tennyson

Swimming Dynamics is about the motive forces that effect change in competitive swimming, especially the interactions between swimmers and coaches. The text is the result of a lifetime habit of asking questions on a variety of topics, both of myself and my colleagues. What follows is an examination of the sport from many perspectives.

These discussions with outstanding achievers started over 30 years ago, and have continued to the present day. Sometimes the same person features in the text more than once, even 3 times, with an interval of many years between each discussion. This exercise in itself provides an interesting study of how changing times influenced their thinking.

Although a host of topics come under review, particularly valuable are the discussions on the 1,500-meter event. Several of the century's most successful coaches express their views on why young swimmers, irrespective of natural proclivity, should develop a good endurance base of early distance training. This nursery exposure also helped many a great champion, through constant and accurate repetition of movements, to develop efficient stroke patterns, including the ability to maintain perfect streamlining within the changing sequences of the stroke.

But success in competitive swimming depends not only on talent, superior training, and coaching, but also on strength of character and a strong desire to succeed. This is why, contrary to usual practice, I have started with the abstract side of the sport and gradually worked toward the realities of practical application. On the way to this objective, the text discusses the origin of the swimming techniques, and also illustrates and describes them in their modern form.

It is only fitting that the modern swimming era will reach its zenith at the 2000 Olympic Games in Sydney, the place where it all started with the "School of Sydney" about 100 years ago. These Games should prove to be a great celebration of the sport of swimming, presupposing that the Olympic organizers, both at national and international levels, will have gained control over the threatening blight of performance-enhancing drugs.

Out of respect for the majority of swimmers who keep the faith by playing the game according to the rules, the epilogue of this book offers a message of hope for the future of the sport in the twenty-first century: "[Those who] continue to develop their skills, strength, and endurance by self-discipline and natural means, rather than by resorting to performance-enhancing drugs, . . . show the courage, faith, and honor that may yet reclaim the sport for those who still believe in its finer values."

                                    C.M.C.
                                    Ottawa, Ontario

✧ ✧ ✧

Shown here is a coach-owned facility presently making a big impact on American swimming: The Meadowbrook Pool, home to U.S. Olympic coach Murray Stephens's successful and widely acclaimed North Baltimore Aquatic Club. The popular Meadowbrook swimming facility is generally regarded as the finest 50-meter pool in Maryland, and is strategically, and surprisingly, located in a secluded nook at the intersection of two major expressways, the Northern Parkway and the Jones Falls Expressway. (Photograph by David Harp © 1998)

ACKNOWLEDGMENTS

Swimming Dynamics was made possible through the direct and indirect help of a great number of people. I express my sincere thanks to all of them, although their number precludes my naming more than a few.

Parts of the text first appeared in the publications listed below, and a detailed source list appears on pages 357-360. A large debt of gratitude and appreciation is due to the editors and publishers of the following journals for their interest and encouragement in granting permission to reprint these materials:

Swimnews (previously published as *Swim Canada,* 1974 to 1996). Publisher and editor, Nick J. Thierry.

Swimming World, Junior Swimmer, Swimming Technique, and *Swim Magazine* published by Sports Publications, Inc. Publishers, Richard Deal and Gerry Rodrigues. Editor-in-Chief, Dr. Phillip Whitten.

Colleagues and Contributors

Over the years help came from many directions, and I thank the following noted personalities for so patiently participating in discussions and interviews. Their fine-tuned antennae, keen insights, fresh perspectives, and articulate voices add immeasurably to the text:

Mike Barrowman, Cal Bentz, Joe Bernal, Mike Burton, John Carew, Forbes Carlile, Sherman Chavoor (deceased), James "Doc" Counsilman, Arthur Cusack, Peter Daland, Donna de Varona, John Devitt, Ray Essick, Don Gambril, Terry Gathercole, George Haines, Penny Heyns, Joe King (deceased), John Leonard, Jim Montrella, Pablo Morales, Jozsef Nagy, Bill Nelson, David Pyne, Ralph Richards, Aileen Riggin Soule, Walter Schlueter (deceased), Mark Schubert, Jonty Skinner, Gus Stager, Murray Stephens, Bill Sweetenham, Don Talbot, Karen Moe Thornton, Nort Thornton, Stan Tinkham, Jon Urbanchek, Scott Volkers, and Michael Wenden.

Resource Specialists

I am particularly grateful to the following who guided me to valuable sources of information, and I extend my deepest appreciation to them all for their expertise, courtesy, and cooperation:

Dr. Linda Borish, Associate Professor of History, Western Michigan University, Kalamazoo, Michigan, who gave permission to quote from her telephone interview with Aileen Riggin Soule (June 16, 1995).

Alan Clarkson, for permission to quote from his book *Lanes of Gold: 100 Years of the N.S.W. Amateur Swimming Association*, Sydney, NSW: Lester-Townsend, 1990.

Dave Kelly, Library of Congress, for source materials on L. de B. Handley and Charles M. Daniels.

Kevin Moccia, managing editor of *The Winged Foot*, the New York Athletic Club, New York, NY, for source materials on L. de B. Handley, Charles M. Daniels, Otto Wahle, and their contemporaries.

Harry Gordon, noted Australian sport columnist for source materials on pioneer swimmers, Cecil Healy and Sir Frank Beaurepaire.

Jozsef Nagy, Jon Urbanchek, and Mike Barrowman for their advice during the course of my describing and illustrating "The Wave Action Breaststroke," which appears in Chapter 2.

The movement sequences in "We Don't Swim in Dry Water" were videotaped using a high resolution video camera (Sony CCD-TR700) and a "Coachscope" underwater housing. The writer acknowledges with gratitude the assistance of Bob Duenkel, the Curator of the International Swimming Hall of Fame for the use of a Mitsubishi P40U video printer. I also wish to thank Raimundas Mazuolis for being such a willing subject, and Coaches Chad Schultz and Greg Tye for their ready assistance during the videotaping process.

Photographs

My sincere thanks go to Preston Levi, director, The Henning Library, International Swimming Hall of Fame and Robert Duenkel, museum curator of ISHOF, for their expertise, and courteous and helpful cooperation on many occasions during a long association, and for providing the large and unique set of photographs from the ISHOF archives that so enhance this text.

The following also provided exceptional photographs, and my debt to these talented people is as great as it is obvious:

Marco Chiesa, renowned photo editor of *Swimnews*; Australian Swimming Inc.; noted swimming photographer, Kevin Berry; photographer David Harp; Marge Counsilman; Coach Peter Daland; Coach George F. Haines; Mike Shafto and *The Star*, Johannesburg, South Africa; the fine photographers of Sports Publications, Inc.; Coach Murray Stephens of the North Baltimore Aquatic Club; Glen Tasker, executive director of the NSW Amateur Swimming Association; and Nick J. Thierry, publisher and editor of *Swim* magazine, an accomplished photographer in his own right.

Cartoons and Illustrations

Robert Colwin for drawing the cartoon, "White Bay Clam Bake" on page 292.

Front view of the wave breaststroke, reprinted from my book *Swimming Into the 21st Century* (Champaign, IL, Human Kinetics Publishers, 48–49).

Editorial Assistance

I have been unusually fortunate in having the ready assistance of Heather Lowhorn, production editor, who brought considerable expertise, patience, and good humor to preparing a long text and its accompanying layout, as well as the quiet efficiency of Julia Anderson, senior project editor, who ensured the book's smooth progress through the final production stages. To them both I express my sincere thanks for their interest and guidance and the excellent job they did.

Last, but by no means least, I owe a special debt of gratitude to my wife, Margaret, for her hard work and assistance in preparing the final draft of this book, compiling the index, bibliography and reference list, as well as typing the annotations to the photographs. Her encouragement, wise counsel, patience, and untiring efforts eased the task.

SWIMMING IN THE LITTLE TOWN OF BETHLEHEM

I learned to swim in the little town of Bethlehem, not in the Holy Land, but in South Africa's Orange Free State. And, indeed, there is a River Jordan that flows by, but I swam in Jordan's waters only after they were purified and piped into the outdoor swimming baths on Muller Street.

Bethlehem was small in the 1930s, with a population of about 5,000, and a grid of 10 streets running north to south and 10 streets running east to west. You could see where the town ended and the countryside began. Bethlehem was a great place to grow up in, and you were never at a loss for something to do.

The Boy Scout troop owned three six-seater canoes which they kept on Loch Athlone, a large dam in the River Jordan. You were only allowed to use a canoe if you could swim. My father gave me money and said, "Buy a season ticket at the baths. Learn to swim, and then you'll be allowed in a canoe."

I stood shoulder deep in the shallow end of the swimming pool, grasping the rails, a weight of water surrounding me. I watched other kids spring lightly to the surface. I tried to copy them, but, each time I stumbled forward, frustrated, gulping large mouthfuls of water, spluttering and gasping for air. On holiday at the sea, I had learned to surf on a small inflated mattress, and I knew the feeling of keeping up in the water. But I still couldn't swim unaided in a swimming pool; the water seemed dead and uncooperative.

One day, Mr. Richter came for a swim. He was a good swimmer. He was tall and thin with blonde curly hair and a mustache, and he wore a pale blue swimming costume with shoulder straps and a white belt. He walked with a swagger, and I thought that this was how good swimmers walked. I badly wanted to learn to swim. If anyone could help me, surely it was Mr. Richter.

I planned my approach carefully because he was sometimes in a bad mood. He was a commercial traveler who covered one of the flattest stretches of country in the world, mile after mile of it, with only here and there, shimmering in the heat, a flat-topped hill to break the monotony. At the week's end, he returned to Bethlehem, tired, dusty, unpredictable. I decided to wait until he had had a swim, and a chance to cool off.

He dove in at the deep end and swam the length of the pool with long, cleaving strokes, everyone watching him. He was the best swimmer in town, even better than Dick Budde, the high school champion. He leaped out at the shallow end, right where I was standing, and I plucked up courage. "Good afternoon, Mr. Richter," I said.

"Hello, young Colwin," he said. "How is the swimming coming along?"

"Not too well," I said. "I can get on top of the water when I'm in the sea, but not in the swimming pool. I keep falling over when I try."

"You need to learn how to float on your back," he said. "Come over here, and I'll show you how."

He stood on the deck, toweling himself as he gave instructions. "Hold your arms out sideways, take a deep breath, and put the back of your head in the water. Try to lie flat on your back as if you're lying on a bed without a pillow."

I tried to do exactly as Mr. Richter told me. I leaned back in the water, preparing to float, but, instead of finding a bed without a pillow, the waters of the Jordan parted to swallow me. "Perhaps they are getting confused with the Red Sea," I wondered, with what was probably to be my last thought as I prepared to drown.

"No! No! No! Not like that! Like this!" said Mr. Richter. He was becoming impatient. "Lie back gently, not suddenly. The water is the softest bed in all the world."

"Yes, my death bed," I thought, with increasing panic. Again and again, I tried to float on my back, but, instead of stumbling forward, now I stumbled backward, as if into an invisible abyss. Chlorinated Jordan water filled my nostrils and seared my sinuses.

"*Himmel-herrgotten-kreuzemillionen-donnerwetter*!" he said, both his patience and teaching repertoire suddenly exhausted. I recognized the word from Konrad Veidt's portrayal of a U-boat commander in a recent matinee at the local cinema. It was the longest cussword in the world, according to the reviewer in the *Bethlehem Express*. It wasn't difficult to sense his displeasure. I decided to make myself scarce.

Later, I was standing in the shallow end when Mr. Willie Israel arrived on the pool deck. He was short and stout and wore a black woolen swimming costume with shoulder straps. He was a local attorney, and known to be methodical.

He folded his towel and placed it on the pool deck. I knew what was coming next, because he always followed the same routine. He would climb down the steps into the pool, take off his thick glasses, and put them on his towel. He tested the water and adjusted to his new environment, then his large, round eyes focused on me. "Oh, there you are," he said. "Are you still performing your ablutions?" It was a standing joke, which he thought I shared. But I didn't; I had looked up ablutions in the dictionary, and knew that it meant ceremonial washing.

"No, I'm not performing ablutions," I said. "I'm trying to stay on top of the water."

"Stay on top of the water?! Anyone can stay on top of the water," he said. "It's staying underneath the water that's really hard. Have you ever tried it? Here, hold the side, bend your knees, and see how hard it is to stay under."

I bent my knees, and sank my shoulders slowly under the surface. Immediately, I felt the resistance of the water.

He noted my surprise. "The deeper you go under, the more the water will push you up. This is the first law of swimming. It was discovered by a certain Mr. Archie Medes, who has been dead a long time now. You keep trying to go down deeper, and you'll be swimming in no time," he said, as he launched himself into midpool with a sedate sidestroke.

Encouraged, I wanted to sit flat on the floor of the pool. I wasn't keen on dunking my face, but I closed my eyes, held my breath, and dropped quickly under. I tried again and again to go deeper, each time struggling against an upthrust of water. By letting air out through pursed lips in a chain of bubbles, I found that I could stay down longer. With growing confidence, I let go the rail as I descended, squinting through half-open eyes, surprised at how clearly I could see.

At last, I was sitting on the bottom, stretched out luxuriously on my underwater couch, hands joined overhead, bubbling out air. I swept my hands downward and returned to the surface and a noisy world of screaming kids. Then down again I went, and as I sat there, no one would have noticed a skinny boy in a red-and-white striped suit, enthralled by his underwater adventures, admiring dappled patterns of reflected light, much intrigued by newfound magic of the water.

Within days, I was floating facedown, and, the next week, I was swimming across the pool, turning my head from side to side, and watching each arm as it came out of the water to see that it was curved, and trying to swim as much like Dick Budde as I could. That was what I admired most about Dick Budde's stroke: the way he brought his arms over in graceful arcs.

I held my arms straight as I pulled, trying to copy the action of a long, straight oar. My muscles developed quickly, especially my upper arm muscles. I was proud of my "new" muscles and glad that I could swim at last. I'll always remember that feeling of accomplishment that learning to swim gave me.

I watched Dick Budde, and noted how he turned his face sideways to inhale each time one arm came over. Then he turned his face back in the water to breathe out. I found that the more air I exhaled, the easier it was to breathe in. This discovery soon helped me to breathe as easily in the water as I could on land, and I swam length after length without tiring. Sometimes I hummed a tune as I swam, and, at other times, in the early morning when the water was calm and not heaving under the weight of many bathers, the water sang its own tune, as it lapped and rippled along my moving body. I swam for the pure enjoyment of it.

Ten years passed before I entered my first swimming race as a pupil at Selborne College, in East London, a port city on the Indian Ocean. It was a 50-meter dash in the so-called "Quanza," a tidal pool on the Orient Beach, where the school swimming sports were held. To my surprise, I won, but all I remember was a period of wild splashing, trying to reach the opposite end as quickly as possible. It wasn't like the usual communion with the water that I enjoyed. I knew that I wasn't doing it properly, and I felt the need to learn to swim well while still swimming fast. I didn't know it then, but this need was to become a lifelong obsession.

At Selborne, I swam for Malcomess House, the same house represented by Jonty Skinner 30 years later, before he went to America and became the fastest swimmer in the world. Across the road from Selborne was our sister school, Clarendon Girls' High, where Joan Harrison, a wonderful swimmer, was a pupil. One day, swimming in the Quanza pool, Joan caused a sensation when she came within 11 seconds of Olympic champion Ann Curtis's 800-meter world record. Later, she was to win the Olympic 100-meter backstroke championship at Helsinki.

The achievements of Joan and Jonty came years after I had left East London to live in the large city of Johannesburg, where I joined the Yeoville swimming club and received the first coaching that I had ever had. By this time, my stroke was so ingrained with faults that correcting them became an exercise in futility for both swimmer and coach alike. I had grown to love the sport and the challenges that it presented, but somewhere along the line, an inner voice had told me (in rather grave tones) that I wasn't exactly destined to follow in the footsteps of my two heroes, Johnny Weissmuller and Alan Ford.

Instead, I set a limit to my ambitions, and decided that my goal would be to improve on my personal best times, and to be the best technical swimmer that my lack of talent would permit me to be. At the end of a long career, the kindest comment that anyone could have made about my swimming, had they spared the time to think about it, would have been that I was a slightly above-average club swimmer. In my enthusiasm to improve, I had become a keen student of the sport, reading everything I could lay my hands on, and I learned about all phases of swimming from my coach, Jimmy Green. I can't remember how he did it, but Jimmy, like all great coaches, possessed the gift of "the nudge," and he quietly nudged me into a career in coaching.

After 25 years, I went back to Bethlehem with my home team of swimmers, and started an annual summer swimming camp there. We trained in the old municipal baths on Muller Street, and swimmers from all over the country, and some from overseas, came to join us and swim in the little town of Bethlehem.

We climbed Stafford's Hill and sat in "Stafford's Chair," the great stone seat on the top of the hill where legend says Colonel Stafford of the Welsh Fusiliers would look through his binoculars at the Boer forces astride the railroad track below. We visited the bushmen caves, and crawled on hands and knees through the long tunnel that led to the paintings of sharks, whales, and dolphins. They were as clear and bright as when I first saw them, and still as fascinating.

One year in early January, Don Schollander, the great Olympic champion, visited us and stayed over at camp, along with fellow Americans, Coach Dave Robertson of New Trier High School, and John du Pont, philanthropist, pentathlete, and marine biologist. That evening, the population of Bethlehem turned out to see Don give a memorable exhibition of the finest freestyle swimming we had ever seen.

As visiting American coach, Dave Robertson gave the commentary, I couldn't help but notice that Schollander was standing right on the spot where I had practiced bobbing up and down, half a lifetime before. For one fleeting moment, I saw Mr. Willie Israel put his folded towel on the deck, climb carefully into the pool, take his glasses off, and smile in my direction. And I could swear that, across the years, I heard a quiet voice say, "Are you still performing your ablutions?"

THE COACH-SWIMMER-TEAM-PROGRAM DYNAMIC

THE INTUITIVE COACH

You'll often hear an intuitive coach say, "Sometimes I know something, without knowing how I know it."

The term "natural athlete" is used to describe an athlete with natural ability, a person who does the right thing naturally, as part of his or her true nature. By the same token, this is also true of the intuitive coach to whom one could safely apply the term "natural coach." Most of the great coaches in the history of our sport have been highly intuitive. Not only do they do the right thing naturally, but they also tend to have a strong innovative streak.

The intuitive coach is in stark contrast to those who tend to coach by a neat synthesis of orderly progressions. Not for them the thrill of the inspired hunch, the sudden flash of insight, nor the sixth sense that tells the intuitive coach that he or she is right on track and should forge straight ahead.

One of the big thrills in coaching, apart from seeing a protégé win the big one, is to spot a youngster with great talent. In fact, there are some who say that if you can't recognize talent when you see it, then you're simply not cut out to be a coach.

In this connection, I remember an old coach renowned for his ability to consistently spot future champions, but who played the horses unsuccessfully. He would bemoan his fate thus, "All my horses graze in the infield. If only I could spot horses like I pick swimmers!"

In the same way as baseball scouts look for players who have what is colloquially known as "a baseball face," so do intuitive swimming coaches know when they have come across natural talent. The intuitive coach has usually summed up a young hopeful long before the swimmer even

1

Left: James "Doc" Counsilman, swimming's great scientist-coach. His well-developed "muscles of intuition" led to many breakthrough ideas that improved the sport. *Second from left:* George Haines, one of the most successful coaches in the history of swimming. This intuitive coach has been described as "unique, self-confident, and calm." *Third from left:* Peter Daland, head U.S. Olympic coach in 1964 and 1972. One of his most noticeable characteristics is his ability to process intuitive information in a flash. Michigan coach Jon Urbanchek once said, "No IBM computer can match him!" *Right:* Don Gambril, 1984 U.S. Olympic head coach, was renowned as one of America's great intuitive coaches. He knew that there was "no single way to success." He used intuition, enthusiasm, and talent to build a great career.

enters the water to display a talent-typical, ghost-like glide and an almost casual arm entry that seems to merely caress the water.

Scientific Talent Detection

Today, it is increasingly common to hear of the application of scientific talent detection methods. To the intuitive coach, this trend is almost as offensive as it would have been had someone tried to teach Rembrandt to paint by numbers.

On two occasions in recent months, I have come across scientific papers on the benefits of a scientific talent identification process that will tell coaches whether or not they are coaching "the right stuff." One scientific article says, "As most coaches would be aware, the scientific research tells us [I love this phrase!] that the important characteristics for sprint swimmers are height, limb length, stroke rate, and power. One of the difficulties in the talent identification process is the problem of distinguishing between current abilities and potential abilities." Good gosh! Who would have thought so! All I can say is that we have come to a pretty pass.

Isn't there anything left for a coach to do without the aid of so-called science!? Nay! Not so. The time is fast approaching when all coaches, especially if they are part of a national program (and

issued with compulsory official certification cards), will actually be told how to recognize talent when they see it. I can just imagine leading coaches, all agog, waiting with bated breath, for the "Talent Identification Officer" to announce the results as to who has talent and who hasn't.

Worse still, it appears that soon coaches will need to abide by what scientific research confirms are the ideal physical and physiological characteristics (forget the psychological!) that elite swimmers possess. And gone will be the days when a coach's heart leapt with joy at the sight of a talented youngster manipulating the water with dexterous ease.

Like Someone Practicing Voodoo

Once I knew a medical doctor whose daughter was training under one of the world's great coaches, and her improvement was quite spectacular. While the doctor was impressed, he was also deeply puzzled because the coach didn't seem to work to any set system or use scientific principles.

Time and again, the doctor muttered, "How does the man achieve such wonderful results? He doesn't even take pulse rates. He's almost like a witch doctor or someone practicing voodoo . . ."

The doctor didn't know that most leading coaches are highly intuitive and use intuition like a built-in guidance system. And, because they produce successful results, they don't feel a need to explain how they do it. When pressed, they will often say, "Well, sometimes I know something, without knowing how I know it." Intuition is a major reason why they are able to make smart decisions and coach consistently well. In fact, they seem to sensitize themselves to their intuition and what it is trying to tell them.

Some people regard intuition as a throwback to an earlier, primitive era before scientific management replaced the "seat of the pants" and "gut feeling" approach. Intuition is often misunderstood, discounted, and confused with the stuff of fortune-tellers, astrologers, and palm readers. Intuition is not the opposite of rational analysis. It is that part of our minds that throws us subtle hints, suggestions, and faint signals (and sometimes not so faint). It's a people-reading device, a trend-spotting mechanism, a pattern-recognition system. *Webster's* defines it as "the direct knowing or learning of something without the conscious use of reasoning."

Qualities of an Intuitive Coach

What qualities or characteristics does an intuitive coach have? Among the main characteristics are good self-image, curiosity, and independence. An intuitive coach is not afraid to experiment. Even when present methods seem to be working well, the intuitive coach, nevertheless, remains open to new experiences and is willing to learn new things about every phase of swimming. In other words, the coach is adventurous, decisive, and able to change old patterns. The characteristics of an intuitive person have also been described as unique, self-confident, and calm.

Unlike an idea, intuition tends to resist analysis and rational probing. An intuitive insight or concept can often turn out to be an unexpected success when logical signs indicate that the concept will probably fail. Albert Einstein once said, "The really valuable factor is intuition." Like Einstein, Sir Isaac Newton worked out his proofs and conducted his experiments to verify what he had first determined intuitively.

It was said of Newton that he owed his success to "his muscles of intuition." It was further noted that Newton's intuitive powers were "the strongest and most enduring with which a man has ever been gifted." For most people, intuition occurs instantaneously and is often over before they realize what has happened, but Newton had the

Left: Australian coach Don Talbot, a great coach who could sensitize himself to his intuition and what it was trying to tell him. *Above:* Australian husband-and-wife coaching team, Ursula (left) and Forbes Carlile. Intuition is the major reason why great coaches make smart decisions.

Kevin Berry photo

International Swimming Hall of Fame

ability to extend that period of immediate know-ing. This was one of the abilities that contributed to his genius.

Can Just Anyone Become Intuitive?

In addition to processing intuitive information, you may find that you tend to have certain types of intuitive experiences. As you become more fa-miliar with the types of intuition that you have experienced, you will begin to notice how fre-quently and in what form they tend to occur.

You may find that you get intuitive flashes. An intuitive flash is a form of intuition in which an image passes through your mind very quickly. You may find that you process information in the form of an inner voice. Or you may have gut feelings. A gut feeling is a form of intuition in which you get a strong physical sensation or an emotional feel-ing about someone or something.

Intuition works best when fed with high qual-ity information and ideas and the desire to find and exploit opportunities. Some coaches tend to forget the competitive nature of their sport. It is important to observe what the competition is do-ing, and then do it better. Using intuition to develop a breakthrough idea is often the result of gathering a great amount of relevant information and then devoting lengthy periods to thinking out the problem.

Breakthrough ideas are most likely to occur when you are calmly, confidently searching for a new and

International Swimming Hall of Fame

Olympic champion Debbie Meyer and her coach Sherman Chavoor. Note the similar facial expression—coach and swimmer with the same mind-set.

better method. Rather than a single magical mo-ment in which the idea arrives fully developed, you may find that the breakthrough idea comes to you in pieces—pieces that you must gradually put to-gether in the best workable order.

No Single Way

The intuitive coach knows that there is no single way of doing things; whatever works, works. You have to have a passion for coaching. It's not some-thing you turn to because you're not good at anything else. I hope that I'm not going overboard by saying that you need to have a talent for it, as well as the enthusiasm with which to express your talent. You can't be cold and clinical and merely scientifically correct. Intuitive coaches are in direct contrast to those who have read the book so thoroughly that, when it comes to the crunch, they do all the wrong things correctly—with disastrous results.

Lest I have given the wrong impression about certification, let me hasten to add that certifica-tion courses definitely meet a need. Much of the information is very valuable and, in fact, most of it is the result of discoveries made over the years by intuitive coaches. The art of tapering is a good example of this, and, certainly, coaches do need to be trained in the generally accepted practices of the profession. This protects the profession, gives it status and prestige, and provides the assurance of capable coaching to employers and the public.

Most of today's leading coaches started their careers as assistants under prominent national coaches in the practical pool deck situation. I be-lieve that, after completing a preliminary certification course, the most effective way of de-veloping young coaches who show talent is for them to serve apprenticeships under the great intuitive coaches of the sport.

Following is a short list of articles on swimming, each by a famous intuitive coach, each a classic of its kind and an excellent example of what intuitive coaching is about. They probably rank among the best articles written on swimming, and should be recommended reading for certification candidates everywhere.

Recommended Reading
"The 'X' Factor in Coaching," from a talk by Dr. James Counsilman, ASCA World Clinic Pro-ceedings, Montreal, 1971. Published by

Left: Nort Thornton, coach of Olympic champion Matt Biondi. "Among the main characteristics of the intuitive coach are good self-image, curiosity, and independence." *Middle:* "The intuitive coach is adventurous, decisive, and able to change old patterns." Coach Sam Herford (left) and Olympic champion Murray Rose, winner of the 400- and 1,500-meter freestyle at the 1956 Olympics, and the 400-meter freestyle at the 1960 Olympics. Herford was an Australian distance champion in the 1930s and helped Rose become a master tactician. Both coach and swimmer had the same intuitive characteristics. *Right:* Mark Schubert's famous Mission Viejo Club in California ran up an American record in the 1970s and 1980s by winning 44 national titles. Coach Schubert used intuition and high-quality information and ideas to find and exploit opportunities.

American Swimming Coaches' Association, 2101 North Andrews Avenue, Suite 107, Fort Lauderdale, FL 33311.

"Sprint Training," by Don Gambril. *Swimming World Magazine*, March 1976. Published by Sports Publications, 90 Bellrock Plaza, Suite 200, Sedona, AZ 86351.

"Evaluation and Opinions on American Swimming—Fall 1992," by George Haines, *American Swimmer Magazine*, Dec./Jan. 1993. Published by American Swimming Coaches' Association, 2101 North Andrews Avenue, Suite 107, Fort Lauderdale, FL 33311.

"Distance Base: Key to Every Event," by Peter Daland. *Swimming World Magazine*, October 1981. Published by Sports Publications, 90 Bellrock Plaza, Suite 200, Sedona, AZ 86351.

❖ ❖ ❖

THOUGHTS ON THE TEAM DYNAMIC

Great athletes come from great teams. It is a cliché to say that "the swimmer makes the team and the team makes the swimmer." However, the statement remains true because every team takes on a joint personality which is an amalgam of the personalities of its members. In successful teams, the momentum of enthusiasm, confidence, and ability takes the team to undreamed of heights.

The team dynamic is often referred to as team spirit, but it is really a changing atmosphere, a combination of the energies—mental, emotional, and physical—that the athletes bring to the group at any given time. It is vital to understand that the team dynamic may assume either a negative or positive form. The role of the coach in ensuring that the team, as a whole, has a positive attitude is obviously important.

If we were to carefully follow the history of any successful team, it would quickly become apparent that a team usually starts from modest beginnings and initially passes through a series of negative experiences before becoming task oriented. The coach needs to develop the trust of each swimmer, reduce the swimmers' levels of anxiety about their ability to perform well, teach the basic skills, and accustom them to training and competition.

Slowly but surely, the swimmers will learn to function as an integrated team and grow in confidence. The coach teaches the team a fresh culture—the culture of competitive swimming, its demands, its moral and physical benefits, and its general positive influence on a swimmer's life.

Gradually, swimmers begin to realize that training is an act of faith, and that conscientious daily practice brings steady results and a newfound pride in performance. This is the start of motivation. Basically, the word *motivation* means to activate, trigger off, or set in motion. Swimmers should be taught that improvement in performance happens to a set pattern. It certainly is not an accidental process or even something magical.

Facetiously, I tell young swimmers that they are not going to wake up in the middle of the night and see their fairy godmother, complete with gossamer wings, standing on the window sill waving a magic wand and saying, "Lo and behold! Now you are a swimmer!" It does not suddenly happen like that.

Improvement is a long and gradual process, requiring patience and persistence. A swimmer should try to do a little better every day in either (or all) of three departments: stroke mechanics, physical condition, and mental attitude. The swimmer learns that over the days, weeks, and months that tiny daily improvements gradually add up to become significant improvement.

Some swimmers eventually become so highly skilled and motivated that they actually develop a certain aura about themselves that may unintentionally intimidate their rivals. This is not to be confused with deliberate psyching out of rivals which, if carried to excess, can only be described as gutter psychology.

I have long been interested in the abstract side of coaching and have always been a keen observer of how other coaches direct their swimmers. Coaches such as Jack Nelson, Don Gambril, Doc Counsilman, Peter Daland, Nort Thornton, Skip Kenney, Richard Quick, and Murray Stephens are born masters of the art of communication. They communicate with their swimmers in many ways other than the spoken word.

One of the most impressive examples of the art of coaching that I have witnessed was a pool deck incident at the U.S. Championships in Indianapolis a few years ago. I was standing behind coach Jack Nelson and a young female swimmer who was obviously distressed after misjudging her race. I could not help overhearing the conversation and the subsequent warm, sympathetic, and encouraging manner in which he spoke to her. I knew that I had observed a minor miracle as coach Nelson virtually reestablished her confidence right there before my eyes!

Great coaches use several leadership styles as they demonstrate a skill, describe a workout item, and allow time for practice, feedback, reruns, reflection, and review. At various times, they will either take direct control of the team or else allow cooperative input, and then, gradually, they allow the swimmers a certain degree of autonomy. This process eventually empowers the swimmers to function successfully on their own with a minimum of coaching intervention as each individual swimmer becomes a self-contained training unit.

Included in a good coach's repertoire are abstract skills such as the ability to scan the team regularly and pick up on nonverbal cues. They know how to bring in the individual swimmer by eye contact, hand gesture, questioning, and divining. The coach is also able to draw out a swimmer who is already talking by eye contact, hand gesture, echoing, questioning, divining, checking for understanding, paraphrasing, and marshaling.

With a deft gesture from one hand, a coach can also shut out someone who is talking, while simultaneously bringing in someone else with the other hand. This is done without any words, like a traffic cop. Or the coach may add words—and question, divine, check for understanding, paraphrase, or marshal what the current speaker has just said, and put this to someone else for comment. In this manner a capable coach keeps a fairly low profile while effectively managing the swimmer's contribution rates, helping the swimmers to discover themselves as well as develop interpersonal learning within the team.

✧ ✧ ✧

SWIM POOLS, CLUBS, AND COACHES

Ready access to swimming pool time and space affects the outcome of most programs.

Swimming coaches around the world work in a variety of systems including state programs, swim clubs, and their own swim schools. The system in which a coach operates often influences results and, where one system predominates in a country, it must affect the entire national standard.

During a long career I have coached in several systems, notably in South Africa, Australia, and Canada, and have also observed programs in other countries. My purpose is not to argue for or against any particular system but to highlight various features. In most systems, access to swimming pool time and space is both a common problem and an important factor affecting the efficiency of the program.

While there is no shortage of good swimming facilities in most countries, large rental fees place inordinate demands on the energies and resources of club personnel. If compromises can be made between the relevant parties, these stresses can be largely reduced. More constructive thought and energy can then be applied directly to improving actual swimming performance.

In Canada and the United States, the swim club system predominates. Parents and swimmers raise the main funding to pay for pool hire, travel, and coaching salaries. The parents employ the coaches and control the club administration with the head coach in charge of day-to-day operations. Like all systems, the swim club has both its strengths and its weaknesses.

While Canada today has perhaps the world's best model of a club system, it is unfortunate that the club system has within it the seeds of its own destruction. Soaring operating costs and consequent diminishing pool time place a heavy burden on already hard-working club organizers.

To meet rising costs, too many people need to be accepted into the program, making it difficult to maintain standards and give adequate attention to the more talented athletes. In addition, the influx of new club members usually results in a mixed membership whose goals are not always exclusively aimed at achieving excellence. After coaching swimmers in my own swim school organization for most of my career, I worked in the Canadian club system for exactly two years. Within that short time there were no fewer than three changes in the club's written constitution. The initial constitution, which stated that the club's aim was "to strive for excellence," was gradually whittled down to a weak-kneed compromise between "recreation and excellence."

Many great swimmers worldwide have been spawned in the swim club system. In the United States, the face of swimming seems to be changing. There are no more "superclubs" such as Mission Viejo and Santa Clara in their heyday. One by one, leading American club coaches are lured to coach in universities. The effects of this migration on the developmental levels of American swimming have been evident for some years now. While recruiting star swimmers for university teams is hard work, no longer do former club coaches have to work all hours and all year. Within the university system they have more autonomy and are not responsible to parents with little background of swimming knowledge. Obviously, there is a need to take a new, long look at the club system, both in Canada and the United States.

In Southern Hemisphere countries such as Australia, New Zealand, and South Africa, the systems are vastly different from those in North America. Obtaining pool time and space can sometimes be surprisingly easy when you are able to strike a good deal with a local pool owner or operator.

In South Africa, I hired pool space from municipal authorities and rented pools from private owners to conduct my swim school activities. In addition, my coaching staff gave learn-to-swim and physical education classes in the mornings at local schools for nominal fees as part of the school curriculum. In return for this service, we received free pool time and permission to charge fees for giving stroke technique lessons in the afternoons and coaching senior competitive swimmers in the evenings.

In this way my swim school chain catered to the aquatic needs of a big population across the eastern suburbs of the large city of Johannesburg. In this system, we first taught the kids how to swim, then we taught them to swim better, and encouraged them to join our junior age-group teams. Over the years, the talented swimmers progressed into the senior ranks, many of them finally reaching world-class status. For more than 25 years, I was my own boss, able to decide my own coaching philosophy and guide and educate the entire group, parents and swimmers alike, in what I believed best to achieve our goals.

Other swim school formats exist in South Africa. Many coaches build their own outdoor swim pools in the backyards of their homes to conduct afternoon learn-to-swim classes with the aid of a staff of assistants. In addition, they contract with local schools, which have their own pools, to give morning swim classes as part of the formal physical education program. In the evenings, the coaches use pool space hired from local municipalities (for a nominal charge of about 50 dollars per season!) to train their competitive teams. This broad contact with swimmers at all levels, from beginners to advanced, ensures a flow of talent through the ranks.

A word of caution when assessing coach-owned and operated programs: With the increased incidence of liability suits in recent years, coaches run a risk of financial disaster should one of their pupils be involved in a serious accident while on their premises.

Another variation on the theme is for coaches to be employed as pool managers of municipal pool complexes. In exchange for sole coaching rights and free on-site housing, these coaches-turned-pool managers often agree to a lower salary for their managerial duties because they are able to earn large incomes from their coaching and learn-to-swim activities.

In Australia, despite the large number of facilities, obtaining the use of a suitable training pool is a difficult problem. Municipal authorities are generally more interested in revenue and the demands of the public than the problems of coaches who want to train competitive swimmers. When allowing coaches to use their pools, they are largely more concerned with what revenue a

coach can raise by way of learn-to-swim youngsters than any ability he or she may have to coach advanced swimmers. The disadvantage of municipally controlled pools, from a competitor's viewpoint, is that recreational swimmers have first preference. Next in line are learn-to-swim programs with competitive swimmers receiving what remains of pool space and time.

Most Australian and New Zealand coaches are entrepreneurs. They need to be in order to have facilities in which to work efficiently. Their main income is derived from fees for teaching and coaching. The majority are financially involved in owning, managing, or leasing facilities, as well as paying staff. Some have shops that sell swimsuits and other equipment. Many coaches build their own indoor pools: utility-type, indoor, 25-meter facilities with limited seating that are certainly not in the same category as the luxurious pools in North America.

It is to their credit that they are prepared to carry large financial burdens to coach their better swimmers throughout the year. Once financial commitments are met, the profit margin is comparatively small; other enterprises would yield better return on capital outlay.

To make their pools pay, Australian and New Zealand coaches are committed to extensive and continuous year-round programs from beginners through "improver" ranks to age group and seniors. They need all this lower level activity to support the top squads, on whom they make very little money because of the extra pool time and space needed. For these entrepreneur coaches, training a top squad appears little more than an expensive hobby. Most coaches find nearly all their waking hours involved in swimming, often to the sacrifice of family life.

In Australia, coaches are very much judged on their merits, and there is a notable tendency for swimmers to move from one coach to another when dissatisfied with their results. In Melbourne in the 1970s, this constant movement of swimmers was known, with typical Australian whimsy, as the "Melbourne merry-go-round." There is strong pressure for coaches to produce good results with their competitive swimmers. Although they do not make much money from training competitors, the results achieved by their star swimmers are "shop windows" which attract hundreds of aspiring youngsters to the more remunerative lower level programs.

There is no comfort zone for the serious Australian coach-entrepreneur who is always judged by his or her most recent results. Contrast this with the situation in some North American swim clubs. Unfortunately, there will always be the coach who feels secure in the certain knowledge of drawing a monthly check, irrespective of results achieved. The problem is compounded by the fact that parents who run the clubs have no yardstick to measure the effectiveness of the coaching staff.

On the other hand, there are many outstanding club coaches who produce consistently fine results with little, if any, motivation and incentive for improvement. Most of the top coaching positions in Canada are taken, and such opportunities rarely become available. Moreover, to build a superclub from scratch is an indomitable challenge. Most talented youngsters are bound to gravitate to the elite clubs before the intended new organization can become reality.

Unfortunately, in all the systems mentioned, there is a high fallout rate of coaches, most of whom are a loss to the sport. Obviously, the coaching of swimming needs to be made more attractive to those interested in pursuing it as a lifetime profession. Many intelligent and capable coaches feel that the average annual salary of approximately 35,000 dollars is not commensurate with their talents, and their perceptions are probably correct. Few coaches seem destined to reach the top salary brackets, reputed to average around 75,000 dollars per annum.

One cannot elaborate on all the components of the Canadian and other systems within this limited space. As stated, my intention was merely to highlight some of the choices and decisions made by others in a variety of circumstances. In studying the inherent difficulties of various systems, it should be noted that, just as most issues are seldom black and white, neither are most good solutions black or white. The reason there are two sides to begin with usually is because neither side has all the facts. Therefore, when the wise mediator effects a compromise, he or she is acting from a sense of respect for the whole truth. If we can identify facts and separate them from personal opinions,

the way will be open to creative thinking and constructive action on the challenges that face swimming in the future.

✧ ✧ ✧

EAGLES DON'T FLY IN FORMATION

How much "think-alike" is right? Perhaps swimming needs more iconoclasts, more people who are just plain unreasonable.

Nothing focuses the mind better than the constant sight of a competitor who wants to wipe you off the map. This perception holds good at all levels, whether it be for clubs, top coaches, or entire nations. If you're not trying to develop better methods than the opposition, it's possible that you could be in trouble. As James Michener once wrote, "It takes courage to know when you ought to be afraid."

I'll tell you what scares me: It's when we all seem to be doing the same thing, happy and content in believing that our methods are proven, accepted, and incontrovertible. This makes me nervous, even though I, myself, may be a believer, if only because I know of no better way. But the sixth sense that hints that all may not be well lingers on.

A Turkish proverb says, "No matter how far you have gone on a bad road, turn back." Now, I'm not suggesting that the sport of swimming is on a bad road. But it is possible that, if we exclude the so-called benefits of pharmacology, designer drugs, and so on, we could be on a slow track. When we place swimming methods into neat pigeonholes and tidy syntheses, there is a danger of becoming too fixed in our approach. And, if we're not careful, this could lead to stagnation.

The Courage to Experiment

Lest you think me an alarmist, consider this example: The history of the sport tells us that the 1930s were a particularly bad time, mainly because we locked into a type of freestyle swimming that, frankly, didn't work. In an attempt to copy the techniques of the successful Japanese swimmers of that era, Westerners adopted a form of crawl swimming that was characterized by a pronounced, overlapping, catch-up arm stroke in which the hands were recovered by rapidly flipping them forward to start each new stroke.

The idea was to ride on the forward arm while the legs performed a deep, wide bicycle kick. Swimmers were told that they would recognize the correct timing of the stroke when they experienced a sensation of "swimming downhill." Well, sad to relate, they swam downhill in more ways than one.

The point I'm making is that it is possible for entire nations to pursue a bad idea to their own detriment, even though the idea initially may have seemed eminently feasible and practical. The trial-and-error process is how we eventually progress, and certainly we should not attribute blame to those whose ideas have failed.

Admittedly, the errors we make sometimes come at a high price, but we shouldn't allow ourselves to become discouraged. An idea that, at first, may appear radical, bizarre, or way-out, eventually may be readily accepted. We should remember that a good creative idea will always collide with an established idea. This can be a frightening experience because the main enemies of creativity are crusty rigidity and stubborn complacency.

The Influence of Nonconformists

George Bernard Shaw said, "The reasonable man adapts himself to the world; the unreasonable man persists in trying to adapt the world to himself. Therefore, all progress depends on the unreasonable man." Perhaps swimming needs more iconoclasts, more unorthodox, independent-minded people who are just plain unreasonable. We need more sharp-eyed eagles, high flyers with the broad vision to view the whole panorama of swimming, where we've been and where we're likely to go. And, we especially need more people who are unafraid to upset the status quo and to challenge our most cherished beliefs.

Eagles don't fly in formation. They rarely flourish within the bureaucracies of centrally controlled national development programs. Bureaucracies are not their natural habitat. Bureaucracy, the rule of no one, has become a modern form of despotism. There, the fundamental skills essential to advancement are how to write a memo; how to survive, master, and even enjoy a meeting; how to

set and achieve goals by means of "management by objectives"; and how to empire build and thus ensure self-perpetuation. The biggest shortcoming of most national sports bureaucracies is their inability to appreciate and encourage the talents of creative people ideally equipped to advance the sport.

Creative Brainstorming

For the best part of a quarter of a century, the annual world clinics presented by the American Swimming Coaches' Association (ASCA) have provided a forum for the dissemination of swimming knowledge, not only to American coaches but to coaches worldwide. It is to the ASCA's credit that many of the important technical advances in swimming have been presented at their well-organized world clinics.

One of the most interesting features of ASCA's clinics has been the panel discussions on set topics by coaches who have had exceptional successes in a particular area. Here is a constructive suggestion for a variation on the panel discussion theme that may promote creative thinking by the best minds in coaching. Select a topic on which most swimming coaches are pretty much agreed; then invite leading protagonists of the method to meet in a panel, not to report merely on what they've been doing, but to propose and discuss possible new variations or improvements to the method.

Selecting a moderator, also a leading expert on the discussion topic, is essential to the success of the experiment. At the end of the discussion, the moderator would be expected to present an accurate précis of all the arguments and suggestions delivered by the panelists.

Another kind of presentation that may lead to creative thinking would consist of a different type of panel. In this instance, a speaker would first deliver a talk on a new method that the speaker is using. Later during the conference, the speaker would be called upon to defend the new idea before a panel of peers, who already will have prepared pertinent questions. Here again, the proceedings will be under the aegis of a competent moderator who would prepare an accurate précis of the proceedings and the final opinions arrived at.

Some Suggested Topics

Topic One: Should short-distance swimmers use power lifting? Power lifting is said to produce some of the fastest power gains possible. For example, in the bench press, it is not uncommon for a total beginner to go from a low of 100 pounds to well over 200 pounds in a few months.

Topic Two: Distance per stroke has been accepted as the criterion for efficient swimming for many years and rightly so. But not much research has been done on the subject. We need to know more about the correlation between stroke length and stroke frequency at all distances, especially the longer distances where muscle fatigue may become a factor. For example, swimmers such as Kieran Perkins change their pace during a 1,500-meter swim and also change their stroke timing.

Topic Three: Body roll in freestyle and backstroke. Does rolling on the body's long axis really improve streamlining? Or does rolling cause retarding crossflow turbulence around the body? How much rolling is necessary in order to bring the large trunk muscles into play? Does the serape effect (starting the pull with the use of hip rotation) really apply to swimming? Is there a different arm stroke for sprinters and distance swimmers? (Until recently, short distance showed a tendency to swim flatter and to use a wider and straighter back pull. Pulling directly backward in freestyle, using predominant drag propulsion, permits the arm to act more rapidly on a large mass of water, but this action is costly in terms of energy expenditure.) Furthermore, is rolling necessary to avoid the so-called impingement syndrome (postural adjustments such as hunching the shoulders slightly forward will permit increased shoulder joint mobility)?

Topic Four: Setting dates for the annual championship program. Should there be fixed dates, as existed in former years, for the Men and Women's NCAA Championships, the Short Course Championships, and the Summer Long Course Championships? There was a time when swimmers had the whole summer to prepare for the Long Course Championships. Do swimmers compete in too many meets? Experienced coaches say that, ideally, they would cut the total of meets by about a third and spend more time on the training buildup. And what about the increase in major international games in recent years? How many major peaks per year should swimmers have at different levels of development? Do inexperienced coaches need guidelines in this respect?

Ask the Right Questions

These suggested topics are obviously subjective and given mainly for example. To bring coaches together in potentially creative brainstorming situations, it cannot be overstressed that the discussion panels should be methodically structured, with great care given to asking the right questions. Panel members should be given the opportunity for prior viewing of the proposed questions to ensure they agree that the right questions, in fact, are being asked.

The composition of the panel should be carefully planned. For example, when topics dealing with biomechanics are under discussion, the panel may be composed of swimming coaches, a prominent biomechanist, and even a fluid dynamicist. In this way, scientists and coaches would work together as a team, and at the end of the discussion, possibly form a hypothesis, derived from asking the right questions, as a basis for future experimentation.

I would like to think that the coaching profession has long passed the time when we tended to be secretive and loathe to discuss our individual methods. The more knowledge we pass on to our colleagues, the more we need to learn in order to keep ahead. Conversely, when we don't pass on what we know, this could be a tacit admission on our part that we have stopped learning and that the concrete has set in our heads.

We should make it a rule to constantly improve on present methods, even if it entails only slight changes or adjustments at first. The old saying, "If it ain't broke, don't fix it!" contains much wisdom. However, there's no harm in stimulating our own curiosity. Don't be afraid to ask yourself, "What if?" Very often, to our great surprise, this is how discoveries are made.

The obvious is something which is never seen until someone expresses it simply. What seems to have been the last word on a subject turns out not to be. We should question everything, even the truths we live by. Granted, there is nothing more upsetting than the clobbering of a cherished belief, but when we become too comfortable with a method, this is a time to be wary, even if everybody else is using it. Remember that discovery consists of seeing what everybody has seen—and thinking what nobody has thought before.

✧ ✧ ✧

LET'S PUT THE SWIMMER FIRST

Earlier this year I returned home to South Africa for the first time in 20 years. To be reunited with family and friends was a powerful, moving, and emotional experience. One of the most pleasing experiences of my tour was meeting former swimmers who had become successful in various fields of endeavor. I was pleased to hear them attribute their happiness and success to what they learned as competitive swimmers. One of them, a highly respected Johannesburg city councilor, said that swimming had taught him the value of team participation, self-discipline, persistence, and hard work.

Although unexpected, I found his comments gratifying because they made me feel I had done more for him than merely teach him to swim fast. I was also surprised to hear his praise because in recent years, I had come to view myself as having been somewhat of an authoritarian coach, to use today's sports psychology parlance. His comment, although welcomed, surprised me and made me think.

I asked myself, "Had I really been a sort of latter-day Captain Bligh, or had I just insisted on maintaining discipline?" I remembered having taught the swimmers that, in the final criterion, the best form of discipline is self-discipline, but if they insisted on acting like babies, I would treat them like babies. Once they showed respect for the team and what we were trying to achieve, I would treat them as adults. This approach seemed to work.

Analysis of my former leadership style led me to think about the tremendous influence coaches wield over developing swimmers. In the last 20 years, the growth of the national development program concept, in some respects, has made it easy to lose sight of the fact that the overall welfare of each swimmer is a very important responsibility.

Too often we find that many people in our society carry a great deal of unprocessed distress because they have been the subjects of oppressive educational methods from the earliest years—both at home and at school—where their needs and rights as young people have not been fully honored or realized. In competitive swimming, they may have learned to swim fast and even become champions, but, in the process, were subjected to a coach's or parent's poor control of anger and demeaning use of criticism. What should have been an enjoyable and educational experience became, in effect, a trial by fire.

One result of this oppression is that in later years they lack certain basic human skills: skills in handling their own feelings, skills in interacting with other people, skills in self-direction and collective decision making. In these instances, there obviously has been a gross deficiency in the range and depth of their education and training.

I believe that, in the midst of learning stroke techniques, the principles of training, race strategies, and so on, there is a need for other important learning objectives if we are to succeed in developing a swimmer's full human potential. By using the sport as a form of leisure-time education, we can show the swimmer how to become autonomous and self-directed.

I see this process as a three-stage cycle of development consisting of direct leadership (or hierarchy and control) in the first instance, then gradually leading to cooperation between coach and swimmers, and finally more autonomy and delegation and scope for the team.

A clear hierarchical framework is needed as the coach outlines the principles in the various swimming disciplines. This phase assumes that the swimmers do not yet have the confidence or sense of complete independence to function with complete effectiveness without the direct control or intervention by the coach. At this stage, it is tacitly assumed that the coach will make all the decisions for the team until a certain level of competence is gained.

Gradually a stage is reached in which the open collaboration of the team members is sought in handling the learning process. The swimmers learn what is expected of them. They learn the basics of the curriculum and they help the coach to cooperatively guide their learning activities. They learn to help each other and, in the process, learn to orient themselves to new knowledge and skills. By learning and building confidence in performing certain skills and routines, they become able to come up with suggestions on how future learning should proceed. This is known as the cooperative phase.

Once team members have developed considerable confidence in implementing the instruction they have received, they clearly have acquired a large amount of knowledge and skill. Now they are ready to enter the autonomous mode in which they will be able to direct much of their own learning. The entry into the autonomous, or self-directed phase of learning, can occur in two ways. Either the coach may give the authority to the team in a hierarchical fashion or the coach may negotiate the transfer in cooperation.

However, autonomy can be seized from the coach by the group should the coach fail to exert his overall authority as leader of the team. There is also a difference between group autonomy and individual autonomy. This may cause conflict in which one team member may disagree with the consensus choice of other self-directing peers. The point is that the group autonomy does not necessarily guarantee the autonomy of everyone of its peers. Therefore, the final controlling authority of the coach should not be abdicated. The main point of developing and leading a team to a certain level of autonomy is to develop a self-containment and sense of self-reliance in each individual team member. This, in itself, is a most desirable educational objective.

✧ ✧ ✧

GOLD THAT DOESN'T GLITTER

How do you develop a swimmer's full potential, and what is a coach's responsibility to each swimmer in a team? These are questions that are not asked frequently enough.

Over a long career, I have seen several examples of swimmers who, for various reasons, have plodded along for years without really being noticed and without making notable improvement. While most coaches may think that they have a good knowledge of every swimmer on the team, this is often not the case. This raises questions as to the compatibility of different types of personalities, and how individual swimmers and coaches respond to each other.

In each instance, the coach has failed to understand the swimmer in all aspects of the swimmer's ability and general personality. Sometimes a swimmer, in utter desperation and at the point of giving up the sport completely, transfers to another team. And, in many instances, the swimmer concerned improved dramatically.

In one unforgettable case, a swimmer who had shown little progress in her previous team transferred to another team and very quickly blossomed into a regional champion. The next year she became a national champion, and within the following two years, was actually selected for the Olympic Games where she swam exceptionally well to finish fourth in an individual event!

The Need for Individualized Coaching

Of course, this was a dramatic case in point, and one that doesn't happen often, but nevertheless, it remains a classic example of how important it is to make sure that you understand every swimmer in your team and that every swimmer's needs are fully met. It points to the need for periodic individualized coaching, and it also calls attention to the coach's responsibility to reduce or eliminate a swimmer's weaknesses while maximizing that individual's strengths.

How do you develop a swimmer's full potential within the context of a team's training program, and what is the responsibility of a coach to the individual swimmer in a team? This is a valid question, and perhaps one that is not asked frequently enough. A wide range of variables arises with any attempt to discuss the topic, but it is possible to identify some of the key components of the question.

One component is the type of training program a team conducts. Ideally, every athlete should start the season by building a strong foundation of endurance work before gradually introducing more speed into the workouts as the weeks go by. With the final stages of the season comes the time to balance endurance and speed in proportions specific to the individual swimmer's racing distance. This approach is more likely to bring out the best in a greater number of swimmers on a team.

However, some teams concentrate almost entirely on so-called sprint programs, while others place almost the entire emphasis on distance swimming. But research shows that too much sprinting dilutes endurance, while swimming long distances only will stunt a swimmer's speed. Not only do polarized programs ignore the need for a well-balanced seasonal program, but often they also ignore the aptitudes and latent ability of individual swimmers. At the very least, some individualized coaching is necessary to find the right balance for each team member.

To develop any swimmer's full potential, it is necessary to study the individual. In large teams this is not always so easy to do. The economics of high rentals for adequate pool time often result in a need to enroll more and more swimmers to cover operating expenses. The bigger a team becomes, the more staff is needed with a corresponding increase in salaries. The larger the coaching staff, the larger and more diverse becomes the range of coaching abilities and coaching styles within the team, often with varying effects on individual swimmers.

Confidence Breeds Success

We have heard the slogan "the swimmer makes the team, and the team makes the swimmer." This means that if each individual swimmer improves, so will the team, and, by the same token, a strong team helps each swimmer to develop to full personal potential. Many swimmers on a successful team are carried along by the momentum of the pack.

The dynamics of the team usually result from a variety of different interpersonal relationships. There are swimmers who "call to the coach"; every aspect of their personalities draws the coach's attention. But there are other swimmers who need to be drawn out of themselves before their individual talents can be revealed. More often than a coach realizes, there will lurk in the money

lanes another kind of gold—the gold that does not glitter.

Although it is often the coach's leadership that sparks the energies of a team, it should be noted that this can only happen if the coach is a strong, confident leader. The old saying that confidence breeds success while lack of confidence breeds failure is very true. Many a talented swimmer will improve in performance under any coach, but in tight competition, all other things being equal, the swimmers of the supremely confident coach usually come through as the winners. There have been, however, instances where swimmers competing under a comparatively uninspired coach have been successful largely because of the examples set by dominant swimmers within the team itself.

Avoiding the Standardized Workout

A coach should avoid the pitfall of the standardized workout. The coach should also avoid the idea that what is good for the champions is good for everyone. This is not necessarily true. Swimmers respond better to training formats that are best suited to the individual. The reason for this preference is not difficult to ascertain. Different personalities, different levels of maturity, the changing physique of a developing athlete are all factors to consider.

In seeking to draw the best out of each swimmer in the team, the coach should avoid using a shotgun method in designing the daily training schedule. In developing novice competitors, the shotgun method may result in temporary improvement, but over the long haul it will not meet the needs of individual swimmers. A few outstanding swimmers will succeed, but many more may fail. The pity is that, in this type of program, swimmers seldom learn to appreciate and enjoy the subtle challenges of the sport. Many young swimmers do not flourish as they should because little instruction is given in stroke mechanics or the whys and wherefores of training, paces, strategies, and so forth.

Balancing Ability and Motivation

The actual design of the training program should meet the needs of the individual swimmer. While natural ability is important, this is not the only factor concerned with success. Motivation is the important, unseen factor in swimming success. Having talent and ability must also be backed up by a high level of motivation. In other words, both ability and motivation will decide the level of success achieved. The amount of ability sets the limits beyond which the swimmer will not be able to go, but the strength of motivation will determine the extent to which the swimmer will make use of the ability that he or she possesses.

A swimmer may fail because of lack of ability or because of lack of motivation. Conversely, a swimmer may be fairly successful with fairly limited ability providing that the swimmer is motivated by intense desire to succeed. When the coach has created desire in a swimmer to the extent that the swimmer experiences the want, wish, or need to strive, the use of motivation has been successful. There is adequate evidence to establish a definite relationship between motivation and ability. An excess of one factor may compensate for a deficiency in the other, and the end result may be an above-average or even superior performance. However, only swimmers who possess both outstanding ability and strong motivation will ever become truly great.

Study Each Individual

Through all the developing years, the coach should study each young swimmer's needs to produce the ideal physiological and technical aptitudes necessary to reach peak performance in each successive season. Every season should start with considerable attention to individual medley swimming and an emphasis on swimming all four strokes. Apart from the conditioning effects of this training, the coach will be able to detect the swimmer's best strokes, as well as the swimmer's potential ability to develop skills in a stroke the swimmer has not swum before. This is important because such an approach will ensure that the coach will not overlook any aspect of talent.

When introducing a swimmer to a new stroke, considerable time—often several weeks—should be devoted to practicing the new stroke because it takes time for expertise to develop. This is particularly true when introducing swimmers to butterfly swimming.

Often lackluster performances may be attributed to accumulative fatigue rather than lack of talent or interest. The coach should not forget that he or she is dealing with rapidly developing young people who often become fatigued by lengthy travel to and from practice sessions, not to mention the inexorable demands of growth.

A training program is not only concerned with the learning of technique and training, but also with providing the swimmer with experiences in surmounting difficulties, in providing the satisfactions that come from achievement, and developing the persistence, confidence, and goal-seeking capacity necessary to achieve his or her potential.

❖ ❖ ❖

SHOULD SWIMMERS BE LEAN AND MEAN OR JUST PLAIN HAPPY?

Should a team be "mean"? Sometimes we hear of formidable teams being described as lean and mean. In the 1980s, Australia had a national relay team proudly known as "The Mean Machine." Incidentally, I once met Mark Stockwell, a member of the Australian Mean Machine. My initial trepidation soon disappeared when I found him to be a very fine and likable young gentleman, which proves that a name can sometimes be misleading.

The dictionary definition of *mean* is ignoble, small-minded, malicious, ill-tempered, vicious, or nastily behaved. These descriptions certainly did not apply to Stockwell. Puzzled, my immediate reaction was to ask myself, "Are we deliberately trying to teach young swimmers to be mean? Or are we merely trying to create an aura around them in which they only appear to be mean? Furthermore, do we want them to be temporarily mean—during a swim meet, for example—or do we wish them to adopt a new persona and become permanently mean?" If the latter is the case, then, obviously, this purpose is at odds with the concept of participating in swimming as a form of leisure education.

My perception is that we generally have not yet come up with a clear concept of exactly what qualities we wish swimmers to develop in the actual competitive situation. Do we want them to be assertive, aggressive, quietly confident, calm and collected, tenacious, determined, unrelenting, formidable, dominating, fear inspiring, and, yes, perhaps even lean and mean!?

Clearly, it is time to take stock of the situation. Over a long experience I have had the opportunity of observing, at close quarters, some of the most successful teams in the history of swimming. One of the toughest and most exciting swim meets that I have attended, the Olympics or otherwise, was the U.S. National Championships in Lincoln, Nebraska, in 1966. Great coaches such as George Haines, Peter Daland, Don Gambril, Doc Counsilman, Jack Nelson, Sherm Chavoor, Soichi Sakamoto, and many other big names were all there with their famous star swimmers. Granted, the competition was tough and unrelenting, and the atmosphere was extremely tense at times, but my predominant impression in the midst of all the excitement was that the swimmers, win or lose, all appeared to be *happy*! With few exceptions, happy coaches and happy swimmers make the most successful teams.

When a swimmer is happy, then it is almost certain that the swimmer is well-balanced, stable, focused, and, generally in control. Being happy need not imply that a swimmer is soft and unable to be determined and tenacious both in training and in the heat of competition. In short, it is possible to be a tough competitor without needing to be "mean."

A happy swimmer is usually also a relaxed swimmer, even in the crucial, decisive stages of a race. Because they are able to relax better, happy swimmers do not usually become anxious, tense, and disorganized.

A very important point is that happy swimmers sleep better. They do not spend the night tossing and turning and worrying about upcoming competition. Because they sleep better, the odds are that they will more readily adapt to the stresses of training and competition.

Looking around me at swim meets, I often observe swimmers, coaches, and parents who, sadly perhaps, do not seem to be having such a great time. They appear tense and anxious and I get the feeling that they have lost much of the fun element of swimming. This is a pity because many of the enriching and pleasurable aspects of the sport have become lost to them.

The first question that arises is, "Can a coach teach a swimmer to be happy?" The next question is, "Should a coach teach a swimmer to be happy?" We have to presuppose that in the first instance the coach is a happy person, because, if the coach is not happy, it is unlikely that the coach can make anyone else happy. Indeed, in the long haul, an unhappy coach is more likely to succeed in making many other people unhappy, not the least of which are the swimmers, and this would constitute a serious situation within the team.

On the other hand, there are many fortunate people—coaches, swimmers, and parents included—who are naturally happy within their own skins. This is a very important point. If you are not happy within yourself, you are certainly not going to make anyone else happy! So the coach needs to be a happy person.

If you are not happy, what do you need to do to become happy? One of the first rules is to not allow outside events to determine whether or not you are happy. The first rule is to establish a system which ensures that you are in control, and that you are not reliant on events outside yourself in order to be happy. In the words of Anthony Robbins in his book *Awaken the Giant Within*, "Set it up so that it is incredibly easy for you to feel good, and incredibly hard to feel bad."

A few months ago, I passed the above inspiring words of advice on to a young swimmer who shall remain anonymous. For various reasons, he had been going through an unhappy and unsuccessful spell. A short while later, our paths crossed again, and I was struck by the apparent transformation in his whole demeanor. To cut a long story short, he told me enthusiastically that he was feeling much happier and his swimming career was starting to make headway again. He told me what he had been doing to become happier. His description was so interesting that I asked him to write it down for the express purpose of using it in this article and, with his permission, it is reprinted here. It goes like this:

Be happy!! Think happy!! Act happy!! Be happy!! Smile!! Smile!! Always have a smile!! Be happy from the inside out!! Let it show!! I am a happy person!! Look at me—I'm safe to approach!! My positive reaction is always guaranteed!! If others look grumpy, negative, etc., they may be sad or even ill, or worried—I feel sorry for them, and so I give them my happy smile!! Sometimes, I make them smile too!! I've noticed now that some people smile back at me and even say hello!! One grumpy-looking man actually winked back at me!! Wow!! Life can be a fun trip!!

May I very respectfully suggest that you try some of the above expedients on yourself and/or your team. The results might even prove to be spectacular. In any event, there's no harm in anyone trying to be a little happier!

❖ ❖ ❖

BEWARE THE PSYCH-OUT ARTIST

This is the season when the voice of the psych-out artist is heard in the land. Who is the psych-out artist? It could be a swimmer in your training lane or from a rival team who, by word, deed, or implication, seeks to demoralize you and prevent you from doing your best. This type of person is out to win by any means, fair or foul. Conversely, there is a milder type of psych-out artist: the cocky, cheeky kid, who by sheer exuberance and self-confidence unwittingly intimidates more timid rivals.

It is well to be aware of the prevailing types of psych-out artists and how they wreak their havoc. Better still, it is wise to know how to counter their often unexpected tactics. The first point to understand is that the psych-out artist is usually a person with a fundamental need to control others, yet is uncertain of being able to win a swimming race on ability and fair play alone. Because the compulsion to win may not be matched by ability and level of preparation, the swimmer reverts to devious and covert means to attain this end. Basically, your average psych-out artist is a manipulator whose tongue is often a more effective weapon than the ability to swim fast.

Often the psych-out artist contrives to appear more calm and confident than he feels. Inside he may be worried, insecure, and unconfident. The only way he can feel superior is to try to make you ruffled, and thus bring you down to his level. Then a surprising thing often happens. He actually pretends to show concern and offers to help you.

At this stage the psych-out artist may appear to be your best friend, and, in a clever and subtle way, will pretend to be interested in helping you, will praise you and place you completely off guard while subtly drawing attention to your negative qualities. In this way the psych-out artist finds your weaknesses, makes you feel vulnerable, and uses this to gain control over you in the competitive situation.

How do you detect rivals who are intent on putting you down and belittling you, depriving you of your confidence, even before you dive into the pool? Don't waste too much time trying to identify them by analyzing their different traits. Instead, if you feel distinctly uncomfortable in their presence, know that this is your first and most important warning sign.

Most perceptive people realize that psych-out artists do not have very high self-esteem. Deep down inside they really feel inferior to others. Usually they hide this behind their displays of overinflated egos. However, it should be known that some psych-out artists could become good swimmers if only they would concentrate on honing their skills and training harder instead of trying to win by unfair and sometimes ruthless methods.

Potential victims of the psych-out artist's invalidating schemes should take heart in the knowledge that a person trying to belittle someone else is very likely to be susceptible to the very same methods were they to be used against him or her. It's an almost amusing fact that most psych-out artists cave in very quickly if subjected to a small dose of their own medicine. Even though doing so might give you some satisfaction, do not do it because you would automatically join their lowly ranks.

What about the phenomenon of recent years, perhaps culled from the professional boxing ring, when swimmers in the prerace marshaling room engage in protracted eyeball-to-eyeball staredown bouts, not unlike baboons attempting to establish troop dominance? My advice to swimmers is not to go along with this game. Refuse to be controlled or manipulated by any would-be psych-out artist by behaving well and concentrating on your upcoming race.

If you should find confrontation unavoidable, then try to treat the entire ploy with faint amusement. If you should have the bad luck of coming up against a master psych-out artist who tries to embarrass you in front of the other competitors, as has been known to happen, then you may have no option but to offer similar embarrassment to the offending person. But don't forget that you may be dealing with a real expert, someone who has been psyching out fellow competitors for years and is probably far more skilled than you will be at your first attempt. Nevertheless, with the benefit of surprise, you may really catch your opponent off balance. Respond this way only when you have no alternative because psyching people out is really nothing more than gutter psychology and a loathsome exercise with no place in our sport.

Rather than seeking to retaliate, set your own house in order by building for yourself an unassailable suit of competitive armor. Seal yourself in your own cocoon of concentration and develop a good knowledge of self, your strengths as well as your weaknesses. Become responsible only to yourself.

Learn to understand your body and also how your mind works in the entire context of training and competing. As you strive to improve and become more and more the fully integrated competitor, you will eventually develop the aura of a confident and seasoned competitor that inspires respect in your rivals. Like hyenas around a lion's kill, would-be psych-out artists will tend to give you a wide berth.

Let's address the problem of the psych-out artist. How should coaches deal with it? First, the enlightened coach should realize that teaching kids to psych each other out is a no-no. Obviously, the coach should set the example. By encouraging youngsters to be manipulative, we are going counter to the ideal of using sports as a form of leisure-time education.

Part of the problem is that sometimes coaches awaken too late to realize that psyching out rivals has already become epidemic within the group. Many youngsters will not be easily motivated to change because they may have developed a set of effective and powerful psych-out mechanisms. In a bad sense, they are coming up winners, and the game has become too successful from their viewpoint to want to change. In sad fact, a few of them may have become irreversible manipulators, but they are in the minority.

The coach should warn against invalidating behaviors during team meetings and explain in detail why such practices are not acceptable behaviors, and how, in the final analysis, they seriously diminish one's personal worth. Parents should also be on the lookout for youngsters who may prove to be victims of the psych-out process. They are often identifiable by a sudden loss of confidence, sinking morale, and a general change in demeanor. Discreet questioning by parent or coach may reveal the source of the problem.

Once a psych-out artist has been identified, try to establish why this person has this problem, then explain why this behavior is not acceptable to the coach or anyone else in the team. Set a time limit in which a complete change is to be effected. Acknowledge that the psych-out artist has a real problem.

The answer in most cases would be to improve the swimmer's self-esteem and to concentrate on improved performance based on fundamental skills and improved physical condition. Hopefully, the offenders will begin to concentrate on swimming faster rather than talking faster.

VALID CRITICISM: AN ESSENTIAL PART OF COACHING

Swimmers often feel devastated when they confuse critical feedback with reprimand.

The very nature of a coach's job is to analyze and evaluate all areas of swimming performance. Giving expert feedback can mean the difference between a swimmer's success or failure. When coaches offer criticism, albeit well-intentioned, they tread a precarious tightrope. On the one hand, they want to help the swimmer to build a positive self-image. On the other hand, they need to be careful that the critiques they offer do not produce an undesirable countereffect.

Even swimmers who outwardly appear tough and self-contained may find criticism hard to handle. People automatically tend to regard criticism as something unfavorable and negative. This is particularly true of criticism offered without the knowledge and background that qualifies a person to criticize, even though the motive may be constructive. Wise coaches understand that young swimmers need sensitive and tactful handling, especially when commenting on their performances.

An important coaching task is to keep swimmers relatively free of unnecessary emotional stress. This is easier said than done because many swimmers are constantly subjected to a variety of stresses in all phases of their lives, at home, school, and at the swimming club. They consider all adults to be constantly on their backs, criticizing and placing diverse demands upon them. As a result, youngsters often become keyed up, stressed, and hypersensitive.

It is natural for people to view criticism as personal and threatening. Because people usually like to hear views consistent with their own self-appraisals, it is natural for them to resist contrary ideas. Patient coaching is required to convince a swimmer that it is possible to dramatically improve simply by heeding the coach's comments.

It is essential that coaches teach swimmers to view critical feedback in a positive light to the extent that there is no doubt as to a coach's intentions. They should understand that criticism presented as an evaluation of performance can be of enormous benefit.

Swimmers should learn that constructive criticism is an indispensable part of our lives that can empower them to make full use of their innate talents and aptitudes. They should also learn that criticism does not imply disapproval or that something must be wrong with them. Once swimmers believe that the coach will offer only valid criticism intended for the swimmers' improvement, an important new stage in the coach-swimmer rapport will have been reached.

A coach's critical comments on a swimmer's performance should always be fair and tempered with praise and encouragement. The manner in which a coach gives critical feedback will affect the desired outcome. If the swimmer feels ridiculed or that the coach is being hostile, impatient, or short-tempered, the swimmer's reaction will tend to be negative. However, when criticism is given in such a way that there can be no doubt of the coach's warmth and sincerity, the swimmer's response will be positive.

When a coach's comments are presented in a patient and tolerant fashion, the swimmer will develop a sense of security as well as increased faith in the coach's ability. It is very important for any youngster on a swimming team to feel the coach's approval, acceptance, and friendship. When a coach provides critical feedback in an expert and constructive way, a swimmer's self-image is heightened by the knowledge that the coach cares enough to correct and improve a particular aspect of performance. Under such circumstances, and even though performance is being criticized, the swimmer can have no doubt that the coach's respect has been earned.

I have mentioned that providing criticism is a part of a coach's professional function. We should not forget that the very nature of the coaching profession entails that the coach is often also at the receiving end of criticism. (This criticism, however, is not always couched in the same careful terms!) It is appropriate for both coach and swimmers to understand the different types of criticism that they may encounter: (1) valid criticism, or justified criticism; (2) invalid criticism; and (3) vague criticism, or criticism that is simply a difference of opinion. The three main types of criticism are self-explanatory. The important point to understand is that for criticism to be constructive, it should be genuinely helpful and should be stated in clear, specific terms so that we can act accordingly if we so choose.

In asking yourself whether criticism is valid or invalid, you should ask whether you hear the same criticisms from more than one person. Do the critics have expert knowledge? Are the critics impartial and unbiased?

There are some coaches who tend to neglect providing feedback, either positive or negative. This is unfortunate because research suggests that feedback is a strong motivating factor in coaching athletes. Careful, well-thought-out criticism takes time. In giving criticism, some coaches tend to criticize before they have effectively explained their expectations (for example, the desired stroke mechanics or the goals of the training program, etc).

Often, the initial description is either too brief or inadequate. In the first instance, it is necessary to set realistic goals and expectations. If coaches fail to outline the expected behaviors that should result from their teaching, they will not have built the foundation on which to base subsequent evaluation or criticism. It is better to voice constructive criticism early to correct faults before they become too ingrained. In the long run, good criticism saves time. Criticism, if thoughtfully presented, encourages both coach and swimmer to learn and grow.

✧ ✧ ✧

SOCIETAL CHANGES AND COMMITMENT

In order for the coach and swimmer to have the same goals, there is a need for clear communication on the level of commitment.

If the 1994 World Championships in Rome and recent statistics are any indication, swimming in America and especially Canada is at a low ebb. Maybe the tide will turn soon, but somehow I doubt it. The sport appears to be in transition, probably due to societal changes and shifts in attitude toward the dedication and hard work required to succeed at the top.

We need a better grasp of exactly what is happening in our sport. Already, the situation is being discussed in both countries. More than likely, we will be presented with opinions rather than facts. And it will come as no surprise to find ourselves looking at problems that are perennial problems that have been around a long time simply because they were never properly addressed in the first instance.

The problems that face the sport cannot be solved by brushing them under the carpet. Neither can they be solved at meetings that seek to reach "consensus" by consolidating the individual opinions of committee members to form a "solution." These problems have remained problems simply because past attempts to solve them were tackled exactly in this manner, rather than by conscientious attempts to carefully examine the facts.

One point should now be clear. We in North America simply have to realize that copying the systems of other countries is no solution. When we copy others, we become followers not leaders. We need to examine every aspect of swimming and then come up with a completely new, fresh approach. And, contrary to popular thought, there is no need to throw big bucks at problems in order to solve them. Often, the best solutions are the simple everyday things that lay right in front of our eyes waiting to be seen.

Today's coaches and their assistants often have to live up to the expectations of a variety of swimmers. There is often a wide spectrum of individual hopes and aspirations within a typical large club. With the money lanes on one side of the pool and the animal lanes on the other side, the implications are obvious.

In many instances, coaches may be expected to look after the needs of every swimmer who wants to try out for the team, irrespective of a swimmer's ability and level of aspiration. The coaches have a widely diversified role spread over groups of youngsters at many levels of ability, often with great attendant pressures.

The situation has a built-in potential for conflict and strain that affect a coach's ability to function at full potential. There is an obvious need to adjust the role of the coach to meet the needs of swimmers and also to meet the coach's personal motivations and ambitions in the sport.

The role of a successful coach relies on the ability to combine winning with generating support, while retaining the flexibility to handle individual swimmers according to their needs. Societal changes are making this aim increasingly difficult. There is a need for a careful delineation of different types of coaching roles, based on each coach's abilities and career goals.

Two-Way Commitment
Not all coaches want to produce world-beaters. Neither do all swimmers want to be world-beaters. It would be an ideal situation were it easily

possible to match swimmers and coaches in various tiers of competition according to their individual levels of commitment. But in a free enterprise society, it is impossible to automatically place swimmers and coaches in such groupings.

The next best approach may well be a process of natural selection in which "like meets like" in the sense that talented and dedicated swimmers who want to reach the pinnacle of the sport, seek out coaches whose programs and known motivations also are aimed at the top. This implies a need for clear communication.

At the outset the coach should outline, in detail, the exact extent of the commitment involved. The coach should make it clear that the word *commitment* implies a pledge to faithfully undertake the requirements of the task. The swimmer then should be given time for thought and consideration before signing on for the long haul.

The time spent in making the extent of the commitment clear to the swimmer is a wise preliminary. Misunderstanding could lead to years of comparatively fruitless effort, and so I stress again the importance of clear and complete understanding of the two-way commitment involved.

The use of the term *two-way commitment* is germane to the discussion. Consider this case in point. Recently, I was told of a top-flight swimmer, supposedly under the direction of a coach dedicated to top-level achievement, who trained by herself in the early mornings, winter and summer.

She was given the key to the pool gate, and she would let herself into the premises to faithfully follow a workout written for her on a small piece of paper. This is an example of what is not a two-way commitment. The case just described is obviously an extreme exception rather than the rule, but it highlights the need for equal commitment by both swimmer and coach. And it does pose such questions as, "How many swimmers are more dedicated than their coaches?" and "How many swimmers are in the wrong programs?"

We need to ascertain, as far as possible, the respective and relative commitment levels of both swimmers and coaches. Perhaps fewer coaches than we think are keen on producing world-beaters. This may be true, or it may not be true. I am merely posing the question. Certainly, we need better information on where a coach's hopes and aspirations lie.

If we don't know the level of a coach's commitment, we are taking too much for granted, especially when planning and funding so-called elite programs. The same is true when we assume that all swimmers are committed to becoming champions. It cuts both ways and indicates the need for clear communication on the subject between swimmer and coach.

Questions on Commitment

The difficulties in obtaining jobs, even for the brightest graduates, may have resulted in many swimmers having to reassess their priorities. Some may choose to quit the sport, while others may reduce their commitment to participation in programs that require less training.

At a time when a return to fast distance training is strongly indicated (and vindicated), we can see how other pressures on a swimmer's time significantly compound the problem. It is clear that we need to develop an understanding of how change in North American society is specifically affecting the young people with whom we work. In short, we need to ask searching, preliminary questions on various levels of commitment prior to engaging in technical and administrative fact-finding missions.

And what about the human factor? To what extent are societal changes reflected in the sport of swimming, and how do these changes affect attitudes, commitment, and discipline? For example, a committed, dedicated swimmer is not likely to infringe on team discipline. Most disciplinary problems seem to stem from less-committed swimmers who have come along for the ride. It certainly saps and drains team morale when coaches and team managers have to deal with swimmers imbibing alcohol or out on nocturnal excursions.

Finally, a survey by sport psychologists aimed at assessing the commitment levels of coaches and swimmers in different types of programs could well yield information extremely valuable to future planning.

❖ ❖ ❖

HIGH SCHOOL SWIMMING IS BIG IN SOUTH AFRICA

Penny Heyns, who in 1996 became the first woman to win gold in both the 100-meter and the 200-meter breaststroke at the same Olympics, is yet another product of the South African school swimming system.

Vodacom, cellular phone and telecommunications giant, recently awarded Penny the richest single sponsorship yet concluded by an individual South African sportsperson. The sponsorship, which includes lucrative incentives should she establish new world records or win major events, is worth more than 1 million dollars.

Penny Heyns first came to the fore as a talented school swimmer in her home town of Amanzimtoti in the province of Natal. Later she joined a group of South African swimmers competing for the University of Nebraska at Lincoln, where more top-flight coaching ensured continued improvement to her present world-beating status.

As an interesting aside, Lincoln is the same city where, exactly 30 years ago, 2 South African girls, Karen Muir and Ann Fairlie, earlier products of high school swimming, won 2 American backstroke titles when competing for their visiting national team at the U.S. Championships. And, by another interesting coincidence, Penny's world-record time for the 100-meter breaststroke in Atlanta, is about the same time as the mark set by Ann Fairlie, for a 100-meter backstroke world record in Beziers, France, shortly before the Lincoln meet. How standards have advanced!

But I digress. Let me tell you about school swimming in South Africa in general, and in the large city of Johannesburg in particular. High school swimming in Johannesburg is an important part of that city's sporting program. In fact, participation in some form of sport such as swimming, tennis, rugby, field hockey, or soccer, is a requisite if you don't want to be considered a ninny.

Their Own 50-Meter Pools

Most Johannesburg high schools have their own outdoor 50-meter pools built by fund-raising and assistance from the provincial government. In many schools, participation in sport is mandatory.

I know of several schools where swimming, for example, is compulsory unless a pupil is excused for medical reasons.

High schools such as King Edward VII, Jeppe Boys' High, Jeppe Girls' High, Parktown Boys' High, Highlands North, Athlone, and Helpmekaar have a rich tradition in producing swimmers who later went on to achieve national and international success. During the summer months, a system of separate dual league inter–high school meets operates for both girls and boys. Many of the country's great swimmers had their first experience of competitive swimming in this system before later coming under the coaching of leading professionals at their respective swimming schools.

Traditional Rivalry

The school swimming season starts in mid-October and culminates in March with a series of big meets at Ellis Park Swimming Stadium, attended on average by crowds of 3,000 to 4,000 shrill, shrieking school children at each meet. For the best part of 70 to 80 years, certainly longer than I can remember, traditional rivals such as King Edward VII and Jeppe Boys' High School, have battled it out for the title of Johannesburg's premier swimming school.

The best swimmers from the Johannesburg area are then selected to compete in the South African Schools Swimming Championships, which are held at a different venue each year. The selection of venue for this important meet follows a pattern of one year at the sea level and the following year at altitude. Most of the South African hinterland lies on an escarpment ranging from 4,000 to 6,000 feet above sea level. Johannesburg, like Denver, Colorado, is located at approximately 6,500 feet above sea level, and so swimmers going to compete at sea level seem to have an advantage over swimmers from the coastal cities and towns.

Four years ago, shortly after South Africa was reinstated in FINA (Federation Internationale de Natation Amateur), swimming's international governing body, I returned to Johannesburg for the first time in 20 years. I attended both the annual Johannesburg Girls' Inter–High School Meet and the National High School Championships in Bloemfontein, where I saw Penny Heyns swim for the first time. The extent to which organized school swimming at all levels kept competitive swimming

Picture by courtesy of The Star

Picture by courtesy of The Star

Left: At Ellis Park Swimming Stadium in Johannesburg, South Africa, where I coached for 25 years, large crowds attended each meet. This picture taken in 1947 shows a junior school meet in progress. Each school's supporters are seated in allocated parts of the stands and are distinguishable by their school uniforms. Parents are seated on bleachers on the pool deck. *Right:* A 13-year-old Ann Fairlie shortly after defeating Ria van Velsen (Netherlands), the reigning European 100-meter backstroke champion, in a 1963 South Africa versus Netherlands dual meet. At the age of 17, Fairlie became the world-record holder at the distance. I coached her since she was 10.

alive in South Africa during the long apartheid years was immediately apparent to me. In Johannesburg, little had changed at the Girls' Inter–High as a continuing lineup of school and city buses disgorged hundreds and hundreds of shrieking, swim-crazy kids, complete with huge mascots, chants, and songs. They stamped their feet on the wooden bleachers, creating a noise not unlike a Zulu impi banging spears on ox-hide shields as they advance to battle.

Schools Promote Swimming

In the 1960s, the Johannesburg Schools' Swimming Association sent a team of boys and girls every year to England and Europe. Many of these swimmers went on to win at the national and international levels, some of them competing on American college scholarships.

The cooperation between professional coaches and the school swimming authorities, not only in Johannesburg but around the country, is an important reason for the popularity and the success of swimming in South Africa despite the fact that there are only about 10,000 registered competi-

tive swimmers outside of school swimming.

The leading professional coaches have always emphasized the importance of giving every assistance to school swimming. Many coaches have working arrangements with the schools whereby they supply coaching staff, at a moderate rate, to teach swimming during school hours in return for free pool time after school ends for the day. This type of liaison also ensures that talented youngsters are encouraged to join swimming clubs and advanced coaching squads.

Identify Talent in the Schools

It is important to identify talent early. Youngsters should learn correct stroke mechanics at an early age so that efficient swimming becomes as easy as walking.

Around nine years is the great skill-learning age. There is an almost dream-like quality about the ease with which children learn motor skills at this age. This is a good age to develop the ability to swim long distances, to practice strokes and develop the endurance base for harder training when older.

Ann Fairlie and I at my International Swim Camp at Bethlehem, South Africa, in December 1966. A few months earlier Fairlie had broken the world 100-meter and 110-yard backstroke records and won both the American and British national titles.

Courtesy of Cecil Colwin

How does an experienced coach recognize potential talent? Usually, a talented youngster is able to perform a new skill after only one or two attempts. Similarly, the talented kid seems to respond more quickly than others to an increase in training workload. I've notice these two phenomena time and again in working with talented children. Other coaches also use these criteria in assessing potential talent. (Not all talented youngsters first come to light in this fashion. Others may be diamonds in the rough destined to shine later.)

Of course, these are not the only indicators. Another good pointer is the way talented youngsters enter the arms in the water at the start of a swimming stroke. They seem almost to nurse the oncoming flow of the water as the hand submerges.

What sort of programs identify promising young swimmers? Joining a swimming club and participating in the various age-group programs is a good way to start. An even better way, of course, is to do what South Africa and so many prominent swimming nations do: encourage swimming in the schools.

Coaches should try to visit neighborhood schools to show instruction films, give talks on the sport, and encourage youngsters to participate. Better still, encourage local authorities to build swimming pools, and include swimming as part of the physical education curriculum.

Let's say it unequivocally: Any country that does not have a strong base of swimming in the schools starts with a distinct disadvantage compared with countries that do.

It should be a top priority to identify and develop as much potential talent as possible. Don't fail to look in the rural areas. This is where tough kids can be found. Some of them become world-beaters. I could cite a few instances of world champions in several countries first discovered in this manner.

To sum up: The first rule of international success is, FIND THE TALENT!

❖ ❖ ❖

PROGRAM PLANNING: THE HUMAN FACTOR

True leadership is concerned with the successful direction of human energies and not administration alone.

When Japanese swimmer Yoshiyuki Tsuruta won his country's first Olympic gold medal in Amsterdam in 1928, his victory inspired the world's first national training program. Japan's coaches, enthused and excited, reasoned that a formal development plan would discover even more swimmers to emulate Tsuruta's Olympic success.

They started a national program to find and train potential world champion swimmers. The result was an almost clean sweep by the Japanese at the 1932 and 1936 Olympics. Nobody expected the Japanese to pose a threat at the Los Angeles Olympics in 1932, and their success took the world of swimming by surprise.

The Japanese success was based on an innovative action program which stressed talent identification, good stroke mechanics, and hard training. The plan was designed and implemented by coaches, without need for a top-heavy administrative structure. Instructional films were made of the world's best swimmers and shown to schoolchildren throughout the country. They experimented with training workloads and found that youngsters could absorb far more hard work than hitherto thought possible.

The Japanese plan was simple in concept and visible for all to see and understand. They were enthusiastic and had a vital sense of urgency. The result was a strong will to win. Their experienced coaches believed their plan would succeed, but they knew that enthusiasm alone was not enough. Energy and inspired leadership were needed to convert plans into action.

The success of the Australian swimming team at the 1956 Melbourne Olympics was another step forward in the growth of the national program concept. Lacking year-round facilities, they took their pre-Olympic preparation out of its normal framework by training in tropical Townsville in northern Queensland for the winter months.

The result of the basic coach-swimmer action program was that Australia won the lion's share of gold medals at the Olympics. Although, like the Japanese program in the 1930s, the Australian approach was simple in concept, it should not be overlooked that their coaches were regarded as among the most innovative in the world at that time. But, most important of all, their coaches and swimmers alike were imbued with a superhuman will to win.

Compared with the simple approach of the Australians, the East Germans meanwhile were developing a centrally controlled training structure in 10 key centers around the country. Their program was founded upon talent identification of a select few who were trained progressively harder over the years. Like the Australians and Japanese before them, the East Germans were innovative. They worked in groups of highly trained specialists: coaches, trainers, biochemists, biomechanists, psychologists, and physicians. It is a pity their successes will be remembered mainly for chemical technologies which enabled them to swim not unusually well, but abnormally well.

When the East German concept of formal development programs spread to Western Europe and North America, a tendency grew to overemphasize the administrative side of planning. There is a difference between real leadership and a management-driven organization which, in crisis situations, begets a bureaucracy that quickly produces reams of statistics, reports, more new plans, and panaceas.

Inevitably, a great deal of window dressing takes place to ensure that they are seen to be doing the right thing even if they are not. This is when activity becomes confused with accomplishment, management by objectives is allowed to run wild, and plans appear geared to machines rather than people. The truth is that there should be a balance between effective administration and skilled face-to-face leadership.

True leadership is concerned with people and the successful direction of human energies to accomplish desired goals. A great leader is one who can do this day after day and year after year, in a variety of situations. Good leaders make it their business to understand the people they work with, relating their individual goals to the main goal of the organization. Many people are capable of designing plans and setting up administrative structures and functions to administer them, but, unfortunately, few understand the human dynamic that translates plans into action. Aristotle said, "With regard to excellence, it is not enough to know, but we must try to have and use it." A common failing of sport bureaucratic systems is to assume that putting policies and systems in place automatically leads to action.

There is a big difference in knowing what needs to be done and actually doing it. Designing behavioral objectives does not guarantee success without the leadership that inspires and energizes everyone to work together to achieve the final goal. Unless you can attract people to your side, they will not behave as you expect. Lack of leadership is usually the problem. Therefore, the first important element in setting a plan on its course to success is the skill level of the people in charge. There is a difference between being a boss, a manager or administrator, and a real leader. Real leaders are more apt to want to persuade people to act and move with them to a shared goal. The end result is a will to win and a desire to belong on the part of all.

Some planners will write a set of objectives instead of trying to form a vision of what it is they wish to achieve. Envisioning the final outcome of a venture should not be confused with the overworked goal-setting process used by followers of the management-by-objectives cult. They have yet to learn that the ability to see some future

Left: At the 1928 Olympic Games in Amsterdam, Yoshiyuki Tsuruta won the 200-meter breaststroke and became the first Japanese swimmer to win an Olympic title. He won the event again at Los Angeles in 1932. Tsuruta's success inspired the world's first national training program when Japan sought even more champions to emulate his success. *Right:* Five members of the 1960 Australian Olympic swim team pictured in Townsville prior to leaving for Rome: (left to right) Neville Hayes, Bob Windle, Dawn Fraser, David Dickson, and Kevin Berry.

happening in the mind's eye is a big step toward achieving at least some significant part of it. Not only does visualizing form a regular part of the preparation of great athletes, it is also used by the best leaders in many fields of human endeavor.

Successful plans start with a vision and not a set of management-by-objectives goals. In fact, management by objectives assumes that writing down what needs to be done is enough for a plan to succeed. But knowing what needs to be done is not the same as being able to do it. As William Shakespeare said: "If to do were as easy as to know what were good to do, chapels had been churches and poor men's cottages prince's palaces."

Once a nation has started to win Olympic medals, how do you maintain the momentum? In any national program, the wave of momentum tends to crest then ease off. It is easier to develop momentum than to retain it. While it is good to keep in touch with basics and to try to retain the core values of an organization, it is a common error for leaders to believe that what was successful in the past will be successful in the future. When this phase of thinking pervades an organization,

momentum starts to slow down. This is because, having achieved what was visualized earlier, we suddenly find that there is no new motivating vision. What worked in the past will not necessarily work in the future, particularly if you try to remain on top merely by massaging and preserving the methods that brought you to where you are. Avoid peering through the rearview mirror instead of looking to the future.

Anyone can hold the helm when the sea is calm, but what happens when results are less than expected, particularly after sets of major games such as the Olympics or World Championships? Under such circumstances many so-called leaders panic and revert to crisis management.

Instead of being able to think in the saddle, they tend to tear down existing plans in the hope that starting afresh will mend the situation.

Experienced coaches know what happens when you try to psych up swimmers who are already psyched. They become tense, disorganized, and perform below par. Similarly, while inspired leadership can generate powerful energies and move people to unexpected success, it also has its limits. In the same way a coach times the psychological peaking of a team with the team's physiological peaking, so should there be a fine-tuning of the emotional level of all personnel as a national plan moves to its peak goals.

Effective leaders have the ability to continually encourage people to accept new challenges and seek new heights, but not to the extent that they become emotionally exhausted. Great leaders have the ability to turn visions into deeds. Not all of them have charisma, but they are able to share their visions with their co-workers, and show them how to accept challenges and overcome obstacles. Above all, they are able to create and sustain the energy that brings an enterprise to a successful conclusion.

❖ ❖ ❖

TAKING STOCK AT CONCORD

When the East German (DDR) swimmers arrived at Concord, California, August 27, 1974, excitement was intense as the scene was set for the "Dual Meet of the Decade."

Their immediate problem was acclimatization. They had rewritten a good portion of the world-record book 3 days before in Vienna. With 10 hours of jet lag and 26 hours of traveling behind them, they were not fresh from their victories.

They arrived at night and had a late dinner. *Verboten* items on the table, tacitly indicated by their sports doctor, were left quietly untouched. Then they went off to sleep in a special wing of their hotel.

They appeared well rested the next morning, a well-disciplined group but still quietly playful. The first impression was of the size of their women swimmers, taller and heavier than the American women. Their pale skins were a marked contrast to the bronzed heroes and heroines of the California swim scene.

Over at the Diablo Pool, their first workout session was a shakedown swim. There was no rigid control over the workout. Swimmers entered the water when they were ready, often after some preliminary horseplay and a few arm-swinging exercises of the Niels Bukh variety.

Despite the apparent informality, their coaches had their logbooks out and were itemizing the swimmers' activities. The swimmers knew what they had to do and left the pool individually as they finished.

They loosened up with easy paddling, getting the vibrations of plane travel out of their bodies. As they progressed into the session, it was obvious that they were trying to get back into the swing of things as quickly as possible. They tried to get the feel of the pool and the groove of their stroking. Their coaches assisted them with small points of stroke technique as they did separate pulling and kicking, as well as full-stroke swimming.

They used the lane ropes often as they changed from one stroke to another, grabbing the lane and giving a little tug to maintain speed as they switched. They also did much ducking under the water with porpoise-like surface dives, obviously trying to become relaxed.

Most of the swimmers exercised on all four strokes. Their breaststrokers sometimes did every alternate stroke underwater to get the feeling of continuous movement. The freestylers allowed their entry arms to glide out in front of them close to the surface of the water. This was apparent in the other styles as well. But, when they competed in the meet, these tendencies disappeared completely.

The DDR backstroke women did pulling drills with the aid of pull-buoy floats. They practiced kicking with wrists crossed, hands clasped and out of the water. The breaststroke women, particularly Karla Linke, had a strong suggestion of dolphin in her overall movement. Their breaststroke arm action was well-rounded and resembled an abbreviated butterfly pull. They kicked very soon after the head lift in the breaststroke. Their strokes flowed in continuous action.

Their butterfly swimmers swam the standard style and Rosemarie Kother used her tremendously powerful back muscles to good advantage. Ulrike Richter's backstroke had a strong similarity to Roland Matthes's—a loose, bent-elbow recovery and a firm, fast pull. She has a fast arm stroke with less shoulder rotation than the U.S. girls. Her leg action was narrow, very supple and relaxed. Richter used a straight-arm posture in the backstroke start and was as fast as Matthes on the turn. With the exception of Matthes, their women swimmers had better turns and starts than their men.

Generally, the DDR swimmers are excellent stroke technicians. For the most part, their women appeared more fluent than the men. Yet, there were some swimmers who displayed dropped elbows and other fundamental errors. Kornelia Ender, the fastest woman sprinter in the world, had a peculiar idiosyncrasy in her left arm entry. Her hand did an awkward wiggle as it reached the water. Her large feet came up very high. She had great foot flexibility. Even her toes appeared to bend at the top of her kick.

The overall impression of the DDR women was their exceptional well-balanced muscular development. My inquiries yielded the information that they used a composite system of weight training.

They maintained that their great strength and larger muscles were the result of strength as well as endurance weight training. Similar to the water training program, their high stress days of weight training were devoted to using heavier weights with low repetitions in a larger number of sets.

For endurance training, they kept to standard sets of 3 with repetitions progressively building from approximately 7 to 10. While they also used specific resistance training on land, they followed a general routine to develop all the major muscles of the body.

For specific arm strength for swimming, they bought large quantities of the centrifugal device (Accommodator Mini-Gym) marketed by Doc Counsilman. They use this machine for strength development with few repetitions. They also used weight training for the development of flexibility with as much extension and flexion in the joints as possible.

As the days went by, their workouts included more pace work and 25-meter and 50-meter sprints at the end of the sessions. They concluded each 50-meter sprint with a fast flip turn. Matthes did a broken 200 pace swim with 15 seconds between 50s in his last premeet workout at the Concord pool. He swam each 50 in 30 seconds.

While warming up, many of the swimmers changed strokes halfway down the lap of the pool.

The more experienced swimmers seemed to be left more on their own. For example, Ender swam easily up and down the pool, gradually getting ready, then called across to one of the team doctors to time her for a 25-meter dash. Other swimmers were systematically put through a few 25-meter sprints by one of the assistant coaches on either side of the pool. Warming up for the start of the first day of competition, Matthes swam a fast 100-meter freestyle in the practice pool.

In the actual meet, the DDR swimmers did exactly what was expected of them, based on their performances in Vienna, and probably the same can be said about Matthes who lost a backstroke race for the first time in seven years. He was beaten by the up-and-coming John Naber. The Germans were cool under pressure, especially on the first day, when they didn't look as good as they did when they hit world-record form in the next session. Their preparation by a well-organized team of coaches and officials was excellent. What we saw at Concord could be described as a synthesis of the DDR approach to sport and swimming, in particular good organization and intelligent implementation.

Good psychology, medical assistance, and nutritional knowledge are all areas available to any coach or nation willing to take the preparation of athletes out of the normal framework. The administrators of sport in the DDR have been efficient and have taken great care to explore all the areas that could prove practical in developing their standards. The lessons of Concord? The DDR claimed from the start that they were out to do their best but not necessarily win. "There will be many other meets in the future," they said. What they did not deny was that this dual meet, midway between Munich and Montreal, would serve as a very useful stocktaking. The United States as well as DDR now both well know their respective strengths and weaknesses.

✧ ✧ ✧

EAST GERMAN SWIMMING

Interview with Gert Barthelmes, Former Secretary General of the Former DDR Swim Federation

CC: I am interested in the method of talent identification used in the DDR.

GB: Our sports system works together with the schools in that the children have swimming classes in the second and third grades. Already, at this time, we are able to identify the more talented, the more capable swimmers, and put them together in a group and train them once or twice a week. And then the best from these groups go forward into the sports centers.

CC: Are the sports centers at particular locations?

GB: We have nine such sports centers in the DDR . . . in the biggest cities in the DDR.

CC: Is it true that families move with those youngsters who are fortunate enough to be farmed into these sport centers?

GB: That's not true as a rule. Most of these swimmers who are chosen for these sports centers, are boarding school students, so they go to the boarding schools nearby. If, however, the parents' professional interest can be connected with this move, sometimes that happens.

CC: So those children who move are those who usually have difficulty in finding a training location, those from small towns or villages, for example?

GB: I cannot really say that because 80 percent of the swimmers come from the big cities, only 20 percent from the smaller towns.

CC: How do you assess the talent of youngsters— by present performance or scientific evaluation?

GB: Both.

CC: Would you please tell me something about your scientific testing? I have heard that you X-ray the wrists of children to assess biological age, for example?

GB: That is not only our method. That's a very common method. To use this in an athletic program is very common. We use this to assess the possible workload we apply.

CC: What other testing methods do you use?

GB: You must realize that we have thousands of children to work with and so we do not have the capacity to do that sort of research with all of them. There are more general ways of estimating who may have more chance of success than others.

CC: So, in other words, when you have a talented athlete who has reached a certain level of achievement, you need to know a lot more about him?

GB: And, of course, you can apply this to early development as well.

CC: The early training of the child . . . is this based on tremendous distances to be covered in training, the development of endurance?

GB: We begin by making sure that they can do all four basic styles, and then we proceed to develop endurance.

CC: What type of competitive program do you have for the development of young swimmers?

GB: Up to the age of 10 we have a competitive system which is based mostly on the localities in which they live. After that they have district competition, pyramided up to the national level.

Interview with Dr. Horst Röeder, a Former Vice President of the DDR Gymnastics and Sports Union

CC: Would you please tell me something about how you train the coaches in the DDR?

HR: The coaches in DDR are state-educated teachers. They were educated at the University for Sports in Leipzig.

CC: When you say "teachers," do you mean that they teach school subjects as well as physical education and sport?

HR: There are two branches. There are those who teach sport and other subjects. For example they would teach sport, German language, and geography. That is one branch in the training of teachers of sport. The second branch is composed of those who teach only sports and later on are involved in training and coaching a sports group or organization. They study for four years.

CC: What subjects do they study?

HR: It is a very comprehensive program. It is 40 percent based on theory and 60 percent on practical subjects.

CC: *Would the syllabus content be basic to all sports and then specializing in particular sports later?*

HR: In general, two years is devoted to basic education and two years to special training. The special training involves detailed specialization in the sport in which the coach will work later on.

CC: *Have your methods been influenced much by the work of Diem, Gersheler, Reindell, etcetera?*

HR: These are the names of West Germans. We have a new family of specialists who have arisen in sport in the DDR. After 1945, we have developed a new generation of specialists—and we have very little contact with the old generation.

CC: *Who are the creative minds in DDR sport?*

HR: You are really asking for the reason for the success in our sport?

CC: *Yes, it is obvious you have done a lot of thinking to raise the level of your sport.*

HR: The first reason is support for sport by the Government, the State. Our leading party is the Socialist Youth Party. They believe they are right in placing great obligation to youth and sport. There is distinct legislation for the promotion of sport in our country. For example, every child in our republic has the right to travel without paying any fee, any due, to take part in sports competitions. This is part of our legislation concerning sport. That is the first reason for our success in sport . . . the very generous support for sport by the State.

CC: *I understand that there is a fund in DDR whereby children pay a small amount of money as their contribution to the cost of sporting activity in DDR?*

HR: That is correct.

CC: *How much is that, if I may ask?*

HR: In North American currency, that would be seven to eight cents per month.

CC: *Then, any child can use any facility?*

HR: Any child can use any facility.

CC: *By appointment or is the facility always ready*

in different programs, depending on what sport the child is officially participating in?

HR: Membership in our sporting program is voluntary and participation in particular sports may depend on the facilities existing in certain cities, towns, or districts. For instance, a small village may not have a pool and then a child has no opportunity to take part in swimming. But there are facilities for other kinds of sport such as track and field, etc.

CC: *Is it true that you have a testing program to test the aptitude of children for particular sports?*

HR: I believe that there is no such program anywhere in the world. Talent is very complex, very complicated.

CC: *Natural aptitude shows up in performance . . .*

HR: Yes, you spot talent in competition. It is empirical.

CC: *When new nations rise to success, people look for the magic . . .*

HR: You are quite right. It is intelligent, hard work.

CC: *May we now continue to the other reasons to which you ascribe the success of DDR in sport?*

HR: The second reason is the special interest of our republic and its youth in sport and in competition. This has a close connection with the first reason. I would like to give you an example. The DDR Swimming Federation increased its membership by 20,000 during 1970–73.

CC: *Are these all competitive swimmers?*

HR: Yes, these are active competitive swimmers and of these 20,000 new members, 95 percent are children. This shows the particular interest of the youth in swimming. We have a growing membership, but our facilities are not growing at the same rate! Unfortunately, we cannot take all those children who want to participate in swimming for this reason.

CC: *The success of your world-class swimmers has created this interest?*

HR: There are now many others who want to emulate the champions. They see it is possible to reach the top by hard work and discipline.

CC: *May I interrupt your explanation of the reasons for your success and ask a question concerning the impressive physical development? Is there a special program you have developed for the muscular development of athletes in particular sports?*

HR: In certain sports we have a special program to intensify the constitutional power of our athletes.*

CC: *Your girl swimmers generally have superior muscular development to any other group in the world. Their stroke techniques are also generally very good.*

HR: There are other swimmers in the world who have similar constitutions. Now, for the third reason . . . we have established, in the last 25 years, a certain kind of organization in sports. This organization is suited to our type of situation. We could not copy any other system. We had to build an absolutely new organization of sport, a system of sport, in our republic. It had to be in tune with our potential and existing facilities. We have a certain orientation to sport in the Soviet Union. But we have a lot of specialties in our country and we have used these in developing our sport.

CC: *In a recent interview with* Swimming World, *I mentioned that I thought the American success in swimming had evolved almost naturally over a period of 50 to 60 years . . . but the DDR has had to methodically plan its rise to success in a comparatively short time . . .*

HR: I am forced to give a diplomatic answer because we cannot praise ourselves!

CC: *Self-praise is no recommendation anyway!*

HR: (laughing) You are right! But every country has its problems. You have them in Canada. The Americans have theirs. We in DDR also have a lot of problems to be solved.

CC: *Let's not use the word "problems" but rather "difficulties" or "obstacles"! If we had no "difficulties," it would be too easy to be interesting.*

HR: (laughing) That is our opinion, too!

When the East German regime collapsed in 1989, and the Stasi *(secret police) files were discovered, revealing large-scale use of performance-enhancing drugs, Dr. Röeder's comment was to prove the biggest understatement in the history of swimming.*

✧ ✧ ✧

LAYERS NOT DEPTHS

"Depth" as a concept in world ranking lists, has been used too loosely and too carelessly. For a swimmer to climb to the top from the lower echelons of the rankings is a rarity, an exception rather than the rule. Future talent should be close to the top to have justifiable expectations of gold medal success.

Most newcomers of outstanding merit usually break into the rankings with an initial placing near the top, within striking distance of the best. In essence, it may be wise not to be smug when a program seems to exalt in having great depth. It depends on what kind of depth you are looking for. Unfortunately, all too often it is found that a promising swimmer in the middle and lower brackets will do little more than promise.

In assessing a country's real strength, it is far more realistic to study actual results and not the promise of things to come. In this respect, it is interesting to note that any country's standing can change very suddenly and unexpectedly. At one moment, a country can be at the top of the heap, and the next moment, because of retirements, be almost back to square one. Australia in 1972 and Canada in 1984 are examples of this.

Overlapping Layers Maintain Momentum

A study of previously successful national programs worldwide shows the real challenge is not in creating the necessary initial momentum, but in maintaining it by continuing to invest in hard work in the pool and being constantly innovative to ensure that a new layer of good swimmers is always ready to move up into place. Unless this occurs, the wave of success tends to crest and quickly fall off. And it should be understood that this doesn't mean having the "depth" that goes down the listing to the umpteenth place, but rather what perhaps can best be termed "quality depth."

The choice of the phrase "into place" is not accidental. It implies that the next layer of swimmers will not move up behind the first layer, but instead will be ready to move into a position that overlaps the first layer. This holds true for clubs as well as nations. This is to ensure that newcomers gain the experience of training with and competing against the champions before the champions retire. In this manner, they will develop the pride in performance that is the foundation of motivation. Most importantly, this type of overlapping layer ensures the continuation, even the improvement, of already established standards.

In the past, most planners of national programs spoke about building a pyramid, broad at the base and tapering to a pinnacle from which the best swimmers would emerge. They reasoned that the broader the base of the pyramid, the higher the pinnacle would be in terms of performance.

In this respect, the superpower nations with their colossal populations would possess an insurmountable advantage over smaller nations. This may have been the case at one time, but it certainly isn't now.

Matching Quality for Quantity

To their credit, it was the Australians who, looking at the depth of the United States swimming

---

Fig. 1 Quality Depth

Based on the official 1994 FINA rankings for 50-meter pools, January 1 to August 28, 1994

Without restricting the number of swimmers per event for each country to 2, as in international competition, I have taken the first 6 placings in each individual event (no relays) and scored as follows: 1st—7 points, 2nd—5 points, 3rd—4 points, 4th—3 points, 5th—2 points, 6th—1 point

MEN		WOMEN	
USA	116	China	114
Australia	65	USA	70
Russia	36	Australia	67
Hungary	18	Hungary	14
Germany	12	Germany	10
Great Britain	12	Costa Rica	7
Sweden	7	Canada	4
New Zealand	7	South Africa	3
France	7	Russia	3
Finland	7	Ukraine	2
Moldavia	5	Great Britain	1
China	4	Japan	1
Brazil	3	Czech Republic	1
Italy	3		
Canada	3		

Total of men's and women's points:

1. USA—186 2. Australia—132 3. China—118

The United States had more than 2 swimmers ranked in the first 6 in 1 event on only 6 occasions, while the Australians had more than 2 swimmers ranked in 1 event on 2 occasions.

program, first said, "What we wouldn't do just to have America's scrap heap. If we can't match them quantity for quantity, then at least we can try to beat them quality for quality." The Australians then proved the validity of this approach with their best-ever success at the Melbourne Olympics in 1956: eight gold medals, four silver, and two bronze, not to mention many others who reached finals.

First the Australians and then the East Germans (albeit with the aid of performance-enhancing drugs), showed there were other approaches to national development that could even the odds.

Now, years later, this philosophy is being followed on an even larger scale as more nations enter the fray.

The East Germans (in their time) nearly always had a group of swimmers at the very top, while their remaining swimmers showed rather insignificantly in scattered clusters way down the lists. These lower ranked swimmers rarely made it to the top of the heap, but remained a kind of residue in the system.

Consider this: In 1986 at the World Championships in Madrid, when the East Germans were

---

Fig. 2 Quality Depth

Based on the World Championships, Rome, September 5 to 11, 1994

Restricting the number of swimmers per event for each country to 2, as in international competition, I have taken the first 6 placings in each individual event (no relays) and scored as follows: 1st—7 points, 2nd—5 points, 3rd—4 points, 4th—3 points, 5th—2 points, 6th—1 point

MEN		WOMEN	
USA	56	China	102
Russia	38	USA	60
Hungary	35	Australia	45
Finland	29	Germany	22
Australia	25	Russia	10
Germany	18	Canada	9
New Zealand	15	Costa Rica	8
Spain	13	Hungary	7
Poland	11	Belgium	6
Sweden	11	Denmark	5
Brazil	7	Italy	5
France	6	New Zealand	2
Great Britain	5	Ireland	2
Japan	4	South Africa	1
Lithuania	4	Japan	1
Belgium	4	Czech Republic	1
Canada	3		
Croatia	3		
Italy	3		
Japan	1		

Total of men's and women's points (first 3 countries)

1. USA—116 2. China—103 3. Australia—70

Fig. 3 Examples of Layer Groupings in the USA, Australia, China, and Canada

From 1993 FINA world rankings for 50-meter pools: 100-, 200-, 400-, 800-meter freestyle

Women's 100-meter freestyle
(Rankings taken up to 118th place)

	USA	AUS	CHN	CAN
Under 0.55	1	0	3	0
Under 0.56	2	1	4	0
Under 0.57	1	0	8	1
Under 0.58	16	8	20	4

Women's 400-meter freestyle
(Rankings up to 112th place)

	USA	AUS	CHN	CAN
Under 4:12	3	0	1	0
Under 4:16	2	3	7	0
Under 4:17	3	1	2	2
Under 4:22	17	5	6	6

Women's 200-meter freestyle
(Rankings taken up to 112th place)

	USA	AUS	CHN	CAN
Under 2:00	1	0	5	0
Under 2:02	2	1	4	0
Under 2:05	22	7	8	8

Women's 800-meter freestyle
(Rankings up to 99th place)

	USA	AUS	CHN	CAN
Under 8:45	7	2	6	0
Under 8:50	3	3	3	0
Under 8:55	16	0	3	5
Under 8:57	5	2	2	1

probably at the peak of their success, their team consisted of only 15 swimmers! Similarly, a look at the present Chinese rankings shows a format similar to that of the East Germans, and at the 1994 World Championships in Rome, China was represented by only 11 swimmers.

❖ ❖ ❖

KEEPING YOUR COOL WHEN ANGER STRIKES

When the tempers of finely drawn athletes become frayed, anger may strike in even the happiest of teams. While venting anger may sometimes serve to clear the air, sudden outbursts may only upset team morale. As leaders and role models, all coaches should know how to keep their cool, and help others to do the same. Learning to control one's emotions is one of the positive spin-offs of competitive swimming.

Angry confrontations often stem from breaking team rules. These rules usually govern pool courtesy, and behavior at practice and meets and while traveling. They are for the good of all members and the smooth functioning of the team.

Rivalry between swimmers, swimming families, coaches, and teams may sometimes lead to jealousy and angry, unpleasant incidents. Sometimes, an already tense situation can be inflamed by irate parents who leap too quickly to the defense of their children before knowing all the facts. Such incidents have the potential to split a team, with rival factions seeking to set the blame on others. It is very important for a coach to be able to manage and control the anger between diverse groups on a team.

Although anger may be triggered by many reasons, specific events, and provocations, it should be appreciated that anger also involves complex feelings. We may express anger in many ways—by becoming annoyed, irritated, frustrated, furious, enraged, and even hurt. Anger that is not managed may lead to a prolonged series of negative or even destructive thoughts and actions.

For instance, a swimmer may feel jealous about the success of a close rival or labor under the misapprehension that the coach has favorites. Veiled anger may show up during that swimmer's circle training with the occurrence of minor skirmishes. For example, a swimmer may obstruct and annoy another while swimming repeat sets. The coach may notice a developing situation and also become annoyed. Then more people become involved and angered.

At this juncture, a wise coach will ask himself, "Why does this swimmer feel the need to interfere with others in the training lane? Why has this swimmer got an axe to grind? What is the swimmer trying to communicate to others on the team? What is the potential threat or loss that would prompt this type of behavior?"

There could be many underlying reasons for the swimmer's behavior. When a coach has a good understanding of the various personalities on the team, sometimes answers may come readily to mind. For example, a youngster who has been spoiled at home may be prepared to go through life believing that everything needs to go a certain way because he or she wants it that way.

Then there are swimmers who feel a need to control other swimmers by taking charge of the way a workout should proceed. A training pace that is too fast (in this swimmer's view) may need to be slowed down, or maybe the pace is too slow and needs to be speeded up. This swimmer believes, "Others on the team will take advantage of me if I am not in control."

The examples above are typical situations that may cause conscientious swimmers to become frustrated and angry with seemingly less dedicated teammates. If not handled wisely, such situations may lead to more conflict and anger within the team.

At times a coach may notice two swimmers having words as a result of disruptive behavior. The coach may choose to ask both swimmers to report after training to discuss the matter. Here it is a good idea for a coach to be able to listen attentively to what angry swimmers have to say and help them to discover healthy outlets. One way the coach can then help a swimmer get rid of negative beliefs that cause anger is by helping the swimmer create a visualization for change.

Ideally, swimmers who have a history of negative hang-ups about the coach and the team should learn to let go of the past, release the hurt for peace of mind, and, in this way, clear the way for a positive future in the sport. It is important for swimmers to know why they get angry and to understand exactly what it is that provokes them.

Once they start to understand some of the factors involved when they become angry, it is possible to develop techniques for handling future provocations. This will help prevent anger from escalating. Swimmers can learn to prevent thoughts that may lead to anger and practice coping skills to increase tolerance to provocative situations.

By assessing whether anger is justified or unjustified, we learn to assess and control our reactions in a more rational fashion. The important point is not to create a problem where none exists. Swimmers should ask themselves such questions as, "Does my anger hurt me or others? Is my anger justified? How can I make my anger work for me, and not against me?"

Before you become too heavily psychological, ask yourself whether you can see some humor in what otherwise seems to be a potentially irritating situation.

For a coach, sometimes having a clown on the team may lighten the load when the going is tough. In this case the coach may choose not to notice these antics. Being able to retain a sense of humor, even when anxious to guide the team efficiently through a workout, may often stand a coach in good stead.

However, at times a swimmer may like to test a coach in a little game of brinkmanship by not entering the water promptly at the start of practice. I once saw how the great Yale and United States coach Bob Kiphuth handled this when a swimmer dove in, swam to the shallow end, and sat down. Kiphuth called across the pool, "John, if you want to take a bath, bring a cake of soap with you!" By introducing a little humor (and a slight put-down), Kiphuth got the workout started quickly.

Another example is the daily routine that Doc Counsilman and Mark Spitz found funny. *The New York Times* reported: "Mark would put his toes in the water and say it's too cold. When he got out of the water, Counsilman would take a leather belt and chase Mark around the pool, into the stands, and finally back into the water."

Finally, may I respectfully suggest that you study the calm, relaxed demeanor of coaches such as Eddie Reese, Deryk Snelling, and other leading figures. Then ask yourself whether you have ever seen them angry. I haven't. Their behavior could be telling us something about their success.

✧ ✧ ✧

MENTAL ASPECTS OF THE TAPER

In this critical final phase of preparation, a positive self-image creates the desire to excel and the quiet confidence to do so.

The literature on the taper is sparse because it relies on such abstract components as keen observation and plain common sense. Tapering can be a simple but successful operation or it can be needlessly intricate and thus doomed to failure. Suffice it to say that, while competition tests the swimmer, the taper tests the coach.

Intelligent planning of the entire training season is critical to the outcome of the taper and the ensuing competition. Ideally, all the skills and disciplines of swimming should merge successfully during the taper: stroke mechanics, pace, strategy, and physical and mental conditioning.

Successful coaches handle the taper with natural insight and careful planning. They guide their teams with ease and confidence, bringing the swimmers to the line in peak condition, both physically and mentally. The athletes are optimally aroused, their concentration is fixed, and they exude quiet confidence as they climb on the block. They have that winning feeling.

Intelligent and sensitive handling throughout the season and into the final taper has prepared each athlete to cope with the unexpected while keeping tension low, even in the thick of the fray. These are the hallmarks of athletes trained by skilled coaches.

Conversely, a poorly planned season may find a stressed-out coach trying to do a season's work in the final three weeks. This is especially true of the psychological handling of the athlete.

Trying to achieve too much too late is a prime cause of a swimmer "tying up," becoming tense and disorganized and unable to function efficiently. The swimmer becomes anxious, and often so does the coach. The swimmer looks to the coach for reassurance only to see his own anxiety reflected in the coach's face. Unless the coach is able to save the situation, the scene may be set for a possible debacle.

Some coaches believe that, if the swimmer emerges stronger and faster from the taper as a result of a reduced workload, a positive mental approach will result. To no small extent this is true, but it is common for coaches to miss the point that physical regeneration and mental approach fall into two distinctly different categories.

For most coaches the main concern lies in how to taper each individual swimmer in the team, rather than the mental approach to the taper. A better understanding of the physiological requirements of the taper exists today than some 30 years ago, but we still have much to learn about the psychological approach.

Relaxation and Mental Motion Pictures

Right at the beginning of the season, the coach should impress upon swimmers and their parents that tension and pressure are the swimmers' arch enemies. Every effort will made to induce a quiet, calm, confident approach to both training and competition. At this early stage, the coach will teach swimmers that their minds should be in control of their activities.

Many swimmers, under the stress of preparation, have trouble sleeping at night. Mentally or emotionally, they are still trying to solve problems that may have arisen in training or at school. Late at night is never a good time to solve problems. Too much motivation, too much anxiety for results, or too much pressure by parents or coach, jams the mechanism.

The swimmers are taught relaxation exercises, and how to think positively, as well as rehearse what they have learned in each daily practice. They will learn that negative thoughts are caused by their own responses and not by external stimuli. Response means tension. Lack of response means relaxation.

Experiments have shown that you cannot have negative feelings when your muscles are perfectly relaxed. Tension in muscles is a preparation for action. Relaxation of muscles brings about mental relaxation or a peaceful, relaxed attitude. Relaxation is nature's own tranquilizer which erects a psychic screen or umbrella between the swimmer and the disturbing stimulus.

It is important to have a clear mental picture of a technique before you can do it successfully. Experiments in various sports have shown that it is possible to improve performance merely by sitting relaxed in an easy chair for five minutes a day and visualizing yourself performing desired techniques.

Swimmers should learn to visualize themselves efficiently performing various skills such as starting, turning, and correct stroke mechanics. They will also visualize themselves going through every sequence of a swimming race from start to finish. They will soon discover the effectiveness of visualization techniques performed before daily practices as well as before competitions.

Gradual Progression

Each daily practice is exactly what it says: practicing all the elements necessary for ultimate success. The important point is that, during the taper, the coach will merely check these items to see that they are correctly performed and functioning properly. The coach should not need to teach these items once the taper has been reached, because they should have been learned already during preceding gradual progressions throughout the season.

In the early season buildup, the skills and disciplines of the sport are taught one by one. At this stage, the swimmers are exposed to practice without pressure. Each layer falls in place, one upon the other, ensuring that the swimmer absorbs each important progression before moving on to the next. This holds true whether it be refining stroke mechanics, improving physical condition, or relating training to the pace of the race.

Gradually, almost imperceptibly, the coach increases the intensity of training swims. On occasions, the coach will even have the swimmers race each other in training to teach them how to remain calm, deliberate, and clear thinking under the stress of competition.

In setting goals, care should be taken to ensure that they are realistic and within reach. If the goals are set too high, the swimmer may become tense and anxious, and the swimmer's level of aspiration is lowered. For example, if a swimmer's best time for the 100 is .57 seconds, the coach should not immediately expect the swimmer to do .55 seconds. Instead, it would place less pressure on the athlete to set a short-term goal of .56.9 seconds, which, of course, would represent the swimmer's new best time. This would be positive reinforcement, and not a situation that immediately sets up unnecessary tension.

As the season progresses, the coach should learn to understand the personality of each swimmer on the team. Sensitive, highly strung athletes may need a careful, restrained approach and constant reassuring, while it may be necessary to drive a more stolid, phlegmatic type. The coach should assess the swimmer's level of commitment and what the swimmer wants from the sport. And, just as important, what is the swimmer prepared to give to the sport in terms of dedication, time, and effort? What are the swimmer's attitudes to the sport?

In every workout of the season, the coach is concerned with three main disciplines: technique, conditioning, and building the swimmer's self-image. Through discussion and observation, an astute coach will gradually form a fairly accurate assessment of a swimmer's self-image.

Self-Image Psychology

Dr. Maxwell Maltz in his famous book, *Psycho-Cybernetics* (1960), refers to a Creative Mechanism that resides within every human being, which "works automatically and impersonally to achieve goals of success and happiness, or unhappiness or failure, depending upon the goals each individual sets for it. Present the Creative Mechanism with 'success goals' and it functions as a 'Success Mechanism.' Present it with 'negative goals,' and it operates just as impersonally, and just as faithfully as a 'Failure Mechanism.'"

The goals that our own Creative Mechanism seeks to achieve are mental images, or mental pictures, which we create by means of imagination. The key goal image is our self-image. According to Maltz, "Our self-image prescribes the limits for the accomplishment of any particular goals. It prescribes the 'area of the possible.' Like any other servomechanism, our Creative Mechanism works upon information and data which we feed into it, such as our thoughts, beliefs, and interpretations."

Most leading coaches have long used Maltz's self-image precepts, either knowingly or unknowingly, and applied self-image psychology as an important and indispensable facet of their work. A positive self-image makes a swimmer want to excel in competition and gives the athlete the quiet confidence and the ability to do so. The coach helps the swimmer to develop a positive self-image by opening the swimmer's mind to the latent powers that lie within. Today it's accepted that a coach can't build a positive approach unless the swimmer has a good self-image.

What do we mean by the swimmer's self-image? In the context of swimming achievement, it's the level of a swimmer's appraisal of his or her individual levels of expertise and achievement in all the skills and disciplines of swimming. Self-image can be extended to include pride in performance, pride in achievement, life ambitions and aspirations, career, studies, and so on.

A coach should make eye contact with every swimmer during the course of the workout and help swimmers develop their self-images by means of positive comment. When a swimmer does something well, the coach should enlarge on it, praise it, perhaps even draw the team's attention to their teammate's new achievement. Gradually the swimmer's self-image will improve, and so will confidence and performance.

The coach doesn't need to praise small progress; it must be something marked, otherwise the swimmer will doubt the coach's sincerity. A coach must be honest in giving praise because this is important to the establishment of genuine rapport and understanding between swimmer and coach. For example, at a meet, a coach will not tell a swimmer that he had turned in a superb swim when, in fact, the performance had been way off form.

The swimmer's respect has to be earned, and sincerity in the coach-swimmer relationship is essential to the process. When this level of confidence and trust has developed, the coach will be able to look a swimmer straight in the eye and say with perfect conviction, "I truly believe you can do this . . . " and the swimmer will go ahead and achieve the goal. When a coach-swimmer rapport has developed to this extent, the scene is set for great team work and outstanding achievement.

When the swimmer steps to the line on the day of the race, a feeling of being in a self-contained cocoon should have been developed. The swimmer feels confident that all the training and guidance received in the program has helped toward becoming a self-controlled swimming machine. The swimmer will have a feeling of his stroke in his muscles. He should know his pace and be alert to the strategic demands of the race as it develops. The coach's final words should be short, easily understood and to the point. They should strike to the heart of the situation that the swimmer is likely to encounter. Once the coach has said what he has to say, he should not repeat his instructions again. His job is done. The swimmer's job is about to start. For both, the moment of truth has arrived.

Chapter 2

SWIMMING TECHNIQUES

THE IMPORTANCE OF VISUALIZATION IN LEARNING AND PERFECTING TECHNIQUE

Visualization is nothing new. I first read about it in 1948 in *The Physiology of Exercise* by Morehouse and Miller. I recently looked up the reference again. The following is an excerpt: "Thinking about muscular performance has been shown to produce an increase in the tension of the muscles that would participate in actual performance. This phenomenon suggests that learning and perfection of skills can proceed by reading and thinking about the technique of the event. Thus a golfer during the winter season may improve his swing by studying texts written on the subject. Divers commonly repeat in their imagination the movements of a new dive before attempting to perform it off the springboard or platform."

Of course, the use of visualization has changed since then, and today's techniques incorporate relaxation, autosuggestion, and even meditation exercises. Starting in 1966 at my swim camps in South Africa, I conducted "talk-ins" in which two or three swimmers at each session were advised in advance that they would be invited to talk for a few minutes on set topics—such as, "What I think about when I'm swimming freestyle," or "What I do on the day of a race," or any other topic—the purpose being to obtain feedback on the swimmer's learning and the concepts that are being formed in the swimmer's mind. This verbalization process is also an aid to visualization, if this is not too much of a contradiction in terms.

The importance of visualization has been stressed by coaches and educators over a long

39

period of time. John Hoberman (1992) describes the work of Etienne-Jules Marey (1830–1904) in his book, *Mortal Engines*. According to Hoberman, "It is interesting to note that, as early as 1883, Marey had anticipated the computer-based technique that today breaks down athletic movements into discrete lines displayed on a screen for analysis in terms of their biomechanical efficiency."

Marey was the world's first visualizing physiologist and he used a technique called photochronography to take pictures of athletes in a series at precisely equal time intervals. According to Hoberman, Marey wrote, "Language is as slow and obscure a method of expressing the duration and sequence of events as the graphic method is lucid and easy to understand. As a matter of fact, it is the only natural mode of expressing such events; and, further, the information which this kind of record conveys is that which appeals to the eyes, usually the most reliable form in which it can be expressed."

Verbal Description

Visualization should be accompanied by verbal descriptions that highlight specific points in technique. I believe it is important to talk to the swimmers often, to ensure that their concentration is focused. Coaches should welcome swimmers asking questions and not take this as a challenge to their authority.

I like swimmers to swim with their heads and not with their bellies. Therefore, before a workout starts, I make a practice of giving a lecture lasting just a couple of minutes. I outline the purpose of the conditioning goals contained in the upcoming workout, and I also touch on one or two aspects of stroke technique that I want the swimmers to focus on and try to accomplish.

There is a motivational purpose to this approach as well. I encourage the swimmers to try to make a little improvement each day in any or all of these three departments: technique, physical conditioning, and developing a positive mental approach. The sum of these small day-to-day improvements adds up to big improvement over the days, weeks, and months.

I will not hesitate to interrupt a workout and bring all the swimmers out on deck to reinforce a point that is not being observed throughout the team. I don't like to interrupt a workout, and neither do the swimmers, but I think the best way to drive a point home is to keep emphasizing it, and I try to do it with good humor. Remember, repetition is the soul of teaching.

Underwater Observation

Because of the distorting effect of light refraction on the water surface, it is difficult to obtain a clear impression of a swimmer's action from the pool deck. Coaches should videotape their swimmers underwater, or at least, find the opportunity to view them through underwater windows.

I use a camcorder frequently, and I have also used one of Marty Hull's "Snooper" underwater video cameras. The camera is attached to a hollow pole that carries a coaxial cable, and it is highly maneuverable. You can obtain views of a swimmer's stroke technique from angles that normally would be difficult to achieve without having to go underwater to do the taping.

In this connection, I strongly advocate the type of videotape session that I am about to describe. About a year ago, I conducted an interesting experiment at a clinic in Mission Viejo. Considerable time was spent carefully videotaping the swimmers underwater. A unique three-way video-viewing and clinic session followed, in which the swimmers, their coaches, and I participated.

First the swimmers were asked to comment on what they saw themselves doing on the video playback. Most of them were surprised to see that their strokes appeared quite different from what they had envisioned . . . a surprise, I might add, that was shared by their coaches. This turned out to be an informative and educational experience. It is worth taking a few hours out of your program to organize a video session of this nature.

Here are some other methods of forming visual concepts of swimming movements. One method that Doc Counsilman recommended was having the swimmers use face masks to observe each other underwater. After observation, the swimmers would describe the other swimmer's stroke. I have copied this method over the years and have experienced very good results.

Johnny Weissmuller first advocated the next method of observation many years ago. Practice your stroke in front of a mirror from both the side view and the front view. A piece of string should be stretched across the mirror to indicate the surface line of the water. Practicing in front of a mirror can be of tremendous benefit in forming a visual impression that leads to greatly improved stroke technique, providing it is done intelligently and conscientiously.

As an additional aid to conceptualization, detailed sequences of the strokes and turns, described and illustrated by the author, are presented in this chapter. There is also a section on how to improve your feel of the water.

✧ ✧ ✧

THE CRAWL STROKE

Overview

The pattern of the crawl stroke varies significantly between individual swimmers. Very rarely do we see two swimmers whose techniques are exactly alike.

Swimmers should be allowed to swim the crawl according to their own natural movement inclination, while still observing the basic fundamentals. The idea is to nudge a swimmer into the ideal stroke for that particular person. This requires intuitive coaching, as well as a knowledge of biomechanical principles.

Phantoms of the Pool

Think of two sailors rowing a boat back to the ship after shore leave. One is fairly sober and the other is quite drunk. One sailor enters the oar and pulls, and the boat glides beautifully. The other sailor, who is four sheets in the wind, drops his oar into the water too soon and destroys the momentum of the glide. In other words, the timing between the two sources of propulsion is out of kilter.

Similarly, when a swimmer enters the hand with a dig-pull and starts the stroke before the other hand has finished its stroke, the momentum being created by the pulling arm is either reduced or destroyed.

To correctly time one arm with the other, the body must first be balanced in the water. Preserving momentum between the end of one stroke and the beginning of the next helps the swimmer develop an invisible run through the water—a slinky, ghost-like, effortless glide. Used in conjunction with good streamlining, momentum is the best way to overcome resistance.

To Summarize

The hallmark of a good swimmer's timing is the way the arm enters the water at the start of the stroke. The hand enters the water slower than the opposite arm finishes the power phase of its stroke. In this way, the swimmer will not put a brake on the momentum created by the pulling arm.

Only when the body is balanced equally on both sides of its long axis during the swimming stroke can there be efficient timing between one arm and the other. When the body is balanced and the arms are intertimed with split-second efficiency, the swimmer is able to maintain the overall momentum of the stroke.

I like to call such swimmers ghost-gliders or phantoms of the pool, as opposed to the spin-wheelers who muscle their way through the water, entering their arms with a dig-pull or a chop-catch. Remember: Visible effort is unproductive effort; it is effort that the swimmer is using against himself.

Head and Shoulder Position, Body Roll, and Streamlining

The position of the head is important. If the head is held too high, as in the older styles of freestyle swimming, the torso and legs will be too low in the water, with a resultant increase in frontal resistance. Instead of swimming with the water level at the middle of the forehead, the modern swimmer keeps the head down, with the waterline at the top of the head. A low head position keeps the hips high and the entire body horizontal to the surface, allowing a smooth, thin stream of water to pass freely under and around the body.

Correct shoulder position also contributes to a more streamlined body position. Hunching the shoulders slightly forward causes a flattening of the thorax and abdomen, thus presenting a smooth, streamlined surface. The slight hunching of the shoulders has another function in that it permits the arms to move more freely in the shoulder joints, and, in so doing, places the arm muscles in a better mechanical position to apply a stronger pull.

However, care should be taken not to exaggerate the hunched position of the shoulders as this could result in loss of power in the arm stroke, and a lowering of the lower back and hips with consequent loss of streamlining. Remember: There's a difference between having a shave and cutting your throat!

The body rolls in the rhythm of the arm action, and the roll is quickly initiated by a long forward reach of the shoulder at the entry of each arm. The swimmer's entire body turns on its long axis, as if the swimmer is fixed on an imaginary spit which runs through the top of the head and down the body.

The rolling action of the body enables the swimmer to develop more power and, at the same time, helps to keep the body as streamlined as possible throughout the stroke. When a swimmer's body rolls on its long axis during a stroke cycle, an important hydrodynamic principle is followed: The use of gradually curved surfaces along the general paths followed by the water flow will minimize resistance.

The roll brings the large trunk muscles into play, particularly during the powerful backward arm thrust at the end of each stroke. The roll also streamlines the hips and shoulders as each arm finishes its pull and exits from the water into the recovery. As one hand finishes stroking , the other is already propelling, and there is no time lag in the continuous rhythmic cycle of the stroke.

Kicking Patterns

Talented swimmers often use a variety of different kicking patterns, even in the course of one race. They may shift naturally from one cadence to the other without even thinking about it. A swimmer may switch from a reduced, very light kick to a six-beat, depending on whether he or she is conserving energy or sprinting to meet a rival's challenge.

Sometimes, as shown in the illustrations on page 43, a stabilizing as well as streamlining effect results from crossing the ankles at certain phases of the stroke (figs. 4, 11, and 12). This action prevents any tendency for the hips to sway in counteraction to the arm recovery, and also keeps the legs tapered close together and well inside the body line. At other times, a distance swimmer, for example, may preserve energy by not kicking at all and by merely allowing the legs to trail as mere balancing agents.

Great distance swimmers, such as Australia's Kieren Perkins, reduce the tiring effects of "over-kicking" by using a subdued kick when swimming the middle and long distances. There is a growing theory that, no matter whether a swimmer uses a two-beat or a six-beat, if the kick is *easy* and at an aerobic level of intensity, then this helps remove lactate.

The key to easy and efficient kicking is to keep the ankles and feet loose and flexible. Feeling the water passing between the toes of both feet is an indication that the ankles are loose and that the feet are performing a supple weaving action. At speed, this motion becomes a powerful whiplash which provides counterbalance and thrust directly inside the body line.

The principle involved in "broken tempo" swimming is that the legs may follow any pattern, just so long as rhythm and balance are not affected. Modern swimming greats are not as style regimented as in previous swimming generations.

The High Elbow Posture

The posture of the elbows during the propulsive underwater stage of the stroke is important. The elbow should not drop below the level of the hand and shoulder at the entry phase, nor precede the hand during the first half of the pull. These faults result in poor leverage, and cause the hand and forearm to slip through the resistance of the water.

Stroke Acceleration

The hand should accelerate as the stroke progresses, because if the stroke finishes at the same speed at which it commences, there will be a general washing out and little true propulsion will be achieved.

As the accelerating arm thrusts powerfully backward, the forward arm slides into the entry at a considerably slower speed as it channels and accepts the oncoming flow of water along the hand and forearm in preparation for the next stroke. The entry of the forward arm is slow in order not to offset the momentum being developed by the propelling arm. A study of the stroke sequences shown here will reveal two different swimming strokes operating at the same time: a slow stroke by the entry arm, and a rapidly accelerating stroke by the propelling arm.

The Crawl Stroke (Side View)—
A Frame-by-Frame Description

Fig. 1 (This figure is chosen as an appropriate starting point to pick up on the continuing sequence of the stroke. This is because the stroke should start efficiently, and any error at this point will cause poor mechanics later in the pull.) The right arm, with elbow set higher than the wrist, is entering the water. The elbow is bent so that the arm is approximately one hand length short of full extension. The left leg kicks downward in a natural counterbalancing action. The left arm, with elbow about to reach maximum bend, prepares to move into the final phase of the stroke. The body is balanced on its left side, but soon the rotation of the body over to its opposite side will bring the powerful trunk muscles into the final backward thrust of the left arm stroke.

Fig. 2 The right arm enters, and in one motion, the entire body has tilted from its left side to a balanced position on the chest. However, the right arm and shoulder will continue to reach forward causing the body to roll onto its right side. Shown here is the right-angle timing of the arms. This is a good checkpoint for accuracy of timing. The waterline is halfway across the top of the head. The head is centered in line with the body's long axis.

Fig. 3 The left arm, assisted by the large trunk muscles, is accelerating rapidly and will soon complete a powerful thrust which will unswirl the water directly backward from the hand and forearm. The left hand is relaxed at the wrist, enabling the palm of the hand to keep planing backward. The leg action remains inside the body line to maintain streamlining. The body, with head down and hips held high, is balanced perfectly on the chest and horizontal to the surface of the water. The right arm nears the end of its forward reach, an action that will finally tilt the body quickly to its opposite side.

Fig. 4 The body has tipped onto its right side. This streamlined body position, parallel to the surface with head down and ankles crossed, enables the water to flow around the swimmer with less resistance. Note the shifting body balance, as one arm recovers and the

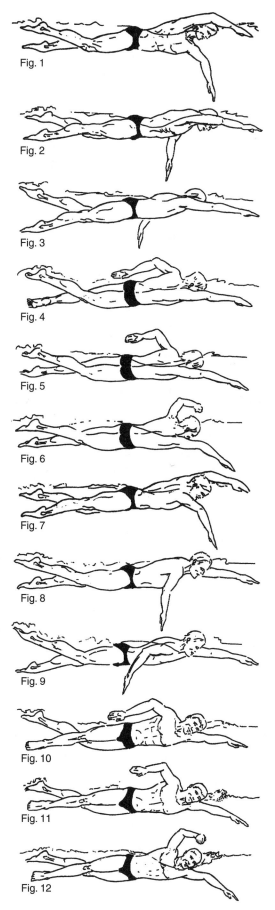

Fig. 1
Fig. 2
Fig. 3
Fig. 4
Fig. 5
Fig. 6
Fig. 7
Fig. 8
Fig. 9
Fig. 10
Fig. 11
Fig. 12

Illustration by Cecil M. Colwin

right arm, with elbow set high, starts to pull. These subtle transitions in body balance are an important part of efficient crawl swimming.

Fig. 5 The left elbow peaks in midrecovery; the shoulder does most of the work in carrying the arm forward. The continued crossing of ankles and feet keeps the legs inside the body line and preserves streamlining along the entire length of the body. The right arm, with elbow still set high, has developed the ideal leverage to apply a powerful pull.

Fig. 6 The recovering left arm and forearm swing around in a smooth circular motion, which will place the arm in a line forward of the armpit as it reaches to the entry. As the left arm recovers forward, the body roll has almost returned to the center position. The right arm, with elbow set higher than the wrist, is now well into the power phase of its pull. This high elbow position is easily attained by keeping the armpit open and pointing the elbow out sideways.

Fig. 7 The left arm is about to enter the water with elbow high, fingertips first, and palm turned slightly outward. At this stage of the stroke, the forearm of one arm is at approximately 45 degrees to the forearm of the other arm. The body is horizontal to the surface and is in an ideal streamlined position. Note the almost straight line formed from the chest down the front of the right leg to the instep of the foot.

Fig. 8. In this transition phase, the body weight moves over toward the left arm as it starts its forward reach. The right arm accelerates into the power phase of its stroke. Note the slight forward hunching of the shoulders with the resultant flattening of the thorax and abdomen. This action also allows the arms to move more freely in the shoulder joints. The leg action continues to be kept well inside the body line. In fact, at this point, a straight line, drawn from the shoulder through the hip joint, will pass exactly midway between the ankle joints.

Fig. 9 With shoulder following, the left arm nears the end of its forward reach. Synchronized with the increasing body roll to the left side, the right arm accelerates to complete its backward thrust at the end of its stroke.

Fig. 10 The body completes its roll to the left side. The right arm recovers with the elbow leading the action. The swimmer inhales in the natural roll of the body without moving the head out of the central axis of the body or changing the level of the waterline around the head. Once again, the ankles cross over to perform a natural streamlining and stabilizing function. Note how the body has remained horizontal to the surface throughout the entire stroke cycle.

Fig. 11 The left arm moves powerfully into its pull with elbow kept high. As the left elbow bends, and the hand moves slightly inward under the chest, water is swirled around the forearm. The body stays in a streamlined, horizontal position, with legs crossed over and inside the body line.

Fig. 12 The right arm swings around in a smooth arc as it prepares to slide into the water along an imaginary line forward of the shoulder. The body weight has moved over the left arm which, with elbow up, has moved into the power phase of its pull.

The Crawl Stroke (Front View)

The arm entry, on a line forward of the shoulder, is slow in order not to offset the momentum being developed by the propelling arm. A study of the stroke sequences shown here will reveal two different swimming strokes operating at the same time: a slow stroke by the entry arm, and a rapidly accelerating stroke by the propelling arm.

The hallmark of a good swimmer's timing is the way the arm enters the water at the start of the stroke. The hand enters slower than the opposite arm that is finishing the power phase of its stroke. In this way, the swimmer will not put a brake on the momentum created by the pulling arm.

The body rolls in the rhythm of the arm action, and the roll is quickly initiated by a long forward reach of the shoulder at the entry of each arm (figs. 1 to 3 and figs. 6 to 9). The rolling action of the body enables the swimmer to develop more power and, at the same time, helps to keep the body as streamlined as possible throughout the stroke.

The roll brings the large trunk muscles into play, particularly during the powerful backward arm thrust at the end of each stroke. The roll also streamlines the hips and shoulders as each arm finishes its pull and exits from the water into the recovery. As one hand finishes stroking , the other is already propelling, and there is no time lag in the continuous rhythmic cycle of the arm stroke.

Stroke Acceleration

The hand should accelerate as the stroke progresses, because if the stroke finishes at the same speed at which it commences, there will be a general washing out and little true propulsion will be achieved.

As the accelerating arm thrusts powerfully backward, the forward arm slides into the entry at considerably slower speed as it channels and accepts the oncoming flow of water along the hand and forearm in preparation for the next stroke.

Fig. 1

Fig. 2

Fig. 3

Fig. 4

Fig. 5

Fig. 6

Fig. 7

Fig. 8

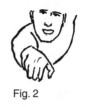

Fig. 9

Fig. 10

Fig. 11

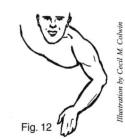

Fig. 12

Illustration by Cecil M. Colwin

THE BUTTERFLY

Overview

More than any other stroke, the butterfly relies on efficient technique. It is often said that a swimmer's butterfly technique is either all correct or all wrong. But some attention to a few key points of technique may cause the beginner to be surprised at the basic simplicity of what, at first glance, seems a complicated stroke to swim.

For example, look at the side view illustration in Figure 2. Notice how the upper arms remain parallel to the water surface as the stroke commences. This is where any number of novices go wrong. They press the arms down too deep, and then wonder why they can't propel without using inordinate strength and power.

Efficient butterfly swimming depends on the accurate synchronization of not only the head action, the arm stroke and the legs, but unlike the other strokes, the body moves through a rapidly changing range of different shapes. The breathing technique, somewhat difficult at first, becomes remarkably easy once the natural rhythm of the stroke is learned and the swimmer becomes able to relax the chest muscles.

As a training stroke, butterfly has great positive transfer value to the other three styles of swimming. Butterfly swimming promotes the skilled use of levers and muscle development, not to mention an improved feel of the water. Once the natural rhythm of the stroke is learned, it becomes an easy, beautiful, and exciting stroke to swim.

✧ ✧ ✧

Side View

Fig. 1 (This figure is chosen as an appropriate starting point to pick up on the continuing sequence of the stroke.) The head drops between the arms as they enter. The chest is pressed forward and downward, and, simultaneously, the hips and the back thighs are pushed upward. The body, thus streamlined, continues its momentum as it slips smoothly under the surface. (The action just described is the beginning of the teeter-totter motion, a unique characteristic of the butterfly stroke, that continues throughout the stroke cycle with the fulcrum centered somewhere near the center of the thighs.) The arms, medially rotated, are almost straight and parallel to the surface. The arms are slightly wider than the shoulders, the hands turned outward at an angle of approximately 45 degrees. The legs having completed their first downward kick, now pause for a split second, as the body continues its run, and the hands compress the water at the start of the next stroke.

Fig. 2 The pull starts with hands bladed outward. The upper arms, from shoulders to elbows, are kept high and parallel to the surface of the water. This position of the upper arms is important because it helps the swimmer to develop powerful leverage and makes the

difference between swimming efficiently and struggling with brute strength. The spreading of the arms allows the body to continue its momentum as the torso is pressed downward between the outspread arms. At this point, the head is down, the hands and forearms are higher than the shoulders and head, and the chest is pushed forward like a soldier on parade.

Fig. 3 The shoulders remain submerged. The hands and forearms are completing the rounded first phase of the pull. Note how the upper arms remain almost parallel to the surface. Pressing the hands downward has been reduced to a minimum, and the hands and forearms are angled directly backward with the elbows still high and close to the surface.

Fig. 4 The elbows reach maximum bend (approximately 90 degrees), and the hands move closer together as they complete the rounded first part of the stroke. The pull remains markedly shallow with the elbows still kept high and moving backward in line with the body. Note the straight posture of the back and how the head is kept in line with the spine. The knees are flexed as the legs start the second downward beat.

Fig. 5 The hands rapidly accelerate as they thrust backward to complete the stroke. The forces developed by the combined mechanics of the arms and the powerful second kick, bring the head and shoulders clear of the surface. The face is directed forward. The chin creates a furrow in the surface water to enable the swimmer to inhale.

Fig. 6 The second downward leg beat is rapidly reaching completion, causing the hips to rise in the water, a motion that facilitates the arm recovery as the hands round out the end of the stroke. The palms of the hands are turned toward the body, and this will help the swimmer lead the elbows into the recovery. The swimmer inhales a split second before the arms leave the water. (Note that the arms do not straighten completely at the end of the stroke. Swimmers should experiment to find the ideal amount of push-back suitable to their individual stroke rhythm, neither too long nor too short.)

Fig. 7 The arms recover with a relaxed, loose swing over the water. The elbows are bent to a lesser or greater degree, depending on the flexibility and strength of the swimmer. A bent-elbow recovery reduces the radius of the recovery action, and, in so doing, often improves stroke accuracy and reduces strain on the upper arm and back muscles.

Fig. 8 The torso, the hips, and the backs of the thighs are at their highest point in the entire stroke cycle. The body is in the high sailing position that results from correct timing. The arms pass in line with the shoulders, and, at this point, the head will drop quickly underwater so that it is submerged a split second before the arms enter. Careful control of the head position throughout the stroke cycle is important to proper timing and body balance.

Fig. 9 The hips start to push upward as the head drops under the water. The hands and forearms submerge last. The upward push of the hips has caused the feet to rise as they start a reacting downward kick.

Fig. 10 The swimmer returns to the position shown in Figure 1.

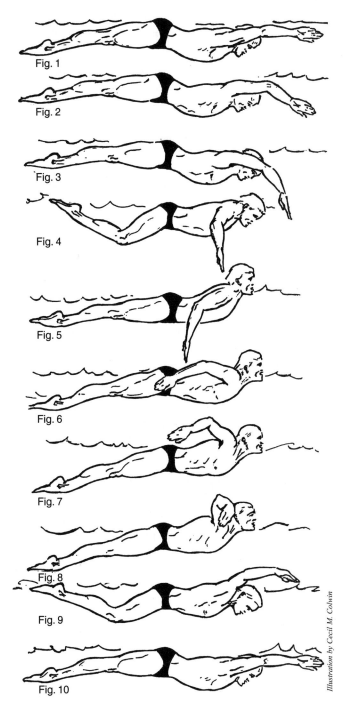

Illustration by Cecil M. Colwin

Front View

Fig. 1 The head is submerged before the arms enter. The arms enter just wide of their respective shoulders.

Fig. 2 The hands blade outward as the rounded first part of the pull commences. The shoulders are submerged. Note the high position of the upper arms and elbows.

Fig. 3 The arms cut inward in a rounded action, the elbows reach their maximum bend (approximately 90 degrees), and the hands come closer together under the waist.

Fig. 4 As the arms extend, the action changes from a pull to a backward thrust. The pull is not deep and the elbows move backward in line with the trunk.

Fig. 5 The stroke finishes, and the hands turn palm inward at the thighs. This action will assist the swimmer to recover the arms with bent elbows leading the action, as in the crawlstroke. The swimmer inhales just before the hands exit.

Fig. 6 As the shoulders clear the surface of the water, the arms start their recovery with elbows bent.

Fig. 7 The swimmer's body has reached its highest point in the stroke cycle. The elbow bend increases as the forearms swing loosely forward in preparation for the entry.

Fig. 8 The head and torso drop under the surface a split second before the arms enter.

Fig. 9 The swimmer returns to the position shown in Figure 1.

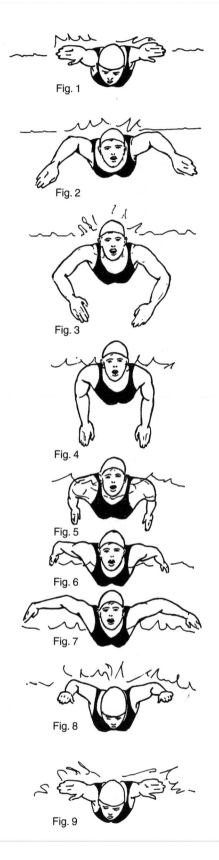

Fig. 1

Fig. 2

Fig. 3

Fig. 4

Fig. 5

Fig. 6

Fig. 7

Fig. 8

Fig. 9

Illustration by Cecil M. Colwin

THE BACKSTROKE

Side View

Fig. 1 (This figure is chosen as an ideal starting point to pick up on the continuing sequence of the stroke.) The swimmer's body is stretched out and balanced comfortably on the back of the shoulders. Note the gradual slope from the shoulders to the hips (iliac crest) which just touch the surface of the water.

Shown here is an important point in timing: The right arm has entered the water a split second before the other arm has finished its stroke. This slight overlap ensures the continuity of the stroke. Tell the swimmer, "An above-water snapshot of you at this stage of your stroke should make it look as if you have no arms!"

As the arm enters the water and performs an initial downward press, the swimmer should have a sensation of moving forward onto it.

Fig. 2 The right arm pull starts in precise timing with the lifting of the opposite shoulder and the quick shift of the body toward the pulling arm. The elbow starts to gradually bend, and the hand turns upward in a slight scooping action. If the stroke is well-timed, the swimmer should have a sensation of the body going past the hand as the arm moves into the pull.

Breathing should be timed so that the swimmer inhales as one arm is recovering and exhalation follows during the recovery of the opposite arm.

Fig. 3 The shoulder leads the left arm into the recovery phase. During recovery, the arm is perfectly straight and will remain in the vertical plane, without any lateral movement, until it has completely reentered the water on a line forward of the shoulder.

The right elbow continues to bend until it reaches maximum flexion (approximately 90 to 100 degrees, depending on the pulling pattern of the individual swimmer). The swimmer allows the wrist to relax, an action which causes the hand to drop back slightly on the wrist. This adjustment positions the hand to push the water almost directly backward.

Fig. 4 The recovery arm, still moving in the vertical plane, passes directly over the shoulder. The right arm, with the wrist relaxed and the hand still angled for maximum effect, reaches its maximum bend. At this point, the arms are almost exactly opposite each other. However, this timing will change once the recovery arm has passed the head, when it will accelerate slightly to be able to enter a split second before the right arm finishes its pull (see fig. 6). The body has reached its maximum roll to the right, and now it will gradually start to roll back to the opposite side in precise timing with the arm stroke.

Fig. 5 The recovery arm, still in the vertical plane, accelerates as it reaches forward to the entry. The hand will enter with the little finger first. The right arm, nearing the end of the push phase of the stroke, accelerates rapidly. The elbow extends, and the hand, still relaxed at the wrist, pushes directly backward in a powerful thrust.

Fig. 6 The left arm has entered, thumb up and at 90 degrees to the surface, as the opposite arm completes its thrust through to the end of the stroke. Note how the shoulder of the entry arm has reached forward without distorting the line of the body, an action that helps preserve the swimmer's continuing momentum. The key to the ideal body position, shown here, is that the arm enters and forms a line with the swimmer's back, a fine point of technique that helps maintain the ideal high position of the hips.

Fig. 7 The right arm finishes its pull with a powerful downward thrust with the palm turned downward (pronated), and driving down well below the level of the hips. The reaction to this vigorous downward motion elevates the right shoulder as it prepares to lead the arm recovery from the water.

Here again, we see the important point in timing: The forward arm, now completing its downward press, has entered a split second before the propelling arm has finished its stroke. This slight overlapping action will ensure that the swimmer's momentum is maintained.

Fig. 1

Fig. 2

Fig. 3

Fig. 4

Fig. 5

Fig. 6

Fig. 7

Fig. 8

Fig. 9

Fig. 10

Fig. 11

Fig. 12

Note: It is not uncommon to note even top swimmers "caught short" with the forward hand not entirely entered, after the opposite hand has finished its stroke. This is a difficult fault to detect, but analysis can be made easier by observing the swimmer from the side and making your own instant viewfinder by pressing the point of your index finger against the point of your thumb. This will effectively isolate the movement for quick observation.

The positioning of the two arms shows the limited range of movement in the vertical plane in backstroke swimming (as compared with the crawl stroke, for example), and this perhaps explains the extra importance of the legs as stabilizing agents.

Fig. 8 Note how the pronounced shoulder lift of the recovery arm is synchronized with the shifting of the body position to the opposite side and the beginning of the left arm pull. Also note how the hand is turned palm slightly upward as the pull commences.

The front of the body should be clear of the water from the chest to the upper abdomen. The front of the pelvis should touch the surface of the water. As the body rolls, the shoulder and part of the upper back will also clear the water.

Fig. 9 The body rolls from the top of the head to the tips of the toes. Note how the legs follow this rolling motion as the body moves from the vertical to the diagonal plane. Allowing the leg action to become too wide will have the adverse effect of slowing down the arm tempo. Therefore, throughout the stroke, the legs should remain inside the body line. (At times, the kick may appear to drop too far below the body, but this is an illusion caused by the changing angle of the body during the roll.)

Fig. 10 The shoulder of the recovery arm lifts as high as possible out of the water, an action that not only reduces water resistance against the shoulder, but also increases the amount of body roll to the opposite side, and sets the pulling arm at an ideal depth to thrust powerfully through to the hips.

Fig. 11 The recovering right arm, still in the vertical plane, increases speed in its reach to the entry. The left arm, nearing the end of the push phase of the stroke, is starting to press downward. The extent of body roll to the left side is clearly shown. Tall, lean swimmers will roll quickly until they are almost completely onto their sides, and, in fact, they tend to spend most of the stroke cycle swimming on their sides.

Fig. 12 The swimmer returns to the starting position shown in Figure 1.

Front View

These sequences show the arm pull from the entry through to the end of the stroke. The pull finishes with a vigorous downward snap of the hand and forearm to a point well below the hips.

Each arm enters, little finger first, on a line forward of the shoulder. The entry is timed so that both arms are submerged for a split second. This action ensures continuous momentum from one stroke to the next. As one arm recovers with lifted shoulder, the other arm presses down into the start of the pull.

The recovery arm moves in the vertical plane throughout, passes directly over the shoulder joint, and then accelerates slightly as it enters.

The hand presses downward, then scoops slightly upward to a maximum elbow bend of approximately 90 degrees, before accelerating rapidly into a final downward snap below the hips. Throughout the pull, the swimmer carefully adjusts the hand posture on the wrist to maintain maximum water pressure on the palm of the hand.

The dotted line through the shoulders is added to show the angle of the torso tilt as the arm reaches midstroke. I have deliberately drawn a swimmer using a moderate amount of roll (approximately 40 degrees), because, unless a swimmer is tall, lean, and lanky, it is probably best to first experiment with a moderate roll. Find how far you can roll without affecting your ability to turn your stroke over continuously.

As your strength increases, you can also try to keep an imaginary straight line through the shoulders to the elbow of the pulling arm, instead of the broken line shown here. This action is particularly suited to swimmers with the muscular strength and power needed to apply the resulting increased leverage on the water.

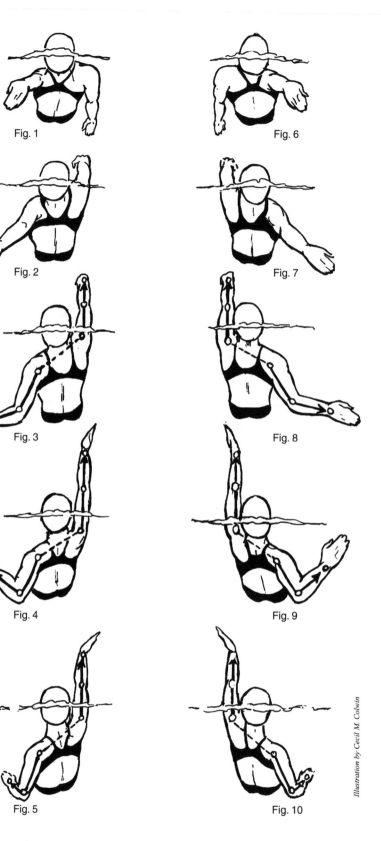

Fig. 1   Fig. 6   Fig. 2   Fig. 7   Fig. 3   Fig. 8   Fig. 4   Fig. 9   Fig. 5   Fig. 10

Illustration by Cecil M. Colwin

Note: The above sequences are diagrammatic in the sense that, in the forward view, unless viewed from a 45-degree angle shown here, one would not see the swimmer's entire torso.

CHECKPOINTS ON BACKSTROKE TECHNIQUE

Backstroke Arm Stroke

Backstrokers can't see their arms as they pull, but, unlike swimmers in the other strokes, they can observe their own body position at all times. This is a beneficial trade-off, but it still doesn't solve the problem of learning to do a stroke you cannot see.

While there are a number of excellent instructional videos available, and also a repertoire of some very good stroke drills for teaching the backstroke arm action and general rhythm, they still don't provide the individual swimmer with the opportunity to form a visual impression of the underwater phases of his or her own swimming stroke.

The use of the video camera, as well as practicing in front of a mirror are useful, but perhaps the most successful drill for providing instant feedback is to practice the backstroke arm action while standing in chest-deep water.

In this way you will be able to turn your head and see the pattern of the stroke as you pull and also be able to rotate your body in time with the arm pull and the recovery.

Basically, the hand follows a down-up-down path through the pull, but you should also try to keep your hand angled directly backward until it moves into the final downward snap at the end of the stroke.

By relaxing at the wrist, your hand will naturally assume the ideal plane for pushing water directly backward. Make the water pressure on your hand stronger as it accelerates through the stroke. Learn to associate the feel of water pressure on the palm of your hand with the visible changing sequences of the stroke.

Now start swimming and practice the actual stroke. Try to make both the feel of the water and the mechanics of the stroke a permanent part of your backstroke form.

Streamlining the Body Position

Keeping a streamlined body position is essential to swimming backstroke efficiently.

Stretch out and try to make your body feel extra long. Imagine that you have become a sleek sculling shell that draws only a couple of inches of water, rather than a rowboat that sits much lower in the water. Remember: The finer your balance, the greater your speed.

Key Points

Except for a slight downward slope from the shoulders to the hips, your body should be almost parallel to the surface.

The earlobes should touch the water surface. The neck muscles are relaxed, and the head floats like a ball on the water. The chin is brought in slightly toward the throat so that, looking down the cheeks, you can just see the tips of your toes.

There should be absolutely no break at the hips. This incorrect position is known as sitting in a tub, and it leads to fundamental faults in your stroke. Some examples: Dropping at the hips causes the flow of water to break up into turbulence around the hips and buttocks. The arm will finish the stroke too deep beneath the surface, and a bobbing action will result from your attempts to extricate your hands.

Dropping your hips may also cause your hand to stop at the side, thus breaking the smooth continuity of the stroke. Finally, if your hips are too deep, your shoulders will be too high, and this will cause difficulty in entering your hand efficiently behind the shoulders. As a result, your arm entry will be too wide as well as too shallow.

Leg Action

The leg action should be kept narrow with the feet inside the body line. The leg action is not really a beat but a very shallow slithering action of the legs during which the swimmer tries to feel the water passing in between the toes. This is a sign that the ankles and feet are relaxed.

At the top of each kick the big toe of each foot merely chips the surface of the water. Instead of creating a sharp splash, the leg action should create a dome of water that follows the feet continuously, neither disappearing nor rising then falling. This is an important sign that the legs and feet are in a streamlined position just beneath the surface and inside the body line.

Note: If your leg action is allowed to become too wide, this will not only pull your hips down in the water, thus reducing streamlining, but will also slow the tempo of your arms.

THE WAVE ACTION
BREASTSTROKE

Following the Wave

In studying the complexities of the wave breast-stroke it is quite easy to be overcome by information overload, so it's important to concentrate on the most important points of the stroke. (See "Key Points.")

In preparing this section, I discussed the stroke in detail with the stroke's leading protagonist, Mike Barrowman, 1992 Olympic champion and 200-meter breaststroke world-record holder. I also spoke to his two former mentors, Jozsef Nagy, who pioneered the stroke, and Jon Urbanchek, Barrowman's coach at the University of Michigan. All three were extremely helpful.

Jon Urbanchek said that the stroke had changed somewhat in the last 10 years since *Swimming Technique* featured 3 articles on the "new breast-stroke" in 1989. Mark Muckenfuss had interviewed Jozsef Nagy on "Catching the Wave," the first detailed description of the "wave action breaststroke." In the same issue, Nagy ("From a Technical Angle") further expounded on the new technique, while Barrowman described the stroke and how he mastered it ("An Athlete's Perspective").

According to Jozsef Nagy, Hungarian inventor of the wave breaststroke, "The point of the shoulder follows the line of a symmetrical wave." In other words, the wave rises and falls in perfect symmetry, and there is no abrupt drop after the breath is taken. (See Nagy's computer-enhanced diagram on page 58 which shows the ideal wave path followed by the tip of a swimmer's shoulder throughout a complete stroke cycle.)

It's also crucial for the kick to fit in at just the right time to help maintain the upper body's forward surge over the water in what Urbanchek calls a catlike lunge.

If the kick comes up too late, the shoulders will drop abruptly creating a sudden trough in the imaginary symmetrical line shown in Nagy's diagram. This is the big difference between the conventional breaststroke and the wave action breaststroke.

Getting the Shoulders Up

A swimmer's first reaction is usually, "How do I get my shoulders and arms up high enough above the water in order to lunge my hands and forearms forward over the surface?"

I passed this question on to Barrowman. This is what he said: "It's critical that the head remain completely down until the hands have finished their insweep and are about to lunge forward. This is because we want to keep the body streamlined as long as the head is down in the water.

"This is the trick to the wave stroke. In the conventional breaststroke the arm recovery is done deep underwater, causing great resistance. But the hollowing of the back brings the whole resistant part of the body out of the water, and leaves almost only the swim suit and legs below the surface.

"As the hands begin the forward lunge, this is the point at which the back becomes convex or humped. This provides a great force forward when done properly, in coordination with the kick.

"This change in the posture of the back is important. You hollow the back, and you sweep your arms in quickly and powerfully to bring the head and torso high out of the water. But you hump your back in coordination with the kick in order to achieve the forward lunge." (Note that in figs. 4 and 5, the back is hollowed, or concave, in figs. 6 to 8 the back is humped, or convex.)

Coach Urbanchek added, "What happens is that the hollowing of the back brings the upper body up high enough so that the swimmer can jump forward. Then the kick comes in."

Center of Gravity

Nagy said, "I discovered that the center of gravity in people who are able to lunge forward remains very constant, four or five inches below the water. It does not go up and down."

Barrowman agreed with Nagy's statement saying, "One thing that's crucial is that throughout the stroke there is very little up-and-down movement of the hips. Certainly some up-and-down movement is unavoidable, but this is the difference between first and fifth place at the Olympics. If the hips move, the center of gravity moves and thus creates more work. If you have any access to U.S. Swimming's data, take a look at their analysis of my stroke in comparison with Rozsa's. This is the biggest difference between us, and most likely the difference of one and a half seconds between us. He did more work due to his hips moving up and down more."

A Discussion with Mike Barrowman

Barrowman says, "The first WR I set was in Los Angeles. Unfortunately, my goggles filled up during the swim. I knew I could swim faster. By the fourth week of taper, 16 days later in Tokyo, I'd lost some of my conditioning, but still had enough to go $1/100$ second faster to break the old record, and the time that Nick Gillingham had set only the day before in Bonn.

"What psyched me up for years was that the Americans would break a record only to see it lowered by Europeans a week later at the European games. I wanted my chance to turn the tables. Plus, I felt that the first record was not a real reflection of what I could do. I wanted to show the world I could do better. The real truth didn't come out for a year when I went 2:11.53. This was a more realistic progression after the goggles episode had messed up my swim in Los Angeles a year earlier."

I asked Mike about his subjective feelings when swimming the wave breaststroke, how the stroke felt to him.

Mike said, "Subjective feelings? Hard question. It never felt good until the day before a race. That was the only time I had the strength to do the stroke correctly. Then it felt great and easy."

I asked him about his intensive medicine ball workouts. My guess was that these workouts must have helped him develop tremendous muscular power and strength.

Barrowman replied that his medicine ball workouts were a critical part of his preparation. "My forearms were the weakest part of my stroke before I used medicine-ball conditioning, and the strongest part afterward. They helped me develop muscle speed, quickness, and endurance. It was an extremely difficult workout when done correctly, nonstop for 50 minutes. It was . . . dreaded."

Barrowman, presently living on Grand Cayman Island in the Caribbean, says that he has taken a break from his desk job and speaking engagements while he finishes writing his 500-page sci-fi book. "I'm enjoying life at its best. I teach diving, drive boats, make underwater videos, and am generally having fun down here before I return to the real world."

Mike Barrowman's World Record Progression
2:12.90 Los Angeles, Aug. 4, 1989

2:12.89 Tokyo, Aug. 20, 1989

2:11.53 Seattle, Jul. 20, 1990

2:11.23 Perth, Jan. 11, 1991

2:10.60 Ft. Lauderdale, Aug. 13, 1991

2:10.16 Barcelona, Jul. 29, 1992

Side View

Fig. 1 At no stage of the wave breaststroke action is the body forcibly submerged. In this frame the body glides forward with shoulders and hips aligned; arms, legs, and feet extended. The shoulders reach forward as far as possible and the upper arms press against the ears to further streamline the oncoming flow of water along the body. The body is flat and ideally configured to achieve the best possible streamlining. This is the basic position, and it will be achieved again in Figure 9.

Fig. 2 The pull starts with the hands facing outward and slightly upward to best engage the oncoming flow. The entire body position remains the same as in Figure 1. Throughout the stroke, the hip movement should be kept to a minimum to save energy and maintain the swimmer's forward movement.

Fig. 3 The first stage of the arm pull closely resembles the start of the butterfly pull. The hands and forearms are about to change direction inward. The swimmer hollows his back, while concentrating on pulling the body forward and not upward. The knees start to bend and spread sideways, but the front thighs remain almost in a straight line with the body.

Fig. 4 With back still hollowed, the head and upper torso clear the surface as the body continues to slide forward. This phase of the action is the key feature of the wave breaststroke. From a streamlining perspective, it is in marked contrast to the conventional breaststroke where the shoulders, the widest part of the body, remain submerged to present considerable frontal resistance. Important: The overall motion is definitely forward and not upward.

The swimmer inhales as the mouth clears the surface.The hands sweep down under the shoulders and continue forward with the forearms following. Although the elbows bend to about 90 degrees as the hands and forearms point forward, the hands are in control throughout, and at no stage do the elbows lead the action. Says Barrowman, "The forearms, led by the hands, are the motion point, not the elbows." To further improve

streamlining, the shoulders are hunched until they almost touch the ears.

Also important to streamlining: The front thighs are kept well in line with the trunk to permit a smooth passage of water under the body. The feet do not hang downward to cause resistance; the toes of both feet are in the same line as the heels.

Fig. 5 The upper arms do not come close to the side of the chest, but follow the hands in front of the chest to reduce frontal resistance. The torso continues to move forward over the surface as the swimmer performs the lunge, the unique feature of the wave breaststroke which enables the swimmer "to follow the wave," as Nagy describes it. In a radical break from the traditional pull-kick rhythm of the conventional breaststroke, the lunge phase takes place between the pull and the kick, so that the rhythm becomes pull-lunge-kick. In this action, the hands and forearms are thrust forward on and parallel to the surface of the water, not above or below.

The heels start to rise in preparation for the kick which will only start when the lunge is about three-fourths of the way through. The kick does not start the lunge, but rather serves to maintain the lunge and keep the swimmer on the surface. Therefore, the kick must be precisely timed or it will break the rhythm of the stroke.

Fig. 6 In the lunge, the swimmer literally throws the body forward and over into the lunge. In performing the lunge, the posture of the back now quickly changes from its arched (concave) shape to an exactly opposite rounded (or convex) shape. According to Barrowman, it is the convex back posture that enables him to apply great force during the lunge. Note the continuing high position of the upper body, shoulders, and arms. Remember, the hands and forearms are thrust forward at surface level.

Accurate timing of the kick is vital to the forward lunge. At the start of the kick, the degree of hip joint flexion is approximately 35 degrees, with the lower leg at almost 90 degrees to the surface.

The feet, barely an inch below surface, are dorsiflexed (everted or turned outward) at approximately 90 degrees to the shin. In this posture they are able to catch the water perfectly. The position of the front thighs in relation to the front of the torso is an important aid to streamlining. A very slight lowering of the hips has helped the swimmer to assume this relative position of the lower legs, thighs, and trunk.

Figs. 7 and 8 The humped, dolphin-like posture of the back, together with a powerful directly backward kick, enables the swimmer to keep moving over the water with shoulders and arms at the surface. There is no downward component at all to the kick.

The feet remain turned outward until just before the kick closes, at which point the ankles and feet are extended to give a final snap to the kick as water is thrust directly backward. The swimmer looks straight down at the bottom of the pool to maintain streamlining during this most powerful stage of the overall action.

Fig. 9 The body, perfectly streamlined, slides forward at the surface. In this position, care should be taken not to permit the legs to drop as this may be considered to be a dolphin kick for which the swimmer could be disqualified.

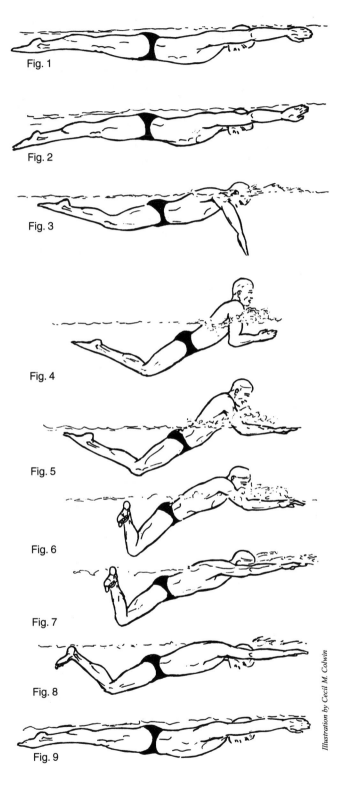

Fig. 1

Fig. 2

Fig. 3

Fig. 4

Fig. 5

Fig. 6

Fig. 7

Fig. 8

Fig. 9

Illustration by Cecil M. Colwin

Key Points

- Unlike the pull-kick rhythm of conventional breaststroke, the wave stroke rhythm is pull-lunge-kick. The lunge is the unique feature of the wave breaststroke. The lunge occurs between the pull and the kick; the hands and forearms are thrust forward on and parallel to the surface of the water.

- The back is hollowed (concave shaped) during the pull and first part of arm recovery (figs. 3, 4, and 5) but arched (convex shaped) during the lunge (figs. 6, 7, and 8).

- In marked contrast to the conventional breaststroke, the head and upper torso clear the surface as the body continues to slide forward. The shoulders, the widest part of the body, clear the surface for better streamlining (figs. 4, 5, and 6). To further improve streamlining, the shoulders are hunched until they almost touch the ears (figs. 4, 5, and 6).

- The swimmer literally throws the body forward and over into the lunge. According to Mike Barrowman, the leading exponent of the wave breaststroke, it is the convex back posture that enables him to apply great force during the lunge.

- The timing of the kick is critical; it only starts when the lunge is about three-fourths of the way through (fig. 6). The kick is directly backward with no downward component (fig. 8).

- Throughout the stroke, the hip movement is kept to a minimum to save energy and preserve the swimmer's momentum (Figs. 1 to 9).

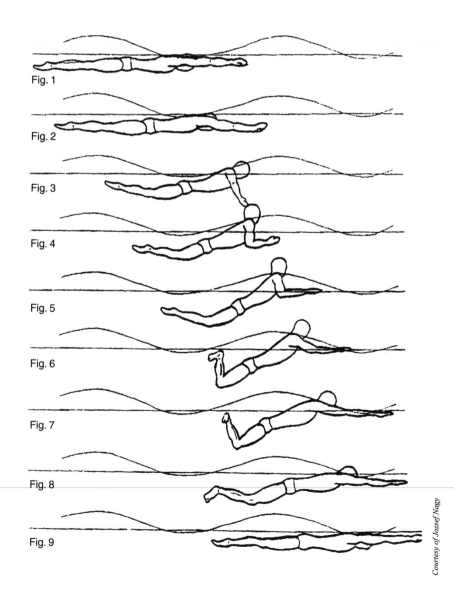

Fig. 1

Fig. 2

Fig. 3

Fig. 4

Fig. 5

Fig. 6

Fig. 7

Fig. 8

Fig. 9

Courtesy of Jozsef Nagy

Front View

Fig. 1 The body is outstretched and streamlined with head down and arms about to pull.

Fig. 2 The pull begins as the hands scull sideways and downward. The swimmer keeps the head down to preserve the body's streamlined position.

Fig. 3 The hands reach the widest point of their sculling action. From here the elbows will start to bend.

Fig. 4 The elbow bend increases as the hands sweep down and inward in a continuing movement that will change direction forward.

Fig. 5 As the hands join, the upper arms and elbows do not come close to the side of the chest. Instead, they follow the hands and forearms forward of the chest to reduce the body's frontal resistance. The swimmer inhales as the mouth clears the surface. The legs and feet are drawn up preparatory to the kick.

Fig. 6 Two important points in streamlining: The shoulders—the widest part of the body—are clear of the surface, and the arms are in front of the chest. The swimmer starts the forward lunge of the arms. The legs are ready to kick, and the feet are turned outward.

Fig. 7 The kick occurs three-fourths of the way into the lunge, thus helping the swimmer to stay up on the surface instead of sinking suddenly. The kick is kept directly backward with no downward component.

Fig. 8 As the legs close, the ankles and feet are extended to provide a final backward thrust on the water. The head is down. The arms and shoulders reach forward as far as possible.

Fig. 9 With arms and legs outstretched, the body is once more in perfect alignment as it slides forward, parallel to the surface.

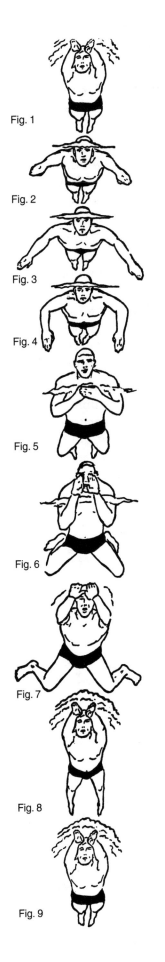

Fig. 1
Fig. 2
Fig. 3
Fig. 4
Fig. 5
Fig. 6
Fig. 7
Fig. 8
Fig. 9

Reprinted by permission from Colwin, 1992, *Swimming Into the 21st Century* (Champaign, IL: Human Kinetics Publishers). 48–49.

THE CRAWL STROKE START

These illustrations show the grab start which is named for the swimmer's initial stance and mechanics on the starting block.

Fig. 1 The feet are positioned carefully on the starting block. The swimmer grabs the front of the block lightly with both hands.

Fig. 2 At the signal, the swimmer grabs hard on the block and pulls the shoulders downward until the head is lower than the knees. This action makes the hips rise and quickly tips the swimmer's center of balance forward over the end of the starting block, without the need for a windup arm swing.

Figs. 3 and 4 The swimmer throws the arms forward as the legs thrust to full extension, thus projecting the swimmer out over the water.

Figs. 5 to 7 As the dive reaches the peak of its trajectory, the swimmer tucks the head under the outstretched arms and pikes at the hips, thus aiming the body at a steep angle to enable it to enter entirely through the same hole in the water. Immediately after entering the water, the lower back is arched, thus setting the body on a course directly forward and horizontal to the water surface.

This clean entry position is in contrast to the old "pancake landing" in which a swimmer either entered at a very shallow angle, or hit the water flat with the whole body at once thus setting up great stoppage resistance.

Figs. 8 and 9 While underwater, most swimmers will dolphin kick for a while with arms extended, before starting the flutter kick just prior to surfacing.

Figs. 10 to 13 The rules restrict the swimmer to 15 meters (16.4 yards) underwater after the start and turn. By that point, the head must have broken the surface. The first arm stroke brings the swimmer to the surface. The other arm is extended forward, but both arms will take up the rhythm of the full stroke as soon as the head breaks the surface.

Irrespective of the distance to be swum, the swimmer should not turn the head to breathe until the swimmer has taken about six strokes and is well into the stroke rhythm.

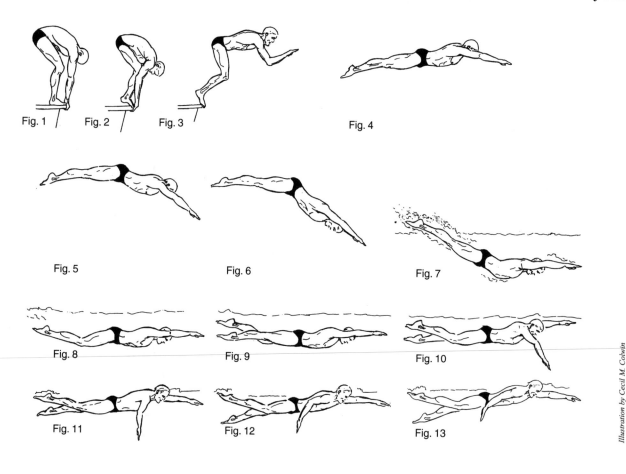

Fig. 1   Fig. 2   Fig. 3   Fig. 4

Fig. 5   Fig. 6   Fig. 7

Fig. 8   Fig. 9   Fig. 10

Fig. 11   Fig. 12   Fig. 13

Illustration by Cecil M. Colwin

THE CRAWL STROKE TURN

Synopsis

In essence, the crawl stroke turn is a gymnastic event in which the swimmer performs a forward somersault with a half twist.

The most important point in effectively performing the turn is to keep the head moving nonstop through the turn and into the push-off. If the head stops at any stage of the turn, momentum is lost and so is speed. In fact, the whole body moves continuously as closer study reveals.

As the hips pike and the legs swing quickly over onto the wall, the head keeps moving. The shoulders turn sharply into the vertical plane causing the body to turn on its side. At this point, the body should be deep enough to avoid pushing off into disturbed surface water.

Throughout the turn, the hands also move nonstop. They assist a continuing body rotation with a powerful reverse sculling motion before thrusting outward to bring the arms to full extension.

Neither do the legs pause through their motion from the initiating dolphin kick to the swing over the head onto the wall. Only the toe tips are placed on the wall and, without hesitation, the legs and feet extend, rapidly thrusting the body out in the opposite direction. As the swimmer pushes off, the body once more assumes a prone position on the chest.

Fig. 1 On the approach to the wall, the head and forward arm dive below the surface. The legs perform a quick dolphin motion which aids momentum while also lifting the hips.

Fig. 2 The head moves nonstop through the turn. The shoulders swing abruptly into the vertical plane causing the body to turn on its side. The arms bend sharply as the hands come together in a powerful reverse sculling motion. The swimmer pikes at the hips as legs and trunk swing over the swimmer's head. The swimmer's directional change is now well under way.

Fig. 3 Without pausing, the legs and feet thrust the body out from the wall using toe tips only and not a flat placement of the heels.

Fig. 4 The arms thrust to full extension as the body returns to a prone position on the chest. As the swimmer planes gradually to the surface before taking the first stroke, the swimmer may use either a dolphin kick or a flutter kick. The swimmer should take 6 strokes before resuming a regular breathing pattern. The rules restrict the swimmer to 15 meters (16.4 yards) underwater after the start and turn, at which point the head must have broken the surface.

Fig. 1

Fig. 2

Fig. 3

Fig. 4

Illustration by Cecil M. Colwin

THE BUTTERFLY START

The illustrations show the grab start which is named for the swimmer's initial stance and mechanics on the starting block.

Fig. 1 The feet are positioned carefully on the starting block. The swimmer grabs the front of the block lightly with both hands.

Fig. 2 At the signal, the swimmer grabs hard on the block and pulls the shoulders downward until the head is lower than the knees. This action makes the hips rise and quickly tips the swimmer's center of balance forward over the end of the starting block, without the need for a windup arm swing.

Figs. 3 and 4 The swimmer throws the arms forward as the legs thrust to full extension thus projecting the swimmer out over the water.

Figs. 5 to 7 As the dive reaches the peak of its trajectory, the swimmer tucks the head under the outstretched arms and pikes at the hips, thus aiming the body at a steep angle to enable it to enter entirely through the same hole in the water. Immediately after entering the water, the lower back is arched thus setting the body on a course directly forward and horizontal to the water surface.

The swimmer is permitted to be completely submerged for 15 meters (16.4 yards) underwater after the start and turn. By that point, the head must have broken the surface. While underwater, 1 or more kicks are permitted (figs. 8 to 12), but only 1 pull which must bring the swimmer to the surface (figs. 13 to 16).

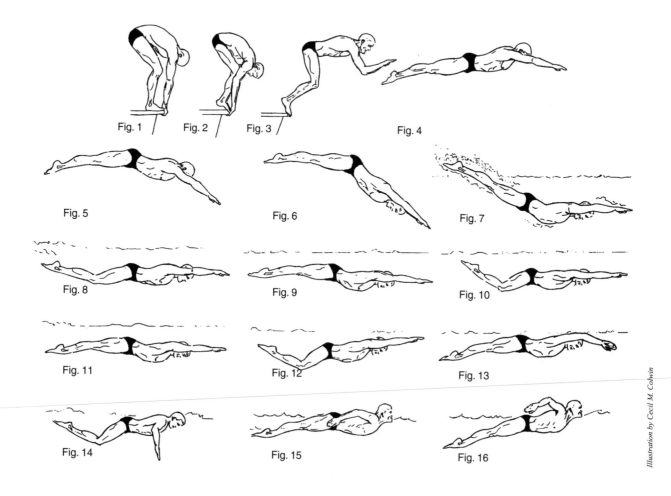

Fig. 1   Fig. 2   Fig. 3   Fig. 4

Fig. 5   Fig. 6   Fig. 7

Fig. 8   Fig. 9   Fig. 10

Fig. 11   Fig. 12   Fig. 13

Fig. 14   Fig. 15   Fig. 16

Illustration by Cecil M. Colwin

THE BUTTERFLY TURN

The FINA rules of butterfly swimming say that "both hands must touch simultaneously at, above, or below the water surface."

Fig. 1 At the touch, the swimmer does not allow the body to come too close to the wall.

Fig. 2 (Note: The swimmer will use the body's momentum to bring the body in toward the wall, and then, by keeping head and shoulders moving out again, will redirect this momentum in the opposite direction.) The touching hand initiates the turn by pushing hard against the wall to push the head and shoulders away. At the same time, the hand on the turning side is pulled back from the wall with elbow well bent and hand parallel to the surface for streamlining. The legs, with knees bent, prepare to move under the body. During this motion, the swimmer inhales in preparation for the push-off and the ensuing underwater swim.

Fig. 3 The head drops underwater as it continues to move away from the wall, while the legs, with knees bent, move toward the wall. The overall impression is of a quick end-over-end movement. The hand that remained on the wall has now pushed itself free and is about to join its opposite member.

Fig. 4 The feet are set lightly on the wall so that the body is deep enough to be able to push off below the disturbed surface water. The arms have joined together and are starting to extend.

Fig. 5 In the push-off from the wall, the body is streamlined with arms and legs extended and head beneath the arms.

The rules restrict the swimmer to be "completely submerged for a distance of not more than 15 meters (16.4 feet) after the start and after each turn," and to "one or more leg kicks and one arm pull under the water which must bring him to the surface. By that point, the head must have broken the surface. The swimmer must remain on the surface until the next turn or finish."

The FINA rule on the butterfly turn says:

"At each turn the body shall be on the breast. The touch shall be made with both hands simultaneously at, above, or below the water surface. Once a touch has been made, the swimmer may turn in any manner desired. The shoulders must be at or past the vertical toward the breast when the swimmer leaves the wall."

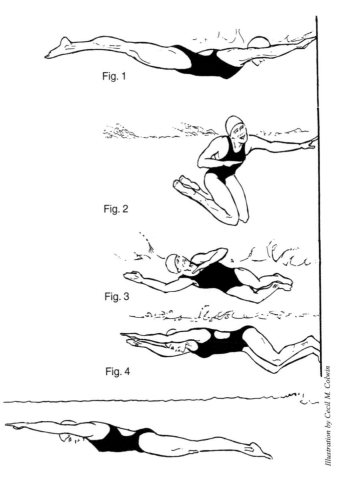

Fig. 1

Fig. 2

Fig. 3

Fig. 4

Illustration by Cecil M. Colwin

THE BACKSTROKE START

Fig. 1 The starting position: The feet are positioned one below the other to avoid slipping and to provide a strong base for the outward leap from the wall when the starting signal is given. The head is erect and the eyes look straight ahead. Pressure is exerted on the fingers and toes to create a spring.

Figs. 2 and 3 The head comes forward slightly as the hands and feet push the swimmer up and away from the wall. Note the fall-back motion of the head and torso, and how the hips start to rise in counteraction to this motion.

Fig. 4 As the body continues to extend over the water, the swimmer drops the hands toward the water surface, an action that further elevates the hips over the surface. The head is aligned with the spine. With the weight of the body out over the water, the ankles and feet are extended to add further momentum.

Fig. 5 The preliminary drop of the arms has resulted in a favorable position for a shallow backward dive clear of the surface. The arms are thrown vigorously out sideways over the surface as the feet and legs complete a powerful thrust from the wall.

Fig. 6 The swimmer enters the water in a shallow trajectory without landing flat on the back, an action that would cause tremendous resistance.

Fig. 7 After a short glide with arms extended behind the head and elbows tucked in, the swimmer starts to kick. The swimmer may do either a dolphin kick (figs. 7 to 9) or a flutter kick (figs. 10 and 11), depending on the swimmer's individual aptitude.

Fig. 12 The rules of swimming limit the swimmer to 15 meters (16.4 yards) underwater after the start and turn. By that point, the head must have broken the surface as shown here. The swimmer commences the stroking action by pulling with the strongest arm first. (In this particular case, the swimmer is left-handed.) Care must be taken to keep the opposite arm submerged and well behind the head as the first stroke is taken, otherwise the swimmer may either come out from under the surface too suddenly or swimming across the lane at a tangent.

The first arm stroke should be close to the body. This action, combined with the streamlined position of the submerged forward arm, will also keep the swimmer moving straight ahead during the breakout into the surface. Once on the surface, the swimmer should not inhale for the first six strokes. This action assists the swimmer to immediately work into a fast tempo instead of a gradual buildup to speed with each successive stroke.

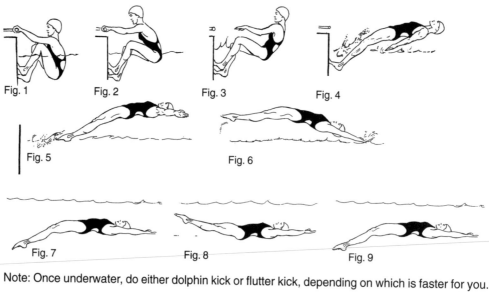

Fig. 1   Fig. 2   Fig. 3   Fig. 4

Fig. 5   Fig. 6

Fig. 7   Fig. 8   Fig. 9

Note: Once underwater, do either dolphin kick or flutter kick, depending on which is faster for you.

Fig. 10   Fig. 11   Fig. 12

Illustration by Cecil M. Colwin

THE BACKSTROKE TURN

Fig. 1 As the swimmer approaches the wall, she starts turning her head and shoulders toward the forward arm. The head will keep moving nonstop throughout the entire motion of the turn. This is the key to a fast turn. Any pause in the head movement will slow the turn.

Fig. 2 The rotation of the body to a prone position is effected by a set of almost simultaneous movements: The head turns facedown. The shoulders and hips turn, assisted by the pulling action of the forward arm. The left arm and left leg swing across the body's long axis.

Figs. 3 to 6 Both arms now pull the body forward and down, aided by a dolphin kick that elevates the hips. The body pikes and somersaults to a position on the back. The hands join together and change their direction to perform a rapid reverse sculling motion to maintain the body's continuing momentum. The legs swing over the head to a deep placement of the feet on the wall that will ensure that the push-off takes place deep enough to avoid turbulent surface water.

Fig. 7 The feet are placed lightly on the wall without touching with the heels. The swimmer pushes off with body well streamlined and arms extended behind the head. The swimmer will use either a dolphin kick or a flutter kick prior to starting the arm stroke. The rules of swimming restrict the swimmer to 15 meters (16.4 yards) under the water after the start and turn. By that point, the head must have broken the surface.

The FINA rule on the backstroke turn says: "Upon completion of each length, some part of the swimmer must touch the wall. During the turn the shoulders may turn past the vertical toward the breast. If the swimmer turns past the vertical, such motion must be part of a continuous turning action and the swimmer must return to a position on the back before the feet leave the wall."

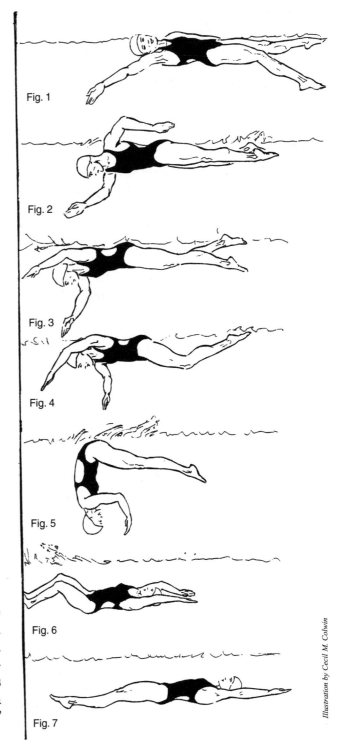

Fig. 1

Fig. 2

Fig. 3

Fig. 4

Fig. 5

Fig. 6

Fig. 7

Illustration by Cecil M. Colwin

THE BREASTSTROKE START

Fig. 1 The feet are positioned carefully on the starting block. The swimmer grabs the front of the block lightly with both hands.

Fig. 2 At the signal, the swimmer grabs hard on the block and pulls the shoulders downward until the head is lower than the knees. This action makes the hips rise and quickly tips the swimmer's center of balance forward over the end of the starting block without the need for a windup arm swing.

Figs. 3 and 4 The swimmer throws the arms forward as the legs thrust to full extension thus projecting the swimmer out over the water.

Figs. 5 to 7 As the dive reaches the peak of its trajectory, the swimmer tucks the head under the outstretched arms and pikes at the hips, thus aiming the body at a steep angle to enable it to enter entirely through the same hole in the water.

Fig. 8 The underwater swimming phase, after start or turn, commences with a short preliminary glide with the body in outstretched and streamlined position.

Figs. 9 and 10 Then follows a long pull through to the hips with another short glide with the arms close to the body.

Fig. 11 The hands are turned palms upward as the arms, with elbows and forearms kept close to the body in streamlined fashion, are extended forward.

Fig. 12 As the legs kick, the back of the head is tucked down in line with the upper surface of the arms to ensure good streamlining.

Fig. 13 The head breaks the surface as the swimmer starts the arm stroke. (The swimmer shown here has lifted the head from the surface well before the arms have separated to start the stroke, and so is safely within the confines of the rule.)

Notes on Figs. 8 to 13 After a start or turn, the rules permit a swimmer to take one stroke completely back to the legs and one kick while wholly submerged. The head must break the surface of the water before the hands turn inward at the widest part of the second stroke.

The full sequence of entry-glide, pull-glide, kick-glide, and breakout, is shown here. Note: Some controversy exists as to the ideal timing for each sequence of the underwater swim. However, a final decision is usually based on what produces best results for the individual swimmer. This approach still appears to be sound coaching practice for every phase of swimming.

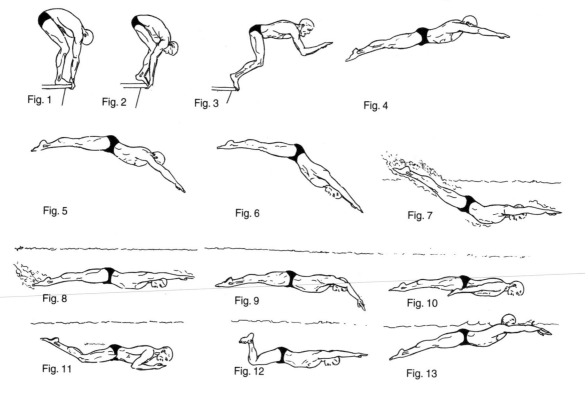

Fig. 1 Fig. 2 Fig. 3 Fig. 4

Fig. 5 Fig. 6 Fig. 7

Fig. 8 Fig. 9 Fig. 10

Fig. 11 Fig. 12 Fig. 13

Illustration by Cecil M. Colwin

THE BREASTSTROKE TURN

The FINA rules of breaststroke swimming say that "both hands must touch simultaneously at, above, or below the water surface."

Fig. 1 At the touch, the swimmer does not allow the body to come too close to the wall.

Fig. 2 (Note: The swimmer will use the body's momentum to bring the body in toward the wall, and then, by moving the head and shoulders quickly out again, will redirect this momentum in the opposite direction. The speed of the swimmer's incoming momentum to the wall is important in effecting a fast turn.) The touching hand initiates the turn by pushing hard against the wall to push the head and shoulders away. The legs, with knees bent, prepare to move under the body. During this motion, the swimmer inhales in preparation for the push-off and the ensuing underwater swim.

Fig. 3 The head drops underwater as it continues to move away from the wall, while the legs, with knees bent, move toward the wall. The overall impression is of a quick end-over-end movement. The hand that remained on the wall has now pushed itself free and is about to join its opposite member. Note the sculling motion of the right hand which increases the speed of the body's rotation, and helps set the swimmer at an ideal depth below the surface.

Fig. 4 The feet are set lightly on the wall well below surface level. The body is deep enough to be able to push off below the disturbed surface water. The arms have joined together and are starting to extend.

Fig. 5 In the push-off from the wall, the body is streamlined, with arms and legs extended and head beneath the arms and balanced evenly on the breast.

The FINA rule states, "After the start and each turn the swimmer may take one arm stroke completely back to the legs and one leg kick while wholly submerged. The head must break the surface of the water before the hands turn inward at the widest part of the second stroke."

The FINA rule on the breaststroke turn says, "At each turn the body shall be on the breast. The touch shall be made with both hands simultaneously at, above, or below the water surface. Once a touch has been made, the swimmer may turn in any manner desired. The shoulders must be at or past the vertical toward the breast when the swimmer leaves the wall."

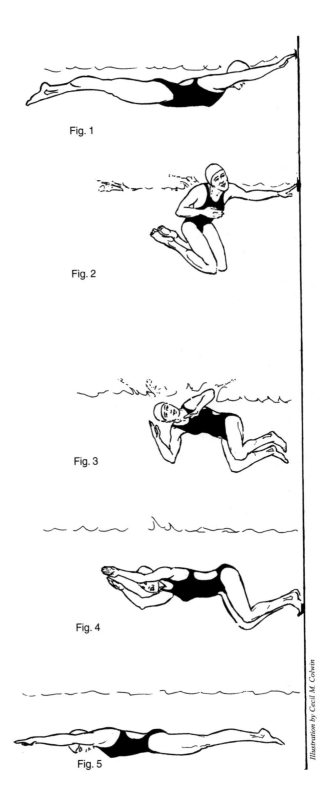

Fig. 1

Fig. 2

Fig. 3

Fig. 4

Fig. 5

Illustration by Cecil M. Colwin

THE BANDWAGON EFFECT

There has always been a tendency to jump on the bandwagons of the leading swimmers of the moment and copy their methods, irrespective of individual physique.

In this respect Rowdy Gaines and Ross Gerry gave timely advice in *Swimming Technique* about not slavishly copying the techniques of Alex Popov. But this same advice could hold good for willy-nilly copying any champion.

Rowdy Gaines suggested that sprinters should not "end up being too long on their stroke" because "not all of us can be Alex Popov." While Ross Gerry, in his article on freestyle tempo, said, "It would be foolish to think that a 5-foot, 10-inch swimmer would have the same stroke length as the 6-foot, 7-inch Popov. If both were swimming at the same maximal speed, the shorter swimmer would certainly need to carry a higher tempo. . . . Long and strong can't be held for long!"

However, while a shorter swimmer is unlikely to achieve the same distance per stroke as a Popov, a Biondi, or a Gary Hall, it has been proved that it isn't absolutely essential to be tall, lean, and lanky to benefit from rolling.

Japanese Introduced the Roll

I'm referring specifically to the successful Japanese Olympic teams of the 1930s. In fact, it was the short but streamlined Japanese who introduced the roll as a part of crawl swimming. Their average height was only 5 feet, 7 inches, yet they swept the boards at the 1932 and 1936 Olympics at a time when Western experts insisted that a flat body position was essential to speed (Cureton, 1934).

Although short in stature, the Japanese had well-rounded shoulders and slender, streamlined torsos and rolled freely from the hips (Beaurepaire, quoted in Kiphuth, 1942). It was also the Japanese swimmers of the 1930s who first realized that it was more efficient to swim with long strokes at a high tempo.

Westerners rushed to adopt the Japanese techniques with the result that swimming progress stalled for many years because the strokes they copied didn't fit naturally to their larger, less flexible physiques.

Hydroplaning Craze

Going back even farther to the 1920s, there was a hydroplaning craze in which everyone wanted to copy Johnny Weissmuller, also known as the Human Hydroplane. Weissmuller, one of the all-time greats, was said to have brought the American crawl to its highest level of perfection. Weissmuller, 6 feet, 3 inches tall and an immensely talented swimmer, swam with his head held very high and his back well arched. He tried to hydroplane, but this is impossible for a human swimmer to achieve under one's own power. Anyway, swimmers of all shapes and sizes tried to emulate Weissmuller's stroke with varying degrees of success or failure.

In 1945, when Alan Ford of Yale broke Weissmuller's 16-year-old 100-yard world record, he was reported in *Life* magazine to have said that he had "practiced until he rolls less than almost any other swimmer." However, Ford admitted to slight shoulder dropping as his arms passed his head which "slows down his speed." At the same time, Ford's coach, Robert Kiphuth, said, "Common faults which I have found in average swimmers are that they roll and let their heads get too low in the water."

Guess what happened then? Why, everyone tried to swim perfectly flat, just like the great Alan Ford. For a whole decade swimmers were coached to swim in this stilted fashion, with body flat, upper arms and shoulder girdle held static, while they

International Swimming Hall of Fame

Johnny Weissmuller was voted the outstanding swimmer of the first half of the twentieth century. He tried to hydroplane by swimming with head held very high and back well arched, but this is impossible for a human swimmer to achieve under one's own power.

Kevin Berry photo

Michael Wenden won the 100 meters at the 1968 Olympics while revving at the incredible rate of 65 strokes for the last length of the pool.

rolling movement includes shoulders, hips, and legs." About this time, Walter Schlueter of the United States was an advocate of rotating the body on its axis and streamlining the shoulders into the stroke.

Bilateral Body Alignments

Howard Firby, one of the greatest stroke technicians of all time, was probably among the first, if not the first, to view streamlining as a continuously changing process during the stroke. Firby coached champion swimmers in the early 1950s (before the Australian resurgence) who flipped from side to side in cadence—back when all the textbooks said don't roll!

Firby recognized the importance of allowing for differences among individuals when coaching stroke technique. Firby said, "A newcomer may be a budding Wenden, a potential Dawn Fraser, a Rick de Mont, and so on. I, then, simply nudge him into his groove through the use of stroke drills—he needn't even know he is being nudged.

"Wenden found success revving at the incredible rate of 65 strokes for the home length of the 100 meter he won at the 1968 Olympics. In my opinion, it was more a display of guts than skill. Spitz needed about 20 fewer strokes per length to win the event in 1972 in a faster time. If Wenden had tried to use the Spitzian style, it is unlikely he would have made the Australian Olympic team. Similarly, if some dolt of an unimaginative coach had negated Mark Spitz's brilliance by forcing the Wenden-type of power stroke upon him, Spitz would never have shone as a freestyler" (Firby, 1975).

Allow for Individual Differences

It should have been obvious that swimming with a flat body position could result in impingement of the supraspinatus tendon during the arm recovery. But, way back in the early 1940s when Alan Ford was swimming flat on the water, my teammates and I all wanted to swim like him. Our coach, Jimmy Green, who had studied under the great L. de B. Handley (one of the pioneers of American swimming in the early part of this century) had us in a quandary by actually being so heretic as to teach us to roll.

He would hold the end of a pencil between thumb and index finger, and roll it both clockwise and counterclockwise saying, "This is how your body

carefully, and almost surreptitiously, turned the head a couple of inches to the side to inhale, all this to avoid the slightest inclination to roll. This was a most unnatural action and, like the preceding era of copying the Japanese technique, the result again impeded swimming progress.

Australians' Technical Breakthrough

Thus it was ironic that in the next decade, Kiphuth's "poor technique items" were to become not only accepted practice, but also one of the main reasons for Australia's rise to world dominance at the 1956 Melbourne Olympics. The Australians made a complete break from the standardized techniques of the post–World War II era. The 1960s and 1970s were to see the greatest statistical all-round improvement in the history of the sport. The lesson the Australians restored to swimming was build the stroke around the individual, and not vice versa.

The Australian technique was one in which the shoulders were not held flat on the surface, as with the American crawl, but were allowed to rotate in time with the arm pull, bringing the more powerful trunk muscles into the action. The action of the legs was subdued but could be speeded up noticeably for sprinting.

According to Forbes Carlile, "The bodies of most of the Australian swimmers in recent years have rolled considerably around their long axis, and this should roll when you swim crawl. Your whole body rolls from the top of your head to the tip of your toes." He had another favorite saying that went something like this, "Streamlining is the unseen factor in swimming. You can build two yachts from the same plan, with the same length, depth, beam, and sail area, and one will give the other a quarter mile on any ordinary wind. What is the reason? Difference in hull design."

What my coach was saying still holds true today for swimmers of various body shapes. Some are cut out for speed while others are not ideally shaped to slip through water easily. Human bodies, like yachts and other kinds of vessels, range the whole gamut of speed potential. In fact, it often happens that, in some locales where there are no coaches, the best swimmer is simply the best-shaped one.

Knowledgeable coaches long ago taught swimmers to simply allow the shoulder to follow the forward arm into the entry, thus causing the body to roll. This was long before such buzzwords as "core swimming" and "power from the hips" were used to describe methods that had first seen the light of day a full 50 years earlier. The difference is that only the very tall, lean swimmers, such as Matt Biondi and Alex Popov, seem able to roll naturally and quickly and completely over onto their sides. In this ultrastreamlined position, with their unusually long strokes, they are able to prolong their momentum, an action once described by Biondi's coach, Nort Thornton, as "similar to skating on a roller blade."

A tall, lean swimmer has only to begin to lift the elbow of the recovery arm out of the water to make the body slip quickly onto its side—the swimmer's body would be hard put to it to do anything else! In fact, did you notice how Alan Ford described the difficulty he had in keeping his body flat when his recovery arm passed the shoulder line? In this respect, he was actually resisting his own natural inclination!

Because of physical characteristics, some swimmers are unable to roll quickly enough to time body rotation with the peak periods of hand acceleration. It is likely that height, buoyancy, average body width, and other such factors, will affect the total time taken to roll the body from one side to the other.

As mention earlier, the anatomical advantages of rolling bring in the large trunk muscles, rather than only the muscles of the upper arm, to result in a more powerful pull. Could it be that it is the more powerful arm pull that results in increased speed, rather than any streamlining "advantage" derived from rolling? In fact, there may even be increased resistance while rolling from the flat central position to a position where the body is completely on its side.

Kinetic Streamlining

Although mainly academic at this stage, there are other factors to be considered that eventually could throw light on unknown factors that might affect streamlining in swimming. The question is: Should all swimmers, irrespective of body type, attempt to roll completely onto each side during a stroke cycle? Rolling may not be the panacea for everybody. In fact, all may not be as simple as would appear at first glance.

In *Kinetic Streamlining* (Colwin, 1984b), I discussed streamlining within the mechanics of the stroke. I described in detail how talented swimmers assume constantly changing body shapes to assist a favorable propulsion-to-resistance ratio.

The aim of kinetic streamlining is to streamline interchanging body postures and configurations in order to reduce resistance and thereby prolong momentum. The moving body is streamlined by (1) rotation about its long axis, and (2) by timing this rotation with peak hand acceleration while maintaining critical postural alignments of the arms and legs as they propel and stabilize.

Changing the Body's Configuration

Each change of body configuration causes a new envelope of streamline patterns to form about the body.

When the body is centered squarely on its chest, it presents greater frontal resistance, like a barge, and the water flow will be deflected almost entirely downward under the body. But when a swimmer's body rolls on its long axis during a stroke cycle, an important hydrodynamic principle is followed: the use of gradually curved surfaces along the general paths followed by the water flow will minimize resistance.

However, it is only when the body is completely on its side that the desired smaller changes in curvature will result. When the body is completely on its side, its configuration will then be narrow enough to deflect the water equally in two directions as the bow of a ship does.

At this point, certain considerations should be taken into account. So far, we have mentioned only two basic body positions: (1) the central, flat on the chest barge-like position, and (2) the final, completely on the side, ideal ultrastreamlined ship-like position. But what about the interim postures of the body as it rolls from the central position to completely on the side?

During this transitional phase, no matter how quickly it occurs, the water flow will not be deflected equally around the body. In fact, it is more than likely that considerable resistance, even increased resistance, will occur during this transitional phase. For example, as the body rolls from center to side and back again, transverse flows around the torso and over the back, as well as on the shoulders, can be seen in freeze-frame, high-resolution videography.

Whatever the case may be, it should be obvious that a chunky, squarely built swimmer of medium height would not be able to quickly slip through this transitional phase from center to completely on the side with the same effortless dexterity as an Alex Popov or Matt Biondi. It seems that each swimmer needs to find the most effective amount of body roll suitable to the individual. It is a big mistake to try to standardize swimming strokes, without regard to individual physique and your natural movement inclination.

✧ ✧ ✧

IMPROVE YOUR FEEL OF THE WATER

When a force acts on water, it causes the water to react in two ways: (1) It flows. (2) It stretches, almost like elastic, except that it doesn't snap back again as elastic does when the force is removed.

To improve your feel of the water, it is important to feel the reacting flow created by your arm stroke, and also to develop the feeling of actually stretching the water as it flows. Once you achieve these two goals, you will be surprised at how easily you will slip through the water.

To become an accomplished swimmer, you should learn to anticipate, control, and manipulate the flow of the water. Most novices tend to use the arm like a blunt instrument, trying to shove the water backward with too much force.

You should appreciate that, in skilled swimming, the arm functions not merely as a propelling instrument, but also as an adroit and sensitive "shaper of the flow." In fact, skilled swimming consists of shaping the flow in an ideal pattern as you apply propulsive force against it.

Before you try to shape the flow, you should know exactly how to anticipate the flow and the direction in which you want to move it. Any object moving through a fluid—whether it be an airplane or a bird in the air, or a fish, a seal, or a human swimmer in the water—always creates an oncoming flow. It is important to always move forward into the oncoming flow in a manner that accepts the flow and does not break it up. This is important especially at the arm entry.

The oncoming flow, which in the crawl hand entry, for example, moves from the fingertips to the wrist and along the arm, is known as distal in its direction. A flow that moves toward the radial bone (or from thumb to little finger) is termed radial; for example, the flow produced when the elbows bend to bring the hands under the body in the crawl, butterfly, and breaststroke.

An ulnar flow moves toward the ulnar bone or from little finger to thumb; for example, the flow produced as the arms extend and the stroke rounds out to the hips in the crawl and butterfly.

A flow is proximal when it moves from the wrist toward the fingertips, as happens in the backstroke when the arm straightens at the end of the stroke (Schleihauf, 1979).

The aim in effectively handling the flow in all the swimming styles is:

1. At the arm entry, to accept the oncoming flow as it moves along your arm from the fingertips to the elbow;

2. Then to swirl the flow around your hand and forearm as your elbow bends;

3. Finally, to unswirl the flow by thrusting it backward off your forearm, hand, and fingertips, as your arm partially extends to complete the stroke.

Now that you know which flows to anticipate and how to handle them, here are a few exercises for improving the sensitivity of your hands as you shape and channel the flow in the desired direction. The hand can be held in a variety of postures while swimming to sensitize fingers, individually or in groups, to the sensation of *moving* pressure.

Keeping the hand closed sensitizes it via *static* pressure. These exercises greatly sensitize the hands to the feeling of moving pressure once the hands are fully opened again and normal swimming is resumed.

Start your workout by doing each exercise for at least one pool length as you warm up. Use care when swimming with only one or a few fingers extended because you can easily injure them by accidentally hitting the wall or prodding a passing swimmer.

1. Swim one length with forefinger extended.
2. Swim one length with little finger extended.
3. Swim one length with forefinger and little finger extended.
4. Swim one length with forefinger, little finger, and thumb extended.
5. Swim one length with fist tightly clenched. (Wearing a fistglove, invented by Scott Lemley, will further sensitize the hand.)

Now continue your warm-up with your hands opened. As you enter your hand at the beginning of each stroke, concentrate on accepting the oncoming flow and feeling the elasticity (or stretch) in the flow. Then, as you bend your arm, attempt to swirl the flow around your hand and forearm. Finally, as your arm extends, unswirl the flow and thrust it backward.

You will notice a pronounced improvement in your ability to feel and manipulate the flow of the water.

✧ ✧ ✧

WE DON'T SWIM IN DRY WATER

We may swim faster when we learn more about how the water reacts. The big problem is visualizing the flow.

What happens to the water when we swim? The answer is we don't exactly know. It's almost as if we swim in "dry water," a phrase coined by Nobel Prize physicist Richard Feynman of the California Institute of Technology.

When we develop a better understanding of what swimming strokes actually do to the water, it's possible we may swim faster. The percentage improvement may be small, but this is how we progress, one tiny step at a time.

Stroke mechanics are rarely analyzed with reference to the water and its resultant flow reactions. Biomechanists claim to be able to calculate the forces that swimmers develop in the water, but the trouble with these studies is that they depend on the premise of "essentially still water." Water doesn't obediently stand still while forces act upon it.

Consequently, some studies may well be flawed because they are based on the mechanics of solids rather than those of fluid behavior. In dealing with a solid, it is generally sufficient to measure the velocity of the body as a whole, whereas the motion of a fluid may be quite different at different points.

Water Under the Action of Forces

Moving water has very different properties from static water, for as soon as a swimmer's hand and the water start moving in relation to each other, another force begins to exert its influence. The force is so familiar that we accept it without second thought, yet all propulsion through a fluid, whether mechanical or natural, depends upon it. The force in question is resistance, or more precisely, the fluid's resistance to motion. Perhaps concentrating on developing resistance on the hands as we propel is more important than whether lift or drag forces predominate at any set stage of the stroke.

The proponents of lift-dominated propulsion and the proponents of drag-dominated propulsion, in one form or another, have continued a lift versus drag argument for nearly 20 years. These arguments are difficult to understand because the very first page of any fluid dynamics text will state that the force on a body moving through a fluid is resolved into two interacting components, one called lift and the other called drag. Human movements are arc-like by nature, and, of course, all swimmers work naturally to push the water backward, so these specious arguments are pointless. It's basic. Instead of belaboring the lift-versus-drag argument, we need to move on and learn more about the way the water reacts when we swim.

On the relatively few occasions when biomechanists refer to the water's reactions to a particular movement, their descriptions tend to gloss over the subject. Such comments will often refer to deflecting water particles rather than dealing with the total reacting flow of water created by each force impulse in the swimming stroke.

Because water does move under the action of forces, we need to understand what effects the forces developed by a swimmer have on the surrounding water, the flow field, as fluid dynamacists call it. One effect of such studies will lead to understanding the relative velocities of the water and the propelling members. This will help show, once and for all, that water does not obediently stand still while a swimmer's body is propelled forward past a fixed position in the water.

Swimmers and swimming coaches understand the importance of good streamlining, ideal stroke patterns, correct timing, distance per stroke, and stroke frequency. But most have little understanding of the effects of their stroking actions on the water. Occasionally, one will hear a coach say, "Pretend you are pulling through soft mud," or "Imagine you are pulling yourself along an imaginary knotted rope, or an invisible fixed point in the water." While these descriptions may create an effective word picture in a swimmer's mind, strictly speaking, they are inappropriate because the propulsive force is not being developed against a solid or rigid resistance.

When a swimmer strokes efficiently, propulsion results from the water's resistance to the applied force. Water changes shape when a force is applied to it. These changes are known as *deformation*, and they appear as flow and elasticity (caused by viscosity). A flow increases continuously under the action of an applied force, however small. A given force produces elasticity, which vanishes if the force is removed, unlike an elastic band which snaps back.

Flow and elasticity are the two characteristics of moving water a skilled swimmer feels and recognizes. Most swimmers are unaware of this. The swimmer isn't stuck in some rigid unyielding medium but creates a continuous dynamic situation within a moving flow that constantly changes. A swimmer should try to feel how the water flows and stretches in reaction to the force impulses applied during the swimming stroke.

Need for Flow Visualization

Neither should we forget that a swimmer, being human and not a machine, will not produce uniform forces within every stroke cycle, or exactly the same stroke patterns from one stroke cycle to the next. We can see that, ideally, the effectiveness of swimming strokes should be analyzed from both the biomechanical and fluid dynamic perspectives.

More can be done to improve our understanding, but because water is transparent, it is difficult to observe its reactions to human swimming propulsion. The ability to view reacting flows has depended upon occasional ideal shadow effects, and aeration caused by accidental air bubbles caught by the hands and feet as they break the air-water boundary at the entry or during the kick. Filming or taping swimmers at top speed, when they inevitably entrap air into the reacting flow and make it visible, has proved to be the most effective method to date.

To make the water's reactions visible by command, as it were, we need to develop a reliable and consistent method of flow visualization. Then it is possible we may obtain the full picture of human swimming, not only the forces developed by the swimming strokes, but also the effectiveness of these forces in the surrounding flow field.

Practical Benefits of Flow Visualization

Analyzing the flow reactions to the swimming strokes can yield three practical benefits:

1. *Understanding propulsion*: Learning how the water reacts to different types of propulsion; for example, pulling straight backward versus pulling in a curved-line path. Each mechanism produces its own distinctive pattern of flow reaction in the water (Colwin, 1985b).

2. *Analyzing propulsion*: Learning to observe and analyze the flow reactions caused by the swimming stroke. An oberver can relate flow reactions to the efficiency of an actual phase of the stroke by assessing the size, shape, and placement of the

vortex patterns (rotating flows) produced in the flow field. When the flow reactions are clearly visible, the trained observer can analyze the net effect of an entire stroke almost at a glance (Colwin, 1985a).

Fluid dynamacists are able to analyze the flows around ships, airplanes, fish, birds, and flying insects without too much difficulty in setting up their experiments. However, it is not yet possible to make detailed and accurate measurements of the flow reactions to the swimming stroke. We lack a reliable method of making the flow visible at will, irrespective of swimming speed.

3. *Improving propulsion*: Learning to recognize through the sense of touch the ideal flow reactions necessary to produce efficient propulsion. This involves a new and unique method of coaching stroke mechanics by having a swimmer associate the feel of the moving water with key phases of the swimming stroke (Colwin, 1987, 1992). (See page 71, "Improve Your Feel of the Water.")

The Energy of Motion
Whenever a swimmer completes a force impulse during the swimming stroke, a ring-shaped vortex is shed in the flow field. What is a vortex? A vortex is a mass of fluid that rotates about an axis. The axis of the vortex may be in almost any plane from vertical to horizontal. A vortex should be circular because a round vortex acts on a larger area or mass of fluid.

A vortex is a form of kinetic energy, the energy of motion. A shed vortex represents the energy produced by the swimmer and "given" to the water. In fact, when you see the vortices produced by the swimmer in the water, you are actually looking at the swimmer's propulsion. You can also see whether the propulsion is efficient or not.

Vortices often become visible to the underwater viewer when a swimmer is moving at top speed and accidentally entraps air into the stroke. If your pool does not have an underwater observation window, submerge wearing a face mask, and ask a skilled swimmer first to swim toward you, and then, later, to swim sideways past you. Vortices can also be seen by a pool deck observer, usually when a swimmer performs the downward thrust of the dolphin kick or completes the outward motion of the breaststroke arm pull.

What Should Be the Ideal Plane of a Shed Vortex?
Refer to the example of the circular vortex and

assume, for the time being, that we have a swimmer who can produce this perfectly shaped circular vortex. Let us orient the plane of this circular vortex at different angles, from vertical to horizontal.

When the plane of this circular vortex is vertical and its axis is horizontal, all the fluid particles the vortex acts on will be moved in the stream direction (the horizontal direction). This will result in ideal direct forward propulsion. When the plane of the vortex is horizontal, or lying parallel to the surface of the water, all the fluid particles that this vortex acts on will be directed downward, meaning that the net force created by the swimmer is upward rather than forward.

Conclusion, if a swimmer's stroke is efficient, the plane of the shed vortex will tend to be vertical or nearly so. The more vertical the vortex plane, the more likely that the propulsive impulse has generated near-maximum forward thrust. If a vortex is distorted or twisted, this is an indication of inefficiency in the stroke or some other fault that hinders efficient propulsion (Colwin, 1985b, 1992).

The Muscles and Sinews of Propulsion
In 1984 (Colwin 1984a), I presented a study on the significance of vortex flow reactions in the swimming stroke. Later I was surprised to hear my report referred to by biomechanists as the "vortex theory of propulsion." This is not a theory but a physical fact—there exists no other way of producing propulsion in a fluid.

Kuchemann (van Holst & Kuchemann, 1942), the noted fluid dynamicist, described vortices as "the muscles and sinews of propulsion," adding that "nothing ever happens without their presence." Without the resistive friction provided by vortex turbulence within a fluid, no tractive force would be provided. This is as true for swimmers as it is for ocean liners. In fact, all forms of propulsion through a fluid, whether by airplanes, fish, birds, flying insects, and so on, depend on the resistive force produced by vortices. Yet, paradoxically, were turbulence not produced by the motion of a body through a fluid, the process of streamlining would be quite unnecessary (Rouse, 1946).

Improving Flow Visualization
Experimental techniques to demonstrate fluid flow have always been challenging. Usually these

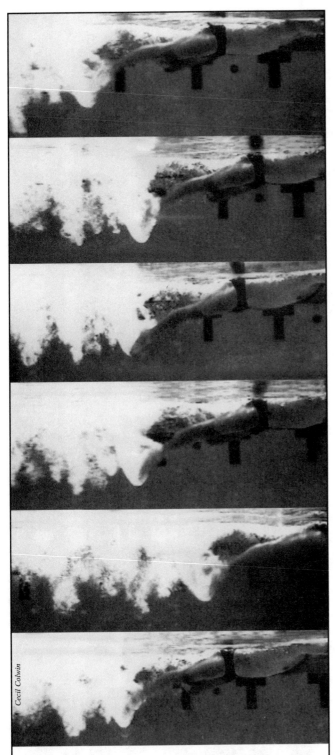

Raimundas Mazuolis practicing his powerful kick on a kickboard. His feet shed large ring vortices, almost in the vertical plane. This is an indication that the swimmer's propulsion is directed almost directly forward.

Cecil Colwin

techniques employ dye streamers or small tracers of some kind, but are typically clumsy and difficult to interpret, particularly if the flow involves vortices.

A novel system developed by McCutchen (1976) to analyze fish propulsion employed polarized light from point sources to create a shadow of a fish and its wake. McCutchen's "shadowgram system" provided just enough information for the observer to easily interpret the flow, but whether such experiments could be replicated on a scale large enough to analyze the flow reactions of human swimmers is unknown.

Nevertheless, by means of a similar test, the reader may obtain an idea of the basic flow reactions produced by human swimmers by simply moving a spoon or any other suitable foil-shaped object through the appropriate directions in a container of water. If you have a strong overhead light and the bottom of the tank is white, you will see the shadow cast by the resulting vortex on the bottom of the tank and be able to note the different reactions produced by straight-line (rectilinear) and curved-line (curvilinear) motions.

Flow Aeration Often Makes the Flow Visible

In wind tunnel or flow tank tests, it is common practice to introduce dye, smoke, or shiny particles of aluminum, into the moving fluid for visual or photographic observation. In the case of the human swimmer, visible agents such as dyes may not be safe.

However, at top speeds, as a result of accidental air entrapment into the swimming stroke, skilled swimmers often display predictable and regular flow reactions, not only from the impulses produced during each arm stroke, but from the oscillating movements of their legs as well. Unfortunately, this method is not practicable at slow or average speed because skilled swimmers rarely entrap sufficient air into the swimming stroke at these slower speeds to make the flow visible.

While it is possible to film or tape the flow reactions produced by aeration of the flow in top speed swimming, much practice is needed to capture the desired effects. Using a high-resolution video camera (Sony CCD-TR700) and a "Coachscope" underwater apparatus, I have found it effective to record swimmers from both side and front

Front view of Raimundas Mazuolis's crawl stroke. The athlete was swimming at slow speed (approximately 28 seconds per 50 yards), and there is only very slight aeration of the flow. The only aeration visible is near the shoulders and this was caused by Mazuolis's splash-type entry.

Here Mazuolis was swimming at top speed (over 25 yards at a rate of approximately 9.5 seconds). There is an abundance of visible vortex flow reactions from both the swimmer's hands and feet. These effects are often a result of high-speed swimming when accidental air entrapment is inevitable.

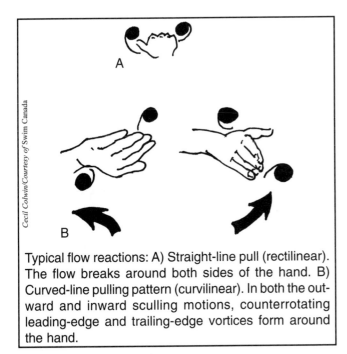

Cecil Colwin/Courtesy of Swim Canada

Typical flow reactions: A) Straight-line pull (rectilinear). The flow breaks around both sides of the hand. B) Curved-line pulling pattern (curvilinear). In both the outward and inward sculling motions, counterrotating leading-edge and trailing-edge vortices form around the hand.

views. The side-view shots are ideal for capturing the placement of the shed vortices, the nearer to the vertical plane, the more directly forward is the swimmer's propulsive effort.

The front-view shots provide a good idea of the mass of water acted upon by the swimming stroke. If each shed vortex is circular and large with a thin circumference rim, this is a good indication. If the vortex is relatively small and twisted or contorted, this signals poor stroke application requiring closer analysis of stroke placement, including inspection of the swimmer's changing hand and arm posture throughout the stroke.

Observing the flow reactions of swimmers moving toward the camera presents a difficulty. When a swimmer pushes off from the wall, the first complete cycle of left arm and right arm pull produces an initial set of vortex rings. However, each new set of flow reactions, produced by subsequent stroke cycles, tends to obscure the previous ones. This superimposition of flow reactions results in a jumbled mass of reacting fluid in the flow field that makes observation difficult.

This difficulty can be solved by zooming in on the swimmer and having the swimmer swim a short distance such as the width of a diving pool. In this manner, when the tape is played back, the images produced by the first stroke cycle will be large enough for clear analysis.

Seeking the Aid of Fluid Dynamacists

A researcher in biomechanics, uncertain of a flow reaction shown in a photograph or series of movie frames, may seek the opinion of a fluid dynamacist as to its significance. The fluid dynamacist, by the same token, unfamiliar with the movement sequences that produced the visible effect, may give an opinion based on the immediate appearance of the flow reaction without knowledge of the mechanism that produced it.

I had similar experiences when I first enlisted the aid of fluid dynamacists. A two-way difficulty existed. It was necessary for me to learn more about the fundamentals of fluid dynamics, while at the same time enlightening my tutors on the subject of swimming biomechanics. As a result, a better mutual understanding was developed.

We need the help of fluid dynamacists to investigate the specific problems of swimming fluid dynamics, not least of all the challenges of flow visualization in a transparent medium. But there are difficulties involved in seeking their assistance. These difficulties are compounded by the fact that few fluid dynamacists have the time or inclination to spend on detailed research of this nature.

Cecil Colwin

Raimundas Mazuolis at top speed (9.5 seconds for 25 yards) showing ring vortex reactions from several stroke cycles superimposed upon each other, thus making analysis difficult. This difficulty can be solved by zooming in on the swimmer and having him cover a short distance such as the width of a diving pool. Vortices are the muscles and sinews of propulsion, and the activity, seen here in the flow field, represents a "history" of the swimmer's propulsion.

Moreover, prominent fluid dynamacists, when asked whether the flow reactions to human swimming propulsion could be analyzed by computer simulation, expressed the opinion that the rapidly changing body configurations of human swimmers almost defy complete analysis.

What is the alternative? The alternative is for as many interested students of swimming mechanics as possible to obtain a basic knowledge of fluid dynamics. They will learn the significance of the distinctive vortex flow reactions caused by different propulsive mechanisms.

Instead of pursuing complex studies, the objective should be to confine early attempts to the most simple dimensions of a problem. The important thing is to make a start. In the first instance, they should learn how to conduct very simple experiments. They will learn how to draw arrows on photographs of a flow reaction in order to assess the speed and direction of the flow. Eventually, they will develop the skill to obtain a satisfactory representation of the flow at any instant.

In time, such experiments would enable coaches to understand more about the effects on the water of their swimmers' stroke mechanics. Their swimmers would learn how best to use the arms as more efficient propulsive instruments that act on a large mass of water with every stroke impulse.

✧ ✧ ✧

STROKE TECHNIQUE OR STROKE PRODUCTION?

Not enough reference is made to the difference between stroke technique and stroke production. In fact, I have never heard anyone make this important distinction in precise terms. It is essential to realize that stroke drills should have a definite purpose. The purpose, however, will vary according to whether you are using drills to teach a beginner the basic fundamentals of stroke mechanics, or aiming to improve the stroke production of a seasoned competitor in the actual racing situation.

At the beginner level, stroke drills should teach the fundamentals of technique: body balance, the

path of the arm stroke, kick, correct timing, and so on. And, if you can teach as much of the whole stroke as possible in one single drill, so much the better. A little later, the beginner will be shown shaping drills that teach the more refined aspects of stroke technique such as hand, elbow, and wrist postures, head-turning mechanics, and so on.

The entire process outlined above can be categorized as "teaching technique" or "coaching stroke mechanics," or whatever you want to call it. However, at the level of the mature competitor, drills should focus on improving the swimmer's stroke output—the efficient use of muscular strength and power in the actual racing situation. In other words, the emphasis is on stroke production.

Very often, the same drills used with a beginner will be used by the advanced swimmer, however, both the purpose and the emphasis of the drills will be different. The drills are now not only concerned with establishing ideal stroke patterns, but also with improving the swimmer's application of muscular strength and power. Stroke drills for mature swimmers will emphasize such aspects of efficient stroke production as well-timed (and adequate) body rotation, stroke acceleration, distance per stroke, and stroke frequency.

Many of the world's leading swimmers use stroke drills regularly because stroke production is an important part of competitive performance. Many top swimmers have their own favorite drills that best serve their individual needs. For example, one swimmer may prefer a certain drill because it aids shoulder joint flexibility, while another swimmer may like a drill because it improves timing between body roll and arm pull.

Other drills will help a swimmer place the stroke in a path where the swimmer is able to secure the most efficient stroke application, the strongest resistance of the water against the hand. Swimmers and coaches need to experiment to find the drills that help the individual swimmer to develop the most productive stroke mechanics.

Many coaches schedule stroke drills into their workouts according to a time slot rather than a set distance. In these instances, where practicable, swimmers should be given opportunity to practice drills specific to their own needs.

Too many coaches neglect to observe their swimmers underwater. While this should be done regularly, it is surprising that so many coaches do not do this at all. Light refraction makes it nearly impossible to coach stroke technique from the pool deck. But the advent of such aids as the "Snooper" make it easy to regularly record swimmers underwater on videotape while they perform their stroke drills.

Finally, this is what John Carew, coach of the great Kieren Perkins, had to say about stroke drills: "Swimming drills are the fastest and most effective ways of molding technique without interfering with other facets of training. One of the things I can't emphasize enough is stroke drills when working on technique. They aid swimmers to get the feel of the water and help toward achieving the correct pattern of your stroke model.

"All stroke drills should be tailored to your model of each particular stroke, rather than a drill some other coach uses. Drills should be effectively incorporated in training sessions. Stroke drills during the taper are extremely important and should be incorporated in at least one session a day. In obtaining maximum results, the intensity and degree to which the swimmers apply themselves determine the end result. The world's top tennis players and golfers all have coaches working on technique daily. I cannot see the wisdom in training and conditioning swimmers who will never reach full potential because of inferior technique."

Remember, it is possible to become an expert at doing drills without improving your normal stroke. You should guard against this happening! Therefore, it is important that every drill should be done with a purpose in mind. The drill should assist the needs of the individual swimmer.

Illustrations

Some of the drills shown here will develop triceps strength needed for stroke acceleration, and producing long strokes without tiring. The breaststroke drill is ideal for developing hand speed and foot speed. There are many other drills that a coach can use, and, of course, still others waiting to be invented by individual coaches and swimmers to suit their particular needs.

Freestyle Underwater Recovery Drill

Purpose: To synchronize the pull with the body roll. The pull and body roll should start at the same time. Also to develop hand acceleration as the hand thrusts through to the end of the stroke.

Fig. 1 The swimmer lies on his right side with his right arm and shoulder extended forward so that his left shoulder is above and behind his right shoulder. His left arm is at his side.

Fig. 2 The body roll starts. The swimmer starts the right arm pull at exactly the same time as the body starts to roll. Strong pressure of the water should be held on the palm of the hand as the body roll starts. This is an important point in timing. The right elbow is kept high by keeping the armpit open while pointing the elbow out to the side of the pool. The left arm reaches forward underwater.

Fig. 3 The swimmer completes the roll through to the opposite side of the body. The swimmer has concentrated on accelerating the right hand through to the completion of its stroke. The swimmer now lies on his left side with the left arm and shoulder extended forward

so that the other shoulder is behind it. While lying in this position, the swimmer completes six sideways beats of the legs before turning back to the other side.

Fig. 4 At the same time as the body roll starts, the swimmer starts the left arm pull, while feeling strong water pressure on the palm of the hand. Maintaining this pressure on the palm of the hand throughout the ensuing body roll will naturally produce a pulling pattern shaped like the letter "S." (Note: Producing this pattern is not the result of conscious effort.) The left elbow is kept high by keeping the armpit open and pointing the elbow out to the side of the pool. The right arm reaches forward underwater.

Fig. 5 The swimmer completes the roll through to the opposite side of the body. The swimmer has concentrated on accelerating the left hand pull through to the end of its stroke. The swimmer has returned to the position shown in Figure 1 and, after performing six sideways beats of the legs while lying in this position, the sequence (figs. 1 to 5) is repeated.

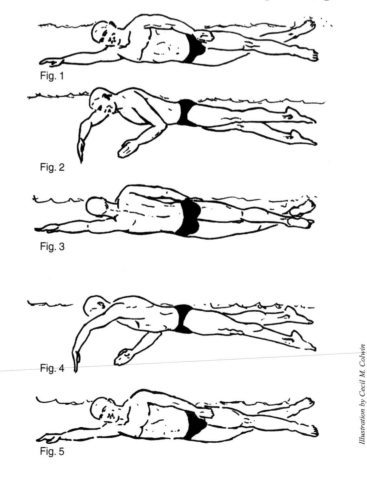

Fig. 1

Fig. 2

Fig. 3

Fig. 4

Fig. 5

Illustration by Cecil M. Colwin

Backstroke One-Arm-Only Drill

Purpose: To synchronize the pull with the body roll. The pull and the body roll should start at the same time. Also to develop hand acceleration as the hand thrusts through to the end of the stroke.

Fig. 1 With both hands at the sides, the swimmer rolls the body to the left, at the same time rolling the right shoulder out of the water.

Fig. 2 Leading with the right shoulder, the right arm is recovered from the water.

Fig. 3 The body roll to the left is almost completed as the recovering right arm reaches over its shoulder to the entry.

Fig. 4 The body is flat on the back as the right arm enters and the hand feels for the pressure of the water on the palm of the hand. All this time the left arm has remained at the side of the body.

Figs. 5 to 7 Here follows a critical point in timing: As the right arm starts its pull, the body rolls back to the left with the hip leading the action. This brings powerful trunk muscles into play as the hand rapidly accelerates to the end of the stroke. From this position the entire sequence will be repeated in rhythm.

Repeat with the other arm after each length of the pool has been completed.

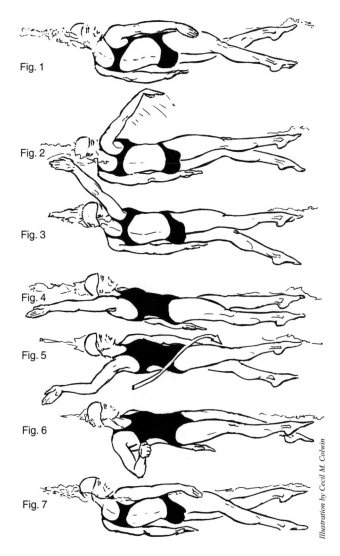

Fig. 1

Fig. 2

Fig. 3

Fig. 4

Fig. 5

Fig. 6

Fig. 7

Illustration by Cecil M. Colwin

Butterfly Thrust-Kick-and-Return Drill

"The highest speeds ever attained in swimming in terms of feet per second, are those measured during the 'flying' part of butterfly."

—The late, great Howard Firby, one of the greatest stroke technicians who ever lived, in his book *Howard Firby on Swimming* (1975).

Purpose: To increase hand acceleration and practice second-kick timing.

Firby also likened the timing of the arm action and the second kick in butterfly to a person trying to pull himself up to the top of a high fence "receiving the distinct advantage of a boost up from a friend on the ground." Firby said that the climber's arms wouldn't have to work nearly as hard as they would if the operation was one of strictly arms only.

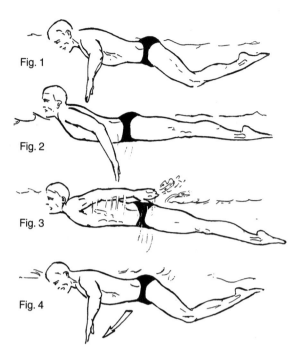

Illustration by Cecil M. Colwin

Fig. 1 The hands are about to thrust backward and outward in an accelerating motion to the end of the stroke, and the knees are bent with the feet at their highest point, ready to kick forcefully downward.

Fig. 2 The combined motion of the hands thrusting backward and outward as the feet drive down hard.

Fig. 3 However, instead of continuing into their normal recovery, the hands stop short, just after they leave the water.

Fig. 4 The hands are allowed to drop back into the water where they reassume the position in which they started the drill.

Figs. 1 to 4 The drill is repeated in regular sequence as the swimmer progresses down the pool. The duration of the drill should be governed by the amount of stress placed on the arms.

CAUTION: The hands should be moved backward AND outward to avoid impingement of muscles against the bony structures of the shoulder joint.

Breaststroke Speed Drill

Purpose: To develop hand and foot speed, two essential elements in breaststroke swimming efficiency.

Figs. 1 to 4 Keeping legs completely extended, do three rapid sequences of arm pull and recovery, and then return to stretched out position.

Figs. 5 to 8 Keeping arms completely extended forward, do three rapid but complete leg kicks. (Note: Extend the legs completely at the end of each kick.)

Next do three complete strokes (not shown here) using BOTH arms and legs in the conventional action. Then repeat in sequence drills, Figures 1 through 4, and Figures 5 through 8, as shown.

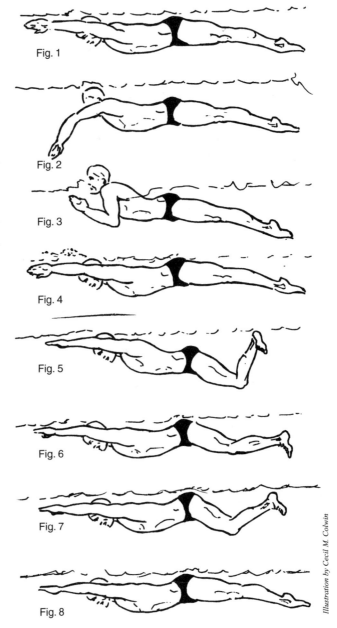

Fig. 1

Fig. 2

Fig. 3

Fig. 4

Fig. 5

Fig. 6

Fig. 7

Fig. 8

Illustration by Cecil M. Colwin

✧ ✧ ✧

"RTR"—RELATING TRAINING TO THE PACE OF THE RACE

When planning for the upcoming season, it is important to set precise goals. To achieve these goals, certain training formulas and ideas should be introduced into the seasonal training schedule.

One goal that should be an obvious inclusion for any coach is to reproduce the swimmers' best times of the previous season by the halfway mark of the new season. The purpose of this objective should be obvious, yet few coaches realize the obvious common sense of being able to attain the previous season's best times before being able to improve further.

If a swimmer has built a good base during the previous season, the previous season's best times will be reached without much sharpening training. At this stage, the work will be mainly aerobic with only occasional forays into anaerobic metabolism. While the early season aerobic base will enable the swimmer to maintain a high average speed through the middle stage of a distance, a certain amount of anaerobic training or sharpening work should be introduced gradually as the season progresses.

Aerobic training is performed at submaximal levels of intensity, the aim being to enable the swimmer to build endurance. The swimmer becomes able to swim farther and faster before lactate builds up in the muscles. A gradual improvement in aerobic fitness enables the swimmer to achieve a higher percentage of race speed before reaching the lactate/ventilatory threshold, the point at which it becomes increasingly difficult to supply energy to the muscles by aerobic means only.

The coach should gradually introduce into the training program certain aspects of race-pace preparation. As a preliminary to this phase of the program, it is useful to schedule effort swims over either the 400-meter or 500-yard distances. The purpose of these swims is to gradually introduce into endurance training a necessary element of speed.

These 400/500 effort swims should be conducted on alternate days, two or three times a week, based upon the coach's assessment of the individual swimmer's ability to handle them.

These effort swims, in a sense, are a type of time trial. The coach asks the swimmers to swim at "fastest comfortable pace," taking care not to make it a flat-out swim. The initial fast swim will be followed by two or three more swims over the same distance, performed at a slightly slower pace, but still at "fastest comfortable" pace, taking into allowance the effects of accumulative fatigue.

The advantage of this type of training is not merely contained in the workout it produces. It also provides a regular check on the swimmer's improvement as the season progresses. This is because the middle distance is a good index of the swimmer's speed and endurance level.

The swimmer's split times for these effort swims should be carefully logged, and when the stage is reached where a swimmer has difficulty in further lowering the 400/500 time, the focus will change to improving initial speed over the 100 and the 200 intermediate distances. In this manner, more and more sharpening work is gradually introduced as the seasonal program expands to include a broader spectrum of different types of workloads.

Gradually, more specific race-pace training will be introduced. Many swimmers do their pace training by means of interval speed training and rested repeat training over shorter multiples of the racing distance, done at a percentage of the desired race pace.

However, it is valuable to introduce workouts that relate more specifically to the pace of the race for which the competitor is training.

Over-the-Distance Training

Broadly stated, over-the-distance swims are twice as long as the distance for which the swimmer has specialized. For example, a 100-meter swimmer should also train for the 200 meter and compete at that distance, too. And so on up the scale. When a swimmer has a good base of over-the-distance swimming, it is often easier to compete at the shorter distance. Over-the-distance swimming provides the endurance necessary to finish a race strongly, especially when competing in the 50-meter course.

Under-the-Distance Training

This method of training has not yet been fully exploited. The pool bulkhead should be moved to provide a 16²/₃-meter course. Swimmers should be encouraged to improve their speed over each of the following intermediate distances on the way to the 100-meter mark: 16²/₃-meters, 33¹/₃-meters, 50 meters, 66²/₃-meters, and 83¹/₃-meters. In training for the 200-meter event, the distances swam are extended to include 100 meters, 116²/₃-meters, 133¹/₃-meters, 150 meters, 166²/₃-meters, and 183 ¹/₃ meters.

Benefits of the Under-the-Distance Training Method

- When sprint swimming 16²/₃-meters, a swimmer can achieve the highest possible rate of speed, learn to improve starting time off the block, and improve on accurately timing the first few strokes out of the dive.

- By improving speed over smaller sections of the racing distance, a greater refinement of pace is learned than would be possible in a larger pool. This method makes it easier to detect the exact stage at which speed starts to slacken.

- The increased number of turns provides extra turning practice, improving the speed of the turn as well as the strength and power necessary to perform it.

- The method enables different breathing patterns to be introduced on each length of the pool.

- The method is an excellent conditioner when used judicially. Short sets of repeat swims, such as 4 x 100 meters with 5 to 10 minutes rest, can be done with great benefit four to three weeks before tapering for a major event (Colwin, 1992).

Building Race Pace

Race pace can be built by repetition sets as follows:

1. 15 x 50 (3 minutes rest)
2. 10 x 100 (5 minutes rest)
3. 6 x 150 (5–10 minutes rest). The last two 150-meter swims should be faster than the swimmer's 150 split recorded on the way to the swimmer's best time for 200 meters.
4. 4 x 250 (10 minutes rest). The last two 250 repeats should be faster than the swimmer's 250 split recorded on the swimmer's best time for 400 meters. (Incidentally, the swimmer's time at the 200 mark will usually accord with the 200-meter pace recommended to the swimmer by physiologists for the purpose of high-lactate training.)

Applying items 3 and 4 during a hard training season can be highly effective in improving a swimmer's times for the 200- and 400-meter events, probably because a swimmer becomes accustomed to tolerating higher levels of lactate around the 150 mark in the 200, and the 250 mark in the 400—the exact stages of the race at which most swimmers start to become fatigued.

All of the above routines are good examples of "RTR"—relating training to the pace of the race.

❖ ❖ ❖

TETHERED SWIMMING

Swimming history has many examples of old methods recycled and used as new. Tethered swimming was first tried 60 years ago.

What is tethered swimming? *Webster's* dictionary describes a *tether* as a rope used for confining an animal within certain limits. If this implies psychological overtones, think of all those animal lanes in training pools around the world.

But back to trace the course of history. Time was when swimmers were trained "under the rod." The mixed metaphor forgiven, it was a case of spare the rod and spoil the swimmer. This wasn't a birch rod, but one used for deep-sea fishing held in the hands of a tall, massive man named Stan Brauninger.

Brauninger, a leading coach of the 1930s, was a whimsical pioneer of training specificity. His philosophy was simple. To swim like a fish, you had to train like a fish.

He stood at the end of the pool, braced against the gutter, plying deep-sea rod and reel as he attempted to land a swimmer. Brauninger's methods were recorded in a 1936 issue of *Esquire* magazine. He had a tough, one hour battle trying to

Coach Stan Brauninger, a pioneer of tethered swimming. "To swim like a fish, you had to train like a fish."

land one Otto Jaretz, the world's fastest swimmer and shatterer of many of Weissmuller's records.

"Jaretz churned the water with all the strength of his magnificent body," relates the article, "but lost ground steadily as the powerful coach continued to reel him in. 'Nice going, Otto.' Brauninger chuckled as he hauled the world champion alongside like a fish.

" 'Hey, Sunny,' the coach barked calling to Adolph Kiefer, Olympic backstroke champion whose lane lines today quell water and control pool turbulence. 'Stretch out and lay back into your stroke—and pull until that rope snaps.' "

Kiefer was whipping up waves in a training harness at the other side of the pool. Swimming backstroke with a long elastic rope attached to a canvas belt about his midriff, Sunny smiled up at his coach, nodded understandingly, and proceeded to follow instructions—literally. He did break that rope.

The article goes on to describe Brauninger's "Aquacademy." The halls of science and learning were situated in the half-million dollar pool of the Chicago Towers Club and were established as an aquatic laboratory for research in swimming and diving.

"The waters of the ultramodern natatorium served as a proving ground for champions—a research clinic that often transforms this year's guinea pigs into next year's champions. Its test tubes, microscopes, cultures and slides are slow motion cameras, dynamometers, training harnesses and stop watches—and 100,000 gallons of solarized water.

"Working hand and hand with his staff, Brauninger does research work, makes analyses, conducts tests and keeps an extensive filing system that holds records of his findings and results of his studies."

In the present all this sounds familiar.

"The most interesting guinea pig from a clinical viewpoint was Adolph 'Sunny' Kiefer who began training at 14 by putting on a training harness and pulling against a steel spring tensionometer until his eyes fairly popped."

Brauninger said that he believed in hard work. "My kids swim a mile every day—sometimes more than that."

Brauninger frowned on calisthenics and other sports. "Nearly every sport but swimming has a tendency to tighten the muscles," he said. "I've found that the best way to build up a swimmer is to have him swim distance so that his muscles are trained for swimming. I never allow my team in a gym. I keep them in the pool where they develop the long, smooth, pliant muscles so essential for a good swimmer. A person with tight muscles tires too easily."

Brauninger proved his point with Kiefer and other great swimmers of the era. Kiefer, the 1930s equivalent of "Redoubtable" Roland Matthes and "Waving" John Naber, ruled world backstroke swimming undefeated 10 ten years.

Tethered swimming training became widely adopted.

In 1950, I was given a "discourager" by coach Harold Minto of the Firestone Country Club of Akron, Ohio, who had trained Jimmy MacLane, the first postwar Olympic 1,500 champion. The apparatus consisted of a canvas harness connected to several yards of elastic aircraft shock absorber cord.

In 1950, South Africa sent only three swimmers to the Empire Games in Auckland, New Zealand, and each swimmer won at least one gold medal. They were all trained on the discourager apparatus.

At Yale University, 1952, I saw scores of elastic stretch bands suspended from the balcony of the practice pool where the great Yale and Olympic coach Robert Kiphuth was a firm believer in their use.

International Swimming Hall of Fame

Adolph "Sunny" Kiefer, 1936 Olympic backstroke champion. An early user of tethered swimming.

Many coaches varied the type of apparatus they used. Some coaches devised harnesses attached to bicycle inner tubes. Others, like Don Talbot, used the type of tubing fitted to underwater spearfishing guns. Santa Clara's George Haines used 202 latex surgical tubing for stretch cord exercises on land.

The application of tethered swimming was fairly uniform. Two different methods were to swim nonstop for a set number of strokes or to swim past a mark on the pool bottom and stay past that point for a specified time.

In the late '50s and the '60s, the use of tethered swimming became sporadic, perhaps because coaches wanted to try other methods such as land training with pulley weights, barbells, isometric bars, and friction or centrifugal exercise machines. The principle of the specificity of exercise became the vogue.

About this time, numerous gimmicks hit the market. Swimmers would arrive at the pool burdened with enough training devices to look like a one-man band.

But by the mid- '70s, the wheel was beginning to turn full circle. Coach Randy Reese at Gainesville, Florida, caused a run on the gutta-percha plantations of Malaysia. Reese was reported to have bought surgical tubing in bulk to be cut into sections of varying lengths.

Reese then set up stretch drills while insisting his swimmers maintain proper stroke form as they swam against the resistance of the tubing for almost any distance.

"We have found that 45 minutes of tube work 3 mornings a week is the equivalent to an hour and a half of straight swimming," he said.

Reese recommends using black tubing. "It seems better than the amber-colored because it withstands pool chemicals, weathers better, and lasts longer."

When you consider that most land exercises involve pulling the arms past the body rather than the body moving past the arms, as in actual swimming, the specificity of much land training is questionable.

Says Australian coach-scientist Forbes Carlile, "A reassessment of dryland training may point to the advantages of tethered or semitethered swimming as a specific strengthening device."

As for the future, have we reached the end of our tether or will high tech produce an automatic fishing reel—a computerized device to free the coach for real fishing?

Chapter 3

FROM THE PACIFIC CAME THE CRAWL

WHY STUDY SWIMMING HISTORY?

In recent years I have often been pleasantly surprised to learn that yet another coaching colleague is a collector of rare books and documents on swimming. The historical literature of the swimming strokes will repay careful study. When we read old books on swimming we learn from the experiences of outstanding teachers and swimmers of other days. In a sense, viewing the past from our privileged viewpoint, we have a sensation of having seen the future, and thus we become able to form a better perspective of the processes of change.

Sometimes, we can almost see the old pioneers taking a wrong turn, and from the history we know it is a wrong turn. Similarly, when the pioneers finally strike pay dirt we indeed learn from our predecessors because we come to understand a little more about the nature of the empirical, trial-and-error, process in developing new methods. An understanding of the older strokes and methods, with an appreciation of their strong and weak points, helps in explaining the reasons why certain strokes and coaching methods have become obsolete and other more efficient ones have taken their place. Then we should ask ourselves, how efficient are the strokes that we are using today? Do we incorrectly think that we have reached the summit of technical development?

The study of swimming history can give even today's experts some powerful clues about possible directions for future development in stroke mechanics. For instance, nearly 100 years ago, history tells us that two different types of freestyle swimming existed—one style for sprinting and one for distance swimming.

Today, true to form, history is repeating itself. When we study today's short-distance swimmers, we see a different stroke developing, a style in which the arms propel by pushing almost directly backward, using predominant drag propulsion, and little curved-line pulling. They are swimming so fast that there simply isn't the time to develop a curvilinear path in the arm stroke. We need to take a new look at the different stroke mechanics of sprint and distance swimming.

But this is just one example. How many people have given much more thought to what David Berkoff showed us about streamlining and dolphin kick propulsiveness when he swam underwater backstroke in the Seoul Olympics? Will students of swimming history 100 years hence smile at us when they observe how slow we were to note the straw in the wind released by Berkoff and his coach?

For instance, are we being neglectful in not pursuing the possibility for a crawl dolphin stroke? Berkoff brought home to us the superiority of dolphin kicking over the alternate flutter kick. Was this a valid clue? Does the idea sound ridiculous to you? Is it any more ridiculous than Dick Cavill's statement nearly 100 years ago, that crawl should not be used for distances over 100 yards? Yes, studying the history of our sport will provide not only a wealth of interesting information, but also a perspective that can hardly be gained in any other way.

◇ ◇ ◇

ENGLISH SWIM COACH EXECUTED FOR TREASON

Let me hasten to tell you that swimming teacher and author Everard Digby was hanged, not for writing about Prince Charles or Princess Di or any other member of the Royal Family, but for actually trying to blow up the Sovereign and the House of Lords with approximately one ton of gunpowder . . . and that all this happened nearly 400 years ago.

Way back in 1587, Sir Everard Digby (to give him his full title) wrote the first book on swimming published in England, two copies of which still exist at Cambridge University. In the custom of the time, Digby wrote the book in Latin. Translated into English the title of the book was *The Art of Swimming*. The Latin title, however, was long and sonorous: *De Arte Natande, Libri Duo, Quorum Prior Regular Ipsius Artim, Posterior Vero Praxin Demonstrationemque Continuet.*

Because Digby's book was written in Latin, its circulation was probably limited to the educated classes of the time. It was not until 1595 that Christopher Middleton translated parts of Digby's book and published them in a manual titled *A Short Introduction for the Learne to Swimme Gathered out of Master Digbie's Books of the Art of Swimming.*

These early books were printed and bound by craftsmen and made to last and be treasured for years as precious receptacles of human knowledge. It is, therefore, no surprise that the French author M. Thevenot, over 100 years later, drew inspiration from Digby's book and elaborated upon it in *L'Art de Nager*. It is an interesting fact that Thevenot's book was published in a number of abridgments from 1696 until as recent a date as 1972!

With the wisdom of hindsight, it could be said that Sir Everard Digby made two big mistakes in his life. First, he should have written his book in English—he may have had a bestseller. Second, he should have kept out of politics—he may have lived longer. As it was, he got mixed up with a notorious gentleman by the name of Guy Fawkes and, together with several other conspirators, concealed 36 barrels of gunpowder in a vault under the House of Lords with the intention of blowing up King James I, parliament and all.

Someone gave the plot away causing most of the conspirators to flee. But not Sir Everard Digby. Anxious for the plot to succeed, his cowardly confreres told Digby that the King was already dead and in this way persuaded him to further implicate himself. A report of the time said that Digby was "run to earth by the sheriff at Hawell Grange."

Digby and seven other conspirators were executed by being hanged, drawn and quartered, which was the extremely barbarous method stipulated for punishing treason. The sentence was that the offender "be drawn on a hurdle to the place of execution, that there he be hanged by the neck but not till he be dead, and that while yet alive he be disemboweled and that then his body be divided into four quarters, the head and quarters to be at the disposal of the crown." (At the risk of wandering too far from the subject, let me tell you that this method of punishing traitors was only abolished in 1870.)

That's the story of what happened to one of England's earliest swimming teachers and the author of the first swimming book published in that country. Finally, it may be of interest that Digby's son, Sir Kenelm Digby (1603–1665) managed to keep his nose clean. He was said to have exemplified the Renaissance ideal of the complete man, and was an English diplomat, naval commander, philosopher, and author. He is not known to have written on swimming, but he did become known as the author of a book on immortality.

❖ ❖ ❖

THEVENOT—THE WORLD'S FIRST SCIENTIST-COACH

Monsieur Thevenot (1620–1692) was probably the world's first scientist-coach, yet he devised comic water stunts to popularize the sport and amuse spectators who came to see him swim.

Here's Thevenot on "How to Cut the Nails of the Toes in the Water:" It is possible to perform actions in the Water; "which one cannot do on land: I myself have often brought my Great Toe to my lips in the Water, which I could never do on land, nor on my bed. You must hold your knife in your right hand (if you are right handed) and take up your left leg and lay the foot on your right knee; there you may take it from the left hand, and with the right cut your Nails without any danger. Then you may also pick your Toes; and if this way has no other use or advantage yet the dexterity of the management may serve to recommend it." So wrote Monsieur Melichedech Thevenot in *The Art of Swimming*, first published in 1696 and regarded as the authoritative book on swimming for over 200 years.

Lest you think that Thevenot was a crazy eccentric, you should know that he founded the French Academy of Sciences, was a distinguished Oriental scholar, and was regarded as a minor celebrity in his lifetime, according to Liana Van der Bellen, chief of the rare books division of Canada's National Library. In addition to *The Art of Swimming*, he also wrote books on travel and navigation as well as a catalog of the valuable books under his care as curator of the French Royal Library.

Thevenot's book throws a clear light on the status of swimming as a sport 300 years ago, as well as the problems of finding safe and hygienic places to swim. First of all, the reader should appreciate that skilled swimmers were a novelty and that they "created admiration in the Spectators of the Swimmer's activity" in similar fashion to the admiration evoked today by the technique of Mary T. Meagher, Matt Biondi, Alex Popov, or the diving genius of Greg Louganis.

In a book that was "very proper for persons to read in these sickly times," Thevenot recommends that people do not swim before "that time of the year which is the best, wherein people follow the Baths, or Swimming for their diversion, or to retain the habit of it; that is in the Month of May, June, July and August, especially in our Climate, where the water is often prejudicial to the Health at other times. There are also some Anomalous Years [Thevenot is probably referring to the periodic outbreaks of plague that ravaged the European continent] wherein it is not healthful to go into the water."

Thevenot prescribes several routines for extricating oneself from weed entanglement and it is safe to assume that weed growth was a constant problem for early swimmers. He gives further advice to would-be swimmers: "The night is also improper for this Exercise; and weeds that may entangle the Feet, are also obstacles among the rest, that ought to deter any prudent person from venturing among them, specially considering, that although you have company with you, yet you may be lost beyond any possibility of help. You ought also to take heed where the grass or weeds be high, for fear of Snakes, or Toads, or other venomous animals, but that it be a plain, even turf, neat and clean, that you may keep your feet so in returning to your cloaths."

Monsieur Thevenot was a distinguished Oriental scholar but still had time to devise comic water stunts.

With great foresight, as well as the benefit of his scientific background, Thevenot proposes that "to determine the business perfectly, recourse ought to be had to Mechanicks, wherein the reasons of the whole are founded. It is easy to find out and determine which motions are best and most expeditious upon all occasions whatsoever, and to demonstrate the truth of them."

Monsieur Thevenot's book is illustrated by "Forty proper Copper-Plate Cuts, Which represent the different Postures necessary to be used in that Art." Thevenot not only teaches his readers how to float in several positions, tread water, change direction, swim underwater, do dog paddle, creep (a crawl-like action), swim like a snake, perform a running sideways (but safe) entry dive, but also how to do several stunts which were probably not only for one's own amusement but also for the entertainment of spectators on the bank.

Thevenot was probably the first to advise the establishment of a coaching profession. After describing what he believed to be the Principles of Swimming, he recommends "Considerations that the Art of Swimming ought to be esteemed, rather than from the Pleasure and Diversion which is commonly proposed by it: insomuch, that besides the interest which particular persons may gain from learning it, and perfecting themselves in it, it seems worth the while to erect Publick Academies, and establish experienced Masters in them to teach it, since the advantages of it may be so considerable. Such persons ought to be fought for and encouraged by rewards, and we are persuaded

that if there was such one expert and dexterous that would publicly profess to teach it, he need want no Scholars nor Encouragement."

◇ ◇ ◇

HOW BEN FRANKLIN COAXED HIS PUPILS INTO THE DELAWARE

Dr. Benjamin Franklin, early American statesman, printer, author, publisher, inventor, scientist, and diplomat, was probably also America's first swimming coach. He would ask his pupils to plunge underwater and try to retrieve eggs which he had thrown into shallow water. In this way, he encouraged his pupils to discover how "the water buoys you up against your inclination. Thus you feel the power of the water to support you and learn to confide in its power."

I can just imagine coach Ben going down to the Delaware, unpolluted then, with a basket of eggs to get the locals waterborne. Dr. Franklin's keen injunctions were followed, however, by a vogue of "bath masters" and self-styled "professors du natacion."

In 1797, one Oronzio de Bernardi published details of his system of "upright swimming" in a book with the imposing title of *Arte de Nadar Compendiade del que Escribio en Italiano.*

Believe it or not, his pupils were claimed to progress in upright position for several miles after only a couple of day's coaching.

Around 1817, General Pfuel of Berlin produced his celebrated treatise which introduced a system of drilling for swimming. Swimming classes were sorted into groups of three. One boy would bend over on all fours while the next boy lay across the first boy's back practicing the swimming stroke. The function of the third boy was to steady the second boy in case he fell off the first boy's back. Got it?

So much for General Pfuel's foolish capers. Now for a look at the methods used in British public schools in the days of yore.

At Clifton, J. J. Sheasby, the swimming instructor, was one of the institutions of the school,

"There was keen rivalry to see who could be the first boy in the water. To be the last boy was another distinction keenly fought for." A two-way race?

According to Mr. C. Dudfield Willis, captain of the Otter Swimming Club in 1890, "successful competitors ran the risk of receiving a flick from Sheasby with a wet towel, which, if successful, was remembered for the rest of the day.

"However, he always gave us a sporting chance, and was deservedly popular, a popularity he enhanced by never reporting a boy without sufficient reason."

Over at Repton, there seemed an ulterior motive behind the aquatic activities of their aficionados. According to Mr. F. G. J. Ford, the old Cambridge cricketer from 1880 to 1886, "we bathed in the Trent below Burton, from which source we got the full benefits [!] of the breweries at times. The cricket XI did not bathe the day before the match." Method in their madness?

Ford goes on to say that at Eton, "swimming was a favorite amusement taught by certain 'cads' who, in a more informal fashion, took new boys out in a boat and threw them overboard.

"George Selwyn, then private tutor to Lord Powis, and afterwards Bishop of Melanesia and of Litchfield, was an Eton swimmer of most remarkable skill. One of Selwyn's recorded feats was taking a running header and diving across the river at Upper Hope."

Unfortunately, the records don't describe fully how he arrived at the other side. This could make the most interesting reading. Probably, at Upper Hope, it was better to travel hopefully than to arrive (Sachs, 1912).

◇ ◇ ◇

FROM THE *HUKI* CAME THE CRAWL

Surfing: A History of the Ancient Hawaiian Sport by Ben Finney and James D. Houston mentions surfing techniques used over the centuries that may throw more light on the origins of crawl swimming.

Surfing: A History of the Ancient Hawaiian Sport follows surfing's time line from the earliest legends and accounts of surfing to the accomplishments of twentieth-century heroes such as Duke Kahanamoku, who was famous as Hawaii's first "surfer-swimmer" to become an Olympic swimming champion.

Over and over again, one reads of the need for quick paddling movements combined with rapid kicking in order to catch the cresting motion of a wave about to break. That the crawl stroke was commonly used in the surging ocean surf of the South Seas there now can be small doubt.

The basic action of the crawl stroke was part of the culture of Oceania. It seems to have been indigenous to the area for hundreds of years, irrespective of the intellectualized versions of the breaststroke, sidestroke, trudgen progressions, to the final modern development of the crawl, outlined so meticulously in the Western world's literature of swimming. Instead, the text clearly shows an inescapable, direct connection between surfing and all the basic elements of crawl swimming that occurred long ago, without any intervening progressions.

The book relates the commentaries of William Ellis, a British missionary who in the 1820s credited the Hawaiians as being a "race of amphibious beings" who were at home in the sea from the time they were born. They lose all dread of it and seem nearly as much at home in the water as on dry land."

Ellis tells how children were taken into the sea by their mothers the second or third day after birth

Dr. Benjamin Franklin, early American statesman, was probably also America's first swimming coach.

International Swimming Hall of Fame

and that there were many who could swim as soon as they could walk.

The Use of Bodyboards

Children first learned to swim by practicing arm paddling and kicking while lying on a shorter board, known as a bodyboard. The use of the shorter board allowed the child to kick as well as paddle, and this fact points to their learning a continuous crawl-type action from the start.

The use of the bodyboard was influenced by the allied sport of surfing; the aim of the method was to have the children swim, or skim (*paka*) on the water rather than in it as in the breaststroke and trudgen strokes.

In a telephone conversation, the book's coauthor, Dr. Finney, told me that there was distributional evidence of this learning method everywhere in Oceania, and that, before the Pacific Islands were settled, people in the

Duke Kahanamoku, famous Hawaiian surfer and Olympic swimming champion.

Phillipines and Indonesia used bodyboards for learning to swim as well as a preparation for learning to ride the big boards.

Bodysurfing and the *Huki*

There are three ways to ride the surf: in a canoe, by bodysurfing, or on a board. In all three methods, timing the precise moment to catch the cresting wave is vital.

The text contains several references that stress the need for a quick sequence of dexterous movements to catch a cresting wave and the ability to use either a wooden paddle, or the arms, as a wave banks to its peak, curls, and starts to break. These observations were made throughout the centuries and are remarkable in the consistency of their reporting.

When bodysurfing, the swimmer has to swim or paddle fast to reach the *kulana nalu*, the place where the wave swells up. In other words, it was essential to be at the right place at the right time to have a chance of catching a cresting wave. Only for a fleeting moment in the life of a wave, as it rolls in from the sea to the beach, does it reach its *muku*, the time when it crests, ready for a surfer to shoot.

If the wave is taken too soon, the surfer will simply be left behind as the wave rolls away underneath the body. If it is taken too late when the wave has broken, the surfer will be unceremoniously dumped into the turbulent foam. At the precise point of catching the wave, the most important skill of all comes into play. It is known as the *huki*, which means to pull, as in paddling with hands, or straining to pull the water back to catch a wave.

As the wave reaches its peak, the swimmer launches forward into the wave's sloping face, at the same time paddling and kicking vigorously to reach a speed as close as possible to that of the incoming wave. The swimmer should take a deep breath so that the head can be kept down until the head and shoulders are positioned squarely to the front of the wave.

All this time, the legs continue to flutter kick until the body is set securely on its course. At this point, the head may be raised to inhale and to see in front. From here on, each subsequent breath may be taken either to the front or by quickly turning the face to the side with as little headlifting as possible.

By keeping the head down and the shoulders hunched, the swimmer will assume a streamlined position in the surf with the water slipping past underneath the body instead of retarding it. If the *huki* has been correctly timed, the swimmer is lifted into the crest of the wave and surges forward in an exhilarating run to the beach.

All the typical components of the crawl stroke occur when performing the *huki* in which a rapid and vigorous bout of pulling and kicking is needed to obtain a secure riding position in a fast-breaking wave. Certainly, the stop-start movements of the breaststroke or trudgen stroke would not have been quick enough to obtain the desired result.

The Kahanamoku Kick

"Several miles down the coast, past Waikiki, there was a break called *Ke-kai-o-Mamala* (the Sea of Mamala). It broke through a narrow entrance through what is now Honolulu harbor and provided some of the finest waves in Kou (an early name for the Honolulu area). The break was named after Mamala, a famous surfer and a prominent Oahu chieftess" (Finney and Houston, 1996).

It was here, swimming in Honolulu harbor in 1911, that a virtually unknown swimmer by the name of Duke Kahanamoku swam the 100 yards in 55.4 seconds, thus unofficially beating the world record of Charles Daniels, America's first great swimmer who had retired only the year before.

However, the officials on the mainland refused to believe that Kahanamoku had not benefited from the tidal waters that flowed into the harbor. Only after Kahanamoku came over to the mainland in the following year and competed in the AAU Indoor Championships, was his greatness fully recognized. Experts who saw him swim attributed his success to what became known as the Kahanamoku kick.

For his part, Kahanamoku could not understand what the fuss was all about and assured questioners that "the stroke was natural to the Hawaiians."

Kahanamoku stood just over 6 feet tall and had unusually well-developed upper arms and thighs. His heavy musculature was probably derived from paddling and kicking his long, thick, 150-pound surfboard several hundred yards out to

where the large waves came roaring in from the open sea.

Having caught a large wave, he would leap to a kneeling position on the board before giving another spring to stand upright. One can imagine that he performed this routine several score times a day when a good surf was running, and many more times this number throughout his career.

It is also interesting to note that there are no records of the Duke ever having received any formal coaching before he arrived on the mainland.

The *New York Times*, February 20, 1916, said, "According to some experts, the Kahanamoku kick originated in the fresh water pools of the East, where a rapid motion of the legs was necessary to overcome the less buoyant fresh water. This opinion appears far-fetched when one bears in mind that Kahanamoku belongs to a race of islanders that have no superiors as swimmers, and that his prowess is probably instinctive rather than the result of any artificial conditions."

The fact is that Duke Kahanamoku had brought the most modern version of the crawl from Hawaii to the mainland despite all the previous knowledge of breaststroke, sidestroke, and trudgen progression accumulated in the swimming lore of Western civilization.

Finally, I questioned Dr. Finney on whether he had given thought to how the crawl had developed in the South Seas. He replied, "No I haven't, but I couldn't imagine anyone trying to catch a big surf while swimming trudgen."

✧ ✧ ✧

LITTLE ALICK "CRAWLED" TO FAME

The crawl stroke, the "glamour" style of swimming, was cradled in Sydney, Australia, but it arrived there in a most inauspicious way.

The year is 1894. A rusty trading schooner from the Solomon Islands slips into dock. On deck with his Polynesian mother and English father is a bronzed six-year-old boy by name of Alick Wickham. His father, a Somerset man, has sold his business in the Solomons and is retiring to Sydney where his son can attend school.

Three years later. The scene is Nelson Bay in Sydney's eastern suburbs. At Bronte seawater pool, a boys' under-10 swimming race is in progress.

Alick Wickham's pipe-stem arms stab the water in staccato rhythm. His feet spin like an electric fan. His head of fuzzy black hair slicks from side to side. Quickly he leaves his rivals who struggle with strange stop-start styles.

"Say, mate," says local coach George Farmer, "just look how that kid crawls over the water." These words are to swimming's saga what "*Veni, vidi, vinci*" are to schoolboy history.

It says much for the Australian "give-it-a-go" spirit that the oldsters bother to watch a nine-year-old boy's stroke technique. It says even more for their inventiveness that the famous Cavill family of great swimmers allow Alick the use of their baths at the Sydney Domain.

They study his style carefully. Soon they improve on it, and Dick Cavill becomes the first swimmer in the world to beat one minute for 100 yards in an unofficial swim. And Wickham becomes the world's fastest at 50 yards as he covers the distance in an unbelievable 24 seconds.

But being the fastest in the world isn't enough for Wickham's new friends. Australians like their sports heroes big and brassy. They note that Wickham is also an excellent diver and so they persuade him to try for the world-record high dive.

The record holder is a gentleman from Chicago by the name of George Clarke. He dove 165 feet from a Chicago bridge. And so it happens that John Wren, president of the aptly named Deep Rock Swimming Club in Melbourne, kindly arranges for Alick to come to his city to try to dive off the 205-feet, 9-inch parapet at Studley Park.

The odd 9 inches or so do not worry Wickham, but the rest of the proposed dive amounting to some 205-foot prompts him to ponder. The day before the dive Wickham accompanies Wren to inspect the special cliff-top platform.

"An ideal spot for diving," is Wickham's casual but wry comment. But Wren glances down and blanches. He makes urgent attempts to be excused for business elsewhere.

The next day, the ticket collectors are busy as 70,000 people gather to watch Wickham attempt the big dive. A bugle sounds. Wickham steps to the platform edge amidst the applause of the multitude. He acknowledges the cheers. Then he crouches.

The bugle sounds again. Wickham plummets in a graceful swallow. He spears the water. A tall vertical splash follows him. Seconds pass. His head appears. Tumultuous applause greets the hero.

Wickham becomes another Australian sporting legend. In great demand at carnivals, he demonstrates the crawl and performs his "South Seas dive." From 60 feet he leaps with body bunched then opens out into a conventional dive a moment before striking the surface. His stunts include a 50-yard underwater swim in which he beats surface swimmers. Then he swims long distances underwater with a polo ball, puzzling his opponents.

Wickham became a champion amateur boxer and a crack footballer. Thirty years passed and his father, old Frank Wickham, died. Then the epic ends. Alick Wickham returned to the Solomon Islands with his widowed mother and was never heard from again.

Back in the 1960s, I tried to follow up the Wickham history in Sydney's eastern suburbs. I searched for his home in Kensington without success. I found the pool where the crawl was first swum, but no other trace of Alick Wickham, one of swimming's greatest legends.

❖ ❖ ❖

THE SCHOOL OF SYDNEY

How the Crawl Was Developed

Ancient artifacts, hieroglyphics, bas reliefs, and other relics tell us that overarm strokes were swum thousands of years ago, particularly along warm ocean shores. Roman writings describe overarm strokes swum by Mediterranean peoples. The literature of other countries contain similar accounts.

Supported by the buoyancy of sea water, any swimmer would be likely to lift an arm from the water on occasion, either to wave or signal to people on shore or to experiment with crude paddling movements. But it is unlikely that the ancients developed a formal continuous overarm stroke complete with flutter kick.

Overarm swimming strokes brought forth connotations of undue splashing and disturbance of the water surface. These facets of swimming were considered undesirable by purists. In fact, travelers from Europe to the Western Hemisphere and to the South Seas had the opportunity to observe native swimmers using overarm strokes, yet despite the obvious speed attained by these unorthodox techniques, they clung to their set ways (Howard, 1849).

Early Opportunity Missed

Resistance to change is evident in the case of the two Native Americans from the Ojibbeway Nation, Flying Gull (*We-nish-ka-wen-bee*) and Tobacco (*Sah-ma*). The pair competed for a silver medal at the High Holburn Baths in London in 1844. According to *The London Times*, April 22, 1844, they "thrashed the water violently with their arms, like sails of a windmill, and beat downward with their feet, blowing with force and forming grotesque actions." Despite the fact that Flying Gull won the race, covering 130 feet in 30 seconds, his stroke was considered totally un-European, and, therefore, unworthy of consideration.

Splashing or plunging the arms into the water was an indication of poor swimming. The idea goes back to William Shakespeare who was probably misinterpreted when he wrote, "An unskilled swimmer, plunging still, with too much labor, drowns his want of skill." Perhaps the great playwright acquired his insight into swimming from the work of his contemporary, sidestroke swimmer Sir Everard Digby, a Cambridge graduate who wrote *The Art of Swimming*, the first book on swimming in England.

Those who witnessed the unusual swimming styles of Flying Gull and Tobacco lacked what scientists call the inspired hunch, and they were probably put off by too much labor drowning in want of skill—despite what the stopwatch had told them. They failed to recognize a good idea, and thus lost the opportunity to put British swimming 60 years ahead of the rest of the world.

The Trudgen Stroke

Alas, the history of swimming, in fact all human progress, is full of tales of opportunities lost. Again, on August 11th, 1873, at the Lambeth Baths in London when John Trudgen brought the double overarm stroke to England from the warm sea waters of the West Indies and demonstrated superior speed, it must have been obvious that his breaststroke-type kick retarded continuous forward motion. Trudgen himself admitted that "there are plenty of men can beat me where I've come from" (Sachs, 1912).

Trudgen adapted the stroke poorly, probably because he was originally a breaststroke swimmer who changed to the double overarm stroke but couldn't swim the new arm action without retaining the breaststroke kick. Unfortunately, no one at the time understood that breaststroke kicking didn't fit naturally with Trudgen's adopted faster arm action, and that a more pliable kick was needed to allow a continuous stroke.

Rare photograph of Cecil Healy at the age of 12 (second on left). Healy was to become one of the great early century Australian swimmers. His reputation "as a competitive athlete and lucid writer was worldwide" (Clarkson, 1990).

Developing a Continuous Stroke

About 30 years later in Australia, a group of innovative swimmers all played a role in developing a more continuous racing stroke, rather than the halting mode of propulsion inherent in breaststroke, sidestroke, and trudgen swimming. This group, whom I like to call "The School of Sydney," included men such as the Cavill brothers (Syd, Arthur "Tums," and Dick), Alick Wickham, Freddy Lane, Cecil Healy, and Barney Kieran.

The development of the crawl in Australia was the result of a series of events, the correct sequence of which is difficult to assess because of the varying accounts on record. However, I have tried to collate them as accurately as available sources permit. The first point to note is that the principles of the stroke were already becoming clear to Sydney swimmers before Alick Wickham

arrived in that city in 1898 as a young boy from the Solomon Islands.

However, Wickham did bring to Sydney the most fluent version of the new stroke that Sydneysiders had seen, and, until that time, the stroke had no formal name. It wasn't called "the crawl" until local coach George Farmer observed it. Another version of the origin of the term crawl stroke was that Dick Cavill, who swam long stretches of a race with his head burrowed in the water, often swam off course, and was accused by a rival of "crawling" all over him (Carlile, 1963).

Tums Cavill's "Legless" Crawl

The same year that Wickham arrived in Sydney, Syd Cavill was making his way to the United States to live there. On his way, he raced a native woman in Apia on the island of Samoa, who swam

Barney Kieran, coached by former Australian champion R. R. Craig, first came to notice when he raced Dick Cavill, the world's foremost swimmer, over 400 yards. Cavill beat Kieran by a touch, but Kieran won in another race over 880 yards. In the 1904–1905 season, Kieran won every Australian title from 220 yards to one mile.

On June 19, 1905, Kieran arrived in London by ship after a seven-week voyage from Australia. Kieran beat Europe's best swimmers and set eight world records from 220 yards to one mile. At Liverpool he won the one-mile championship of the River Mersey by 300 yards.

At the end of 1905, he won the Australian 220-, 440-, and 880-yard championships in Brisbane, setting records in each event. On the third day of the championships, he suffered an acute appendicitis attack and died within a few days after surgery. He was only 19 and at the peak of his fame. Thirty thousand people attended the funeral of Australia's great boy champion. In 1906 the Kieran Memorial Shield Contest was inaugurated by public subscription as a memorial to him. The Shield is still awarded to the state associations whose men swimmers gain the maximum number of points in both individual events and team races at the Australian championships.

the crawl stroke naturally, but without using her legs at all. She gave him the toughest race of his life. Syd wrote home to his brother "Tums" (Arthur) describing the event, whereupon Tums immediately started practicing with his legs tied.

Tums then challenged Syd Davis, a prominent swimmer, to a one length race (33 yards) in which he would swim with legs tied while Davis was to feel free to use both legs and arms. To everyone's surprise Tums won the 5-pound bet by winning in the then respectable time of 20 seconds. However, in a subsequent race using his legs as well, Tums was unable to beat Davis. The lesson learned was that the trudgen kick actually inhibited the continuous action of the crawl arm stroke.

Freddy Lane, the first swimmer to cover 100 yards in one minute. Swimming in Manchester, England, on July 24, 1902, he beat his countryman, Dick Cavill, and Britain's finest swimmer, J. H. Derbyshire, to accomplish this feat. Later that same year in Leicester, Lane officially became the first to break one minute for the 100 yards with a time of 59.6 seconds.

Dick Cavill, the youngest of the Cavill brothers, then only 14, was present when Tums beat Davis, but refused to believe what he had seen. Back in the privacy of their home pool at Lavender Bay, near where Sydney Harbour bridge now stands, he timed Tums several times. Tums swam without the use of his legs, and then again using the full stroke. Tums really was faster when swimming with his legs tied. Then the experiment was repeated, this time with Dick acting as the guinea pig. The evidence was irrefutable; the trudgen kick definitely retarded progress (Sullivan, 1927).

The Crawl in Competition

Dick Cavill set out to find the ideal kick to synchronize with his crawl arm action. Then he remembered Alick Wickham's straight-legged kick and decided to experiment with vertical kicking. He tried the new stroke only a few days later in the New South Wales 100-yard championship. The lad created a minor sensation when the amazing speed of the new stroke brought him to the 50-yard mark fully 5 yards ahead of the field. Then the rigors of the imperfectly learned action caught up with him, and he was passed by a speedy swimmer by the name of Bishop.

In 1899, at the age of 15, Dick Cavill won his first state title, this time cautiously swimming the distance using part sidestroke and part trudgen. He then concentrated on learning to swim complete races with the trudgen before returning to improve his crawl swimming ability, using a vertical kick which eventually became his famous two-beat action. However, according to Cecil Healey, who was not only a great swimmer but also a prolific and eloquent writer on the sport, Cavill was "by no means a great stylist, and his stroke was a crude arrangement consisting largely of splash"(Carlile, 1963).

South Seas Influence

On the other hand, Alick Wickham was acknowledged as a fine stylist. He had a very powerful kick that was a six-beat at the start of his career, but which he was said to have reduced to a two-beat (according to the prevailing fashion?) after he had been swimming for a few years. Wickham was very fast for distances up to 75 yards after which point he faded badly. This was a difficulty encountered by most of the pioneer crawl swimmers who took too many strokes before inhaling. Cecil Healy is credited with developing a more relaxed method of swimming the crawl by rolling the body slightly and turning the face sideways to inhale, instead of lifting the head forward. He also introduced a regular breathing rhythm within each complete stroke cycle (Kiphuth, 1942).

What were the points of contact with the Polynesians that clearly establish linkage between the Islanders and the competitive swimmers of Australia? Probably there were many contacts never annotated, but the arrival of young Alick Wickham from the Solomons is well recorded, and so is the episode of Syd Cavill's race with the native woman in Apia. But it is not well-known that, before the end of the nineteenth century

International Swimming Hall of Fame

Three members of the famous Cavill family: (left to right) Percy, Arthur (Tums), Dick. Percy won a so-called World Championship over a mile and 440 yards in England in 1897. Arthur won a bet in 1898 by swimming a race at Rushcutter's Bay Baths in Sydney with his legs tied while swimming a continuous crawl arm action. Dick was the first man to swim the crawl in championships. Officials were reluctant to recognize his times as records.

"Professor" Fred Cavill, head of the large Cavill clan of champion swimmers, was said to have visited the islands of the South Seas where he observed the native stroke. He supposedly taught it to his sons on his return to Australia, but this version of the crawl's origin is difficult to verify and somewhat doubtful.

A little-known story concerning Alick Wickham is that, although crawl swimming was said to be indigenous to the Solomon Islands, Alick learned the flutter kick only after observing swimmers in Colombo on the island of Ceylon. If this is true, and there's no reason to doubt it, the incident probably occurred while traveling to Ceylon as a youngster on his father's trading schooner. Of further interest is the fact that Alick Wickham had an elder brother who attended school in Sydney before Alick arrived there, and who swam the crawl there on "numerous occasions. Possibly, because he was not a speedy or polished demonstrator, no particular notice was taken of him" (Beaurepaire, 1942).

Well, then, where did the crawl originate? There can be little doubt that the crawl was indigenous to the Polynesian Islands, particularly the technique of the flutter kick which fit ideally with the continuous overarm action. Both the flutter kick and the arm stroke probably came naturally to the islanders when they were bodysurfing and trying to catch the surge of cresting ocean waves. But it was the Australians who systematically adopted and adapted the crawl to the needs of formal competitive swimming. The technique they developed took the world by storm. Although the crawl was at a comparatively elementary stage of its evolution, it completely changed the nature of speed swimming.

Four Classes of Crawl

The early crawl was basically a stroke for swimming short distances and was too tiring for prolonged effort. Again, according to Cecil Healey, one of the great Australian swimmers whose reputation as a competitive athlete and lucid writer was world wide: "There are two distinct methods of crawling at present, and its exponents can be said to consist of four classes, namely, those who breathe regularly and those who take four or five strokes before replenishing their lungs; and those who strike with the right arm, left leg alternately and vice versa; and those who have an independent leg action.

"Exponents who do not breathe regularly lie flat, with head down, shoulders square, face submerged and use a short paddling action. The effect of keeping the head lowered is to float the legs as high as possible, the body thus lying in a horizontal position near the surface, which enables it to skim along. Undoubtedly, great speed can be attained this way, but holding the breath for the length of time necessitated causes the physical exertion to become more acute and exhausting. Under the latter conditions, those who swim as described show a great slackening off in their rate of progress after 100 meters have been covered, compared with what they are capable of doing up to that distance" (Kiphuth, 1942).

A Fatiguing Stroke

From Healey's description we know that the early crawl came to be swum in a variety of ways. A few swimmers allowed their legs to drift behind them. Some varied indecisively between a two-beat and a continuous flutter kick. Others had difficulty shedding the remnants of sidestroke and trudgen kicking learned in childhood, and thus they adopted a hybrid crawl, which for some was remarkably successful.

The early crawl stroke was crude and ungainly, consumed energy rapidly, and was used mainly for a fast finishing burst. Several swimmers could cover 50 yards using crawl throughout, but not many could maintain the tiring action for a full 100 yards. Dick Cavill, the first man to swim crawl in championships, would start a 100-yard race using the crawl, then switch to the trudgen stroke for most of the distance before reverting to crawl to produce a speedy finish.

There was no doubt that, speedy as it was, the crawlstroke became more fatiguing the farther it was swum. Barney Kieran, a brilliant teenage swimmer, went against the trend, believing that the crawl was only good for sprints. He developed his "amble crawl," an almost lazy, loping style of double overarm swimming—in fact, a type of trudgen stroke—with the intention of trying to relax more while still exerting effort.

Freddy Lane, on the other hand, achieved great international success, swimming a double overarm trudgen with a narrow straight-knee leg action. To Cecil Healey, however, goes the credit of advocating the pronounced two-beat kick that came to be accepted as the hallmark of the Australian crawl, as it became known around the world.

The famous Domain Baths in Sydney had seating for 3,500 spectators and was the scene of many spectacular encounters including the 1924 match races between Arne Borg (Sweden) and Andrew "Boy" Charlton (Australia) over 440 and 880 yards. Charlton won both. It was here on a 1915 visit to Australia that Duke Kahanamoku amazed Australians by swimming 100 yards in 53.8 seconds.

Cecil Healy won the 1905 Australian 100-yard championship in 57 seconds. The following year he finished third in the 100 meter in the unofficial Olympics in Athens. In 1912 in the Olympic 100-meter final, he was narrowly beaten by Duke Kahanamoku of the United States.

Courtesy NSWASA

"Flying Squadron Relay Team." Seated left to right: Cecil Healy, Alick Wickham, and Reginald "Snowy" Baker. Standing left to right: Theo Tartakover and Freddy Lane. This team held the world 500-yard relay record for 5 years and included three famous pioneers of crawl swimming: Wickham, Lane, and Healy. Baker was proficient in 29 different sports and won the heavyweight silver medal for boxing at the 1908 London Olympics.

Difficulties of Analysis

No one was certain which method of crawl swimming was the correct one. To their surprise, people eventually realized that crawl swimming permitted a great deal of individual latitude. Uncertainty about important aspects of crawl swimming prevailed until the 1960s when Doc Counsilman's research improved understanding of crawl fundamentals.

The early stroke was not a pretty sight, and, at first, was difficult to analyze. To the uninitiated it was a jumble of scurried movements. The ability to breathe regularly was a hit-or-miss affair, depending on the hopeful chance of gulping air somewhere amidst a rapidly rotating arm action. The first crawlers wanted to develop a stroke that

provided continuous propulsion without the stop-start motions of the trudgen and sidestroke. Drawing the legs up to perform a trudgen kick made the arm stroke pause, and so they concentrated instead on turning the arms over quickly and continuously.

The components of the early crawl stroke were not always assembled in the best working order, often resulting in premature fatigue. The splash and thrash of the crawl horrified traditionalists who regarded speed swimming as an art form requiring skill, grace, and elegance. They looked askance at the crawl stroke, this intrusion from Australia, in the far-off reaches of the Empire and thought it a freak stroke and an abomination, a passing fad that, given genteel tolerance and patience, soon would fade from memory.

Cavill Takes the Crawl to England

Even in his native Australia, Dick Cavill found officials not always ready to sanction his record-breaking swims. And in England, then home of many of the world's greatest swimmers, skepticism of the world records set in Australia existed side by side with keen interest to see Cavill and his countrymen in action.

A month after the South African War ended in May 1902, a steamship from Australia carrying Dick Cavill, Freddy Lane, and other Australian swimmers, rounded the Cape of Good Hope, halfway on its seven-week voyage to England. Swimming in Manchester on July 24th, 1902, Freddy Lane beat Dick Cavill, and Britain's finest swimmer, J. H. Derbyshire, by the narrowest of margins to become the first swimmer to cover 100 yards in one minute. Two weeks later Cavill showed his true form when he cut Lane's record to 58.8 seconds, a time that had to remain unofficial as it was recorded in a handicap race. Later that year in Leicester, Lane officially became the first to break one minute for 100 yards with a time of 59.6 seconds.

During their English tour, the two Australian crawl swimmers, Cavill and Lane, won four national titles between them. Lane captured the 100 and 220 while Cavill took the 440 and 880 yards. To their credit, the British experts became loud in their praise of Richard Cavill and his Australian crawl. Said one leading reporter, "Cavill adopted a stroke entirely new to the English critics. He kept his head entirely under the water and extended his arms forward under the water, his kick being a revelation to our swimmers" (Cureton, 1934).

An English newspaper report quoted in the *Sydney Referee* said, "Cavill's marvelous crawl-stroke called forth the admiration of everybody present. His head is low in the water, and he breathes by snatches, every five breaths or so. His arms extend wide and sweep under the chest."

A more vivid account of Cavill's stroke was given by McArthur Moseley of Leeds, the President of the National Amateur Swimming Association, who said, "Generally known by the appropriate name of 'Splash Cavill' when he is swimming, you see a lot of splash but little of Cavill. One might be pardoned for mistaking him for a screw propeller that received a galvanic shock but the rate he struggles through the water is little short of a miracle. He uses a sort of revised double-over-arm of the trudgen variety. To describe it scientifically or even minutely is impossible."

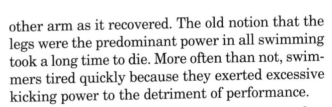

The historic Randwick & Coogee Aquarium Swimming Pool in Sydney where Barney Kieran took 2 seconds off the 200-yard world record on January 25, 1905. Kieran's world records in 1905 were 200 yards in 2:13.6, 220 yards in 2:28.6, 300 yards in 3:13.8, 440 yards in 5:19.05, 500 yards in 6:10.6, 880 yards in 11:29.8, and 1 mile in 23:16.8.

The New Glamour Stroke

What had once been termed the freak stroke of swimming became known as the novelty stroke of swimming. In the following decade the crawl stroke was to achieve a new status as the glamour stroke. However, it was a long time before it was refined sufficiently for use over the longer distances. Even Annette Kellerman, who won the Australian 100-yard championship in 1902 using the crawl with a scissors kick, and who later became a world-renowned distance swimmer, advocated using the trudgen stroke for all distances over 100 yards (Kellerman, 1918).

The early crawl swimmers had difficulty in conserving energy. Their breathing techniques were generally poor, and they kicked inefficiently. They quickly became breathless because they used the awkward method of lifting the head forward to inhale. Neither had they acquired the subtle knack of relaxing within the stroke. They didn't know how to apply effort to the pulling arm while resting the other arm as it recovered. The old notion that the legs were the predominant power in all swimming took a long time to die. More often than not, swimmers tired quickly because they exerted excessive kicking power to the detriment of performance.

With the wisdom of hindsight, it is easy to understand how the crawl pioneers took a long time to free themselves from the rigidity of the older styles of swimming. For years there remained a tendency to swim crawl in the same precise fashion in which breaststroke, sidestroke, and trudgen were swum. A precise number of leg beats was prescribed for each arm cycle, irrespective of individual aptitude or whether a swimmer was "leg-talented" or not. The classic style came to be the six-beat crawl in which there were two major beats and four minor beats for a complete cycle of both arms, but the ease and fluency of the modern crawl took a long time to evolve (Colwin, 1969).

Worldwide Interest Develops

After the Australians had shown their wares in England, worldwide interest in the new crawl stroke slowly developed. The word "slowly" is used advisedly because intercontinental travel was possible only by steamship, and a round-trip from

Australia to England took over three months. For example, Freddy Lane, who competed in England and Europe in 1899, 1900, and 1902, spent on average three months at sea each year. During each long ocean voyage, he tried to stay fit by training in the ship's small canvas swimming pool.

Despite travel difficulties and slow communications, there grew an exchange of information that resulted in the crawl spreading from Australia to Europe and to the American East and West Coasts. The next generation of swimmers, nurtured in the crawl as their beginning stroke, swam it in more facile fashion. Young children proved it possible to easily cover long distances with the crawl, succeeding where the oldsters had failed. This period produced the first significant exchange of technical ideas between nations. Swimming development entered a new era, and the world of international swimming was never to be the same again.

◇ ◇ ◇

THE CRAWL BECOMES A DISTANCE STROKE

Children are taught the crawl from the start and break records with it at all distances.

The Pacific Islanders are believed to have swum with natural overarm strokes for centuries. But the first exponents of the crawl in Western culture, with the possible exception of Alick Wickham, were "converted" sidestroke or trudgen swimmers. Because they hadn't learned the crawl as their first stroke, their neuromuscular systems were not attuned to the complex motions of an entirely new technique. Famous authorities, both in Australia and America, advised against using the crawl for distances over 100 yards because they thought it too strenuous. They maintained that the trudgen stroke would yield better results.

Some American coaches were reluctant to give up the wide scissors kick of the trudgen stroke. A leading Chicago coach, Frank Sullivan, tried to adapt the crawl for use over distances longer than 100 yards. He developed a stroke that was characterized by a series of flutter kicks added to the wide major kick of the trudgen.

He pioneered the trudgen crawl in America, probably after studying the successes of a new crop of Australian distance swimmers, led by the boy-genius Barney Kieran. Sullivan developed three prominent champions who used the trudgen crawl, Harry Hebner, Perry McGillivray, and Richard Frizelle.

Later, Sullivan's trudgen crawl was to merge into the type of continuous crawl as used by Daniels because, when the wide kick was used on both sides of the body with the small flutters in between, it became the double trudgen crawl. This stroke became the balanced action of six beats to the arm cycle as used in the American crawl, and it was easy to see how the early American crawl came to be swam with two major and four minor beats (Handley, 1914).

Youngsters Learn the Crawl from the Start
Despite subsequent refinements that made the stroke easier to swim, the crawl didn't become second nature to swimmers until a whole new generation of youngsters had learned the crawl as their first stroke. Increasing numbers now swam the crawl stroke over longer distances.

They learned better timing to provide intermittent periods of activity and rest within the stroke. They learned to relax one arm in recovery while the other applied power, and to relax the opposing muscles to avoid the rigidity that had hindered earlier exponents of the stroke. Soon, the crawl made great advances in America as a competitive stroke for all distances.

The Crawl as a Distance Stroke
Charles Daniels, at the end of his remarkable seven-year career, had reduced the 100-yard world record by nearly four seconds to a final mark of 54.8 seconds. But it is possible that his 220-yard world record of 2:25.4 was a more meritorious swim, if only from a technical standpoint. He swam the first 100 yards using the crawl, then covered the next 50 with the trudgen stroke before reverting to the crawl to complete the distance, a feat that first showed the potential of the crawl as a distance stroke.

With the help of his coach, Otto Wahle, and the renowned authority, Louis de B. Handley, Daniels figured out what parts of the stroke worked well and what parts needed improving. Together, they brought the crawl to a new high level of efficiency and showed the world that it was not merely a freak sprinting stroke.

Individuality in Crawl Swimming

Also to Daniels's credit was his realization that the crawl could be swum to suit the individual swimmer. He said, "No two men swim it alike and each indulges in a little experimenting of his own. This will gradually lead to progress, and it is probable that, as the men discard the inefficient details in favor of the more efficient ones, the different varieties will condense into different strokes from which the best will eventually be picked" (Daniels, 1919).

Most swimmers used a continuous kick, but over a distance the cadence was slower than that used in sprinting, often resulting in a beautiful free-flowing action such as enthusiasts had never seen before. Other kicking techniques were developed that combined easily with the crawl arm stroke, and they too provided a more free-flowing action.

In 1910, when Daniels retired after a shining career that completely changed speed swimming, many swimming enthusiasts were copying the American crawl that he had refined and popularized. Using a long arm stroke and slight body roll that permitted breathing on every stroke, more and more swimmers were soon swimming the crawl effortlessly for mile after mile.

A New Generation of Crawl Swimmers

The American National Championship meets of 1912 saw the distance events captured by swimmers who swam the crawl stroke all the way. James Wheatley captured the national quarter-mile title, Gilbert Tomlinson took the half mile, Bud Goodwin won the mile in record time, and Michael "Turk" McDermott won the 10-mile championship. Young lads tutored in the crawl from an early age, their muscles naturally tuned to crawl movements, tackled every distance with telling effect.

Particularly meritorious were the performances of the slightly built 15-year-old from Philadelphia, Gilbert Tomlinson. He won the half-mile championship from an exceedingly good field, came second in the mile while beating the record of 25:36.2, and also finished second in the quarter-mile championship. Tomlinson's achievements prompted much comment among the sport's followers. The truth was brought home to them that if a mere stripling could use the crawl to break the record for a mile swim, no coach should be allowed to claim that the crawl was too strenuous for grown men.

The *New York Times* of September 14, 1913, said, "The teachings of the last few months should not be overlooked by those coaches who are still in doubt. If they will cut through the tight lashings of conservatism and break away from foolish tradition, the sport will profit by it. Let them prescribe the crawl from the very beginning to their new recruits, and they will soon find that they can turn out faster and better swimmers for all distances. There has been entirely too much skepticism of new methods in the field of swimming."

The next few years brought remarkable performances with the crawl stroke. It was not only being used over the short sprint distances but also over the longer swims of 10 or more miles. The greatest feats of combined speed and endurance ever accomplished stood to the credit of swimmers using the American type of crawl.

❖ ❖ ❖

THE DANIELS DYNASTY

Charles M. Daniels, the first great American swimmer, is virtually forgotten, but he had the stuff of which legends are made.

Charles M. Daniels of the New York Athletic Club, born in Buffalo on March 24, 1887, was the first of the great American swimmers. His performances had a big influence on speed swimming in this century. Daniels was a highly successful athlete, a superstar to use today's parlance, and an intelligent, observant, and creative man who revolutionized the art of swimming fast.

A man of outstanding physique and patrician bearing, Charles Daniels had an air about him that commanded respect. In his swimming prime, he weighed about 200 pounds and stood 6 feet, 3 inches. Photos show that he wasn't bulky but had the lean, rangy, whipcord, symmetrical physique that was to typify many of the great crawl swimmers who came after him.

Daniels adopted the Australian crawl and refined its basic elements to create a new stroke with an independent leg action. This stroke, faster and less tiring than the Australian crawl, came to be known as the American or independent crawl, and it set crawl swimming on course for the rest of the twentieth century. When the Helms Sporting Hall of Fame was established in the 1950s, Charles Daniels was retroactively selected as the "North American Athlete of the Year for 1909."

Unusual Talent Immediately Recognized

Charles Daniels learned to swim when he was nine years old, but didn't compete until the winter of 1903. In the spring of that year, he had placed himself under the instruction of Alex Maffort at the Knickerbocker Athletic Club, who soon had his young ward making good time. In December of 1903, Daniels covered 100 yards in 1:08. For a novice this was unheard of.

When the Knickerbocker Athletic Club closed down, Daniels was accepted as a member of the New York Athletic Club where his progress was unusually rapid. An article praising his ability appeared in the *New York Athletic Club Journal* (March, 1904): "C. M. Daniels, aged eighteen, a mere stripling, worsted veteran swimmers and made eight new indoor swimming records for all distances from 150 yards to 300 yards." (Note: It was then the practice to keep a set of records for all the intermediate distances. These records were referred to as intermediates, and were not accorded quite the same prestige or always recognized internationally as were the classic distances such as the 100, 200, 400, etc.)

A Natural Athlete

Only a year after taking up competitive swimming, Charles Daniels became an Olympic champion. He won two titles at the 1904 St. Louis Olympic Games, and became the first American to win an Olympic swimming medal. Shortly after this triumph, a photograph of Daniels with a complimentary article about him appeared in the *New York Athletic Club Journal.*

The article said, "Among the many marvels of muscular strength, agility, staying power and courage which have been developed under the Mercury Foot banner, none is more interesting than C. M. Daniels, the phenomenal swimmer who within a short period has leaped from the ranks of the unknown to a solitary pinnacle of championship, holder of a world's record and world-wide fame as an amateur swimmer.

"The excellent picture of Mr. Daniels which appears in this issue of the *Journal* shows an ideal physique for a swimmer, although the great strength that must exist in the youthful body is unrevealed. The face is that of an idealist and looks more like that of a poet than the stern countenance of an athlete who struggles for physical supremacy."

Daniels's athletic ability was not confined to swimming. As a schoolboy he excelled at diving and rowing, competed in track in the mile and half mile where he won a few prizes. As a 15-year-old, he won the Junior Pistol, Revolver and Rifle Shooting Championships of America at Madison Square Garden. He could broad jump over 20 feet, high jump over 5 feet, 9 inches, was a "cracking good" baseball player, and also a fine hurdler.

Daniels's obituary in The *New York Athletic Club Journal* (August, 1973) said that in later life, Daniels surprised his friends, "who were not aware that he possessed any skill at the shooting traps, when he smashed 23 of the 25 flying blue rocks, lacking only one of the number credited to the winner, Mr. Fred Hodgman. "Danny" also had a record of 226 in the high score bowling tournament at the NYAC, was a wizard at billiards, and also the club's squash and bridge champion."

The Crawl "Arrives" at the NYAC

Some writers say that the crawl arrived from Australia "via the back door" when Syd Cavill began coaching the San Francisco Olympic Club in 1903, and that swimmers in the eastern states only learned about the elements of the stroke some years later.

However, that same year Louis de B. Handley, 29-year-old captain of the NYAC team, received newspaper clips from Australia, describing the Australian crawl. Handley discussed these articles with Gus Sundstrom, the NYAC instructor, and leading swimmers, Otto Wahle, Budd Goodwin, and Joe Ruddy. (Otto Wahle, besides training himself, was guiding Charles Daniels, who had recently joined the team, and was to continue coaching Daniels throughout an unparalleled career of national and international successes.)

The group noted that the main feature of the Australian crawl was a very fast alternate arm action with a two-beat leg kick that was synchronized with the arm stroke—as one arm pulled downward the opposite leg thrashed downward with a pronounced bending at the knee. Actually, this deep-knee flexion couldn't really be called a kick, it was a continuous thrashing of the lower leg only, from the knee downward, with the feet moving in the vertical plane. There was more knee bend than in the modern crawl stroke. The energy consumed by the continuous heavy thrashing motion of the feet, combined with irregular breathing, and a very fast and tiring arm action, resulted in a stroke too strenuous to hold for long.

The NYAC swimmers noted the rationale behind the Australian crawl. Because the trudgen technique of drawing the leg up sideways resulted in a stop-start arm action, it was better either not to kick at all, or if one did use a kick, it was advisable to kick only in the vertical plane. However, once they entered the water to try it out, Handley was reported to have said that he and his clubmates had "tried unsuccessfully to get the hang of it."

As soon as they tried to copy the mechanics of the stroke, they found that their legs would start to sink. Then it dawned on them that because the stroke had been invented by saltwater swimmers around the shores of Sydney Harbour, it wouldn't work as well in the less buoyant fresh water of the NYAC tank. Instead of a two-beat kick, it was obvious that in freshwater they needed some other action that would support the aft-body.

Sundstrom's Swordfish Glide

A few days after reading the Australian news clips, Sundstrom came up with the answer. He gave an exhibition of what he called the "Swordfish Glide." (With some imagination the outstretched arms, hands together with thumbs locked, looked like a swordfish.) With his face submerged, Sundstrom shot across the pool, with his feet fluttering up and down in a very propulsive drive. The next year in 1904, two leading NYAC swimmers, Jack Lawrence and Olympic

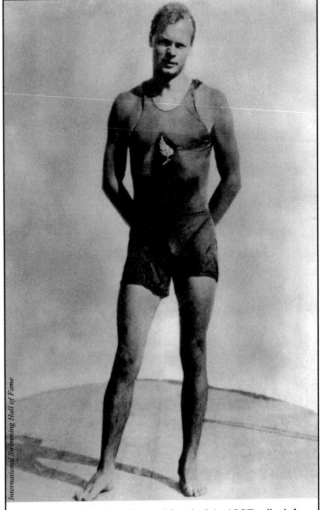

International Swimming Hall of Fame

Charles M. Daniels (born March 24, 1887, died August 9, 1973), was the first of the great American swimmers. Daniels set crawl swimming on course for the rest of the twentieth century.

swimmer G. Van Cleaf, combined the flutter kick with double overarm strokes to break the American 50-yard record, covering the distance in 26 seconds.

At the end of 1905, when Daniels finally started to devote his full attention to crawl swimming, he too adopted a flutter kick by adding two extra beats to his already established two-beat kick. In effect, Daniels swam a four-beat crawl at the start of the crawl-swimming phase of his career. When swimming at top speed, however, he appeared to add yet another two beats to his action. His stroke then became a full six-beat independent crawl, that is without the pronounced two major and four minor beats that occur when the legs are consciously timed with the arm action.

Some years later Daniels said, "Mr. Gus Sundstrom, instructor of the New York Athletic Club, was indirectly responsible for the introduction of the crawl stroke into America. He introduced a stroke called the swordfish stroke in which the body was propelled through the water by a continuous drive of the legs.

"He has more leg drive alone than any man I have ever seen, but not only bends the ankles back and forth, but says that it is by doing it that he gets his wonderful speed. A few of the American swimmers move their ankles a little, but most of them keep them rigid. A few of the Americans have adopted the Australian stroke, with its wide and synchronous thrash, but have added a fluttering of the feet which makes the action continuous. With a few exceptions, the arms and legs are working independently and the thrash has a narrower scope, the legs being opened less" (Daniels, Handley, & Wahle, 1919).

Both L. de B. Handley and Otto Wahle were a great influence on the development of Charles M. Daniels and what was to be known as the American crawl. However, Daniels was to spend two more years—1904 to 1905—developing his power and expertise as a conventional trudgen swimmer, before taking up the Australian crawl and modifying it to suit his own needs, with results that echoed around the world.

Daniels's American crawl was distinguished from the Australian crawl by a faster leg kick than the arm stroke. There was no conscious timing between arms and legs. For the first time in the history of swimming, a stroke was used in which the legs were independent of the arm stroke, resulting in a more relaxed, free-flowing action. The new American crawl still needed refining to make it easier to swim over longer distances, but with each succeeding year of his competitive career, Daniels's action became more polished, and other swimmers, particularly the very young, were able to copy his stroke and swim farther without undue strain. Eventually the old Australian crawl, the ancestor of the new modern crawl, became obsolete.

Olympic Swimming Championships, 1904

Meanwhile on the West Coast, Syd Cavill had been teaching the Australian crawl—very likely for the first time in America. One of his pupils was J. Scott Leary who finished third to Zoltan de Halmay (Hungary), and Daniels in the 100-yard freestyle at the St. Louis Olympics in 1904. (Yes, the distance swam was 100 yards and not 100 meters!)

de Halmay, who won the event, was one of the great swimmers of the day and was to become the only swimmer to win a medal in five Olympic Games. It is interesting that de Halmay swam a double overarm stroke with trailing legs—a type of crawl—as far back as 1900, the same time the crawl was being developed in Australia (Carlile, 1963).

It is not known whether Scott Leary swam part of any distance using the crawl stroke at the St. Louis Olympics. Nevertheless, Daniels, swimming the trudgen, became America's first Olympic champion in winning the 220 yard and 440 yard in 2:44.2 and 6:16.2, respectively.

The swimming events at the St. Louis Olympics were a strange affair and completely different from the Olympics of today. For example, the competitions were a mixture of events between individual athletes, nations, and even club teams. The final points standing for the meet were New York Athletic Club, 40; Germany, 32; Hungary, 17; Olympic Club of San Francisco; 16. A certain piquancy was added to the proceedings by a telegram from the steamship *Bulletai* in San Francisco harbor. The telegram said that a former champion, F. J. Black, was coming to the World's Fair to represent Australia in the Olympics, but Australian officials had never heard of him. In fact, no Australian swimmers competed in the 1904 Olympic Games.

The swimming events began on Monday, Sept. 5, in the pool of the U.S. Life Saving Corps, which was surrounded by an immense crowd. As expected, C. M. Daniels won the Olympic 220-yard and 440-yard titles and broke a world record in the 220-yard event. Due to a faulty stopwatch, however, his world record of 6:16.2, set in winning the 440-yard event, could not be recognized.

No Australian Swimmers at the Olympics

Australia did not send an official team to the 1904 Olympic Games in St. Louis largely because these games, like those of 1900, were regarded as sideshows for World Fairs, and also because of resistance to the idea of sending athletes overseas at the public expense.

It had been suggested that Dick Cavill and Cecil Healy could make up the Australian swimming contingent, but *The Bulletin* of Sydney said, "The proposal is one that cannot be too strongly condemned . . . the export of Australian athletes can serve no useful purpose. We don't want to encourage young men to go in for athletics that they may eventually be sent globe-trotting at public expense. . . . This sport business threatens to produce a huge crop of sporting parasites, traveling round the world in search of prizes and medals while living on the charity of the people" (Howell & Brooks, 1988).

The swimming facilities at the games were severely criticized by the Hungarian contingent: "The swimming events were held in an asymmetric lake in the grounds of the fair, and the swimmers were unable to keep to the right direction, because of the asymmetric banks.

"In addition, the drifting turn markers made their situation even more difficult. The starting line was a raft which had been thrown together for that purpose and, at the start, it sank under the weight of six to eight men, and what was more discouraging was the fact that, with every dive it slid backwards" (Howell & Brooks, 1988).

Daniels Breaks the 100 Record

On Saturday, January 13th, 1906, Daniels became the first American swimmer to set a world record at a standard distance when, in the same evening, he twice broke the world 100-yard record of 58 seconds held by the Australian, Dick Cavill. The *New York Athletic Club Journal* recorded the historic event as follows: "Swimming in the New York Athletic Club's 25 yard pool, C. M. Daniels added to the fringe of triumphs on the Mercury Foot banner, a new world's swimming record. He covered the 100 yard distance twice in the one evening in hitherto unequaled figures. In his first swim, Daniels touched in 57.6 seconds, eclipsing the mark of 58 seconds made by Richard Cavill. The American mark, 61.4 seconds, was made by Harry Le Moyne."

Careful Timekeeping

The *Journal* went on to say, "When the result was announced, there was great excitement, and Harry Buermeyer, referee, at once made tests of the watches used by the timers. The excitement increased when Daniels, in the final heat, covered the distance in exactly 57.6 seconds once more. This was a remarkable exhibition of consistency and strength. In his first trial heat, Daniels used the old style trudgen stroke alone, and the fact that he made a record without using the crawl stroke was in itself remarkable.

"In the final heat, the champion made use of a combination which he had thought out for himself. He combined the crawl leg work and the double overarm so that he had the greatest possible drive.

"Daniels' time was submitted immediately to the record committee of AAU on January 17th, and the time of 57.6 seconds was unqualifiedly accepted and now appears in the record book of the AAU as the fastest 100 yards ever covered by an amateur swimmer."

Record Application Rejected

Unfortunately, Daniels's new mark was not ratified internationally. The English swimming authorities did not allow the record because it was made in a handicap race. Barney Kieran, the great Australian swimmer who had broken every world freestyle record from 220 to the mile, suffered the same rejection as Daniels when his times were sent from Australia for ratification by the English Amateur Swimming Association (ASA), then the ruling body of international swimming. Kieran was a great swimmer, far ahead of his time, and many of his marks remained out of reach for 10 to 15 years. Yet when FINA, the International Swimming Federation, was formed in 1908, only Kieran's 500-yard record was officially recognized, although there was little doubt as to the authenticity of his other records.

Handicap races were quite the vogue in those days. The slower swimmers started first, and the handicapper walked behind each remaining swimmer shouting out the time off the ticking stopwatch. The rest was simple, when your handicap time was called, you started and chased after the swimmers who had left before you. One of the chief objections to records set in handicap races was that swimmers receive an unfair advantage because they are able to have "pacemakers." In the cases of both Kieran and Daniels, however, subsequent events were to prove them both capable of breaking world records and beating the world's best, pacemakers or not.

Handley Describes Daniels' Swim

L. de B. Handley commented on Daniels's record swim in the *New York Globe* on January 15, 1906: "The most marvelous part of the whole affair was Daniels' repeating in 57.6 after a very short rest in the final heat of the race. It may be added by way of information that in the final performance, when Daniels started, the water was already churned up into seething waves. Daniels was fouled in the third lap, and beat his man handily so he did not even have to exert himself at the finish. The New York A. C. pool is 75 feet in length, which is the length prescribed by English and Australian rules.

"It is worthy of note that since going the 100 yards in 59.6 last December, Daniels has yielded to the entreaties of his coach, Otto Wahle of the New York A. C., and former mile champion of America, and taken up the famous Australian crawl stroke. He tried it in Saturday's race, and many attribute to this his sudden and unexpected display of speed.

"From start to finish Daniels seemed to positively crawl over the water, with half his body exposed. He used his usual long, clean, powerful overarm stroke, with a peculiar combination of scissor and crawl leg movement. He would give a great scissor kick with every other arm stroke, and would wiggle his feet up and down fast between times. Unlike most of our crawlers, who keep their feet under water, he lifted his left leg high above the surface, and then slapped down hard with a great splash.

"The wonderful form shown by Daniels must in part be attributed to the constant and indefatigable care with which Mr. Wahle has attended the development of that talent which he discovered in our young prodigy several years ago."

Daniels Versus J. Scott Leary and H. J. Handy

Now Otto Wahle focused Daniels's attention on the American National Championship meet to be held in the club's pool February 21–24 in 1906. Entries were coming in from all parts of the United States. Daniels's recent swims had captured the public imagination, and it was anticipated that spectators would completely fill the tiered three balconies that surrounded the club's new pool.

It was reported that H. J. Handy, of the Central YMCA of Chicago, was training hard for his first meeting with Daniels, since he had reached the rare form that had enabled him to break so many records that winter, and it was thought that these races would eclipse all previous ones.

The swimming committee of the NYAC also tried to have J. Scott Leary, the Syd Cavill–trained swimmer from San Francisco, present at the meet to give Daniels a good race for the 100-yard championship. Leary was the holder of the United States straightaway 100-yard record, which he had set at Portland, Oregon, the previous year. It was thought that he would force Daniels to break the world's tank record of 57.6 seconds.

The Swimming Marvel of the Country

The March 1906, issue of the *New York Athletic Journal* reported, "By far the most interesting race at the afternoon session February 22 was the American 100 yard championship in which Daniels, wearing a heavy swimming suit, covered the distance in 58 seconds, equaling the world record made by Dick Cavill at Sydney, New South Wales, in January, 1904. Daniels swam 100 yards in 57³/₅ seconds in the club's tank recently, but the English swimming authorities took exception to the record on the grounds that it was made in a handicap race.

"As predicted by all who are keen on aquatic sport, the club's swimming carnival was a magnificent success—in fact the greatest event of its kind known in the history of sport. Records fell at every hand, the lion's share going to C. M. Daniels, the swimming marvel of the country. Daniels was not pressed at any time during the carnival, and to the ordinary observer it looked as though he easily could have done better. During the four days of the carnival, one world record and 12 American records were put to the credit of Daniels' name."

Daniels—How Do You Do It?

In 1906, Daniels was using the crawl technique regularly, improving at a faster rate than he had done before. This was the year in which he established his world supremacy as a sprint swimmer. Shortly after Daniels's record-breaking spree in the American championships, the *New York Tribune's* swimming specialist wrote, "Daniels uses a stroke that is a combination of the well-known trudgen and the new Australian crawl.

"He seems to have acquired the knack of so blending them as to develop great speed without the loss of any energy. The crawl, although used in Australia for some years, is comparatively new in this country. Its value lies in the use of the legs and feet, not only for keeping afloat, but for propelling purposes as well. The scientific application of force in the water is the secret of speed, and while natural ability counts, Daniels owes his success largely to proper coaching and careful and constant study. Much could be written about the evolution of the stroke, but enough now to say that, as far as can be judged, it is the best yet devised."

Daniels, a World-Beater

The *New York Athletic Club Journal* of August 1906, was ecstatic over Daniels's two great victories in Europe the previous month: "Hats off and a ringing cheer to C. M. Daniels! By his repeated victories over the best swimmers of the world he has brought great fame both to himself and our club, and his name will go down in history as the greatest swimmer America has ever produced.

"Daniels' crowning achievement, the winning of the 100 yard English championship, July 12, was easily accomplished according to cable dispatches; the American beating Healy of Australia by two yards. The time was 0:58$^{2}/_{5}$ seconds, or three-fifths of a second faster than the old English record which was held by Halmay.

"Previous to winning the championship, Daniels swam 100 yards in an invitation race in 0:57$^{3}/_{5}$ seconds, and will probably be credited with a new world's record by the English swimming authorities. The *Journal* hopes to be able to give its readers a detailed list of Daniels' triumphs in the September issue.

"The Bath Club International Swimming Contests were held July 2, at Dover, England. In the 120 yard scratch, C. M. Daniels won by one and one-half yards in 1:12 beating the Australian Cavill's record by one-fifth of a second. Cecil Healy of Australia was second, and Zoltan de Halmay, Budapest, was third."

1906 Olympic Victory

Eight days after winning the English 100-yard championship on July 20th, 1906, Charles Daniels captured the 100-meter Olympic title at the Athens Olympic Games. Daniels defeated his old rival Zoltan de Halmay, Cecil Healy of Australia, and the best of the Englishmen, including Jarvis. Daniels led from the start and eventually touched a winner by 10 feet in 1:5$^{3}/_{5}$ seconds.

Daniels' First Contacts with Australian Swimmers

The *New York Globe* said that it was "hard to see where Daniels gets his great speed from. There seems to be no visible effort above water; only a steady rush with the body under, mostly submerged, with now and then a lazy kick of the foot out of the water. The secret is the crawl—the stroke that is being copied by boys in every swimming hole in America. Perhaps Daniels and his great stroke will

Early picture of Charles Daniels, circa 1903, when he first joined the New York Athletic Club. A 1904 issue of *The Winged Foot* described Daniels as follows, "The face is that of an idealist and looks more like that of a poet than the stern countenance of an athlete who struggles for physical supremacy."

be the means of making America a leader among the swimmers of the world."

This stroke was used as a result of studying news clippings from Australia and subsequent interpretations made by Daniels and his clubmates before they ever made personal contact with any of the leading Australian swimmers. Daniels is said to have "studied the crawl stroke of the Australians at the 1906 Olympic Games in Athens, where he saw Cecil Healy use it. He practiced it assiduously at home and perfected a style entirely of his own" (Cureton, 1934).

Daniels, with the advice of Wahle, developed his own version of the crawl. While he was definitely influenced by what he learned from the Australian technique, it is doubtful that he commenced studying it as late as 1906, as claimed by Cureton. To the contrary, Daniels probably made his first personal contact with one of the great Australian swimmers a year earlier in 1905, when he met Barney Kieran, Australia's 19-year-old wonder swimmer (Beaurepaire, 1942). Beaurepaire does not state exactly where Daniels met Kieran in 1905, but the odds are that the venue was either at the English Championships, where Kieran won the 220, 440, 500, and 880, or later that same year during Daniels's visit to France and Germany.

Although Kieran was a trudgen swimmer, he showed Daniels and H. Julin, the Swedish champion, and other leading swimmers, the principles involved in the Australian crawl (Beaurepaire, 1942). It is worth noting that, although Kieran was technically a trudgen swimmer, he observed the new Australian crawl principle of not drawing the knees up, preferring instead to keep to a very narrow trudgen kick, like so many of Australia's golden age (Carlile, 1994).

In his book, *Australia at the Olympic Games*, Harry Gordon wrote that "1905 was the year in which Kieran competed in England, won four English titles, and broke world records from 200 yards to one mile. A month after returning from his European tour in November 1905, and a triumphant two days in which he won six Australian titles, Kieran died on December 22, 1905, after an appendix operation in Brisbane where he was competing in the championships. His funeral in Sydney was attended by 30,000 mourners. . . .

Cecil Healy's Influence

"Cecil Healy's preparation for the 1906 Olympic Games in Athens was hampered by a late departure from Australia, which left him very little time for training after the long sea voyage, during which he had no opportunity to swim. He was beaten in the 100-meter freestyle by the American, Charles Daniels, and the Hungarian, Zoltan de Halmay. For Healy, and for Australia, there was some comfort in Daniels' acknowledgment, after his win, that he owed much to instruction he had received a year before from the great Barney Kieran.

"It is very likely that Healy also gave some pointers on the Australian crawl to Daniels, but he was such a modest man that he would have given all the credit to Kieran. It was written of his 1906 continental tour (in "The Lone Hand," March 1916) that 'he went to much trouble teaching the crawl stroke to swimmers from other countries, where it was practically unknown. . . . Listed among those he taught were Meyboom of Belgium, R. Andersen of Sweden, Haynes of Scotland, and Kurt Bretting of Germany.'"

Healy was killed in action in the Somme in 1918, serving as an infantry officer in charge of a machine gun unit. A gold medalist in 1912, Healy was the only Australian Olympian to die in war (Gordon, 1994).

A Two-Way Trade

What did Daniels learn from his meeting with Healy? And, conversely, what did Healy learn from Daniels?

My guess is that their exchange was a two-way trade because both men were observant, analytical, innovative, and articulate. In addition, they were both open-minded and eager to experiment with their individual crawl techniques.

Healy learned from Daniels how to improve the continuity of his stroke by making certain adjustments to his leg action. I also believe that Healy showed Daniels how to improve his breathing technique, by "turning the head sideways to breathe, and bringing the shoulders much more into play by a rolling movement of the hips, which reduces the strain on the body, acts as a propelling force, and brings about a gliding motion" (Kiphuth, 1942).

Sprint and Distance Techniques

Healy's observations on head-turning mechanics and the body roll were indeed remarkable for the time. As we will see, they enabled Daniels to breath more regularly and swim in more relaxed fashion; factors which enabled him to swim the crawl farther and farther into the racing distance.

Healy, it appears, had also stumbled on the fact that, indeed, there could be two different crawl techniques: fixed shoulders and flat body for short-distance racing, and bodyroll with regular breathing for the longer distances. In fact, these are points of technique that present-day coaches, and possibly biomechanists, too, would do well to consider.

And what did Healy learn from Daniels? According to reports of the time, Healy observed Daniels's American crawl flutter kick, and moved away from the stylized, and synchronized, two-beat kick of the Australian crawl. He did this by first lengthening his arm stroke, and then introducing a fluttering of the feet between the two leg drives. These changes enabled him to obtain a continuous thrash without reconstructing his stroke entirely.

The Handicap Season

Why meet organizers persisted in framing elaborate handicap races with Daniels as the main attraction, is difficult to understand, because surely they knew that any world record set in a handicap race stood little chance of recognition. Even Daniels's coach, Wahle, who was also the club's official handicapper, announced, "If C. M. Daniels wins often in the handicap season, he will have to move through the water close to record time."

Back in America at the beginning of 1907, Daniels was soon in fine form, when the handicap season started at the New York Athletic Club. On January 12, 1907, swimming off scratch (the last swimmer to leave) in the 200-yard handicap, Daniels came within 1.6 seconds of Barney Kieran's world record of 2:13.8. Daniels's swim was also notable for the fact that he swam the first 100 using the crawl, and became the first swimmer to beat 60 seconds (59.6 seconds) for the 100 on the way to the 200. Daniels then changed to the trudgen stroke for the next 50 before reverting to the crawlstroke to finish the race.

At the 1907 American Championships, Daniels had four firsts in the individual events plus a relay first. Then in a 1,000-yard match race with H. J. Handy of Chicago, Daniels broke all the middle-distance records once more. Two nights later, he not only bettered these figures, but he set up a new American record of 23:40³/₅ for the mile, shaving seconds and fractions of seconds off previous records for all intermediate distances. This iconoclastic performance gave Charles Daniels every American record from 25 yards to a mile.

Daniels in the Lion's Den

In September of 1907, Daniels was back in England competing in the English Championships at Manchester. Daniels was anxious to do well because word had reached him that the British were skeptical about his world 100-yard record of 56.0 set in New York in 1906.

However, Daniels was defeated in the 220-yard championship by his old rival, Zoltan de Halmay of Budapest, immediately after his arrival in England. His friends claimed that the ocean voyage and change of climate had affected Daniels. This explanation was not immediately accepted, but the critics soon had reason to change their minds.

Competing in the 100-yard English Championship on September 8, against de Halmay and England's fastest 100 swimmer, J. H. Derbyshire, Daniels took the lead with his remarkable start, drawing away at once to win handily. Daniels clipped two seconds off the mark he had set in Richmond, England, the previous year, finishing in 55.4 seconds to set a new world record for the distance.

Commenting on Daniels's success, the *New York Times* said, "The record is especially gratifying to Daniels' American friends here, for the reason that Englishmen, in spite of the fact that he held the English record for the distance, were disposed to question his world record of 56 seconds made in his home tank at the New York Athletic Club. Now that he has beaten that phenomenal time before the eyes of the most capable timers in England, there can no longer be any question that he is the greatest swimmer who has ever raced in the world."

Daniels then embarked upon a strenuous tour of England and Scotland, winning 24 of the 25 races in which he competed.

Incompetent Officialdom

On January 20, 1908, Charles Daniels was in record-breaking form in the water carnival held to mark the opening of the New York public school baths. The *New York Athletic Club Journal* of February 1908, said, "Considering that Daniels' appearance was advertised as the feature of the occasion, it is incomprehensible how the officials could have made such as a blunder as to station the timers at the wrong end of the pool. As a result of this inexcusable folly, Daniels lost the credit of two new world records on a technicality.

"In his trial heat of the 60 yard swim, the NYAC man covered the distance in 24³/₅ seconds, which would have wiped out his old record of 25¹/₅ seconds, had it not been that the timers of the race were stationed at the end of the pool opposite the finish. Again, in the 200 yard handicap, Daniels was timed in 2 minutes, 9²/₅ seconds, a most remarkable time and one which, if allowed, would clip nearly 4 seconds from the record of 2:13 seconds established by Barney Kieran of Australia."

Trigger Happy Starter

While Daniels had an Olympic record and at least two world records turned down as a result of incompetence by officials, in 1908 at the Olympic Games in London, he nearly lost an Olympic title for the same reason.

Daniels's victory in the 100-meter swim was indeed hard earned. He was pulling a jersey over his head when the starter, without the slightest warning of "get ready," fired his pistol. The other contestants had a clear lead of 6 yards before Daniels had plunged into the water. Under the circumstances, his win was almost miraculous. Daniels won 12 first prizes while in England that year.

Kieran's Record Broken

One of the last performances of Daniels's great career was on March 26, 1910, at Pittsburgh, when he won the AAU 220-yard freestyle championship, and clipped three seconds off Barney Kieran's world record for a new mark of 2:25²/₅. His time was seven seconds faster than the American record.

Note: Kieran's record was probably an unofficial record because, as mentioned earlier, only Kieran's world record for 500 yards, set on August 25, 1905, was recognized by FINA when it was formed in 1908. In all probability, prior to 1908, the Americans and the Australians, tacitly if not outwardly, had continued to recognize world records set by their swimmers, despite the English governing body's rejection of their record applications.

Daniels' Legacy

Shortly after Daniels's retirement from competitive swimming, the *New York Times* paid tribute to his great contribution to the technical side of competitive swimming in this 1911 article: "A prominent Sydney waterman said recently that, when Cecil Healy returned home after racing Daniels in Europe, he set out at once to lengthen his arm stroke and to introduce between leg drives a fluttering of the feet which enabled him to obtain a continuous thrash without reconstructing his stroke entirely. A flattering tribute to Daniels and indirectly to American instructors.

"Possibly other countries followed the same line of reasoning that we did and so we reached the same conclusions, but that we were the first to swim the crawl with a long reach and separate timing of arms and legs is incontestable. The newspaper and magazine clips of 1905 and 1906 contain ample proof that we were even then comparing our ways with those of others and trying to show why they should give better results. We have had no occasion since to revise these views.

"Our experts maintained from the start that the crawl was not a freak sprinting stroke, but one which would eventually prove its superiority for all around swimming. Even today Cavill says that it should not be used over distances greater than 100 yards, and this in spite of Daniels' having created a world record of 2:25²/₅ seconds for 220 yards with it. A ready explanation offers itself of this difference of opinion.

"In timing the legs with the arm drive as Australians do, there is experienced a heavy drag as soon as the speed of the arms is decreased. If the action of the arms and legs is independent, instead, a slow continuous thrash can be indulged in which not only keeps the swimmer underway while the arms are recovering, but also ensures the maintenance of the proper position of the body in water throughout the stroke, thus avoiding all check of the forward impetus.

"This is why so many of our crawlers have been able to hold the stroke over distances as great as several miles. Lack of facilities for outdoor work has really been the cause of the slow progress in distance swimming in this country, but if the improvement has been gradual it has been nevertheless consistent and it will not be long now, before a new crop of speeders is heard from. The next Olympics will tell the tale. Even without the great Charles Daniels we should have a relay team of furlong swimmers able to hold their own against all foreign nations, and the longer distances will come next."

In the century's first decade, the infant crawl stroke was a tiring technique, useful for short sprints only, but Charles Daniels had the foresight to predict ". . . it is very probable that eventually we will use the crawl for all distances." His prediction came to pass, and Daniels lived to see the day when crawl swimmers such as John Kinsella, Mike Burton, and Stephen Holland, were nearing the 15-minute mark for the 1,500-meter distance, an average speed of nearly 60 seconds for each 100 meters—less than the world record for a single 100 meters in Daniels's heyday.

When Daniels died on August 9, 1973, he had the satisfaction of knowing that many an accomplished exponent of the American crawl had followed in the tradition he started, including such great swimmers as Duke Kahanamoku, Johnny Weissmuller, Alan Ford, Walter Ris, Clark Scholes, Steve Clark, Don Schollander, and Mark Spitz. And scores of other singularly talented men and women, not only American, but from around the world, had swum the American crawl to reach the Olympian heights.

✧ ✧ ✧

WHERE DID DANIELS MEET KIERAN?

When Charles Daniels captured the Olympic 100-meter title from Cecil Healey and Zoltan de Halmay at the 1906 Athens Olympics, Daniels credited his win to the instruction received in the year before from Australia's great Barney Kieran. The intriguing question, however, is When and where did Charles Daniels first meet Barney Kieran?

In the article "The Daniels Dynasty," little mention was made of Daniels's activities in the year

1905 for the simple reason that no information was available. The records of the English championships for the year 1905 showed that Kieran had indeed competed, and, in fact, had won the 220-, 440-, 500-, and 880-yard events, while Zoltan de Halmay, the 1904 Olympic 100 champion, had won the 100 yards in 59.0 seconds. No mention is made of place winners. While it is possible that Daniels placed in the 100, his favorite event, no record of this existed.

However, I have been able to piece most of the story together. The account starts with two excerpts from the *New York Athletic Club Journal*. A March 1904, article mentions how, despite "the long, cold winter of 1904, the natatorial miracle-worker, young C. M. Daniels, continues to mystify people on the bank who thought they knew what fast swimming was before they saw Daniels perform." Then, in the December 1904 issue, we note that Daniels obviously has decided not to experience another long, cold winter, because the article reports that "C. M. Daniels, the club's great swimmer, who holds all the American records up to 500 yards, and the world record for 220 yards, sailed on November 4 on the Minnehaha for an extended tour of Europe, during which he expects to compete with all the leading foreign swimmers.

"In England Daniels proposed to challenge Billington and Derbyshire, the leading English tank swimmers, and to meet them or any others in as many matches as might be arranged. He will travel through Germany and France, and will meet the best swimmers of those countries. Then he will go to Spain, Algiers, and Egypt for the winter, returning to England next spring, where he will compete in the English Championships.

"When Daniels left he was swimming faster than ever before, as was shown by a trial November 3 in the club's tank. He made 100 yards with ease in 1:02²/₅, the record being 1:01²/₅, and it is expected that he will return from his foreign tour with many international honors." (Note: These times were swum using the trudgen stroke. Daniels did not take up crawl swimming seriously until December 1905.)

After leaving America, as far as available records of the time are concerned, Daniels appears to have just dropped out of sight. I received no replies to my requests for assistance from the English

C. M. Daniels' World Records When He Retired in 1910

Distance	Record	Country	Date
100 yards	54.8	USA	4/7/10
100 meters	1:02.8	USA	4/15/10
150 yards	1:32.4	USA	7/8/08
220 yards	2:25.4	USA	3/26/10

authorities as to whether Daniels had competed in the English championships in 1905. I grasped at one last straw by asking Dave Kelly, of the Library of Congress, Washington, DC, if *The London Times* carried any record of Daniels's competing in the English Championships in 1905. The next day, he sent me five historical excerpts from *The London Times*.

The London Times, **June 12, 1905**
CAMBRIDGE UNIVERSITY S. C. v. OTTER S. C. The visit of the London Club provides one of the May Week entertainments. Additional interest was manifested in the meeting owing to the fact that C. M. Daniells, [name misspelled] the American amateur champion, would compete against the Light Blue captain (B. T. Verry), who has during his residence at Cambridge, carried all before him. Daniells, however, proved too strong for the Cantab, and won both the 50 yards and quarter-mile race. The result was a victory for the Otters by 2¹/₂ points to a half. Daniells won the 50 yards race by 2 yards in 28¹/₅ seconds, and the quarter mile by 40 yards in 7 min. 15 secs.

The London Times, **June 19th, 1905**
SWIMMING. ARRIVAL OF THE AUSTRALIAN CHAMPION. On Saturday afternoon, Mr. B. B. Kieran, the amateur champion of Australia, arrived at Tilbury on board the Royal Mail steamer Oratava. Mr. Kieran, who comes to England at the invitation of the Royal Life Saving Society, will be the guest of that body during his stay in this country. At present he is the holder of all the Australian championships from a furlong to a mile and the holder of the world amateur records at all recognized distances from 200 yards to a mile. His first

attempt to gain national honors will be in the one mile amateur championship of England at Highgate Pond on July 1; but before that he will swim at the Oxford and Cambridge meeting at the Bath Club on Monday next, and at the Otter's Club meeting on the following night. On July 8 and 10 he will take part in the races for the King's Cup at Blackpool, and later he will compete in most of the English amateur championships. In the King's Cup race will be Mr. Daniels, the amateur champion of America, who is also now in England.

In the same issue of *The Times* was a report of a meet in which Daniels competed:

OXFORD UNIVERSITY v. OTTER S.C. In the 50 yards race the University were represented by E. G. Morris, Hertford, and the Otters by C. M. Daniels, the holder of the American championship for 100 yards, 220 yards, and a quarter of a mile, and H. L. R. Jacobs. The race resulted in Daniels getting home a yard in front of the other two, between whom there was a dead heat.

The first meeting between Daniels and Kieran probably took place at the Oxford and Cambridge "swimming matches" on June 26th, 1905.

The London Times, **June 23rd, 1905**
SWIMMING. OXFORD v. CAMBRIDGE. The Oxford and Cambridge swimming matches will take place at the Bath Club on Monday next, beginning at 8:30. Mr. B. B. Kieran, the amateur champion of Australia, and Mr. C. M. Daniels, the amateur champion of America, will, at the invitation of the president of the Bath Club, Mr. W. H. Grenfell, M.P., give an exhibition of swimming during the evening.

The London Times, **June 27th, 1905**

SWIMMING. THE INTER-UNIVERSITY MATCHES. Feat by Mr. B. B. Kieran. Some remarkable swimming by B. B. Kieran, the Australian amateur champion, was the feature of the inter-University swimming meeting held at the Bath Club, Dover-street, Piccadilly, last night, in the presence of the Duke and Duchess of Connaught, Princess Patricia of Connaught, Prince and Princess Henry of Plesh, Mr. W. H. Grenfell, M.P., and many old Blues. The members of the University clubs had invited Mr., Kieran to give his first display in this country at their entertainment, and the young Australian readily consented to make an attempt to lower the 600 yards record, which in England is 8 min. 3 sec., and in America 8 min. 25 sec. As soon as Mr. Kieran started it was evident that in him Australia possesses the best swimmer known to the world. Though he is only 18 years of age, his pace is remarkable, gained principally through a wonderful leg kick. He covered the distance in 7 min. 42²/₅ sec. in the most easy fashion, and could easily have beaten the record by several more seconds.

Note: No mention whatsoever is made of C. M. Daniels, whether he was present, gave an exhibition as advertised, or whether he competed against Kieran in the 600-yard record attempt. The next mention of Kieran and Daniels again being on the same program was in *The London Times,* July 10, 1905.

The London Times, **July 10, 1905**

SWIMMING. RACE FOR THE KING'S CUP. Three years ago the King presented a cup to the Royal Life Saving Society for International competition. In the first year of its institution the contest took the form of ordinary swimming races, and those England won; but last year the conditions were altered, two life-saving races being substituted. In the first race the men had to swim a quarter of a mile in clothes and to carry a supposed drowned person for the last 40 yards of the distance. The second race was one of a 150 yards in clothes, the subject being carried for the last 25 yards. In that year, H. Johannson, of Stockholm, won on points. The first of this year's races took place at Blackpool, on Saturday afternoon, in the presence of a very large crowd of spectators. It was the quarter mile race and was made especially interesting by the fact that D. Billington, of Bacup, the English champion, J. Daniels, the American champion [name again incorrect], and B. B. Kieran, the Australian champion, were among the competitors. The race was a struggle between Kieran and Billington. When the subjects were reached Kieran was leading, but Billington proved more adept at carrying his man in the water and won by 10 yards. W.W. Robinson of Liverpool, the holder of the English breast-stroke amateur championship, was a bad third. Time 9 min. 35 sec.

Note: Although this was the first occasion when Kieran and Daniels were actually reported to have been in the same place at the same time, it is fairly safe to say that the historical occasion when Barney Kieran explained the principles of the Australian crawlstroke to Charles Daniels occurred either at the Oxford versus Cambridge meet at the Bath Club in Piccadilly, London, on June 26, 1905, or at the King's Cup competitions at Blackpool on July 9, 1905. The important point is that we now have a very good idea of the approximate time frame during which their meeting took place. And what happened to Daniels in the unusual lifesaving race? If Robinson finished "a bad third," was Daniels's finish even worse? Perhaps he was overcome by cramps, swimming in the Irish Sea can be a very exhilarating experience to those accustomed to swimming in heated indoor pools. Nevertheless, whatever may have transpired in any actual swimming competitions they had, the subsequent discussion between the two talented youths was an important landmark in the history of swimming, and particularly in the development of the crawl.

Although Kieran was a trudgen swimmer, he understood the principles of crawl swimming. He is said to have passed these principles on to the young American champion, who thereupon started experimenting with the new stroke.

Although Syd Cavill, one of the pioneers of the Australian crawl, had been coaching at the San Francisco Olympic Club for some time, and Australian travelers had also passed on what they knew of the crawl, the meeting between the two national champions was the first actual swimmer-to-swimmer link between the Australian crawl and the person who was to modify it and create the American crawl, a new stroke that became so successful at all distances that eventually the Australian crawl became obsolete.

When he returned to America, Daniels incorporated the principles of the crawlstroke to suit his own movement pattern, as well as the less buoyant freshwater conditions in which most Americans competed. The almost instant result was that Daniels improved at an even greater rate than he had done before. On January 13, 1906, he became the first American to break the 100-yard world record with a time of 57.6 seconds. Over the next four years, Charles Daniels steadily improved on this time until his world record stood at 54.8 seconds on April 7, 1910, a few months before he retired at the end of a legendary career.

✧ ✧ ✧

DUKE KAHANAMOKU—THE GENTLEMAN SWIMMER

Swimming is a way of life in Hawaii, and the overarm stroke was swum there for centuries, but the greatest of the Hawaiian swimmers learned the finer points on the mainland in a crash course, only weeks before the 1912 Olympics.

One day in 1911, a year after Charles Daniels, America's first great swimmer, had retired, his former coach, Otto Wahle, then President of the American AAU, received a very unusual letter.

In it the Hawaiian Swimming Association applied for recognition of a 100-yard world record of 55.4 seconds set in Honolulu harbor by a young swimmer with the sonorous name of Duke Pao Kahanamoku. The application was accompanied by affidavits saying that Kahanomoku had received no benefit from the harbor's tidal waters. But the AAU's officials were not convinced.

Instead of accepting the record, they invited the Hawaiians to enter Duke in the AAU indoor championships in Pittsburgh early in 1912. Duke was assured of being selected for the Stockholm Olympics if he repeated his form.

The Hawaiians were excited at receiving the invitation. The colorful Hawaiian party caused quite a stir when they arrived in Pittsburgh, and everyone was impressed by the fine physique and gentlemanly bearing of the tall, bronzed youth from the Hai Nalu Boat Club of Honolulu. When Kahanamoku hit the water in the 220-yard championship, the experts gasped at his great natural speed.

But his stroke was rough, and he had no experience of swimming in a tanked pool. He set off like a frightened horse. He had no idea of pace. He had two speeds: flat-out and stop. At 60 yards he had gained a lead of three body lengths, but at the 120-yard mark, he was so exhausted that he had to be yanked out of the pool.

Surprisingly, Duke wasn't discouraged. In fact, when he recovered his breath, he shook his head and laughed at his own misfortune. The mainlanders were soon to learn that Kahanamoku was a man of remarkable character. Throughout his career, no matter the circumstances, The Duke, as he came to be called, remained an immensely likable, relaxed, happy, gentle, and fun-loving person.

The Duke was quick to learn. He realized that his stroke was far from efficient, his start and turns were a severe handicap, and, to cap it all, he knew it was urgent that he learned to spread his energy evenly over the distance. A few days later, he competed in Chicago, and, despite fumbling his turns, he redeemed himself to some extent by winning the 100-yard title. In the 50-yard event, however, both his start and turn were poor, and he failed to gain a place.

However, the AAU officials had seen enough of the Honolulu youth's raw speed and power to convince them that he had, in fact, equaled Daniels's 100-yard record in a straightaway swim, and he was awarded the open-water record. As a result, he was also included in the American Olympic team.

Wahle thought it urgent to teach Kahanamoku as much as he could safely absorb within the limited time before the Olympics. He arranged for

Duke to receive a crash course of instruction at the University of Pennsylvania in starting and turning, and entering his arms cleanly instead of hitting the water forcefully.

A canvas pool was erected on the deck of the *S.S. Finland* in which the U.S. team sailed to Stockholm. The Duke soon became popular with the other swimmers, and they took turns at helping him master various points of technique. But no one did more than team manager Otto Wahle in smoothing out Kahanamoku's style, and The Duke benefited from the knowledge and experience acquired by Wahle during his years of coaching Charles Daniels.

One would have thought that being coached by so many people within so short a time, and only a few weeks away from the world's major swim meet, would have resulted in The Duke showing the classic symptoms of paralysis by analysis. To the contrary, he learned new skills almost immediately, a sign of true natural talent, so much so that he is said to have shown more technical improvement in Stockholm than during any other stage of his career. When The Duke returned home, he was swimming what had become known as the classic American crawl.

In Stockholm, he adopted new tactics. Instead of taking the lead immediately, he allowed his nervous energy to carry him down the pool, letting his rivals set the pace to the halfway mark. Then he would strike, increasing his lead with each successive stroke.

In the first heat of the 100 meters, The Duke brought the spectators to their feet when he set a world record of 1:02.6. In the semifinal, the new Olympic star further reduced the mark to 1:02.4. In the final, he defeated the great Australian swimmer, Cecil Healy, to win the Olympic title in 1:02.6.

With the possible exception of Johnny Weissmuller, Kahanamoku did more than anyone else to popularize swimming around the world. In 1915, The Duke traveled to Australia where he spent three months swimming and surfing, and he soon captured the hearts of that country's sports-loving people.

He won the New South Wales 100-yard title, thrilling the crowd with a spectacular new world record of 53.8 seconds. Later, the *New York Times*

said of this swim that "The Duke's stroke is so slow that the Australians thought that he was stalling and not trying when he created his world record. They were astounded to learn that the Hawaiian had established a new record, for they had been fooled by the easy precision of his form, which was much cleaner than that of even their star performers. The slow, easy movements of Kahanamoku from the hips to the tips of the fingers were markedly in contrast with those of all the men who have competed against him in his important races."

Perhaps the greatest compliment ever paid to Duke Pao Kahanamoku came from Otto Wahle: "There is one thing I will always admire about Kahanamoku. He is a great swimmer, but he is even higher in my esteem as a gentleman. On the trip to Stockholm in 1912, he rendered every assistance to the Olympic Committee, proved a modest, retiring sort of fellow, and attracted everybody to him through his good nature.

"His smile became famous among us, for it was golden if ever a smile was. Duke is a striking personality, and even now I can see him lined up at the start ready to dart into the water. His long shining black hair and his copper-colored skin blend in harmony, and altogether he would make a model worthy of any sculptor's chisel."

A JAPANESE SWIMMER WAS ONE OF SWIMMING'S GREAT VISIONARIES

Sixty years ago, Katsuo Takaishi accurately predicted most of the fundamentals of the modern crawl stroke.

When Katsuo Takaishi reported for the start of the 100-meter freestyle final at the 1928 Amsterdam Olympics, he was dwarfed by America's 6-foot, 3-inch Johnny Weissmuller, and another 6-footer, Stefan Barany, the Hungarian champion.

Weissmuller, the reigning Olympic champion, was the acknowledged "Prince of Waves," the greatest swimmer who ever lived. Smiling, supremely confident, the engaging Weissmuller sauntered onto the deck, cracking jokes with

International Swimming Hall of Fame

Katsuo Takaishi (Japan), in dark swimming suit, takes the lead at the start. It was not uncommon to see a "staggered" start, such as shown here. Many swimmers had not yet been taught the difference between motor mindedness and sensory mindedness when starting. Note the primitive conditions, lane markers, and "starting blocks."

friends and admirers. Behind him, incongruous, almost apologetic in this company of giants, came the tiny scholarly-looking fellow with a little beard.

People looked at each other and asked, "Surely he isn't the legendary Takaishi, said to be Weissmuller's biggest rival for the title?" But, as Takaishi limbered up, the crowd watched, goggle-eyed. The tiny athlete was not just extremely flexible, but almost completely double jointed. The spectators applauded the far Easterner's short display of gymnastics. Takaishi grinned with amusement, waved, and bowed slightly in the direction of the stands.

The swimmers came to the line. The scene was dramatic. Eight finely tuned athletes crouched for one suspenseful moment. The pistol cracked, the swimmers hit the water, and the Olympic final was underway. Weissmuller and Takaishi took the lead, barreling down the stretch, swimming head to head.

Weissmuller swam with back arched, head and shoulders high, while the fish-like Takaishi swam lower in the water with unbelievable initial speed, his powerful strokes making him look a much bigger man. One thing was certain: The great Weissmuller was in for the race of his life.

Deep shadows at the far end of the pool made it difficult to see clearly, but Takaishi appeared to head the field into the turn. Then, after a long push-off, Weissmuller's long brown arms appeared flashing in the sunshine. Using his height to advantage, Weissmuller had gained almost a body's length over the valiant Japanese, while Barany had edged into second place. Over the last 20 meters, Barany pulled away from Takaishi, but was unable to sustain his sprint as he tried to catch Weissmuller, who touched first equaling his own Olympic record of 58.4 set in the semifinals.

Remarkable Insight

The Amsterdam Olympics marked the highpoint of Katsuo Takaishi's brilliant competitive career, but few people know that the modest Japanese champion was a keen and able student of swimming. Takaishi had a remarkable insight into the niceties of the sport, an intuitive feel probably far in advance of what any latter-day certification program could have developed in him. Sixty years ago, long before the advent of scientific analysis, he predicted most of the fundamentals of the modern crawl stroke with uncanny accuracy.

Here are some of Takaishi's farsighted comments on various phases of crawl swimming, as published in *Swimming in Japan* (Tokyo: International Young Women and Children's Society, 1935).

The Arm Entry

Takaishi believed that the arm entry was the key to producing an efficient stroke. Moreover, the way the swimmer entered the hand in the water was also an indication of whether or not a swimmer had talent.

Takaishi said, "There are a few who have the opinion that the pressing movement of the arm at the beginning of the stroke is of no use or can even be detrimental for increasing speed, but the writer believes that this very movement decides whether one is a good swimmer or not. A good swimmer must learn to press the water skillfully.

"It is better to let the arm into the water before it is completely extended. If one extends the arm fully before letting it into the water, the time for pressing will be too long." Despite Takaishi's advice, most Western swimmers continued to enter the arms by reaching out over the water prior to entering the hand, and it was not until the 1950s that the Australians reintroduced the method of entering the hands just ahead of the preceding bow wave.

Body Roll

At a time when swimmers were urged to retain a flat body position in order to keep resistance to a minimum, Takaishi recommended that "both shoulders [should] draw ellipses while swimming. One of them should be lifted when the other is dropped. Accordingly, the upper part of the body should roll to both sides, but the position of the body does not change.

"This movement is called rolling the body and it has a very close relation with the crawl stroke. If one swims without rolling the body on the longitudinal axis he must swim in a very unnatural position, such as pushing the head above the surface of the water or floating the upper part of the body by sinking the legs deeply in order to breathe easily."

Stroke Tempo

Takaishi realized that rolling the body brought into play the large trunk muscles. He said: "If one tries to stroke without rolling the body, the power required is produced only by the muscles of the arms and shoulders, but when the rolling of the body is added to that of the arms the force will be greatly increased. But one must understand that there is a limit even for rolling, as too much will destroy the form or will slow down the stroke. Rolling the body is necessary and the power produced by it greatly strengthens the stroke when it is combined with the arm movements. This strength is increased according to the degree of rolling, consequently it is natural that the more one rolls the body, the larger the arm movement becomes. The larger the movement, the slower the tempo of the stroke."

Stroke Length and Stroke Tempo

With amazing prescience, Takaishi made what are probably the first references in the literature on the subject of stroke length and stroke tempo: "The best method of speed swimming for a fixed distance is to swim with the largest and strongest stroke and with as high a tempo as possible. However, it is difficult for a swimmer of

Johny Weissmuller (USA) on left, Olympic 100-meter freestyle champion, 1924 and 1928, with Katsuo Takaishi (Japan). Takaishi was one of swimming's first great visionaries.

limited power and strength to enlarge his stroke without dropping his tempo. Thus, we must consider the limit of rolling. In considering this it is important to decide whether the rolling suits the swimmer or not, for on this decision rests whether he will succeed. This limit cannot be decided uniformly for every person. It is very difficult to find the limit of rolling which is most suitable for each individual. If one rolls the body too much, he is compelled to let the arm stop while pressing on the water before it commences the catching movement.

"In short," said Takaishi, "the maximum of rolling is when the power gained by that rolling is all applied to that arm movement and each arm carries on its stroke without wasting time and energy."

Stroke Acceleration

Fifty years before scientific research on the subject, Takaishi appreciated the importance of hand acceleration as an important factor in stroke efficiency. Takaishi put it this way: "It is the power of the finishing movement of the arms which actually increases the speed. Consequently, the finishing movement should be done very quickly and strongly." Amazing!

In his day, Takaishi's writings may well have been pooh-poohed, scoffed at, and classified as merely anecdotal, but science has since proved him right. The pity of it is that Takaishi's writings were virtually ignored by Westerners (to their detriment), only to be revived many years later. Takaishi was living proof of the old adage, "Be right too soon, your word will be ignored. Be right too late, and everyone is bored."

✧ ✧ ✧

THE 50-YEAR SAGA OF THE BREASTSTROKE RULES

No other stroke has undergone so many changes as breaststroke. The arms and legs were meant to be kept completely submerged in breaststroke swimming, but in 1934, some swimmers found a loophole in the rules that allowed them to recover their arms over the water, thus creating the butterfly. Although the butterfly eventually emerged as a separate event, it took nearly 20 years to return orthodox breaststroke to its original form.

But what happened then? Swimmers found another loophole in the rules that enabled them to swim underwater for most of the race. It took from 1956 to 1987 to finally define breaststroke as the surface stroke it was intended to be.

The saga of the breaststroke rules lasted a total of 50 years, and although the memory is gradually vanishing, there are many lessons to be learned from the political and technical bungling that adversely affected the growth of the sport, and the careers of many individual athletes.

By studying the course of these events, swimming legislators can avoid making the same mistakes, while still encouraging innovative athletes and ensuring that existing swimming techniques are performed according to the intention of the rules.

Enter the Butterfly

Like many crawl swimmers switching to breaststroke, young Henry Myers felt restricted by the resistance caused by the stroke's underwater arm recovery.

He thought, "Why not pull right through to my hips with both arms, and then bring them forward over the water like a double freestyle arm recovery?"

The result was amazing. Myers, swimming his so-called butterfly stroke, soon found he could beat his club's best breaststroke swimmers in short practice swims.

Because only the kick resembled breaststroke, it seems unlikely that Myers's original intention was to invent a new style of breaststroke or to circumvent the existing rules. Perhaps he thought he had produced a sort of novelty stroke that was really only half breaststroke and that his escapade would be good for a laugh.

Only after close study of the breaststroke rules did Myers find to his surprise that the new stroke complied with the rules in every respect. And he was probably even more surprised when his coach, W. W. Robertson of the Brooklyn Dragon Swim Club, encouraged him to try out the stroke in the 150-yard medley event at the Brooklyn Central YMCA swim meet in December 1933.

Myers's entry into the event was to set the whole world of swimming on its head. He became the first person to swim the butterfly in competition.

Myers was seeded in the first heat with the favorite, Wallace Spence, the American medley champion. Spence took the lead at the start but Myers soon caught him halfway down the 25-yard pool, and quickly pulled away. The crowd was taken aback by Myers's odd-looking stroke. They couldn't figure out what was happening. At the end of the breaststroke leg, Spence was about 3 yards behind, but he slowly overtook Myers to pass him before the race finished. Spence was to say later that he thought Myers had been swimming freestyle.

Coach Robertson showed the rule book to the puzzled officials to prove that Myers's odd-looking stroke did not contravene the rules. Myers wasn't disqualified, and this set the precedent for using the butterfly breaststroke, as it became known.

A reaction soon started that was to continue for many years after Myers's retirement from competition. The central YMCA's magazine in a vitriolic article, made disparaging remarks about "the sportsmanship of young Myers who observed the letter but not the spirit of the breaststroke rules."

Still, there were others, carried away by enthusiasm and imagination, who acclaimed butterfly as the most sensational development in swimming in recent years. They emphasized that it met the requirements of the breaststroke rules at every point. One can only wonder what would happen today if anyone was suddenly to attempt to introduce so drastic a departure from accepted technique.

Butterfly Grows in Popularity

On March 2, 1934, in a novice 100-yard breaststroke race at an AAU meet in Harrison, New Jersey, the new stroke was used again in competition. Before the start, the local officials were told that two swimmers, Henry Myers and Kenneth Stevenson, were going to introduce a new type of breaststroke that had been approved by New York officials. The officials were told the stroke was currently in use in New York meets, and that what was good enough for New York should be good enough for New Jersey.

The officials, loathe to start a controversy with the New York officials, agreed not to disqualify the stroke. Consequently, both Kenneth Stevenson and Henry Myers used the butterfly, and the finish was 1—Stevenson, 2—Muntz, 3—Myers (Kiputh, 1942). Butterfly breaststroke soon grew in popularity through school, college, and national competition in the United States. People began to take it seriously, and some even claimed to have originated it.

The outstanding early exponents of the stroke were Kaplan and Friesel. The stroke was first used in intercollegiate swimming in a specially arranged dual meet between the University of Michigan and an all-star City College of New York team. The new stroke was used by Lester Kaplan against John Schmieler, who was the National Intercollegiate breaststroke champion. Kaplan left the champion well behind for the first 3 lengths of the 25-yard pool, but was unable to maintain his pace over the final length.

The early breaststroke swimmers used butterfly breaststroke for only 3 to 6 strokes on each length. However, more and more swimmers developed the ability to fly the whole 220-yards, and Jack Kasley set world records in 1936 for the 220-yard, 200-meter and 200-yard events. The National Intercollegiate record very quickly dropped from 2:30 to 2:22 (Mann & Fries, 1940).

The Butterfly Advantage

Why did the discovery of the butterfly breaststroke create such an advantage over the original style of breaststroke swimming? The difference was in the fact that a swimmer could almost double the length of the arm pull used in the conventional stroke, and that the arms could be recovered over the water with less resistance than used in pushing the arms forward underwater to start the new stroke. Another advantage of the butterfly breaststroke was that the overwater recovery allowed the swimmer to raise the head to inhale.

It should be pointed out that, prior to the "invention" of butterfly breaststroke, there were breaststroke swimmers such as 1928 and 1932 Olympic champion Yoshiyuki Tsuruta, and his contemporary, bronze medalist Teofilo Ildefonso, who both used underwater breaststroke techniques. They pulled through to their hips but recovered their arms forward under the water.

While Henry Myers was the first swimmer to use the butterfly arm strokes in continuous sequence, it is interesting to note that each time Ildefonso swam into the turn, he used a single butterfly arm recovery as he reached for the wall, and so did breaststroke world-record holder, Erich Rademacher of Germany.

A note concerning Erich Rademacher: On a visit to the United States in 1927, Rademacher caused much protest when he gained a considerable advantage by bringing his arms over the water in a double arm recovery as he went into the turn, and also when he touched at the end of a race. It is significant that Rademacher insisted, even at that early date, that this in no way infringed the rules of breaststroke swimming. Nevertheless, at the Amsterdam Olympics the following year, Rademacher played safe by not using this technique (Oppenheim, 1970). On this occasion, however, the tables were turned. Rademacher, swimming on the surface, could not match the prolonged underwater swimming of Tsuruta, who won the Olympic title in a world-record time of 2:45.4, even though Rademacher was recognized as the faster swimmer of the two swimmers, when swimming the surface stroke (Dawson, 1987).

Half Breaststroke or Half Butterfly?

Nearly 60 years later, it is difficult to understand why officials were in such a hurry to press for the acceptance of a new stroke that looked so little like the breaststroke, even though it met all the requirements of the rules.

Increased speed, of course, was the main reason. People were jubilant at the discovery of the butterfly breaststroke because it sped up the sedate breaststroke. Furthermore, the orthodox breaststroke had never really been a popular event in the United States.

In many European countries, it had been revered as the traditional stroke as well as the first stroke taught to beginners. In fact, it was known as "the school stroke" in the Netherlands, and was reputed to be the only stroke swam in Iceland.

Historical analysis shows that American officials appear to have overlooked one important fact: Although the new butterfly stroke complied with the breaststroke rules, by no stretch of the imagination could it honestly have been described as the breaststroke that had been the traditional stroke in Europe for three centuries. At best, it could have been said that it was either "half breaststroke" or "half butterfly," take your pick.

Surely, some official at the time would have had the sense to hold up a hand and say, "Hey, stop! Can't you see that this stroke is not breaststroke? Don't you realize that what we have here is a completely different stroke altogether? It's obviously the result of a loophole in the rules, and it would be grossly unfair to take advantage of it. This new stroke should be recognized as such, and given its own set of rules."

At the same time, to preserve the intended form of the traditional breaststroke, wise officials could have prevented a lot of trouble by closing the obvious loophole in the breaststroke Rule 34, by simply adding a few words that said, "The hands must be kept under the water surface and recovered forward from the breast." But, as I have said, the wisdom of hindsight is a wonderful thing.

Butterfly at the Berlin Olympics

On March 19, 1934, the United States AAU wrote to the FINA Bureau seeking an "urgent opinion" on whether "a swinging or throwing the arms instead of the rounded and outward sweep of the arms under the surface of the water was legal or not." This was obviously an initial move to have the new butterfly breaststroke accepted

Action picture of Kevin Berry (Australia), 1964 200-meter butterfly Olympic champion, who won in world and Olympic record time: 2:6.6. In 1962 Berry broke 10 world butterfly records.

at the forthcoming 1936 Berlin Olympics. The immediate result was that the FINA Honorable Secretary, "owing to urgency," cabled his "personal opinion" that "according to the existing rule, such swinging or throwing of the arms was legal."

In 1936, FINA announced that "the so-called butterfly-breaststroke, including an over-water-recovery of the arms was not contrary to Rule 34 of the FINA and that it would be permitted at the 1936 Berlin Olympic Games."

However, it seems that this was, in effect, only a temporary permission to use the stroke in the 1936 Olympics, because FINA's announcement warned that the meeting of the FINA Congress of the Federation, scheduled for August 16, 1936, after the Games had ended, would be asked to decide whether or not the "butterfly stroke" was desirable.

Apparently, even at this early stage, some swimmers were either accidentally or intentionally inserting a dolphin kick on completion of the breaststroke kick. FINA saw fit to accompany its announcement with a quaintly-worded statement that swimmers "using the fish-tail leg drive constituted by a downward whip of the legs in a short quick flip after the completion of the rounded and outward sweep of the feet, being contrary to the aforesaid Rule, will be prohibited. Any swimmer using it will be disqualified."

After the Berlin Olympics ended, FINA resolved that the butterfly breaststroke be admitted in international competitions under breaststroke Rule 34.

1938–1946 Alterations to Breaststroke Rule 34

In 1938, two years after the Berlin Olympics and a year before the outbreak of World War II, what was to become known as "The Breaststroke Saga," or the "Saga of Rule 34," started in earnest when FINA voted on a proposal to ban the butterfly. After a long debate, the motion was supported by four votes out of seven, but because a two-thirds majority was required, the motion wasn't carried.

At the same meeting, at the request of Max Ritter who was representing the AAU, it was unanimously resolved to prohibit up-and-down leg movements in the vertical plane.

In October 1946, a new section (f) was added to Breaststroke Rule 34: "A swimmer must swim, when on the surface, either orthodox (conventional) breaststroke or butterfly stroke throughout the race. These strokes must not be alternated." This muddle-headed ruling, in essence, confirmed that something was radically wrong, and that basically, the two strokes belonged in different events.

FINA and the IOC

After the 1948 Olympic Games, the FINA Congress accepted a proposal by the Amateur Swimming Union of Australia that "butterfly-breaststroke and orthodox breaststroke be considered separate events, as they represent two distinct styles of swimming, and should not be

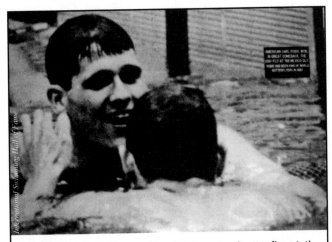

Carl Robie (USA) won the 200-meter butterfly at the 1968 Mexico Olympics in a great comeback after ruling this event in 1962.

swum in the same competition." Proposal passed by 42 votes to 31. The Congress asked FINA to work out the details. The FINA Bureau, however, voted 7 to 3 to veto the Congress ruling (O'Connor, 1948).

This action brought an immediate protest from Harold Fern, Britain's Bureau representative and a former president of FINA. Fern, who had presided at the Congress meeting, said he felt strongly "about keeping faith with the FINA nations, and that, unless the Bureau change their decision in the next meeting in Italy in September, it means the butterfly stroke will be used at Helsinki against the wishes of the majority." Fern pointed out that the European League had already decided to make butterfly and breaststroke two different events for the forthcoming European Games in three years time. Fern added that this action was "unconstitutional" and a postal vote was taken. By six votes to three (the Hungarian representative did not reply), FINA again decided to retain the butterfly. Mr. Fern, believing that a grave injustice had been done by this ruling, circulated the following resolution with the support of the English ASA: "The ASA Committee submits that the FINA Bureau's ruling on the matter of the breaststroke over-rides the decision of Congress in a manner which is quite unwarrantable. The Committee accordingly records a strong protest against the action of the Bureau" (O'Connor, 1949).

Up to this date the butterfly breaststroke controversy had been the center of many bitter arguments, but this one even threatened to cause a split in FINA.

Although the Congress had voted to separate the butterfly-breaststroke and orthodox breaststroke, because the IOC would not allow additional events in the Olympic Games, the real effect of the vote would have been to ban the butterfly breaststroke.

IOC Adverse to New Events

Max Ritter, American Honorary Secretary of FINA, was the main force behind the veto. He pointed out that thousands of swimmers had taken up the butterfly, and if it was banned it would cause an uproar in the United States. Mr. Ritter said, "The members of Congress were too tired to understand what they were voting for when they banned the butterfly."

Max Ritter had a meeting with President Edstrom of the IOC, on August 9, 1948. During this meeting Edstrom told Ritter that the IOC "was adverse to increasing the Olympic program, as also the national Olympic Committees considered it a hardship to increase the Olympic teams for financial reasons."

Ritter, on the basis of these facts and other important implications, felt compelled to point out this situation to all the Bureau members. He did so in a letter dated August 11, 1948. He requested consideration of the earlier decision taken and an early reply of all members so that a final ruling could be drawn up and communicated to the affiliated nations.

By September 22, 1948, the answers from the Bureau members were received, one member failing to send his reply. Six Bureau members voted to draw up rules for breaststroke, grouping under (a) orthodox breaststroke and (b) butterfly breaststroke, thereby retaining these two strokes as breaststrokes. Three Bureau members were of the opinion that the butterfly should be listed as an entirely new stroke and that the only the orthodox stroke should apply to breaststroke. Based on this decision of the FINA Bureau, there followed yet another detailed list of rules for the two strokes which were to be swum in the same event! At this point, the rule makers of FINA had reached a new high in obfuscation.

The *FINA Bulletin* of January 1949, mentioned how the Bureau members had discussed in detail the Congress's mandate to the Bureau to draw up rules for the orthodox breaststroke and the butterfly. The article said, "It was not clear to some members if the intent of Congress was to separate these two strokes under the names of breaststroke or to create an entirely new stroke called butterfly. In this meeting the majority of the members seemed to favor the latter course and rules were drawn up accordingly. On later reflection it was felt that it was possibly not the intention of Congress to create an entirely new stroke with butterfly, but still to consider butterfly as a breaststroke, although separated from the orthodox stroke." This apparent confusion could well have been the result of language difficulties, and the problem of ambiguous translation among the representatives of so many nations.

IOC Again Refuses New Events

At a meeting with the IOC in Copenhagen, May 12–13, 1950, the final 1952 Helsinki Olympic Program was submitted for approval to the IOC by the Finnish Organizing Committee. The FINA Bureau requested an additional event for butterfly, however, the IOC "refused to add new competitions to the Olympic program."

As a result, FINA asked the IOC to consult with international sports federations "before future final Olympic programs were approved by the IOC." FINA said that no program can be permanent and that the natural development of a sport must be taken into consideration. The FINA Bureau said that it "considered this to be a very vital question, but recognizing the great extension of the present Olympic Program, pledges itself to cooperate with the International Olympic Committee in any curtailment of the program that might prove necessary in the future."

In a FINA meeting in April of 1952, there was a proposal by Hungary saying that, "breaststroke should be separated from butterfly stroke as these are two different styles which should not be swum in the same competition." This simple statement hit the nail on the head. At the same meeting there was a proposal by Iceland along the same lines, saying that "a definite distinction should be made between breaststroke and butterfly stroke, and that the two styles should be kept entirely separate in international contests." At the same meeting there were similar proposals by Japan and Spain while Sweden, for some imponderable reason, went back to square one, by suggesting that "orthodox breaststroke and butterfly shall be considered the same stroke and that a swimmer should be allowed to change from one style to another during the race."

In December 1952, a letter from the president of the IOC was read to a FINA meeting regarding the necessary reduction in the number of participants at the Olympic Games. Japan and Iceland proposed that the number of events be increased to include breaststroke and butterfly for men and women. The vote was carried by 52 to 38. The meeting also agreed, by 39 votes to 33 (it looks as if 18 people didn't vote on this!) that, if the IOC would not allow this increase, then the event should be breaststroke.

After 21 Years Butterfly Becomes a Separate Event

FINA announced in December of 1954 that the IOC had agreed to the inclusion of butterfly events in the 1956 Olympic program, with the provison that a maximum of three competitors for men and three for women from each nation "be entered for the combined breaststroke and butterfly events." It should be noted that prior to this announcement, the IOC had been requested by the Honorable Secretary of FINA to consider the introduction of two butterfly events into the Olympic program. The IOC president had pointed out that the committee which had considered the reduction of the Olympic program had strongly recommended that no new events should be accepted.

In June 1956, entries for the breaststroke and butterfly events at the Olympics were limited by the IOC to only three competitors to be entered in breaststroke and butterfly together. Furthermore, the IOC said that these three competitors would be entitled to compete in both styles. This statement showed that, after so many years, the IOC still did not understand that the breaststroke and butterfly were essentially different strokes that should have been separated long ago. The truth is that the IOC had been too concerned with its own priorities to consider the developmental needs of one particular sport.

The 1957 to 1987 Underwater-or-Not Saga

After the 1956 Olympics, where several breaststroke swimmers spent most of their time in underwater swimming, a new saga of rule making ensued as attempts were made to eliminate underwater swimming. This bout was to last for the next 30 years.

In February of 1957, the FINA International Swimming Technical Committee (ISTC) recommended to Congress that no underwater swimming be allowed in breaststroke and butterfly events.

Apparently the big problem facing FINA's rule makers was the semantics of describing when a swimmer's head was, or was not, submerged under the surface.

First, it was ruled that part of the head should always break the surface of the water. This resulted not only in a stilted action, but in the swimmers having to hold their heads too high, thus reducing the body's streamlining. Some swimmers were even disqualified when their heads disappeared under their own bow waves.

The result was a big debate as to when a swimmer's head was "above the general water level." This rather nebulous description was later changed to read the head should "always break the surface of the water."

It was hoped that the FINA Congress in Moscow during the 1980 Olympics would solve this problem. The ISTC had proposed that "part of the head should break the surface of the water during each complete stroke." Instead, the Congress decided that "part of the head shall break the surface of the water throughout the race." This decision was really no different from the old rule.

Salvation came from an unexpected source when Howard Hanson, an Australian coach writing in the Australian Speedo magazine, *The International Swimmer*, said that the remedy suggested at the Moscow meeting of FINA "was worse than the original complaint." He offered the following solution: "A part of the head or body shall be above the general surface of the water at least once during each arm stroke. This would effectively prevent underwater swimming and make judging possible." Using wording not much different from that suggested by coach Hanson, FINA finally got it right on February 15, 1987, when the breaststroke head rule was changed to read, "During each complete cycle of one arm stroke and one leg kick, some part of the head of the swimmer shall break the surface of the water."

In February 1957, FINA rejected a peculiar proposal from West Germany that either a breaststroke kick or up-and-down movements of the legs and feet in the vertical plane be allowed in the butterfly. Had it been accepted, this proposal would have been a regressive step.

In December of 1963, seven years after the butterfly had become an accepted event, FINA made the curious announcement that "a mixture of frog-kicks with dolphin-kicks in butterfly and with crawl-kicks in backstroke shall be allowed, even in one and the same race." After closer scrutiny, it appeared that what FINA was actually saying was that butterfly swimmers could either use breaststroke or dolphin kick, and that backstroke swimmers could use either an inverted breast-stroke kick, dolphin kick, and presumably by "crawl-kicks" they meant an inverted flutter kick, but your guess is as good as mine.

✧ ✧ ✧

QUESTION: WHEN IS A STROKE NOT A STROKE?

ANSWER: WHEN IT'S A KICK!

A loophole in the butterfly rules permits swimmers to swim underwater using the dolphin kick for long indeterminate distances. The end result is a large helping of underwater kicking served up with a soupcon of butterfly. In fact, some swimmers, particularly in the short course events, have become so highly skilled in this art that they cover a good part of the so-called butterfly event while swimming underwater.

Now and again, when they surface to swim a few strokes of butterfly, we are reassured that we are actually watching a butterfly race, but obviously the whole production has become a travesty of what the rules really intended it to be.

Innovators Deserve Credit

Innovative swimmers and their coaches have shown the advantages of swimming well beneath the complicated wave-making resistance produced at water level, and they deserve full credit for their contribution to our knowledge of human swimming propulsion. After all, competitive swimming, to a large extent, is all about the quest for speed. This should be encouraged, but within the intention of the rules.

Now, it is not for the swimmer or the coach to philosophically ponder the intention of the rules. In fact, if a loophole exists, they have every right to take advantage of it, especially at a time when statistics would otherwise show an overall flattening out in human swimming performance.

The word *intention* is, or should be, the main point to all rule changes. The questions to be asked in setting a new rule should be: What is the intention of the rule? Will the new rule achieve what

it intends to achieve? Does it say so with absolute clarity, and without any chance of misinterpretation? Last, but not least, are there any loopholes that would permit a swimmer to do other than what the rule intends?

When we ask ourselves, "What is the intention of the rule?" it would be wise to study the historical background of that particular rule, to see how changing events (I'll explain the term "changing events" in a moment) may have allowed loopholes to become evident to those wishing to take advantage of them.

"Changing Events": Historical Background

After FINA had moved to make breaststroke a surface stroke, with only one arm pull and one kick allowed at the start and at turns, a meeting was held in 1957 to discuss these new rules. FINA said that "there had been some misunderstanding in a few countries as to the decision of the Congress concerning the butterfly stroke." The following clarification was adopted: "At the start, at the turn, and also during a race when a swimmer is in the underwater position, he may be allowed to make one or more leg kicks."

The purpose of this clarification was probably twofold:

1. Someone may have pointed out, in those early days of learning the dolphin butterfly, that not all swimmers were capable of returning to the surface after a dive or turn with only one kick to assist them. Some swimmers needed to do two kicks underwater, and sometimes even three kicks were needed, when a swimmer had accidentally gone too deep at the start or at the turn. Also, younger swimmers, or swimmers of smaller stature and weaker physique, might have needed more leg kicks to resume surface swimming. (Incidentally, "leg-kicks" is typical of some of the quaint terms used by FINA's experts over the years. Can one kick with any other part of one's body? If so, there may exist yet another loophole in the rules!)

2. Some swimmers at that time were using a technique in which they did a sort of porpoise dive under the surface as their arms entered the water after each recovery. At this stage, the swimmer's whole body followed through

this "hole" in the water, and often there were three kicks underwater, one kick as the arms stretched forward in a sliding action, and two more kicks during the actual pull, as the swimmer surfaced again. In present-day swimming, of course, the stroke technique of the event has changed, and, in effect, as a result there exists an obvious anachronism (and a loophole) in the butterfly rules that apparently was never detected, and therefore not updated, to accord with the modern intention of the rule.

It seems that the lawmakers were trying to make provision for the two contingencies mentioned above, but, in doing so, their wording was allowed to become too loose, thus leaving a loophole in the butterfly rule which still exists today, albeit in slightly modified form.

SW 8 Butterfly Rule

SW 8.1 "The body must be on the breast at all times, except when executing a turn. The shoulders shall be in line with the water surface from the beginning of the first armstroke, after the start and after each turn and shall remain in that position until the next turn or finish. It is not permitted to roll onto the back at any time."

SW 8.5 "At the start and at turns, a swimmer is permitted one or more leg kicks and one arm pull under the water, which must bring him to the surface."

Encourage Innovation

From the above, it must be clear that the original intention was not to permit a stroke in which the leg action was to become entirely separated from the complete butterfly stroke and used on its own for large portions of a racing distance. In fact, in all fairness, few could ever have envisioned the modern development of prolonged underwater kicking invented by a few enterprising and innovative swimmers and their coaches.

We do not want to see the sport enter another protracted period similar to the 50-year breaststroke saga.

One has only to log on to the Internet to read of young swimmers seeking advice on how to do the underwater fishtail technique. This is fine, and prolonged underwater swimming is a new and interesting development that should be pursued,

but continued innovation should be encouraged in exhibition events, conducted outside the existing program, and researched under the supervision of exercise physiologists and medical personnel. Certainly, it should no longer be a part of the butterfly event, or any other established event, because the end result could easily become the development of another multiyear saga, typical of the breaststroke-butterfly controversy that ruined the careers of many swimmers who were talented in one stroke only.

Distinguish Between Surface and Underwater Events

The time has come for the rules to make a clear distinction between swimming on the surface of the water and swimming beneath it. If you study the history of breaststroke and butterfly, you will see that there has always been a tendency to return to underwater swimming when the rule governing the surface stroke became too well defined for comfort.

What I am saying is that the time has come for underwater swimming to be banned in all four existing styles of swimming except for short prescribed distances after performing the start and turn, as in the breaststroke and backstroke rules. If this does not happen, the result may well be a travesty of the intention of the rules that govern the existing strokes.

Such a distinction would preserve the four main styles of swimming in their entirety, and in the manner intended by the rules, although, obviously, the present rules do not state their intention clearly enough. While breaststroke and backstroke have now been well defined as surface strokes, except for short, restricted periods underwater permitted at the start and turn, the question arises, why should the same restrictions not apply to freestyle and butterfly?

Legislate "Crawl," Not "Freestyle"

The rule says that, "Freestyle means that in an event so designated the swimmer may swim any style, except that in individual medley or medley relay events, freestyle means any style other than backstroke, breaststroke, or butterfly."

In effect, freestyle, although it has long supposed to have been the stroke in which anything goes, has not seen anywhere near the amount of change such as has occurred in breaststroke and butterfly. However, as the other three strokes become more clearly defined, there is a danger that the inherent nature of the crawl stroke (let's be frank, and call it crawl) may lose its original intention of being a surface stroke. There is also a danger that it may also become a parking place for all sorts of extraneous techniques that legislation may eventually bar from the other three strokes.

So why not define "freestyle" as "crawl stroke" and as a stroke that is "swum on, or in, the surface of the water in prone position, with alternating arm recoveries over the water performed in the continuing sequence of left arm, right arm recovery." And do the same with backstroke, except, of course, that it should be typified as a stroke that is swam on the back.

And, if a swimmer can comfortably and effectively perform a surface dolphin kick, or any other kick, in time with the strictly legislated alternate arm actions for these two strokes, then good luck to him or her!

Are we now faced with the possibility of another FINA-type protracted debate over whether swimmers should be allowed to cover ever-increasing distances underwater using the dolphin kick or newly developed fishtail kick? Are we in for more bungling and dithering such as the swimming world experienced during the 50-year saga of the breaststroke-butterfly rules? It's time that the opinions of professional coaches, who deal with stroke techniques every day of their working lives, should be sought by the FINA Technical Committee.

WANTED: EXHIBITION EVENTS FOR UNDERWATER SWIMMING

Innovative techniques should be recognized, encouraged, and developed through closer study.

New techniques with a potential for speed, such as underwater dolphin and fishtail kicking, should be encouraged but not permitted to remain an event within an event. The choice FINA faces is whether to continue to permit the traditional strokes to be adulterated, or whether to preserve them in their intended form.

FINA doesn't seem to realize that underwater swimming is not just a way to get around the rules. Athletes have discovered new facts about speeding up human propulsion through water. But the trouble is that these swimmers do not have the appropriate "testing grounds" for developing their newfound expertise.

Instead of considering underwater swimming merely as an interesting spectacle, or at worst, an intrusion into the established events, FINA should show some positive leadership in this matter by placing these new techniques in separate events for experimental purposes—call them "experimental events."

Provision should be made for additional "unlimited" exhibition events to be included in some meets for the purpose of showing the swimming public potentially faster methods of swimming, either above or below the water surface, and thereby encouraging further innovative developments in our quest for speed. Perhaps, at first, these exhibitions should be over a short distance, either 25 or 50 meters.

Furthermore, there is a growing body of opinion that believes the time has come for FINA to draw a distinction between surface swimming and underwater swimming. To some extent, this already has been done in breaststroke and backstroke, but similar restrictions to the duration of underwater swimming at the start or turns should now be extended to butterfly and crawl.

Responsibility to Learn from the Past

My purpose in writing the two previous sections, "The 50-Year Saga of the Breaststroke Rules" and "When Is a Stroke Not a Stroke," was to document the historical facts of how FINA blundered and dithered in an amateurish way for 50 years before it finally got the breaststroke rules right.

Over this long period of time, FINA's continued political and technical bungling has adversely affected the technical development of the sport as well as the careers of many individual athletes. In fairness to FINA, the problem caused by their piecemeal approach to rule making was compounded by the IOC's reluctance to increase the number of Olympic swimming events. (This may pose the question as to why the IOC's influence on swimming should extend to the periods between the Olympics, but of course, the answer doesn't take much guessing. He who pays the piper plays the tune.)

The FINA Technical Committee could learn from both past and recent history. By doing so they could avoid repeating the same mistakes. They would learn the importance of encouraging innovative techniques while ensuring that these techniques accord with the intention of the rules.

Innovations should fit naturally into an existing event. They should not be permitted to be swum in events to which they bear little resemblance. For example, swimming underwater for long indeterminate distances, no matter what anyone may say, is NOT the butterfly as we understand it to be, but a travesty of what the rule—"two kicks or more"—intended it to be. Indeed, it is the result of a loophole in a rule that was carelessly worded by FINA in the first instance.

Piecemeal, Band-Aid Legislation

Murray Stephens, 1996 U.S. Olympic coach, and coach of Beth Botsford, winner of the 100-meter backstroke in Atlanta, said, "FINA historically has always tended to respond to innovation and experimentation in a ponderous and deliberative manner, instead of first reviewing the history of an individual stroke's development in order to clearly determine what the intent of a proposed new rule should be.

"More often than not, FINA chooses to legislate in a piecemeal and Band-Aid fashion on each new problem as it arises, instead of trying to assess, with foresight and clarity, the broader implications of any rule change for all the four traditional strokes of swimming."

Leading coaches and swimmers say that innovation has been the underlying theme and reason for the continued development of our sport, and it should continue to be encouraged. However, they all agree that there is a vast difference between swimming on the surface of the water and underneath it. Although extended underwater dolphin kicking has already been limited in the backstroke rules, for some peculiar reason, FINA has continued to permit this admixture of long indeterminate spells of dolphin kicking in what is supposed to be the butterfly event.

Granted, it is expected that Australia will soon move to have a limit set to underwater kicking in butterfly, but this typical FINA piecemeal approach will probably result in freestyle (a.k.a. crawl) becoming a dumping ground for new ideas that wouldn't pass muster in the other three strokes. Therefore, no time should be wasted to ensure that the use of underwater dolphin techniques in both butterfly and crawl is limited to the breakout from the start and the turns, as already exists in backstroke. And, exciting and extremely interesting as these underwater techniques have proved to be, separate experimental events should be staged to encourage and promote their development.

All are agreed that the innovative techniques of swimmers such as David Berkoff, Daichi Suzuki, and Misty Hyman should be recognized, encouraged, and further developed through closer study in separate events.

The Intention of the Rules

Competitive swimming, to a large extent, is all about the quest for speed. This should be encouraged, but within the intention of the rules.

Beth Botsford (left), Coach Murray Stephens, Anita Nall. In the 1996 Olympics, Botsford won gold in the 100-meter backstroke and 400-meter medley relay. Nall is a former world-record holder in the 200-meter breaststroke. In the 1992 Olympics, she won a bronze medal in the 200-meter breaststroke, silver in the 100-meter breaststroke, and gold in the 400-meter medley relay.

Pablo Morales, a law graduate and an Olympic butterfly champion, says, "I agree that some guidelines in this regard should be set, and, of course, I'm all for removing ambiguities in the rules, and for removing loopholes in rules, and sticking with the intention of the rules.

"If anything, my legal experience taught me that you can't always look at the words. You have to look at the legislative history and the intention behind the words to determine the meanings. I think there shouldn't be loopholes, and I think the intention of the rules needs to be stated so that people won't take advantage of the rules, or perform in a way that is clearly against the intention of the rules.

"A lot of legal books have a section for legislative history that talks about the intention of the rule itself.

"I also agree that innovative techniques should be saved for exhibitions or competitions outside the four recognized strokes. Innovative techniques should be saved for exhibitions, etcetera, only in situations where the innovative technique falls outside the intention of the rule. This, of course, presumes that such intent has been expressed and disseminated, which we know has not usually been the case. So, essentially, and maybe this has already been said, I believe the problem is not the innovative technique, which I would generally encourage, but the lack in some cases of a clear statement, and enforcement, of rule intent."

Legislate the Four Strokes as Surface Strokes

Murray Stephens said, "I agree that a 15-meter underwater rule for all strokes, including crawlstroke, is appropriate and long overdue. In other words, all four of the traditional strokes, breaststroke, crawl stroke, backstroke, and butterfly should be clearly legislated as surface strokes.

"The dolphin, fishtail, or butterfly kick motion of the legs and body has proved to be an enduring addition to the world of speed swimming. I believe that it has been correctly added to the overarm action that we call butterfly. But, a stroke such as backstroke does not deserve, or need to be confused with butterfly by having large amounts of distance covered by dolphin kick. Short course backstroke has been transformed into

another event by this usage. The back flutter kick should be the defined kick for backstroke.

"In like manner, any underwater footage of international breaststroke events reveals both men and women adding significant dolphin foot and leg actions to the end of the breaststroke kick prior to the hand separation. Breaststroke kick, after much preliminary piecemeal legislation, is now clearly defined in the rules and this should remain the enforced standard."

Coach George Haines, the most successful coach of Olympic swimmers in the history of swimming, says that the designated distance allowed to dolphin or fishtail off the dive and off the push-off at the turns should be legislated fairly. "For example, and these suggested distances may not meet with agreement from everybody, but just for example, the dive start in the 25-yard or 25-meter pool may result in a 12½-yard, or 12½-meter halfway rule, and then they have to swim the rest of the way on the surface. And the push-off from the wall, in a 25-yard or 25-meter pool, should be 12½ yards or 12½ meters."

Haines says that the underwater segments in long course would differ slightly. "The dive in the long course could be 20 to 25 meters, and off the push-off could be 20 to 25 meters, but, whatever distance is designated or legislated, you should not have to count strokes. In other words, take out this business of counting strokes and make it a certain distance off the dive and off the wall at the turn, just like backstroke."

Haines said that, although "it took a long time to convince the powers that be, breaststroke swimming, as it is now enforced, seems to me to be more than fair. Allowing the head to go under the surface to streamline the body took a long time to become law, so leave that rule as it is. Breathing every cycle in breaststroke covers the need to be on the surface, according to the rules. The current rules governing the dive and the turn in breaststroke are also quite adequate."

Pablo Morales said, "The one thing that I must express a concern about, is that I wonder if that would stifle innovation. For example, what was called the "Berkoff Blast-Off" really opened our eyes to streamlining and underwater work. As a result, it's now limited to 15 meters. A person who can emphasize and do those 15 meters

Aid to FINA?

John Leonard, Executive Director of the World Swimming Coaches' Association (WSCA), also Executive Director of the American Swimming Coaches' Association (ASCA).

Cal Bentz, head coach of the University of Nebraska, suggests that coaches deal with new ideas by selecting a panel of coaches whose charge it would be to review creative and innovative ideas submitted to them by other coaches. "The panel could determine the viability of creative ideas becoming legitimate additions to our sport and make recommendations to our coaches' body for ratification and support. I believe the panel should be made up of many of the great minds of past and present which certainly should include those representing the purist's position, as well as those who support the creative position. The panel could release periodic reports and recommendations to the coaching body which would allow us all to examine their work, and draw our own conclusions about the direction in which competitive swimming should move."

John Leonard, Executive Director of the World Swimming Coaches' Association (WSCA), when questioned on his reaction to Coach Bentz's suggestion, said, "Cal Bentz has come up with a very progressive idea. His suggestion goes to the heart of the matter, because it would draw on the views of coaches who walk the pool deck every day. Such input would give us the cumulative views of leading coaches worldwide, and their professional expertise can then be delivered to FINA to facilitate the work of its Technical Committee. This would be the next best thing to having a permanent representative on the FINA Bureau, an objective toward which WSCA continues to strive."

effectively off the start, is going to be put in a very good position.

"Berkoff taught us a lot about what can happen whenever somebody sort of takes the rules, and I don't know if bending them is the right word, but just innovates within the given rules. I think that's a good thing. But I think there should be a distinction between surface swimming and underwater swimming. However, I don't want the rules to be so inflexible so as to discourage innovation."

George Haines agreed with Morales in that "backstroke, a surface stroke, already has been toned down as a result of Berkoff's amazing underwater dolphin on his back which was more of a backstroke event underwater than backstroke on the surface. Thus the rule change. Butterfly, backstroke, and crawl, should have similar rules.

"In the past, the tumble turn was first accepted, to be followed by the tumble turn with no touch in freestyle and backstroke and they were great innovations. So the streamlining of underwater swimming in backstroke, butterfly, and crawl should be allowed, but should be limited by certain restrictions.

"I don't see why a crawl swimmer or a backstroker has to be restricted by what type of kick they use if they're limited in how far they are permitted to go underwater. If you legislate 12½-yards or 12½-meters in a 25-yard or a 25-meter pool, that's half the pool. Those guys are going to go underwater half the pool anyway. So what difference does it make if they use a flutter on the back or a crawl flutter?"

Coach Nort Thornton, coach of Matt Biondi and many other great swimmers, said, "I have a little bit of a problem in that I hate to take away the opportunity for people to be innovative, and to look for new ways to go. We're always trying to get swimmers to streamline, and to come off the wall and run their streamlines out, and if you get somebody who does this so exceptionally well, it's almost as if you're penalizing them for being able to do what you're asking them to do. But you definitely have to have some sort of common rule that will encompass all the strokes, and so I think that bringing in a 15-meter underwater law for all the strokes is probably a pretty good idea. In this way, everybody would be on the same page all the time, and they would know what the rules are, and they would not be trying to circumvent them.

"Another way of looking at it is that you've got physiological limitations on the length of the body. For instance, the taller person is definitely at an advantage, and, in underwater swimming, the shorter person is able to take on a taller type individual and be more successful. So, in a sense, you don't want to limit it to hereditary qualities. You don't just want to have the whole Olympic final to be all tall people. That would limit the sport. So I think you've got to leave somewhere for people to be innovative. A lot of the swimmers who are adopting underwater kicking are short people.

They've found a way to compete better against the taller swimmers."

Coach Cal Bentz, head coach at the University of Nebraska, said, "Why not simply extend the current backstroke rule to cover butterfly and freestyle races as well? I suggest including butterfly and freestyle in the same application of the 15-meter rule since they each gain a similar advantage while employing the dolphin kick underwater. I would exclude the breaststroke pull-out from the application of the 15-meter limit after the start and turn. Since the breaststroke pull-out allows only one pull and one kick off the start and turns, and, since it is a more deliberate and slower action it is easier to judge, and should not be restricted by the 15-meter rule."

Pablo Morales on Monofinning

"I've taken part in the sport of fin swimming over the last few years. It's great, and I enjoy it. The feeling that I get in fin swimming is a feeling that I was never able to create swimming without fins. As a competitive swimmer, I spent the better part of 10 years training to experience the sensation of speed through the water, and the feeling of water flow over the body at increasing velocities, and putting on the monofins gives a feeling of speeds of up to 30 percent faster than I have ever experienced before.

"Fin swimming gives one a great, great feeling of fluidity and power that I admire so much. I've had the good fortune to watch the World Championships last summer in Hungary, and to see the best in the world. As I've said, there's such a grace and a fluidity and, at the same time, a combination of power and speed that makes it a very beautiful and exciting sport to watch.

"I didn't compete at the World Championships, but I have competed since then. To tell you the truth, I am not on a par with the best. It just really showed me that someone who is a world-ranked classical swimmer, a world champion butterflyer, whatever, can't expect to put on a monofin and think that they're going to be up there with the great fin swimmers, because the great fin swimmers grew up with fin swimming. That was their sport. They weren't classical swimmers. They developed and grew up with fin swimming, just as I grew up as a classical swimmer. So they know how to operate the fin, and how to maintain the proper motion to get the most out of the fin. They don't swim butterfly arms action at all. In fact, to actually stroke will slow you down."

Asked if fin swimming was done underwater, Pablo replied that it was done on the surface with a snorkel, and the rule there is that at least one part of your body must remain on the surface at all times, and the snorkel is included as part of your body.

"Then there's another class of events, which is the immersion in which you actually hold a scuba tank out in front of you. It's a modified streamlined tank, and you hold it out in front of you. I don't think the streamlined tanks are specially designed for the purpose; they just sell different types of tanks, but they do seem suited for monofinning."

Fin swimming has been in existence for about two decades, and they've held eight World Championships so far. It's an IOC-recognized sport, although it hasn't been part of the Olympic Games yet.

Experimental Events to Encourage Innovation

"You definitely don't want to discourage innovation because this is where we all came from," Thornton said. "I agree with the idea of exhibition events. Such strokes as dolphin kicking in its various forms, back dolphin, underwater dolphin, even the sideways dolphin, or fishtail, deserve an opportunity to be seen in separate races, 50 meter events, with or without equipment. Some could even use monofins. Obviously, there is already some monofin swimming around the world. It's already pretty well established and very popular, and this may well be another way to introduce another event into competition."

Stephens believes that underwater 50-meter experimental events, with and without equipment, deserve an opportunity to be seen. "Dolphin kick would be a strong contender for this competition. Back dolphin, underwater dolphin, and breaststroke dolphin need to be separated from the stroke events."

Haines said, "The underwater propulsion being developed by coaches and the swimmers with specific talents is very interesting." He points out that streamlining has always been a major factor in generating speed from the dive into the water, and from the push-off at the turn. Haines believes that "the dolphin kick, or the fishtail on the side, is now a part of swimming fast. Any rule to govern this innovation should be fair to all the strokes involving this type of propulsion. Changes should not be so drastic that they allow one individual athlete to be completely dominant."

"Innovation should not be legislated out, Haines said. "If you're going to have those 50s only as exhibitions to help promote innovation, that's fine. I don't think Misty Hyman, and others like her, should be completely legislated out of what they can do to go fast. She's a good athlete, and as she gets stronger, she'll be able to do that thing underwater even faster."

"Crawl," and not "Freestyle"

Although freestyle has long supposed to have been the stroke in which anything goes, in reality it has not seen anywhere near the amount of change as has occurred in breaststroke and butterfly. Nevertheless, as the other three strokes become more clearly defined, there is a danger that the inherent nature of the crawl stroke (let's be frank, and call it "crawl"!) may lose its original intention of being a surface stroke. There is also a danger that it may also become a "parking place" for all sorts of extraneous techniques that legislation may eventually bar from the other three strokes.

Pablo Morales says, "I agree that freestyle shouldn't be literally a 'free' style to do whatever one wants to do. It should be determined to be crawl." In saying this Pablo is quite correct because the FINA rule simply says (did I say "simply"?!) that "freestyle means that in an event so designated the swimmer may swim any style, except that in individual medley or medley really events, freestyle means any style other than backstroke, breaststroke, or butterfly."

This is yet another example of FINA's classic gobbledygook. What is FINA trying to say? If a swimmer may swim "any style other than backstroke, breaststroke, or butterfly," what exactly is the swimmer permitted to swim? Work through this rule using the process of elimination, and eureka!, we find that "freestyle" can only mean "crawl", so why not call it "crawl" and have done with it?

Why not define "freestyle" in the future as clearly being the "crawl stroke"; a stroke that is "swum on, or in, the surface of the water in prone position, with alternating arm recoveries over the water performed in the continuing sequence of left arm, right arm recovery." And do the same with backstroke except, of course, that it should be typified as a stroke that is swum on the back. (Note: Attention to FINA's poorly worded turning rule is long overdue.)

Incidentally, the term "crawl" should also be used in any new description of the four strokes to be used in medley swimming. Otherwise, if a loophole is left by retaining the "freestyle" description in that medley definition, it could happen that some super swimmer, not too fatigued at the end of the freestyle leg of a medley swim, may resort to—guess what?—underwater dolphin or fishtail kicking!

On Dolphin in Crawl

Haines spoke at length about swimmers that are beginning to do dolphin kick in the freestyle event. "This freshman girl at Stanford . . . she dolphin kicks underwater, and she goes about two-thirds of the way underwater, and comes up, takes about three or four strokes, and takes a turn. I don't get that. I don't see that at all because eventually you're going to get a Misty Hyman, some super-athlete who can really do that dolphin kick, and that takes the times recorded under the recent past rules right off the books. I really believe that we have to legislate against this happening. The distance swum underwater has got to be restricted. In backstroke now, they can only go 15 meters underwater, after that, they've got to be able to swim backstroke. If 15 meters is good enough for backstroke, it's good enough for crawl, and it's good enough for butterfly."

Haines said, "The same off the starting block in crawl, or freestyle, they should be restricted to a certain distance underwater; after that, you've got to be able to swim crawl."

Would It Be Fair?

"What happens if someone breaks Mary T. Meagher's butterfly records swimming underwater fishtail; would that be fair?" asked Haines. The only way they're going to avoid this is, well, you take Jenny Thompson beat Misty Hyman this year already (in Gothenborg). Jenny Thompson didn't go underwater, she preferred to swim on the surface. And so Misty Hyman really hasn't got a lock on this thing yet, and, before she does, if they restrict the distance she can do underwater, let's say that, in the 25-meter pool, she has to be up and going at $12^{1}/_{2}$ meters, she's not going to get any advantage. At the same time, she's going to be able to do the same thing off the walls, then she has to be up and swimming.

"If I thought they could get away with making the backstrokers use a back flutter, and making the freestylers always use a flutter when they push off the wall, it would be fair. But a flutter kick comes in all sorts of variations, drag kick, two-beat, four-beat crossover, etcetera. You can't start legislating all that. You've just got to call all those different types of kicks flutter kicks."

In the final criterion, Haines, who has had more swimmers inducted into the International Swimming Hall of Fame than any other coach, does not appear optimistic about FINA's ability to bring about immediately effective rule changes to the sport of swimming. He said, "Anyway, no matter what we say, it's going to take FINA another 21 years to do anything about it. You mentioned that FINA should discuss rule changes in the context of all the strokes, and how changes in one rule may or may not affect another stroke, or have relevance to it. That's exactly what they should do, and that's what they have never ever done. When you take a look, and put down all the names of people who have been on FINA over the past 30 or 40 years, two thirds of them have never ever had anything to do with coaching or instructing people, so how in the hell can they interpret? That's why it's taken them so long."

Note

Was it coincidence that, shortly after the preceding article appeared in the August 1997 issue of *Swimnews*, the FINA Technical Committee (at its meeting in Perth, Australia, January 1998) saw fit to legislate freestyle as a surface stroke?

The new FINA freestyle rule effective March 6, 1998, reads as follows:

SW 5.3 Some part of the swimmer must break the surface of the water throughout the race, except it shall be permissable for the swimmer to be completely submerged during the turn and for a distance of not more than 15 meters after the start and each turn. By that point the head must have broken the surface.

Chapter 4

SWIMMING THE 1,500 METER: THE BLUE RIBBON OF SWIMMING

WHATEVER HAPPENED TO THE DISTANCE BASE?

Can the slump in North American swimming standards be partly due to less importance being placed on having a good distance background?

There was a time when distance training for all swimmers was almost a religion. This era also saw some of the most dramatic improvements in the history of the sport.

Every leading coach believed in the benefit of a distance swimming background, and they pointed to the fact that most distance-trained swimmers were able to swim multiple events at maturity.

They preached the gospel that a good swimmer should be good at all distances. They proved that the broader the base of the endurance "pyramid," built over all the developing years, the higher would be the pinnacle of achievement.

Young swimmers were encouraged to swim distance as soon as they had acquired a good basic swimming stroke. Only after many years of the long, slow, progressive buildup were swimmers gradually introduced to training for specific events.

Building the Endurance Base
Constant repetition of correct movements at slower speeds helps to build ideal stroke patterns, while short sprints tend to cause stroke deterioration.

At high speed it is hard to detect the faults in a swimmer's stroke. At slower speeds a stroke fault becomes magnified, and easier to detect and correct.

Furthermore, most young swimmers simply haven't the musculature to handle a lot of sprinting. Distance swimming, rather than incessant

International Swimming Hall of Fame

SHANE'S COLLECTION OF MEDALS
IN 1969 AT THE AGE OF 13

Shane Gould, 1972 Olympic champion and one-time world-record holder at all freestyle distances, is shown here at the age of 13. She was brought up on a steady diet of distance training.

sprinting, is more compatible with a young swimmer's normal growth and development.

Swimming strength and endurance, especially for young males, takes years to develop, and submaximal, prolonged swimming is the proven way to achieve this. Sprint swimming, on the other hand, is too intensive to permit enough sustained work to develop endurance.

This is not to say that endurance swimming does not build muscular strength and power. It does. But the process is slower and marked by a more gradual increase in work intensity. It wisely takes into account the inexorable demands of growth on the younger swimmer.

The goal is to gradually learn to swim a little farther each day, while perfecting stroke and developing rhythm. Not only does distance swimming build strength and endurance but it also develops a stroke characterized by a machine-like rhythm. Most of the time, the swimmer is asked to swim at his or her fastest comfortable pace.

Historical "Big Drops" in the World Record for the 1,500-Meter Freestyle Event

July 8, 1923, Arne Borg (Sweden) reduced the world record of George Hodgson (Canada) from 22:00 to 21:35.3—a drop of 24.7 seconds.

January 30, 1924, Arne Borg reduced his own world record by 20.3 seconds to 21:15.0.

July 15, 1924, Andrew Charlton (Australia), at the Paris Olympics, reduced Borg's two-day-old world record of 21:11.4 by an amazing 1:04.8 to a record 20:06.6.

September, 1927, Arne Borg "did a Charlton" by reducing the world record (20:04.4 set by Borg on August 18, 1926) by a gigantic 57.2 seconds to a record 19:07.2.

Over a period of little more than four years, Arne Borg took nearly three minutes off the world record for 1,500 meters. But it must be noted that the times recorded by swimmers such as Charlton and Borg were a mere saunter when compared with the driving pace set by today's stars. In fact, it is probable that the swimmers of that era did not do much, if any, special training for long-distance events. One can only guess how much faster they would have swum using today's methods.

In the post–World War II era, the tendency toward big drops in the world 1,500-meter records has continued although, in the last two decades, the definition of a "big drop" has had to be revised—if this is not a contradiction in terms—because of a natural leveling off effect.

The following shows the margins by which a few of the great 1,500-meter swimmers have reduced the world 1,500-meter record during the course of their careers:

Hironoshin Furuhashi (Japan) 39.8 seconds

George Breen (USA) 26.1 seconds

Murray Rose (Australia) 57.7 seconds

John Konrads (Australia) 41.9 seconds

Michael Burton (USA) 54.1 seconds

Stephen Holland (Australia) 41.69 seconds

Brian Goodell (USA) 8.49 seconds

Vladimir Salnikov (URS) 7.64 seconds

Kieren Perkins (Australia) 8.70 seconds

The Influence of John Carew and Kieren Perkins on the 1,500-Meter Event

Asked to comment on the present-day status of the 1,500-meter event, Don Talbot, head coach of the Australian Swimming Team, said, "The swimming speeds of Kieren Perkins and other 1,500-meter swimmers of today border on the unbelievable. Not too long ago a sub–15 minutes was thought to be phenomenal, and I suspect that we have not yet seen the last of the 'big drops' in this event.

"Salnikov, of course, led the way with his incredible 14:54.76. He trained in the traditional way—big yardage with not much special work.

"Today's 1,500 swimmers do not do as much yardage—although it's still a lot when compared to the swimmers in other events—but now they pay much more attention to speed work in all phases of their preparation. I believe this approach is what Kieren Perkins and his coach, John Carew, have brought to 1,500-meter swimming today. The swimmers who are presently able to go sub–15-minute swims are those who have adopted the philosophy of John Carew for 1,500-meter swimming.

"Oddly enough, however, this approach does not seem to suit female swimmers and perhaps the less mature males also. In fact, the performances of female swimmers across the board have definitely deteriorated over the last 3 years or so. This is another story however, and far too complex in nature to deal with in a few short sentences."

A youngster who can handle a steady diet of distance training soon develops the confidence and determination to swim a respectable 1,500 freestyle, not just in training, but in competition as well. And, furthermore, a swimmer's times over the 100 will also start to improve, without a formal sprint preparation.

Start young swimmers on distance training, and you'll soon be surprised at how well they adapt, and how quickly their times will drop, usually with a minimum of sprint work.

Coaches will find that a thorough background of distance swimming helps youngsters to more fully realize their endurance potential at maturity. When a swimmer is older and ready to concentrate on specific events, the necessary speed endurance will be there to enable any racing distance to be covered at the fastest constant speed.

"As the Young Twig Is Bent . . . "

Forbes Carlile, the great Australian coach said, "As the young twig is bent, so will it grow." By that he meant that the younger a swimmer started distance training, the greater would be that swimmer's eventual ability to adapt to hard specialized work.

In fact, years ago when I first learned the value of distance training for young swimmers, I was amazed at how quickly young swimmers took to this new program, while older swimmers, to their embarrassment, were slower to adapt, and, in fact, were having great difficulty in doing so.

As a result, I saw a new generation of potentially more successful swimmers developing right in front of my eyes, and, soon they were able to push the older swimmers every inch of the way over the longer distances. The truth of Carlile's philosophy on the importance of early distance training needed no further validation.

Carlile called his program "speed through endurance" after the philosophy of German track coach, Ernst van Aaken. And Carlile's approach proved its merit with great swimmers such as Shane Gould, Karen Moras, Jenny Turrell, Jane Lockyear, and many others. Particular proof of his method was Shane Gould's success in the early 1970s when she broke every world freestyle record from the 100 to the 1,500.

Carlile's endurance training program was based on two simple components. The first was improving the swimmer's ability to swim distance (prolong the activity), and the second was to increase the speed of the established distance (increase the speed of the prolonged activity.) Carlile kept the duration of each training period constant. He conducted 11 two-hour sessions a week, and the aim was not to increase the duration of each practice but to have the swimmers try to cover more distance within the given period.

Yards per Minute

Dick Shoulberg (1983) said that there has been an unnecessary tendency to increase the amount of training time instead of concentrating on improving the speed of the long-distance training swims. He said that the key to distance training is to increase the number of yards per minute, not the number of minutes per day.

Dick Jochums (1982) said that coaches are too wrapped up in the yardage syndrome, and that the true definition of work is the yardage times the intensity of the effort at which the work is done.

It is significant that most of swimming's most successful coaches—coaches such as the late Sherman Chavoor, Don Gambril, Peter Daland, George Haines, Don Talbot, Mark Schubert, "Doc" Counsilman, Dick Jochums, Nort Thornton, and Dick Shoulberg—all had a philosophy that was distinctly distance oriented.

Without exception, most of the great swimmers they produced were able to swim multiple distances because they had developed the necessary distance base from an early age. Their swimmers were able to compete in several events a day against tough competition, not only in freestyle but also in the form strokes and the IMs.

The late Sherman Chavoor always insisted that a great long-distance swimmer could swim a good time at any distance. For example, Mike Burton was a great distance swimmer, the 1,500-meter Olympic champion, and world-record holder, yet he was an NCAA record holder in the 500-yard freestyle in 1970 and a fast 200-yard freestyler.

Burton was a good sprinter, too, with a ranking of seventh in the world at one time. Chavoor said that Mark Spitz was also a good distance swimmer who at one time missed the 1,500-meter world record by a scant four-tenths of a second.

In 1969, Mark Spitz won the NCAA 500-yard freestyle, another example of how easy it is for a distance-reared swimmer to move up or down the scale (Colwin, 1992).

Swim Up, Swim Down

George Haines said that over-the-distance training is good conditioning for all events. He maintains that "it is easier to come down to shorter races with more stamina if you train over the distance and then be able to swim the 1,500-400-200 in the Olympics as Kieren Perkins of Australia did, and Brian Goodell did in 1976."

Haines said that "when a 100 swimmer stops training for the 200, the 100 effort suffers, and the same happens to the 200 swimmer when he gives up training for the 400, etcetera. We must remember that it is easier to drop down to the shorter races during taper time if you have a good over-the-distance base."

Haines said that Australia's Kieren Perkins is "the perfect example of what over-the-distance training will do for you. The Australian swam in the 200, 400, 1,500, and has a best time of 50.0 for the 100."

Peter Daland is another authority who points out that most of the great swimmers were adept at the 1,500, and were able to swim down and set world records in the shorter events. To those who question the value of distance training for sprinters, Daland says that "all the past mileage enables the sprinter to swim the last 10 meters very, very fast."

On the subject of maintaining speed in a distance program, Daland insisted on all his swimmers doing some fast work every day. His

Forbes Carlile's speed through endurance philosophy proved its merit with great swimmers such as Shane Gould and Karen Moras. In 1972, Gould broke every world freestyle record from 100 meters to 1,500 meters—a feat never equaled before or after.

sprint swimmers also used weight training while swimming distance to maintain their speed. Daland said, "Strength is power is speed."

Daland's swimmers did about 30 percent of their distance workouts on pulling. He said, "Pulling relates to stamina as kicking relates to speed. Sprinting speed can be ensured by some really hard kicking, as kicking relates more than the arms to sprinting.

"In swimming, the big question really is: How many fast miles did you swim? You can swim 20 miles a day, and it wouldn't mean anything. You can swim 10 miles a day, and it would be more significant than the 20. It's not how fast you swam, because you might swim fast and go only 1,000, but how many fast miles you swam. That's the idea you want to implant in your swimmers, even with the distance base. If the distance base is going to bring on a lot of lap swimming, forget it" (Daland, 1981).

Base Training Like Money in the Bank

Nort Thornton (1987) draws a distinction between what he calls "base training" and "sharpening training." Thornton describes base training as "that inner basic strength of the athlete that produces a performance without specific muscle adaptation for that event as the result of years of training, overall stamina and conditioning. Such a base is usually best built by long, slow distance training at a pace well within one's capacity for a long period of time."

On the other hand, Thornton (1987) describes sharpening training as work that "adds muscular and neuromuscular efficiency to the circulatory efficiency gained from the swimmer's base training. Sharpening training involves numerous repetitions of a short distance at a racing pace or faster."

Thornton makes important comparisons between the respective values and effects of base training and sharpening training. He says that base training, by its very nature, can only be developed at a slow rate, but its effects are long lasting and not easily destroyed. Thornton says that swimmers who have built a good distance base are able to swim at a high level even after a great reduction in their training levels.

Thornton says that, while sharpening training may often produce spectacular results within a short time, by the same token, the training effects achieved may not last longer than three months. Thornton warns that sharpening work, if continued too long, can result in a sudden slump in performance.

Finally, Thornton (1987) said that base training and sharpening training could not be combined for optimum results over a long period of time. Fast sharpening work quickly depletes a swimmer's reserve. Thornton makes the classic observation that ". . . base training is like money in the bank, while sharpening, when done properly, is like taking out the accumulated interest. When done improperly, sharpening is like draining one's financial reserves."

✧ ✧ ✧

CECIL COLWIN DISCUSSES THE 1,500 WITH JOE BERNAL

An interview at the U.S. Long Course Championships at Indianapolis in 1984.

CC: You coached Bobby Hackett to his outstanding achievements in the 1,500-freestyle event in the 1970s. How did you become interested in coaching?

JB: I was introduced to coaching swimming when I swam at the Badger Swim Club in Larchmont, New York, under coach Jack Collins.

CC: He is the father of John Collins, coach of Olympic backstroke champion, Rick Carey?

JB: Yes. We used to be flown out every summer to train with Doc Counsilman and I guess that the two most influential people in the early stages were Jack Collins and Doc Counsilman.

CC: How much time did you spend there?

JB: We went for about a month and half each summer for about five summers. I became very interested in Doc's approach to coaching. Jack Collins, I guess, emulated quite a bit of what Doc did and so I was constantly bombarded with the scientific aspects of stroke analysis and stroke mechanics. Later in my development, I came in contact with people like Ron

Ballatore, Don Gambril, and Dick Jochums, and from them I learned other aspects of coaching. There were also fine coaches, such as Frank Elm and Sherm Chavoor, who were major influences in my coaching development.

CC: *Apart from your own innate ability, you were really lucky to have contact with some of the greats of coaching. Some of those names are strongly associated with the development of distance swimming. Would you agree that they influenced you?*

JB: Yes. Doc always had great 500-yard and 1,500-meter freestylers. Dick Jochums and Don Gambril also. Sherm Chavoor was one who had fantastic success in distance coaching . . . Mike Burton and many others. These people had a great influence on my approach to the coaching of distance swimmers.

CC: *I remember back in August 1973, at the national outdoor championships in Louisville, Kentucky, you told me that you had a very promising young lad in your team by the name of Bobby Hackett. Even at that time, he was the fastest in his age group in the world at 1,500 meters and you were predicting big things for him.*

JB: Yes. I remember that well. In fact, not too many people had the same confidence that this young man would develop into a distance swimmer because of his size.

CC: *He was a very big youngster . . .*

JB: He was 6 feet, 2 inches and usually weighed about 185 pounds when racing fit. We tend to sometimes stereotype distance swimmers as being of a certain physique. There were other large people, like John Kinsella, who were very successful. At that early stage, people thought Hackett was too big to become a good distance swimmer

CC: *You started coaching by forming your own club?*

JB: Yes, I have a club called the Gator Swim Club. When I became the coach at Harvard, I moved the club up to Boston and now it's starting to develop into a second generation. It is having great success now.

CC: *Is it a year-round club or just a summer club?*

JB: It's a year-round club directed in the same

way as in our previous program in New York. It's the same as Mission Viejo or FAST or any of the other swim clubs in the USA.

CC: *So you train the Gator Club in the afternoons and the university team in the evenings?*

JB: No. It's the other way around. We train the youngsters in the evenings and the university team in the afternoons. And they come in the mornings before the university swimmers.

CC: *Now back to your early interest in training distance swimmers. What was your early philosophy on the subject?*

JB: Well, my early philosophy was very much what was in vogue at that time. And that was that distance swimmers had to cover 20,000 to 24,000 yards per day. And, if you did a lot, even more was better. But, I didn't see that the amount of time and distance was proportional to the results achieved. So I changed my approach—especially when I had five young men, one of them Bobby Hackett, who had a flair for distance swimming.

CC: *What were the names of the other lads?*

JB: We had Paul Fallot, who usually took second in our area to Bobby Hackett, Frank May, Bobby Crush, and Jeff Stylen who had a great deal of success in the area. The most prominent, of course, was Bobby Hackett. I found that the more yardage I gave him, the worse his performances became. He had natural speed. No matter how much we trained him for negative splitting, no matter how much we worked descending sets, his initial speed remained the same. No matter how easy he tried to go out at the start of a race, his early speed would still be there. Contrary to what was considered to be the accepted way to train distance swimmers . . . that is by coming back faster in the second half of the race . . . negative splitting . . . we tried to even split the race. The most important race that he ever swam was the 1,500-Olympic final up at Montreal. His last 400 meters in that race was 3 minutes 58.8 seconds which was faster than his middle 400 and Bobby Hackett, contrary to the label that he had: "He can go out fast but he can't bring it back," showed very well that he could bring it back.

CC: *What were your impressions of that classic race between Goodell, Holland, and Hackett? I'd like to hear your point of view.*

JB: It was very clear. We kept a very close eye on what Brian Goodell was doing and what Steve Holland was preparing to do.

CC: *And Paul Hartlauf?*

JB: I must say that we never considered him to be one who was going to be in contention. But I must say that Paul did a fantastic job by putting himself in contention. He swam a superb 1,500 meter at the Olympic trials. His coach, Jack Simon, did a good job with him. I also think that they made a big error at the Games by trying to get into the media, throwing their hat into the ring by saying they were as good as Brian Goodell, Bobby Hackett, and Steve Holland. Psychologically, where they got beaten was that the talk always was about Goodell, Hackett, and Holland and that must have affected them. If they had swum their race accordingly, he could have been the bronze medalist.

CC: *By coming in as the underdog with no one expecting him to do anything?*

JB: Exactly right, but I think that both the coach and the swimmer felt that they were not being considered as anyone of credibility in that 1,500 freestyle. In the heats of the Olympic 1,500 he set a new Olympic record. He swam a real tough 1,500-meter freestyle. In reality what Paul Hartlauf should have done was to swim a smooth 1,500, get into the final with everyone else, then swim his race; and I'm quite sure that he would have been able to repeat the performance that he had at the Olympic trials at Long Beach and probably come in as a bronze medalist. He tried too hard in the finals to go out with Bobby, and consequently he fell off the pace.

CC: *Talking about swimmers who could have been in the reckoning for the Olympics, I was very disappointed that Tim Shaw didn't make it in the final analysis coming up to the Montreal Olympics, especially when we saw his great swims at Concord, California, in 1974 and during the immediate period thereafter.*

Coach Joe Bernal discusses the classic 1,500-meter Olympic final at the Montreal Olympics, 1976, when Brian Goodell, Bobby Hackett, Steve Holland, and Paul Hartlauf battled for Olympic honors.

JB: Tim Shaw was a fantastic swimmer. For a swimmer, at one period of time to hold the world record at 200, 400, and 1,500 in the same year is a great accomplishment. However, I think that he was a person who started to feel the pressure of two young swimmers coming at him; one of them, Brian Goodell, in his own back yard in California, and then, all of a sudden, another 14-year-old from the other side of the country, Bobby Hackett. That created a tremendous amount of pressure on him to stay at the top, having these people come so close to him every time out. That wearing-away process caused Tim to fall off the high schedule that he had. Psychologically, it started to have an effect on him. The 1,500 race, as we know, and competitive swimming generally, is a great psychological game. But to stay at that level in distance swimming is particularly demanding. You must have a tremendous ability to concentrate and focus in on what you are doing. Once you start to look around over your shoulder and have doubts, then the whole game goes down the drain.

CC: *It's almost like a chess game in the water—it's a test of the whole person.*

JB: I fully agree with that, if you want a race that's going to test all the ingredients, all the fibers that make up the personality of that individual, then the 1,500 race at a high level, like at the Olympic Games, certainly will bring out every bit of information you want to know about that person.

CC: *You've got to know your own energy distribution and your own pace, your own stroke as well as have a good idea of your rivals' pace and tactics, what their moves are likely to be. The 1,500 really is the blue ribbon of swimming.*

JB: Personally, I think that the greatest master of the 1,500 event, over the years, had to be Murray Rose who could control the pace of the race by what he did. In this way, he was able to control the other swimmers, too.

CC: *What would you say was his control technique?*

JB: Establishing himself as the dominant figure in the event and perhaps being the early leader, but then backing off and controlling the rest of the swimmers to swim at his pace.

CC: *By using subtle changes of pace . . .*

JB: Yes. And he could do that extremely well. I studied the many swims in which he had the uncanny ability to be able to control his heat by picking up the pace, slowing it down, testing the other swimmers' strengths, seeing if they would go with him.

CC: *Whether they responded to his pace changes?*

JB: That's right. He could test the other swimmers, and, once he sensed that they were weakening, he would put in an extra fast lap and start to open water on them.

CC: *When his rivals stopped reacting to his subtle pace changes, it was a sign that they were losing concentration?*

JB: Yes. He was breaking their concentration and preventing them from swimming their own race and, all of a sudden, they were trying to accommodate themselves to what Murray was doing.

CC: *Causing them to force their pace?*

JB: Absolutely. We basically did exactly that at Montreal. The difference between the silver and the gold medals was the fact that Bobby Hackett was the youngest 1,500 swimmer there. He was only 15 years old and turned 16 on the last day of the Olympic Games. The difficulty we had was having Bobby being able to introduce a four- to six-beat kick on the last 150 of the 1,500.

CC: *Change to a six-beat kick?*

JB: Yes. And, if you review the films of the Games, you will see that Brian Goodell was able to turn from a two-beat to a four-beat to a six-beat at the end, and Bobby was not able to maintain the rate of speed that he needed to come home.

CC: *He needed a six-beat kick?*

JB: He needed a six-beat kick, and he didn't have enough time as he developed to be able to learn that. Later on in college, he was able to do a six-beat, and I dare say that, if the motivation wasn't taken out of the heart of the swimmer by not going to the 1980 Olympic Games because of the boycott, you would have seen Brian Goodell there, Bobby Hackett, and Mr. Salnikov all fighting it out. And I would say that we would have seen a super performance from Brian Goodell and Bobby Hackett.

CC: *Who do you think would have won out of Goodell and Salnikov?*

JB: (laughing) Out of Goodell and Salnikov!? Bobby Hackett!

CC: *We would have come to that question afterward!*

JB: I would say that between Salnikov and Brian Goodell, Brian Goodell would have won. I've seen Salnikov over the years, how he developed; we watched him training at Mission Viejo one Christmas with Brian and Bobby, and I would have to say that, if it came down to an equal basis on a given day, at the Olympic Games, whether it was in Russia or

Timbuktu, that Brian Goodell would have beaten Mr. Salnikov.

CC: *And Hackett would have beaten Brian Goodell!?*

JB: I'm afraid that Bobby Hackett would have been totally ready with all the necessary things in his arsenal to make sure that the last 150 meters would be different from Montreal.

CC: *I know that when you say a thing you really mean it. So this brings me to the next question on the aspect of speed in the 1,500. It is speed that really provides the ability to be combative, to dictate tactics and dominate the race?*

JB: I fully agree with you. Over the years the fact that great 1,500 freestylers could dominate the event was based on the fact that swimmers like Murray Rose could go out as fast as they needed to control the race. One fellow that I think was one of the greatest distance swimmers was Mike Burton. And Mike did not back off in the first half. In fact, when many of the critics would talk about Bobby Hackett going out too fast, two of the people who came forward and said, "My goodness. The man is swimming it properly for the kind of swimmer that he is" were Mike Burton and Sherm Chavoor. [They] stepped forward and said: "Absolutely! The proper way!" I mean Bobby Hackett just had natural speed. No matter how much we backed him off, he was fast.

CC: *Mike Burton had a certain measure of speed, enough to win the Olympic 400-meter freestyle at Mexico City in 1968. But, basically, he was more of a one-speed swimmer and had to establish that one speed from the start of a race. He had to swim a pretty solid race, being in there right from the start.*

JB: He had to go out as fast as he could to maintain the pace because if he wasn't out there, he would just start to fall off the pace. But, once he established his pace, he could maintain that rate of speed. That was the type that Mike Burton was. Now Brian Goodell was the type who could go out light and come back faster and he had a great deal of success. I personally feel that speed is the ingredient

that is going to dictate what can be done to the whole 1,500. At the 1976 Olympic trials, Bobby Hackett set a world record going out at the 800-meter mark with a foot touch. That made quite a few people stand up and take notice and he was able to swim the fastest 1,500 meters he had ever swum in his life.

When we went up to Montreal, we very specifically calculated on spreading through the Olympic Village that Bobby Hackett was going to break the world record again at the 800 and nobody dared to go out with him because, if they tried, they would pay the penalty in the second half. And Steve Holland came in saying that he was going to break the world record and we very precisely challenged the Australians, even to the point of suggesting that they might like to take on a few wagers, that that was not going to happen. What we were looking to do was to slow up the first 800 and everyone followed Bobby Hackett for the first 800. This was an indication that we had established our dominance by having the reputation for speed. With the speed that he possessed he was able to establish what he wanted to do in the first 800. Now I would say a very important thing that you need in the 1,500, contrary to what many people feel, is speed.

CC: *Now looking at Salnikov, what would you say has been his contribution to the 1,500 event?*

JB: One of the greatest contributions that Salnikov has made is to show that 1,500 freestylers can last a great deal of time, contrary to what may be believed in our country. In the United States, many people think that 1,500 freestylers may only last maybe three years or four years, that the wearing away process on the athlete is so great that they cannot maintain a high level of performance in the 1,500-meter freestyle. I think that you could probably say that Salnikov, lasting from 1976 at the Olympic level, to this point, 1984, shows the amount of endurance created and the amount of resilience that can be developed.

People fail to realize that Salnikov was a finalist at the 1976 Montreal Olympics. He was in lane eight and people don't even remember that he was a finalist. He has continued to swim at a high level for almost eight years now.

CC: *How have training methods for the 1,500 changed over this period?*

JB: They've changed drastically. In fact, I changed my training methods with Bobby Hackett. We concentrated on doing shorter distances at race pace. On a daily basis, we would go double workouts, covering about 16,000 meters and a great deal of that was more quality-type work in which we would take a unit where we would ask for as close to race pace as possible.

✧ ✧ ✧

CECIL COLWIN DISCUSSES THE 1,500 WITH MIKE BURTON

An interview at the U.S. Long Course Championships at Indianapolis in 1984.

CC: *I saw you set your first 1,500 world record in the U.S. Outdoor Championships in Lincoln, Nebraska, in 1966. Your time of 16 minutes 41.6 seconds reduced the world mark by a big margin. Perhaps you could start by talking about your development up to the stage where you set your first world record?*

MB: I started swimming with Arden Hills in 1962 and one of the things that Sherm [coach Sherman Chavoor] did was something I kind of liked because it was an incentive for me to get out of practice early! Many of our practices ended with a 1,650 or a 36-lap swim which was a 900, and things like that. I went rather fast just so that I could be the first one out and dressed.

CC: *Did you train mainly in the 25-yard pool?*

MB: We trained in pools of several different sizes in the summertime but, in the wintertime, we trained in the 25-yard course only. Endurance was the main ingredient. We would go through just a horrendous workout, a very tough workout, and Sherm would say, "OK. Last race, a fast 66." He would try to make a 1,650 sound shorter by calling it a fast 66. Of course, a 66-lap swim is a total of 1,650 yards.

And so we would do that, and I'd finish and get out and be dried off and dressed before the next guy on our team would finish. It was an incentive for me, and I just worked my way into this type of program. Eventually, I started swimming better and better at the Nationals until, in 1966, I won my first National Championship.

CC: *You mentioned not feeling as tired as your teammates; were any physiological tests done on you to assess the reasons for your superior endurance?*

MB: No, not really. I never had any physiological testings done on me and about the only thing that happened that was unusual was when I made the Pan American team in 1967. We went to a physical in Minneapolis prior to leaving for Winnipeg. The doctor was checking my heart and found a heart murmur.

CC: *Systolic or diastolic?*

MB: I'm not really sure but it had been there since I was born so it wasn't anything to worry about. My own doctor had found it when I was about 16 years old so it was just an idiosyncrasy, just one of those things. It wasn't anything to worry about but I'd never gone through any real type of testing. They didn't do it at UCLA because there were no facilities for it. And neither did the Arden Hills Club have any testing facilities. So we never got into that.

CC: *Did you hurt when you swam all those long distances in training? Sherm said that you did, but that you hid this fact from your rivals because, if they had known that you also got tired now and again, it would have given them encouragement.*

MB: Well, I always felt that when I swam the 1,500 or 1,650, I had to be tired by the time I hit the 400 or 500 mark and the remaining two-thirds of the race were actually done in a state of fatigue. I was always very tired by that point but usually . . . in fact, at the beginning of my career, when I first started winning, when I got to that point, I was so far ahead that it didn't matter how tired I was, and the idea was to keep the pressure on for every 100 meters or every 100 yards and try to keep the race-pace going.

Sports Publications, Inc.

Mike Burton: He took nearly one minute off the world 1,500-meter record during his career.

World Record Progression

Mike Burton's world-record progression is marked with *.

16:41.60* Lincoln, Aug. 21, 1966 (Burton's first world record which bettered the existing record of 16:58.60 held by Stephen Krause, 1965)

16:34.10* Oak Park, Aug. 13, 1967.

16:28.10 Guillermo Echevarria, Mexico, at Santa Clara Jul. 7, 1968.

16:08.50* Long Beach, Sept. 3, 1968.

16:04.50* Louisville, Aug. 17, 1969.

15:57.10 John Kinsella, Aug. 23, 1970.

15:52.91 Rick de Mont, Aug. 6, 1972.

15:52.58* Munich, Sept. 4, 1972.

CC: *When you felt fatigue, where did it hit you, your arms, your legs, your breathing, or generally all over?*

MB: Just all over. Legs, arms, everything, and I had a two-beat, crossover kick, and so I didn't use a lot of leg power in my swimming, but I still tried to kick hard, especially in training. The main thing was that you had to hurt all over and once you started going and got past that 500, it had to start hurting there and you had to continue to swim under a certain amount of stress.

CC: *When you really got tired, did you actually enjoy testing yourself to see how much fatigue you could endure?*

MB: I'm not sure that I enjoyed it, but it was important to me to try to always swim the best I possibly could. Even now, I tell the swimmers whom I'm presently coaching that if they're swimming a distance race, they should keep trying to put a little more pressure on each successive 100 during the race as it progresses. In that way you are able to maintain an even pace.

CC: *You are trying to build all the time, but, really, it's a delusion in that the pace stays the same, but fatigue increases.*

MB: Yeah. That's exactly right, and it's like a major buildup swim.

CC: *You had a two-beat kick. When you had to increase speed or overtake someone, did you increase your kick to a six-beat or did you just kick harder with your two-beat?*

MB: I just kicked harder because I always felt uncomfortable with a six-beat. In practice, I sometimes tried to imitate Don Schollander. Back then, we used to look at him and say: "He has the perfect stroke." He just really looked pretty in the water, so fluent, but I always felt so uncomfortable when I tried to kick faster like Schollander.

CC: *So you were unlike Murray Rose, Olympic 1,500 champion at the 1956 Melbourne Olympics, who could switch the tempo of his kick from two-beat to four-beat to six-beat?*

MB: That's right. I couldn't do that. Roy Saari could do that real well. He went from a trudgen to a nice six-beat and Murray Rose also could do it, but . . . I don't know, I wasn't that coordinated or it just didn't feel right to me.

CC: *Did you do much stroke counting?*

MB: Only during some of our tapers. We would count strokes and try to lengthen out our strokes. But, in the actual race, the only things I was really concentrating on were the number of laps I had done or the number of laps I had left to do and I had to concentrate on where everybody else was in the pool. I always maintained a constant surveillance on where everybody else was placed during the race.

CC: *Also, you were judging your energy output?*

MB: Yeah. Pretty much, because I was trying to go a little faster with each 100.

CC: *Did you feel that you had a reservoir of energy that you were rationing out as you swam?*

MB: I never even thought of it that way. Most of the time I was saying to myself, "I've got to go faster on this 100, faster on this 100, faster on this 100." I knew that I was going to run out eventually, but it didn't really matter when—as long as I was far enough ahead to get to the finish first.

CC: *Did you try to time your energy output so that it ran out just as you touched at the finish?*

MB: Yeah. And sometimes it worked, and sometimes it didn't, but usually I never felt that last 100 or 150, 200 or so, anyway.

CC: *When you say that it didn't work. You mean that you had something in reserve or that you really had to fight to be able to finish?*

MB: Usually it was a fight to finish. I hardly ever had enough in reserve so that I really felt great coming home.

CC: *Did you have difficulty in holding your stroke, keeping it under control?*

MB: No. I think that, due to the training we did under Sherm's direction, holding the stroke was never a problem because if you can do it enough in practice, then it works fine in a race.

CC: *Did you note the number of strokes you took in early season and then compare this with your number of strokes per lap when you were in peak form?*

MB: No. We never really did that.

CC: *Did you compare your stroke rate with your lap time?*

MB: No.

CC: *What did you know about the 1,500 before you took it up as an event? Did you know about the swims of Ford Konno and those other great swimmers in the history of the event?*

MB: I knew absolutely nothing. When I first arrived at Arden Hills, I was a backstroker and I was also a sophomore at high school. That was my first year of high school swimming and, one particular afternoon at a dual meet, the high school coach needed someone to swim the 400-yard freestyle, and he put me in it. And I swam it and broke the district record.

CC: *What was your time?*

MB: (laughing) It was something like 4 minutes 12 seconds.

CC: *You won't forget that, will you?*

MB: (still laughing) No!

CC: *That 4:12 was considered very promising. How old were you then?*

MB: I was 15. So, when Sherm saw the time he thought it pretty good and so he started entering me for the 1,500 and 1,650 and events like that. And, when I'd made the 1,650 time to go to the National Championships, I did it at the San Francisco State College pool in 1964. I swam the race and didn't even realize that I'd made the qualifying time. When the race was over, Sherm said, "How would you like to go to Bartlesville, Oklahoma, to swim in the Nationals?" And I said, "That will be great." But, up to that time, I really didn't know anything about the history of the event or who had swum it before but I did compete against Murray Rose, Roy Saari, and Bill Farley and people like that.

CC: *Murray Rose was a great tactician. Were you able to match him tactically?*

MB: Er! (laughing) No way! Because when I swam against them, Murray Rose and Roy Saari were always in the middle of the pool and I was always in an outside lane or in the heat previous to that. I remember at the Los Angeles Invitational in 1964, I think it was, I was in lane eight and they were in the middle of the pool.

CC: *You were just an up-and-comer then?*

MB: (laughing) Yes! Really up-and-coming I remember, after the race people were saying, "Who's that guy in lane eight who went out so fast?" I remember Murray saying something to the effect, "You know, you really go out too fast to swim this race!" . . . something like that.

CC: *Do you think that was an attempted psych-out?*

MB: I don't know. I never really thought much

about it. It always felt good to me to go out fast and so I really didn't think about it. I just figured, "One of these days, I'm going to get him, and I'm not going to die. I'll be there!"

CC: *Did you experience any of Murray Rose's subtle changes of pace? He used to do that to test a rival's concentration.*

MB: When Murray retired in 1964, I had only swum against him a couple of times and those were at the Los Angeles Invitational and in our National Championships. I think that I was probably too young and naive then to realize what he and Roy Saari were actually doing in a race.

CC: *Would you like to discuss your main rivals during your swimming career and your big races against them?*

MB: Probably the biggest rival I had was John Kinsella. He was about 6 feet, 3 inches and just a hulk of a guy, even when he was 16 years old, and we swam against each other in Mexico City. We had some very good races prior to that, and probably the biggest and most exciting was in Los Angeles when he touched me out by two-tenths of a second. And we both broke the 16-minute mark for the first time. That was a tremendous race. I had just come off knee surgery in April, and we swam in August. It was a tremendous event. Some of the other ones . . . Graham Windeatt of Australia at the Munich Olympics, 1972 . . .

CC: *Graham passed you in that race. What was your reaction to that?*

MB: Well, in that particular race, again, I went out fast and, at about 400 to 500, when I was starting to feel fatigue but still trying to maintain the pace, Graham came shooting by me.

CC: *What part of the lap was that?*

MB: That was on the way down to the turning end, probably on 600, I think.

CC: *Did he try to catch you on the blind spot going into the turn?*

MB: Well, he got me about in the middle of the pool actually because I was breathing to the left. He went by me pretty quickly and, as he started to go by, of course I moved over as close as I could to his side of the lane, hope-

fully, to draft off him, but he got about a half a body length or so ahead—maybe a body length—and we stayed right there for quite a while.

CC: *For how long?*

MB: Until about 300 to 400 meters to go.

CC: *Do you think that he perhaps killed himself by passing so quickly?*

MB: I think so, because if you look at the splits, I was holding a constant 1:03 plus and Graham, when he went by me, dropped to something like 1:02 low . . . real fast.

CC: *He had to do this, otherwise, there's no way he could have gone by—you would have been warned.*

MB: That's right. Yes, he passed me very quickly, and he held 1:02s for a couple of 100s then he dropped back to 1:03s. We had about 300 to 400 meters to go and I realized that I was catching him. The thought went through my head, "I think I'm doing it on the turns." Actually what was happening was that he was slowing down gradually and so I tried to hit my turns even harder, as well as putting on more pressure between the walls. And it worked out to where I gradually caught him and passed him and then, once I got past him, I moved over to the opposite side of the lane to get away from him so that I didn't pull him along in my wake.

CC: *Up until the 1972 Olympics you had deliberately*

"Probably my biggest rival was John Kinsella," said Mike Burton. Kinsella reduced Mike Burton's world 1,500-meter freestyle record of 16:04.5 to 15:57.1 on August 23, 1970. Both Burton and Kinsella broke the 16-minute mark for the first time in this race. Kinsella won by two-tenths of a second.

Graham Windeatt, another of Don Talbot's all-time great distance stars and one of Mike Burton's biggest career rivals.

"He was really tough to swim against," said Burton of Rick de Mont.

gone into a sort of quiescent period, resting up so as to be ready to make a big pre-Olympic training effort?

MB: I was still doing the same amount of hard training. I was getting older, naturally, and I got married in 1969 and the younger kids were actually getting tougher. Some people thought I was on the decline because guys like Kinsella and Rick de Mont were coming up and just getting tougher all the time. They were really tough to swim against.

CC: *Who was the toughest swimmer you ever raced?*

MB: I think it was Kinsella. He was, for his time—and it wasn't a real long span—he was actually the toughest competitor I ever had.

CC: *In what way? What makes you say that?*

MB: Because he was willing to go out with me and hang on. A lot of the other guys, like Rick de Mont at the 1972 Olympic trials, he swam his normal race . . . he went out fairly easy and descended from there and, of course, flew by me at about 800 meters, but Kinsella was always willing to challenge right from the start. I give him a lot of credit for that.

CC: *What were your impressions of the 1,500 meter at the Montreal Olympics in 1976?*

MB: I enjoyed watching that race an television. It was a great race. Steven Holland and, of course, Hackett and Goodell and Hartlauf, Paul Hartlauf. All the swimmers were doing a tremendous job.

CC: *How would you have liked to have raced against Goodell, Hackett, or Holland?*

MB: (laughing) I don't think that I would have!

CC: *Why not?*

MB: Just because of the way Goodell swims his race—the negative split and the descending 100s, and things like that—and he's so fast over that last 100 or so. It's just unbelievable.

CC: *Come on. Mike, let's assume that it was possible to reverse the time machine a little. How would you like to race today's top 1,500 swimmers?*

MB: I don't know.

CC: *That wasn't a fair question?*

MB: It's a tough one to answer. When you consider the success that I had—I really enjoyed that! And it was a lot of fun and I wouldn't have done it any differently. I imagine that, if I could have the same amount of success today as I had then, then yes. Sure, it would be great!

CC: *Today's top swimmers have introduced a real speed element into the event.*

MB: Yeah. Well, I think all the kids have—they're so much faster, talent wise the speed they have—and we're getting better athletes into swimming all the time. They've got that speed and it's just great to watch.

CC: *Speed gives them a real competitive edge.*

MB: Oh yeah! I think that they can be much better tacticians today than I was and even better than Murray Rose was back then.

CC: *What did you think of Steve Holland's swimming?*

MB: I liked it because he was the kind of guy who was similar to my style of swimming. He would go out and he would hold the pace but it would be a very, very fast pace. I liked his coach, Laurie Lawrence, very much and I enjoyed watching his protégé swim.

CC: *Would you say that a one-pace swimmer like Holland really has to get out very fast and set the speed standard for the race? If he starts out too slowly, he could have problems achieving the time needed to win.*

MB: There's no question about it. If you are an even-pace swimmer, then you've got to set the pace for the entire field.

CC: *You've got to be a solid type of swimmer.*

MB: You've got to be really solid, right from the gun. We always like to think that we are going to be able to pick up the pace coming home and so forth, but what usually happens is that you only got a little faster and that's it. The guys with the great speed, the Goodells, the Salnikovs, and the people like that, they can really come home and do a fantastic job over that last 400 meters.

CC: *Do you think it possible for any one to develop speed?*

MB: I think so. If you have the right kind of athlete, one who's fairly talented, I think you can develop speed.

CC: *It also depends on one's attitude.*

MB: The best I could do for 100 meters was 54 high and a 47 low over 100 yards. Back then that wasn't too bad, but I never really ever swam these distances shaved and tapered unless it was on a relay.

CC: *Have you seen Salnikov swim?*

MB: I haven't been able to see him swim too often. He was in an 800 last summer [1983] in an invitational meet at the Los Angeles Olympic pool. I watched that on television but I haven't been able to watch him too often. I don't get away to all the big meets as I used to be able to do. I'm coaching now in Des Moines, Iowa, and we're just starting a team there and it isn't ready yet to travel to the big meets.

CC: *Do you foresee the nature of the 1,500 event changing?*

MB: I don't know that it is going to change a tremendous amount. I think it is going to get faster. It's always going to get faster.

CC: *Do you think that less mileage and greater intensity in training may result in faster times?*

MB: I don't know. I really don't. I kind of think that just as much mileage and more intensity will produce faster times. You may find that the kid who is prepared to go the same amount of yards at a more intense level could be your next world-record holder.

CC: *How much of this is psychological? In any particular era you may find swimmers all around the same time.*

MB: Oh! I think these psychological barriers are set up for us such as when Roger Bannister went under four minutes for the one-mile run, things like that. The psychological barrier, once someone does it, then everybody does it. And so I think that these psychological barriers certainly enter into it in our sport as well.

CC: *During the peak of your career did you make up your mind that you were going to do times that were way ahead of the others and set new standards for your event?*

MB: I always felt that I was going to be able to do that simply by the way I felt in practice— what I was doing in practice and, quite often, I was able to predict the time I was going to do prior to swimming it in the event.

CC: *Was this the result of a mental effort as well*

as a physical effort—feeling the speed of your body in the water?

MB: I think so. There was mental concentration on how I felt during the warm-up, the type of training I had done previously, how I felt during the taper and the 100 repeats that I did in the warm-up at race pace. If these felt OK then I could come very close to predicting what I was going to do in the race.

CC: *Would you care to comment on the great coaches in the 1,500-meter event?*

MB: I think that Don Watson was fantastic with John Kinsella, and George Haines could always get Mike Wall to be there as the person who would score points and make an international squad and make the Olympic team as an alternate. Mike Wall's basic problem was that he could never quite get over the hump to be a winner. He could always be there to score a point. I think that all of our coaches can do a good job of coaching the 1,500 and, of course, my coach, Sherm Chavoor, taught me everything I know. We worked well together and that was just a neat experience really and it was one where I totally respected what he had to say and what he asked me to do.

CC: *He said that you were his guinea pig.*

MB: Yes, that's true. I don't resent that at all. It was positive, very positive. We had success together and I did the things he asked me to do out of total respect because he is a great man and I admire him very much. You know the other coaches, Peter Daland, George Haines, and Don Talbot are fantastic in the things that they have done with some of their swimmers.

CC: *What would you say is the reason for Peter Daland's success in coaching swimmers for the 1,500 meter?*

MB: Well, I think that Peter, when he was coaching Murray Rose at USC, either he learned it or he picked it up, they were doing some over-distance training—3,000s and items like that. Well, that's where Sherm picked it up, the 3,000s, we started doing those.

I think that Coach Bob Horn at UCLA is a coach who is little known in the swimming world. We started some things there, one I particularly remember was that as a freshman at a UCLA practice, I did my first broken 1,500s. It went very well. Coach Horn said, "I want you to hold 1:03s with 10 seconds rest after each 100." Well, I started off and I was going 1:02s and 1:01s. I could never do a 1:03! It was too slow! Those broken 1,500 swims transferred quite well to the actual race situation.

CC: *What splits did you produce in the race?*

MB: I ended up doing 1:02s. It was just an invitational meet over at USC. It wasn't any big deal but I did my best time. So it worked out very well. Bob Horn is not coaching swimming any longer. He is just coaching water polo. Of course, Mark Schubert is a tremendous distance coach as well. He's fantastic. The things he's done with Brian Goodell and Tiffany Cohen and people like that, are just amazing. One has to respect what he has achieved. You always relate success with what the coach's protégé has done. Perhaps he's had the good athletes to work with, perhaps not, but we do know the ones he has had in the distance events!

CC: *Mark Schubert has done a great job.*

MB: Well, you can look at the National Championships. For example, he hasn't got just one girl or one boy in the 1,500 or 1,650. He has got several, and some of them are the winners, and the others are up there scoring points and doing a tremendous job.

CC: *They are the gold that doesn't glitter because they drive the champions to success.*

MB: (laughing) That's very well said. Yes, I always feel that competition breeds success and they've got this sort of competition in their animal lane, or maybe two animal lanes, in which their top distance swimmers train. They can perform at a much higher level than many other kids who don't have that competitive edge within the daily practice. So that makes a big difference.

Now, Don Talbot, I've always admired Don Talbot because he is one of the great coaches who would always come up and talk to me after my races and just congratulate me and discuss what I had done—also the things that he has done with his swimmers to get them to perform. This has always been kind of neat. Many times, as swimmers, we don't really get into finding out what the other coaches are doing in practice. Don was always free to talk to me, and it was a very nice relationship as a competitor to be able to talk to another competitor's coach.

❖ ❖ ❖

CECIL COLWIN DISCUSSES THE 1,500 WITH SHERMAN CHAVOOR

An interview at the U.S. Long Course Championships at Santa Clara, California, in 1986.

CC: *When did you first start coaching the 1,500-meter event seriously?*

SC: I started serious work on the 1,500 about 1962, although previously I had always coached swimmers for this event. I was very impressed by the Japanese swimmers, Furuhashi and Hashizume, when they swam at the Coliseum in Los Angeles in 1950.

On the way out to the 1,500 meter they broke the world record for the 800 meter. In talking to their coaches and watching them swim, I learned that they covered exceptional distances in training. I liked the way the Japanese trained and I remembered what they did so that, when I came to coach my great Mike Burton, who was always like a robot, I would tell him to do this and he would do it. I had been unable to find youngsters prepared to apply themselves to do this hard kind of work. But Mike Burton took to it. He always pressed himself to swim farther and faster—over-distance work. As I've said before, he was my guinea pig. When Mike proved what could be done, I really started working hard on my youngsters. I'd have them swim 1,500 meters in training about three times a week.

CC: *What was your rationale in having your youngsters swim over-distances?*

SC: I was a track man in high school and college and I did some amateur boxing. I could never understand why the coach would train us for the mile by making us run only three-quarters of a mile. Why not the last lap? And why did professional boxers do only 2 or 3 rounds instead of 15 rounds? It always bothered me. Why shouldn't boxers over-box and runners overrun? Why, for example, shouldn't runners do five miles in training in order to run a fast mile? It seemed a very simple concept to me and yet no one seemed prepared to do over-distance in training.

CC: *Did you encounter psychological resistance to this new concept of training?*

SC: Yes. Very much so. All the youngsters didn't want to swim over-distance. They felt that I just wanted to give them a long distance training program so that I could sit and rest or read a book or something! They would say: "Gosh! The coach is lazy. He won't give us sprints!" They wanted to do just sprints, but I know that you could do both because, when you've mastered swimming distances, the ability to sprint would come eventually—particularly with the youngsters who were not very strong when they were younger. Debbie Meyer was a very thin girl, and so were many of the other youngsters I had. Mike Burton wasn't a very strong boy when he started. I felt that we could go to the Nationals on a distance program rather than sprints. You had to be a rather big, strong, tough high school boy or girl to be a good sprinter.

I felt that you should start with distance first and then you can always cut down in distance once you are big and strong and you come to the college age. Mark Spitz was a great distance swimmer. He came within four-tenths of a second of breaking the world record in the 1,500 meter. Later, after he went to Indiana, he cut down to 200s. Many swimmers start out now on over-distance and reduce their distances later, but I had a lot of early opposition because they didn't want to swim so far. Mike Burton, my guinea pig did, and, because of his success, it didn't take long for the other youngsters on my swimming team to do the same thing because they wanted to go to the Nationals. Not only my youngsters started working over distance, but other coaches eventually were able to encourage their youngsters to train the same way.

CC: So Mike Burton was the first person on your team to really take to your over-distance program?

SC: I've had other persons on a distance program but they didn't take to it. Burton was the fellow who first took to it. I'd say to Mike Burton, "Let's go three 1,500s," and he would do it. He was the first one who started to really put it over.

CC: And Mark Spitz was one of several others who started off with a good distance base.

SC: Yes, Mark Spitz and Johnny Ferris and all my great swimmers swam distances from 25 yards to 3,000 yards. Mark Spitz was a very good distance swimmer.

CC: What was his daily average in early season?

SC: He would go about 10,000 yards to 11,000 yards up to 14,000 yards.

CC: And then in midseason?

SC: Well, you've probably heard rumors that I very seldom tapered my swimmers.

CC: You coined the phrase, "It takes guts to taper."

SC: (laughing) Yeah! It takes guts to taper and so we tapered when we boarded the plane to go to the meet. That was about four days before the meet started. That was about it.

CC: That was for sprinters as well?

SC: Sprinters as well. Who's to say if I'm right or wrong? Some were very successful with it. Some of them were not. Only now, when we are older and wiser, do we try to plan for the individuals. I'm always skeptical though. Jeff Float, one of my present stars, wants to taper more, taper more, and I don't want him to. I say, "Never mind. I think a three to four day rest is plenty."

CC: Do you find the younger kids losing their feel of the water if they taper too early?

SC: Yeah. I think so. So much of it is psychological. These youngsters go to college and they get some lazy coaches who want to take time off towards the end of the season and they taper the kids off longer than I think they should. And, when the youngsters come back

from college to our USS programs, they think they know it all. I was talking to Mitch Ivey the other day, and he was talking about these college coaches. When the kids come back, they think they know it all.

CC: You are saying that, in some cases, college coaches have a negative effect on kids who developed in the clubs?

SC: Well, I think so, particularly through the older kids. Don't get me wrong. There are coaches and coaches. I'm not debunking any of the college coaches, but if you don't have the horses already given to you, whether it be swimming, basketball, or football, you're not going to win. If the coaches don't have the horses already developed for them, they are not going to win. Unless the kids are developed for them, they are not going to do much developing.

A famous sports writer in the *San Francisco Examiner* said, "The college coaches are lucky. They put a little polish on their diamonds, and they become famous because of some club coach, some high school coach, who has made these diamonds." What do we mean by a little polish? Actually just normal maturation. The youngsters get older and stronger. They become better. The psychological effect of swimming for their university does something very, very important. And, yet again, don't get me wrong, I'm not debunking the college coaches, but if you don't have the horses, you're not going to win. Yet, college coaches have different problems with the swimmers. The kids are not with their parents, and so the college coaches have their problems, too.

CC: Is the distance swimmer at a disadvantage in a college program as far as training and competition is concerned? Do college coaches prefer swimmers who have more speed and can handle multievents?

SC: If you're a great distance swimmer you can move along at just about anything. Mike Burton was a great distance swimmer and yet he was an NCAA record holder in the 500-yard freestyle in 1970. And was a heck of a 200-yard freestyler. He always made the team at 200-yard freestyle, and he was NCAA champion at 200-yard butterfly, also in 1970. So, if you're a great distance swimmer, you can move along into just about anything. And you have the example of Mark Spitz winning the NCAA 500-yard freestyle in 1969. Conversely, Burton was a good sprinter, too—seventh or eighth in the world was a good sprint.

CC: *Let us come now to the finer points of training for the 1,500-meter event. At the beginning of the season, how would you go about defining some goals if you were training a top 1,500 swimmer?*

SC: We do a lot of pulling, developing the arms by placing a tube around the ankles. We do over-distance in that or, in lieu of that we do a lot of weight training to strengthen their muscles. Constantly, we do 30 by 100 with short rests. My present crop of swimmers go 30 by 100 on a minute. They have to hold 55s or 54s, and that's an easy way of getting them into good shape. And, as we go into the season, instead of having them go on the minute, I have them go on 58 seconds—even as low as 57s. We also do 50s.

CC: *How often do they swim unbroken 1,500s?*

SC: I always have them do two or three 1,500s a day. And then, a couple of times a week, I have them do 3,000 nonstop.

CC: *Just to get the feel of continuous swimming, otherwise there may be some doubt in their minds as to whether they can put it all together in a nonstop swim?*

SC: We do straight swimming as well as broken swimming all the time. We do a combination of both. And, while we are doing the straight swimming, the clock is on, and I time their 100s ever so often. And, of course, they can see the clock themselves and know their pace.

CC: *You said that you did quite a few long, unbroken swims. Your habit of giving your swimmers 3,000 and 5,000 long, unbroken swims was copied worldwide.*

SC: Yes, we did. My philosophy in any sport is over-distance, overdo, overwork. Run in the sand. Then get on the flat and you'll really move. Psychologically as well as physiologically, the concept was sound.

CC: *What is your feeling as to how often they*

should race the 1,500 event during a season?

SC: Well, it varies. The younger swimmers race it every three weeks, every two weeks, if we can.

CC: *At top speed?*

SC: Yeah! Debbie Meyer broke world records for a long time every time she got into the pool. Of course, she was an exception, but people like Mike Burton and Debbie, later on in their careers, would go five or six 1,500 races a year, at the maximum. They proved that they could handle this quite well. It doesn't work with all swimmers. It's the same old story; I may develop some good swimmers who become world champions, and you may develop some world champions out of swimmers I couldn't make work. If you had them, you might make world champions while I could do nothing or little with them, or vice versa. It depends on the personality of the coach and the swimmer and how they are able to relate to each other.

CC: *What are your ideas about tactics in the 1,500 race? Sometimes, you swim for time and you have no need to worry about the opposition. But there are times when you need to swim a tactical race. What are your views on tactics?*

SC: Well, I've never given that much thought because all my distance swimmers have won so easily! I always made them go out hard and fast and make their rivals try to catch them. If a rival was good enough to stay with you, then you put in a couple of fast turns to try to lose them psychologically—make the other kid say, "Gee, this guy's too good for me." You need to have some tactics, but for a long time, we outdistanced, outswam everybody. But toward the end of the careers of Mike Burton and Debbie Meyer, we had to use some strategy by putting in good, fast turns, maybe 5 to 10 of them, one after the other, gaining half a yard with each turn. Pretty soon the other youngster would say, "Holy smoke! I guess he's too good for me," and just sort of give up. I always tell my youngsters, "When you hit that wall, act as if it is a hot iron. Get off the wall in a hurry. That way you can gain a yard on the opposition and really destroy them." Don Schollander was a master of that. He would do a couple of fast turns and, pretty soon the other kids would be saying, "Forget it. I'm not going to win."

CC: I saw Don Schollander do that to John Nelson in the U.S. 400-meter championship in Lincoln, Nebraska, in 1966.

SC: Yes, I remember that.

CC: Do you recommend a long push off the wall in a distance race or do you prefer them to push off a little short to conserve energy?

SC: It all depends on individual physique and the strength of the swimmer's legs. If you have strong legs, you get a good push-off. A long glide is fine as long as your momentum doesn't stop and you keep going.

CC: You don't think that is unnecessarily tiring?

SC: No, not at all. You train for that. You should practice hard, fast turns when you're training. A turn is part of a race.

CC: Do you like your swimmers to speed up in the turns, not only because of the distance to be gained, but because the blind spot going into the turn makes it easier to break away without being noticed?

SC: That's one reason. It's difficult sometimes for your rival to see you but the big thing, of course, is that if you can gain 2 to 3 feet with each turn. With 10 turns, you've got 30 feet on your rival. That alone can win a race.

CC: What are your views on changing pace to test whether your rival is losing concentration or not? Murray Rose used subtle changes in pace and, when his rival began to be slow to respond or react to these pace changes, that was when Rose would start to break away. Do you have any similar tricks of the trade?

SC: Well, I watched Murray Rose swim and there's no question that he was a great swimmer, and no question that Roy Saari was a great swimmer, and they would play cat and mouse together, which I thought was wrong. I wish I could have coached Murray Rose and Roy Saari. I would have coached them the same way that I coached Mike Burton. I feel that they would have been a hell of a lot better swimmers than they were.

CC: Would you have had them go out faster from the gun?

SC: No question about it. I proved that. Roy Saari would play catch up, but one day in 1966, he let Mike Burton get out in front, and Mike Burton finished the race 25 yards ahead of him. That broke his back. When I saw Rose and Saari swim together, I always felt that lying back until the last 100 to 200 yards was a mistake. "Go out hard and get him right at the beginning," was my motto. As I said, I wish that I had coached these two fellows at the height of their careers.

CC: What would you say is the danger margin in distance swimming in how far you can let the other swimmer get away from you? A body length and a half or any set distance where you are cutting it really fine if you need to close with a sudden challenge?

SC: Well, being the nervous type that I am, if anyone is one foot ahead I get panicky! But, seriously, you fall half a body length behind, and the other fellow is in as good a shape as you are, unless you are real strong at the end, you are going to get beaten. I like them to swim neck and neck!

CC: Let's say you have layed back in the race for a while, and now you've decided that you are going to make your effort. That effort should be made gradually and not so late in the race that it is incapable of achievement?

SC: If you get behind in a race early—of course, I get all panicky and wonder, "Holy smoke! What's happening!?" Graham Windeatt did that to Mike Burton. Mike Burton had a lead in the 1972 Olympics, and Graham passed him. That scared me. But then I think Graham tried to pass Mike too rapidly. But this was at the end of Mike Burton's career. He wasn't doing so well due to the fact that he was 25 years old. Then I was very pleasantly surprised when Mike Burton caught him and Windeatt died.

CC: Looking at Salnikov and the way the 1,500 is being swum at the present time, do you detect any significant change in 1,500 tactics?

SC: Well, for one, Rick de Mont and other people were doing negative splitting. Negative splitting, negative swims, I say. But it works for some youngsters. Here again, there are others trying to do it the way I thought was good.

I think they're going back to it—going out hard and holding it. I've seen evidence that they're doing that.

CC: *So you don't like negative splitting in the 1,500?*

SC: Not at all. I like my swimmers to go out hard and say "catch me."

CC: *There's one school of thought that says that the time at the 750-meter mark ideally should be about half of the final time for the complete 1,500-meter swim. In actual fact, many coaches could predict their swimmer's final time from the 750 split. What is your opinion on that?*

SC: Well, every day I learn about swimming and I've seen that. But you know that Mike Burton, Debbie Meyer, and Vickie King, all these great swimmers I had in the distance events, they were so far ahead of everybody. But, since that time, many coaches have caught on, and they're using different tactics. As you say, at the 750 mark they can predict what their swimmers are going to do, and I think you're right.

Mike Burton wasn't a great, great athlete like Spitz or, say, a Debbie Meyer. Burton won on guts. I don't think that he would have made it in this era of swimming, but I think that Debbie would have. Also, Mark Spitz still would have.

CC: *You really don't believe that Mike Burton would have made it in this era?*

SC: I don't think that he had that great natural ability. No.

CC: *So he did it all on sheer guts.*

SC: He had a lot of guts, determination and he was so far ahead of the field. Our distance training program was so far ahead at the time and that's how he won.

CC: *Do you think that he really hurt in a race or did he have an unusually high tolerance to pain?*

SC: Oh! I asked him about that, and he told me that he would hurt, and I said, "Don't go broadcasting that to too many people because they might think that 'Mmm! Next time I'll get him!'"

Mike Burton in full cry. "He had a lot of guts, determination, and he was so far ahead of the field. Our distance training program was so far ahead at the time and that's how he won," said Chavoor, Burton's coach.

International Swimming Hall of Fame

CC: *So you let the "iron man image," if not myth, live on.*

SC: That's right. No question about it.

CC: *Do you think that it was a myth?*

SC: No, I do think he was hurting, and I said, "Don't go tell people you're hurting. Just say, 'Oh well, just another race.'" That would give an impression of "next time I'm going to murder you anyway." You see, some of the other guys were beginning to catch on a little bit, and their times were closing. So I would tell them to act as if nothing was going on, and after a race, look as if you're not even puffing hard.

CC: *In other words, walk to the change rooms with nary a puff and then collapse inside.*

SC: (laughing) Yeah! That's right!

CC: *Did he say where he hurt? His lungs, his arms and legs? Did he pinpoint a specific part of his body?*

SC: He said that his legs and shoulders would hurt.

CC: *And he was a two-beat kicker.*

SC: Yes, a two-beat kicker.

CC: *So he really must have been pressing with that kick.*

SC: Yeah! But don't forget that he had a scar about six inches long on one leg and he couldn't use that leg very well.

CC: *What caused that?*

SC: He was hit by a car while riding a bicycle.

CC: *Was that before he became a swimmer?*

SC: Yes. That's why he took to swimming, because the doctor told him, "The only sport for you is swimming." In fact, he walks with a limp to this day.

CC: *He was one of the early swimmers to do the two-beat kick. Did you make any effort to change it?*

SC: Yeah! Then, of course, others came along like Karen Moras, Shane Gould, and Shirley Babashoff. Debbie Meyer, however, was a six-beat kicker.

CC: *Debbie Meyer didn't slow to a two-beat kick in the 1,500?*

SC: No. She was pretty consistent. Of course, in Mexico City she couldn't do that, drag her legs, she just wanted to win. At the Olympics you don't go for world records. You're just out to win that gold. That's what she was trying to do.

CC: *And, she felt that a two-beat kick would slow down her particular style of swimming?*

SC: Yes.

CC: *Did you allow Mike Burton to just develop his own natural and individual style of swimming?*

SC: Before Burton came to me at Arden Hills, they used to kid him about being a woodchopper, the way his arms would go flying over the water. But Mike had a marvelous underwater stroke. He pulled just perfectly.

Coincidentally, he had a brother who also was a good swimmer. Doc Counsilman couldn't distinguish between them because their styles were so similar, probably something to do with having similar hereditary factors.

I didn't worry too much about what Mike did above the water compared with what he did under the water. It came naturally to him. Later on, when he was swimming thousands and thousands of yards, his above-water movement also became more controlled.

CC: *What are your general views on stroke technique with special reference to distance swimmers?*

SC: All youngsters should have good stroke technique. I was just talking to my friend, Walt Schlueter, who is a great stroke technician, and he said that Debbie Meyer was a great swimmer because she had a perfect stroke. I believe him because I emphasize good stroke technique with younger kids. As they get older, I'm not going to worry too much about stroke technique because maybe they can't change once they are set in their styles. The main thing is to get into great shape. This also helps offset stroke faults which have become too ingrained to change.

Sue Pederson pulled to the left a little bit and I didn't worry about that. I got her into great shape to offset that. Two baseball pitchers pitch underarm, but they are champions.

Coached by Chavoor, Debbie Meyer held 400-meter, 800-meter, and 1,500-meter world records in the 1960s. The roll of the entire body on its long axis is clearly seen as well as the inhalation in the body roll. The arm is recovered loosely with high elbow and relaxed hand and wrist.

Theoretically, you are supposed to pitch overhand, but both of them are champions. So it depends on the individual—how much guts they have and the extent of their desire to get there first.

CC: *So most kids have had their stroke instruction before they come to you?*

SC: I've taught 6- to 8-year-olds proper technique. But, during the last 15 to 20 years, they've come to me out of age-group programs, pretty well developed at the ages of 10, 11 years old. We do make some slight changes, but we don't work a heck of a lot on stroke.

CC: *How many swimmers did you have on your team at the time when Burton and Spitz were swimming so well?*

SC: About 150 swimmers. We always took 20 to 30 swimmers to the Nationals. And we took 36 to the Olympic trials in 1972.

CC: *How many assistant coaches do you have?*

SC: Two or three.

CC: *To take these swimmers to the Nationals did the parents just pay their share of the travel expenses or did you find it necessary to have fund-raising projects?*

SC: We had very little fund-raising. Swimming is an expensive sport. The clientele we had at Arden Hills, other than a few, could afford it.

CC: *You just told them that air tickets and hotels would come to a certain figure?*

SC: Yes. That's right. We still do that.

CC: *You weren't really involved in any fund-raising, bingo nights, and so forth?*

SC: No, Arden Hills is a swimming and tennis club which I own, and it's really my main business. That's where I make my living. Swimming coaching, of course, is my hobby even though I've spent up to 60,000 dollars of my own money on the swimming program. It's an expensive hobby, but one which I enjoy because somebody has to work with youth.

CC: *Let's move away now from the background to your program and your great swimmers and get your impressions of the other great postwar 1,500 swimmers whom you've had the opportunity of observing.*

SC: I remember Jimmy McLane the 1948 Olym-pic 1,500 champion. He was one great swimmer. I was thinking the other day when I was looking at the results of the 100-yard freestyle how Alan Ford swam the 100 yards in 49.6 seconds back in 1945, and now it is 42 seconds. I thought, "Gee, that was 40 years ago. We haven't made a heck of a lot of improvement in the 100 compared with the distance events."

But if Jimmy McLane was swimming today in the same type of program as the present champions, he would have been a hell of a swimmer.

CC: *What did you think of his technique? He had a very strong six-beat kick.*

SC: I remember that he had a very strong kick. He wasn't very big in the shoulders.

CC: *He had broad shoulders but he was very thin.*

SC: Yeah! He had skinny shoulders. That always surprised me. I thought he would be bigger. When I first saw him I thought, "Is that Jimmy McLane?! He's such a little squirt!" (laughing) Compared with the image I had of him, you know.

CC: *Yet, when he started, he was a 13-year-old winning national 1,500 championships and 3-mile open-water swims and beating grown men by big margins.*

SC: Yes, I remember that. He was a good swimmer. I still remember John Marshall of Australia. He was an excellent swimmer, very good. At one time, he held every world record from 200 to the 1,500. He, too, with modern training techniques would have made it in today's swimming. I always felt that, if Johnny Weissmuller had swum today, he still would have been world champion.

CC: *Ford Konno was the 1,500 champion at the Helsinki Olympics in 1952. What were your impressions of him?*

SC: Very smooth. He had stroke mechanics down real well. Of course, he had a great coach in Sakamoto. It's kind of funny. I was going to Europe, and this airline official saw my USA Olympic bag, and he asked, "Are you involved with the Olympics?" I said, yes, I was. He said, "Do you know Ford Konno?" I said, "Yes, very well." He said, "Well, he's my uncle." I said,

"Well, I'll be darned." And so he upgraded my ticket, put me in first class instead of second class.

CC: That shows yet another hidden benefit of swimming.

SC: Yeah! I thought Ford Konno was really good. He was as smooth as glass. He was good.

CC: Did you see the classic race at the Melbourne Olympics in 1956 between George Breen and Murray Rose?

SC: Murray Rose had great conditioning, but Breen didn't have the conditioning that Murray Rose had.

CC: Do you think that George made a mistake by setting a world record in the heats?

SC: Oh, yeah! I think he did. You're not going to psych out a guy like Murray Rose. He was also too strong for him. People will do that in time trials; just do real well and go off in a final. Mind you, I've seen them win as well! But Murray was too strong for that.

CC: Do you believe that George Breen really went out to psych Murray Rose by setting a world record in the heats?

SC: Knowing Breen, I thought he did. It's no reflection on Breen. He's a nice person. He probably thought, "I have to get him some way." (laughing)

CC: Was there much tactical maneuvering in the race itself?

SC: I thought there was a lot of maneuvering six months before and again in the race.

CC: In what way did it happen six months before?

SC: It was just the atmosphere between the Americans and the Australians as to who would win the 1,500, the way people were talking about the big race coming up in the Olympics. People were saying, "Breen is going to do this. Rose is going to do this."

CC: Did you know that George Breen counted his strokes in training?

SC: That always puzzled me. I never had any swimmers count their strokes. I don't know why they do it. Maybe their coaches have them do it. I don't care about that as long as the swimmers get there first.

CC: According to George Breen, he learned after the race that his coach, Doc Counsilman was talking to Charles Sylvia during the race and he said to Sylvia, "George isn't going to make it because his stroke count has gone up."

SC: Well, Doc Counsilman is a great coach. I've never used the method of counting the strokes. I never have. I still don't see the importance of it, and he's a great coach who has had great success. And I never had Mike Burton or Debbie Meyer count their strokes. They just moved their arms fast to get there first.

CC: Which of the Olympic 1,500 swims has stuck most in your memory?

SC: Well, naturally the one that stuck most in my memory was when Mike Burton, now an old man of 25 years, won the 1,500 at the Munich Olympics in 1972. He was not supposed to win it. de Mont was the favorite. He might have won it. He might not have done. Who's to say? Mike Burton won the race. He felt a little bad because de Mont wasn't there.

CC: What was your impression of the 1,500 at the 1976 Montreal Olympics with Brian Goodell, Bobby Hackett, and Stephen Holland fighting it out?

SC: Goodell was a great swimmer and so was Holland. The race was a dog fight! Again, great preliminary interest had grown around the Olympic 1,500, six months before everyone was wondering who was going to win the race. Everyone here was hoping, of course, that it would be an American lad. But I had a lot of confidence in Holland. I thought Holland was a very well-trained youth. He seemed to have an objective. He wanted to get there in a hurry.

CC: You were talking about getting out fast. Steve had the disadvantage of not having great initial speed. He seemed to have had two speeds: flat out and stop!

SC: That could have been. I didn't know Holland too well other than that he was one great swimmer. He may have had a bad week at that time. Who knows?

CC: What was your impression of Bobby Hackett?

SC: I'd watched Hackett swim for a long time. He was a great swimmer. He was a big strong boy. Perhaps he would have been better suited to the 400.

✧ ✧ ✧

CECIL COLWIN DISCUSSES THE 1,500 WITH MARK SCHUBERT

An interview at the U.S. Long Course Championships at Indianapolis in 1983.

CC: *You coached 1976 Olympic champion, Brian Goodell, and Goodell's contribution to 1,500 swimming, if you want to call it that, was the introduction of great speed to the tactical approach to the event.*

MS: My philosophy in training swimmers for the 1,500 is, first of all, that it is very important to give swimmers a very good endurance base when they are young. We try to train all our very young swimmers in endurance swimming, giving them a lot of endurance training in practices as opposed to speed training. As they become older and stronger, then we start to introduce the speed element into their training.

I feel it important that swimmers train primarily by using descending sets. This teaches them to increase their speed at the end of a race. It's also important that swimmers work on negative splitting in individual practice swims. We put emphasis on negative splitting in 90 percent of our training.

I also feel it is important that distance swimmers do speed training and sprint training. We also emphasize teaching all our swimmers to be able to do a six-beat kick. Many times in races, you'll see our swimmers at the beginning of a race, maybe the first 1,300 to 1,400 meters, using a two-beat kick but switching to a six-beat kick over the final 200 to 100 meters.

CC: *What approach do you use in teaching them to convert from a two-beat to a six-beat kick? Just plenty of work an the kickboard?*

MS: Yes. We do a lot of kicking. Also we have a very good technique program. Walt and Nancy Schlueter are our stroke coaches, and all our swimmers report to them for stroke work. And one of the things they work on is sprint swimming using six-beat technique. We do technique work also with the two-beat and, of course, most of the training is done using a two-beat kick. But, at the end of the sessions, we finish up with 25-yard sprints working on the six-beat technique.

CC: *Do you do many pace-simulated 1,500s?*

MS: We do many 1,500s throughout the season but most of them are done in sets of two to five in descending manner.

CC: *Always negative splitting?*

MS: Always negative splitting, always descended. Most of our actual pace sessions are done with 1,500 swims broken at the 50, 100, or 150. These are done at race pace, sometimes with a short rest, sometimes with a longer rest, and sometimes with an easy swim in between the pace work.

CC: *What rest do you give between each 1,500?*

MS: Normally between the 1,500s, I try to keep them on a fairly challenging interval. If we go a set of as many as 5 by 1,500, what I'll do is descend the intervals. But, for the better 1,500 swimmers, we might descend the intervals perhaps from on 18 minutes to on 17:30, on 17:00, on 16:30—something like that—for some of our better ones.

CC: *Do you encourage the idea of active rests between swims?*

MS: Sometimes we encourage them to do active rest swimming, sometimes we don't because I think that occasionally it's good to do some quality work without a preliminary active rest in order to simulate the race situation.

CC: *You mentioned that you do negative splitting all the time. Do you try to teach them other kinds of pacing in case of unexpected tactical situations arising in the race?*

MS: I think it very important that a good distance swimmer has a bag of tricks, so to speak, a number of tactics that can be used. Therefore, I encourage my swimmers not to always swim the same tactics in every race so that they are not pegged as a certain type of swimmer. We actually do sets in which the swimmer goes out very fast at the beginning or working the middle of the distance or just working the end so that they can develop different tactics. Also, it's sometimes important in a 1,500 to practice sprinting for 200 meters or so to try to pull away from another swimmer or break another swimmer. These are things that need to be practiced in order for them to be performed well.

CC: *Do you teach them how to get the measure of their rivals? The kinds of things to look for, certain ploys to use so as to dominate the race?*

MS: I think education is very important, and that's why I always try to attend as many major championships as I can to observe other swimmers and learn how they swim their races and how they can be beaten. And I certainly try to educate my swimmers to the race tactics that they use. We always discuss before hand how the race will be swum and what they can do to perhaps upset the other swimmer in the middle of the race.

CC: *So you make a point of studying the rival swimmers, their split times, their personalities, their strengths, their weaknesses?*

MS: I think it's more important in distance swimming than anything else to know the other swimmers inside out and to know exactly how they swim—their races, their history, how they became successful, if they've had a bad race and why they had a bad race—because tactics play such a big important part of distance swimming. If a race is to become tactical, then you like your swimmer to be as educated as possible or as smart as possible. Murray Rose was probably the distance swimmer whom I respected the most for being a great tactician, and I like to try to teach my swimmers to be as tactical as possible.

CC: *One of the exciting things about the 1,500 is that it is a test of the whole person, not just your strength and endurance but also your generalship, your ability to apportion your energy, measure your reserves, distribute your energy evenly so that you've used the last just as you finish the race. What are your comments on the premise that the 1,500 is a test of the whole person?*

MS: I definitely believe that the 1,500 is a test of the whole person and, therefore, training is very important because the better you train, the tougher you become mentally, and you won't be scared of a tough situation. If the pain comes you won't be scared of it. You'll attack your race even harder and try to break through the pain barrier. Also, one of the reasons why we've been successful in developing tough distance swimmers is because we've developed a very strong training group, people who train together and do hard series and hard weight training together, and support each other and this gives them a lot of confidence.

CC: *Earlier, we were talking about tactics. Do you prefer any particular set of tactics—being in the lead or challenging closely, perhaps pushing a rival to go out faster than intended, breaking his back a little?*

MS: My preference would be for my swimmer to be in the lead over the first 500 and swim away from the field. Unfortunately, that doesn't always happen. I just always like to have the feeling that my swimmer is going to be the best over the last 500, and whatever the race strategy is, I want him to feel good enough over the first 1,000 to know that he can be very aggressive and on the offensive in the last 500.

CC: *If a swimmer is going to lead at the start, where would he begin to move away—just after the first 50?*

MS: Again, it's individual for each swimmer. The coach must know his swimmer, what his strengths and weaknesses are as well as knowing the field. In different races you have to make the move at different times, keeping in mind what's best for your swimmer and what would be the best strategy for defeating the rival swimmer.

CC: *What 1,500 swimmers impressed you before you developed Brian Goodell, your first great champion? And what did you learn from them?*

MS: Probably the other two swimmers who impressed me the most were Mike Burton and Rick de Mont. I studied the way they trained and also the training methods of their coaches, Sherm Chavoor and Don Swartz, and really learned a lot about race tactics. Rick de Mont was the swimmer who first got me interested in negative splitting and swimming strongly at the end.

Certainly, I also had a great deal of respect for Steven Holland and was lucky enough to have the opportunity of coaching him for a year. But, I think that Steven Holland, when he was with Laurie Lawrence, probably made the biggest breakthrough in the last 10 years in distance swimming. He brought the world record for 1,500 meters down from the high 15 minutes to the low 15 minutes. He was probably the swimmer, in the last 10 to 15 years, who improved the art of distance swimming more than anyone else.

CC: *Very few people have given him credit for that and, of course, it's quite justified. What do you think helped him to slice off those big chunks from the 1,500 time? Was it the result of a different approach to the event or his natural physiological aptitude?*

MS: Well, I think that it was probably a combination of both. I have never trained a swimmer

Rick de Mont and his coach Don Swartz. "Rick de Mont was the swimmer who first got me interested in negative splitting and swimming strongly at the end," said Schubert.

who had the aerobic capacity that Steve Holland possessed. He had very little speed but he did have the capacity to just keep going. Also, he was very tough mentally. I'll never forget the race at the first World Championships in Belgrade 1973, when he not only flipped at the 1,500 but also at the 1,600! He obviously had put himself into a mental trance and had just blocked out the field and was going to just keep swimming regardless! He was bound and determined to set a pace and stay within it and not let anyone else come close to him. That was one of the most incredible 1,500s I've ever seen!

CC: *Something similar to a runner's high. On occasions like Holland's great swim in Belgrade, you realize that the 1,500 is the real test of the whole person, the blue ribbon of swimming.*

MS: Absolutely! I had a lot of respect for Steve, and when Brian Goodell raced him in the Montreal Olympics, 1976, I was very aware of the fact that the way for him to beat Steve was for Brian to stay as close as he could and then for Brian to use his speed over the last 200. And that worked out to be a very successful tactic.

CC: *You mentioned Steve Holland's lack of speed. A swimmer who lacks speed really has to start out as fast as he can go at the beginning of a race and swim a very solid race. Do you think that Steve didn't do that in the Olympic final?*

MS: I think that Steve swam an excellent race in the Olympic final. I don't feel that the 1,500 was the best distance for Steve. The 1,500 isn't really and truly a total endurance race. It's not long enough. I think that Steve would have felt better in an hour's swim or something of that nature—something longer. Steve would be better by far than anyone else in the world in such an event but the 1,500, where you can use more speed and swim a little bit anaerobically at the end of the race, is an event that works very well for someone like Goodell or Salnikov who have speed and are also successful over distances like 400 meters.

CC: *George Haines has told me that he watched Salnikov from high in the stands and that,*

International Swimming Hall of Fame

Steve Holland (Australia). "When he was with Laurie Lawrence, Steve probably made the biggest breakthrough in distance swimming. He brought the world record down from the high 15 minutes to the low 15 minutes. I have never trained a swimmer who had the aerobic capacity that Steve Holland possessed," said Schubert.

"If you are looking at Salnikov, you're looking at Brian Goodell."

MS: Yes, there is a similarity between Brian Goodell and Salnikov, both physically and in the way that they swim the race. Salnikov likes negative splitting. He likes to use his speed at the end of the race. I think that's what makes him so dangerous. Certainly, one of the things that has been truly amazing about Salnikov is the way he has been able to dominate the world since 1980 and I have to give him a lot of credit for that.

CC: *To what do you attribute his dominance?*

MS: I think that he received great coaching from Igor Koshkin. I also feel that he has had every possible opportunity in the Soviet Union as far as training is concerned, and obviously he has great motivation, being a national hero. Basically, I think that he is very tough mentally and able to get himself ready for competition and, obviously, he has found ways to avoid the staleness that comes from the long, hard training required for swimming the 1,500 meters.

CC: *Which is a real factor one has to beware of . . .*

MS: Yes.

CC: *He seems to have had adequate competition in Europe to push him to those fine performances.*

MS: He has had a lot of competition right in his own club. Swimmers who are world ranked in distance events, and certainly some of the swimmers from Yugoslavia, like the Petric brothers, have given him challenge, some of the East German swimmers as well. Maybe that has been the problem in the United States these last few years; we haven't had enough people going fast enough to really challenge our best. It seems now that we are getting some young distance swimmers who are doing a better job, and we are starting to improve again.

CC: *If you have a whole group of these fast, tough kids and put them together in training—misery loves company—and they'll work until their eyes pop out!*

MS: Yes! Basically human beings push themselves only as hard as they need to do to win and, if you don't have the competition in the distance races, I don't think that you're going to get the top times. The kids are only going to swim fast enough to win. It's tough to push yourself to a truly great world-class performance if you are swimming against weaker competition.

CC: *Once the depth of participation starts to improve then so does the general standard and, in particular, the caliber of the athletes who emerge at the top. Now, I'm going to use your last statement as an opening to ask you this question. Do you think that Goodell could have beaten Salnikov had they both been at their physical peaks in the same era?*

MS: I think that Brian Goodell at his peak which was about 1976, probably had the ability to go just as fast as Salnikov is going now (1983). I don't know that he was in good enough shape or had trained hard enough in 1980 to beat him in the summer of 1980, but, of course, with the boycott being announced in January, there was a true lack of motivation, and I think that's probably what hurt his training that year.

CC: *It would have been a terrific race.*

MS: It's a tough comparison to make, but I do know that Goodell never lost in a head-to-head race with Salnikov. One time I remember was at UCLA when they swam a 1,650-yard race, and Goodell beat him by nearly 50 yards. So I know that Brian was a tough competitor and I have a lot of respect for Salnikov as well.

CC: *How do you foresee the 1,500 event developing in say the next four years or so?*

MS: You know that I would have predicted that we would have been under 14:45 by now. Unfortunately, the men's distance races haven't seemed to progress as quickly as perhaps we could have expected. One of the reasons is that when you get somebody like Salnikov doing so well for so many years, an aura develops around him, similar to the aura Tracey Caulkins seems to have had in the United States, and the other swimmers seem to think that they are unbeatable. Sometimes this seems to hold the event back a little bit. In the years 1976 to 1980, I think that this is what happened in American distance swimming because Goodell had developed this kind of aura. They couldn't beat him and so the times didn't seem to improve. If we can make the event more competitive and get four or five swimmers near the world record, then we could see some real breakthroughs.

❖ ❖ ❖

CECIL COLWIN DISCUSSES THE 1,500 WITH DON TALBOT

An interview at the author's home in 1984.

CC: *Would you agree that the 1,500-meter freestyle event is the blue ribbon of swimming?*

DT: As far as I'm concerned it is the blue ribbon of swimming. Certainly, I love the event, always have. I have a special admiration for the qualities of the 1,500 swimmer that goes beyond anything I may feel about successful swimmers in other events. I guess that these qualities are epitomized by swimmers such as Murray Rose, John Konrads, Bobby Windle, Mike Burton, and other great 1,500

swimmers whom I've seen do tremendous swims at major competitions such as the Olympics. They've received great ovations while standing on the podium after winning their events, simply for being tough guys. I must admit that I like a tough guy.

CC: *When you mention the ovation they receive, I've noticed that the winner of the 1,500 always seems to receive the greatest acclaim from the crowd.*

DT: I think that, if you were to do a survey through the crowd, you would find that the 1,500 swimmers are given the biggest ovation because people appreciate the amount of work and sheer courage that they've put into the sort of performance that have led them to victory. Certainly, I agree with you. I think that what does happen is that the true followers of swimming give the ovation. They are the initiated. The uninitiated are the people who recognize, say, the 100-meter swimmer as the fastest swimmer in the water.

CC: *Why is that so? What do you believe the 1,500-meter swimmer has that the others do not have?*

DT: Not only is he a tough guy, he has to work a lot harder and to me there's something special about a man who has to do that. And I'm not denigrating the 100-meter swimmer. He is gifted with speed and talent, but he has problems very different to those of the 1,500-meter swimmer, but I just happen to have a greater affinity for the 1,500 swimmer.

CC: *In addition to being a person who works harder, what other qualities do you look for in the potential 1,500 swimmer?*

DT: The first thing that I look for is that the swimmer has to like the event. Some swimmers will tell you that they like the event, but they don't swim as if they like the event. And I feel that it is this attitude that tells me, "Yes, this swimmer has a talent for 1,500 meters." There are many swimmers, competing in sprints and short events, generally, who have a talent for swimming the 1,500 meter, but they don't like the event. They are not psychologically oriented to it. Therefore, when the crunch really comes in the last 300 or 400 meters, they are going to fail. This does not mean to say that they can't be good 1,500-meter swimmers, but I'm talking about the great 1,500-meter swimmer.

I think that, after I've got the liking for the event out of the way, then I would say characteristics such as endurance, stroke technique, economy of stroke. These are the things that go toward it, and they are the finessing of the event, if you like. But I think that I've got to say . . . well, I don't have too many "characteristics," as you can hear.

CC: *What about being a strategic swimmer, assessing your rivals, planning and pacing your race accordingly?*

DT: I think that a great 1,500-meter swimmer, despite what a coach may say, and despite what others may say to him, will do these things intuitively. You don't need to tell them how to swim a 1,500 meter, they feel it. That doesn't mean to say that you can't help them and you can't guide them. Certainly, you can. But, when a decision has to be made to go or to lie back or to take it out hard or to do whatever, then the great 1,500 swimmers instinctively feel that.

CC: *It's interesting that you should say that because I'm thinking specifically of the 1976 Olympic 1,500 final in Montreal when Goodell won in world-record time. Compare that race with Mike Burton's greatest races in which he got out in front and, according to Sherm Chavoor, said in effect, "Catch me!" Sherm also said, "If you negative split, you get a negative swim! As you well remember, this was an exceptionally tactical race, several sets of individual tactics all going on at once. And, prior to the race, Bobby Hackett, had announced that he was going to break the world record at the 800-meter mark, trying to slow down the rest of the field. In the race Goodell lay back for a while and watched the field. In the light of what you've just said, do you think all this was wrong?*

DT: Well, I can't say it was wrong. Goodell won the event. After all, that's what we're all aiming to do.

CC: *You can't argue with success.*

DT: No, you can't.

CC: *Do you think that there is a tendency by many coaches to overcoach the 1,500-meter event?*

DT: I don't know what other coaches do. I can only say that I never attempted to do that. Anyway, I don't think I did. I always believe that in swimming any event a very large degree of decision has got to be left to the swimmer. I provide parameters, say, for a swimmer to operate within. I think that Goodell won that event in the way he thought best, and it may have been the way the coach thought best as well. He may have thought that this was the way in which he could beat the other swimmers in the event, particularly Steven Holland from Australia, whom I coached in his early years, and so I know a little bit about him. I might make the comment too that, with other coaches' kids, I really have 20/20 vision, particularly in the hindsight department. Having that sort of vision in foresight is very difficult, and I don't know what I would have advised in the same situation. But, I still believe that, despite what a coach says, a swimmer in the 1,500 event particularly, and almost any event, probably more in the 1,500 than any other event, will know how he is feeling and what he should be doing and make the decisions that are appropriate for him.

CC: *Judging from Goodell's interview with* Swimming World *shortly after the race finished, it is obvious that his effort in the Montreal 1,500 was largely intuitive. He lay back for the first 500 and then decided that he had better start to make his effort. He said that at one stage, he was becoming concerned about his ability to catch up.*

DT: Well, he might have said that, but he did catch them. Who is to know? If he had taken out the first 500 faster, then he may not have had the back end he wanted to have. It depends upon a lot of things. That may have been a characteristic of his swimming.

You see, Sherm's comment about negative split, negative swim may have been appropriate in one respect. I mean negative split swimmers can still win, but I would say that, if a swimmer wins in an event with a negative split, then he hasn't been against talent that is good enough to extend him. That's my belief. Somebody will beat the negative-split swimmer eventually, if he continues with that tactic blindly. I can't be a critic of Goodell and his swimming in Montreal. He's a great swimmer.

CC: *Neither was I inviting you to criticize him. I was merely seeking an objective comment.*

DT: I've got to go with the swimmer's decision, and, possibly, the coach's decision, too, to swim it that way. It was the right one, I think.

CC: *Let's talk about your career in coaching great 1,500 swimmers in which you've made a great contribution. Your first great 1,500 swimmer was John Konrads who came to the fore in the late 1950s. His best time was 17:11, wasn't it?*

DT: (laughing) Your memory's better than mine. Yes, it was something like that.

CC: *Did he improve when he went to the United States?*

DT: I don't know whether he did or not. As a swimmer he may not have. I feel that John didn't handle the American system well.

CC: *Why not?*

DT: I think it was partially culture shock. Particularly at that time, cultural differences between the United States and Australia were absolutely tremendous. They are not so big now. Australian swimmers going to the United States now do not have that problem. But, at that time, I think that the system of comradeship, team spirit—it was just foreign to the Australian way. In Australia, it was every swimmer for himself. And, having to meet certain deadlines, keep grade point averages, even though John was a good student academically, being expected to produce every week in a dual-meet situation was something he just wasn't used to.

CC: *He did win the 500 and 1,650 in the NCAA Championships.*

DT: Yes. He swam very well, but I feel that he didn't show his best in the States. Some Australian swimmers did, but there were other Australians at that time who didn't either. In fact, the only Australian swimmer in that era who really did great was Murray Rose.

There were no others who did very, very well.

CC: *Did Murray Rose improve his time in the States?*

DT: I think that Murray Rose did, but I'm not sure.

CC: *Do you think that Murray Rose contributed to the Americans' knowledge of 1,500 swimming?*

DT: I think that he contributed to the world's knowledge of 1,500 swimming. Certainly, he has been credited with being a great tactician. Certainly, a great swimmer, many people classify him as being the greatest 1,500 swimmer ever. I would qualify that by saying . . .

CC: *Certainly the most colorful!*

DT: Certainly colorful and certainly one of the most . . . well, he certainly knew how to swim the event. While he met my measure of being a great 1,500 swimmer in that he liked the event, I think that he liked the event because he could play with it and achieve his ends. When Murray Rose swam the 1,500, it was a cat-and-mouse swim always, I felt. I don't think we ever saw the best of Murray Rose either. But I think that about a number of other swimmers as well. I feel that the U.S. did learn a lot from him, watching Murray Rose swim. He showed that in the 1,500 meter, if you were fit, it didn't really matter how you swam the event. And that's why, getting back to Goodell's swim, I believe that Goodell's swim was also a cat-and-mouse swim, and he knew what he was doing. Murray Rose always knew what he was doing. Very seldom, when I saw Murray Rose swim, did I feel that he didn't know where he was or what he was going to do.

CC: *Candidly, I was a little disappointed to hear you say that the best 1,500 swimmers are intuitive because one of the reasons I like the 1,500 race is because of the chess factor—it's like playing chess.*

DT: (laughing) Well, yes, it is, from the swimmer's point of view. We like to think that we contribute an awful lot to the plan, the technique, and strategy of the race, and, to a certain degree, we do. But I've seen swimmers go in—I've had swimmers of mine go in and completely ignore what I've said and win the

Murray Rose. "He showed that in the 1,500 meters, if you were fit, it didn't really matter how you swam the event. Murray Rose always knew what he was doing. Very seldom when I saw Murray swim did I feel he didn't know were he was or what he was going to do," said Talbot.

event! And, by the same token, I've had them go in and completely ignore what I've said and lose the event.

CC: *Give me two examples.*

DT: (laughing) No! No! All right, I think that probably the best example was in Tokyo at the 1964 Olympics—not with Bobby Windle who won the event, but with Alan Wood who was third. Alan certainly didn't swim the event as I wanted him to do, and had he done so, I felt that he might have been able to win the event. His swim was too tentative. He had been swimming very well. I had asked him to go out much harder. He already had a third place medal for the 400-meter freestyle in his hand at that stage. I think that he didn't swim that 1,500 as confidently as I wanted him to do, and so I feel he only ended up with the bronze where he could have had the gold.

CC: *The other example?*

DT: John Konrads, in only a minor swim, a state championship in New South Wales, where I

asked him to do something, to go out at a certain speed, he was telling me that he didn't think that he could do that. He didn't do it.

CC: *He went faster?*

DT: Yes, and he broke the world record. Oh, well! That was that! It made me a good coach.

CC: *Coming back to Bobby Windle—had Roy Saari been in the 1964 Olympic 1,500, do you think Windle still would have won?*

DT: I think that Bobby Windle would have still won. Bob Windle was a racer. In fact, you may not recall this, but he was eliminated from the 400-meter freestyle at that Olympics because he had to time trial. He drew the first heat and again, tactically, he swam the race wrongly, and I've got to take the blame for that myself. He listened to me, and he shouldn't have done!

I told him to win the event and not worry too much about the speed and he missed qualifying by a tenth of a second. I believe that, if he had been in the 400 final, he really would have frightened the daylights out of Schollander. But I don't want to take anything from Schollander, but certainly, Bobby Windle wasn't there. Alan Wood was the bronze medal winner, and Alan could not see Bob Windle at all over 400 freestyle.

CC: *You're an exception to the saying that: "You hear all about a coach's successes, but you rarely hear about his failures!" You're not scared about talking about your failures as well! Failure is the name you give experience.*

DT: They're the awful truths! (laughing) And, not only that, I didn't look at a failure as a reflection on your ability to coach. I think, just as you were saying, failure to me was always a learning experience. I won't do that next time. I'll do this or I'll try this approach. And for me that always worked, and I've taken that approach with all the swimmers, but I don't like to talk about failures either. However, I hope that I'm experienced enough to know that any success you have, particularly with any great swimmer, is because you're darned lucky, and Counsilman was probably the first one in the world to make that claim. I agree with him wholeheartedly. You're lucky to get a Windle. You're lucky to get a Konrads.

CC: *George Haines has said the same thing, and other coaches, too! Coming back to Murray Rose, Sherm Chavoor said to me that, if he had coached Murray, he would have been an even greater swimmer because he wouldn't have allowed him to be so tactical.*

DT: You know that I can coach someone else's kids much better than I can coach my own, and I don't mean that to be derogatory of Sherm. I think that he is right in what he feels. The truth of the matter is that this may not have been the case. I think that the 1,500 meter, more than any event, results in a very significant rapport developing between coach and swimmer. The rapport that Sam Herford had with Murray Rose was something that I believe no other man probably could have developed with this swimmer. If a different approach had been applied, it might not have worked.

CC: *Murray Rose, competing in a masters event recently, swam faster than he did in his competitive heyday.*

DT: Yes, that was darned good!

CC: *Have you studied the swimming of Vladimir Salnikov?*

DT: Only from a distance, but I have read some of the workouts that he has done and watched him swim on two or three occasions, and I'm terribly impressed.

CC: *Why?*

DT: Sherm would love to coach the guy because he goes out from the start.

CC: *Each 400 under four minutes . . .*

DT: I might add that any coach would like to coach him. I feel that he is showing himself probably to be the greatest 1,500 swimmer who ever lived. He has completely dominated 1,500 swimming for two or three years, like no other 1,500 swimmer has done.

CC: *According to Joe Bernal, Salnikov has proved that the 1,500 swimmer can have longevity in the event.*

DT: Yes, that's right, and particularly in the American system, that's not accepted, but it is in the Australian system.

CC: *Mark Schubert said to me that Salnikov has created an aura around himself of being unbeatable, not intentionally so, but an aura does exist around him in the same way that an aura existed around Brian Goodell of being unbeatable. Where do we go from there?*

DT: Well, I think that the first swimmer who realizes that Salnikov is beatable will beat him.

CC: *He has been beaten a couple of times by Jeff Float, a Sherm Chavoor protégé, and Boric Petric of Yugoslavia.*

DT: Yes, but I mean when the chips are down. When he is fully prepared and ready, they

John Konrads (Australia), 1,500-meter freestyle Olympic champion in Rome, 1960.

Bob Windle (Australia), 1,500-meter freestyle Olympic Champion, Tokyo, 1964.

won't beat him. But, when they realize that he can be beaten under equal conditions of preparation—someone believes that he can be beaten. You see Steven Holland had that aura but he was beaten eventually and he was beaten at a critical time.

CC: *Steve Holland probably did more for the 1,500 than any other swimmer in terms of time improvement over the distance.*

DT: Yes, maybe he did, although John Konrads really improved the 1,500-meter record dramatically over the space of a very few months. Getting back to the Salnikov aura, I think that all great athletes create that aura. In fact . . .

CC: *They propagate it.*

DT: Yes, and unconsciously a great swimmer capitalizes on that. Murray Rose had an aura about him and certainly Dawn Fraser too in the 100 freestyle.

CC: *Sherm Chavoor said that Mike Burton used to feel the pain terribly and so Sherm told him, "Don't let them see that you're puffing hard. Wait until you're out of sight in the dressing room."*

DT: That's right, and I agree with that, and I feel that this is why many coaches make the comment that those people hurt the sport. In one way they do. I can't contribute to the fact as to why they do but, in one way they do, because people say, "I can never beat Salnikov. He's too good."

CC: *Do you think that Salnikov is so far ahead because he is so superior physiologically? Or is it just that he has done the work to achieve superior adaptation?*

DT: I don't believe that physiologically . . .

CC: *Such great differences exist . . .*

DT: The differences exist, obviously, but they said that about Konrads, and look how they've knocked the daylights out of his times. And, certainly, 10 years from now, we'll look at Salnikov's times and say, "Huh!" Physiologically he probably does have something. He is also operating in a period within a nation that is very, very advanced, I believe, with the sport science support of the athlete. In North America, we virtually do nothing. We talk a lot about it but we don't do it.

CC: *In track and field, the Soviets have been very advanced for a long, long time.*

DT: Yes, yes. And I think that is happening there in swimming. So who knows what they are doing!? What about physical strength and development? What about the strategies of swimming the event? All of those things, I think, are pretty advanced there, and I think that Salnikov is probably maximizing his potential to say 98 percent whereas the rest of the world achieves say 90 percent of potential. And I think that this is probably making him a great swimmer. Yes, he may be superior, and certainly, he is superior as far as I'm concerned because he appears to like the event any way. That makes him superior in my opinion.

CC: *Do you see any swimmers in North America, or elsewhere in the world, of whom your instinct as a coach tells you could possibly develop into rivals to Salnikov?*

DT: Just straight out, no. But, remember that I'm not coaching on the deck now, and when you're not on the deck coaching, I think that you lose touch with the fine honing of an athlete and the critical points that indicate to you that a swimmer may have great potential. You know the way a swimmer handles workouts, the way he reacts when he is obviously overtired. When he stresses himself, how does he finish his event? What sort of feedback? How does he talk to you when he is in those stress conditions? What is his capacity to handle work? Until you work with an athlete, you can't tell that. How does he learn when you talk to him about technique? Does he listen to you? Is he a fairly tractable sort of man? These are factors that a coach measures. So I can't tell you, but if you spoke to some of the other coaches, they might say that they have people who could challenge Salnikov.

CC: *Do you think that there has been any great advance in the training of the 1,500 swimmer?*

DT: Personally, I think no, although some people may want to argue with that.

CC: *Do you think that there is a greater emphasis on the pace?*

DT: I think that there is a greater understanding of pace. When you begin to talk about lactate thresholds, then I think that you are really getting down and measuring better whether or not you are actually working aerobically, whether or not you are working to the capacity of the swimmer. So I think that there have been big improvements in that direction, but at this stage, this isn't even available to every coach, even though we've been talking about it for a while. In fact, very few coaches have access to lactate testing on deck in swimming programs when they are needed.

Generally, the programs that I see are the same as they ever were. I think that, psychologically, the preparation of the athlete now is much better. There are many more sports psychologists around who are talking to the athletes on how to think about their events and this has a big application to the middle-distance and the distance swimmer. A coach always has to be a psychologist. Even when John Konrads started, we talked about these sorts of things but we did it then by gut feeling. Now there are certain measures that can be talked about and practiced to improve performance and they are known pretty well by every good 1,500-meter swimmer. In these areas there has been improvement.

CC: *Elaborate on these a little.*

DT: I'm talking about imagery, seeing yourself swimming.

CC: *Envisaging a fatigue state . . .*

DT: That sort of thing. In other words you are mentally preparing yourself for what happens. Therefore, you are building a defense against it happening and the progression into the event is not so severe upon the athlete. It doesn't come as a shock.

Coach Don Talbot with two of his Olympic gold medalists. On the right is Bob Windle, who won the 1,500 meter in Tokyo (1964), and in the center is Brad Cooper, winner of the 400 meter in Munich (1972). Cooper's gold came after the disqualification of the man who touched first, Rick de Mont (USA). "I think that a great 1,500-meter swimmer, despite what a coach may say and despite what others may say to him, will do the right things intuitively," said Talbot.

CC: *Today's swimmers know more about what is happening to their bodies when they exercise and when they experience pain, fatigue, and learn to endure the torment induced.*

DT: It's a little like going to a dentist who says, "I'm going to do this next and you'll feel this." He prepares you for it. But, once upon a time, they just jabbed you and you leaped out of the chair because you weren't aware of what was going to happen.

CC: *What about the use of psychology to lower the so-called time barriers?*

DT: What I really believe is that we impose psychological limits. I even believe that now concerning Salnikov's performances. He has probably reached his psychological limit. He may go a little bit faster. We want somebody now who doesn't see Salnikov's performances as a psychological limit, to push himself through it. And he will then do the physiological preparation and testing, etcetera, that will help him achieve a better performance.

✧ ✧ ✧

WILL "THE OLD SWIMMING FACTORY" PRODUCE AN OLYMPIC CHAMPION?

Vic Centre's Daniel Kowalski may turn out to be the main contender for the 1,500 gold in Atlanta.

A week before the 1996 Australian Olympic trials in Sydney, I returned to Melbourne where I coached in the early 1970s. On Batman Avenue, the traditional center of swimming in Melbourne, I came to the Olympic Pool, where, in 1956, Australian swimmers had reestablished world ascendancy in their first at-home Olympics. There, for one exciting and dramatic week, bronzed young athletes such as Dawn Fraser, Murray Rose, and Jon Hendricks, fresh from their training camp in Townsville, Northern Queensland, brought the crowds to their feet with cheers that raised the rafters.

Alas, what was once a shrine to true Olympic endeavor has been vandalized over the years, and is now converted to an exhibition hall. The giant stadium, where thousands lined up daily to see the training sessions of Australia's greatest team ever, is now a sad, gaunt sight.

Across the road from the old Olympic Stadium is the Vic Centre, formerly the open-air Beaurepaire Pool, named after Sir Frank Beaurepaire, the man mainly responsible for bringing the 1956 Olympics to Melbourne, and whose outstanding swimming career lasted a quarter century (1906 to 1930).

Because Melbourne's climate is notorious for having four seasons in a day, most of Melbourne's swimming pools are built indoors. Before leaving for the national championships, we coaches would bring our swimmers to Beaurepaire for a few outdoor sessions to sample the fresh air.

The old pool is now housed indoors, and it still wouldn't win architectural awards. Not by chance is the Vic Centre known as "The Swimming Factory"; it is strictly utilitarian, a place plainly planned for making swimmers through industrious effort.

The kindest thing one can say about the Beaurepaire Pool, in its new guise as the Vic Centre, is that it serves its purpose and is a tribute to the Australian gift for ingenuity. Along the walls and ceilings of the pool, fat, brightly colored ventilation tubes lend a surreal effect.

"Where do I find Bill Nelson?" I asked. "Up those steps on the other side of the pool," said my guide. High in the air, I saw the coach's office, a large box attached to the far side wall, looking for all the world like an oversized dovecote.

Access to the office is by climbing three flights of steep iron steps. Carrying a heavy bag and rapidly approaching anaerobic threshold, I finally made it to the coach's roof-top eyrie. Seated in a neat office, complete with computers and training records, sat Coach Bill Nelson and his young assistant, Robert Iannazzo.

Daniel Kowalski

Nelson told me that he had coached Daniel Kowalski since November 1994, but had first met him at the Australian Institute of Sport in 1990, when Nelson and David Pyne, the Institute's head physiologist, had conducted a national talent identification program.

"At that stage, Daniel was a fairly good freestyler, and also a good backstroker, and 200 fly swimmer with good technique. He already had an excellent physique and a fine mental attitude. He was all set for a great career.

"Because it was only a 7-day camp and Daniel was one of a group of about 23 swimmers, there wasn't time to form in-depth opinions. We had a brief opportunity to talk about different things, but we never had the chance to really get to know the swimmers as well as we needed to. But we kept in touch with Daniel, as we did with all the kids who came to the camp."

At the 1994 World Championships in Rome, Don Talbot told Nelson that Daniel Kowalski wanted to move to Melbourne to train with him.

Nelson said that, on moving to Melbourne, he had resigned himself to the fact that it was going to take a while for him to put swimmers on the national team. "So I was delighted by the fact that Daniel wanted to come to Melbourne. But, it was a sensitive situation because when you are on a national team, you have the responsibility to do the right thing by the coach who is not there, and to look after the swimmers to the best of your ability.

"When Don asked me to meet Daniel, I did so, and briefly said to him, 'I am here to do a job, and you are here to do a job. When you get home, you think about it. Then, if you still want to go ahead, give me a call.' And I left it at that.

"When I returned home, Daniel rang up and said that it was something he wanted to do. I suppose the hardest thing for someone in that situation was to decide what he was going to do, and where he was going to live. So I spoke to my wife, and she said that Daniel was welcome to stay with us until he was ready to move on.

"Kowalski has now stayed with the Nelson family for 18 months. He gets on very well with my three children, Jae, Ele, and Kye. He gets on well with my wife, Joanne. We really don't have too many problems mixing the swimming side of it with the family life at home. I try to give him his space, and he knows to give me mine. And it works out well. He likes to be in a family setting. I know his parents. They are a tight family; for him to be happy he really had to be in a family environment."

Fine Stroke Technician

Daniel Kowalski is a polished stroke technician. He must be one of the easiest swimmers in the world today. There is no visible effort in his stroke. Visible effort is unproductive effort; it's effort the swimmer uses against himself.

With typical understatement, Nelson says, "Daniel's got a good technique. Like everyone else, sometimes he'll get a little bit lazy on a few things, but he's one of those people who wants to be a student of the sport. There's nothing that he wants to leave to chance. He leaves no stone unturned. So if I say something to him, I know it won't go in one ear and out the other. He'll take it in, and do his best to do it.

Daniel Kowalski is an intelligent young man, mature for his age. I heard that Daniel had won additional fame as a TV quiz kid, and I asked Nelson to comment on this.

"Daniel went on this nationally televised quiz show, and ended up winning it. He was pretty happy because he beat some politicians and media personalities. This was a different sort of pressure. It also gave him the opportunity to feel good about himself. If swimmers feel good about themselves, then they'll swim fast.

"You're not just trying to mature them as swimmers, but you're also trying to mature them as people. The thing about international sport is that it is all about pressure, being able to withstand it, being able to apply it."

Training Methods

Nelson said that the type of training, the stroke mechanics, and the emphases placed on his swimmers are probably not much different from anyone else's. "We try to cover the full spectrum of the heart rate range, and the lactate range, and our program is carefully planned and methodical. But, at the same time, if I think something needs to be changed, then I'll change it on the day.

"Obviously, the key sets for Daniel are similar to those for any other distance swimmers; his overdistance work, and certainly his MVO_2 and threshold work are the key themes. Kowalski is fortunate in that he has natural speed, and can handle a variety of training without losing his speed. About two or three times a week, he tries to do a certain amount of work, about 3,000 meters, as close to race pace as possible."

Nelson divides the program into four-week periods. "Basically, I have an endurance week, a quality week, a sprint week, and an adaptation week. These four weeks are cycled into a format depending on the individual group, and their responses. I usually work three weeks on and one week off, every fourth week being an adaptation week.

"The off-week is an adaptation week devoted to recovery. What I usually do is keep the main sets at the same intensity, but half the usual distance. So, if we're going 3,000 meters of MVO_2 work, we'll come back to 1,600 or 2,000 meters during that week. I allow the body to just catch up after what it has been through, but, at the same time, not allow it to go into a full rest state. Our MVO_2 work varies between each of the individual groups, and it also depends on each individual swimmer."

Nelson said that Daniel Kowalski would do something like 30 x 100 on 1:30, and he would hold anywhere from high 57s to low 58s. His heart would reach about 20 below his maximum, which is in the 172 to 176 range.

The Coal Miner's Son

Bill Nelson's father was a coal miner, and so was his father before him. From an early age, Nelson took it for granted that he would spend his life at the coal face. At 16, he left school and was apprenticed by the Australian Miners' Federation. For 4 years, he worked 7 hours a day at the coal face, 4 kilometers below ground. "Working in a mine taught me the value of team work. The older guys drummed this into me," says Nelson.

Like many young Australians, Nelson soon heard the siren song of the surf. He spent the next two years traveling around Australia riding a surfboard on the professional circuit.

Nelson became keen on coaching swimming when teaching a small group of kids at a school near his home in Miyuna Bay, New South Wales. This led to a job as assistant to Eric Arnold from 1983 to 1987, when he moved to Tamworth to become the town's first professional coach.

He stayed there for only 12 months because "the people there didn't understand the need to pay a professional for his work. With a wife and a young son to support, the situation wasn't financially viable. Although not my most rewarding experience, it provided an insight into dealing with people, and how, when things don't go their way, how callous and rude swimming parents can be."

Nelson returned to work in Eric Arnold's program in preparation for the 1988 Olympics. "We had some kids from Singapore who made their national team for the Olympics, and Donna Proctor, a 400 medley swimmer, made the Australian team. She was more Eric's pupil than mine; I was his assistant coach."

In 1988, Bill Nelson was appointed assistant coach to Bill Sweetenham at the Australian Institute of Sport in Canberra. When Sweetenham left for Hong Kong in 1991 Nelson took over Sweetenham's part of the program, until after the World Championships in 1994, when he moved to Melbourne to be head coach at the Vic Centre Club.

"Especially at Kowalski's level of achievement, every workout is highly individualized," says Nelson. "The whole thing with coaching is that it is highly individual. I hand out my training plan to anyone who wants a copy of it, because I don't think that drawing up a schedule represents the art of coaching. It's the interpretation of that plan that counts, and how you convince the swimmers with what you want to do."

Nelson believes that the coach has to build the training program around each individual swimmer. "Don't try to put a swimmer into the training program. Plan the program around the swimmer. That becomes a difficult thing to do in any program when you have a big team. But that's the art of coaching. It is this that distinguishes people who really want to coach from those who only do it half-heartedly, with insufficient regard for each individual swimmer."

In Nelson's experience each swimmer has favorite workout sets which may vary with time. They find the type of workout that really works for them. This provides a yardstick to measure progress by repeating the same type of set on another occasion.

For example, at the end of a training session, after seven kilometers of freestyle and separate kicking, Kowalski may do three 200-meter swims in a descending set of 1:56.2, 1:55.2, and 1:53.5.

"The key is to do the work that you know is going to stimulate the response you want, but, at the same time, the workout must be put across in a way that will challenge each swimmer. It's got to be enjoyable for them to meet those challenges, and the stimulus you're trying to give to the swimmer comes in a variety of ways. It's a matter of finding those different ways."

I commented on the rivalry between Daniel Kowalski and Kieren Perkins. Nelson said, "They respect each other, and, in fact, Daniels said, after Perkins had swum his way into the Australian team, that Perkins had shown a lot of character."

Nelson says that there's an interesting relationship between Kieren Perkins and Daniel

Kowalski, and even Glen Houseman. "I think it has been built up over a period of time, and it carries over into Daniel's swimming, how he handles himself leading up to the meet, during the meet, and after the meet. It says a lot about Daniel's character."

"This probably sounds strange, but going into the 1,500 at the Olympic trials, Daniel was wishing that Kieren would also be on the team. He knows that, for Australia to be successful at the Olympics, Kieren has got to be a vital part of that team, and Kieren has got to be swimming well.

"But, at the same time, Daniel knew that he had to go out and do the things I set him to do. Although the time wasn't what I wanted, and what Kieren and Daniel, or John Carew wanted, as I've said before, it provided a great race. I don't think that anywhere in the world there would have been a better 1,500 race than what those three guys did on Saturday night. That caliber of tough, hard racing has got to help us as we go into the Olympics."

A Test of the Whole Person

"It's OK to have a closely contested race over a 100, a 200, or even a 400, but over 1,500 it is a test of the whole person. And it shows a great insight into what those two guys are about. So there were some very positive things that came out of that race. It stood both of them in good stead, leading up to Atlanta in 12 week's time."

Nelson said that many people look upon swimming as an individual sport, but it's only individual when they stand on the blocks. "You must create a team environment, and it must be conducive to excellence. This is important to me as a coach because it helps everyone to swim to the best of their ability."

Asked if Daniel would stay with the 1,500, or move down to the 400, Nelson said that Kowalski would stay with the 1,500. "He loves the 1,500. When you look at the times on the board, there are certainly people who are closing the gap, but, by the same token, Daniel hasn't reached the level that he wants to achieve. And he certainly hasn't reached what I think him capable of doing."

Nelson said that Kurt Eldridge looks a good prospect. "Kurt has been around for quite a while. He spent time at Cal Berkeley with Nort Thornton,

and then came back to Australia. He is a very, very tough competitor. There are kids such as Grant Hackett, the 15-year-old, who went a 15:30.63. There are a few kids like them knocking on the door, and that's good for our sport."

Nelson continued, "After Atlanta, Kowalski, who has only just turned 20, is keen to go to the World Short Course Championships, and, from there, he is at an age when Sydney 2000 certainly is not out of the question."

"Daniel is very keen to keep going, and for him, his swimming has entered a new era. He is enjoying his swimming more. He accepts the challenges. He has always accepted challenges, but I think he is more interested in the challenges. It's not a case of 'I've got to do this because it's being thrown at me.' He tries to really be part of what is happening, and if you've got someone like that, who is open-minded, then the future looks good. Daniel has put in the hard work, and he is about to reap his rewards."

❖ ❖ ❖

SWIMMING THE 1,500 OUT FAST

John Carew was looking for a swimmer to prove a pet theory; then Kieren Perkins, a skinny 8-year-old, came along.

Coach John Carew of Indooroopilly, Queensland, nursed a notion that the ideal 1,500 swimmer should be able to swim fast from the start and change the pace at will.

Carew's interest in the 1,500-meter event stemmed from his friendship with Sam Herford, who coached Murray Rose, one of the greatest tactical 1,500 swimmers of all time. "Sam taught me a lot about stroking and coaching in general. I learned a great deal about Murray Rose's technique, and I liked the concept of relaxation within the stroke," says Carew.

Back in the 1970s Carew coached Stephen Holland as a young lad. Under Laurie Lawrence, Holland later went on to win World and Commonwealth Championships, finish second in the 1976 Olympic 1,500 meter, and break 12 world records. "Steve was one of the greatest, but he had one weakness. Although a tough, courageous athlete, he lacked early speed. In those days, the 1,500 swimmer would go out slowly for the first 100, and then race for 1,400. Steve couldn't change to a six-beat kick in the same fashion as Murray Rose. Steve had a higher body position and a faster stroke rating than Murray Rose, and could hold a fast, steady pace throughout, but he couldn't shift gears."

Over the years, Carew would say to his wife, "If only I had another chance to coach a swimmer with the ability to swim the 1,500. This time I'd make sure to teach him to go out fast." For nearly two decades, Carew sought a talented youngster to prove his pet theory. Then, one day, malleable material arrived at Carew's small indoor pool in the unlikely form of a skinny eight-year-old boy.

"When I first saw Kieren Perkins, he wasn't a good specimen at all. He wasn't tall. He looked undernourished, actually. He was down on one shoulder, and he was fatter on one side of his body than the other. But he was a good kid, a willing kid, and I wanted to help him. He didn't show any promise at all until he was 13."

Changing the Pace

At 13, Carew introduced Kieren Perkins to distance swimming. "I tailored Kieren's stroking to a faster rating, brought him to a higher body position in the water, and increased his body roll a little, but still kept his head fairly low."

Carew developed Perkins's ability to go out at a set speed, and then maintain it. Carew came in for more than a little criticism because he insisted on Kieren swimming the race fast from the start. "Everybody said I was doing the wrong thing," he said.

Carew taught Perkins to change pace by changing both his arm timing and kicking cadence. "I taught him to change up from a two-beat to a six-beat kick, and then down again to a two-beat, until he learned to change pace as needed. Of course, you know the results of that. Suddenly, the days of swimming the 1,500 at one pace were over. I attribute Kieren's success in large measure to his ability to change pace. Kieren goes out from the start and he just keeps going."

Timing the Arms

Carew says that Perkins changes both stroke length and timing during the course of a race. In this way, the triceps muscles don't become too fatigued by constantly using a long push backward.

Carew said, "Timing refers to the position of the pulling hand when the other hand enters. When Kieren is doing a two-beat kick, he advances his timing by increasing the amount of overlap between his arms so that his hands are brought closer together in front of his body. When Kieren sprints and switches to a six-beat kick, he retards his timing by bringing the pulling hand further back before the other hand enters. When his right hand enters, his left hand will be level with his shoulder. This is the timing that Dawn Fraser used when sprinting. Arm timing is what I call "the swimmer's gear box." Distance swimmers use advanced timing, while middle-distance swimmers use semi-advanced timing. Two hundred meter swimmers use a timing between middle distance and sprint timing. One hundred meter swimmers use a retarded timing."

Timing the Kick

Kieren Perkins concentrates on relaxing within his stroke. "When his right hand, for example, pushes backward, he kicks downward with his right foot, and allows the other side of the body to relax completely." Carew says he has seen swimmers who pushed back with one hand, but kicked down on the opposite side of the body. "Bobby Windle, who was one of our great distance swimmers, did this. But I don't like it because it destroys your hip position which is most important to forward movement.

"Kieren's shoulders probably roll about 50 degrees, and his hips roll about 30 degrees. However, I think he should have about the same hip roll as he has shoulder roll. Getting the hips into place steadies the body for the pull.

"When Kieren does a two-beat kick, he floats his legs and crosses his ankles over as the body rolls to the other side. It's really a two-beat kick with a crossover."

Early Progress

Kieren Perkins first came to national notice at the age of 13, when Carew entered him in the Queensland 400 Meter Championship. Carew said, "I trained him like a distance swimmer for this event, and he went 4:09 in a 50-meter pool. Up to this point, he hadn't shown anything at all. This was in 1987, and it was the first race that he won. It was very good, and I was very pleased with that."

Carew believes strongly in the value of stroke drills. "I cannot see the wisdom of training and conditioning swimmers who will never reach full potential because of inferior technique. I can't emphasize enough how stroke drills aid a swimmer to get the feel of the water and set up a correct stroke pattern. For example, we practice sculling drills once a week during the season, and once a day in the tapering period."

Carew said that Kieren had developed a good technique by the time he was 14, but his speed was nonexistent. "He couldn't break 30 seconds for 50 meters. To increase his speed, I set short programs of 5 kilometers duration which emphasized quality speed work. Half of his workouts were in my 20-meter pool at Indooroopily, and the remaining sessions were in one of the only two heated Olympic-sized pools in Brisbane.

"The total distance per session covered by Kieren Perkins was increased by one kilometer each year. The aim was to train at race pace, and faster, as often as possible, the goal being to teach the body to buffer lactate and hold glycogen stores."

Example:

1st year—5 km per session, 55 km per week

2nd year—6 km per session, 66 km per week

3rd year—7 km per session, 77 km per week

4th year—8 km per session, 88 km per week

Heart Rate Sets

Carew says that Kieren's maximum heart rate is 180 beats per minute, and when he is fit, his resting heart rate is 38 beats per minute. His heart rate sets range in distance from 1,200 meters in the early season to 3,000 meters in the last 12-week cycle.

"While doing heart rate sets, swimmers should aim for a consistent 10 beats below the maximum heart rate. A period of 2 seasons is needed for physiological gains to occur. Sprint swimmers should do 2 heart rate sets per week over a total distance of 2,000 meters. Distance to middle-distance swimmers should do 3 heart rate sets per

week over a total distance of up to 3,000 meters for the 1,500-meter swimmers.

"The use of heart rate monitors is essential for the accuracy of these sets," said Carew. "The Treffene model in my opinion is the best. Test sets should be organized once a month. From these the coach is able to monitor fitness gains."

Example of Perkins' Heart Rate Set

Time	H/R	Time	H/R
:58.1	160	:59.3	130
:57.8	157		
:58.5	167	:58.8	143
:58.2	155		
:58.9	167	:58.2	153
:57.9	164		
:58.2	167	:58.5	150
:58.5	157		
:58.0	168	:58.3	159
:58.4	162		
:58.2	166	:58.0	155
:58.4	163		
:58.5	163	:58.0	145
:58.4	160		
:58.1	167	:58.4	159
:58.8	166		
:58.4	168	:58.2	164
:58.8	161		
:57.6	171	:57.6	162

Going Out Fast

When Carew first tried to make Perkins go out fast in the 1,500, he would lose his stroke rhythm because he couldn't hold the pace. "But we persevered, and at age 15 he went 15:48, and he made the Australian team for the Commonwealth Games in Christchurch."

Once again, Carew was the butt of much joking when he maintained that Kieren would go under 15 minutes. "I came out and made this statement, and people thought there was something wrong with me, but I knew he could do it. I could just about estimate what time he would do. He finished up going 14:58.

"Kieren will tell you this himself. I've been able to tell him, within a second, what time he will swim, every time he has broken a world record. When Kieren swims certain times during the taper, I can correlate these closely to what he will do in competition. You see, I think he would have swum a 14:30 plus, 14:38, 14:39, in Rome, but he disobeyed my instructions at the Commonwealth Games in Victoria. I asked him to go out and break the world 800 record, which I knew he could do."

Carew didn't want Perkins to break the world 1,500 mark in this race. "But as he went through, and knew he had broken the world 800 record, he just kept going. I can't blame him for this, I suppose, but the effect of the swim tore him down. I couldn't give him the required work between the Victoria meet and the World Championships in Rome. There were only about five weeks between the two meets. So we got the 400-meter record instead. When he swims two fast 1,500s within such a short time, his body really feels the effects.

"A top 1,500 swimmer should only go for a fast time about twice a year at the most. The 1,500 really tears Kieren down. This is because I don't permit Kieren to touch weights; I only allow him to use cords."

Carew says that, after the Commonwealth Games in Victoria, it took Roger Fitzgerald, the team physiotherapist, one week to get Kieren's body back into shape again. "That's how much effort he puts into it. After swimming that 14:50 in the 1,500 against Hoffmann in the World Championships at Perth, Kieren didn't eat for three days. He was sort of torn down, and didn't want to eat. He puts that much effort into it that it tears him down."

Pace and Strategy

Carew says that Kieren Perkins is probably one of the best athletes he has ever seen for focusing. "He can stand up on the block, and I'll tell him the plan, whatever it is: 'You've got to go through the 150 in so-and-so, and you've got to go through the 400 and the 800 in so-and-so,' and he'll focus on that.

"Kieren wouldn't know who was in the race with him because I've always taught him that way. I feel that, if you start thinking about other people, then you've lost the plan. You're in there to do a job. You're in there to swim the time. So you don't want to know who's in the race with you."

Carew works on teaching concentration. "Kieren is very good at it. He just relaxes and thinks about what he has to do. What time he's going to go through in. If we are going to have a go, I never talk to him about it a week or two weeks before. I don't give him time to get nervous about it. I don't tell him what I have in mind until just before the race. I always give him his instructions just as he goes into the marshaling area. If I say 'go for it,' he knows that I just want him to swim to win.

"Kieren doesn't need a lot of time to psych up. I just say, 'I want you to go through in this time. I want you to be through the 400 in this time. I want you to be through the 800 in this time.' So he'll get up on the block, and he won't know who else is there. He wouldn't know who is in the race with him. It wouldn't even worry him. He has his plan, and he can really focus on that plan. He's nearly a complete sportsman, I feel."

Kieren's a Racer

What does Perkins think about during the less than 15 minutes he usually takes to cover the 1,500?

Carew says, "Well, he really focuses on what he has to do: his stroke, his turns, and, of course, he's got to focus to push himself through the pain barrier, which he can do."

Asked if he ever spoke to Perkins about the pain barrier, Carew said, "No, no, I don't discuss things like that with him. Except at the Olympic trials last week, as he was going out on the deck, I said to him, 'I want you to take it out the way you normally do. I want you to put pressure on these people early, and let them know that you are there.

'Now, if you fail, and you start to lose at the 1,000, then I'm to blame, not you. I'm the one that's telling you to do this, and you're going to have to dig deep in the energy barrel, and you'll have to show a lot of character. Just swim your normal race, and if it goes wrong, then I'm to blame, not you.'"

On the topic of giving it a go, Carew says, "When Kieren is in there, he's a racer. Like Haylie Lewis, she's a racer. And these two get in there to race, see. I don't have to give them pep talks. You know, it's something I don't have to do.

"Sometimes Kieren concentrates on swimming for time, as he did in the Commonwealth Games in Victoria. I told him to break the 800 record, but he went out and broke the 1,500 mark as well, and, of course, my remark to him was, 'What did you do that for?' And he said, 'Well, I felt that good, I thought I'd go for that, too.' And I said, 'Well, you've just destroyed our plans for Rome.'"

I suggested to Carew that perhaps Kieren had thought, "I may not feel this good ever again, or not for a long time, I may as well make hay while the sun shines."

Carew replied, "Well, I suppose he was right, if a world record is in the offing, he should go for it. I couldn't very well castigate him for swimming a world record. It was just that I had planned, and I've always felt—I don't think I'll see it now—but I've always felt that he would go into the 14:30s."

Carew believes that Kieren would have been able to reach an even higher peak in Rome had he used the Commonwealth Games 1,500 swim as a preliminary effort on the way to a world record at the World Championships.

"I thought he could go 14:30 at Rome. With the extra work, this would have had him right. It wouldn't have torn him down, if he had just broken the 800, and then gone on from there to just win the race."

A Second Father

Carew says that he and Perkins never quarrel. "We have an agreement. We have a fine line; I'm the coach, and he's the pupil. And he does as I say. He calls me Mr. Carew, which he doesn't have to do, and that to me is a mark of respect. He just keeps a fine line between us.

"I said to Kieren, 'Look, I'll become friends with you when you've finished swimming. At the moment we have a role to play. You're the swimmer. I'm the coach. You have to do as I say, but if you lose that respect for me and don't think things are right, then you have to go somewhere else.' So we play our two roles, and this is something that goes straight down the line. I play my role as a coach. He plays his role as a swimmer. He never contradicts me on anything."

Carew says that Perkins is never temperamental. "He knows me. Well, he's been with me since he was 8, and he knows that if I get annoyed, you keep out of my way, and that you just don't argue with me, you just do it. He knows that I'll rationalize later on, but there can only be one boss. You can't have two."

Carew says that he is probably like a second father to Kieren. "You know he comes to me for a lot of advice, personally, and in all ways, and I think you've got to really care for the athlete. You're not a coach if you're going to use them just to get your name up there. I care for him, and so I try to do the best I can for him."

Carew doesn't know Perkins's future plans. "We'll see what happens at the Olympics. I've told Don Talbot that I think we haven't given ourselves enough time for the distance swimmers. I think we should have another month. You see, Kieren has been sick this week, and so he has only been in the water a couple of times. That's another week we've lost.

"However, I think he'll go quite well at the Olympics, as long as we don't have any more setbacks. I think he'll swim well, because he's been in the water a long time. We never get out of the water. If he goes on holidays, he's in the water three times a week. That's all in his favor."

✧ ✧ ✧

WHAT MAKES KIEREN PERKINS GREAT?

Dr. Ralph Richards talks on the physiology of double Olympic 1,500 champion, Kieren Perkins, and the importance of having a long-term consistent training plan.

Dr. Ralph Richards says that Kieren Perkins is a superbly talented, and well-conditioned athlete, with a great fighting spirit that saw the young Queenslander fight his way into the 1996 Australian Olympic team in the 1,500, the last event of the last day of the Olympic trials in Sydney.

At the Olympics, Kieren once more cut it fine—very fine—when he qualified last into the final of the 1,500. But, against all expectations, Kieren, in a display of courage and tenacity, swam from the outside lane, to a spectacular and historic Olympic victory, which sad to relate, was completely overlooked, or ignored, by the American media.

Says Richards, "John Carew has done a marvelous job with Kieren over many years. Not just one year, but many years. I think Kieren has been with

John for about 10 years, which is good because there's been a lot of continuity in the program.

"Now, having paid tribute to Kieren's great fighting spirit, the reasons that I think Kieren Perkins is the great athlete that he is, are several.

"First, there's a very fine aerobic component in his ability to produce energy. This means that he uses his aerobic component to support his anaerobic capabilities. If you look at Perkins's world-record splits for his 1,500, the first 200 meters he was out in 1:52+."

Great Early Speed

"Now an ordinary athlete, going out that fast, would have a huge accumulation of lactic acid, but because Kieren has a well-developed aerobic system, he's able to remove lactate as well as produce it concurrently which means he's able to generate a lot more early speed without the detrimental effects of lactic acid buildup. His removal rate is tremendous."

Richards says that Perkins has a larger than normal heart with very good stroke volume, and a very well-developed circulatory system. "He probably has very good buffering capacity. But the ability to remove lactate has to be associated with his long-term aerobic conditioning, that has gone hand in hand with the integrated approach of also doing anaerobic speed work."

Richards believes that a young swimmer should also do speed work, and that it is a misconception that children do not accumulate lactate. He says that children accumulate lactate, but they accumulate it at a different level, and their removal rate is different.

Richards added that they rely more heavily on aerobic energy supply to sustain the demands of competition, no matter what the time frame is. A 10- or 11-year-old, swimming a 100-meter race, still uses more aerobic energy to complete that 100-meter race than a 19- or 20-year-old.

CC: *In other words, they are getting rid of the lactate much quicker than an older swimmer?*

RR: Yes. That is correct. At least, I believe it to be correct. As that swimmer matures, the problem that inhibits this ability is that they develop more muscle mass. Now you notice

that Kieren is very lean, and very streamlined. Not having excessive muscle mass is really a benefit to him.

People will say, "Muscle mass is related to strength." It is, but only to a certain degree. Also strength is a qualitative thing as well as a quantitative thing, and Kieren does a lot of good work that John gives him to develop the kind of muscle strength and power that he needs over the period of time it takes him to swim the 1,500.

It's always a matter of balance and determining the characteristics that need to be emphasized in a particular individual. Some individuals will need more muscle mass, because of their explosive capabilities. But, generally speaking, the rule of thumb is that you want the highest power package in the most streamlined design possible.

CC: *Would you say that Kieren is a freak of nature, or an athlete trained to be somewhat ahead of his time?*

RR: He's not a freak of nature. He's normal in every respect, his personality and most of his physiology. No, I don't think that Kieren is unique. I think there may be a lot more Kieren Perkinses out there, but they've never had the unique set of opportunities that Kieren has had.

CC: *Such as the opportunity to train with one good coach for a long period of time, such as 10 years.*

RR: Well, sometimes it's one coach that provides that opportunity. Sometimes it's one continuum of philosophy, and if we train enough of our coaches to understand these processes, it doesn't matter whether it's a single person who does it, or many people who influence a swimmer during a career, but the philosophy must be consistent.

I will say that Kieren has had the tremendous advantage of having a coach who has a very good model of what he wants to achieve in terms of technique, range of motion, energy supply qualities in his athlete, and he has worked very hard in taking a long-term approach to achieve those results.

If we think back, when Kieren emerged on the scene, which was at the Auckland

About Ralph Richards

Dr. Ralph Richards is the Coaching and Development Coordinator for Australian Swimming Inc. Richards completed a Doctoral Degree program in Human Performance Studies from Indiana University in 1982, under the direction of James "Doc" Counsilman. Over a seven-year period at Indiana University he served as a research assistant and helped Counsilman run summer camp and club programs.

During his senior coaching career Richards placed swimmers on Olympic, Commonwealth Games, World Championships, and Pan Pac teams. Richards was the head coach of the Victorian State Team on their tour of China in 1985, an assistant coach on the 1988 Seoul Olympic Team, and headed Australia's altitude training program in 1992. He coached backstroker Nicole Stevenson throughout her age-group career and took her to a World Short Course record in the 200-meter backstroke and Olympic bronze in Barcelona as a senior.

Prior to his present appointment Richards has held the following positions in Australia: director of the National Sports Research Centre of the Australian Sports Commission, senior women's swimming coach at the Australian Institute of Sport for three years, head swimming coach of the South Australian Institute of Sport for two years, head coach of the Melbourne Vic Centre Swimming Club for six years.

Commonwealth Games in 1990, where he finished second and broke 15 minutes for the first time, I think he was only 15 or 16 years old. That effort was already the result of several years of developmental work that John had put into him.

This is the kind of developmental work that we are trying to show all our coaches, and say, "Hey, this is the process that you should be going through, and, then if you happen to find someone who has a higher degree of talent than Kieren has, you can pull all those elements together, and you will have a champion athlete. But, if you have someone who has very average characteristics, you can still improve their performance level dramatically."

CC: *There are quite a few great distance swimmers who started off as backstrokers. Is this coincidental, or is there some connection with developing a strong shoulder girdle, or what?*

RR: I worked with Daniel Kowalski when he was an age grouper, and, at that time, we thought he would become a 200 backstroker. I have some really good underwater photographs of Daniel as a 12-year-old backstroker! My theory on this might be a little bit radical. Talking from a personal perspective, back in the late 80s I was the first national event coach for Australia, and many top backstrokers were under my tutelage. I think that one of the things we overlook when we're developing swimmers to swim a particular stroke is that different muscle groups are used, and they're used in different sequences.

Richards says that freestyle, being the fastest performance stroke, tends to put an emphasis on the anterior muscles, and this, in turn, may develop a muscle imbalance.

"For this reason, backstroke is a very good complementary exercise to freestyle. You can develop muscle balance by doing other things. We encourage our coaches to do diagnostic work, and work with physiotherapists so that we have well-conditioned, well-rounded muscle balance, in both the anterior and posterior compartments. It doesn't necessarily have to be done by swimming backstroke. You can do it in the gym. You can do it a lot of different ways."

Chapter 5

THE PIONEERS OF WOMEN'S SWIMMING

FIFTY WOMEN STARTED A WORLD-FAMOUS SWIM CLUB

In 1917, the year in which women won full suffrage in the state of New York, about 50 young women from the business world of New York banded together to promote interest in swimming among women. In December of that year, they formed the New York Women's Swimming Association (WSA), an organization that was to popularize women's competitive swimming around the world. In its heyday the WSA was the undisputed world leader in women's competitive swimming. It is said that the WSA won more national titles than any other team in the history of American swimming.

The purpose of the founders of the WSA was to encourage women to learn to swim as a safeguard against the danger of drowning, urge them to practice for recreation and physical improvement, and provide them with competent elementary and advanced instruction at rates low enough for as many as possible to participate. There followed an amazing growth of interest in swimming among American girls and women.

Less than a decade before, the great majority of women hadn't known the first thing about swimming. They looked upon swimming as a pleasant accomplishment, desirable no doubt, but not really essential. Little effort was made to teach women to swim, very few acquired proficiency, and, as for organized competition for women, it simply did not exist. American girls were hopelessly outclassed by their rivals of other nations.

But within a brief period the situation changed. Educators came to realize that swimming was not only a means of protecting life, but the most enjoyable and beneficial form of exercise. This caused most girls' schools and colleges to build pools and make swimming a compulsory course. Heads of clubs, YWCAs, social settlements, recreation centers, and other organizations began to appreciate the value of swimming for pastime and physical culture. They encouraged its practice more and more.

Probably the greatest factor in fostering this striking progress was the national standardization of aquatic competition for women. From the time the AAU undertook to supervise women's swimming, women were able to strive officially for championship and record laurels, thus providing even more incentive to develop expert skill.

This opening of opportunity furthered the cause of swimming in more ways than one. Girls immediately sought competent coaching and began to train faithfully and intelligently. They improved rapidly. Then the newly produced stars came into the public eye with increasing frequency as water carnivals steadily grew more popular. As a result, girls and women throughout the United States were given practical demonstration of the efficiency of the modern stroke, as propounded by swimming's maestro, Louis de Breda Handley, for nearly 40 years the amateur coach to the highly successful Women's Swimming Association of New York. This competition proved highly motivating, causing a greater influx into the ranks of devotees.

The outcome was that, in a short amount of time, America rose from the rear ranks to be the foremost nation in women's competitive swimming. The percentage of women able to swim efficiently became larger in America than anywhere else on earth. American women swimmers won undisputed international leadership at the Olympic games in Antwerp, where they won four of the five championships at stake, shattered every Olympic record, and scored more points than the representatives of all other countries put together.

Handley Promoted Crawl Stroke for Women

"Girls and women who seek instruction in swimming should not be misled into believing that old-fashioned strokes are best for them," said Handley. "Unfortunately, quite a few of our teachers still cling to methods of bygone days and do not advocate the modern strokes, except for competitive purposes, which is a great mistake."

Handley said that every prospective swimmer should realize that the up-to-date strokes used for racing could not have brought success and become accepted in competition had they not afforded greater speed and endurance than their predecessors.

Handley said, "Now greater efficiency from the identical fund of energy can mean only one thing, . . . reduced effort. Obviously then, these newer strokes will enable girls and women to utilize more adequately their natural resources and either cover a given course faster, or last longer in an unlimited swim, than earlier styles.

"The extent of the progress may be gauged from the fact that American girls hold virtually all the world's swimming records for women today, while six years ago our national marks were so far behind the latter as to be a source of merriment to foreigners.

"It is interesting to note, too, that women have actually played a prominent role in the evolution of the American swimming stroke, now recognized universally as superior to all others. And we of the WSA may take special pride in the fact, because from the ranks of our organization stepped forth the history makers.

"Many are taking credit nowadays for introducing the six-beat double trudgeon crawl, our standard national stroke, the stroke which must be held largely responsible for the world supremacy attained by the United States in swimming. As a matter of fact, two of our own girls, Claire Galligan and Charlotte Boyle, were first to use it successfully in competition. At the time they took it up, experts did not believe it could be held advantageously for distances longer than 100 or 150 yards.

"Indeed, before our girls ever displayed it in racing, letters asking for opinions concerning it were sent by a local coach to the leading men swimmers and instructors of the entire country and not one favored it. All declared it entirely too punishing for the middle and long distances; all spoke of the four-beat, with either single or double rhythm, as the only stroke for courses of 25 yards and upward. And these expressions of opinion are still on record in black and white, furnishing incontestable evidence.

"Claire and Charlotte provided the earliest proof of the value of the six-beat with double rhythm in the 500-yard championship of 1918 in Detroit. Claire took the title, while Charlotte, who was swimming her first race longer than the furlong, finished third, a bare touch behind Olga Dorfner of Philadelphia, the former record holder.

"This was in April. That summer both did wonderful work with the new stroke, and Claire, among other achievements, hung up a world's record for 880 yards which remains untouched to this day. Nor is there the least doubt, despite other claims, that the brilliant feats of our two champions led men and women stars everywhere to try the stroke, and so brought about its general adoption eventually."

Note: Claire Boyle, acclaimed as America's first woman to win an Olympic title, was actually of Canadian parentage. Her father, who was known in his youthful days as "Klondike Jim," later became Sir James Boyle, having been knighted by King George V for rescuing Queen Marie of Romania from the Romanian troubles of 1914. Queen Marie, for the interest of royalty buffs, was originally Marie of Edinburgh, granddaughter of Queen Victoria. I ascertained this information in a recent conversation with master swimmer Mrs. Aileen Riggen Soule who, as 14-year-old Aileen Riggen and one of Handley's first female stars, was the first women's Olympic springboard diving champion. Later, at the age of 18, she became the only female in Olympic history to win medals in both diving and swimming—silver in the 3-meter springboard, and bronze in the 100-meter backstroke.

❖ ❖ ❖

HANDLEY STOOD FOR MORE THAN WINNING AT ANY COST

"Good sportsmanship is greater than victory" was the motto of the Women's Swimming Association of New York, and "Fullerton's Ten Commandments" was their code.

Louis de Breda Handley's WSA swimmers held 51 world records, won over 200 AAU Women's National Senior Championships, and 30 National Relay Team National Championships. And Handley never received a penny for coaching them!

Not only did he teach the WSA women to swim fast and well, but he continuously and persistently instilled in them respect for the amateur code, and the sport they represented. Today, Handley probably would be unkindly regarded as a naive, laughable, and even pathetic, anachronism. Nowadays, the word amateur, is generally interpreted to mean a person without professional expertise. But, at the turn of the century, an amateur was one who pursued sport for the thrill of it, not to mention the challenge of good, clean competition. Yes, believe it or not, the athletes of yesteryear competed merely for the enjoyment and love of the sport . . . and without being paid or subsidized. In those days, this behavior had something to do with an ideal that was known as the Olympic spirit . . . remember it?

By the early 1920s, the WSA of New York had become "the most prominent club of its kind in existence, and the undisputed leader in national and international water sports for women." Despite the fame achieved by the club's swimmers, their mentor, L. de B. Handley, always warned that "the girls should not lose their sense of proportion when success began to crown their efforts in competition. Good sportsmanship is greater than victory," he said. This became the club motto, emphasized over and over again. It was displayed on the pool deck; it appeared repeatedly in the *WSA News*, and was even prominently displayed on the club's stationery.

Handley's Advice to the Ambitious

Handley believed that water sports were "most enjoyable and profitable, providing one follows them in the proper spirit." However, he felt that, if undue importance was attached to success, so that victory became the paramount consideration, and defeat left "a feeling of disappointment and humiliation, then the zest goes out of the game and it no longer represents pastime and recreation, as it should."

Handley said that it was natural to like to win, and moreover, every contestant should devote all efforts, both in practice and competition, to achieve success. But the athlete who would derive the greatest pleasure and the most benefit from racing, was the one who, having done her best, was "able to accept victory modestly and defeat smilingly, taking each as a part of the

The Code of a Good Sport

When Hugh Fullerton, a well-known sporting editor, featured an article on good sportsmanship in *The American* under the title "Ten Unwritten Commandments of Sport," it caused a minor sensation. Handley promptly reprinted the article in the *WSA News* saying that "these laws should model everyone's conduct; they are handed down by tradition and should be obeyed by all sportsmen if they wish to live up to their good names."

Fullerton's Ten Unwritten Commandments of Sport
1. Thou shalt not quit.
2. Thou shalt not alibi.
3. Thou shalt not gloat over winning.
4. Thou shalt not be a rotten loser.
5. Thou shalt not take unfair advantage.
6. Thou shalt not ask odds thou art unwilling to give.
7. Thou shalt always be ready to give thine opponent the shade.
8. Thou shalt not underestimate an opponent, nor overestimate thyself.
9. Remember that the game is the thing, and that he who thinketh otherwise is a mucker and not a true sportsman.
10. Honor the game thou playest, for he who playeth the game straight and hard wins when he loses.

(Footnote: It is likely, that if Fullerton had composed his Ten Commandments at the end of the twentieth century, instead of at its beginning, he would have moved Commandments Numbers 5, 9, and 10 to the top of his list.)

game and looking on the sport merely as interesting play."

Handley stressed that parents could do a great deal to help on this point. He said: "All too often, unfortunately, they are so eager to see their daughters win, so unreasonable and downhearted when they fail to do so, that they influence the youngster's attitude most unfavorably, at times to the extent of making the sport a task instead of play."

Handley said that this was the most regrettable in that it was not within the scope of every swimmer to become a champion, nor even a star of exceptional ability. Handley said: "In swimming, as in every other branch of athletics, champions are born, not made. Special natural gifts, not in build and strength, but in watermanship, are essential to the development of a champion. These gifts are vouchsafed to a very few only and all the coaching, all the acquired skill in the world, will not make champions of the others.

"Let none be discouraged if one fails to attain front rank in short order. Frequently latent ability does not develop at once. Usually it takes years for a potential champion to learn to exploit one's natural resources. Moreover, though it is not within the ken of all to become topnotchers, any normal girl or woman may acquire sufficient skill to enjoy competition, win prizes and laurels occasionally, and improve her health and physique the while. Practice and perseverance will accomplish this every time."

Difficulties in Learning the Early Crawl Stroke

It should be remembered that, all the time, Handley was doing pioneer work in developing the crawl stroke. Among members of the public, there was no real knowledge of how the crawl should be performed.

They knew that this was a novelty stroke that provided unusual speed, and they had a hazy idea that one should try to keep the arms going round and round nonstop, while at the same time fluttering the feet up and down in an alternating action. But, how was one to breathe amidst this welter of flying foam? The prime thoughts in the minds of most beginners were: "Breathe! Survive! Get oxygen!"

The result was that many early crawl swimmers breathed in so much air with each gasp, that there was little room for more air when the next chance to inhale came around again. This was the main problem in learning the new crawl stroke; most swimmers didn't know how to breathe regularly. When they did manage to gasp air, they not only took in too much, but forgot to breathe out. They "blew up" and quickly became fatigued. When swimmers finally did manage to learn basic breathing technique, they often had difficulty pacing this fast new stroke that consumed energy so quickly. Instead of trying to spread the pace evenly over the distance, they started off too quickly, became breathless, and had to stop frequently to rest.

Even the Champion Stopped to Breathe

In the early days of swimming crawl at distances over 100 yards, it was common to see even good swimmers having to stop to regain breath as a result of faulty breathing and poor pacing.

Such an incident was reported in the March 26, 1921, *Detroit News* account of the National 500-Yard Swimming Championship, contested between three national champions, Margaret Woodbridge, Charlotte Boyle, and Helen Wanwright:

"Miss Woodbridge retained her title in 7:33 2/5, a time that was not a record. But it was Charlotte Boyle who finished second, who was the heroine of the race. At 300 yards, Miss Boyle was in the lead. She set a new world's mark at this distance when she covered it in 4:21 1/5. From the 300-yard mark on to 375 yards, Miss Boyle held her lead. Then suddenly she stopped.

"She continued the race, but not until she had lost yardage. Miss Woodbridge was fully 10 yards in advance of the New York girl when Charlotte started after her rest.

"At 400 yards Miss Boyle again stopped swimming, even longer this time than she did at 375 yards. Miss Woodbridge was now well out in front. With but 50 yards to go, Miss Boyle cut loose with a sprint that was sensational. She quickly narrowed the gap separating her from Miss Woodbridge, but the distance was too great to be overcome in such a short length and Miss

Woodbridge won by a two-yard margin. At the 400-yard mark, Miss Woodbridge set a new record for that distance, her time being 5:57⁴/₅.

"At the conclusion of the race, and after the swimmers had gained breath, Miss Boyle was closely questioned as none present understood her actions in twice stopping while the race was on. Miss Boyle explained that she was unable to get air into her lungs.

"The final stage of the race witnessed Miss Boyle's most sensational performance. She swam that final 50 yards as though she was starting a 50-yard sprint. At the conclusion of the race, she was given an unusual ovation by the spectators, who recognized in her feat a performance of most extraordinary merit."

The Action of the Head in Swimming

Handley was among the first to appreciate the difficulties encountered by novices in learning the crawl breathing technique, and also in attempting to pace themselves effectively and economically. Accordingly, he made a point of writing on these two topics. Handley's descriptions may seem quaint to the modern reader. But remember that these could well have been the first attempts at accurate analysis ever made. Here follows Handley's advice on the crawl head action:

"In swimming the modern crawl stroke, the action of the head affects to a large degree the action of the entire stroke, and it is all important to use it correctly. It should be held erect always and merely twisted for the purpose of breathing, never raised or lowered, nor bent toward either shoulder."

Handley said that the head movement should be timed accurately with the movements of the arms, "so that it would turn to inhale throughout the recovery of the top arm (that on the breathing side) and kept straight, in normal position, throughout the recovery of the other arm, while one exhales underwater. Moreover, it should not be turned to inhale until downward pressure on the water has been applied with the under arm, nor turned back to normal until pressure has been applied with the top arm.

"A mechanical way to ensure its correct carriage is to look at right angles to the body, along the surface, throughout the recovery of the top arm, then to shift the glance forward, straight ahead, as one turns it back to normal. After breathing, and during the whole recovery of the under arm, the eyes should be approximately at water level."

Handley on Learning Pace

On the question of learning pace, Handley advocated that time trials should be few and far between, because they "serve no particular purpose and have a disturbing influence on the mind of girl and women contestants."

However, he believed that "swimming under the watch when going at moderate speed is decidedly profitable." Handley said that this method "helps to develop ability to judge pace and this is one of the most valuable accomplishments of the competitor, for it provides knowledge of how fast a gait one may hold over any given course without fear of tiring before the end."

Handley maintained that the perfect pace is one that distributes the swimmer's fund of energy evenly throughout the course being covered, so that she reaches the finish unexhausted, yet without an excess of reserve power.

Handley said, "It is through such a pace that a swimmer best exploits natural resources and makes the fastest times. Tricky contestants often try to get the best of a feared rival by sprinting and slowing up alternately, a method that sometimes succeeds against a nervous antagonist, but the system affects performances invariably. The swimmer who holds a steady gait will develop a maximum of speed and improve her chances always."

Handley said that it followed naturally that one should not be influenced by the actions of opponents in racing. "Quite frequently some opponent will set out at an untenable pace, and those who try to keep up with her inevitably must tire before completing the course. Again, a fast sprinter engaged in a middle- or long- distance race may hold back in the hope that the rest of the field will do the same and afford her the chance to win out in the final dash. But the girl who swims her own race, regardless of what others may do, never makes a mistake. She may not win, but she will display the best performance of which she is capable."

❖ ❖ ❖

THE PIONEERS OF WOMEN'S SWIMMING

Charlotte Epstein's Women's Swimming Association of New York, coached by L. de B. Handley, put women's swimming on the map worldwide.

Annette Kellerman, of Australia, one of the first great women's swimming champions said that women swam more gracefully than men, and that, "what is more, they can swim with almost as much strength, and, at least in distance swims very nearly equal men's records." She whimsically added: "I am not trying to shut men out of swimming. There is enough water in the world for all of us. But as men can indulge in so many other sports where women make a poor showing or cannot compete at all, swimming may well be called the women's sport" (Kellerman, 1918).

Annette Kellerman's comment was followed, in December of 1917, by news of Charlotte Epstein's founding of The Women's Swimming Association of New York.

Charlotte Epstein was the administrative genius behind the success of the WSA, and the debonair L. de B. Handley was its coaching genius. Together they were to change the face of world swimming. Epstein was a court reporter by profession and a remarkable organizer. "Eppie," as she was known to club members, was to prove a dynamic and driving force. She started the club in a little pool at the Hotel Terrain in Brooklyn. Lucky for those days, the pool also happened to be chlorinated.

Eppie spent much of her spare time attending to the logistics of running the WSA. As the membership grew, it became necessary to spread the club's activities to several venues. She was constantly busy finding more pools to hire, as well as the finances to pay the rentals involved. Eppie arranged the team travel to swimming meets, everything from local competitions to national championships. Eppie loved nothing better than to plan train trips to swimming meets, and it was said that she knew the train schedules to major cities by heart.

In 1932, Charlotte Epstein was appointed the assistant manager of the United States Women's Olympic Swimming Team, the first time a woman had been appointed to this position. She was an expert at everything she did, meticulous to a degree, but always maintaining a close rapport with the swimmers on the team. "She always went on the trips as chaperon-manager," said 89-year-old WSA master swimmer, Aileen Riggen Soule recently. "We would go to Buffalo, Toronto, and Philadelphia to compete, have dinner, and come home on the train. In Detroit we would stay overnight. As the manager, Eppie was on the sidelines, helping all the young people" (Borish, 1995).

"Eppie and I were good friends. The chaperon and the youngest one roomed together. I was 14 years old in 1920 at the Olympics. In 1924, I roomed with Eppie for one week in a hotel outside of Paris. We needed time to practice, and it was about an hour's drive to the pool in Paris. We were frantic. I had to swim as well as dive, all in one hour. I was in the 100-meter backstroke, as well as the diving. The week before the contests, we got nervous about this lack of time, and we asked if we could stay in Paris and get up at dawn before the pool was really open to anyone. Eppie was always there at workouts at 5:00 AM."

A Fine Leader and Source of Encouragement

Not only was Epstein a wonderful administrator, she was also a fine leader and source of encouragement to every girl on the team. Riggin Soule said: "The United States Olympic Committee wouldn't take children to the Olympics. Helen Wainwright, Helen Meany, and Aileen Riggin were the three youngest members competing, 14 and 15 years old, and this seemed to cause great commotion with the officials. They said there was absolutely no way they were going to take children to the Olympics.

"They had several meetings about this, and they said that they would take the next highest rated women in our place. Our manager, Charlotte Epstein, and other women went to the committee and lodged a complaint. They had a bitter session, but finally we won, and the committee members said they would allow us to go.

"During this time of about a week, we packed and unpacked our steamer trunks. We wanted to represent our country and wanted the wonderful trip to Europe. Then Eppie called and said 'pack again.' We got our passports, and were measured for our uniforms at Spaldings.

"Eppie was always around, an inspiration to all of us. Mr. Handley knew all about swimming. But Eppie knew the manipulations of all the plans, who would compete, where to go. Eppie was terribly important to me. Swimming coach Mr. Handley was too. She was a great influence. My parents thought she was great. She was a very good companion. She was always way ahead of everybody. Eppie could talk us into competing. 'Get points for the club, get in there and dive and never quit, never show off,' these were some of her axioms. 'Behave and have a dress code, compete no matter how you felt.' She was understanding and kind. Eppie was wonderful company, she knew so much. I was one of her most avid pupils. They were great people to look up to; Mr. Handley and Eppie were role models. A great team together."

◇ ◇ ◇

THE PROGRESS OF WOMEN'S SWIMMING: EARLY HISTORY

To understand and appreciate the challenges, as well as the obstacles that the pioneers in women's swimming had to overcome, it is necessary to backtrack a little.

In 1838, a London writer had written, "There is no school of natation for ladies in our smoky metropolis; nor do I think that English ladies in general will ever take to the amusement of swimming, which, however, might prove useful in an emergency."

His words proved prophetic. Forty years later, the steamboat *Princess Alice* sank in the Thames with almost 350 women on board. Only one could swim. She saved herself by swimming to shore. The others drowned.

In 1854, a French lady writer pronounced that swimming was not for women. "It is a purely masculine exercise, which will be detrimental not only to women's beauty, but will take away her gracefulness."

However, "around 1860, some recognition of the advantages of swimming by women was manifested, and it is interesting to note, that at the Ilex Club's Entertainment at the old Lambeth

Baths in 1861, ladies were admitted as spectators for the first time in London"(Sachs, 1912).

When the *Badminton Library Book of Swimming* by Archibald Sinclair and William Henry was published in June of 1893, it was considered the most complete and up-to-date publication with regard to swimming. But it made only two sparse references to women's swimming. The first comment was: "There are not many lady swimmers who bathe in open fresh water, privacy being somewhat difficult to obtain," and the second referred to ideal ladies' "bathing dresses."

"The best material is Turkey twill. The costume should be tight fitting, and, if considered desirable, can be made with knickerbockers and a short skirt; but for speed swimming, the absence of the skirt is desirable. The costume should be trimmed with the club colors, and made neatly but not elaborately. Waterproof caps are worn by many ladies." These comments, and an illustration by S. T. Dadd of ladies bathing from a stage at the seaside, comprised the only notice taken of swimming by women in what was supposed to be the most advanced book on swimming yet published.

The "University Costume"

The quotations and the illustration were so out of date that it was surprising they were reproduced in the 1908 edition. However, Sinclair and Henry said in their later work that "privacy for women's swimming is no longer so urgent, and the university costume is by no means confined to the male sex nowadays—indeed, any girl having any pretensions to being a swimmer adopts quite naturally and judiciously what is known as the university costume."

What was this much talked about university costume? It was a full-length "bathing suit" with shoulder straps and a short skirt, usually for both men and women, the upper legs were covered by what could best be called leglets, or short cuffs that extended a few inches down the thighs. (In the 1920s, the skirt was often dispensed with in the manufacture of men's racing suits.)

The university costume was usually made of black- or blue-colored wool the dye of which often ran, causing significant discoloration of the swimming pool water. For this reason, the WSA of New York, permitted only gray-colored bathing suits to be worn.

In addition to carrying and absorbing a significant amount of water, university costumes often had the additional disadvantages of crinkling and riding up, and also of chafing the chest and shoulder areas. For racing purposes, university costumes were later made of cotton, or, as time progressed, a type of silk.

Inadequate Early Women's Swimwear

Annette Kellerman was not only a great swimmer, but also a pioneer in protesting the negative social attitudes and dress restrictions placed against women's swimming. On the subject of the inadequate, cumbersome, and inhibiting swimwear that women of the time were expected to wear, Kellerman said, "While woman as compared with man is endowed by nature with many advantages as a swimmer, Dame Society has bequeathed her serious handicaps. The bathing girls of our popular beaches only a few seasons ago wore shoes, stockings and bloomers, skirts, corsets, and a dinky little cap; all she needed was a pair of rubbers and an umbrella and she could have gone anywhere and in any weather. But thank heaven in the last two or three years styles have become more sensible—and in my opinion more decent—though some prudes continue to call them indecent (Kellerman, 1918).

"But when a woman enters the water clad in Mother Grundy's conventional wardrobe, she invites troubles galore. Skirts or flowing robes are fairly feasible garments for walking, and are used by a large majority of the world's population, both male and female. Such an enveloping garment hangs from the widened region of the hips, leaving the legs sufficient free play for the vertical motion of walking. But in swimming these conditions are radically changed. In walking the knees can be kept comparatively straight; in swimming the breaststroke they are thrust sharply upward the chest. Moreover water is 700 times as heavy as air, and to attempt to drag loose, flowing cloth garments of any sort through water is like having a Biblical millstone around one's neck.

"There is no more reason why you should wear those awful water overcoats—those awkward, unnecessary, lumpy bathing suits—than there is that you should wear lead chains. Heavy bathing suits have caused more deaths by drowning than cramps. I am certain that there isn't a single reason under the sun why everybody should not wear lightweight suits. Any one who persuades you to wear the heavy skirty kind is endangering your life.

"The bathing suit problem might fairly be summarized in this way. There are two kinds of bathing suits: those that are adapted for use in the water, and those that are unfit for use except on dry land. If you are going to swim, wear a water bathing suit. But if you are merely going to play on the beach, and pose for the camera fiends, you may safely wear the dry land variety."

Strong Feelings About Mixed Competitions

In England, when the first ladies' championship was held, the Amateur Swimming Association almost immediately broke into camps. "Certain male members of the ASA were solicitous about the decency and the womanhood of the female competitors, a course of action that was deeply resented by some of the women themselves as well as by their male supporters" (Sachs, 1912).

"Seeing that the competitors would necessarily be attired in racing (i.e., skin-tight) costumes, it was assumed that they, or at any rate some of them, would prefer to compete in the semiprivacy of a female audience, but the majority would have none of such restrictions, and it was decided that the contest could take place in the presence of a mixed assemblage. The fact that such a

Annette Kellerman (Australia), one of the first great female swimming champions, was also a pioneer in protesting negative attitudes and dress restrictions placed against women in swimming.

International Swimming Hall of Fame

decision would disenfranchise those who shrank from the ordeal of exposing themselves in such a manner was ignored by the 'whole hoggers,' although it was obvious that the title of championship would be a misnomer under the circumstances, and that victory in a contest that was not open to everybody would be shorn of its full value (Sachs, 1912).

Later, clubs that had a "ladies' branch" wanted to stage mixed competitions in public. This led to strong feelings, and to remarks in the press directed at men in the ASA. The result of this controversy was a compromise in which the ASA law was changed to read: "No mixed races or competitions shall be permitted at meetings where the public are admitted."

While there were many female competitors who "were willing—nay, anxious—to thrust themselves forward in the public gaze," there were still greater numbers who were "content with a less exuberant display of their powers" (Sachs, 1912).

There were some who expressed the belief that there was a tendency to exploit females in a swimming bath in order that a gate may be attracted, and that this was a retrograde step in connection with amateur sport. "These public exhibitions in baths are moreover prone to confine the sport to a certain class of swimmer—the class that has no qualms about being stared at in a wet university costume, and they therefore tend to retard one of the objects the ASA has mostly at heart—the spread of the knowledge of swimming" (Sachs, 1912). With equally convoluted reasoning, the author went on to say, "Competitions in public, or any competitions at all, between the sexes are opposed to the true interests of sport because they can seldom be serious, even when indulgent handicapping equalizes the chances to some extent. [This last statement seems to indicate that "mixed swimming" was assumed to mean that men and women were to compete against each other in the same events.]

"Those who object to women's swimming confine their opposition to the appearance of female swimmers in a public covered bath, and they do so on the grounds of decency, as well as in the interests of the sport itself. Mixed bathing in sea, river, or lake, from machines, shore, rocks, or house; family bathing in a bath, and all such arrangements as these, come under another heading altogether; it is by their use that the fullest and healthiest enjoyment is obtained from the finest of exercises. And they differ in every aspect from the dictum of those reactionaries who tell us that in order to compete in a championship our female kith and kin have to submit themselves to the scrutiny of those who pay for the privilege in the confines of a bath. It has been said that the ASA is not a society for the protection of public morals, and that is literally correct, but one of its manifold duties is to see to it that the amateur sport it governs is kept clean and decent, and that the first of its objects, to promote the art of swimming amongst both sexes, is thoroughly carried out, i.e., that its benefits are not withheld from those who desire decency when competing in a bath. Moreover, I venture to hold the view that every member of the Association, and every member of society, is constituted a protector of morals, and those who support the promotion of women championships and mixed races in a public bath, whilst at the same time objecting quite definitely to allowing a female relation to compete in a like manner, are surely taking up an untenable attitude" (Sachs, 1912).

Australian Women Swimmers Gambol Unseen and Unmolested

Australia was experiencing the same controversy as New York City. The first swimming pool in Sydney, Robinson's Baths at the Government Domain, was built in the 1830s in a secluded area, with separate baths for men and women. John Hood, a journalist of the time, commented, "The ladies are safely secure from all intrusion and they can gambol unseen and unmolested."

In 1884, *The Saturday Magazine* said, "Where there is so much bathing, it may naturally be supposed that there are good swimmers, and Sydney is celebrated for them. There are many young men who think no more of swimming out in the sea a mile or more and back than a stranger would of taking a walk that distance. Men and women, boys and girls all, more or less, indulge in this healthy enjoyment."

In his book, *Lanes of Gold*, Alan Clarkson wrote, "In 1912, a Reverend Adamson spoke at a Methodist conference and was reported in the *Argus* as saying, 'No modest women can be associated with mixed bathing and no man who respects the

opposite sex could take part in it. I know arguments will be raised against me. Some excellent men have told me they have been associated with the practice of mixed bathing, enjoying it in the company of their daughters and wife. But another gentleman told me that his wife absolutely refuses to be associated with the practice of mixed bathing. Married women ought to take up a strong position in this matter. If some of them who bathe could hear what is being said about them, they would be startled.'"

Fannie Durack, Annette Kellerman, and Mina Wylie Pioneer Women's Swimming

Despite the continuing controversy, the New South Wales (NSW) Swimming Association held its first state championship for women in the 1901–1902 season. At this meet three swimmers emerged, Fanny Durack, Annette Kellerman, and Mina Wylie, all of whom were to become legendary figures in the history of women's swimming, not just in Australia, but also worldwide. During her career, Fannie Durack set 11 world records, as well as several others, that failed to be recognized because the record applications never reached FINA for endorsement.

The NSW Women's Amateur Swimming Association was formed in the season of 1905–1906. From the moment of the association's establishment, no males over the age of three were allowed at women's swim meets, this included family members.

A costume worn by Annette Kellerman in one of her many movies. This outfit is on display at the International Swimming Hall of Fame.

Courtesy of Kevin Berry

The first official state titles for women were held at the Lavender Bay Baths on April 7, 1906. Only two events were held—the 100-yard freestyle and the 100-yard breaststroke (McDonald, 1993).

At the Olympic Games in Stockholm, 1912, in the first-ever swimming event for women, Fanny Durack won the 100. Mina Wylie was second, with Jennie Fletcher of England in third place. It should be noted that both Fanny Durack and Mina Wylie were not included in the five-strong Australian team and were only allowed to participate after a public outcry and a petition by the women of Australia. In his book *Australians at the Olympics*, Gary Lester wrote, "Swimming officials relented and Durack, with her sister Mary as chaperon sailed with the team. Three weeks later, Mina Wylie, then 15, joined the team with her father who paid her fare to Stockholm."

Both Durack and Wylie had to overcome seemingly insurmountable odds to even take their places in the 1912 Stockholm Olympic Team. Rose Scott, the president of the Women's Swimming Association resigned her position in protest against the two swimmers being members of a mixed team, and denounced "any female who swam under the gaze of males" for fear of having her "modesty hopelessly blighted."

Fiery Durack Makes Her Feelings Known

In 1918, men who had resisted the inclusion of the two women in the 1912 Olympic team, took their revenge when they threatened to suspend Fannie Durack and Mina Wylie for traveling to America to compete without official sanction. They were forced to return for fear of losing their amateur status.

The two women ran into trouble again the following year when they toured America, this time with official sanction. They were angered by claims that their coach was a professional. "They were told to get rid of him or return home. They defied the criticism and stayed on for early success. As their tour progressed they were shunted from one city to another with hardly any time to recover.

"This annoyed the fiery Miss Durack who made her feelings known. With a pool packed to see the Australians battle against the cream of American swimming, Miss Durack calmly announced

she was not going to swim. Flustered officials warned her she faced suspension from all future events if she did not swim. Fanny decided then that she would swim—before the start time of her race! She dived in, swam a leisurely 20 meters, then climbed out and said to officials 'I swam, didn't I?' "(Clarkson, 1990).

A photograph of Fannie Durack, Mina Wylie, and Jenny Fletcher at the Stockholm Olympics shows an amazing array of swimsuit designs. Durack was clad in what looked like a heavy woolen suit with a voluminous skirt with leggings that stretched well down the thighs. Mina Wylie's suit, possibly homemade, was apparently designed for ultramodesty, according to the maxims of the day. It fitted around the shoulders and upper arms, complete with cap sleeves, in much the same manner as a woman's summer dress. However, the similarity to a dress ended at the legs, where the "dress" sprouted long leggings that reached almost to the knees. The English woman's suit resembled Mina Wylie's to some extent, except that it didn't feature cap sleeves to protect the upper arms from view.

Crowd of 3,000 Sees Bleibtrey and Boyle Beat Australian Visitors

On August 17, 1919, the headline in *The New York Times* proclaimed, "Australian Yields to American Girl. Miss Bleibtrey defeats Miss Durack in record time in quarter-mile swim. Sets new national mark. Miss Boyle also finishes ahead

Fanny Durack (Australia) became the first women's Olympic champion when she won the 100-meter freestyle in the Stockholm Olympic Games in 1912. Her father paid her ship fare to Stockholm.

of Mermaid from Antipodes and beats Miss Wylie in dash.

"Miss Ethelda Bleibtrey, sensational 17-year-old swimming star of the Women's Swimming Association of New York, yesterday accomplished the crowning feat of her career when she captured the women's national AAU quarter-mile swimming championship title. In annexing the title, Miss Bleibtrey, swimming a remarkable race, erased the existing American record for the distance and administered an impressive defeat to Miss Fanny Durack of Australia, who has heretofore been regarded as the world's greatest woman swimmer. Miss Bleibtrey swam to the title in 6:30 1-5, displacing the record of 6:39 3-5, made two years ago by Mrs. Claire Galligan Finney. Mrs. Finney, winner of the title last year, did not defend her laurels yesterday.

"There was no questioning the superiority of Miss Bleibtrey. The young local star, who already holds the national 500-yard title and record and the metropolitan 440-yard title, judged her pace well from the start, and finished, after a thrilling struggle, about 5 yards ahead of Miss Charlotte Boyle, the Sea Gate swimmer, who holds several sprint swimming titles. Miss Durack was third, less than a yard back of Miss Boyle, after being beaten in a bitter tussle for the place position. Miss

Eleanor Uhl of the Meadowbrook Club, Philadelphia, the only other starter, finished fourth.

"The race furnished the leading competition in an attractive card conducted by the Women's Swimming Association at Manhattan Beach. A crowd of 3,000 crammed every available point about the lagoon where the mermaids fought for supremacy.

"With Miss Bleibtrey's convincing victory there broke forth a spontaneous volley of applause which has seldom been surpassed at a swimming meet in this country. The crowd, largely composed of women, broke out as if at a given signal and filled the air with their shouts. To an individual they were thrilled by the superiority of Miss Bleibtrey over Miss Durack—the superiority of the American girl over the foreigner.

"Spectators slapped one another on the back, jumped into the air with glee; women fondled and hugged one another, and sometimes—in mistake or out of pure, unexalted joy—the man nearest them. Women officials of the meet forgot everything in the excitement of their unleashed joy while they showered hugs and kisses unstintedly on Miss Bleibtrey. Pandemonium reigned without hindrance."

Bleibtrey Visits Hawaii, New Zealand, and Australia

In February 1921, The *WSA News* reported that "Great news had come over the cables from Australia that Ethelda Bleibtrey had established a new world's record of 1:4.2-5 seconds for one hundred yards. This performance displaces her own previous world's record set in Honolulu. Since then we have had no reports of her performances, but several letters have been received telling of her cordial reception in New Zealand and of the great kindness being shown her throughout the tour.

"Unfortunately, Fannie Durack, for many years acknowledged to be the world's greatest swimmer, has retired definitely from competition, so Ethelda will not have the hoped-for opportunity to again measure strokes with her. But several of the younger and newer Australian swimmers are doing remarkable work, and she will probably have to extend herself to win the various championships and other events in which she is scheduled to compete.

Charlotte Boyle (left) and Ethelda Bleibtrey, both swam for the Women's Swimming Association of New York. They created a sensation in 1919 when they defeated Fanny Durack of Australia in the Women's National AAU quarter-mile championships. Miss Bleibtrey won the title in a record 6 minutes and 30 seconds.

"Speaking of Ethelda's tour in New Zealand, she seems to have had a rather strenuous, if enjoyable visit there. She writes on the subject, 'I have just completed my engagements in New Zealand and we are back in Auckland, awaiting a boat for Sydney. We took in Wanganui, Palmerston, Fieldings, Napier, Hastings, and Christchurch, besides Auckland, so you can realize how we've been moving. Usually it was a two-day exhibition for me, then we'd rush off the same evening to the next city, that I might swim there on the following afternoon. No chance to rest or train anywhere. The result is that I am swimming awfully, completely off form. I consider myself lucky to have won all races here, under the circumstances, for there are two girls, Violet Waldron and Guithra Shand, doing the 50 in 29 seconds, world-record time.'"

Australians Praise Ethelda Bleibtrey

Bleibtrey completed her successful tour in New Zealand and Australia, where she made a big impression. Not only did press reports and letters from prominent Australians give her credit for being "the greatest swimmer, woman or male, ever developed," but they spoke also in glowing terms of her fine sportsmanship and engaging personality.

The Australians said that Norman Ross, Ludy Langer, and George Cunha, who had visited earlier, were graceful, beautiful swimmers, but that Ethelda Bleibtrey outclassed them all. Said one prominent official, "The enthusiasts of Sydney have been carried off their feet by the perfection of her stroke, and, too, by her sportsmanship, graciousness, and attractive personality. Almost overnight she has become a universal favorite."

A local newspaper said, "Miss Bleibtrey is the most obliging champion we have ever met. Her sportsmanship in starting in the 220-yard championship on the night of her arrival, after the long sea voyage from New Zealand, was wonderful. Any other champion would have demanded a few days to recover from the trip. But she is a charming girl too. She puts on no side, and assents readily to any proposal put forward. We have found her everything we could wish for. Miss Bleibtrey has displayed generous sportsmanship in helping our lady swimmers to learn the methods she uses. Miss Bleibtrey is a great swimmer with a perfect stroke; she is a good sport also."

International Swimming Hall of Fame

Olympic champion Ethelda Bleibtrey completed a successful tour of New Zealand and Australia in 1921 during which she set a world record of 1:04 for the 100-yard freestyle.

The following was taken from an Australian social column: "Ethelda Bleibtrey is a real girl—a girly girl. [This comment was probably made in the spirit of the times, but it was not one that would have gone over big nowadays!] Her fine, open, smiling countenance, her manner generally, and the ease with which she approaches strangers, have won her many friends. At the Domain Baths on Wednesday she chatted with the girls all around her as freely and as easily as girls might who had known one another all their lives . . ."

" 'That's some girl!' remarked Mrs. Chambers, secretary of the Ladies' ASA, as we discussed the visitor, and she meant what she said. Miss Bleibtrey was agreeable to everything, willing to do anything to make amends for her late arrival, due to the disorganization of the oceangoing boats. 'Oh! what a relief it is to meet such a woman,' sighed Mrs. Chambers.

"Miss Bleibtrey's grace of manner is reflected in her stroke. It is the poetry of motion. When she is doing her best she does not look to be using any extra effort. She achieves the maximum of speed with the apparent minimum of exertion . . . If personality and ability as a swimmer count for as much as they should Miss Bleibtrey will prove a wonderful attraction.

"Miss Bleibtrey is a great swimmer, a choice specimen of the American athletic girl, and she has a most attractive personality. She will be as popular in this country as she was across the Tasman. Clad in a white satin skirt, cream jumper with blue edgings and broad sailor collar, a blue tam-o'-shanter on her white locks, her sleeves revealing shapely, sun-bronzed arms, Miss Bleibtrey looked a champion in more ways than one. Her manner is frank and unaffected. She is modest also and much prefers to talk of the deeds of others than of her own wonderful performances. There is about her not a trace of the conceit one might reasonably expect in so great and so young a champion."

✦ ✦ ✦

A VINTAGE YEAR FOR WOMEN AT THE HALL OF FAME

The year 1993 was indeed vintage for women at the International Swimming Hall of Fame (ISHOF) as such great names as Mary T. Meagher, Tracie Ruiz, Virginia Hunt Newman, Lillian MacKeller, and Alice Lord Landon, were honored. In a very real sense, the aquatic achievements of women were highlighted.

Cohost of the ceremonies with 1976 Olympic champion, John Naber, was Donna de Varona, double gold medal winner at the 1964 Tokyo Olympics, and former holder of an unprecedented 18 world records. As a consultant to the United States Senate, Donna was a moving force in Congress's passage of the 1978 Amateur Sports Act and the landmark Title IX legislation for equal sports

Dawn Fraser (Australia) coached by Harry Gallagher throughout her outstanding career, achieved the unique feat of winning the 100-meter freestyle gold medal at three Olympics. Fraser was the first woman to beat 60 seconds for the 100-meter freestyle. For longevity as a top-level swimmer, as well as for outstanding achievement, Dawn Fraser is generally acknowledged as the greatest woman swimmer of all time.

opportunities for women. As a leader in sports and fitness, Donna served under two Presidential Commissions: President Ford's Commission on Olympic Sports and President Carter's Women's Advisory Council.

At the ISHOF Honors Weekend I had the honor of sitting next to Alice Lord Landon—at 92, swimming's oldest surviving Olympian. As she watched China's tiny female divers sweep the boards at the Hall's Aquatic Extravaganza, Alice was in a veritable wonderland. Over and over again, she expressed amazement at the progress made by women in all four aquatic disciplines.

Granted, over the years, both men and women have dramatically improved the actual techniques of swimming, but women have faced an even greater challenge in the strong initial social resistance to their participation in the sport. This early prejudice extended not only to their appearance in public in "swimming costumes" but also to their using the same swimming pools as men.

Watching the amazing display of synchronized swimming by 1992 Olympic champions, Sarah and Karen Josephson, and the flashback video of Mary T. Meagher that was shown as part of the induction ceremony, one could not help but think of the great contributions women have made to aquatics. Their rise to their present position of respect wasn't easy. In fact, they had to fight every inch of the way for aquatic emancipation.

When the first ladies' championship distance of 100 yards was instituted in 1901, it was assumed that the women would prefer to compete in the semiprivacy of a female audience. But the majority would have none of these restrictions, and it was decided that the contest could take place in the presence of a mixed assemblage.

Annette Kellerman, the famous Australian pioneer swimmer, diver, and early swimming movie star, wrote a book titled *How to Swim* in which she gave sage advice on women's swimwear. "Where swimming is engaged in as a genuine sport and not as a mere excuse for social diversion, the very best society permits and approves of the close fitting swimming tights, or of the two-piece suits commonly worn by men.

"Perhaps you will say that in your locality the one-piece tights will not yet be tolerated. In that case get one-piece tights anyway and wear over the tights the lightest garment you can get. It should be a loose sleeveless garment hung from the shoulders. Never have a tight waistband. It is a hindrance. Also on beaches where stockings are enforced your one-piece undergarment should have feet, so that the separate stocking and its attendant garter is abolished."

Kellerman offered the view that fewer women than men became proficient swimmers because they did not want to wet their hair. Kellerman said that to keep their hair dry women swam with their heads out of the water, thus distorting balance and causing neck strain, "both drawbacks to good swimming." Kellerman advised women swimmers to wash their hair in fresh water and borax immediately after coming out of a salt bath. She added that "a brisk rubbing of the scalp with a rough towel will dry the hair. Do not go around with your hair damp and dripping until it dries naturally. Wearing caps keeps the hair out of the eyes and protects it as much as possible.

"Never forget to take with you a large box of talcum powder. This simple little adjunct is worth its weight in gold in a bathhouse. A great many women dislike bathing because they say it is hard to dress afterwards—their clothes "stick." All this is done away with by using talcum. Use it profusely, all over the body, and dressing after the swim will be a pleasure, instead of a task."

In her hints to would-be women swimmers, Annette Kellerman touches on the dangers of alcohol. "Indulgence in alcohol after a bath is the worst possible thing. Of course in a case of heart exhaustion, or fainting, or any of the unusual things that may happen to a person unaccustomed to the water, alcohol might be used—but not for the chilly feeling that sometimes follows a bath. Exercise is the cure for that. Just three minutes of a brisk moving around, running, jumping, or simple calisthenics will cause the blood to circulate rapidly. Do not use alcohol internally" (Kellerman, 1918).

In 1927, L. de B. Handley wrote in his book *Swimming for Women*, "Strict dieting is not necessary

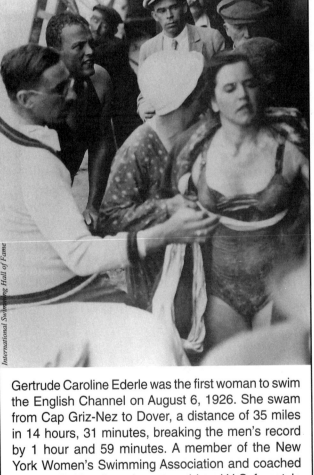

Gertrude Caroline Ederle was the first woman to swim the English Channel on August 6, 1926. She swam from Cap Griz-Nez to Dover, a distance of 35 miles in 14 hours, 31 minutes, breaking the men's record by 1 hour and 59 minutes. A member of the New York Women's Swimming Association and coached by L. de B. Handley, she set world and U.S. freestyle records for distances from 100 yards to 880 yards and was a member of the U.S. Olympic team in 1924.

in training for swimming. Plain, wholesome food may be taken plentifully, for a little surplus weight increases buoyancy and makes for imperviousness to cold water, and is therefore actually an advantage.

"Girls and women, however, need to be cautioned against their almost universal inclination to overindulge in sweets. Ice cream and the more simple chocolate confections will do no harm if used in moderation, but sodas, sundaes, rich candy, and fancy pastry should be taboo altogether. They play havoc with condition.

"Eating heartily shortly before entering competition not only affects one's efficiency in racing, but is extremely dangerous. Light, easily digested food may be taken no less than two hours in advance, but only in small quantity.

"A general complaint which must be guarded against is worrying in anticipation of a contest. Even the most experienced and mature competitors are inclined to fret at the approach of an important race and some girls allow themselves to grow so nervous and restless that they waste energy and strength quite unnecessarily. The remedy is to keep the mind off the coming event by engaging in occupations of sufficient interest to prove absorbing and seek to be busy constantly with work or recreation. Idleness is chiefly responsible for worry.

"The belief seems widespread that girls should refrain from all physical exercise the day before a contest, in order to store up vitality for the morrow's race. But the wisdom of this practice is open to question. Punishing work should be avoided, of course, but a comfortable, easy swim will prove more beneficial than harmful, not only on the eve but on the very day of the event. It will help to limber up the muscles without drawing on reserve power in the least degree.

"Regular massage serves no particular purpose where girl and women swimmers are concerned. A plain rubdown to activate the circulation before a race, or after swimming in chill water, should be the extent of a woman contestant's indulgence in this line."

So there you have it. Women's swimming certainly has come a long way. And when you study the performance records of a swimmer such as Mary T. Meagher, it is not too difficult to see that women could have won Olympic titles in the men's events not so very long ago. . . .

Chapter 6

THIRTY YEARS OF DISCUSSIONS WITH LEADING FIGURES

DISCUSSIONS WITH DR. JAMES "DOC" COUNSILMAN

Recorded in Lincoln, Nebraska, 1966, at the U.S. Outdoor Long Course Championships.

James Counsilman's successful Indiana University teams won 17 consecutive Big Ten titles and 190 dual meets while losing only 6. In addition, his teams won 7 Outdoor and 4 Indoor National AAU Championships. He was head coach of the two most successful United States men's Olympic teams, 1964 and 1976. In 1976 the United States men swimmers won 12 of 13 possible gold medals. Counsilman's work as a researcher contributed greatly to the development of modern techniques in training and stroke mechanics. At the age of 59 he became the oldest man to swim the English Channel. These discussions cover a wide range of topics including training, program planning, scientific research, and analysis.

CC: *Do you feel that the size of the large squads in American swimming militates against completely educating the youngsters in stroke techniques?*

JC: The thing that suffers is the work that should be done on stroke. This is the biggest problem, probably, that is facing our country right now. It's pretty obvious as you get out and you see some of our better swimmers and watch the contestants in the finals. Some of them are getting there through brute strength and conditioning and they, no doubt, would be much faster if they had a little better stroke technique.

CC: *Isn't it possible to give this technical instruction in the class situation?*

JC: We have had to do this in a class situation; almost as if you are teaching a beginner's swimming class. In other words, we here at Indiana University worked with a small group of boys. This summer vacation I've worked with 12 swimmers. Ordinarily, I work with about 20, so I don't need an assistant. We do a lot of underwater photography, but this is an exception.

CC: *Do you have any sort of age group program attached to your university activities and, if so, on what basis is their stroke instruction?*

JC: We have an age group team of 180 swimmers at Bloomington Swim Club and what we have done here, experimentally, is to conduct it as a class situation. We have the kids line up. We show them swimming movies. We explain what we expect of them. We get them in the classroom and take them in the pool and we teach them just like you would a beginning class. As you've mentioned, we have certain drills. We have out-of-water drills and we use isometric contractions for instance in the elbow bend. How much elbow bend should they have in the crawl stroke when the hand is halfway through the pull?

CC: *What are your views on motor learning in this educational situation?*

JC: There are certain steps in motor learning that we have simplified. You have to visualize, verbalize, and feel. So we make the kids visualize it by showing them pictures, by having them look at their elbow bend as they do an isometric contraction. And then they help each other so we have the visualization, the verbalization, in their own words, so they can say it to each other.

And then we get them in the water and have them feel it. There are a lot of drills with which we are experimenting. For instance we have the kids bring down face masks so that they can watch each other underwater and they tell each other how much they are bending their elbows. There has to be an approach

to stroke mechanics but I don't think this is the beginning. The beginning is to learn how to do it properly. We still have a lot of coaches with stroke ideas which are completely ridiculous—like you swim backstroke with a straight arm. We have a lot of books published in the United States in which they say the backstroke should be swum with a straight arm pull. Well, we start our beginners on a straight arm pull but, after they learn that, then we go to bending the elbow. Still, some of our top coaches in this country are so busy coaching their 200 kids and being administrators that they don't have time to learn all these things. It's a really complex problem, but I think the start is to learn what's right and work out the drills and so forth.

CC: *Would you mind outlining a little about your motivational approach?*

JC: The other night you talked about spending a lot of time with your kids. I too have always worked with small groups and the kids come over to our house frequently and I'm very close to my swimmers. We enjoy working with 20–30 swimmers, but to be merely an administrator in which there are 200 swimmers—if I ever have to get to that to win . . . then I think I'll give up swimming coaching because I like the personal touch with the kids. I just cannot see or understand the administrator approach to swimming coaching.

We try, as much as possible, to have a lot of fun in our workouts. Quite frequently we have a kickboard throwing contest in our outdoor pool. The boys will challenge me to throw the kickboard. I'm the world's greatest kickboard throwing expert. I can throw it 50 meters almost every time. I use a sidearm fetch, but sorry, I can't tell you more about this as it is a professional secret!

We quite frequently get bored with training and we'll go out spelunking—going exploring in the caves. We have certain games like pom-pom-pull-away. If the boys do very well in training and make the time I may set, we may play these games. You put a towel in the pool and the two opposing teams try to stop each other getting the towel across the pool and it actually sometimes gets a little rough! Frequently, I will set up goals for them and if they swim and make the goals, then I give them a handful of jelly beans. We do this nearly every other day. Quite frequently, we have what we call jelly bean day. They will go half mile at their own stroke and I'll set a goal for them. It usually is their best time and, if they do better than that, they get a pound of jelly beans. We have a lot of fun, but we could only do this if we had a small group. You cannot do this with a group of 200.

CC: *On the question of training, would you agree that different systems of the body need different periods of time to adapt?*

JC: I know the heart cannot be conditioned in just a matter of a few weeks. The heart takes months and even years of conditioning, and it takes a long time to condition a swimmer for the 1,500. Whereas the muscles can be conditioned for a 100-meter swim in a relatively short time. I think this is one of the things we will learn through physiological research—the type of work we should use. For instance, we feel that the heart should be conditioned for a long period of time, so we start the season with nothing but heart work, which means slow interval training with little pressure on the swimmers. We do 50s, 100s, and 200s mostly because most of our swimmers compete at 100 and 200, and we also do some fartlek training or speed play just like the track people do.

This is all preseason work and, as we get further into the season, we reduce the total distance of training and we increase the amount of rest we are giving the kids. We try to go a little faster and go more into what I call repetition training, or training where you are swimming at race speed and, of course, you have to cut down your distance. For instance if you were racing 200s, then you might concentrate on 50s and 100s at racing speed or better. We refer to this as repetition training.

CC: *In the research field can you relate your experiences of testing the maximum oxygen consumption of swimmers in actual swimming?*

JC: At Indiana we have done quite a lot of oxygen consumption tests in all-out swimming efforts. Dr. Syd Robinson and Bruce Still have found that we obtain amazing amounts of oxygen consumption—it almost rivals some of those that they have run into on the treadmill runs. I don't have the figures here but I do know that George Breen, years ago, was close to what they had done with Roger Bannister, the first four-minute miler, on the treadmill in an all-out run.

We have difficulty keeping our stroke mechanics the same with all that apparatus but we have a track that goes up and down the pool so they can swim. We should have something in publication very shortly on Kevin Berry, Bob Windle, and Chet Jastremski.

CC: *What equipment do you use for measuring oxygen consumption during actual swimming?*

JC: We actually use the Douglas bag carried on a pulley directly over the swimmer as he swims up and down the pool.

CC: *Does the mask over the face, while swimming, not have an inhibiting effect?*

JC: It certainly does but we don't know how else we can do it otherwise. It's not a good way to do it but it's better than stationary swimming. Many of the studies have been done with stationary swimming and collecting the air. It's very hard to swim in a stationary position—they get much more resistance— so what we've done is construct a long cable and we put some rollers on this and we pull the bag up and down the pool as the swimmers are swimming. In this way, they are at least moving—they try to swim at an all-out speed—but it's very difficult because of the interference of the equipment. It's better than any of the other methods.

✧ ✧ ✧

Recorded at the U.S. Short Course Championships, Gainesville, Florida, April 1982.

CC: *What happened to the mileage syndrome? Swimmers were cramming more and more miles into the allocated training time to develop aerobic endurance. What about the need to look at a more specific type of endurance, namely speed endurance, or the pace of the race? Perhaps pace is the key word. What do you think of the mileage syndrome and where are we now in this respect?*

JC: Well, in talking to many coaches and swimmers at this meet, one can see that many of them are de-emphasizing the tremendous yardage we used to do, such as 20,000 a day. To give you an example, I talked to Tony Corbisiero's coach, Don Galluzzi. He said that Tony, during a winter will never go more than 15,000 yards. I talked to Dick Fadgen. He coached the 16-year-old boy who swam here and made the finals, and he swims only about 12,000 in the winter and goes up only a little in the summer.

And in talking to many other coaches, I think they're right. Most of them are starting to move a little away from the aerobic work in which one just swims a lot of yardage, the main goal being to train endurance into the person.

CC: *There comes a stage when a swimmer needs to be able to tolerate a certain amount of lactic acid in the muscle.*

JC: Yes, most of them are going more to what we call anaerobic lactate work where they swim at a very high level, working over the anaerobic threshold; in other words, very specific to the race for which they are preparing.

Talking to the various coaches, one can see also three definite different trends, different methods of training. Number one for the sprinter: Some of the better sprinters are doing as little as 5,000 to 6,000 a day. The middle-distance swimmers, the stroke swimmers, the 200 and 400 swimmers—they're going a little bit farther. And then the distance people are going up to 16,000—although some are still getting the proper balance for an integrated type of workout. I think we need to learn a lot more about the individual. Just now the mileage syndrome, of course, is being downplayed, and I think that we are becoming more specialized in the particular events that we are swimming. I think that this is good and that we are just

following what runners have been doing for years.

CC: *Do you think that we will ever find a selective basis for applying the workout?*

JC: Well, I think that there are many individual differences in kids. I don't think we recognize this sufficiently. I don't think that we are placing enough emphasis on the individuality of the swimmer, not only psychologically, but also physiologically. For instance, Roger Madruga could take 20,000 meters a day and not feel it too badly, neither in terms of boredom or physiological fatigue. But, as he gets older, this will become more important, and probably, he too will want to go to a much shorter distance program, which if it is too short, will not bring him success in distance events. So there is no standard answer. You've got to individualize workouts. I think the way we have to do this is to break our teams into three groups when we deal with world-class swimmers.

CC: *I view the situation sometimes with concern. Young kids training for two hours in the morning before school, two hours after school, many of them seeming to carry residual fatigue from day to day. I wonder whether, perhaps, three to four months of the year shouldn't be devoted to twice-daily training, developing a basic endurance background, and then going to once-a-day training with more specified work?*

JC: A lot of swimmers are turned off by the demands of a program that makes them be there twice a day and to put in all of their effort in one aspect of life. I think that this drives many kids out of swimming. So we're torn between two things—working them real hard and making the program palatable. Now we have seen in the United States a constant decrease in the number of swimmers at the age group level, and I think this is due, of course, to these tremendous demands on the kids—early morning workouts, afternoon workouts. If they go out for soccer, they spend an hour and a half and the costs are paid by a team sponsor.

Now, on the other side of the coin, there is no short formula for getting into shape, particularly for the distance events. So we really have a conflict here. We have to make the program palatable without crippling it by offering a very short training program. This is the problem we're faced with. There is no short answer to getting into shape. We still have to put in the yardage, but you're right. By having a season shortened a little bit in terms of the very intense training, starting off three times a week, then once a day, working up to our intense level of training where we go twice a day and then a taper.

So I think the answer is to tell the kids that there are times in the year, maybe three or four months of the year when we are going to expect an awful lot from you. We're going to have you in twice a day. The rest of the year we're going to lay an aerobic foundation. You're going to swim distance. You're going to do strength work. That may make it more palatable.

But to look at it and say, we're going to have to shorten the distance you swim, isn't the answer. We're competing against the Soviets and East Germans and the various countries where the kids don't have to go to school for a couple of years, where they are state supported. And I don't think we're going to be able to stay in the same ball park with them in terms of distance events if we shorten distance training. Sure, for the sprint swimmers we can shorten it. But the distance swimmers will still have to put in the yards.

That's where specialization is important and we must expect more from the distance swimmers and a lot less from the sprinters. A very small percentage of our group, maybe 10 or 15 percent at the most, would be distance swimmers, primarily because of their physiology not because of their personality.

CC: *This comes back to one of your earlier statements and this is that we need to know a great deal more about the individual swimmer. And I wonder when you have these teams of 100 to 200 kids in the water, whether there isn't a large scrap heap, largely because some kids may escape notice completely. There may even be a diamond in the rough among them.*

JC: The answer is to use the talent we have, develop it to a higher level through better coaching, better analysis, better screening methods. There is an awful lot of talent wasted, particularly in the distance events because many age group programs are centered around the sprint. We've discussed this at our Olympic committee meetings, our U.S. aquatic meetings. Everybody says, "We've got to get more kids out." Well, let's be realistic. We're not going to get more kids out. There are more sports that we have to compete against.

What we have to do is capitalize on the talent we have, scientific analysis of what it takes to be a good swimmer, also better training methods and better stroke mechanics. All these things are going to help us. But just to say that we have to get more kids out is not realistic. We're going to get fewer and fewer as other sports expand.

CC: *You raise two points on which I'd like to question you. First, you say we need to specialize more. Are you saying that the talented youngster should zero in on one or two specific events?*

JC: I think not at the very beginning. But as they get to be 14 or 15, you know pretty well whether a kid is a middle-distance, a sprinter, or a distance swimmer. Now he can move up or down and you can use him in different events on your team to help your team do well. But we still need to identify, physiologically, who is a great distance swimmer, who is a sprinter, and who is in between. We have a lot of measures which will determine this. They are not secret. One would be their explosive power. If you get a person with a lot of explosive power, either by measuring with a vertical jump or on a biokinetic swim bench, he can pretty much be categorized. One of the things we have to do—just like the East Germans and the Soviets—we have to capitalize on the talent that we have. We have to train them better and learn more about this complicated thing we are dealing with, the human body.

CC: *When you talk about testing, you can spend a lot of money on testing. Do you think that you can focus on key factors that could show up the majority of the things you need to know and the rest would depend on a coach's empathy?*

JC: The first measure we should test is what the individual is good at. Everyone knows here's a guy who is very explosive, swims a good 50 and can't swim a 1,500. The coach knows better than anybody whether a swimmer is suited for distance, middle distance or sprint just through the times recorded at the various distances. Everybody else going the same distance, using the same training, the sprinters will stick out and so will the distance swimmers. The ones in the middle won't show up as much but that's true of anything following a normal curve.

Then we should get into more testing. For instance, we've found out that one pull on the biokinetic bench correlates .93 with the time for 100-yard freestyle. Well, there's a good measure because it measures explosive power.

CC: *That test was done by the American Swimming Coaches' Association? Is that correct?*

JC: Yes. Dr. Costill, myself, and Rick Sharp did the same experiment, and we found that in a homogeneous group—that is at the same level of swimming, at an international level or national level—they're all very similar in stroke mechanics. There's very high correlation.

If we start getting into muscle biopsies, that's pretty complex and costly. So this is a much better method than going into the muscle and counting the slow-twitch and the fast-twitch fibers. I don't recommend that. There are other methods that can be used. Pulse rate hasn't worked out to be a real good measure of anything so we should drop that as a predictor. But by taking the variables that correlate highly with distance or sprinting, we can pretty much classify the swimmers. As I mentioned, the coach already knows whether this is a drop-dead sprinter or whether this guy has endurance and no speed. So it's no problem. But we should continue to do research, take physiological measurements but not expect to use these as standard testing devices.

CC: *Have you made any personal observations on physiological testing in East Germany and the USSR?*

JC: I get some of their publications and I'm familiar with what the East Germans are doing with the blood lactate in terms of training load. I believe that lactate has limited applications.

CC: *Why do you say limited?*

JC: To measure lactate depends on where you take them and how you take them. The coach knows the training load better just from his normal observation. Nobody has yet proved that really high quality . . . We can get very high lactate by doing a few 50s real hard or we can do 30 by 50 moderately and get the same level of lactate, so it hasn't really proved to be a good measure.

Now, if we get into the pH, we'll find a different thing. The pH is important. There are a lot of possibilities that we haven't tested, but to continually test VO_2 max and all of the things we've been repeating for years is a waste. We need new approaches, a little creative thinking on this, and we need to work with the coach. In this country the coach and the scientist don't work together.

CC: *They work together in very few countries.*

JC: Right. But they are starting to work together much better now in the USSR. East Germany has been trying it for years, but I'm not too sure they know a lot that we don't know.

CC: *In attempting to bridge the gap between coach and scientist, many scientists say, "We haven't got the time, we haven't got the funding." Sometimes, with all due respect, their attitude is patronizing. The coach's response is, "The scientist tells us what we've done already rather than what we should be doing." So there's obviously quite a bit of bridging to do in terms of mutual respect.*

JC: I think we have just started to cooperate in the last few years and there's going to be confusion and a lot of conflict between the coaches and the researchers, but progress will come. First of all, the coaches don't have the background in physiology, and the scientists don't have the background in training. They also don't have the practical experience. Suddenly we are seeing more former swimmers become interested in exercise physiology and biomechanics, so I expect a major contribution in the future to come from ex-swimmers. A few coaches now are also becoming well qualified in exercise physiology and biomechanics and they will contribute also. Slowly, we're getting together, and there's more of an overlap. The future looks brighter.

CC: *Earlier you were talking about applying the anaerobic aspect of training more specifically in the future. Do you think the coach will learn more about the efficiency of this approach by the stopwatch or by consulting with the scientist or both?*

JC: It must be from both. So far we've just used trial and error, and we've done a lot just by intuition, and it has worked out better than working with the scientist. But the coaches are now starting to apply some science. The problem in the United States is that our coaches don't have a good background, not due to their fault or lack of interest, just through the poor training they receive in college, the poor science background that they bring to college. If I lecture in Japan or Taiwan, and I start talking about the Bernoulli Principle, the coaches have such a good science background, they know what I'm talking about. That's why I say I blame a lot of it on the very poor science background obtained in our high schools and colleges. We've de-emphasized science in the last 20 or 30 years.

We've much better coaches than the Japanese or the Germans from the psychological and motivation aspect. We've been good promoters and we understand training, not from a scientific aspect, but through trial and error. We're much better coaches, but our coaches don't have the scientific background that they have in foreign countries due to what I would say is our lousy educational system insofar as science is concerned.

CC: *I'd like to discuss the educational training of coaches. In Canada there is the certification program which raises some doubts as to*

whether it will achieve its goal. Many people come out and attend the courses and receive certificates, but, simultaneously with the program, there does not appear to be the development of jobs for the people once they are trained. To me it seems the apprenticeship type of program, in which a profile of a student coach's ability is developed, is a better idea. What science core subjects should be studied while, at the same time, following an apprenticeship course in the practicalities under a master coach? I think that seems to be the best approach at this stage of coaching education development for coaches. Have you any comments on that?

JC: I think you're right. You have to learn the practical aspects and then you understand the problem, and if you have the scientific background and the tools to solve those problems, then you have what's needed. Some of our worst coaches have been researchers, former swimmers who are primarily eggheads, who want to do something in biomechanics or something in exercise physiology. They go into a situation where it takes a lot of personality and motivation to coach. Well, many of these very intelligent introverts get into such a situation and do a lousy job—not all, some do a very good job. But the main thing in coaching is personality, the ability to motivate. Secondly comes scientific knowledge.

CC: *What about the ability to improvise, to innovate?*

JC: Well, this would be included in the personality, the creativity of the individuals.

CC: *And the imagination?*

JC: Right. And it's like the X factor we were talking about.

CC: *Your mythical Frank Zilch* [see p. 273].

JC: Yes. We are going to have to combine the two. It will be a long, slow process. The researchers have to come up with practical applications of research instead of doing a mathematical model for stroke mechanics.

CC: *Putting it all into a neat synthesis in neat pigeon holes . . .*

JC: Right, and something which they express in

scientific terms that is not applicable in the pool. We want to know how much you bend your elbow, if you keep your elbow high, we want to know how your hand should accelerate during the pull. These things are important to us but, if a coach reads *The Biomechanics of Swimming, 1, 2,* and *3,* some 90 percent of it is worthless to him. It's just strictly research, but that's the way research always is. Research pays off in a small percentage, 5 percent at the most, so let's not be impatient, but stay with it. Let's stay with the research and see if there's anything we can apply to our swimming methods, training and biomechanics and psychology. We almost expect too much. We think research will give us all the answers. It doesn't work that way.

CC: Do you think that coaches are finding as much talent in American swimming as they used to?

JC: Right now we are at an all-time low for real talent in the pool. Times haven't improved significantly. We have a little talent here and a little talent there but we are not drawing the talent we formerly did, and I think its primarily because we don't have the number of swimmers out.

The number of swimmers is decreasing steadily at a rate of about 10 percent a year.

CC: To what do you attribute that?

JC: Mainly to other sports that are more attractive—soccer, gymnastics, football . . .

CC: And their media coverage?

JC: Yes. And we are never going to get that type of coverage again.

CC: What about getting up at 5:00 in the morning and twice-a-day training?

JC: This is what I was talking about when I said we must make the sport more palatable. It's not a very palatable sport in many respects.

CC: You take a parent who works hard in a very demanding job, and until a child is old enough to go alone to early morning workouts, how many are keen on getting up before 5:00? And they may do this for the best part of six years, and go to swim meets that last all day for a few days, and after six years or so, when the swimmer is about ready to do really well, the parents, and perhaps the swimmer, too, may have become tired of it. Some feel that it's just too much.

JC: That's true, but I've also encountered another situation. Some parents love it, but I have found that a lot of parents, particularly the mothers, spend a lot of time taking the kids around, taking them to the pool sitting around during the workout, spending four or five hours a day. This is an observation I have made, and I found it to be very revealing. Such parents hate being home. They hate housework. They push the kids, even though sometimes the kids aren't good, because it gives them a release from the home, they seem to hate being home.

CC: That's an unusual observation.

JC: I believe many kids who are kept at it, even though they don't have talent, are in swimming because of their parents. And once again, to get down to it, we have to use the talent we have. Ideally the age-group program should be primarily a screening program. If a person doesn't have the talent they should not be encouraged to stay in the program either by the parent or by the coach. Take up the violin, ice hockey, or whatever. But in another way, we need these people in the program. We need their money so we can keep our jobs. You can't coach the top 10 and not have 150 kids on your team. And so a lot of them are kept on for financial reasons, and it is a good opportunity for them to exercise; it's not a complete loss. But such swimmers should not be put in a position in which their self-esteem is harmed or they slow down the top few.

There's no single answer to it but, in all fairness, it's often not good for the kid to be the last kid on the team always. He or she would be better off finding status elsewhere.

✧ ✧ ✧

DISCUSSION WITH FORBES CARLILE

Recorded in Sydney, Australia, July 1967.

Discussion with Forbes Carlile on long-term development, distance training, and tapering. Carlile was the head coach of the Carlile Swim Club in Sydney, Australia, a graduate physiologist and lecturer at the University of Sydney, and pioneer in scientific training. He was an Australian Olympic coach in 1956 and Olympic coach of the Dutch Olympic team, 1964, and Australian coach at the first World Championships, Belgrade, 1973. His swimmers set nine world records and Shane Gould became the first swimmer of the modern era to hold all FINA-recognized freestyle records from 100 to 1,500 meters. His book, Forbes Carlile on Swimming was the first to deal with the concept of tapering, a term originated by Carlile and Professor Frank Cotton and includes Carlile's research into the historical development of the crawl stroke.

CC: The organization of your swimming program at Ryde and Pymble is most impressive. Would you care to elaborate on your program?

FC: Our program has grown out of the need for good instruction from an early age and the need to train advanced swimmers the year-round. The result is that we now employ more than 45 staff during the summer. Of course, the majority of these are part-time, teachers at school, etcetera. Much of our training, summer and winter, is done at the Pymble Indoor Pool, 25 meters. Then we also use the Ryde Swimming Centre during the six-month summer. The great trouble outdoors is the cold water. Some of our swimmers just can't handle water less than 68 degrees and will train almost continually indoors.

CC: You have observed swimming in America extensively, and no doubt have very strong ideas on how Australia can match, or, rather, attempt to match, the depth in American swimming?

FC: We quite obviously cannot hope to match the depth of American swimming. I cannot see how any country of 12 million can hope to do this. However, this does not mean that we cannot develop a handful of world-class performers. The fact is that we are, and perhaps in a greater proportion than our relative populations would suggest. I believe that

whereas the USA has developed its swimming very much on the efforts of individuals and with individual enterprise, countries like Australia and European countries, less affluent than America, must have national programs of training sponsored directly or indirectly by the government. In Australia our swimming officials have been complacent and have left things to the professional coaches. They have not set out any blueprint for national development. Now we are paying for their complacency.

CC: Can you see Australia converting to interclub national championships in the near future instead of the present interstate basis?

FC: It has been a bone of contention with me for years that the club system is the way to stimulate the maximum of individual effort which, even with a national plan, is still very important. National championships, on a state basis, from my observations of the American system of club representation, do not hold as much interest and stimulus to excel. Our system has been going since the turn of the century and our Australian officials, isolated from world swimming trends, are traditionalists and very slow to learn. Only recently could an Australian make a national record when he went overseas! In Australia, a schoolteacher teaching beginner swimming is a professional! Coaches are still not given votes or a voice in the administration of swimming. International swimming teams are still sent away without coaches! The rest of the world has not much to learn from Australian administration of swimming. But I digress . . .

CC: I liked your ideas on the advantages of starting youngsters in competitive swimming at an early age. What do you think the future benefits of this procedure would be?

FC: In my book, written more than five years ago, I referred to the young twig's adaptation being molded by early stress. Nowadays, I am keener than ever on this idea, despite having a rather depressing time in the Netherlands as national coach with the Medical Committee there dead set against my ideas. This is the benefit of coaching in one's own club and not being answerable to a national committe—one can follow one's own ideas and convictions. Future benefits of swimming young and training young? In my view the whole future of competitive swimming lies in this. More and more, those who start old in swimming, at say over 10, and get to the top will be the exceptions. The future will prove how right I am. Give me the keen mother with a 4- or 5-year-old who has the swimming bug. They might be a damn nuisance now and then, but these are the children whom we find are succeeding. Even if they don't make outstanding competitive swimmers, we still believe that the physical and social benefits of training and competitive swimming are worthwhile. If they have not the aptitude to make it, then it has still been worthwhile.

CC: *What are your views on the exercise workloads these very young swimmers can safely tolerate? Have you formulated any findings on the physiological capacities of these children?*

FC: I don't know, but I do know that we have 6- and 7-year-olds who have been brought along steadily who can outtrain many older swimmers, even champions. The young twig can be bent a great deal. We learn from empirical experience. We seem to have learned that the youngster can be asked to do all that the older swimmer can do, providing he is taken along gradually and not rushed into it. Better for the coach, not the parent, to call the tune, of course. The parent, admittedly, does ask too much in the way of success. But, we still need the keen parent!

CC: *What is your basis for teaching stroke technique to the very young competitor? Is this done in a large class or individually?*

FC: We spend hours—by we, I mean our staff— on the youngsters just out of the learn-to-swim group. We call them tadpoles and they often have three 45-minute lessons a week at $1.50 per lesson in groups of up to 10, until they are good enough to get into the squad which trains daily and at a cheaper rate.

CC: *What is your feeling about the future strength of Australian swimming? Your age group program certainly seems to hold great promise for the future.*

FC: Frankly, I would rather discuss the future of our teams at Ryde and Pymble than the future strength of Australian swimming, over which I have very little control. I am not particularly impressed with our age-group system, at least considered against the American system. In New South Wales, for instance, the standard of officiating at this time is not good. Swimmers cannot be told their times by timekeepers, no meet summaries of results are issued, even for important meets. There are often not enough officials, but it is no use washing our dirty linen here. Maybe things will take a turn for the better. I am surprised to hear you praise our age-group system in Australia. When the leading state, New South Wales, will not hold 400-meter freestyle events at a state championship level for under 12s— although we have youngsters, boys and girls, under 5 minutes at this age—then I don't think we can be too proud of our system. Perhaps our program in other states looked good compared to South Africa! I'll bet you have the same conservatism and brakes on progress as we have here. We have too many officials who have retired on the job and whose hobby seems to be debate and holding the status quo.

CC: *Jim Counsilman has discussed extensively with me his ideas on the need for a reliable predictor of when a swimmer is moving into a state of failing adaptation. Have you done any, new work in this field?*

FC: You know that the concept of failing adaptation, introduced by the Canadian, Hans Selye, has been of fascination to me for many years and, at one time, I was much concerned in physiological testing in this field. The thing is that this laboratory work cannot be carried out effectively by the full-time coach. I have chosen of late to coach. Nevertheless, I believe that here is the field for our next step forward. We are saturating our swimmers with hard year-round training, starting young. I am inclined to think starting young is the key, as I have already said, and that the body usually can adapt, and we don't have too much use for such tests. However, we clearly must eventually get this on to a scientific basis.

CC: Have you given any thought to permitting swimmers to have a mild form of taper after say a week of very hard work to aid adaptation? If so, do you feel that this might result in being able to curtail the tapering period which follows the end of the hard training season? It would also have the advantage, psychologically, in enabling the swimmer to know, at regular intervals, where he is in terms of improvement made. Would you like to comment on this supposition?

FC: About 15 years ago, I wrote a paper on the hypothesis that a 3-day cycle of hard work, followed by a brief recuperative period, would best effect adaptation. In point of fact, we just about do this in our training at Ryde, but I must say that it is played by ear. Of course, the point is that individuals must certainly all have varying capacities so that no plan of training can be more than a rough guide. Of course, the key is to be able to measure the exact adaptation capacity and then budget accordingly. This must be some time in the distance, and I don't think I will be around then, somehow.

Beyond doubt, tapering is very much an individual requirement. I fancy that the word was first used in connection with training as long ago as 1946 when the late Professor Frank Cotton, my boss at the University of Sydney, and I sat down for a conference on terms to use in training. We decided on tapering for the easing-down process and on basic for easy swimming. Sometimes I feel that the use of these concepts in the context of modern training, as we know it now, are inhibitive to progress. Nowadays, when some of my pupils ask when they taper, I pretend that I don't know what they are talking about. When Karen Moras at 13 can swim 9:38.8 sees for 800 meters right in the middle of 35 miles a week training, I begin to wonder! I tell the swimmers that we don't know what basic swimming is, that we have not got the time to go slowly. The old concepts were all right in the context of training in those days, but other factors, like year-round training and starting young, have changed the complexion of things.

❖ ❖ ❖

DISCUSSION WITH ARTHUR CUSACK

Recorded at Scarborough, Queensland, July 1967.

Arthur Cusack was an Australian coach for the 1956 Olympics in Melbourne in 1956. He also coached the Commonwealth Games team in Perth in 1962. Cusack coached David Theile, the Olympic backstrock champion in Melbourne in 1956 and in Rome in 1960.

CC: You coached world-record holders David Theile and Pam Sargeant. Would you say that if a swimmer hasn't a good kick, his chances of becoming a top backstroker are limited?

AC: No. Pam Sargeant had a first-rate kick. Theile did not. I had considered altering his kick until I saw an underwater film of it at top speed. It synchronized effectively, so I made no effort to increase its depth. I left it alone.

CC: What would you say are the technical points necessary for good backstroke swimming?

AC: A flat planing trajectory, where possible. Good use of the head and neck for direction. Even and rhythmic movement and entry of the arms and hands. Correct use of the length of the arms underwater to enable the greatest possible pressing surface of hand and arm to be brought to bear in the sweep of the arm. Synchronized leg work to avoid upsetting the balance in the water and to assist with the movement through the water. Even breathing, certainly not on every stroke.

CC: What specific strengthening exercises would you prescribe for backstrokers both in and out of the water?

AC: I use calisthenics, isometrics, isotonics, and [a resistance machine] on the land. Use of all these is governed by age, time of year, time available for training and proximity to a major meet. In the water I use arm work, single arm work, and belt work—canvas belt round body, attached to end of pool by rubber rope. With Theile I used a special set of exercises which I devised myself and in which he used light weights ranging from 5 to 15 pounds.

CC: *What proportion of a backstroker's water work would be done on backstroke?*

AC: That depends on circumstances. Pam Sargeant from Townsville did 70 percent of her work freestyle with some medley work thrown in. Once she came down to me for holidays she switched to backstroke, with a little freestyle and medley. David Theile did 50 percent backstroke and the balance was medley and freestyle at which he was adept. Anne Nelson, who did a great deal of her training in Brisbane, switched her work to suit the density of the crowd of recreational bathers.

CC: *What method do you use in teaching the backstroke start and turn?*

AC: Land demonstrations using the swimmer and working through each section of the movement in very slow time. Practical demonstrations by more able squad members. Films and photos and line drawings. Incidentally, I teach my backstrokers to sink into the water at the start and not to pull up and out of it. Theile taught Anne Nelson to start and turn. Nelson taught Sargeant. Sargeant taught . . . etcetera.

CC: *Theile's turn was a controversial point at the Melbourne Olympics, 1956. Would you please elaborate on his technique?*

AC: Theile's turn was controversial in Melbourne, but caused little discussion in Rome. This furor was due to so many people deploring something different and better. This particular turn was used by Adolf Keifer. It was described in Professor Armbruster's book *Competitive Swimming* and was illustrated reasonably well in Kiphuth's and Burke's book *Basic Swimming*. We took advantage of all three, worked systematically at the turn, practiced flexibility and speed, and that was it. Theile forced his hand deep down the wall. He threw his head back and down and arched his back so that he could look along the turning arm. This action lifted his hips which he flexed, throwing his legs and feet toward the turning hand. This swiveled him

off the wall. He placed his feet against the wall with legs well bent, ripped his hands to full arm extension behind his head, and pushed off hard, commencing his kick as he left the wall.

CC: *Do you experience any difficulty in training backstrokers using circle formations in that the backstrokers are continually bumping into each other?*

AC: No, but normally I try to work backstrokers and breaststrokers together. I find that in all strokes poor swimmers collide often, good swimmers seldom, if ever.

CC: *Many backstrokers finish their races poorly, particularly in judging their approach to the end wall. What method of finishing do you advocate?*

AC: The swimmer maintains normal position as the flags are passed. The number of strokes from sight of flags to the end should be known and should be constant. The flags having been sighted, the swimmer commences to count. On the final stroke the body and neck are stretched back. The arm sweeps back lower than usual over the water. The fingers contact the wall and the wrist and elbow bend. The muscles taunten and the limb acts as a shock absorber. The other arm is kept out of sight. Should the hand miss the wall, the arm is locked behind the head and the feet kick hard to drive the swimmer into the wall. The hand and arm are locked at full arm extension and are at 12 o'clock.

CC: *Do you think that male backstrokers will eventually adopt a flatter body position in the water? After all, the freestyle swimmers have long ago changed to a more horizontal posture in the water, rather than the high head and upper trunk position of Weissmuller.*

AC: Believe it or not, I have always advocated a flat trajectory and have modified it to suit body types and length of neck and its position in relation to the shoulders.

CC: *How do you teach arm timing to novice backstrokers?*

AC: Much as I teach starting and turning—with practiced land work, a lecturette, a reasonable demonstration, and the use of single arm work and separate pulling practice with the arms.

✧ ✧ ✧

DISCUSSIONS WITH SHERMAN CHAVOOR

Recorded at the U.S. Long Course Championships, Lincoln, Nebraska, August 1966.

Sherman Chavoor was one of the most successful coaches in U.S. swimming history. He produced three of the greatest swimmers of all time: Mark Spitz, Mike Burton, and Debbie Meyer. A millionaire, Chavoor owned the Arden Hills Swimming and Tennis Club from where he produced a long line of champions. His swimmers set 83 world records and 131 American records. At the 1968 Olympics (Mexico City) and the 1972 Olympics (Munich), his swimmers collected 16 gold, 2 silver, and 3 bronze medals. Chavoor coached for 32 years and was the 1967 U.S. Women's Pan-American Team Coach, 1968 and 1972 U.S. Women's Olympic Team Coach, and received the 1968 ASCA Coach of the Year award.

CC: We in South Africa are particularly interested in hearing something about your famous prodigy, Sue Pederson. Would you be so kind as to provide some background to her career?

SC: She started swimming when she was 6 years old, had 28 national records when she was 8 years old, first 10-year-old girl to break the minute in the 100-yard freestyle. At the age of 12, she recently did 1:02.2 for 100 meters in the long course. She has done 4:40 for 400-meter freestyle, and at Bartlesville, Oklahoma, she went 18:29.0 seconds for 1,650 yards. She's gone a 1:58.2 seconds for 200-yard freestyle, 2:17.0 seconds for 200-yard individual medley, 55 seconds flat for 100-yard freestyle, and about 1:14 seconds

for the 100-breaststroke. Her biggest problem right now is her weight problem—she thinks nothing of eating 10 or 11 candy bars a day! I try to make her realize that diet and sleep all go with training—very important. Perhaps in a year or so she may develop an appreciation of these factors—if it's not too late!

CC: What type of training routine was she doing when you first started her, and then again, say at about 10–12 years of age?

SC: Well, we did a lot of kicking and pulling—not so much pulling in her case because she's a big, strong girl. As I said at the coaches' meeting the other night, we overswim them at distance. If she's going to race a 400, I'd have several 800s, 1,500 yards and, of course, the usual sprints. I would do the same thing with Mike Burton and Debby Meyer who are very good freestylers. I swim Burton several 3,000-yard swims a week. As Susan gets better, we increase her workload to 8 or 10 miles a day during the summer. In wintertime, perhaps 6 to 7 miles a day.

CC: Would you say then that yours is essentially a distance program?

SC: We lean toward distance swimming.

CC: Do you think that shorter multiples with shorter rest, greater intensity, might not also produce similar results?

SC: Probably, I'm sort of experimenting at this stage, and you might be right.

CC: Do you feel that they find a better rhythm by swimming so much distance?

SC: I think so with my present group. Perhaps if I changed the program they might go better. I think all coaches should experiment. I might change my mind after this meet!

CC: In what fields do you think that swimming will improve—conditioning, psychological approach, technique?

SC: Everyone talks about psych, getting psyched out, it's a big factor, I think. Psychologically, if our kids relaxed a little more and if you get the parents off their backs, the parents leave the coaches alone, they might improve better. Even more important, if the parents would leave the swimmers alone! Some of the parents want their kids to be national champion today, not next year or the following year. They simply don't realize the effect they have on the swimmer.

✧ ✧ ✧

Recorded at the U.S. Long Course Championships, Indianapolis, 1984.

CC: *How did you get into swimming?*

SC: I thought I'd make the military my career. At the officers' club they needed someone to help with the swimming. I volunteered to help. I knew nothing about swimming, but this fellow there taught me a little about it. And so I coached a little team, and I sort of liked it.

After the war, I was originally going to a little school near Berkeley to teach, but I stopped at Sacramento, went to the YMCA there to work out, and there was a little swimming team. So I started coaching this little team, a little hobby it became. I also taught school and became the school superintendent.

Because I liked to coach youngsters, I started my own club, The Arden Hills Swimming and Tennis Club. We have 1,000 members who pay 500 dollars to join. I chose to coach as a hobby, as a fun thing.

We drew some pretty good swimmers just by chance. We had Debbie Meyer, Mike Burton, Vicki King, Sue Pederson, and, of course, I had Mark Spitz at the beginning. He moved to Santa Clara and then came back to me the last four years.

Arden Hills has had over 100 world and American records, 19 gold medals, and I coach now to work with youth because youth is our future. They will become doctors, lawyers, statesmen, and help save our great country and the world. There are a couple members of our swimming team who are now doctors. Maybe they'll find a cure for cancer—save your life and my life. Luckily I'm well fixed financially through my investments so I coach as a hobby.

CC: *So your motives are altruistic and you enjoy coaching?*

SC: Oh, yes. You have to work with youth. It keeps you young! It's fun! My daughter asks me, "Why have you been successful as a coach, all these world records and 19 gold medalists?" She's a clinical psychologist and says, "Dad, you're mean to the kids as far as making them work hard, discipline. The kids know you want punctuality and so forth, but they know inside you love them, and that's the key to making them good swimmers. They want to work for you because they believe in you and they want to come back because you like them."

CC: *Discuss your coaching philosophy. Do you use any particular techniques in your coaching? Are you distance-oriented?*

SC: As you probably know, my superstar, Mike Burton revolutionized swimming all over the world in 1963 by the over-distance.

CC: *What is called speed through endurance?*

SC: Yes. We did things with him that no coach had ever done. Medical doctors questioned me about him, and said "We know what you are saying, but we don't believe it." They came to Sacramento. They saw how far Mike Burton swam in training.

I even went to Australia and demonstrated there. They wouldn't believe it until Mike Burton proved it. Then came Debbie Meyer who broke all the world records. You can always sprint coming out of a distance program.

Mark Spitz held the world records at 100, 200, and 400 freestyle, but he also came within four-tenths of a second of breaking the world record at 1,500 meters.

Many coaches like to get my swimmers because I overdistance them. As they get older and stronger, they can come down to the shorter distances and sprint.

CC: *There seems to be a tendency now to cut down on the training mileage, introducing more quality to the work.*

SC: People started copying Mike Burton, Debbie Meyer, all my distance champions, and these people went as high as 25,000–30,000 a day. We did the same thing. I thought the average body could take 17,000–18,000 a day, and so we hold it at that.

Now I don't believe in too much quality stuff at the beginning of the season. I believe in short rests and quality maybe a month before we start tapering for a big meet. That has been my philosophy. It has worked, but I don't care how great a coach you are, if you don't have the horses, you're not going to do anything.

I've been lucky, I've had this great, great material. But I have some of the greatest swimmers I've ever had now, some of the young swimmers coming up in the program now. But the kids are spoiled these days for this reason. The kids are coming from the higher socioeconomic group because it costs lots of money to go to the meets and so forth.

They're spoiled because they've been all over the world, and you can't hang a carrot in front of them anymore. Mike Burton came from a poor family, and he loved to travel. Debbie Meyer loved to travel the same way.

CC: *Today's swimmers do a lot of travel outside of swimming trips.*

SC: Yes. I can tell my kids, "Hey, you do well, you'll go to Florida; there's a big meet there." They say, "We've been there."

It's not the same motivation any more. Many coaches say they find the same thing. I find here in the United States that some of the better swimmers want to go to the clubs that are high pressured and have a lot of good swimmers so they can compete with them.

When Mike Burton swam with me, he was the only good swimmer I had until I developed more. Now the kids will go to Mission Viejo and Texas—a lot of good swimmers going there to fight for survival. That's why American times are coming down, but those Germans and Russians are hard to beat.

CC: *What do you think of specializing in particular events the same as the East Germans are said to be doing?*

SC: I believe that because it's too hard to coach youngsters in an individual medley—all our strokes.

I've got a tendency to work on butterfly. I've had five world records in butterfly and freestyle. The IM and backstroke and stuff I don't work as much as I used to.

I believe in what the Germans and Russians are doing. It certainly has become too hard to be versatile these days, in my opinion. We have a rare exception like Tracy Caulkins, but even then, I think she is going to have to start specializing pretty soon because everybody's catching up.

CC: *What about Rowdy Gaines and his sprint freestyle, he's extending his distances to the 400 meter and the 500 yard.*

SC: Well, of course, if I'd had Rowdy Gaines when he was a little boy, he would be swimming 500s right now and probably winning because he has great ability. I think he could have made it easier had he started when he was younger. He would be able to swim anything from 100 to 1,500 like Shane Gould could.

CC: *How about discussing Mark Spitz? Was he such a complex personality to train? I must admit I admire the way he got up and dusted himself down and tried again after the 1968 Olympics in Mexico City. Then he came up with great results in the Munich Olympic Games.*

SC: Mark came to me when he was nine. That was for three years, then his parents moved to the Bay Area. I sent him to Laurabelle Bookstover, but that didn't work out very well because she changed pools.

So I said, "Why don't you go to George Haines?" Which he did.

At Mexico he was very young and got needled because he was Jewish. In my book, I wrote that he was needled and harassed and that hurt him. He got into a tussle with George Haines, then came back to Sacramento, and I handled him differently. He was interested in cameras and stereos. So was I. He came to my house all the time, and we discussed those things but very seldom discussed swimming.

I'd say, "Well, Mark, let's finish our workouts and go see about cameras and stereos." I used the adult approach, and my good friend George Haines admitted that I perhaps handled him better than he did at an older age.

CC: *What do you think of U.S. chances in swimming at the Los Angeles Olympics?*

SC: I think the men will do pretty well, but I think the East German girls will rip us apart. That is my feeling right now, but of course Americans are Americans, and they have a lot of guts. They've proved that in war, and they've got guts, and they'll fight.

Going by the times and so forth, it seems the Russians and the Germans have more to gain because of what they receive after they win. They get houses. They get cars, better food, better clothing. Here in the United States it's all the same. I do think we're in trouble in swimming more so than we've been in the past.

✧ ✧ ✧

DISCUSSIONS WITH
PETER DALAND

Recorded August 1966, at the Los Angeles Athletic Club, Los Angeles, California.

Courtesy of Peter Daland

Peter Daland coached two of the most powerful United States teams ever in Olympic competition: the 1972 men's team that won nine gold medals and the 1964 women's team that won six gold medals. He also guided American teams to impressive victories against East Germany and the USSR in 1971, and at the World University Games in 1973. Among the world-class swimmers he has coached are John Naber, winner of 4 Olympic golds and 10 NCAA titles; U.S. record holders Dave Wharton and Mike O'Brien; Olympic stars Murray Rose, Jeff Float, Joe and Mike Bottom, and Bruce and Steve Furniss.

CC: *Do you think swimmers could reach a state of fitness where hard workouts don't hurt anymore? If so, could this be a new concept in total fitness?*

PD: I do believe that this is possible but it takes the exceptional swimmer, exceptional from the point of view of physical ability to resist physical wear and, perhaps, even more exceptional, of being able to take it mentally. On my current squad, I have a boy whom I believe could adjust to this, but he's 1 out of 65.

CC: *How would you decide what tempo of stroking a swimmer should adopt?*

PD: I think the stroking tempo depends on 1) the distance to be faced; 2) the physique of the swimmer—whether he or she is large or small, long armed or short armed; 3) on the style of the swimmer. By style I don't just mean where the hand goes in the water, but I mean whether it's a kick swimmer or a pull swimmer; 4) finally, on his or her condition at the moment.

CC: *Would you say that there is definitely a balance between the amount of purchase a swimmer should handle and the rate of tempo he swims at?*

PD: Yes, I would say there is. For example, strong short-armed people, who can get a very powerful grip on the water and who can hold the water all the way through, can afford to turn over fast. A rather long-armed, weak individual, who is not able to hold the water powerfully in a fast stroke, would just have his hands slip through the water and should definitely observe a slower tempo.

CC: *What expedients do you use in motivating your swimmers?*

PD: I think motivation of swimmers has to come from many different sources. What I try to do more than anything else is to teach the swimmer to motivate himself by presenting a series of challenges to him and showing him how he can best answer these challenges. After a swimmer has had several years of experience of this, he begins to put up his own challenge and come up with his own answers.

CC: *Do you find difficulty in keeping a swimmer charged up mentally, year in and year out? Especially after he has arrived at the top?*

PD: It's a very real problem, and I think the only way of handling it is to present higher and higher goals. And when the highest goal has been achieved—the Olympic Games, an Olympic medal, perhaps even an Olympic first—perhaps the only thing left is just to swim for fun. And once you've sold this, your swimmer can go on into maturity.

CC: *Do you think it good or bad to keep them at a high psychological level for long periods of time or do you advocate an easing of pressure only, using psycho-peaking in line with physical peaking?*

PD: I am very opposed to frequent psychological peaks just as I am opposed to frequent physical peaks. I feel that an ideal season would be a gradual buildup to a summit performance, psychologically and physically, with perhaps one or two minor peaks, psychological and physical, on the way. However, these must be subordinated to the ultimate peak.

CC: *What value do you attach to breath-holding drills in training?*

PD: I think there is great value in working swimmers hard when they are short of breath. After all, in the flat-out race, if it is, let's say, over 100 meters, for the last half, the last third, or maybe only the last quarter, there will be a rather desperate situation on the respiratory system. And the more you condition people to operating at maximum under adverse conditions, adverse breathing conditions, the better they are going to do.

CC: *What balance would you use between interval swimming with long rests and short rests? What percentage of your seasonal workout and your daily workout would be short rests? Long rests?*

PD: Well, that's a little difficult to answer because of the different phases of the season, people in different stages of development, and people swimming short and long races. But speaking in very general terms, I would say that the sprinters perhaps would do one-third short rests, two-thirds long rests, and the distance swimmers might do the reverse. But this would be a very general statement.

CC: *Do you think that a swimmer training under long rest conditions only would keep or lose form?*

PD: I think that his speed would increase but his stamina would decrease.

CC: *Do you feel that modern procedures tend to longer workouts and more mileage than is really necessary to reach peak form and that, perhaps, a more concentrated type of workout would assist both sprinters and distance swimmers to reach form? After all, the longest race on the program at top level is 1,500 meters with elapsed times of approximately 17 to 19 minutes—men and women's events. [Note to reader: Keep in mind this was recorded in 1966!]*

PD: I think an answer to that might be as follows: The 100 swimmer is going to swim, let's say, a mile and a half each day at training. If the 100 swimmer is going to swim $1\frac{1}{2}$ miles, shouldn't the distance swimmer swim at least 5 miles since the ratio between their events is 15:1?

CC: *Do you think that it is really necessary for a 100 swimmer to swim a mile and a half?*

PD: Well, I think it certainly is in the beginning and . . . yes, I do! I think that, if you swim less than that, the last 30 meters is greatly weakened.

CC: *What form of land training do you advocate?*

PD: I think that one of the greatest strides forward in our world of swimming in the last 10 years has been through the use of controlled weight training, and this is used almost everywhere. It started, perhaps, with Bob Kiphuth's book published in the early '40s on pulley weight work and free exercises. James Counsilman, Indiana University, further developed it with his work with barbells, doing pullovers, and then he went into the isometric and isotonic phases of work. Donald Gambril, Los Angeles Athletic Club, has come along with the Exer-Genie which is a pint-sized pulley weight machine which, perhaps, in many areas is even more effective than pulleys. I think that any of these is certainly going to increase physical strength, and I do believe that weight work should be maintained throughout the season to within a few days of a climax meet.

CC: *What are your predictions for next week's National Championship meet?*

PD: At Lincoln, Nebraska, this coming weekend, if pool and weather conditions are favorable—and, of course, I have no way of predicting these elements—but, if they are favorable, then I think we are going to see one of the greatest swimming meets of all time. There are a number of reasons for this. The most important reason is that in almost every event, there is a mass of world-class competitors all ready to jump at one another's throats!

Included in this group will be the South African National Team which already distinguished itself in the Los Angeles Invitational without rest and which should now be very fit and well rested. I think, looking beyond this, as far as your South African group is concerned, that we can look forward to continued relations, and we must ready ourselves over here every time your boys and girls are able to come and visit us. We know they are going to be fit, and even jumping right off the plane, you are going to give us a good run and might very well be taking us.

CC: *Would you care now to make a few remarks about your view of the present world picture in swimming?*

PD: I want to make just one remark about the world picture. Our competition in the Soviet Union in early July [1966] certainly convinced us that the Russians have arrived in this sport. The Australian performances in the Empire Games in Jamaica have certainly brought them back into the picture all the way. I think that the American situation for the Mexico City Olympics will not be an easy one. It will not be a Tokyo situation and I feel that the Australians and Russians as well as many other countries are going to give America an enormous challenge. I hope that we are able to answer it.

CC: *Are you prepared to say a few words about the role played by the professional coach in American swimming?*

PD: One of the happy phases of our American swimming is the fact that the professional enjoys a very high position, and I think that this has not only been of benefit to the professional, but it has been of benefit to the sport and swimmer as a whole. Over 50 percent of the leading administrators in American swimming, by this I mean members of national committees and local committees, are professional coaches. Our honorary officials, on every occasion, seek the advice of the professionals. This is something that has benefited swimming enormously, and I believe that this is one of the major reasons for our current success.

CC: *Are your officials paid for officiating at various meets?*

PD: Our practice in this area, Southern California, is to have a paid referee and a paid starter. We have found that a paid official in a striped shirt, similar to the soccer officials, definitely commands the respect of the athletes and keeps officials, coaches, spectators, parents, and athletes under control. We like the system very much. Our officials do an excellent job and take a great pride in their work.

CC: *Are amateur officials paid for officiating at meets?*

PD: The other officials, timers, judges, clerks, and so forth, are honorary, and they fit around the two paid officials. I must add that, unfortunately, this practice is not observed all over the country and, as a result, in many areas, we still have spotty work which causes great criticism.

CC: *Do you have any liaison bureau or advisory council whereby new ideas for improvement of the sport, technically and administratively, can be disseminated?*

PD: No, we just have our various coaches' associations and officials' associations, usually local, and they come up with various suggestions. As far as rule changes are concerned, we have our local committees, and we often borrow from the national collegiate body which administers high school and university.

CC: *What can you tell me about the numbers of people competing in American swimming in the various associations? What are your numbers? How do you attract your talent to age group meets? Do you advertise? Do you keep a tally of the numbers of people coming into the sport? Where they are located?*

PD: I can only give you some rough figures. There are about 10,000 in the Los Angeles area and about 8,000 in the San Francisco area. It's been estimated that there are something upward to 500,000 competitors in the United States. This is the result of a survey made about two years ago [1994]. Swimmers are introduced to the sport usually as a follow-up to various instructional programs in clubs, swim schools, etcetera.

❖ ❖ ❖

Recorded at Indianapolis, U.S. Long Course Championships, 1984.

CC: *As a pioneer in American swimming, what would you say have been the main trends during the last 30 years?*

PD: Certainly the biggest single factor changing American swimming has been the development of age group swimming which began around 1950.

CC: *When did the results of this program show up?*

PD: They showed in 1956 when Sylvia Ruuska, an age group product, won the bronze medal in the 400-meter freestyle in Melbourne. The first real depth effect was in the 1960 Olympic Games.

CC: *What about the upsurge of swimming in California?*

PD: I think California showed up in the late '50s. A number of age-groupers started breaking world records in 1957, '58, '59. One of the things that took place throughout the U.S. was we multiplied our swimming population by about 10 between 1956 and 1964. Little meets soon became huge meets. For example, in our district, where there had been a senior meet with usually one heat, sometimes two, the same meets even with qualifying standards, soon came to 10 and 12 heats. The age group program was developed locally by swimming committees. In places like Texas, Florida, northern and southern California, it was promoted mainly by age group parents, upper-middle class people who had taken over the leadership role.

CC: *Let's trace the development of superclubs.*

PD: If you go back to the 1920s, we had superclubs like the Illinois Athletic Club or the New York Athletic Club. Most of them were downtown athletic clubs. In the '30s, it spread around the country: the Indianapolis Athletic Club, the Riviera Club, clubs in Honolulu. Then in the '40s and '50s we started seeing the development of smaller clubs in suburbia, outside the central cities.

CC: *As the youngsters became older, there was a big influx of swimmers into the university programs.*

PD: Of course, university swimming benefited from the dynamic age group program beneath it. Before long, there were many hardworking age groupers in the college ranks and this caused a revolution in the size of college teams and competitions and the number of good swimmers. Athletic scholarships have been present for the last 50 or 60 years but became more numerous in the 1950s and 1960s. Finally, in the mid-'70s, a financial crisis in the college system caused a severe cutback. Forty percent of the financial aid in nonrevenue sports was summarily removed by the NCAA. The majority of college swimmers in America are not now on athletic scholarships.

CC: *Men's participation in NCAA swimming has given them an edge against foreign rivals for many years in Olympic competition. Do you see the same process taking place in the rapidly developing NCAA competition for women?*

PD: I think what it means is women will have an incentive to continue beyond the age of 17 or 18 because there will be a reward. At the same time, our universities will develop outstanding teams with fine coaches.

CC: *Do you see this program developing to the same prestige as the men's?*

PD: I think you'll see this in swimming as much as you'll see it in other sports. I don't think it will ever have quite the same aura simply because they don't swim as fast.

CC: *You really believe that?*

PD: Yes, I do.

CC: *What about the excitement of the meets as an incentive?*

PD: Even sports with women's professional teams will not outdraw men in the same sport.

CC: *Do you think we'll get to the stage where there'll be combined men's and women's teams competing in dual meets?*

PD: It already exists in many places but makes the meets very long.

CC: *You are known as a master tactician, especially in dual-meet competiton. It's been said that you like to come into a meet as the underdog, but very often, you're in a position to deal out surprises. What's your secret?*

PD: Well, I have no secrets and, in fact there are no secrets in swimming because everything, like truth, will be out and others will know about it. Perhaps I study the opponent more carefully than other coaches. Therefore I have more knowledge of the teams we are competing against.

CC: *Have you reached the stage where you assess dual-meet results with a computer to consider team composition at the NCAA Championships?*

PD: No, I don't think you can do that because dual-meet results don't necessarily relate to the NCAA results.

CC: *The rules of NCAA competition permit the coach to announce and enter swimmers just before a particular event?*

PD: That's correct, but it's considered foolish to announce names just before an event.

CC: *Does the coach have to think on his feet and make name changes suddenly?*

PD: Most coaches don't make name changes during the first part of the meet but change at halftime when they go down and talk to the team and assess what happened in the first half.

CC: *Changing one event may require corresponding adjustments further down the program and could lead to difficulties if you make just one mistake?*

PD: Very often a coach will go into a meet and have two or three options in mind and when the battle unfolds will decide which of his options is in order.

CC: *Do you have these program formats in front of you?*

PD: Sometimes. I would certainly have them in the swimmers' minds so that they know if so-and-so wins the backstroke then so-and-so will swim the breaststroke.

CC: *Do you feel that some kids become unstuck at dual meets by becoming too excited?*

PD: I have noticed through the years that when the adrenaline levels get very high as it happens in a very dramatic dual meet the swimmer pays for it later in the day. Maybe later in the meet, because for every action there's an equal and opposite reaction. We very often have meets where, in the first part of the meet, we were very excited and very high. We come back in the second half and couldn't get off the ground.

CC: *So you prefer to induce in your swimmers an attitude of quiet confidence?*

PD: I tell them to pay attention to what they're doing. Don't get too excited and above all, eliminate mistakes because the mistakes of other swimmers usually decide who wins the race.

CC: *You are involved with preparation for the Los Angeles Olympics?*

PD: Yes, I'm the Competition Chairman for swimming.

CC: *How do you see the relative strengths of the leading swimming nations shaping up?*

PD: Off the top of my head, I would say the U.S. looks like the dominant power in the men's division. The Soviet Union and East Germany will be in for a number of medals, perhaps some titles. There are always the good Australians who come popping up in the Olympic year. Sweden is particularly strong and greatly enhanced by American college training. On the ladies side, East Germany looks like the leading power with maybe the U.S. second, although our girls are, in my opinion still quite difficult to predict. It's difficult to know how well we'll do.

CC: *The U.S. coaches are assigned to various events now?*

PD: Yes. For the first time, we are really going to

use an efficient coaching system. The head coach will control the overall operation and specialty coaches will work on various areas like breaststroke, individual medley, and so forth. These men and women have already been appointed, know their jobs and have started to assess America's talent in their respective areas.

CC: *You haven't mentioned the Canadians. Is that an oversight or for a particular reason?*

PD: No, I wouldn't slight the Canadians for the world! Canada is one of the major powers and recently the greater strength seems to be in men's swimming. Traditionally, Canada has been a great power in women's swimming.

CC: *The feeling in Canada after the recent short course championships is that the country is on a resurgence.*

PD: Well, I don't think the country faded out. I think Canada has done awfully well for a country with less than 30 million people.

✧ ✧ ✧

DISCUSSION WITH DONNA DE VARONA

Recorded at the U.S. Long Course Championships, Lincoln, Nebraska, August 1966.

Donna de Varona was the Olympic champion in the women's 400-meter individual medley in Tokyo, 1964. One of the most versatile swimmers ever developed, she has been rated in world top 10 rankings in all 4 strokes simultaneously. A popular television sports commentator, she is a member of the President's Advisory Council for Physical Fitness.

CC: *How did you prepare for individual medley races?*

DdV: I always tried to break up everything I did into all four strokes. If we did, say, 4 by 400 meter repeats, I would go a whole 400 meters butterfly, 400 meters backstroke, 400 meters breaststroke, and 400 meters freestyle. But, if I was swimming against the freestylers that day and I wanted to see how I could do freestyle, then I would go two repeats in freestyle and then I would go two repeats at 400 meters individual medley. Or, let's say, we were doing 2 by 400 meters, then I'd go 200 butterfly, 200 backstroke. The next 400 meters, I'd do 200 meters breaststroke and 200 meters freestyle. I'd do a lot of block work. That means I'd dive in and do a 100 butterfly, wait 10 seconds, then do a 100 backstroke, wait 10 seconds, do a 100 breaststroke, 10 seconds, then a 100 freestyle. Then we would add up our time. We would do the same thing on 200s where we would do 50s instead of 100s.

CC: *I suppose you lay great emphasis on quality in your workouts?*

DdV: In our sprint workouts we did a lot of quality. We always sprinted at the end of every workout to keep up our speed. As we reached better shape during the season we would do more quality work. Cut down, maybe, the number of sprints, but times would have to be better, and we would sometimes cut down the rest period.

CC: *Yet still maintain the quality?*

DdV: Yes, we would try to cut down the rest period yet still maintain quality swims for most of the season. George Haines stresses quality most of the time in our workouts.

CC: *Did you time all stages of the workout?*

DdV: We would do 800s, say three 800s, and we would time every single 800 whether it be pulling only or kicking.

CC: *I believe George has great variety in his workouts?*

DdV: Yes, one would go to work out and think it was fun. The thing about George was that he never did the same workout twice. He is very good at knowing how to handle the swimmers. This is his talent, too, because he would take a large team, such as ours, and know each individual and how to train him. If there's a day when he is off form, an individual swimmer wouldn't have to do quite so much work, but next day he would have to make it up—but he would know how to handle that individual swimmer!

CC: *How did you come to participate in competitive swimming?*

DdV: I started swimming in our age-group program. I started swimming in a 3-lane, 20-yard pool at a YWCA, and I think the thing about swimming or any form of athletics is that you have to have something inside to be successful. I've seen so many cases where a swimmer, a basketball player, a baseball player, doesn't have any right physically to be out there winning but he's got the stuff that's inside.

CC: *This desire, determination, is something that has to be built up goal by goal.*

DdV: That's right. You can't just start out and say you're going to the Olympics. You have to start out and aim for a time a little bit ahead of what you think you can do and just keep working. Of course, George makes this aim a lot easier. He gives you the confidence, he makes you work, he makes you realize that you can't get it without the work.

CC: *What did you think about before your big races? Did you become somewhat temperamental?*

DdV: I thought about all my big races. I'd swim my race days ahead of time over and over again in my mind and I'd swim it right before! My father was an athlete himself. My parents wouldn't let me get away with being a little snippy if I was on edge before a big race, but they tolerated any nervousness I may have had.

CC: *And when the race started?*

DdV: When I dived into the pool I thought about my stroke, when to breathe, and not to hold my breath too long! If you do, you won't have enough oxygen and your legs will get tired and you won't be able to bring your race home again. You think about changing from one style to the other in individual medley, you think about rhythm, you think about coming off that wall, taking sprint strokes, and then relaxing into your stroke. You think mostly about technique all the time—pace and technique.

CC: *And what about the stages of the race that really hurt?*

DdV: Of course when you are hurt enough that's the time you've got to push the hardest.

CC: *And tactics?*

DdV: You have to be tactical, especially in my race, the medley. When I was weak in breaststroke in 1962 and 1963, I had to swim a tactical race. I had to go out and make sure I was ahead by two body lengths by the time the breaststroke leg came because my main competitor was strong in the breaststroke. I think the main thing, though, is like I said before, when a swimmer is great he must remember that be has to think the whole time. The people he meets on the way up, he will meet on the way down, too. He should watch other swimmers. If he is around the pool deck, he should watch and see how their strokes are. That's how I learnt at the beginning. I'd go to a pool and watch everyone swim, and not just the surface stroke—that's not what is important—it's what the swimmer is doing underneath the water that counts.

CC: *Did you always have the feeling that you were destined to be a champion?*

DdV: I was never that confident before I went into a race! I was always saying to myself, "If you put the work behind it, you can do it. There's no way that you can be beaten if you use your capability, you use your head, and you don't become overconfident and relax and you get in there and think the whole race."

CC: *Have you always found swimming to be fun, or were there times when you found the tension almost unbearable?*

DdV: Yes, I always found swimming fun and, now that I've retired, I still take a swim every day. There were times, before a big race, when I felt like running away! But the times when I felt like running away, were the times I remember the most. Three minutes later, after winning the race, I was highly elated! In life, if you are going to do anything, you have to be that way. Anything that you get—the harder it is, the more you appreciate it!

✧ ✧ ✧

DISCUSSION WITH
JOHN DEVITT
Recorded in Sydney, Australia, July 1967.

John Devitt, 100-meter Olympic champion, 1960, and former world-record holder for the distance. Devitt was captain of the victorious 1956 Australian Olympic team, as well as the 1960 Rome Olympic team and the 1958 Cardiff Empire Games team. In all, he was elected captain of Australian international swimming teams on seven occasions. He is vice president of Australian Swimming Inc. At meetings of the FINA Congress, Devitt has twice successfully argued on behalf of Australia for retention of a four-year ban for swimmers who tested positive for steroid use.

CC: *You are very active in promoting the New South Wales and Australian age-group programs by way of commercial sponsorship and through administrative channels. What are the aims of these programs?*

JD: The aims of the programs are to produce a very strong base in order to achieve a high standard of swimming through to the apex which is Olympic Games competition. We do this on a basis of sponsoring various swimming competitions from the district age groups through to the metropolitan areas then on to the state and national championships. This is a very important phase in the promotion of swimming and we feel that in Australia we must delve deeply to produce the widest base possible to give our swimmers the chance to progress to championship level. Various organizations such as Speedo and Shell are very active in this phase, joining recently with Nestlés, in the promotion of swimming. We feel that the only way that

the sport can progress is to have active commercial backing. This seems to be readily forthcoming at the present time and the people who are sponsoring the championships are most cooperative in their efforts on behalf of swimming.

CC: *Would you please outline the various age groups and events in your age-group calendar?*

JD: The ages which are usually conducted in Australia are the even age groups. I mean by that 16, 14, 12, and 10. In one particular competition we have also 8, 9, 11, and 13. The aim of these various age groups is to produce even competition throughout the country. The first of October is the date on which the calendar is commenced. People who, for example, turn 12 on the second of October, compete for that season in the under-12 bracket.

The events are confined, as closely as possible, to the Olympic events. This means that almost all freestyle—events from U 14 upwards would be 100- to 400-meter freestyle. Butterfly, backstroke, and breaststroke are held at 100 and 200 meters, except in the younger age groups, which would probably cover 50 and 100 meters. Individual medleys are swum for U 12, 14, and 16, and there is a move at present to organize U 10 medleys. Relays are a very important part of our competition and, while we do not in most states go below the U 16 age groups, Tasmania is far advanced at the present time by having medley and freestyle relays in the U 12 age group.

In summing up, I am confident that the events conducted are most constructive to producing the base that I mentioned earlier. However, I feel that we can still further add to the list of events as we cannot obtain the competitors for an event until we make the event possible for the competitors to compete in.

CC: *Would you please describe your winter age-group activities?*

JD: Winter age group is now conducted in four states: West Australia, Victoria, Tasmania, and New South Wales. Queensland is preparing a basis for larger winter programs. There is a move afoot to eventually conduct national championships in a winter program, but at the present, it is confined to individual states. This consists usually of time trials at various swimming centers in these states culminating in winter state championships. The events are not as widespread as in the summer, but they cover most of the competitive distances and provide constructive competition.

CC: *What are the incentives provided for these age-group youngsters?*

JD: With the standard of swimming in Australia at such a high level, a qualifying standard has to be placed on the competitors to compete at national level. Therefore, the number of age-groupers are mostly limited in the national junior championships as only people of a high standard may compete. New South Wales appears to be the only state which is organizing an incentive for the swimmers and in 1966, an age-group team was selected from the winter championships to go to New Zealand. In 1967 a team went to Fiji to participate in an age-group competition. This has proved a great incentive, limited in size, but still incentive for the youngsters to compete during the winter.

CC: *My observations of your age-group plan indicate that you should have some wonderful international prospects coming from these programs. Would you agree that the heaviest emphasis in Australian swimming seems to be on age-group development?*

JD: There has been quite a tremendous surge towards age-group programming particularly since 1962. Although there were many people advocating this development at an earlier stage, it was about 1962 when the program really began its forward impetus. The program has developed from a point of view of commercial sponsorship. Your statement is true, but I am confident that the older age groups have not been neglected, and I feel that we have a very balanced swimming program for all ages in Australia.

CC: *On whom do you call for the administration of this program? The same officials connected with senior swimming?*

JD: Yes, all officials who conduct swimming meets in Australia, and they must be registered officials who have to sit for an examination. They do this in the categories in which they wish to officiate at the various swimming meets, but to be a referee, they must pass all these examinations before they can achieve this position. They must study hard, and they are then rostered per swimming meet and, perhaps, have four or five swimming meets every year to which they are allocated.

CC: *Is your age-group program bringing many new officials into the sport?*

JD: Well, like all countries, no doubt, we have the wastage problem. People are coming in at approximately the rate at which the swimmers and their parents leave the sport. Parents are usually the most profitable as far as the swimming associations are concerned because, while their children are swimming, these people become swimming officials.

CC: *Is the age-group plan unearthing promising new coaches as has been the position in the United States?*

JD: Yes, new coaches are coming to the fore. We have far more coaches than we had 10 years ago and our position in 10 years time will make it seem that we have very few coaches now! Younger coaches are constructing their own indoor heated pools and are thus enabled to work a year-round program. They can now start with learn-to-swim enthusiasts, teach them the fundamental strokes, take them through stroke correction, and then enroll them in their training squads. It is now possible, as never before in Australia, to start with one coach and continue your whole swimming career with this person.

CC: *Will you please describe the organization of the Australian top 10 age-group rankings, as published in* The International Swimmer?

JD: This is a personal ranking and the organization of it is that people send in to *The International Swimmer* the listing of their particular swimmers. This is done in all freestyle events from 100 to 1,500 meters, 200 and 400 individual medley, the 50-, 100-, and 200-meter butterfly, backstroke and breaststroke, also the various relays. We collate these times and publish them once every year. The aim of this ranking is to discover the best swimmers for the season. It can be done anywhere providing three small but very important rules are adhered to. It must be in competition, with a scratch start, and it must be in a pool. The swimmer must state his age and have the time officially signed by a swimming official.

DISCUSSION WITH RAY ESSICK

> Ray Essick was the executive director of United States Swimming for 21 years and retired in 1997. Ray Essick graduated in physical education from the University of Illinois where he studied under the famous researchers, Dr. Thomas Cureton and Dr. Bill Heusner. After 20 years as a college coach, Essick stepped away from coaching and went into administration. Essick discusses the many facets of administering the gigantic United States swimming structure.

CC: How did you get started?

RE: I graduated in physical education from the University of Illinois. I was fortunate to study under Dr. William Heusner and Dr. Thomas Cureton. As you know, both men have a history of interest in swimming. They stimulated my interest to go into coaching. After 20 years of coaching, I was fortunate to find a position in our swimming organization that permitted me to step away from coaching and go into administration.

CC: You were head coach at Harvard before you moved into administration?

RE: Yes, I was at Harvard University for three years and prior to that at Southern Illinois University for seven years. I was a high school coach for eight years and have also coached in YMCAs and country clubs, so I have experience in most phases of coaching.

CC: What contact did you have with international swimming before you became executive director?

RE: First, of course, in preparing swimmers to succeed internationally or to make international teams. I've taken teams overseas on tours and I was the U.S. men's coach at the 1971 Pan American Games. To serve on the swimming Olympic Committee helped me obtain a pretty good idea of the international program.

CC: Until recently, you were based at the AAU headquarters in Indianapolis. You moved to Colorado Springs as a result of a big change in the structure of United States Swimming. Expand on this change.

RE: As you know, in our country there has always been a challenge about who will administer our amateur sports and have the final say. We have several strong lobbying groups in amateur sports. President Ford, in response to some of these pressures, appointed a commission to investigate administration of amateur sports, especially the Olympic sports. I believe he appointed the commission in 1976. In 1977 President Carter responded to the commission by endorsing the Amateur Sports Act. In 1978, it was approved by Congress and amateur sports were determined to be autonomous and separate from any overall governing body. The sports act said that a governing body could hold only one international sports franchise. Sports governing bodies were given two years to implement the law. At that time we were the Competitive Swimming Committee of the Amateur Athletic Union which held the USA membership in FINA. In the summer of 1980, United States Aquatic Sports was given the franchise and the membership in FINA. We in the United States Swimming decided to rent a space from the AAU. In the fall of 1981, we decided to relocate our national headquarters in Colorado Springs where Olympic Committee facilities were available to us.

CC: How is the new office organized?

RE: We have five divisions at our headquarters. Our business division handles accounting and bookkeeping. Our information services division is headed by Randy Hart, who takes care of all our publications and our radio, television, and media materials, as well as keeping statistical records of our sport. Our local services division is headed by Carol Alexander who is responsible for the 60 different swimming committees that make up United States Swimming administratively. Selden Fritschner is our technical director, taking care of our national teams and providing liaison between coaches and many of our meet managers. There is also a promotions division and my personal office as executive director.

CC: *I'm particularly interested in an elaboration of your technical side and what importance you attach to it.*

RE: United States Swimming has had technical success, but I don't think we've ever had our planning formalized. We're at the point now where we have a planning committee which is composed of five coaches, one athlete, two lay people, and the chairman of our sports medicine committee. These people meet regularly and discuss long-range technical plans. They have direct input to our board of directors, the highest elected group in United States Swimming. Their chairman, by election, also sits on our board. The Technical Planning Committee goes to the Board of Directors for the implementation of their ideas by the various standing committees in our structure.

CC: *Who appoints the Technical Planning Committee?*

RE: The lay people and the chairman of the sports medicine committee are elected by the House of Delegates. The coaches are elected by the United States Swimming Board of Directors from a list of coaches recommended by the American Swimming Coaches Committee. The athlete is elected by the United States Swimming Athletes Committee.

CC: *What is the purpose of having the lay people on the committee?*

RE: I think it is to give an overview. We have people who are in officiating or administration and there is certainly more to the technical aspect of swimming than the mere planning of competition, research, or team structure.

CC: *What do you mean by that?*

RE: We have the personnel necessary to help achieve a balance in the total program—maybe a coach doesn't have the perspective—and I think the tunnel vision of some coaches has to be balanced out.

CC: *By the presence of two lay volunteers?*

RE: By the presence of somebody who is not in the coaching profession.

CC: *Tell me about your sources of funds and how you raise funds from the corporate sector.*

RE: Our program traditionally has been funded from membership fees and that is still a major source of funding. However, for 10 years we've had excellent support from Phillips Petroleum. They have a tradition of involvement with amateur sports and involvement with youth. We've also developed a corporate program with Arena and a corporate program with McDonald's for our junior Olympic and age-group programs. They have an awareness of amateur sports and the necessity of corporate money for our survival. So we have the corporate money, the major revenues from membership, we get some money as the outcome of television, some funds from the USOC and, surprisingly, no money whatsoever from the federal government.

CC: *How did you go about seeking support from McDonald's?*

RE: I don't think there was any great secret or insight to create this support. As you know, the McDonald's corporation has constructed and contributed a swimming pool for the 1984 Olympic Games in Los Angeles. The donation of the pool and promoting the sport are very important to them. It turned out to be a wonderful marriage, because our goals are parallel and overlap the goals of McDonald's and their market.

CC: *How do you raise funds from the corporate sector?*

RE: Part of my philosophy has been not to attempt to delve into areas where I have no knowledge but seek out people who do have the expertise. As a result, we retained a marketing and public relations firm to assist us with the marketing of our sport and the sale of television rights. They do the business end of sponsorship.

CC: *Who first approached McDonald's?*

RE: Surprisingly they approached us and the result was their sponsorship of the junior Olympic program. John Naber works as a spokesman for McDonald's and the junior Olympic program. He attends meets giving out awards in a standard public relations program but he doesn't really do a great deal of clinic work.

CC: *I'm impressed with the amount of time you spend on the deck. You're in the stands; you're with the coaches; you're with the swimmers and the officials. You seem to be wherever I look.*

RE: It's very important for any administrator to stay in touch with the sport and its roots. That's where I came from—coaching, physical education. I find it distracting now that our staff has grown and my administrative responsibilities have grown. It's at the point where I feel I don't get out enough and stay close enough to the sport. I force myself to do this. This is a power base if you wish to talk about it politically. It's very important to have the support for the projects that we wish to pursue. Our power base comes from the coaches and the people who actually conduct swimming in this country.

CC: *Do you feel there's a risk in structuring administration in such a way that it becomes difficult to keep the program flexible?*

RE: I don't think that is ever going to happen in this country because administration must be responsive to the coaches. One of the criticisms of ourselves is that sometimes we are too flexible, not allowing us to predict what's going to happen from day to day. We find, if you keep goals and objectives too static, then it's easy to get hung up too much in the management concept rather than adapting to what you need. So I think adaptability, the ability to think on your feet, and avoiding a bias to structure for structure's sake are important in our program.

CC: *I get the impression in American swimming*

that leadership comes from nearly everyone involved. It's a democratic process rather than the national office sending it down to the lower ranks. It appears to be a continuous contribution from every key figure, whether coach, swimmer, or official.

RE: I think that's a significant fact. I think that as United States Swimming matures as a separate administrative body, after 90 years caught up in the AAU, we'll be able to see what we need to do. One thing I can guarantee is the direction of the program comes from the grassroots. Those people tell us what to do and we try to refine it. It's important for me to know the feelings and hear the needs of the grassroots, and then I can respond. For example, two years ago, our House of Delegates determined that each local swimming committee should have a coaches representative. We now find in some swimming committees the predominance of people are coaches and these people are telling us what to do. They are elected. You can be a coach and be elected to any position in United States Swimming. We don't tell people what to do. We don't sit up at the top and have it filter down. It comes up to us and we have to try to adapt and adjust and do the very best we can because we're responsible to them. They are not responsible to us.

CC: *Do you believe in four-year plans and things of that nature? I've noted over the years it never really happens just like that. Usually the target year is so far ahead that, when the time arrives, none of the original personnel are still on the scene to be reminded of whether their plan was successful or not.*

RE: Let's say an annual meeting is very flexible! I don't think we'll ever have a static four-year plan or the like. There are different ways of achieving our goals and we evaluate them regularly. We are never going to get stuck with a four-year plan just for the plan's sake.

✧ ✧ ✧

DISCUSSIONS WITH
DON GAMBRIL

Recorded in August 1966 at Los Angeles, California.

Don Gambril, one of the all-time greats of American coaching, started his career in Southern California in the early 1960s where he produced a number of world-class athletes at all distances from the 100 to the 1,500 meter, before moving to Harvard. Don Gambril was head coach of the highly successful American team at the 1984 Los Angeles Olympic Games. Gambril discusses great athletes, national planning, and the importance of continuing psychological preparation. Among his famous swimmers are Sharon Stouder, Gunner Larsson (Sweden), Jonty Skinner, Patti Caretto, and Jean Hallock.

CC: *How were you able to build your squad, in less than seven years, into one of the major squads in the world?*

DG: I started in 1959. Actually I had a little competitive background—not very successful, I might also add! I was involved primarily in American football, in college, and when I was hired as a schoolteacher, I was given an additional sport in the spring, and that sport was swimming.

As things went along, I decided to start a summer training program for my swimmers, to make my school team a little better. We had no girls on the team. Around 1959, we picked up a couple of girls, very important to start out with, a couple of girls named Sharon Stouder and Jean Hallock, both of them at the time young age group swimmers. Sharon was known nationally, but Jean was not. This was the nucleus of the squad.

CC: *What do you consider to be the most important aspects of team building?*

DG: I think that in building a team one has to prove oneself capable of coaching. I think that too many mistakes are made by coaches that are beginning by trying to assemble a top team to begin with. I think that you have to prove yourself capable of handling such a team and the only way to do this is to build your own swimmers. As you build your own team you are going to pick up talent, as it were, that will come one way or another. One thing I have always tried to be personally is ethical on any swimmers that have transferred to my team. I think that this is a good sound foundation for a club and, if you are just around recruiting or stealing swimmers from everybody else, why you are going to have to live in a house you're building, and it's not going to be a very happy one.

CC: *What advice would you give the inexperienced coach just starting out on his career?*

DG: As we started our team, I was very inexperienced and, fortunately, I was able to learn enough each year to keep one step ahead of the swimmers I was coaching! I think that this is about all coaches all over the world can hope to do—that is, keep ahead of the swimmers they are coaching—because I feel each year, if I had only known last year what I know now—look what I could have done with my team last year! And, as you look at the records, you feel the same way—wishing that you just could have had that swimmer going that fast a year ago, and he would have had the record, and he would have been in first place.

CC: *What about a coaching philosophy, drive, and direction to the building of the team?*

DG: Anyone, in any position, building a squad, needs to have some firm thoughts, philosophy in building and training towards whatever their goals happen to be. First of all, I think that the most important thing in building a team is, as I mentioned, ethics, and this is on the part of the coach and the squad he is building. You've got to have some strong moral character to the squad and to the program. And then, ever important, and you'll hear me mention this time after time, is team morale. You touched on this this morning about your squad and the things they do. I think that every coach has to coach within his own personality and has to play upon the emotions and personality of his squad members.

CC: *Do you agree that it is asking for trouble to set down certain irrevocable rules in managing your squad?*

DG: As one tries to build a squad, if you set down certain guidelines that you're never going to vary from, you are going to enter problems and very shortly. You are going to run into the swimmer that cannot conform to the guidelines you have set out through one reason or another. Maybe it's physical, maybe it's mental, maybe it's economic—whatever it is. Each case, each incident, everything that crops up, should be handled as an individual case and, what might be held true one time, may not be the way you want to rule another. I'm always in favor of being nothing but fair-minded, and I think the fairest way to the individual is to treat each case as a single incident—not to necessarily set a precedent. Some precedents you may set up and later on you would have to rule on the same precedent.

CC: *Would you please elaborate on your ideas on team morale?*

DG: The team morale, once again, is the most important thing, I feel, in workouts, in preparing for meets, in your relationship with your squad. We do all sorts of things to encourage team morale. As I told you this morning, no matter where you are coaching, where you are working—anywhere in the world—you've got handicaps. The one in Los Angeles that I face, and my squad faces, is the geographical area. I have swimmers that drive as far as 54 miles one way to workouts on city streets, which means they drive 108 miles to single-day workouts and over 200 miles to twice-daily sessions—unless they can stay with a teammate and drive home in the evening. This is a handicap. The boys and girls get out of school at 3:30 PM and, by the time we can assemble from varying distances they travel, we start the workout at about 4:45 PM, work a half hour on deck exercises, Exer-Genie work, an hour and thirty minutes in the water, and that gets us out of there by 7 PM. So it's

time to change and get clear, so they are out of it by 7 PM with an hour's drive to face before they can start their homework and other things they have to do. We do not train twice a day except in the summer.

CC: *How does your summer program operate?*

DG: In the summer, our schedule runs almost continuously, and we do train seven days a week and I feel that this is best after several varying circumstances, over a period of years. The last three years we have trained on the following schedule: In the winter we train two hours a day, in the summertime we train twice on Monday, once on Tuesday, twice on

International Swimming Hall of Fame

Sharon Stouder, coached by Don Gambril, won three Olympic gold medals in 1964. She set an Olympic record in the 100-meter butterfly that stood until 1972. She was second in the 100-meter freestyle—a touch behind Dawn Fraser—thus becoming the second woman to beat 60 seconds.

Wednesday, once Thursday, twice Friday, twice Saturday, and once on Sunday.

CC: *What are your reasons for this?*

DG: The reason is that we can't get the pool Tuesday and Thursday evenings. This has worked out very well for us. I'm not saying that we are going to stick to this. We may pick up additional workouts, especially for the distance swimmers, in the next couple of years. But, the two workouts and one workout off, two workouts, one workout off system has worked very well for us. I've noticed that our swimmers never get as tired at the end of the week the way they used to be. We used to work five days a week, twice a day, maybe once on Saturday, then have the rest of the weekend off. Well, Friday and Saturday nobody could move they were so tired. By Monday, after being out of the water two days, they had lost the feel of the water. They came back, they wouldn't be any good to work out on Monday. So, therefore, we would get, maybe, Monday evening through Thursday evening, pretty good workouts, but the rest of the workouts were, more or less, a waste of time. So this, I think, does have merit, to miss a workout in the middle of the week occasionally so that you can keep going at a more intensive rate.

CC: *We all agree that workouts have to be planned in keeping with team morale. What are your feelings on this subject?*

DG: Workouts always have to be planned around the morale of the team. There was a time, in fact, until this year, where for over two years I wrote out our workouts religiously. At the beginning of the week, I would write them out for the entire week and we would stick right to the workout. And this worked very well. We had great success with it. But, later and particularly this year, it seemed like it wasn't working so well, and I began to wonder if maybe I shouldn't change. We did change this summer, and I think it was a change for the better. The change this summer being mainly that I had in mind the amount of work we are going to do for each workout but, as to exactly what we were going to do, I determined it by the way the squad was performing and, if there was a day where everybody seemed kind of grumpy and weak and not doing too well, well, then we would switch to something like relays or motivation workouts. If there was a day when things were clicking real well, then we would really pour it on them!

CC: *I don't think the fact that you have so many girl distance swimmers in your team can be attributed to the long arm of coincidence! Do you care to elaborate?*

DG: Last year in the United States National Championships, we got five out of the top six places in the 1,500 meters—first, third, fourth, fifth, and sixth. We weren't so fortunate this year. But, I think that one of the reasons we have this is that we do have a world-record holder in this event, Patti Caretto. A lot of the younger swimmers that are her size are performing and, every time they see something she does in workout, they try to do the same thing and do it faster. Some of them, actually, at times, repeat better than she does now, and so they are all shooting for her, the people that are in her category. This is why I think we have a good distance program.

CC: *I believe that you returned from your visit to Russia, as coach to the American team, with some very interesting impressions of swimming in that country.*

DG: My first impression of Russian swimming was that it is highly organized and scientific—just as most of their other facets are today including their outer space, track and field, and all other forms of athletics. They went into the 1956 Olympics primarily as observers and in 1960 had no finalists in swimming. By 1964 they did have one Olympic champion, one second place, and one third place, all in breaststroke, as it were. Now we find them in 1966 nearly ready to take over second place in the world in swimming by my way of thinking. I feel that, by 1968, they will be very close to the United States and, possibly, have surpassed Australia as number two swimming country. By 1972, I feel they will have an excellent chance of being number one in swimming. I feel this to be true after witnessing the type of program that they are running.

CC: *Do the Russians appreciate the importance of a strong base in age group programs?*

DG: Yes, they have gone to age group swimming. What they have done is to pattern it after the United States program. Then, of course, they have tried to use scientific methods to make improvements. They have 1,100,000 swimmers registered now. This is the information I was given.

CC: *Do they have a national coaching program?*

DG: They have two coaches, considered their chief coaches, one for the age group and one for senior swimming. They are actually administrators and do no coaching, but rather set up the program. They had, at the swim meet we attended, 12 national coaches, all having attained this rank by coaching a swimmer to a national championship in Russia.

CC: *Is there any specialization in swimming at school?*

DG: Their sports program for schools is set up primarily by the interest of a parent or family wanting a child to do ice skating, fencing, or whatever it might be, then put them in school. In sports school, they go through the regular academic subjects each day, but then they are with other boys and girls that are also training for the same type of sport, whether it be swimming or ice hockey, etcetera. So from the beginning level of school, they are thinking and being brought up in this atmosphere; thinking of their sport, working on tactics, thinking of conditioning and training and motivation towards this particular end. Therefore, you have groups of swimmers all over Russia going to these schools, and in summer, they take them to training camps, maybe in the Ural Mountains, maybe along the Volga River—wherever it might be—for their holiday season. There they will receive free clothing, food, and so forth while they are training. Once they reach a certain level there is absolutely no expense to them for training.

CC: *Quite a comparison with conditions obtained in the rest of the world, isn't it!!?*

DG: Comparing this with the United States and our own club, our swimmers are paying from 32 dollars to 47 dollars a month for training as well as their entry fees and all the other costs to and from workouts, and you can see how they are going to overcome us simply by great numbers, if nothing else. They have 250 million people in their country—about 50 million more than we. They have facilities, and these facilities are made available for training throughout the day to the coaches. In the United States, we have plenty of facilities—there is no lack of facilities—our problem is getting into them. Most of them are recreational facilities, and we get into them only in odd hours and then have to pay a high toll to get in.

CC: *What are their research programs yielding as far as new training programs are concerned?*

DG: They are doing a tremendous job scientifically. As we got off the aircraft at 11:30 at night, two scientists were there and rode back with us to the hotel in the city and were already interrogating me as to methods of training, wanting to know if they could film our workouts, wanting to know if they could interview me, interview the swimmers. They did this very thoroughly, collecting all the material and data they could! This alone will not make swimming champions. They take this, however, and analyze it and incorporate it with the ideas they have already come up with. One of the things we noticed in the competition, however, and something that enabled us to win several races, was their lack of racing knowledge and tactics. This is something that one can't learn in a book or just through observation or talking to someone—something has to come through experience! As I see it, their biggest handicap now, and the thing that is going to hold them back for a few years possibly, is not having enough top-level competition to provide the experience they need. They will get part of this, of course, in international meets, like the one we've just completed; they will get more of this in European championships and Olympic Games, but there is nothing like actual competition with top level competitors to develop this sense of tactics and racing strategy.

❖ ❖ ❖

Recorded at the U.S. Long Course Championships, Indianapolis, 1984.

CC: *Where do you think American swimming is headed?*

DG: We had a big setback last year at the World Championships in Ecuador. We feel this was due partially to the lateness of our trials, poor planning. Also our athletes were disillusioned by the cancellation of the 1980 Olympic Games. We are aware that we were almost rudderless and did not have a major plan. We're striving to get organized so we have more to do with planning the future instead of letting it happen through the efforts of coaches, a lot of swimming talent, and accidental happenings. We're trying to bring more design into our program.

CC: *When that happens, American swimming will be even more dangerous to its rivals because it is a giant that has tended to just grow and grow.*

DG: If you look at the results of East Germany from a country of 18 to 20 million and what we are getting out of a population of 220 million, then it can be seen that we are not doing the job that we could.

CC: *To what do you attribute that?*

DG: Part of it is a lack of planning. But I think much of it is a lack of control. We certainly don't want and will never have the type of control that East Germany has. We will always have mavericks who are not going to fall into our plan. I don't think that's going to change, and I'm not sure that I would want it to change. But by design, we can at least do a better job to ensure total representation of the country.

CC: *What about your pre-Olympic planning?*

DG: The staff is selected now and we've had two meetings to begin to formulate our plans for the location of the training camp and how we are going to divide team responsibilities. We have a large, very experienced staff, most with Olympic or Pan-Am experience. The organization from the Olympic Committee is good as it has always been in the United States. Of course, having the Games in the U.S. will save us the planning problems of setting up a field kitchen in a foreign country.

CC: *Tell me about your development camps.*

DG: One is the Olympic development training camp for junior national level swimmers under 12 at Colorado Springs each year. Starting this year another series of camps will be sponsored through U.S. Swimming Olympic development funds. The original idea was to have 10 to 20 of these camps around the country, each with 20 boys and 20 girls. They will be organized to run the same workouts so that training data can be computerized. We'll try to motivate talented people and see that they are in good training programs. The main thing is to identify the talent, make the swimmers aware of their talent, and hope they will seek their own training levels.

CC: *Do you see any really bright new prospects?*

DG: Tammy Thomas was tremendous at the women's indoor meet, breaking all of Jill Sterkel's records. Obviously, she could be a sprint talent for us within 14 months.

CC: *What do you think of the East Germany tendency to train swimmers for specialty events? Do you think there is merit in doing the same thing in the United States?*

DG: East Germany is having great success. I can give you case studies of success in the U.S., too. Charlie Hickox was a backstroker through his entire career in the '60s. Then Roland Mathes comes along and seems to be unbeatable. Hickox changed his event to individual medley in the 1968 Olympic year and won two gold medals plus a silver in the backstroke. Gary Hall changed events through his three Olympics. Sometimes specializing can be good. Right now with Tracy Caulkins, one of the most versatile swimmers in history, her only chance to really do something is to specialize. Pick an event and go for it.

CC: *Conversely, is there comparatively more rapid turnover among the East German girls?*

Patty Caretto, coached by Don Gambril, set seven world records in the long-distance freestyle during the 1960s. Her specialty was the 1,500 meter in which she revolutionized distance swimming with her continuous windmill arm stroke and two-beat leg action.

DG: That might be. They certainly continue to spring new young swimmers on us who come up awfully fast but don't stay on top or stay in the picture too long. American swimmers spread their events. When we recruit athletes for our college programs for example, we're seldom interested in the swimmer with just one event unless the athlete is good enough to be national champion. You can't build a very strong team if you put all your scholarships into recruiting just a few people for a few events. They have to be able to swim multiple events and help in relays. This is one of the reasons why our distance swimming suffers. If you sign a distance swimmer, he can only help you in one or two events.

CC: *Do you think the distance swimmer is at a disadvantage in the college program especially when working toward the Olympics? Often they can't put in the time because of scholastic obligations. Perhaps in Olympic year, they should train with their home clubs.*

DG: That could be. It depends upon the individual, the academic major and the school year. In my experience, the person who trains without studying or working part-time will find that a tremendous amount of pressure builds. Many of our top people do take off for the last quarter or the last semester to prepare for the Olympics. That's not just distance swimmers but people like Mike Burton and Mike Bruner. By taking a full year off, you just sit around all day and climb the walls. If all you're doing is training twice a day, and you've got 10 months to go before the Olympic trials, it's a long time and a lot of pressure. It's much better, I think, to have it broken up into a college season where you're training hard and getting the background work anyway. It is essential for a distance swimmer to train long course. Many schools don't have a long course facility.

CC: *Do you think the pressure cooker of college swimming is an advantage going into the Olympics?*

DG: I think it's good for the most part. There are still individuals who get to the end of their careers, the Olympics let's say, and still choke. But generally, the people who come through our program have been through high pressure programs for their entire careers, and the result is that the pressure at the Olympics isn't as much as at our own Olympic trials. It's not that there aren't great competitors from the other countries, but just making our team is a big relief. They can go on and feel good about the Olympic competition. It's certainly much tougher now in the Games than it was a few years ago. There are many countries producing great swimmers. It's going to be difficult for a single country to dominate as we have over the last two decades.

CC: *What about the frequency of competition?*

DG: Certainly we have a very extensive competitive program. One of the things a competitor in the United States learns is to take some losses on the way to an important win. Some people never learn do that and can't absorb that loss.

CC: *The youngster who can get up after a defeat, dust himself down, and continue on to success, has undergone a toughening process.*

DG: That's true. A prime example is Mike Burton. He didn't swim well until the championship. He would take defeat after defeat and then come back at the championship and break the world record. With confidence in himself and his coach, he was able to accept the fact that "losing today to win tomorrow" was part of the approach.

CC: *What are your views about a yearly training plan?*

DG: The East Germans and the West Germans apparently test the lactate system and rely on it quite heavily to trace a swimmer's conditioning. It must give them a lot of insight where we, by comparison, are really flying by the seat of our pants. We take a look at swimmers and, from how well we know them, decide if they need more work, what kind of work, or whether they need rest. We're really guessing. They have a lot more information and feedback than we do. Still granting them that, I know there's a lot of mental approach to it, and that's just as important as all the scientific information that you get.

CC: *What is your viewpoint on peaking?*

DG: If you're looking at a swimmer's career, year by year, season by season, the most important thing is to keep a swimmer going through continued progress. It comes back to one thing and that's motivation. If you're going to train all year for one competition, then you've got to have some way to keep the swimmer motivated 365 days to make the approach for that competition. Little steps along the way, I think, make it easy even though you're still planning for the one major effort. Motivation is so important, because every day you're out there writing the workout, but the effort from the swimmer counts far more than what you've written.

✧ ✧ ✧

DISCUSSIONS WITH GEORGE HAINES

Recorded at Lincoln, Nebraska, U.S. Long Course Outdoor Championships, August 1966.

In a remarkable career George Haines has been a U.S. Olympic coach on many occasions: 1960 U.S. women's coach, 1964 U.S. men's assistant coach, 1968 U.S. men's coach, 1972 and 1976 U.S. women's assistant coach, and 1984 men's and women's assistant coach. In 1980 Haines was appointed head coach for both men and women, but the United States did not compete in the Moscow Olympics. He was named ASCA Coach of the Year in 1964, 1966, 1967, and 1972. Between the years of 1957 and 1974, his Santa Clara Swim Club won a remarkable total of 43 national titles; developed 55 Olympians; and won 33 Olympic gold medals, 11 silver medals, and 7 bronze medals.

CC: *How do you organize your workouts?*

GH: When we train in a 50-meter pool, we have something like 55–60 swimmers, and this means we must use circle training. We train mostly 50s, 100s, 200s, 400s, even distances, so that we can go from opposite ends of the pool and, in doing this, we use circle training. We have huge training clocks at either ends of the pool, and we time everything we do. We time the total workout. The swimmers know exactly what they are doing—whether its swimming, kicking, or pulling. We try to keep control of the workout by using the training clocks.

CC: *Do all your youngsters do the same workout in training?*

GH: Basically, most of the time the swimmers are doing the same workout but, right before the

Nationals, a month to a month and a half before the Nationals, we divide up into three groups. We may have about three lanes of distance and middle-distance swimmers on one side of the pool, then the 400 and 1,500 swimmers in the middle of the pool, and then on the other side, we'll have all the sprinters, the 100 and 200 swimmers. Then we'll change the workout so that they are all doing different things, because the sprinters have to be cared for as well as the distance swimmers at this point.

CC: *Do you plan your workouts very far in advance or do you do them off the cuff on the actual day of the workout?*

GH: Most of the time I try to plan my workouts two to three days ahead of time, but I've always had the feeling that you have to do the workout with regards to the swimmer and how he feels on a particular day. I think if you plan the workouts three weeks or a month ahead, you can run into trouble, because you find you become stereotyped, and the swimmers become bored. You can get too tired, well, you think you have the workout planned and you must carry it out. We try to plan the workout about a day ahead, and sometimes we'll even change it right in the middle of the workout! I'd change my ideas because the swimmers may not feel as well as I think they should.

CC: *Do you do much stroke correction work and, if so, I suppose it is done probably in the off-season?*

GH: We don't do anything different with regard to stroke work than anyone else and, as long as we can have our training going on, using the training clocks, and I don't carry a stopwatch, I feel that between each flight I can get to individuals and try to work on their strokes. However, our stroke work is done mostly in the fall of the year when we come back to training after our layoff; we do work quite a bit of time on stroke. We have a bench at the side of the pool, and I get this individual out that I want to work with, and put him on the bench and have everyone else listen, and we go over the stroke. Then we get them back in the water and have everyone take turns in trying to demonstrate the strokes. We try to do as much stroke work as possible throughout the year without taking up too much time because, after all, conditioning does mean a lot, too.

CC: *Do you conduct a novice group of competitors as well as your National Championship team?*

GH: Well, we have about 240 swimmers on our swim club so that means we have a group of about five to six years old up through to our senior group, we have here at the Nationals, and the oldest person is about 22 to 23 years old. We do have what is called a novice or beginning group, and then we have the in-between or intermediate-type swimmers who are just leading up to the senior squad, and then we have our senior squad. Here in the United States, as you know, we are all broken down into age groups. I have two assistant coaches, and they do a fantastic job with our young swimmers, and so I have to give them a lot of credit for the buildup that we have in our young program.

CC: *What role do the parents play in your setup? You seem to be on a friendly, relaxed footing with those parents present here at the championships and that seems to be contrary to the coach-parent relationship that exists in many squads where the parents are usually anathema to most coaches and considered just a necessary evil.*

GH: I feel that the parents play a real necessary role in swimming. You bring 41 swimmers to the National Championships—someone has to raise the money. We have quite an active parents' association, and they have done a great deal of work to ensure that we have the money. They play a necessary role in our squad. I feel that I have to get along with the parents, if I'm going to get along with their children, and I've got to know them as well as the swimmers. We have a real active parent organization which does a fantastic job, and they know where they stand with me, and I know where I stand with them. I have my problems just like everyone else, but most of the time we get along real good.

CC: *In what directions do you think swimming will improve? What will be the next big*

International Swimming Hall of Fame

George Haines on Don Schollander: "One big thing that makes Don so much better than anyone else—when he gets tired he is able to control his stroke, think about technique, and not let himself go and flail."

forward stride in the advancement of our sport.

GH: Well, of course, as you know, we are finding out that these swimmers can take more work, but I think that, psychologically, we have to work on the swimmer's mind and get him to believe that he can do a lot more. Once they get into condition, I really feel, that well over 90 percent of what they do as far as success is concerned is in the head. If they begin to believe that they can do things, well, they will go ahead and achieve these aspirations.

CC: *What are your ideas on interval training? Do you believe in long rests, short rests, or, if you believe in a combination of both, and in what proportions?*

GH: I believe that we have to have a little bit of both but, once we get into good condition after the early season training where we've done a lot of quantity swimming with short rests, most of our training is done with quality type swimming where we have a little bit more rest, and we are asking more out of a

swimmer. We are asking better times in practice and I like to put it this way: We train most of the time in a slight state of fatigue because if you don't, you are never going to build up a resistance to fatigue and oxygen debt. To me this is very important, because a swimmer has to perform in a meet of any kind in a slight state of fatigue—at least at one point of the race—and I think the more you train like this the more you become accustomed to it. They begin to learn how to take pain and how to feel their stroking, to control themselves when they are swimming in pain. This is the way we try to operate all year round.

CC: *Approximately how much quality work would you do early in the program?*

GH: We do a lot, even in the early program, but we get into more and more quality swimming as we get closer to the National Championships. What I mean by quality work is that you give long rests between the repeats, and we are then justified in expecting the swimmer to perform much better than earlier in the year. We try to perform at pace or near the pace they are going to swim when they go to the Nationals. Two or three weeks before the Nationals, we do a lot more dive swimming. We get out of the pool and start from a dive and try to swim at or near the pace they are aiming for in the championship. This is what I call quality swimming.

CC: *Would you like to outline Don Schollander's approach to racing, his ideas of pace and why and how you think he was able to meet John Nelson's redoubtable challenge in the 400-meter final after Nelson broke Don's world 400-meter record in the morning heats?*

GH: I think he won the 400 simply because he might be a better swimmer than Johnny Nelson at this stage—and Nelson is a great swimmer. He likely won the race because he is probably a little bit more mature, but I think the tactics he used in this race were a lot different to anything he has ever used before. Normally, he goes out quite easily and then swims the second half of the race almost as quick or as fast as the first half. But this time we decided before the race that he had to make Nelson swim early in the race—try to make him force himself so that he didn't have quite so much left or wasn't so strong at the end of the race. So our objective was to go through the 200 a little under 2:03 and he went through at 2:03, or just slightly under. His 100 meters time was probably a high 58 and then he came through the 200 in about 2:02.8 or 2:03 flat, which was very good. Then he tried to force the issue a little bit more in the third 100 to keep bringing Nelson out so that he wouldn't have much left. He did it perfectly and John tried to close on Schollander in the last 100 but he didn't have enough left to do it. Tactically, the idea was to make John swim and not let him lie back. Don did a perfect job and I think that it was probably the best job of pacing he's ever done. The same thing was true in the 200; he tried to get him out, make him come out with him and then try to break his back a little bit in the third 50 and he did. Don was just able to get home faster in the last 50 in each one of the events. I think that, tactically, he did a beautiful job.

CC: *Do you believe his superior stroke technique helped in any way?*

GH: I think this is the one thing that makes Don so much better than anyone else; when he gets tired he is able to control his stroke, think about technique, and not let himself go and flail. He does have a beautiful stroke and he's able to control it even when he's tired. This certainly is an advantage. He does have the most efficient stroke of any boy I've worked with and I think that Greg Buckingham, the other boy I had in there, along with Mike Wall, have outstanding techniques also. I think this has helped our swimmers in this meet a great deal, especially the freestylers. I think that our technique of all trying to be as much like Don as possible—everyone is individual and different of course—but I think that Don's technique has helped him a great deal, and I do feel that he probably would have swum better in the 400 had he not gone to Russia, but I think that trip was important and we did allow him to have the time out of the

program to do it. It was just fortunate that he had quite a bit of training background, was able to go to Russia, come back and perform as well as he has done. I do feel that he would have been much better this summer had he not gone to Russia because, in our training, he has done better than he has ever done in his life. His repeat performances in practice have been much, much better than in 1964 before he won the Olympic titles.

CC: *I hope you are going to have him up there for the 1968 Olympics so that we can see some of the greatest middle-distance swimming of all time.*

GH: I think that if these other swimmers keep putting the pressure on him, he'll have to

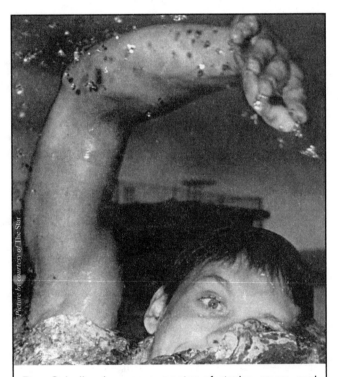

Picture by courtesy of The Star

Don Schollander was a master of stroke, pace, and strategy. Except that by today's standards he probably held his head too high, his stroke perfectly combined all elements of rhythm, control, and equal balance of form and pattern of movement. One of the clues to his unusually slow stroking and smooth power application is shown in the broad, propelling surfaces of hand, forearm, and upper arm. At the 1964 Olympics in Tokyo, Schollander, the first to win four gold medals in one Olympics, thrilled the water world with victories in the 100- and 400-meter freestyle, and his team work in the relays. He set three world records and four Olympic marks.

be great in 1968—much more so than he is today. I do feel that, since this boy has established goals and principles and high morals, he'll do it and, in 1968, he'll be the one to beat. Incidentally, I hope South Africa will be back in the Games and we certainly feel that politics have nothing to do with sport—competitive swimming or any other sport. I think you have a fantastic squad coming out of South Africa and those backstrokers are something to behold and, in fact, I think I've got a lot of good ideas just watching them swim. Got to go back and teach my girls how to swim like girls and not like boys!

✧ ✧ ✧

Recorded at the U.S. Long Course Championships, Indianapolis, 1983. Haines discusses his new role as a women's college coach.

CC: *Congratulations on Stanford winning the women's NCAA championships. It seems to me that you could be starting a new dynasty, this time in women's college swimming.*

GH: Well, that sounds easier than doing it! But I think that we have a good chance to be in the top three each year. Stanford is a great school. Our program is very good and that will help to recruit good people.

CC: *You've coached at the high school and club level, and for the past decade mostly in college. Now you are concentrating on women's college swimming. It has to be very challenging.*

GH: The history of women's college swimming has not been very good. With athletic scholarships, older female athletes are now staying in the sport and that will eventually help American swimming a great deal. I feel there is a much higher level of swimming yet to be achieved by women.

CC: *What are the difficulties to overcome in order to emulate the performances of the men's American college program?*

GH: Historically, American women have retired before they reach college age, mostly because the scholarships were just not there. Now, this has all changed. We will keep more of the older girls in their prime in the sport. Also, the team concept will become more prevalent, and within three to five years, we should be as strong as the men's program.

CC: *How do you recruit swimmers for your team?*

GH: Stanford is a great school with a solid academic reputation. That is really the main reason people come to study at Stanford. Swimming is secondary. I try to attract great athletes with a solid academic interest. Actually, it's quite easy. If they have high test scores and good grades, they are top prospects. It's very expensive to study at Stanford. We can only afford to keep them on scholarships for four years, so we're looking at the academic-athlete types.

CC: *Do you find it difficult to find sufficient athletes who are also good students?*

GH: I haven't found it to be so here. When I was at UCLA it wasn't difficult either. The average grade point of my incoming girls last year was 3.8 with 4.0 being 100 percent. They are straight-A students. This makes it easier to coach, as you don't have to worry about them going to class and being eligible.

CC: *Do swimmers have time problems in university?*

GH: Budgeting time is very important, but swimmers have learned a great deal of self-discipline as a result of their years of training.

CC: *What type of athlete are you trying to recruit?*

GH: First, I expect them to be very strong academically—good marks, that's the first requirement. Second, that they come from a club program that has a great background of training and that have good techniques. And third, that they are going to train during the summer. Summer training is crucial in maintaining a high competitive level.

CC: *When you say "train in the summer," do you mean train with the home club or with you?*

GH: I hope they return home to train with their coach. This is the person who developed them. There would be no point in staying at Stanford if they had a good home program.

To stay at the international level, swimmers now have to train almost throughout the year. It's the same as before they came to college. We do have a program for those who end up not having a place to go to.

CC: *How do you cater to swimmers who were used to over five hours of daily workouts?*

GH: By and large I think we handle it well. We obviously can't train the same hours, but we make up for it by training at a higher intensity. We do more quality work. We ask for a little more effort in their swims. We can probably get almost four hours in daily, and we have three very hard days of weight training.

CC: *Would you describe the weight program in detail?*

GH: Our weight room is within 150 yards of the pool. It is an outstanding facility. We're able to work for an hour, and give extra attention after that to our sprinters. The distance and middle-distance groups will do a basic circuit, with low weights and high repetitions. The sprinters work on strength building with free weights, a lot heavier weights, with low repetitions.

CC: *Have most of the girls done weight programs before?*

GH: Most of them have had some form of circuit training. Not usually as sophisticated as the program we are able to provide due to our range of equipment. We have Universal gyms, Nautilus, and free weights. We use the Isokinetic Swim Bench extensively.

CC: *Anything special for sprinters?*

GH: I believe they not only have to do heavy weights for strength, but they have to be on some kind of a circuit where they have to do very fast repetitions. That is to learn quick hands.

CC: *What type of free weights do you do?*

GH: We have six strength coaches at Stanford. I talk to them a lot about using weights. As a result we don't do any free weights where the weight has to be lifted over the head. I do like the bench press and side raisers. One of the most important exercises is what I call the power clean. You bend over, lift the weight, pull it up to your shoulders and hold it and maybe do squats or something. But no lifting directly over the shoulder. I also like lightweight dumbbells, 5 to 10 pounds. I believe tendinitis problems are caused by lifting heavy weights over the shoulder.

CC: *Is there a high incidence of shoulder problems?*

GH: There is great deal of shoulder problems in the U.S. I believe we can reduce the problem with a proper circuit program and some specific exercises.

CC: *Shoulder problems can also be caused by incorrect swimming technique.*

GH: Lack of proper technique is a major cause of injury. For instance, backstrokers are particularly susceptible as they swim flatter and they pull out to the side. This puts greater pressure on the bicipital tendon. Most backstrokers don't roll enough, and so they end up causing more pressure on that tendon.

CC: *Should freestylers roll more, especially as it's faster to be on your side?*

GH: I certainly believe in that. Both Don Schollander and Mark Spitz rolled a lot. With a proper head position you can roll all you want. Poor technique in freestyle is caused more by faulty breathing and head position than body roll. As a matter of fact, in 1964 when Schollander touched out Bobby McGregor at the Tokyo Olympics, we spent a lot of time working on finishes where you do not keep your shoulders flat and reach for the wall. If you roll in and you're on your side reaching for the wall, you get about two extra feet.

✧ ✧ ✧

GEORGE HAINES SPEAKS OUT ON THE UNITED STATES 1996 OLYMPIC TRIALS

"We have to go back to the 10-, 11-, and 12-year-olds," says Haines. "Mark Schubert should write up the program that he used to develop all those great young distance swimmers. He'd make a lot of money selling it!"

A pall of gloom hung over the recent U. S. Olympic trials. For the first time in 76 years, not a single

American record was set. In fact, 20 of the 26 events produced slower times than those recorded in the 1992 trials.

Without dramatic improvement the once mighty American team may appear before a home crowd in Atlanta as underdogs to the Australians, Europeans, and Chinese. Only four gold medals are predicted: Jeff Rouse in the 100-meter backstroke, Tom Dolan in the 400 IM, and two mens' relays.

Present in Indianapolis was retired Olympic coach George Haines who said: "Older athletes don't like to hear coaches of my age say that we're going downhill, especially when the facts show that older athletes have very little chance of making it to two Olympics.

"Only about five to six percent manage to repeat by going to the Olympics twice" said Haines. "For example, just look at the percentages between 1992 and 1996; swimmers such as Tom Jager, Melvin Stewart, Anita Nall, Summer Sanders didn't make this year's team, and Jenny Thompson, who won two golds in 1992, only managed to qualify for a relay. Of course, there always are exceptions like Jeff Rouse, etcetera."

"Who is this guy, Haines?" newcomers to the sport may ask. The quickest answer is to simply say George F. Haines is not only one of the most successful swimming coaches who ever lived, but is famed as one of the sport's all-time great motivators.

As coach of the renowned Santa Clara Swim Club in the '60s and '70s, Haines's swimmers achieved the remarkable tally of 43 national team titles, no fewer than 55 Olympians, and 33 Olympic gold medals, 11 silver medals, and 7 bronze medals. And, moving into the '80s, 6 of his college swimmers made the 1980, '84, and '88 Olympic teams. Not a bad record at all.

Haines remains as fit, dynamic, and charismatic as he was in his coaching heyday. Put it this way: He is far from being your run-of-the-mill old-timer engaged in the luxury of idle anecdotage. To the contrary, "King George" doesn't sound out too often. But when he does, the wise take time to listen. Haines's astute comments on American swimming today could well apply to other countries, too, especially those who mistakenly think that to throw enough public money at a problem is to solve it.

Haines said that many articles on swimming often blame the predominance of sprint events in the college programs for the decline of American swimming. Club coaches say that the college coaches are only interested in recruiting swimmers who can score in sprints.

Over-Distance from an Early Age

Haines said, "We have to sell the club coach that it is everybody's fault. It isn't just the college coach's fault, it is your fault as well. It's long been an accepted fact in many leading swimming countries that, if you don't know who your potentially great distance swimmers are before they are 16, you can kiss them good-bye. If you have not selected athletes to be distance swimmers by the time they are 15 to 16 years old, you cannot expect the college coach to develop distance swimmers."

As an example, Haines mentioned that he had first seen Brian Goodell, who was later to win the 1,500 at the 1976 Montreal Games, when he was only 10 years old, and at the time had told his mother that he would be one of the best. Haines added, "Under Mark Schubert's coaching, Goodell went on to become one of history's great distance swimmers. In fact, Mark started a great tradition of providing a good basic distance background to all the very young swimmers at Mission Viejo.

"Everybody should be in an over-distance program from the time they are 10 upwards. It's easy to see who the sprinters are. You can tell that right away. But, if you don't get good athletes to participate in distance events, they'll never get good," said Haines. "It is easy to come down to shorter races than to go up.

"I can reel off name after name of great short-distance swimmers who started by swimming distance events, and then swam down from these longer distances. The examples go right back to Duke Kahanamoku and Johnny Weissmuller in the 1920s, then in the 1930s and '40s, to Jack Medica, Clark Scholes, Wally Ris, and Alan Ford, and then more recently to Tom Jager, Rick de Mont, Don Schollander, Mark Spitz, and Matt Biondi, who all started as distance and middle-distance swimmers. You have only to look back in history to see the number of swimmers who were good at distances and became great at the shorter distances."

Haines added, "The moment Matt Biondi stopped training for the 400 and 200 in training, his 100 and 50 ceased getting better. Here, at these trials, you could tell by the falloff in time between the first and second half of a swimmer's race that many swimmers had an insufficient background of distance work in their preparation. Amanda Beard had a falloff [difference] of 3.48 seconds in her second 100 of her 200. Almost all the other breaststroke swimmers had a difference of 5 seconds or more. However, Tom Dolan's splits were really impressive!"

Haines said, "The writing has been on the wall for a long time. Jeff Float, a member of the 1984 Olympic team, and the winning 800 freestyle relay team, called me after my return from Indianapolis, and said that his 1984 time for the 200 freestyle still would have made the team. A statement like that brings the truth home to us. There's no point in hiding it." (Note: Jeff Float swam for Sherman Chavoor at the Arden Hills Swim Club in Sacramento, and also for the University of Southern California.)

Get Back to Big Teams

Haines said, "Recently, I was talking to Nort Thornton's son, Richard, and he commented that in the 1960s and 1970s, when American swimming led the world, eager-to-learn coaches from many countries came to visit us. It's ironic that today many of those countries have swimmers who can now beat ours. They train like we did prior to 1980."

Quipped Haines, "The Exer-Genie and the swim bench have given way to the lactate machine. Now I'm not saying there's not a place for science, there is. You can learn a lot from lactate testing. I learned a lot from Bill Heusner on interval training, and I learned a lot from Doc Counsilman, but now Doc says, 'They've gone goofy over science; they're not doing enough work between blood tests.' However, the results produced by Jon Urbanchek at the University of Michigan suggest that American coaches should take a good look at both his program and its work ethic."

Haines expressed the view that "the leadership is spending a lot of money in promoting the older athletes, but we have to go back to big teams with large numbers of swimmers. Initially, I was one of those against the national training center concept, but I'm not sure now that I'm still against it, but they need to improve on it by adding a co-coach, who is distance oriented to encourage more aerobic training, to enhance Jonty Skinner's sprint-oriented program. I've mentioned this to Jonty and I think he agrees. At the moment, I think they are spending a lot of money on only eight people, but Jonty had eight swimmers at the trials, and five of them made the team, so you can't knock that. But, as I say, Jonty needs a co-coach who is a distance-oriented person.

"One of the problems we have today is that no one wants to coach big teams," said Haines. "In fact, one guy, whose name I won't mention, came right out and said that big teams wouldn't work today. But, team training, or racing in practice, is not something to take lightly."

Racing in Practice

"Mark Schubert is the coach who showed the value of training in a big team where the distance swimmers compete against each other in training. But, nowadays, when swimmers get a little older, they don't want to train with the age-groupers any more. It's nice to train with only two or three swimmers in a lane. Often, the college swimmers don't want to go home because the pool is too crowded."

Haines said that there was a great deal to be said for having top swimmers race each other in training. "But today everyone wants to do their own workouts in the training camp, and they blame the Olympic coaches for interfering with their own schedules set by their home coaches," said Haines. "The club and Olympic coaches must come to a common ground on training.

"Our Olympic team could improve a great deal between now and Atlanta if they could race against each other more in practice—breaststroke swimmers competing against each other, backstroke swimmers versus each other, butterfly versus butterfly, etcetera." said Haines. "They could put in some great and valuable sessions in 3½ months. When Olympic swimmers train together like this, they really start to put it together, and they make the coaches' eyes pop out. I think we have a good team but they need more race training, to race more in practice with good people, 2 or 3 times per week."

Said Haines, "The Santa Clara Swim Club trained swimmers in stroke groups. Race-pace training happened a great deal. Eight men and eight women made the 1968 team to the Mexico Olympics through racing each other in practice. At Montreal, the 1976 men's Olympic team, after a great training camp of racing each other, was the best ever."

Haines said that the trials should have been held a little later. "Indianapolis was cold. It's not natural to swim fast when the weather is cold. It would have been a lot better to have had the trials at the end of April or early May. Finally, I think it vital that everyone should get on the same page in trying to improve our sport. You can't improve a national program with club coaches versus college coaches, and vice versa. There are a few great programs to look at for guidance, and we need to share our theories on training. Get on the phone to each other."

✧ ✧ ✧

DISCUSSION WITH JIM MONTRELLA

Recorded at the U.S. Long Course Championships, Indianapolis, 1983.

Jim Montrella, whose experience spans over 30 years, was the highly successful coach at Lakewood Athletic Club in Los Angeles where he developed several world-record holders. Later he continued his winning streak as women's swimming coach at Ohio State University. Montrella maintains that we have come to rely too much on exercise physiology and what we perceive to be the specificity of training, instead of getting back to the meat and potatoes of our sport. Like Mark Schubert, he believes in going more mileage and doing it more intensely.

CC: *To what extent are you and your wife, Beverly, involved with United States Swimming?*

JM: I'm the head coach of Ohio State University's women's swimming team and my wife is the assistant coach. She coached at Mission Viejo for a number of years. We are both on the United States Olympic Swimming Committee. She is the assistant manager for the 1984 U.S. Olympic swimming team. We love the sport. We've gained much from it and want to give back as much as possible.

CC: *Let's talk specifically about your work with the American Swimming Coaches' Association. Is there a move to transfer the headquarters to Colorado Springs, the same venue as United States Swimming, the governing body of American swimming?*

JM: The ASCA board of directors voted to pursue the possible move and/or merger with United States Swimming because we thought it could have a positive impact for coaches and swimming in the United States.

CC: *Why?*

JM: We noticed a tapering off of membership in ASCA and a tapering off of new ideas. We feel the way USS has developed since breaking away from the AAU that a partnership would possibly be more conducive to better swimming.

CC: *Again, why?*

JM: To improve the opportunities for more coaches to become involved, not only professionally and technically, but administratively as well. To have a stronger impact on the decision-making process of USS. We are not ready to consider a merger with USS if our wishes cannot be accepted. One of the great things we have in this country is that our coaching association has been a separate entity. We have become a very powerful lobbying body over the years and we think that ability has paid big dividends. To dilute that to become a part of USS would be to no avail, in fact, a great deterrent to U.S. Swimming. So we're waiting to see what we can come up with.

CC: *You've coached some great women swimmers such as Susan Atwood and Ann Simmons. What do you think of the present standard of women's swimming in the United States?*

JM: We certainly reached one of our lows in 1976. Had we competed in 1980, I think we would have redeemed ourselves a little. In 1983, I have a great concern for women's swimming because we are not up to par at all. Most of us thought the women's NCAA Championships this year would be an outstanding meet and it was not. The same is true of this U.S. championships here in Indianapolis.

CC: *What is your criticism of the women's 1983 NCAA?*

JM: The criticism is that most of our great swimmers did not swim fast! The level of swimming at the top end, the first, second, third, and fourth places did not produce fast times. We were going faster four to six years ago.

CC: *Actually faster four to six years ago?*

JM: Some events were faster, and in some events the depth was faster.

CC: *To what do you attribute this?*

JM: To attribute it to any one thing would be unjust and unfair to all the coaches and swimmers in the country. One misunderstanding was thinking that women's athletic scholarships would be a cure-all for our slump. The thought that our men have been strong because of a great collegiate experience carried over to the women. This generalization has not proved to be true. When women's college programs first offered grants-in-aid, many of our women retired somewhat in the college ranks and did not train as intently as they had in club programs.

CC: *In other words there was a tendency for them to come in for a soft landing?*

JM: Yes, I think that still exists today. I don't believe we are training hard enough. Our college girls must accept the necessary responsibilities to ensure professional achievement later in life and also accept the responsibility to train much more intensely if, in fact, they want to be competitive at the international level. I also think, and I'm sure this will come under criticism by some, that our college coaches have not only undertrained some of our girls but also over rested them during the season for dual-meet performances. Therefore, we did not get the championship meet performances they were capable of doing.

CC: *Why should this exist in women's swimming and not in men's?*

JM: I think it does exist in the men's program but definitely not to the same extent. Many of our men's performances have been great at the conference championships. Good swimmers have gone on to improve and the competition has been even better at the NCAA.

CC: *How much blame, if any, should be attached to the people running the university programs?*

JM: Blame is the wrong word. I don't think it's a matter of blame. Physically. the women are capable of much more. Mentally and emotionally, they are more stable and secure. We know their performances can be good. But many were not expecting or used to some of the work that was necessary to continue in the college program. I don't think the girls and the coaches were committed to the fact that more training is necessary to be competitive internationally. We must reevaluate where we are and then reestablish what our commitments will be and make sure that we progress to those commitments.

CC: *What are your views on foreign athletes participating in the NCAA Championships and being rewarded with scholarships?*

JM: I've got two philosophies. One, in our sport and in the Olympic movement, everyone deserves the opportunity to compete. If you think of it in terms of a broad Olympic movement, everyone deserves that opportunity. Their country of origin has nothing to do with the concept at all. The more narrow philosophy, possibly a selfish one, is that I personally would like to see great opportunity for our own girls because we've taken a back seat internationally. When I see girls from other countries get grants-in-aid, the first thing that enters my mind is to question whether someone in our country is losing an opportunity to be very competitive at an international level.

CC: *Where do you think training methods are heading? Have there been new developments?*

JM: The greatest new developments have been in the area of research in exercise physiology. We've been able to learn an awful lot from the exercise physiologist. However, too many coaches, and I have to admit I was one, put too much faith in research and not enough effort in the meat and potatoes of our sport—training intensely, swimming more. As a matter of fact, I had a discussion recently with Mark Schubert, comparing notes on training sets. We chuckled because we both realized we had tendencies to be the meat-and-potatoes type of coach, going more mileage and doing it more intensely. We never came up with unique ideas to break the boredom but we both had world-record holders. At the present time, I believe too many of us are trying to be too nice, too good, too understanding, wanting to break boredom to such an extent that we have not trained the athletes hard enough. Researchers have published and gained credibility as if they had all the answers. It's been like a pendulum swing. We've begun to rely too much on some research and what we perceived as specificity of training. I believe we've got to get back to swimming more.

CC: Do you think people really understand specificity?

JM: The word has been overplayed, misunderstood, used, and misused. Specificity has caused us to believe everything we do must be specific to a given time, given stroke mechanics. We overlook that the water is an unnatural environment. If everything we do is specific to time, speed, or relative power, we are working improperly and not becoming at-one with the water. Rather, we are fighting the water.

CC: Some swimmers don't have a very good feel but the way they handle the water suggests they have come through very heavy land programs.

JM: I think you're right. There has been a movement towards more strength and power development on land expecting the carryover to be in the water. I believe this has helped short-course swimming and the shorter races. Quite frankly, too many college coaches have relied on strength to be able to muscle through the water instead of finesse through the water.

CC: Do you mean weights are used as a shortcut to get fit quickly and save time?

JM: No, not so much to save time but certainly to gain strength. To break the boredom, we offered a lot of land programs. These supplements were accepted as complements to swimming fast, as necessities instead of options. I think that has been one of our shortcomings.

CC: There's a tendency in Canada to throw everything but the kitchen sink into the program. But you've probably noticed with many of the great swimmers you've developed that your most successful seasons have been when the program was relatively simple so you could see where you were at a glance.

JM: You are very right. Many times we introduce so many variables into a program that it's almost impossible to go back and analyze and evaluate. I think we need fewer variables and more controls.

CC: You talked about being nice to swimmers and offering them training variety so they don't become bored. But swimming can be boring when you're gazing at the bottom of the pool all the time. If you understand your body, what you're doing with your body, and what you are trying to develop in your race pace as you move towards competition, it can be made interesting without great variety.

JM: I agree with you 100 percent. If we give certain thought processes and mental patterns to our swimmers on how to accomplish a given part of a practice, it can be more advantageous than introducing many strength variables or drills, tubes, buckets, tethering devices, all the things you've heard over the last few years. By getting them to use their heads rather than using their bodies in so many different ways, we will progress faster.

CC: I think if you use similar types of workouts, similar sets fairly frequently, it is easier for a swimmer to gauge improvement. However, even this becomes boring so you can't stay too long with one particular pattern of workout. The main thing is to keep the pattern fairly simple and recognizable so the swimmer can chart improvement in key areas such as endurance and speed.

JM: I agree with you. At the Ohio State University, we do not repeat the same set within a period of eight weeks. But there are given times we can use on a proportional basis to measure progress. An example would be 20 by 100 on 1:10. A week later, we may go 10 by 200 on 2:20. It's the same total distance but, if the 200s are faster proportionately than the 100s, then we know that we've improved. I think this concept can breed development and oneness with the water.

DISCUSSION WITH
WALTER SCHLUETER

Recorded at the U.S. Long Course Championships, August 1966, Lincoln, Nebraska.

Walter Schlueter of the Arizona Desert Rats team, Phoenix, Arizona, was one of the great stroke innovators of the twentieth century. He produced swimmers on every Olympic team from 1948 through 1972. His swimmers set 15 world records, 51 American and senior national records and won 35 national AAU Championships. His teams won 2 U.S. AAU National Team Championships with the Chicago Town Club in 1950, and the Multnomah Athletic Club in 1961. He was the originator of short-rest broken swim training, and was responsible for the early stroke development of 2 great stylists, Don Schollander and Marilyn Ramenofsky.

CC: *I say this not to flatter you, but you are known as a fine stroke technician. Do you prefer coaching any particular style?*

WS: My favorite stroke has always been freestyle and, of course, from freestyle you often develop fine butterflyers. I think this may be my weakness in that maybe I spend too much time on stroke and not enough on training, I don't know.

CC: *Have you developed any new progressions for developing freestyle for instance?*

WS: One thing that I think may be of interest to you is that we do all of our kicking on our sides and I believe you do this, too?

CC: *Definitely so, but not a tremendous amount of it.*

WS: Well, we don't either. We do a maximum of 400 meters a day. Like you, we have them kick a set number of beats on one side then move over onto the other side and do the same there, too. We do a lot of streamlining in freestyle. We do not swim flat. I try to get the feet to constantly turn and that's why we practice so much on our side.

CC: *Do you make this movement or does it happen within the rolling of the body on its long axis?*

WS: Well, I think you just said it!

CC: *What is your reason for kicking on the side?*

WS: Because I feel that I can't get into the push phase of the stroke if I can't move my hips out of the way. In other words, when I'm trying to finish the push, if my body won't turn, well, I can't complete the stroke. We believe that propulsion is governed by the size of the paddle and, probably, the amount of acceleration you can get with that size paddle. So, we try to start the pull from zero velocity, constantly building it up to maximum.

CC: *Do you feel that certain individual swimmers should deliberately lessen their purchase in order to develop higher tempo?*

WS: No. We try with all of our 100-meter swimmers to have the same approximate turnover as the 1,500-meter swimmers. I have a little boy here, a 15-year-old, Blair Driggs, who has gone 17 minutes 58 seconds for 1,500-meter freestyle. He's going to compete in this meet, and he's also swum 59 seconds for the 100. His turnover is almost identical at both 100 and 1,500. This is one of the things, whether you know it or not, we worked with Schollander. I had

Schollander from the time he was 10 years old until he was 14. His stroke was built exactly as we were talking about, on a constant long turnover.

CC: *And the head position, does that vary from individual to individual? Where do you like them to have the waterline?*

WS: I like the waterline right about the eyebrows. What we do is to ask the youngsters to do this to get the right idea on this position . . . put the thumb here at the throat and stretch the neck forward until the forefinger is at the chin. This will give you the normal position. I ask them not to look at the bottom of the pool but to see where they are going, in front.

CC: *The head position at the time of the inward breath. How do you time the inward breath with the stroke?*

WS: We believe that the breath should be delayed until the hand is finished pushing—just before it starts to recover— we turn the head and then we want the head to lead the shoulder back!

CC: *You don't time it on the forward arm at all?*

WS: No. And the reason we don't is because if the swimmer is rotating the body on its axis, there is no weak side, there is no bad side breathing, both sides are exactly the same. The head position we use, the head is always so high that, as they take their normal streamlined position, all they have to do is just turn their heads . . . they don't have to lift them or do anything. Also, in training we use a lot of breathing every three strokes and every five strokes breathing patterns.

CC: *Concerning the kick, do you impose any set pattern of kicking when arms and legs are combined in the full stroke?*

WS: We subdue the kick. Let me say this: We stress and stress kick but, when we start the arms, the legs must do what they want to do. We don't force the legs in.

CC: *With regard to the side kicking patterns— we've been doing exactly the same thing at a distance of 13,000 miles!*

WS: I said this to my wife yesterday when I read your article. We do this because we want the legs to turn to help *balance* the body so the swimmer can breathe and complete each stroke. We feel that the propulsion mainly is going to come from the arms but, if the legs start to counterbalance each time, then I can't get the streamlining of the shoulders into the stroke.

CC: *What are your views on timing the arms in the crawl stroke?*

WS: I don't think there is such a thing as opposition. I mean, with one arm recovering through the air and the other one pulling through the water, I don't think it is possible to get absolute opposition.

CC: *Yes, but do you try to have one arm overtake the other so that, as one arm enters, the other is halfway through the pull? Would you agree that this is the key to the timing?*

WS: I think the key to my timing is for them to understand that through the pull phase you are increasing your acceleration, and maximum acceleration comes through the push phase, and I think that is where my timing is.

CC: *You believe, as I do, in putting over colorful language in order to paint a word picture in their minds?*

WS: Because I deal with 7 to 10 to 12 years of age youngsters. When I coach my college team I don't talk in the same terms. My terminology, my communication, has to be different! But this is the key, this is what I love to do. I love to teach them from this early age.

CC: *Have you any other stroke drills that you would like to discuss?*

WS: We do what you did in backstroke—both arms back then one stroke pull—but I've never tried it three in a row like you do. This is different. I'm going to try it. I'm going to steal that!

✧ ✧ ✧

DISCUSSION WITH
MARK SCHUBERT

Recorded at the U.S. Indoors Short Course Meet, Gainesville, Florida, 1981.

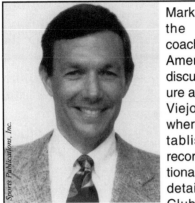

Mark Schubert is one of the most successful coaches in the history of American swimming. He discusses his 13-year tenure at the famous Mission Viejo Club in California where his swimmers established an American record by winning 44 national titles, describing in detail the Mission Viejo Club structure that resulted in the club becoming known as The Swimming Capital of the United States. In 1997, Mark Schubert was inducted into the International Swimming Hall of Fame as an Honor Coach.

CC: Your club is unique in that it is sponsored by real estate developers. Is that correct?

MS: Yes, we're sponsored by the Mission Viejo Company. Basically, their sponsorship includes the facilities. We train in three privately owned recreational facilities—two with 25-yard pools, one with a 50-meter pool, and two warm-up pools.

CC: Did you sell the concept to the promoters or did they approach you?

MS: No, the promoters built the facility for the homeowners, and I was hired as the age-group swimming coach for the 100-member team in 1972. At that time the 50-meter pool was under construction and we started the senior program September 1972. Within two years, we turned the program to a serious orientation and developed an age-group program to feed the senior program which was geared to national competition.

CC: How did you find the age-groupers?

MS: We have a tremendously big learn-to-swim program fall and spring. We bring out about 200 young swimmers, ages 4 to 8. The basic requirement is they have to be able to swim 25 yards. Then we teach them the 4 competitive strokes in a 4-week lesson setup. They have the choice, if they are interested, to join the competitive program.

CC: Do they pay fees to be taught to swim?

MS: Yes, a 40-dollar fee for one month. The dues for the team are 30 dollars a month for residents and 40 dollars a month for those outside the community.

CC: Do you pay pool rentals?

MS: The pools are provided free by the recreation center as part of their sponsorship of the team.

CC: Do you have all the training and teaching time you want or do you have to leave some time for recreational swimming?

MS: We certainly have to work our training and teaching time around the recreational set of members. Our 50-meter pool is available for our total use from September through the middle of June. From June to September, we have the pool from 5 AM until noon and from 5 PM as late as we want.

CC: How are the coaches' salaries and travel expenses covered?

MS: The coaches' salaries are covered by the fees paid by the swimmers. Traveling expenses are provided by the booster club which raises about 70,000 dollars a year. Traveling expenses to the Nationals are provided both through U.S. Swimming, with their sponsorship by Phillips Petroleum, and by the Mission Viejo Company. Mission Viejo also sponsors swimmers who place in the top 16 at the Nationals, giving them motel expenses and food during the Nationals.

CC: Tell me a little more about your fund-raising activities.

MS: We sell advertising for our major meets and our annual program. Swimathon is also a great part of fund-raising. We run about 10 major meets during the year with our own concessions. There are numerous small activities such as dinners, raffles, and things of that nature.

CC: You must have a very well-organized parent body to run the meets and participate in other activities.

MS: Yes, and I'd have to say that the enthusiasm of the parent group was there before I arrived. I think we've built on that enthusiasm and that's probably been one of our biggest pluses.

CC: *Tell me about the motivation behind the Mission Viejo Company.*

MS: Mission Viejo is a very unique community in Southern California. Los Angeles being what it is, quite a megalopolis, it's very difficult for a community to have an identity. The first identity that Mission Viejo had was the swimming team and now kind of being known as the swimming capital of the United States. I feel there is a lot of community pride, and the company likes that because any type of community pride also helps sell homes. So this is why they've been enthusiastic.

CC: *Do they keep evaluating the situation in terms of dollars and cents?*

MS: They certainly do. They reevaluate it every year. We have to submit a budget and it's scrutinized and basically it's a selling job by the club and the booster club every year. But the company has been extremely supportive.

CC: *Tell me how you direct a staff to look after such a large number of swimmers. Exactly how many swimmers do you have?*

MS: The number ranges from 35 during the winter to 500 in the summer We have a tremendous influx of age-group kids and we try to hold a percentage of those and make them more serious year-round swimmers. Our staff consists of 12 coaches. The head age-group coach is Pat Burch who's been with me for 8 years and has done a tremendous job of developing talent. The age-group coaches report directly to him and he reports to me. I have a senior staff of 5 coaches, and we direct the junior national and senior national programs. We have about 165 senior swimmers in the summer and about 100 in the winter.

CC: *Do you meet regularly and coordinate your efforts? How much of the effort is individual and how much within a set framework of the club and your personal philosophy?*

MS: We have weekly meetings. Pat and I have worked together for so long that we have pretty much an ingrained philosophy. We direct a certain amount of overall philosophy but I've always felt that it's important to give your assistant coaches independence. Their creativity is brought into the program so they can feel they are an integral part of it. I don't set programs for the coaches. I give them a general outline of what I want to see. I want basic things done with strokes, breathing patterns, and training attitudes so swimmers are indoctrinated in our program from the age-group level.

CC: *When you say you give them a general idea of what you want done, do you say, "We want this type of stress done today, endurance or speed endurance, or some specific work, or just an easy type of day?"*

MS: Well, more than a day-to-day outline. It's a seasonal outline. We try to make our training groups progressive stepping-stones in intensity so the athletes aren't burned out at a young age. I feel the most important thing in age-group swimming is for the swimmers to really enjoy it.

CC: *Do you give your coaching staff individual opportunities for professional development?*

MS: Yes, we encourage them to attend as many clinics as possible. We have numerous outstanding clinics in Southern California. Occasionally, the club sends them to national coaches' clinics.

CC: *What about an age-group philosophy?*

MS: We feel it's very important to bring the kids up with the idea that swimming is fun—not train age-group swimmers twice a day, year round. We do train the top age-group swimmers twice a day in the summer but again, there isn't a lot of pressure as far as attendance is concerned. We make a great deal of compromises with the age-groupers if they want to participate in other activities. Soccer is very important in Mission Viejo. So are football and baseball. To keep the swimmers in the program, we allow them to do this and don't force them to make a choice at a young age.

CC: *You said you discuss seasonal training emphasis with your assistants. How do you view the various phases of your season?*

MS: We have a Junior Olympic Championship in March and in August. Within each season we have an endurance phase, say for two months, a speed and endurance phase for two months, and then a quality phase for about six weeks.

CC: *What type of work would your age-groupers do?*

MS: At the bottom of our program, they would train for 45 minutes, 3 days a week and progress to an hour, 5 days a week. Then it's another group for an hour and a half, 5 days a week. There's another group 2 hours a day, 6 days a week. Finally, the top age-groupers would be going 2½ hours, including some dry-land work, 5 days a week. Once they have developed to senior swimming, this is determined by our local senior swimming standards, they are assigned to the senior program. Larry Leibowitz is the junior national coach in charge of developing the age-groupers into senior swimmers. He has about 65 swimmers in his charge and has an assistant coach with him. We have sprint, middle-distance, and distance programs just as we have in the national team. It's his responsibility to train these swimmers and teach them all the rigors of the senior program. They must attend 8 workouts a week. We offer double workouts 5 mornings a week, taking Wednesday morning off, double workouts on Saturday, sometimes an optional workout on Sunday. We get into a more rigorous land program at that level.

CC: *When you mention your dry-land program, it's appropriate to ask how you break down the time frames of your workouts.*

MS: In the junior national program, the swimmers train from 5:30 AM to 7 AM. They train dry-land from 3:30 PM to 4:30 PM and then swim 4:30 PM to 7 PM. This varies depending on the events and distances they are going.

CC: *What type of dry-land work are you doing?*

MS: It's a 6-day-a-week program. We do isokinetic work on Monday, Wednesday, and Friday and we do weight training on Tuesday, Thursday, and Saturday. The isokinetic work is based on the biokinetic swim bench and mini-gyms with various sets depending on the event. The endurance athletes will go long periods—

perhaps 2 minutes exercise with 30 seconds off. The sprinters will go maybe 12 to 20 seconds with 15 or 20 seconds off. In the weight training cycle, we gradually build our intensity to fairly heavy weights. That tapers off as the season progresses. With the distance swimmers, we do high repetitions on Nautilus and Universal equipment.

CC: *How do you blend your land-training taper with your swimming taper?*

MS: I think rather successfully the last year and a half! We've changed our program and tapered our weight program instead of taking them off the weight program the last three weeks. I used to take them off weights totally and found they were losing strength. I think we've had a lot of success tapering the dry-land program similar to the way we taper the swimming. For instance, we're doing mini-gyms until the day we leave for the Nationals. So they have about three days before the big meet when they are not on some type of dry-land program.

CC: *You have so many great athletes training together—do you find problems at times of athletes being incompatible with each other? I've always felt having great athletes train together is the best way to develop a good program and make mediocre athletes into good ones.*

MS: That's human nature and any coach is going to face the challenge. I've always felt having great athletes train together is the best way to develop a good program and make mediocre athletes into good ones. If there is a secret to our success, this is certainly one of them. It raises the level of the kids who don't have a lot of faith in themselves. I've seen amazing things happen when kids come into our program and train with a Brian Goodell or a Jesse Vassallo and find out they're human just like everyone else. All of a sudden, they'll decide, "Well, maybe I can be great, too!"

CC: *When you have three or four swimmers in the finals in the Nationals, you've got to avoid any impression of having favorites. How do you handle a tricky situation like that?*

MS: I always try to coach each athlete as an individual. I'm very honest with them and tell them pretty much the strategy of the others so there are really no secrets, and they don't feel I'm trying to play one against the other or anything of that nature. For example, in the 500 freestyle at this meet, the women's 500, we were fortunate enough to go first, second, and third. I felt each of the girls had definite strengths and weaknesses. I tried to point out to them how they could capitalize on the strengths, how I thought the race would develop, where they needed to be, and what they needed to do to capitalize on their strengths to win.

CC: *How do you discuss race tactics?*

MS: I feel every swimmer should go into a race with a plan. A true champion will be able to handle any type of situation. Train your athletes to go into a race with a plan and follow it until it's obvious a change needs to be made. The athlete who can be flexible, maybe change his tactics, is the one who's going to be successful.

CC: *It's often said there can be eight swimmers in a race of almost equal ability, but there's only going to be one winner. That's the person who arrived at the pool believing more than the others that he was going to win. That edge also belongs to the swimmer who can react to the unexpected as the race develops. This requires imagination, too.*

MS: Absolutely. I think this can be a minor problem with all the visualization and mental training. I know that a good example of flexibility was Brian Goodell in the 1,500 meter at the Montreal Olympics. His plan was to be even at the 800 and then totally control the race. Well, he wasn't even in the race until the 1,300 mark. So it went totally against what he thought would happen. If he hadn't developed the flexibility and mental toughness, I think he would have been an easy third. I feel human nature shows you there are a number of ways to be successful, and every person has his own method. I think you have to stay somewhat flexible and try to develop your program around the strengths of your athletes. Make them feel you're doing absolutely what's best for them.

CC: *You've won nine National Championships in a*

row. *How important is it for you to keep winning team championships? Could you reach a satiation point as far as motivation is concerned?*

MS: We love winning the team championships. A big part of our program is the team motivation. That's from the little kids right on up. We try to make every kid feel as much a part of this National Championship as the national champion himself. Every season is different. We have new kids to work with and the kids with experience still have new challenges. We are just trying to get each kid to accomplish his goals. I think that with a team such as ours, if we can be successful with 75 percent or 85 percent of the kids, then the national championship is a result. But I look at each season as a new challenge.

✧ ✧ ✧

DISCUSSION WITH JONTY SKINNER

Recorded at the U.S. Long Course Championships, Indianapolis, 1982.

Jonty Skinner, head coach of U.S. Swimming's International Training Center at Colorado Springs, is a former world-record holder in the 100-meter freestyle (49.44 seconds). Skinner talks about the important elements of short-distance training. He says, "People can dream and people can believe, but they're not the same things. Believing is simulating what you want to do in practice—knowing that you can do what you want to do."

CC: *Let's talk about your career as a sprint freestyler in the United States.*

JS: If you compare me with American standards, I didn't have the background, being able to swim only four to six months of the year in South Africa due to the lack of all-year facilities. The thing that worked well for me was that I was really a distance-oriented swimmer when I was younger and competed in more distance events. During the first summer I was here, Coach Gambril sent me to a real distance-oriented coach. I went into a program that was 18,000–20,000 meters a day. It gave me the base I needed and after that I could really sprint all year round.

CC: *How do you personally relate the distance background to sprinting? Does it help you to hang in there on the last 10 meters?*

JS: I'm not sure of the relationship. The 100 is not really a sprint. No one can sprint a 100 yard.

CC: *It's a fast swim.*

JS: Yes, so to speak. You know I always swam my race, not with

International Swimming Hall of Fame

Jonty Skinner, center lane, on his way to a world 100-meter freestyle mark of 49.44 seconds in Philadelphia on August 14, 1976. This beat the 20-day old mark of 49.99 seconds set by Jim Mongomery at the Montreal Games, July 25, 1976.

the intention of negative splitting, but thinking in those terms. I felt that I wanted to get down halfway through the race and feel easy and then come home. That's where I won a lot of my races. I was never really out ahead at the 50. I would outswim them on the way home. I'd always look for a split difference of 1.2 to 1.5 seconds.

CC: *And to swim as fast as you can—not flail as fast as you can?*

JS: Correct. You can't swim faster than you can hold the water.

CC: *So you concentrate on a strong push-back?*

JS: Yes, on good control. Every day at the end of a workout I did four or five 50s that I called accelerating 50s. I would start out swimming as I felt like it—80 percent to 90 percent to 100 percent—making sure that I kept control all the way through. I'd say taking 40 strokes at 80 percent, 40 strokes at 90 percent, maybe 38 strokes at 100 percent.

CC: *Feeling the pressure out, establishing your stroke, and then building?*

JS: Yeah. A lot of sculling drills, working on a sculling feel. You know some athletes, you can't teach them the concept that you don't pull straight back to go straight forward. It's

more the angle of your stroke—the pressure you apply to the water, the feel. The other thing that helped me was to take elastic tubing, take it down to the end of the pool, and let it pull you at swimming speed to get the feel of what it is like to swim fast, when you swim shaved, tapered and sharp. You swim like that maybe once or twice a year, and the only way you can simulate it is to do that in practice. The only other way I could simulate coming home was to go out underneath the water—hypoxic training—without depleting your physical reserves and sprint back in semioxygen debt.

CC: *In other words, feeling your stroke out. Feeling the water along your whole body, being at one with the water, perhaps even hearing the way the water moves.*

JS: Yeah! These are the things that I have a hard time teaching my athletes. I'm looking each season to develop drills to help them learn those skills—acceleration, sculling drills, feel drills—anything to simulate the race is good. Anything I could do to simulate my race, I felt was very good, very beneficial.

CC: *What are the key points of a short-distance race?*

JS: One has got to understand that it is not a sprint. It is a sprint, but it isn't. No one can go flat out; it's got to be a controlled race. You've got to swim like a distance swimmer. Every day, every practice toward the end of the season, a distance swimmer should be going pace, pace, pace. A sprinter can't do pace, but he can simulate it. Every day he wants to work on some part of the race—a weak part or a strong part. Whatever it is, there should be some work done every day to simulate the race. You just keep building the confidence and develop the ability to control the overall stroke by doing those little bits and pieces.

CC: *You've said that you concentrate on keeping your stroke long?*

JS: You've got to be conscious of distance per stroke. You can't count your strokes while you race, but you can count them in practice. In a race, I just get locked into what I'm doing.

CC: *What do you think of when you race?*

JS: In my best races, I didn't think of anything. They just happened. I did a lot of preprogramming work when I trained. When I went to bed, I preprogrammed what I wanted to do when I trained the next day or what I wanted to do in a meet. In my best races, I just climbed up there and it just happened.

CC: *So you freed your mind from your body and let instinct take over?*

JS: Well, it's not instinct. Your mind can act as a computer. It does control you physically. A lot of people have trouble adapting to it. I mean I'd never been faster than 51.0 and all summer I believed I could go 49. I knew I could. I trained for it. I did the splits. I simulated it. I swam slow in the heats because I knew that I didn't have to swim that fast. Yet, when I climbed on the blocks for the final, I knew I was going to go that fast.

CC: *Your belief becomes stronger and stronger and finally what your mind conceives and believes, happens.*

JS: I agree. I mean you have to feel it internally. You have to feel it inside yourself. People can dream and people can believe, but they're not the same things. Believing is simulating what you want to do in practice, knowing that you can do what you want to do.

✧ ✧ ✧

DISCUSSION WITH GUS STAGER
Recorded at the U.S. Long Course Championships, Lincoln, Nebraska, August 1966.

Gus Stager followed the great Matt Mann as coach of the University of Michigan. Stager's many great swimmers included Olympians Carl Robie, Dave Gillanders, Dick Hanley, Gill Farley, the Wardrop twins (from Great Britain), and Juan Bello. Stager was one of the coaches of the 1960 Rome U.S. Olympic team that broke the Australian stranglehold. In 1967, in Winnipeg, he coached the winning U.S. Pan Am men's swimming team. At the first 1973 World Championships in Belgrade, his U.S. men's team won first place.

CC: *Perhaps you would like to tell me about your program at Michigan University.*

GS: Well, I followed Matt Mann and you know Matt and his vast reputation at Michigan. Our program is very much the same as his. We've made some changes and some have been pretty drastic but, basically, Matt was always a believer in work, and my concept of swimming is pretty much the same. I believe in a lot of work.

We have a relatively new facility, about 6 years old, which has the largest indoor capacity in the United States. We seat about 2,700 spectators. We have a diving well and it's the first pool in the United States to have a tower, a 10-meter tower.

The swimmers at Michigan are encouraged to work out at least twice a day, as much as they can throughout the week. When we reach the peak part of the season we often ask them to come back in during a break in their studies, sometimes in the evening or, perhaps, around 10 o'clock and spend maybe half an hour with us and do some short interval repeats. There are occasions when we will even go to three workouts a day. They will be brief workouts.

CC: *What type of workouts do you believe in?*

GS: Of course, we all use the interval training, I've been most successful with work that's been on a 1:1 work-rest ratio and this is perhaps the basic part of our program. For short-course work I am most enthusiastic ... well, let's say, the basic part of our training will be interval 100s.

Carl Robie and Bill Farley often break down to a 1:$\frac{1}{2}$ work-rest ratio—they will swim for a minute and rest for 30 seconds. Of course, we do normal work that other teams do. We have done a lot of split interval work and then again we'll do a lot of rest time trials. In other words, we'll do ten 100s and give them 10, 12, or 15 minutes rest between each 100 and, along the way, we'll get a good 100 out of them.

CC: *How do you think that there will be advances in the mental approach to the sport?*

GS: You're nailing me with a question I haven't had time to think over! I think that, in other countries, we may get an advance in the future when they get more on a team basis but, basically, swimming is an individual sport. Along the way, the swimmers learn the team effort, the team spirit, the team feeling, and this is one area, I think, that we are able to capitalize on. The swimmer doesn't necessarily need to be a team man, but, the fact of team competition swimming for the Los Angeles Athletic Club or the University of Michigan or a high school, certainly has an effect in bringing out, in many instances, better performances.

What perhaps is more important than the team aspect is that the swimmers we have here in this meet, the record holders, the Don Schollanders, the Steve Clarks, the Carl Robies, the Roy Saaris, all the great swimmers, are certainly individually oriented and

can swim a marvelous race at any time they have to, and the team effort on them doesn't seem to be too important, but, what does make it important in relationship to the team, is that you have someone competing against them, representing their team, and they will strive harder to win the race and, as a consequence, very often push these young men to better performances.

✧ ✧ ✧

DISCUSSION WITH DON TALBOT

Recorded at the author's home, 1984. This discussion took place while Talbot, the Australian coach, was working in Canada as executive director of Canadian Swimming.

Don Talbot is the most successful coach in the history of Australian swimming and has produced many of the great swimmers of the modern era. He was the first director of the Australian Institute of Sport, and is now head coach of Australian Swimming as that country heads toward the 2000 Olympics in Sydney, Talbot's home city and the scene of his greatest successes. Talbot talks about his early years in coaching, how the Australian Institute of Sport came to be founded, and the Australian swimming ethos in general. He was inducted in the International Swimming Hall of Fame in 1979 for his contribution to the sport.

CC: *How did you come to be interested in swimming?*

DT: I swam as a kid. My first recollections of swimming actively are around 1948. I swam until 17, when I went to teachers college. I quit swimming at that point. I came back and began to teach. My coach, Frank Guthrie, asked me if I'd be interested in becoming an assistant coach for a program he was conducting at Bankstown pool in a western suburb of Sydney. He offered me the grand sum of 14 pounds a week, the equivalent of 28 dollars. I jumped at it because I needed the money. That's how I got involved with coaching.

CC: *How did Guthrie go about teaching you to coach? How did you get your first experience?*

DT: I don't think he went about it in a formal way. He just said, "There's a group. You take them and coach them how to swim. If you run into problems, come and talk to me." So, occasionally, when I did run into difficulties, particularly with what to do with stroke technique or what program to give, I did talk to him. I have no recollections of any major discussions with him. I think that the state of the art at that time was that virtually anybody could coach. I think if today's conditions had existed then, I may never have got into coaching. It was easy to walk from in front of a blackboard in school onto the deck and begin to coach. I had some teacher training, but none of that was in physical education to any great degree. I certainly had no background in physiology. Anything I did in that area was something I worked on myself. I happened to be always interested in physiology, but I came into coaching with the credentials of being a swimmer, not of very great note, and a teacher, trained in primary school education. It virtually said that if you could add one and one to make two, you were good enough to teach school. It was with only that background that I entered coaching.

CC: *What subjects did you teach in school?*

DT: I taught general courses but I gravitated towards physical education because I was very interested in that area. I was naturally interested in coaching right from the start. I remember that, after school hours I started coaching track and field before I got involved with Guthrie's swim program. I was teaching this kid to high jump. At that time the western roll had been adopted instead of the scissors style of jumping. We used to just jump over the bar onto the ground. There were no landing pits, no sand. I told this kid, "We'll try to introduce the western-roll style for the championships meet. It's a month away. You'll have enough time to learn it." After about four days he was getting it right, but he broke his wrist. That put an end to my career as a high jump coach!

CC: *What stroke did you swim?*

DT: I was an individual medley swimmer. I won the IM state championships. It was just before butterfly was really in vogue. In those

days it was butterfly breaststroke, the fly pull combined with the breaststroke kick. I was one of the first to use it. The dolphin kick was not allowed at that point. My best strokes were free and back. I did better in backstroke than anything else.

CC: *So you came to your early coaching career with some interest in physiology and some practical experience of the strokes. How long did you work for Frank Guthrie?*

DT: I worked with him for one year. He came to me then and said, "I'm leaving to coach in a new pool. You can come with me or you can stay here." I didn't know what to do. I didn't have confidence in myself. Guthrie said, "I'll fix up the lease at the pool for you." He used to pay five pounds a year [$10] for the coaching rights at the pool. "I'll fix it for to you stay here," he said. At that point I had built up a small squad which included Jon and Ilsa Konrads. I had taught them how to swim. They were just beginning to show up pretty well as young age group swimmers.

CC: *You were working with them while part of Guthrie's team?*

DT: Yes. I still have some films taken at that time. Guthrie tried to recruit them to go with him to his new pool about 15 miles away. Luckily, for me, their parents said, "They're going to

What a way to start a coaching career: Don Talbot with the fabulous "Konrads Kids." Left to right: Coach Talbot, Ilsa and John Konrads. Over a two-year period, they slaughtered all the world middle- and long-distance freestyle records.

stay with Mr. Talbot. He's taught them to swim and we feel an obligation to him." At the same time I had some other kids like Neville Hayes [silver medalist in the 200 fly at the Rome Olympics in 1960]. Soon after, the likes of Kevin Berry and Bobby Windle joined the squad. It was a tremendous period for me. At the start, I didn't know it was going to be so. The dice were loaded in my favor! Guthrie had said, "If you work here, you'll be successful." In retrospect, when I think about it, there were a lot of young kids there at the time. Today, it is a city of half a million but, at that time, there might have been 50 or 60,000 people and it was growing rapidly. The type of families that lived there would have their kids go to school with no shoes, not bothering even to comb their hair, with the seat out of their pants. To keep them out of mischief their parents would send them to the pool to swim. I used to charge them 4 dollars per month for coaching. That would be around 1951 or 1952.

CC: *You were learning from the kids at the same time that they were learning from you?*

DT: Well, I'll tell you. I was flying by the seat of my pants. There was no question about that. I knew nothing about coaching. I think now, in retrospect, I must have had a feel for it. Knowing so little, or virtually nothing about coaching, turned out to be a plus. In fact, I hate to admit it, but a certain coach of that time said, "He doesn't know anything about coaching. He's fluked it. He's been very lucky." It was just around the time that the Konrads kids really made their breakthrough. I resented that statement at the time. But now, looking back, there was a lot of truth in it. I felt the only way to win was to get kids to work hard. I also had a dream. I wanted the kids I coached to be the best in the world. Through them I would become the best coach in the world. That's what drove me. I got going in the beginning doing programs and workouts that were much more than anyone else was doing anywhere in the world. Of course, I didn't know that.

CC: *You felt that the kids could take it?*

DT: I was looking at them, and they were happy.

International Swimming Hall of Fame

"When John Konrads broke his first world record in the 800 free, I began to find out through all the interviews what other people were doing. We were doing sometimes twice as much!"—Don Talbot

Their parents were not complaining to me when I talked to them. I always believed it was important to bring the parents into the program, unlike other coaches who like to keep them at arm's length. I think on many occasions, with the collaboration of the parents, I have won kids over to change their attitudes. I still have John Konrads's logbook for about 1956–57 and he was swimming 6,000 or 7,000 meters, sometimes in a day. I was absolutely stunned when I found out that this was more than anyone else in the world was doing.

CC: *Was this in each session or the total for the day?*

DT: No. Sometimes he would get to that in one session. I don't remember what he would total in a day. When John Konrads broke his first world record in the 800 free, I began to find out through all the interviews what other people were doing. We were doing sometimes twice as much! I couldn't believe it. Even today I am astounded. It was as if I had discovered a new way. I was isolated in the area where I was. I also didn't know anything about the state of the art. I wasn't inhibited by the constraints that physiologists had put on us. I was responding to my own judgment. It might have been wrong. I might even have hurt some people, but the results were all around me. I prefer to think that I was right.

CC: *You were going by your subjective feeling as to what the kids could take?*

DT: Yes, not so much by what they told me but how they were behaving. If a kid would come to the pool down and tired and generally off, I knew they couldn't handle it. If they were up and bubbly, fooling around and they wanted to josh you a little bit, that would be an indicator that the kids were OK. I certainly didn't get any complaints about the kids being too tired or not being able to cope. I never heard anything from their schools either. I just assumed that everything was alright.

I was criticized a great deal at the time for working people too hard. It was said that I would cause kids a permanent physical damage. I never could believe that. In fact, one heart specialist accused me of doing heart damage to his son. Fortunately, I had some allies who said that was plain nonsense. It turned out this kid had a congenital problem anyway, and they should have known about it before sending him to train with me.

CC: *Did you have the swimmers medically examined at the start of training?*

DT: None of that. Just didn't know anything about it. It wasn't the state of the art in the 1950s! Nobody knew that, certainly not in Australia. Quite frankly, I doubt that it is even done today.

I was very interested in what people did in swimming throughout the world. In fact, I remember when Alex Jany, the French world-record holder in the 200 freestyle, came to Australia. His time was around 2:07. I was swimming around 2:35 and couldn't understand how someone could swim that fast. Guthrie took us down to see him do a time trial. Jany did a 2:09. I remember thinking that, while he might be a great swimmer, he didn't look that great and that anybody should be able to do that.

Eventually, when I became a coach, it just made me more determined. I was going to

get swimmers to do these sorts of things. I just pumped work into people without much rhyme or reason. It was a matter of subjective judgment, based on observation and the way the kids were behaving.

My working day was about 15 hours, with workouts before and after school. The school authorities felt I wasn't really able to handle the teaching load. But I felt it helped me. I learned to understand the whole spectrum of swimming.

CC: *The stress that the child is under, with school work, budgeting time, a child's life in general?*

DT: Yes. And I always had an interest in physiology and psychology. I read anything I could find on those subjects. There wasn't too much readily available at that time.

CC: *What made you interested in these two areas?*

DT: I was interested in personal fitness and in physical performance.

CC: *Did you have much exchange of opinion with other coaches during the early stages of your career?*

DT: You have to remember that when I started coaching I was 19 years old. When I had my first world-record holder I was about 21. I ran into a lot of trouble. Some of the great names in Australian swimming even accused me of killing swimmers off—that with all the hard work I demanded I was doing nothing to promote interest in the sport. I was alienated from the others in the sport. I was a very young man in a sport that was considered an older man's profession. The prevalent feeling of the day was that you could not be a good coach until you had been in the game for 20 years.

CC: *And paid your dues?*

DT: Yes. And paid your dues, so to speak. It just made me more determined. I was going to beat the hell out of everybody. I really did not have any exchanges with other people for about the first 10 years of my coaching career. It was somewhat mutual. I didn't want to talk to anybody. I got most of my ideas from reading, mainly American publications as that was the only source of anything at the time.

CC: *Did you travel overseas to observe other methods?*

DT: Never had any money to do that at the time. My first outside experience was in Cardiff, Wales, at the 1958 Commonwealth Games. I had to borrow money to go there. Remember, at this time in Australia, a coach was a freelancer. You had to run your own business. Nobody gave you a regular salary.

CC: *There was no government support for sport in those days?*

DT: None whatsoever. In fact no support from your club. Funds were generated by charging your swimmers. When I returned from Cardiff I had literally two cents in the bank!

CC: *Did you remain in contact with Frank Guthrie after you went your separate ways?*

DT: Actually we became rivals. He was one of the big names in Australian swimming. The others at the time were Harry Hay and Sam Herford [Murray Rose's coach]. Generally speaking there was antipathy right through the years until Guthrie's death. I respected the man, but I don't think that we ever met when we were not fighting about swimming or something that was going on.

CC: *I heard it 24 years ago so no harm will come of telling it now. The other Aussie coaches used to refer to you as "the bantam cock." Did you know that?*

DT: No, but I wouldn't be surprised at all! It was they who created a situation in which I felt I had to fight.

CC: *Let's talk about facilities and the transition in Australian swimming when coaches decided they had to do something about training all year, rather than only during the summer months. Coaches had to raise funds to build their own indoor pools?*

DT: The first indoor pool built by a coach was Frank O'Neil's pool at Pymble; it's a northern suburb of Sydney in a very wealthy area. He was not one of the great coaches in Australia. His main interest was the monetary gain. He made people realize it could be done. He eventually talked to me about my renting the facility from him as he was planning to move away. I refused, as I didn't know anything about running a pool, and I felt it would distract me from my coaching.

Eventually Forbes Carlile being more astute, leased the pool, and went on to produce some really great swimmers. Now this stimulated me, Forbes being a great rival. I also had to do something about getting more water. I tried to convince people to have some outdoor pools heated, but without success. In the end, with the assistance of somebody who was a big help in my life, I found sufficient financial backing to build a pool. It was in Hurstville, a western suburb of Sydney, about five miles from my outdoor pool. But it wasn't until 1968–69 that Australians managed good winter programs. Training camps in the tropical part of Australia would be too costly except for the Olympic Games which 9 out of 10 times would be out of season for us. We had these camps in Townsville and later in Scarborough in the state of Queensland. Before the 1960 Olympics in Rome, I spent 3 months in Townsville getting swimmers ready for the games.

CC: *The Australian system has been facetiously called the feudal system. Professional coaches were not allowed on amateur committees, etcetera, nor on the pool deck during meets. How do you contrast that with the present situation in Australia?*

DT: I wish I could say it was dramatically different. It troubles me to have to say it, but still today there are many things not good about Australian swimming. But, with all the great swimmers there, Australia is like a sleeping giant. If they ever get organized, Australia will be a great swimming nation once again.

CC: *What is holding up this organization?*

DT: I would like to say in one word, administration, but I think there is a problem also coming from the coaches. The coaches and administration are so far removed from each other that a dialogue between them is almost impossible. During my three years at the Australian Institute of Sports [1980–83], I tried to bridge that gap. I tried as hard as I could with the AIS coaches, the administration in Australia, with people I know very well and with whom I enjoy a good relationship, to get them to work together in the interest of better Australian swimming. I failed. I don't see any improvement since I have left.

CC: *You say you failed in bringing together the professional coaches with the volunteer officials to work together for the good of swimming?*

DT: In our best days there always existed this animosity, but everyone had Australian swimming success as the goal. Now the athlete has been forgotten while the two factions are fighting over control of the sport. Until they realize the swimmer is the meat between the sandwich, I don't think anything will happen in Australia. The raw material is still there, and the AIS has given them the best sport science anywhere in the Western world, maybe as good as in the Soviet Union or the GDR. It's not being utilized in the right way. It's very sad.

CC: *What was your role at the Institute?*

DT: I was recruited back to Australia to help establish the Institute. It was a government plan as a result of Australia's poor performance at the 1976 Olympics, which was repeated again at the 1980 Olympics, the boycotted games. My job was to set up an institute which eventually would serve all sports. It started out with only eight sports, and of course swimming was one of these. I was to set up a system in which the best conditions and the best support staff could be recruited from anywhere in the world. If a swimmer wanted to be great, wanted to have the benefits of modern coaching techniques from the best coaches in the world with support from sports psychology, biochemistry, and biomechanics, you name it, that's where they would come. The theory is sound, and in actual practice it did go very well. One problem was the lack of planning in the early stages. The Institute grew as the whim of one politician who wanted to improve Australian performances internationally.

CC: *What about Alan Coles visiting all the similar centers throughout the world? Was that not preliminary planning?*

DT: Purely pigeonholed paperwork! Not only Alan Coles but John Bloomfield had written papers for the government. Nothing was ever implemented. One high-powered politician made it all happen.

CC: *Yet it somehow worked. The Brisbane success at the 1982 Commonwealth Games was proof of that.*

DT: In spite of all the criticism within Australia it worked. But it's not really accepted in the society as it should be. Curiously enough, there are only two sports who do not believe strongly in the worth of the AIS. They are the old established sports of swimming and track and field.

CC: *Some Australian coaches felt that the money spent on the AIS should have been shared equally with funding for the development of sport generally?*

DT: Without getting into a big discussion on this subject, I feel the development of sport in Australia is well handled.

CC: *Does developmental swimming take place in the school system? I know that there are no rules or resentment against national or state champions competing for their schools, such as exists in some Canadian schools.*

DT: School swimming is a very important part of Australian swimming. In fact, not many people have noticed this, but our best years were when school swimming was very strong.

CC: *I remember Sam Herford telling me that scores of buses would arrive at the North Sydney pool to disgorge thousands of youngsters, participants and their supporters, for the annual high school championships. He likened it to a super Cecil B. de Mille production.*

DT: I think that's a good analogy. I think the standard of swimming in the school system today is not what it once was. It definitely has affected the overall Australian standard. It should be examined. It could have some lessons for Canada. There really isn't any serious school swimming in Canada. The lifestyle of the swimmers is not established in the Canadian schools. It's different in Australia and the United States. There is a spontaneity that comes out of school swimming, when it is fostered and promoted properly, that is invaluable. It is an overlooked area in Canada. I think a greater effort could be made to make sure that a good program exists in all levels of the school systems.

❖ ❖ ❖

DISCUSSION WITH
KAREN MOE THORNTON

Recorded at the U.S. Long Course Championships, Indianapolis, 1983.

Karen Moe Thornton was one of the greatest butterfly swimmers in history. As Karen Moe (her maiden name) she won the 200 fly at the 1972 Munich Olympics, and after having retired, returned in 1976 to finish fourth. She set five world records in the event between 1970 and 1972. She started coaching in 1978 at the University of California at Berkeley. She said, "I enjoy coaching at this level. I don't think a lot of coaches understand what it is like to be a woman in college trying to continue a competitive career. I felt that it was here that I could make my impact."

CC: Would you please give me a little of your background as a competitor? You were a world-record holder in butterfly.

KT: Right. I swam mostly in the early '70s. I was a member of the U.S. Olympic team in 1972 and 1976. At Munich in 1972, I won the gold medal in the 200-meter butterfly and was fourth in the 100. In Montreal in 1976, I was fourth in the 200 fly.

CC: When did you start your coaching career?

KT: Right after the 1976 Olympics while I was in graduate school at UCLA. I was coaching a club team. In 1978 I started coaching at the University of California at Berkeley.

CC: Do you prefer coaching at the university level?

KT: I enjoy coaching at this level because I feel this is where one can have the biggest impact. I feel this is important as I don't think a lot of coaches understand what it is like to be a woman in college and trying to continue

a competitive career. I felt that it was in this type of environment I could make my impact.

CC: What makes it different for women as compared to men, prejudice or tradition?

KT: The main difference is that most females start training earlier, at 12 or 13, while most males don't really start pushing it until 15 or 16. It has to do with the age at which you mature physically. By the time a woman starts college, she's invested a lot more time than most of the men. At that point swimming has to be more interesting, requiring a different type of motivation to keep women in the sport a little longer.

CC: That's an interesting point. A number of coaches used to be of the opinion that any girl, upon reaching 17 or 18 and involved with a social life, diminishes her chances for further swimming success. It was precisely because of this that a significant number of coaches would work their female swimmers to a physical peak much earlier than they should have done.

KT: I agree. This probably contributed to a shortening of their careers. Women mature physically in their early 20s—just like men do. With swimming being a pretty technical sport, which many people often forget, the more you know about the sport, the better you can train and the more you can improve your technique. It takes a lot of time to develop these skills.

CC: It would seem that we haven't seen the best male or female swimmer yet. They tend to retire before they reach full maturity.

KT: I also agree with that. There is a tendency to stress conditioning too much, especially at an early age. Many never reach their maximum strength potential or fully develop their techniques because they get so tired investing all the hours in training.

CC: Do you notice that a great number of swimmers have a tendency to swim a slightly different style each year?

KT: It's hard to keep improving your technique without constant work. I think that a lot of swimmers who don't have continual stroke work just slip into some of their earlier bad habits.

CC: *The point I was getting at is that as the body is still maturing, leverage is applied in a slightly different way.*

KT: The stronger you get, the better you can control your limbs, especially people with long arms. Many youngsters with long arms are not strong enough to handle an efficient stroke. As they become stronger they can become more efficient, if they keep working on it.

CC: *How do you see women's swimming progressing with their entry into NCAA competition. Will it develop a higher profile?*

KT: The fact that scholarships are available for women to help pay for their education is going to be another kind of motivation to keep people swimming. I would like to think that with more people staying longer in the sport, they will have the opportunity to continue to improve. We will have to wait to see if that really happens.

CC: *Eventually there will be a certain social tinge towards it as there is with the men's program. It's the thing to do.*

KT: Right. It's become more accepted with more and more girls in high school planning to swim through college. I'd like it to have the same status as for the men.

CC: *Do you think that women collegiate swimmers remain as motivated to train as hard as they did previously?*

KT: At some universities that attitude is predominant. I think it really depends on the program. In the best programs there is no way you can come in and slide because the training is too hard and the pressure too great. There is too much asked from each athlete.

CC: *Would you agree that European women have tended to swim further into maturity than Americans?*

KT: It's a question of status. But like European men, their women have the same trouble in getting an education and continuing to train. Their educational system is just not set up for that. That has to be the reason why so many Europeans come here for their education.

CC: *It certainly happens in men's swimming. Do you think women's programs will recruit from outside the U.S.?*

KT: It's starting already. European swimmers want to have good programs while continuing their education. It works both ways.

CC: *Are American universities screening potential swimmers elsewhere in the world?*

KT: Probably every swimmer in the free world.

CC: *How do you feel about recruiting. Do you enjoy it?*

KT: I don't really enjoy it, mostly because it takes so much time. That time could be better spent with the athletes I have. I try to tell the prospective student-athlete as much about the school and the program, and let her make the decision. Often decisions aren't made based on logic or their needs. I wouldn't want anyone to spend four years at my school who wasn't going to be happy. I want them to understand what they're getting into and to make sure it's what they're looking for.

CC: *Do you talk with their parents?*

KT: I first approach the athlete, because they're pretty independent and like to make their own decisions. Of course, the final decision will be influenced by the parents and the coach. Parents are usually concerned about the academic reputation of the university or the particular department in which their daughter is interested. They seldom ask about training programs.

CC: *Do you find it difficult for people from a variety of backgrounds to adjust to their new team situation?*

KT: It's always difficult. But that's what makes college athletics so exciting. It's a kind of microcosm of what the real world is like—people coming from different backgrounds with different attitudes and working together, trying to get along. I think it's a good way to get used to dealing with people in an environment that's maybe more secure and with more support than what they'll face when they're out of school.

CC: *Coming from a variety of different programs, do the athletes find it difficult to adjust to their new program? Do you allow some aspects of their old program to be continued?*

KT: It's important to take the good from each person's program because your own program will improve. We talk with each of them about what they were used to, what they like, what didn't work in the past. Each year our program continues to evolve and hopefully improve as new athletes come in.

✧ ✧ ✧

DISCUSSION WITH STAN TINKHAM

Recorded at the U.S. Long Course Championships, August 1966, Lincoln, Nebraska.

Stan Tinkham's 1956 U.S. Olympic team was the only one ever coached by a 24-year-old and most of the swimmers came from his own club. Though the Australians dominated the Melbourne Games, Shelley Man, one of Tinkham's home pupils, became the first female Olympic butterfly gold medalist. According to Tinkham's International Swimming Hall of Fame citation, "From 1954 through 1958, the Walter Reed Army Hospital team, coached by 22-year-old Army Private, Stan Tinkham, dominated the U.S. Senior National Championships, winning every event but diving at one or more times during those four years."

CC: *I believe you conduct a family athletic club. How does a club of this type operate?*

ST: Basically, we have a family swim club or family athletic club in Arlington, Virginia. The youngsters of the families are members of our club and there are quite a few individual members too. Our swim team is our main product and we have approximately 144 swimmers all totaled including the age-groupers and the seniors. We have actually a hard-core unit of 30 workers, real hard workers, who compete on our senior team, and the remainder in the program we have building up to the senior.

CC: *When you say a family club, do you mean this is a form of limited liability company?*

ST: No, it's just a unit whereby we were able to build the pool, have the pool, and operate it. Basically, it was built through subscriptions by the families and through the backing of two business associates—and, with the support of the families, we opened the doors with about 100 families and more families came in. Our basic family cost is 300 dollars for the initiation fee and then we have a monthly charge of 15 dollars per month. This includes all coaching and all use of facilities. We have classes in swimming, synchronized swimming, and diving. If a family moves to another area, it may not sell its shares—it is strictly a lifetime fee—it's good for whenever they move back to the area but it's not transferable nor salable.

CC: *What are the dimensions of the pool?*

ST: The pool is of the standard American indoor dimensions: 75 feet by 42 feet. The general price of the pool itself would be about 30,000 dollars. The building and improvements made we value at 250,000 dollars. We do have a 20-yard course which we have just built about 2 years ago.

CC: *How did you interest people in this project? Did you already have an existing team?*

ST: We did have a team which was the basis of the Walter Reed team which left the Walter Reed Hospital in 1958 and from there we went to the Potomac Swimming Association. Our membership is primarily based, however, from the North Virginia area where there are 44 teams in a league which is called the North Virginian Swim League. These swimmers practice only during the summer. In the total Washington area, there are about 300 outdoor pools and we draw talent from these.

CC: *Would you mind elaborating a little on your conditioning program?*

ST: I think that to be in the national picture here, one must swim a minimum of 6,000 meters a day and preferably between 9,000 and 10,000 meters a day. I think, with this work, conducted along sound principles and with enthusiastic youngsters, this would be the formula. I am afraid that our ideas, here in the United States, have become somewhat stereotyped on the basis of repeat distances. By that, I mean 2 or 4 by 1,500 meters a day or divisions of that such as 8 by 800 or 16 by 400 or something of this nature with the distances going downward as the proximity of the meet draws near. I personally have had more fortune with sprinters and individual medley swimmers and like to vary my strokes more and my distances more than following a strict stereotyped plan.

CC: *What type of workouts do you do? Do you do sprint-type workouts to reach the distances you mentioned or middle- or long-distance workouts?*

ST: We try, to a great extent, to do a repeat workout every other day. Our first workout of the day would be 3,000 to 4,000 meters and this would be a repeat workout with 16 by 200 meters or 8 by 400 meters and then, on the other or alternate day, we would do an awful lot of individual medley like 100-meter repeats with, say, one length butterfly, one length freestyle, one backstroke, one breaststroke, then one length freestyle kick, and then one length freestyle, and variations of the strokes such as right arm and then left arm only, kicking only and pulling only.

CC: *What are your views on rest intervals? Do you believe in long rest intervals, short rests, or a mixture of both? Working in oxygen debt for a great part of the workout?*

ST: I think it is best to work in oxygen debt. We have a very limited use of a pool and, therefore, we have little time for rest intervals. We have to be out of the pool by 8:30 in the morning and we have to do this work just back to back with very little rest.

CC: *What are your views on the mental approach to competitive swimming?*

ST: As far as mental approach is concerned, obviously the swimmers have to have competitive form instilled into them and I think the higher this desire to succeed the more the swimmer will succeed. I hate to see a need in a person

although some people do need to succeed to be happy. I hate to see this because I feel that swimming is a game and should be maintained as a game. The better swimmers who get something out of the sport will strictly be in it because it is interesting, enjoyable, and a challenge. But, the youngster who is in it just for notoriety, is obviously fulfilling a need and, obviously, this should be filled. But I feel that the youngster who has the talent and ability and really enjoys the game, is going to be more successful in life.

✧ ✧ ✧

DISCUSSION WITH GENNADI TOURETSKI

Recorded at the ASCA World Clinic, San Diego, 1996.

Gennadi Touretski, former head coach of the Australian Institute of Sport, is coach of Alexandre Popov, the 1996 Olympic 50- and 100-meter freestyle champion. In 1968, Gennadi was USSR national 400 and 1,500 freestyle champion. He competed for 15 years, first as an age-grouper, then took part in 10 national trials, but twice missed Olympic selection by narrow margins, finishing third in the 1968 trials for the Mexico City Olympics and fourth in the trials for Munich, 1972. Says Touretski, "The most important factor in coaching is to be yourself. A lot of coaches try to copy other coaches or other programs. There's a lot of discussion on whether a coach should be scientific, or whether one should coach swimming as if it's an art. Every coach should find a personal way of coaching, the way that is best for oneself because, first of all, coaching is the art of communication.

The Logic of Excellence

Touretski said, "If we look at the logic of how we achieve excellence—it doesn't matter in what field, in mathematics, in culture, in politics—the way is very simple: from information to knowledge, from knowledge to experience, from experience to wisdom, and then to excellence.

"We meet older coaches such as Joe King and John Carew, who started coaching elite athletes later in life, and they have more wisdom. With these people wisdom is quite a natural thing. A coach doesn't have to have an inferiority complex because someone else is more scientific. You just have to be yourself, and be sure that what you are doing is good for the people you are coaching. It doesn't matter how many swimmers you have, 30 or 40 or one, to be yourself is the most important thing."

Elaborating on the difference between the science of swimming as compared with the art of coaching, Touretski said that, in terms of art, this is the art of communication, an ability to open yourself to others.

Different Psychology

"Now, if you compare athlete and coach . . . I was a swimmer for a long time, and I reached a turning point when I decided I wanted to be a coach. Very quickly, I realized that I had to decide whether I could change from the psychological approach of a swimmer to that of a coach.

"The psychology of the athlete is absolutely different, because a coach has to be ready to give everything . . . maybe we should use a very simple term like the coach should be a giver, but the athlete, by nature, is a taker. He takes information from the coach, and this is a natural thing because he accepts what the coach gives him. And to make this step from athlete to coach, we have to change our psychology."

Touretski says there is one word, partners, to explain the communication between himself and Alexandre Popov. "We are partners, but there is a certain distance between us. For example, last week I moved into a house which is 30 meters from Popov's home, but still I don't bother him. I think we should respect our personal lives, what is going on outside the pool, so if I want to watch him, I tell him at the pool or I call him."

Asked about Popov's future plans, and whether Popov would continue swimming if he fully recovers from the knife wounds he suffered in a Moscow street attack on August 25th, Touretski replied, "I'm sure he will, but I will be surer to say tomorrow when he is released from the hospital . . . tomorrow his federation will make a presentation for Alex."

Good Liaison

Touretski said that he and Popov have a good liaison with their national federation, to the extent that the federation has given Popov total freedom to choose the competitions in which he wishes to enter. "They said that if the national trials were not included in our preparation plan, Alex could go wherever he wanted. This is very good because it shows they trust me and they trust him. However, we decided that it would be better for Alex to compete in the trials because there were no other suitable competitions. So he competed in his national trials, and he clocked 48.8. He did very well."

Touretski said that Popov usually races over the 100-meter distance about 100 times in a year. "That's average. But this year we couldn't do it. We had no competition."

Surprised, I questioned Touretski closely on this topic, and the conversation went like this:

CC: *He swims the 100 a hundred times?*

GT: Yes.

CC: *In one year?*

GT: Not less. He does not less than one hundred starts. We have a special calculation of average results, so . . .

CC: *You're talking about competitions?*

GT: Competitions, yes.

CC: *He goes to meets?*

GT: He has no less than 100 starts in the 100.

CC: *And that means, he may do two 100 races in the one meet.*

GT: Yes, it looks like he does one hundred 100s, 10Ks with a speed of more than 2 meters per second.

CC: *That's good training.*

GT: That is also learning the skill of racing the 100. That's the most important thing, because we had no opportunity before the Olympics. We had a lot of competition last year but we hadn't enough competition in the Olympic year.

Preparing for the Race

Touretski said, "This is based on the psychology of the coaches in Australia with elite athletes. They are afraid of competition. They are afraid to be disappointed. They are afraid to break the communication and get a negative atmosphere in the school. But I think this problem is only in the minds of coaches but not in reality.

"The race is the goal and meaning of preparation. That's the most important thing. This is the most effective type of training. If we have this good balance of recovery and training, we can achieve results.

"We can use very simple logic: If you want to measure any coach or any training method, there are four stages: training, activation, stress, recovery. Training is mostly aerobic and anaerobic threshold work. Activation, this is MVO_2. This is the Australian method, MVO_2. Now stress, well, that is high-intensity training, or competition, then recovery.

"I asked one coach in Australia about one very successful swimmer, why she didn't do well as expected, and he said, 'She didn't train.' I said, 'What did she do?' 'She did heart rate sets.' Activation. That's why they've gone up, then they've gone down."

Seeking Competition

I asked Touretski whether he made a point of seeking top competition for Alex. "Is Alex always swimming against top competition? Do you seek competition against Gary Hall, or to swim against the fastest he can find at a certain stage of the season?"

Touretski said, "Organizing competition is quite difficult because it depends on many factors. You mentioned Gary Hall . . . well, Alex is the best in the world, so if there is a good condition for this swimmer to compete against him, they may contact Alex's manager at IMG and ask if he will be available.

"This is another factor if you want to compete with a swimmer like Alex in a particular event, televising and all the attendant details. This is a professional area, so I don't want to touch this. This is not my business."

On the question of how many top races Popov needed to get into shape to produce his best performances, Touretski said, "I think this is the business of every federation—to prepare a competitive plan for the national team and its members. That's the most important thing. They have to decide what kind of competition they need.

"I say what I need but Don Talbot may say no. Or we could compete, let's say, in Santa Clara, but he has his own model, and I don't want to criticize so what I say is only my opinion. While I prepare good athletes, there are other people who must make the decisions and they are responsible for them.

"That's why I think, first of all, we should start a plan. We need to plan, and if we plan, we'll realize what the objectives are, and by what means we can achieve this goal through training and competition, and things like that."

Thoughts on National Planning

"If you want to know my opinion on what should be done about national planning to make swimming successful, imagine me as head coach of Russia, or any other country. The first thing I would do would be to start looking for talented coaches. I would do everything to prepare these coaches. Give them information, everything.

"Next, I would bring them together, not to challenge each other, but to get them together, not as one squad, and not as the national team, but just to start doing things together in the direction of developing this particular sport in the country. Let's say it's a part of the culture, to do something outstanding for the country, like, let's say Canadian hockey, the best in the world, or Canadian ballet. I don't know about the ballet, but Canadian hockey is well-known.

"I like Don Talbot. He tries to encourage the coaches personally, and that's what he did for Scott Volkers; that's very, very good. I think the success and ability of the head coach to bring coaches together and train them is very important.

"Let's get together. Let's make our swimming the best in the world. Well, probably it is not a good idea to be a shadow of American university programs, but to do something of our own, something together. This should be the most important thing, to move in that direction.

"To achieve these objectives you need to have very clear minds, and very talented people. I think every country has such people, and then these people should decide how many competitions they need, and who should be there.

"The problem of countries like Canada and Australia—America hasn't all these problems because they have a whole lot of swimmers and coaches—but swimming in Australia is still not so big, and the problem is that Queensland competes against

Michael Klim, Gennadi Touretski, and Alexandre Popov shortly after their successes at the 1998 World Championship in Perth.

New South Wales, and all together, they compete against Canberra. Why?"

Asked how he would solve the problems he had mentioned, Touretski said, "First of all you should decide what you have to do. As soon as I start to do it, I will find a way how to do it, because I do not know the culture, for example, of different countries so good. This is my opinion: I know how to do it in Russia, even I mention how to do it in Australia. That's what I've been doing for a long time, but when I first came to AIS, I said, 'People, we have a very high level of tension of kids. Where is it coming from?'

"It's coming from the competitive situation between coaches. We can never be successful as a country while we just compete against each other, and this is the main goal. We have to compete against America too, we have to compete against Russia, we have to get together and compete against them. We have to help each other, and in this way we will have a perfect team spirit."

On Training Coaches

I asked what he thought was the best way to train a talented young coach, certification or be-

ing apprenticed to an experienced older coach?

"I don't think there exists one way. There can be different ways. I think if you have someone like a head coach, he has to realize that there can be different ways. A top athlete can be prepared at home, in a university, or in a special center. It depends most on whether you have a coach there, and talent, sooner or later will come to the top. But you need to have a coach there.

"Alex Popov does 2,000 kilometers every year, having not less than 100 starts. This means that he does 30 competitions a year. This is the only way to go to achieve perfection."

A Clear Mind

Asked whether Popov, as a sprinter, was temperamental and, at times, perhaps difficult to train, Touretski replied, "Alex does the whole mental work himself. I merely give him the framework, because his creative abilities are so great. As a coach, that's probably what I've most helped him to develop."

Touretski says that Popov has such a clear mind that he doesn't have difficulty in concentrating. By the same token, he doesn't talk strategy with Popov. "I try to avoid this kind of talk because I don't want to interfere with his natural way, although, some time ago, I did show him some strategies. As I mentioned in my lecture, we did all the pre-Olympic work in March and April, and later we didn't speak about the Olympics."

When I mentioned that John Carew was the same with Perkins, and that Carew had told me that he doesn't say too much to Perkins, Touretski said, "That's the Golden Rule. If you start speaking to the athlete, it means that things are not well, and that soon things probably will not be good, and that's important to remember."

Touretski said that a coach must use different strategies with kids than with older swimmers. "Jim Fowlie was once surprised when, one day after a training session, we had some kids come to the pool, and he saw me working with them. He said: 'Gennadi! You don't look like a national coach when you laugh and jump up and down like that!' Yes, but I did it that way because that's how I coach younger kids, and I enjoy doing it."

Chapter 7

GREAT PERSONALITIES PAST AND PRESENT

JAMES "DOC" COUNSILMAN: THE TALENT IS THE CALL

Each man has his own vocation. The talent is the call. There is one direction in which all space is open to him. He has faculties silently inviting him thither to endless exertion. He is like a ship in a river; he runs against obstructions on every side but one, on that side all obstruction is taken away and he sweeps serenely over a deepening channel into an infinite sea. He has no rival. For the more truly he consults his own powers, the more difference will his work exhibit from the work of any other.

—Ralph Waldo Emerson

He is the preeminent visionary in the history of swimming, and his work has left an indelible mark. True, others have made major discoveries, but none over so wide a spectrum as James Counsilman of Indiana University. Taking the science of swimming, from the birth of the sport to the time of Counsilman, what he has contributed has been much the better half.

Before the advent of Counsilman, swimming coaches didn't take sports science too seriously. Most scientists weren't very good at explaining themselves, and their work was generally thought to be too technical, and of little practical value. Frustrated, they withdrew into esoteric language, referring to the public as laymen, and developing obscure terms from which a naive secret society feeling of superiority was derived.

Counsilman, however, wrote simply as well as accurately. He understood the sport, had an intuitive feel for it, and was immensely creative. He was a former national champion, a successful coach, and trained in scientific investigation by the best in the field. He was one of the few who knew how to ask the right questions.

The word went out that Counsilman's stuff really worked. Coaches started to read his papers on interval training. They learned to control work-rest ratios and develop a swimmer's speed and endurance. Then, when Counsilman published his work that first explained how the laws of physics govern stroke mechanics, they read that too, applied it, and found that their swimmers swam more efficiently.

And, all the time, Counsilman continued his research. He directed his mind to a methodical and unrelenting analysis of swimming techniques in a manner never before attempted. The quality that sets the scientist apart is perhaps the persistence of his curiosity about the world. He slept only five hours a night throughout his career. He coached his team, and he also spent hours—deadly, difficult hours—his keen, inquiring mind extracting information from the data and forming workable concepts.

His swimming teams improved, and so did the teams of those who adopted his concepts. The coaches knew that Counsilman was one of them, a scientist but also a coach, and a great one at that. He was twice American Olympic coach (1964 and 1976). The 1964 team won all but two gold medals and over half of all medals; the 1976 men's team won all but one gold medal and three-fourths of all medals. At one time or another, his swimmers had set world records in every single men's event, a record unequaled by any other team. When Counsilman retired in 1990, his teams' win/loss record at Indiana was 286-36-1, and his swimmers had won seven long course national team championships.

Early Years

James Counsilman has always had an implacable curiosity. As a boy, Jim, as he was known, loved to watch fish slip through water. He was fascinated by all kinds of swimming motions in nature. He even caught snakes and put them in water to see them swim. This was not all. He and his brother, Joe, collected a variety of pets until the basement of their home resembled a small menagerie. The outcome of their interest in animals was that Joe became a veterinary surgeon, and Jim became the coach-scientist who uncovered the secrets of human swimming.

James Edward Counsilman was born of German-American parents in Birmingham, Alabama, on the 28th of December 1920, the younger son of Joseph and Ottilia Counsilman. He was two years old when his parents separated, and his mother returned with Jim and his brother Joe (3½), to her home town of St. Louis, Missouri.

The small Counsilman family arrived in St. Louis, poor and desperate, destined to face years of hardship and privation. But Ottilia Counsilman, a staunch member of the Missouri Lutheran Synod, was a woman of strong principles, great drive, and indomitable spirit. The eldest of a family of 12, she had known little else but hard work from the age of 13, when she took a live-in job with a German family as a younger child's companion.

In her prime, Ottilia Counsilman was a tall, stately, chestnut-haired, Wagnerian figure, dignified and intelligent. She faced hardship with self-sacrifice, and cheerful, perennial optimism, often encouraging her two sons by saying, "God helps those who help themselves." Working as a cook in a nearby hospital, she earned enough money to lease two apartments. She kept half of one apartment for the family living quarters, and then leased the remaining 1½ apartments to roomers.

Becomes a Swimmer

Together with Baron, a black Labrador retriever, the two brothers spent their boyhood rambling the 1,400 acres of nearby Forest Park, the site of the 1904 St. Louis World Fair and Olympic Games. One day, they were wading in the park's fish hatchery when Jim stepped into a hole and nearly drowned. He had been in a similar incident years before and was scared of the water. But now he knew that it was urgent he learned to swim, and he taught himself at the age of 13.

A year later, Jim won a place on the high school swim team. He also became a fine high school track-and-field athlete, covering 440 yards in 54 seconds, and leaping 5 feet, 10 inches in the high jump. He had wanted to be a diver, but he broke his ankle, so decided to focus on swimming.

Now keenly interested in swimming, he read the autobiography of Captain Matthew Webb, first man to swim the Channel. Webb's feats inspired Jim.

He developed into a fine swimmer and a national champion. He went on to become one of the great figures in the history of the sport. And, like Matthew Webb, he accomplished his own first when he became the oldest man to swim the Channel.

Ernst Vornbrock—A Profound Influence

In 1938, at Maplewood, Missouri, Jim Counsilman won his first important swimming race, and caught the attention of Ernst Vornbrock, the coach at the St. Louis Downtown YMCA. Vornbrock, a tall, thin man, with a large nose, didn't look the typical swimming coach, but he was an excellent mentor who believed in self-discipline. He was a quiet, modest man, and a talented violinist. Through his study of music, Vornbrock had learned the importance of self-discipline and practice, and he carried the precept into coaching.

Vornbrock came into Jim's life at the right time. His mother had toiled hard and long to support her family, the two boys had always been trouble-free and dependable, but the influence of a strong male figure was never more needed. By comparison with his school friends, Jim was at a disadvantage. Vornbrock saw this, and soon took a keen interest in the young man, in whom he discerned the character and talent that leads to success.

Vornbrock became a big influence in Jim Counsilman's life, so much so that, 30 years later, Jim was to dedicate his epoch-making book, *The Science of Swimming*, to "My coach, the late Ernst Vornbrock." Vornbrock helped Jim to improve his self-image, and discover the potential that lay within him. A year before meeting Vornbrock, Jim had graduated 113th in a class of 116, and was in the depths of despair. He had shown promise in mathematics, an indication of conceptual ability, but his teachers overlooked his strong points instead of using them as positive reinforcement. This failure to perceive his innate ability resulted in Jim never thinking of himself as smart.

But Vornbrock was devoted to helping kids improve their self-esteem, and become better adjusted. A highly intuitive person, Vornbrock treated Jim like his own son and taught him to think positively, and to always finish what you start. Vornbrock introduced him to classical music, and the arts in general, and even allowed him access to his collection of classical records. Jim learned to appreciate classical music. He still remains an opera enthusiast, and Puccini's operas, "Turandot" and "Madam Butterfly" are his favorites.

The Depression Years

Jim Counsilman graduated from high school in 1937 in the middle of the Great Depression. The next three years were tough, but his swimming and his attitude improved because of Vornbrock's coaching and friendly interest. Jim had inherited his mother's tremendous drive, and he found employment wherever he could get it. One week he would work as a packer for Singer sewing machines, while the next week might find him climbing poles and wiring up domestic telephones for 20 dollars a week. And, all the time, he attended workouts, walking two miles there and two miles back again, to both early morning and evening practices.

In 1941, the United States national outdoor championships were held in St. Louis. This was a break for Jim Counsilman in more ways than one. Had the championships been held elsewhere, he

James Counsilman was a national AAU champion in the 200 meters and the 220-yard breaststroke in 1942, and Big Ten champion and NCAA runner-up in 1946.

couldn't have afforded the travel expenses. Jim finished second in the 200-meter breaststroke event. He swam the distance by alternating between orthodox breaststroke and the hybrid butterfly-breaststroke, a combination of butterfly arm action and breaststroke kick.

At the meet, Coach Vornbrock introduced Jim to Mike Peppe, coach of the Ohio State University. There were no scholarships in those days, but Mike Peppe took an interest in Jim, and found him a job as an elevator operator in the Statehouse (State of Ohio governmental building), where he earned 40 cents an hour, which bought a full meal in those days. At the same meet, Coach Peppe met a great young Hawaiian swimmer by the name of Keo Nakama, and he arranged for Jim and Keo to room together in the International House at the Ohio State University.

For three years Jim gave his mother 5 dollars a week for the household, but she saved the money and returned it to him when he left for college. Thanks to his mother's sacrifice and hard work, and thanks to Coach Vornbrock's paternal interest, at last Jim Counsilman's world was opening up. When he left for college, Jim thanked Vornbrock for all he had done for him. As Vornbrock smiled at the tall, young athlete, he remembered the words of the philosopher, Jacques Barzun: "In teaching you cannot see the fruit of a day's work; it is invisible and remains so, maybe for 20 years," and, in his heart, Vornbrock knew that he would hear more of his departing pupil.

Leaves for Ohio State

Jim enrolled in a BA course, majoring in forestry, but later switched to a science degree in physical education. In April 1942 he competed in the National Short Course Championships, in Columbus, Ohio, and won the 220-yard breaststroke event, setting a new national AAU record in the process.

In June 1942, Coach Hal Minto invited him to train with him at Cuyahoga Falls, Ohio, to prepare for the National Long Course Championships. He was not to know that the pool was filled with artesian well water, and that it was "as cold as ice." Neither did he know that, at Cuyahoga Falls, he was to meet Marjorie Scrafford, his future wife and lifelong companion.

After winning the national 200-meter title at New London, Connecticut, in August 1942, Marjorie and Jim started dating. Then he returned to Ohio State, only to be called up for military service in early March 1943, a week before the Big Ten Conference meet. Although he wasn't to compete in the Big Ten for the first time until 1946, Jim was not about to delay his marriage. He and Marge were wed on June 15, 1943. Jim left for Europe on active service in January 1945.

The U.S. Army Air Corps

Jim signed up in the U.S. Army Air Corps, and scored in the 99 percentile in the IQ tests. During his training, Jim learned about the Bernoulli effect, and later he was to relate it to swimming. Although he is not talkative about his actual military service, it is on record that, between January and May 1945, when the war in Europe ended, Jim flew no fewer than 32 missions as a B-24 bomber pilot. He was awarded the Air Medal with Oak Leaf Cluster. While bombing the railroad marshaling yards in Innsbruck, his plane's landing gear was shot out, and he flew the plane over the Alps to crash-land near Zagreb in Yugoslavia, saving the lives of his crew. For his courage Jim Counsilman was awarded the Distinguished Flying Cross.

First Coaching Experience

Discharged from the Army Air Corps in August 1945, Jim returned to his studies at Ohio State, and was appointed captain of the championship-winning swimming team in 1946 and 1947. In 1946, he won the Big Ten Conference 200-yard breaststroke title, and took second in the same event to Charles Keating in the NCAA Championships.

In those days swimmers were allowed to coach while still competing, and Mike Peppe, impressed by Jim's personality and knowledge, asked him to be his assistant. The former bomber pilot made a strong, mature leader to whom the swimmers reacted with enthusiasm. And he kept a log, just as he had done in the Air Corps. He recorded every workout, from the day he started coaching. Years later, he was to say, "The most valuable research I ever did was contained in the daily training log of every workout I set in my career."

In 1946 the Ohio State team, which had a number of great Hawaiian swimmers on their roster, went to Hawaii for the summer to train under the legendary coach, Soichi Sakamoto. Sakamoto taught Jim that swimmers could train much harder than most people thought they could; in fact, every aspect of the Hawaiian experience made a great impression on him.

Later Jim said, "Sakamoto trained the swimmers hard, but he was a kind, gentle person, and he never screamed or hollered. If you did something that he didn't like, he would become quiet, but he was not vengeful or vindictive. Sakamoto never won a place as a coach on a United States team. He wasn't a politician, and he was never really recognized, even when he had the majority of swimmers on the team. At least, he should have been selected as the distance coach."

Swimming Research

Jim Counsilman graduated from Ohio State in 1947, then went to the University of Illinois to study for a master's degree under Professor Thomas Kirk Cureton, regarded as the father of swimming research. Cureton's pioneering research made prolific contributions to understanding physical fitness. He was one of the first to undertake the physiological measuring of champion swimmers. Cureton was known for his ability to make students think. He challenged them, stimulated their curiosity, and their desire to investigate, saying, "If you end up upsetting tradition, why that's fine."

Jim admired Tom Cureton for his original thinking, and not being afraid to upset tradition. He respected Cureton's individualism and drive. Cureton taught him how to apply the laws of physics to human movement, how not to be afraid to try new methods and make radical changes. Said Cureton, "We are not out to prove statistically how infallible a particular method is but to broaden our field of knowledge." In this stimulating environment, Jim's mind ranged far and wide, speculating over unsolved problems in the new field of competitive swimming.

Jim always had the knack of being in the right place at the right time, and of making the right choices. Tom Cureton was involved in studying the effects of weight lifting in the training of athletes. Jim was working as assistant to Ed Manley, the varsity coach, and he experimented with weight training for the swimming team.

However, Jim's main focus was on preparing his master's thesis, "A Cinematographic Analysis of the Butterfly-Breaststroke," which included a comparison between the breaststroke whip and wedge kick actions. In this study, he pioneered the use of the motion camera as a scientific instrument for analyzing swimming techniques.

He discovered that underwater photography, to be successful, required plenty of light and clear water, and Jim found the ideal venue at Silver Springs, Florida, where he obtained the use of a specially made underwater tank. Among the first subjects in his underwater studies were such great swimmers as Adolph Kiefer, 1936 Olympic backstroke champion; Wally Ris, 1948 Olympic 100-meter champion; Keith Carter, national butterfly champion; Bowen Stassforth, 1952 Olympic silver medalist in the 200-meter butterfly; and George Breen, 1,500-meter Olympic bronze medalist, 1956.

First Olympic Champion

Completing his master's degree, Jim went to the University of Iowa, on Cureton's advice, and Cureton drove him there to meet C. H. McCloy and W. W. Tuttle, important names in exercise physiology, a science then only in its infancy. Years later, Jim would say, "Both these men were also good biomechanists. They were great pioneers, and I can't say enough in their praise. In retrospect, much of the material they were publishing was a bit naive, but, nevertheless, very good for the time."

While preparing his doctoral dissertation, Jim was assistant coach to David Armbruster. In 1948, Jim coached Iowa swimmer, Walter Ris, to the Olympic 100-meter freestyle title at the London Olympics. Head Coach Armbruster was busy building a boat in his garage; so it was Jim who coached Ris all that summer. Ris's Olympic victory gave Jim a great deal of confidence.

Jim Becomes Doc

Jim completed his doctorate in August 1951. His dissertation, "The Application of Force in Two Types of Crawl Stroke," was a continuation of Louis Alley's early work on the crawl stroke. Jim stayed one academic year longer at Iowa, then accepted a post as assistant professor, and head swimming coach at the State University of New York at Cortland.

He taught tests, measurements, statistics, and physiology, coached the swimming team, and junior varsity soccer. The university administration, anxious to publicize the qualifications of its staff, insisted that personnel of doctoral status should be addressed as "Doctor." But Jim's students, somewhat less formally, addressed him as "Doc." So Doc he became, and Doc he remains, to this day.

Cortland was exclusively a teacher's college, and not a place where one would expect to find Olympic-caliber talent. But one day Doc spotted a freshman with obvious feel of the water. He had also seen him on the soccer field, and Doc knew that the young man had never swum competitively, but Counsilman told him that, with hard work, he could break world records. Three years later, George Breen won a bronze medal in the Melbourne Olympic Games, and broke three world records in distance freestyle.

Breen's unorthodox two-beat crossover crawl kick was criticized by traditionalists who maintained that the correct leg action in crawl swimming was the six-beat kick. In 1957, Doc was the first to describe and explain the two-beat crawl, and it became standard for most distance swimmers.

Doc experimented with weight training. He held a landmark symposium of weight training experts at Cortland State in 1954 that helped to dispel the fallacy that weight training made swimmers muscle-bound. The Australians were making big strides with new training methods, and it was significant that George Breen, a weight-trained athlete, was one of the few non-Australians to challenge them.

George Breen confirmed what Doc had learned from Coach Sakamoto in Hawaii, namely that swimmers are capable of adapting to large amounts of hard work. At Cortland, Doc soon made his mark. In 5 years his team won 35 of 40 meets, and 4 conference titles. Not only did he coach his team to win, but he always encouraged his swimmers to reach for their full potential in all aspects of their lives. Ernst Vornbrock had taught him well.

Home in Indiana

By the late 1950s, Doc's reputation as a coach and researcher was well established, and, when Coach Robert Royer became ill and had to retire from his post at Indiana University, Frank McKinney urged the university to hire Doc. Doc thrived on being in the thick of competition, and it was natural that he jumped at the chance to enter the big leagues.

Doc came to Bloomington in 1957, and two outstanding swimmers, Frank McKinney and Frank Brunell, came to swim for Doc at Indiana. Soon others followed. Don Watson, coach of the outstanding Hinsdale High School, who had trained under Doc at Iowa and was a close friend, encouraged swimmers such as John Kinsella, Scott Cordin, John Murphy, and many others, to go to Indiana. From Australia came Coach Don Talbot's outstanding stars, Kevin Berry and Robert Windle, both of Olympic gold medal fame. The momentum was so great that, at the 1964 Olympic trials, at Flushing Meadows, New York, seven of the eight finalists in the 200-meter breaststroke, led by the great Chet Jastremski, came from Doc's team.

Although barred from competing in the NCAA's from 1961–1963 because of rule infractions by the university football program, Doc kept morale high and the team continued to compete at a high level in the Big Ten and AAU championships. Ted Stickles broke seven world records in the individual medley event during his career, and, in fact, during those years, it was calculated that Indiana teams could have defeated the rest of the world in a head-to-head competition.

A list of swimmers who swam for Doc reads like a who's who of swimming greats: Mark Spitz, Jim Montgomery, Gary Hall, John Kinsella, Mike Troy, Charles Hickcox, Don McKenzie, Chet Jastremski, Tom Stock, George Breen, Mike Stamm, Alan Somers, Ted Stickles, Larry Schulhof, John Murphy, and many others.

Coaching Philosophy

Doc's coaching philosophy was influenced in several ways by the late Ernst Vornbrock who aimed to help swimmers achieve their full academic, athletic, and social potential. "Maturity in coaching is important; not only should the coach be aware of one's own basic needs, but also of those of the team, and when the two coincide, the coach usually has a very sound philosophy."

Doc warned about getting caught in the trap of

seeking to develop champions only. "You don't have to sacrifice the rest of the team to develop the exceptional few," he often said. "Develop a state of mind that concerns itself with everyone on the team. Then you will have more than your fair share of champions, and fewer champions will have a distorted idea of their own importance."

Doc's swimmers gloried in hard, intelligent work, and they attached a stigma to those who didn't pull their weight. Doc was a born master of group dynamics; he used positive thinking, ritual, ceremony, and tradition to bond swimmers into tough, enthusiastic, successful teams. But, above all, Doc was a fine inspirational coach, as sensitive to the aspirations and emotions of the swimmers as a photographic plate is to light.

There is insufficient space to list all the fine achievements of individual Indiana swimmers. There were many all-time firsts, the most notable of all being Mark Spitz's seven gold medals at the 1972 Munich Olympics, and Jim Montgomery's 100-meter Olympic freestyle win in Montreal, 1976, when he became the first swimmer in history to crack 50 seconds for the distance.

Doc readily admits that he learned a great deal from the talented swimmers he coached. "For example, Mark Spitz taught me a lot," he says. "Great swimmers usually have an innate sense of how they function. They seem to know instinctively how hard they need to work, and when they need to ease off. There's no need for the slave-driver approach to coaching. By respecting the swimmer's perceptions about his swimming, and by good communication, a coach can develop the sensitivity to understand the swimmer's basic needs."

Over 20 years, about 18,000 kids have attended Doc's annual swim stroke clinics. He taught his assistants the importance of a positive approach to stroke instruction, and how important it was not to jump in with criticisms of a young swimmer's stroke, but rather to praise the good points about it. Doc believes that too few coaches look at their swimmers underwater. "It is imperative to do so," he said.

"I don't think that I ever wanted to change a talented swimmer's stroke. The better swimmers do the right thing automatically. Only occasionally do they need a nudge in the right direction.

Many a good swimmer with an excellent stroke has been ruined by a coach who knows little about stroke mechanics. Sometimes it's difficult to tell whether a swimmer is successful because or despite of his stroke mechanics."

Doc allowed the swimmers to take part in decision making. Before finalizing the schedule for the following year, he would discuss it with the team. Sometimes, he let them choose their own events in dual meets, write the team workout, and also decide where they would train at Christmas.

The success of Indiana's swimming teams became a tradition in the Hoosier State, and twice the team was given a dinner by the governor of Indiana. And, if this were not enough, once a year Marge Counsilman invited the team home for lasagna.

Doc's Jelly Bean Day was another traditional occasion. Once a season, every swimmer was timed for 800 meters, using his particular competitive stroke. A pound of jelly beans was awarded to every swimmer making standard times. This became such a tradition that the stands were half filled with spectators, and the results were published in the local newspaper.

Scientific Method

Doc had an excellent training in the scientific method. His advice to students was, "Outline your topic clearly and discipline yourself to stay within the limits of your subject." Doc realized it was important not to become a mere recorder of facts; one should try to penetrate the mystery of their origin.

Doc once said that true understanding in any area of science is always preceded by a series of responses involving three stages—Stage One: Curiosity, Stage Two: Confusion, and Stage Three: Comprehension. Doc added that coaches and scientists are constantly challenged by this triad of learning. "The process can be stimulating, but it is often frustrating and annoying because the light at the end of the tunnel often seems very distant."

Doc said that a study often shows that a certain method is the best, while another study directly contradicts the first one. "The more we discuss the questions, and research them, the further we push ourselves into the second stage, that of confusion. Finally, after dwelling for some time in this stage, we begin to develop some understanding and venture into Stage Three, that of comprehension.

"I doubt that any intelligent scientist-coach believes he ever enters fully into Stage Three on any subject. As he starts to comprehend some concept or principle, he becomes aware of new unanswered questions, and the cycle of the triad response begins all over again. The perceptive scientist has come full circle and enters again into Stage One as the cycle repeats itself."

Doc believes that we keep progressing by evaluating change objectively. He warns, "Don't paint yourself into a corner; people write something and they are scared to walk away from it." He has an antidoctrinaire nature which precludes him from swallowing systems whole. He believes that putting methods into neat pigeonholes, to synthesize them, leads to stagnation and not progress.

Doc's contributions to competitive swimming are legion. There was hardly a phase of the sport that escaped his attention and was not significantly improved by his influence. His groundbreaking research covered a wide field. In the area of exercise physiology and conditioning, he published papers on a wide range of topics: interval training, strength training, isokinetic and biokinetic exercises, hypoxic training, altitude training, and so on.

Underwater Stroke Analysis

Doc's first interest had been in kinesiology, the science dealing with the study of body mechanics and the prescription of exercises for developing specific muscle groups. This interest started in high school when he saved up to buy a small Argus camera for 10 dollars, and asked a school friend to photograph him in various phases of the high jump. Little did he know that this modest start was to grow into a photographic odyssey spanning more than half a century, in which he was to become the consummate artist of underwater photography, who also pioneered the use of the movie camera as a scientific instrument.

With the wisdom of hindsight, it's hard to believe that only 40 years ago, coaches didn't know the exact answers to such questions as, where and how should the hands enter the water? Should the pull be bent or straight? What should be the path of the hands in the stroke? Should the stroke be short or long, slow or fast?

His early attempts at motion film analysis of swimmers started with the use of an old aircraft movie camera that, according to Doc, "looked as if it had been through both World War I and World War II!" Using outdated film given to him gratis by the university athletic department photographer, he could shoot 5 or 6 swimmers in slow motion with each 100-foot roll. The film still cost 6 dollars per roll to process. Then he would take the film home to study it. In typical painstaking and implacable fashion, Doc gradually solved the problems of underwater photography: light refraction, image distortion, and the use of grids to measure stroke velocity and acceleration.

Last but not least, the big difficulty was the design of an underwater camera housing that was both waterproof, and easily maneuverable. Before perfecting an ideal camera housing, Doc wrote off two expensive movie cameras that were ruined by leakage, and his basement shelves still carry umpteen experimental housings that failed to meet his needs.

Lest it be thought that Doc had access to only the most expensive testing instruments, it should be known that he was a master at devising ingenious makeshift equipment. He followed the precepts of Ivan Pavlov, the Russian scientist, who said, "Accustom yourself to the roughest and simplest scientific tools." Doc cleverly contrived a unique system of underwater strobe light photography, and used it to show, for the first time, the true nature of human swimming propulsion.

He attached a battery-powered flashing light to the midfingers of a swimmer's hands, and had him swim in complete darkness, before flashing a strobe light to make a single picture that showed where the hand was at a given point. Because he left the shutter open throughout the entire swim, he obtained pictures of the flashing light, before and after the strobe was fired, and thus was able to work out where the hand was at other points in the stroke cycle. Doc's underwater photography completely revised the understanding of stroke mechanics. Using this method, Doc eventually produced the first complete analysis, not only of stroke mechanics and the forces developed, but also of the actual propulsive mechanisms used in swimming.

The Bernoulli Effect in Swimming

There was a time in the 1960s and the 1970s, when *Swimming World* published at least one breakthrough article by Doc every year. Readers, and coaches in particular, developed the habit of quickly scanning the pages of each new issue, seeking new articles by Doc. Even his Indiana swimmers were caught up in the anticipation, and one day they appeared on deck in bright new T-shirts inscribed "What's up Doc?"

Each new discovery was released to the swimming public in sequence to aid the process of concept formation. First he showed, by means of underwater trace-light photography, that swimmers used curved-line sculling patterns, and did not pull in a straight backward line, as commonly believed. Only in his next paper did he reveal his major discovery, namely that swimmers propel mainly by means of lift propulsion (the Bernoulli Effect).

Later, he expanded this work to show how good swimmers have acceleration patterns that are interrelated with lift propulsion.

Mentor to the World

Doc published over 100 papers on various aspects of swimming research. His interest extended to swimming pool design, antiturbulence lanes, and building thousands of the first specially designed pace clocks for interval training.

He visited no fewer than 24 countries. A constant stream of coaches from over 37 countries came to Bloomington to interview him, and often to stay and complete studies under his guidance. Then they went home to spread the Counsilman gospel.

In 1968, his classic book, *The Science of Swimming*, showed the value of a scientific approach, and was reprinted 22 times. The book had immediate credibility because its author was also an outstanding coach at the pinnacle of his career, with a long and illustrious record of producing world-record holders and Olympic champions.

In 1977, he published another best seller, *Competitive Swimming Manual*. An outstanding feature was the series of underwater action sequences of Mark Spitz, Gary Hall, Jenny Turrall, Kornelia Ender, and dozens more of the greatest swimming stars of the 1970s, from the United States, Australia, and East Germany. This collection remains the finest photographic record of the stroke mechanics of great swimmers.

Competitive Swimming Manual included an important section on the psychology of coaching. The eminent George Haines paid Doc a fine compliment when he said that Doc had the ability to bring together matured star swimmers, from a wide variety of backgrounds, and then coach them to even greater improvement. Doc aptly fits the great Australian swimmer, John Devitt's description of a great coach: "A great coach can take a good swimmer and make him great, and he can also take a great swimmer and make him greater."

The X Factor

Doc sometimes adopted a folksy way of putting his message across. His talk at the ASCA World Clinic in Montreal in 1971 on "The X Factor in Coaching" remains a classic. He spoke about a mythical coach, Frank Zilch who, hard as he tried to become successful, lacked the X factor. Doc explained the X factor as the ability to recognize the important things in coaching, and to work on them, and to minimize the unimportant.

"The great coach must have two basic abilities—he must be a good organizer and a good psychologist," said Doc. "The good organizer will have the large team, will attract the good swimmers from other teams, and develop the Mark Spitzs and Gary Halls of the future. The good psychologist will be able to handle the parent problems, get along with the city council, and be able to communicate successfully with the swimmers—he will have the super teams.

"The good coach today needs only an elementary knowledge of conditioning physiology and stroke mechanics. He does not need these to get the job done. However nothing remains static, and in the future these two areas will become more and more important."

Doc Emulates Matthew Webb

No one knows when Doc first started to nurture the idea of swimming the English Channel, not even Doc himself. He had joined the masters swimming movement when it started in the early '70s, and soon made a mark for himself in its ranks. Marge Counsilman noticed that he was spending more and more time swimming in Lake Monroe near Bloomington. He had decided to swim the English Channel. Marge didn't think this was a good idea, but try as she did, she was unable to dissuade him.

Doc engaged the services of Tom Hetzel, a renowned coach of Channel swimmers, and Hetzel recommended that Doc build up to a 10 mile swim twice a month—to begin with. Then, a month before the Channel attempt, he was to have reached a stage where he could cover an average of 100 miles per month. During this time, Doc could be seen regularly swimming up and down Lake Monroe, with one of his students motoring close by in an escort boat.

Hetzel, a shrewd psychologist, warned Doc, "You need to stop thinking in minutes and seconds, like a competitive swimmer, but rather in hours— hours and hours. That's the biggest mental hurdle every Channel swimmer must overcome. The Channel swimmer also needs to not let unexpected

Courtesy of Marge Counsilman

In September 1979, at age 58, Doc, who was coached by Tom Hetzel, became the oldest person to conquer the English Channel. He is seen here preparing for a workout in Dover Harbor.

events get him ruffled." In August 1979, shortly before he left for England, Doc attended the American Long Course National Championships in Fort Lauderdale. He took the opportunity to do a 16-mile, nonstop swim in the sea in extremely hot conditions.

In England, there were disappointments; on two successive days, the swim had to be called off because of unfavorable weather. This was a concern because there were only a certain number of days in which a swimmer could catch the favorable neap tides. Doc spent the waiting time in his hotel room writing his lecture papers for the ASCA World Conference, to be held in Seattle the following month.

Waiting for the word to start the swim brought Doc to a highly psyched-up state. When the great moment came on September 17, 1979, he set off at dawn from Shakespeare Beach, swimming a steady 70 strokes per minute. Aboard the 26-foot fishing boat accompanying him were Marge; Tom Hetzel; two television photographers; a *Sports Illustrated* writer; an *SI* photographer; the official observer, Ray Scott of the Channel Swimming Association; and the fishing boat captain, Reg Brickell, and his two sons.

For hour after hour, except when feeding, he plodded along, arms pulling and recovering in a steady crawl stroke, and purposely breathing late to avoid inhaling seawater. He needed all the physical strength and endurance, so conscientiously developed during the preceding months. His implacable will compelled him to continue, despite accumulating exhaustion and threatening seasickness.

When an unexpected tide threatened to drift him miles off course, his naturally cheerful disposition surfaced; he thought of his colleagues back home who had told him to his face that he would never make it. He also thought of the media people onboard the fishing boat, all of whom expected him to finish. "I'll show them," he said to himself, and kept on stroking.

He tried to keep his mind occupied by thinking back to highlights in his life. He remembered his boyhood days in Forest Park in St. Louis. Instead of thinking of the time he nearly drowned in the fish hatchery, he remembered the Charles Lindbergh exhibit near the main gate, that he had visited so often. "Ah yes!" he laughed to himself, "Lindbergh flew The Spirit of St. Louis across the Atlantic. The least I can do is to swim The Spirit of St. Louis across the English Channel."

Hetzel had warned Doc to expect the unexpected, and it happened when an undermanned Russian trawler appeared, coming straight towards him. The captain of the fishing boat radioed the trawler to warn them that a Channel swimmer was in the sea in front of them. But the trawler was under the control of an automatic pilot while the crew was below deck taking coffee, and it kept coming straight at him, almost to the point where it would have been too late to avoid him. In desperation, the fishing boat radioed to shore, and only then did the trawler get the message, and take avoiding action.

Later, Doc appeared to be losing concentration when he suddenly seemed to be swimming out into the North Sea, but this was an illusion caused by the fishing boat suddenly veering to avoid an exceptionally heavy swell. Marge, who had been seasick the whole way, was frightened for Doc's safety, but knew that trying to stop him would be a waste of time.

Hetzel had arranged a set of signals with Doc: he had three hats which he was to change at certain intervals, and when he changed his hat for the last time, that was to be the signal that Doc had only three more miles to go. Toward the end of the swim, the worst fear of most Channel swimmers appeared about to happen when the weather took a sudden turn.

The rolling swell suddenly became a violent chopping sea that threatened to engulf Doc. The wind whipped up, and it was obvious that Doc was very tired. It was feared his core temperature could drop so low that his brain would stop functioning properly, and he would start hallucinating.

At that moment, however, Tom Hetzel changed hats for the last time, indicating that there were only three more miles to cover. Doc remembered Ernst Vornbrock and how he had taught him: "The most important thing in life is to always finish what you start." Doc started swimming with renewed determination.

Finally, just at sunset, the oldest man to swim the Channel found himself wading ashore. He heard cowbells. Then he saw a herd of cows, and realized he was in the midst of a farmer's pasture. He thought, "What an anticlimax, no one to welcome me, only cows." The tide had caused him to miss the traditional finishing spot at Cap Gris-Nez, and he landed at Wissant, 13 hours and 7 minutes after leaving the English shore.

The news of Doc's swim spread rapidly around the world. Doc and Marge flew straight from London to Seattle. When Doc entered the conference room at the ASCA World Conference to give his talk, over 1,000 colleagues rose spontaneously and gave him the ovation of his life.

On their way home, when Doc and Marge arrived in Chicago, an Indiana University plane was waiting, sent specially to bring them home. At Bloomington airport, before the mayor and the university president could reach them to extend their official welcome, their grandson, overcome by impatience, broke ranks and ran onto the tarmac to greet them. There was a motorcade parade. Nearly the whole student body and most of the townspeople lined the streets to welcome them and show their joy. In every respect Doc had finished what he had started.

✧ ✧ ✧

THE GEORGE HAINES STORY
Haines has witnessed more than 50 years of swimming history, and often been an important part of it.

George Haines is one of history's great swimming coaches. He is also one of the most popular coaches who ever trod a pool deck.

Haines likes people, and it's easy to see that people like him, too. It's not surprising that he attracted swimmers from every point of the compass. Not only did he draw them in, but he made many of them great. In fact, he has had more swimmers inducted into the International Swimming Hall of Fame than any other coach.

Haines took the pressures of top-level coaching in his stride. Throughout a long career, he remained relaxed, outgoing, good-natured, and free of hang-ups. While Haines kept firm discipline in his teams, he never lost his sense of humor.

George Haines, left, receives the high points trophy on behalf of his Santa Clara Swim Club at the Leandro Relays in 1967. Presenting the award is coach Dave Beaver of the San Leandro Beavers Swim Club.

His swimmers were relaxed and confident, just like their charismatic coach. They sported one of the cleverest T-shirt slogans that I ever saw. It said a lot in two words: "By George!" It also meant "best in the world."

It was commonplace to see a Santa Clara swimmer step to the starting block, look over at George, and give a wink. George would smile and wink back. Then the race would start, and yet another "by George" product was on the way to a championship medal, or perhaps another world record.

Nowadays, Haines has become one of swimming's most entertaining and beguiling raconteurs. To hear him talk about impact people is something to remember. He talks about other great coaches, great swimmers, their achievements, and the lessons he learned from them.

Not for him the intellectualizing, or the now customary buzzwords about blood lactates and the like. Instead, Haines speaks with the natural quiet authority of a great intuitive coach who has done

it all. Haines's stories, told in the flat, flinty tones of his native Midwest accent, are tinged with wry humor and a sharp eye for human foibles.

Early Influences

Haines has witnessed over 50 years of modern swimming history, and often been an important part of it. The Haines saga started in Huntington, in northeast central Indiana, where Haines was born. As a schoolboy there, he came under the spell of Glen Hummer, coach-mentor at the local YMCA. "He was a great, great man," says Haines. "His techniques were ahead of the time. When Hummer died, I felt as if an arm had been cut off."

There is an interesting parallel here with the early history of Haines's great contemporary, Doc Counsilman. Two of the most successful swimming coaches of the twentieth century were inspired by outstanding mentors at the local Y.

In Counsilman's case it was Ernst Vornbrock, coach at the downtown YMCA in St. Louis, Missouri, who turned Counsilman's life around during the Great Depression and set him on the road to success. Glen Hummer and Ernst Vornbrock were two of a kind, and American swimming owes much to their indirect influence.

Even before he became a swimming coach, Haines learned the value of a good early distance background, because Glen Hummer first trained him to be a 1,500 swimmer. (Haines was later to become the conference champion in the 50 freestyle at San Jose State College in California, a big drop from swimming the 1,500!)

Peter Daland tells a little-known story about George Haines's early years: "When George got out of the service in 1946, he hadn't swum for three years, and was badly out of shape when he got back into training at the Huntington Y.

"Glen Hummer took George to a meet at the Indianapolis Athletic Club and said, 'It will be good training for you to swim the mile,' to which George replied, 'Yeah, right.'

"Matt Mann had brought his Michigan swimmers to this meet, because competition was restricted just after the war had ended, and people had to search far and wide to find competition. And so it turned out that George found himself swimming in the same meet as the mighty Michigan swimmers.

This historic photo features many great names in swimming. Taken at the 1957 Hawaiian Open Championships. This annual meet was popular for many years. Front row, left to right: Coach Soichi Sakamoto, Dawn Fraser, Nancy Ramey, Chris von Saltza, and George Haines. Behind Sakamoto's left shoulder is Lorraine Crapp. Behind Ramey is Carin Cone. Behind von Saltza is Jane Wilson. Behind Haines is Shelley Mann. Robin Moore, the sprinter, is upper left in the top row.

"After George finished the 1,500, and was climbing out of the pool, Matt Mann called him over, and said, 'Young man, you have a marvelous stroke. You have excellent technique.' And George was smiling, and feeling pretty good. Matt Mann continued, 'But there's one problem.' George said, 'What's that?' Matt said, 'You swim in the same place too long.'"

When reminded of this story, George laughs and says, "Matt Mann was a great guy. I loved Matt Mann and Bob Kiphuth, they were both great gentlemen."

Ann Curtis and Charlie Sava

During the war Haines joined the Coast Guard, and was stationed in San Francisco. He was billeted in a barracks that had once been the Simmons Mattress Company's shipping and receiving depot. Haines said, "I was there three years. I saw guys going out to the South Pacific, and they would come back three years later, and say, 'Are you still here?'

"I taught survival training to people who were going overseas at Crystal Plunge Pool for the Navy, the Marines, as well as the Merchant Marines. I ran the program with a great U.S. swimmer by the name of Fred Taoli who was in the Navy."

Haines described how Ann Curtis, America's first great postwar swimmer, trained at Crystal Plunge under Charlie Sava. Haines said, "I thought Sava had unbelievable talent. He was the first coach I saw using wall pulleys." Charlie Sava took regular wall pulleys and placed them alongside the pool. Haines said, "He had the number of pounds painted on the weights, and then he attached one end of a tether to the weights, and the other end to a belt around Ann Curtis's waist. She swam against the tether for what seemed like hours."

Tethered swimming, in Haines's opinion, is nothing new. "Doc Counsilman once showed me a book, written in the 1,800s that had a couple of paragraphs on tethered swimming. It's just another case of what goes around, comes around.

"Charlie Sava and Ann Curtis were great impact people in the '40s, and, of course, at the first postwar Olympic Games in London, Ann Curtis won gold medals and anchored the winning freestyle relay team."

Tom Haynie and Charlie Walker

Haines said that, in the 1950s, he learned a great deal about rest and taper from the Australians. About the same time, Haines met a good swimmer by the name of Tom Haynie who swam for the University of Michigan.

"He was a great freestyler," said Haines, "but a kind of a wild character, and he didn't become as good as he could have been. Later he coached at Stanford and I can remember a clinic that he gave at San Jose State in 1952 where he talked about streamlining the crawl by rolling the body on its long axis."

Haines said that he was so impressed that he asked Haynie why he didn't write a book, and he said, "No, I'm too busy coaching." I asked George Haines the same question. Haines smiled and said, "Guess, I've also been too busy coaching and never found enough time.

"What I'm saying is that certain people make impacts on you as a coach and as a swimmer. I used to listen to Charlie Walker, my coach at college, and then we used to take our teams up to Stanford and have dual meets with them—later Jim Gaughran was the coach there and so on—but, at that time, Tom Haynie was an impact coach to me. I learned a lot from the man about freestyle—get your hands under the body, roll the body on its long axis, your hips control the roll."

Haines said that he still had the paper that Haynie presented at the 1952 clinic. "It's in my box in the garage, where everything else is. But I can still remember him talking about that."

Chris von Saltza

"One of the great American impact swimmers, after the 1940s, was Chris von Saltza, and I had the good fortune to coach Chris from the time she came to Santa Clara for a tryout in December 1955. In June of 1956 she broke the American record by about nine seconds in the 500-yard freestyle."

At the Olympic trials for Melbourne, Haines said that Chris von Saltza was 12 years old, and pushing off the last turn in the 400 meters, she was coming second. "At the 475, I thought, 'Good gosh! She is going to make the team!' But I really didn't want her to. But, anyway, she dropped back to fifth place as the bigger and older girls went by her. She came in fifth. She was 12 years old."

Haines said that Chris's father, Dr. von Saltza, came up to him, pulled him behind the bleachers, and said with a sigh, "Oh man! Am I glad she didn't make the team."

Haines added, "You know why? We thought it would have been too easy. She didn't start swimming until December 1955, and here she was nearly making the Olympic team in August or late September of 1956 to go to Australia.

"So we were both praying that she wasn't going to make it. I was glad to hear her father say it, too. He said it first. He was also a great person.

"So she didn't make the team, but she continued to develop and became one heck of a swimmer," said Haines. He claimed that von Saltza would have been great in any era of swimming. "She was about 5 feet, 10 inches or 5 feet, 11 inches, weighed about 140 pounds. I wouldn't want to say she was about 140 pounds today, she'd probably punch me," quipped Haines. "I see her once in a while. She lives in Sacramento. If she was swimming today, she would be right there with the big guys."

Haines said that Chris von Saltza had great technique, the desire, everything. "She had good body roll. She kept her hands under her body as she pulled. She was fantastic."

Value of Rest

In 1959, Chris von Saltza was the first American girl to break 5 minutes for the 400 meters. The Australian and world record was 4:46+ held by Lorraine Crapp. Said Haines, "We learned about rest and taper from the Australians, but I also learned something about rest from an incident in Chris von Saltza's career, and I'll tell you about it in a moment."

Haines said that the idea of shaving down was introduced by the Australians, and they kept it a big secret over there. "They wouldn't tell anybody about it, and they waxed us. Not only were they better swimmers, but they had the little edge of shaving. They were the first group to do it."

Haines described how, when von Saltza came down with a bad case of ptomaine poisoning at the 1960 Olympic trials in Detroit, she had inadvertently taught him the value of rest. "She came down with this bad case of poisoning, four days before the meet, and I thought, 'My gosh! She's never going to be able to do it.'

"We put her in a room by herself, and she stayed in bed for two to three days, and finally brought the fever down. Her dad, who was a doctor, showed up, and he knew a doctor in Detroit who came out to the hotel, and took care of her. But she wasn't in the water for three days—never got out of bed. We fed her, and that was it. She'd just go back to sleep."

Haines described how von Saltza, after being sick in bed, and only having had the chance of loosening up the day before, said, "I want to do a dive 50 just to see how I feel, to see if I have any strength."

Haines said, "I think she did her best time or something, and here I am, giving her heck, because I think she's burning herself out. Prior to the meet, Chris had done 4:53+ for the 400, but the next day she went 4:44.5 and broke the world record. And, so I prayed from then on, that everybody would get sick when we go to the Nationals, and we could put them to bed to rest for a few days. It's true that you learn more from great athletes than you ever teach them."

Steve Clark and Matt Biondi

On the subject of men freestyle swimmers, Haines said that Steve Clark was one of the great impact swimmers he had trained. "Steve Clark started swimming in Los Altos when he was eight or nine years old. He came to Santa Clara, and he and another guy, Eddie Townsend, both had to stand close together to make a shadow in the high sun, they were so damned skinny."

Later, Steve went to Yale, where he swam a new American 100-yard record of 46.7 seconds in the NCAAs.

Yale's Payne Whitney Exhibition Pool was like the Taj Mahal of swimming. It seated 1,500 people in plush seats around an elevated amphitheater that circled the pool. More world records were broken in it than anywhere else. It was here that Bob Kiphuth, the great Yale coach, reigned like a demigod. He protected every aspect of the pool as if it was a holy shrine.

Haines said, "The first time I ever visited there was when I was a young coach. I started to step out onto the pool deck. I was wearing my regular street shoes, and I heard Kiphuth shout, 'Hey kid! Go back and get a pair of rubbers.' I said, 'Yes, sir! Yes, sir!' and went back and put rubbers on.

"But the worst thing you could do was to go from the pool deck to the amphitheater by climbing over the banisters. This set Kiphuth into a terrible

rage," said Haines. "Anyway, when Steve heard that he had broken Jeff Farrell's American record of 48.4, he was so excited that he forgot the rules. Up he goes, over the banisters, to where his mother was sitting.

"She was knitting, for gosh sake! Maybe it was crocheting! 'Hey Mom,' Steve calls, 'I went 46.7.' His mom says, 'Is that good, Steve?' Steve had the perfect parents, let me tell you!" added Haines.

Haines classifies Matt Biondi as "one of the great impact swimmers and a real Hall of Famer.

"Matt went 41.8 for the 100 yards. He still holds the record. The reason he went 41.8, and the reason he went his 48.4 world record for 100 meters in Korea, was that the guy was training over-distance; he was training for the 500, he was training for the 200, he even swam the 500 in dual meets, and he was our greatest 200 swimmer. But, as soon as he stopped training for the 200, and the over-distance, he never ever, even in the 50, swam as fast again.

"He never swam 48.4 again because he quit training for the 200, and it was really sad for me to watch the Olympic Games in 1992, and to see that our best 200 guy, with 1:36.2 or 1:37, whatever it was, wasn't on our relay. He didn't swim the 200 so he couldn't qualify. But Matt was a great impact swimmer for our sprinters."

Schollander, Spitz, Saari, and Roth

Haines talked about two other impact sprinters, Don Schollander and Mark Spitz, both of whom he had trained. "Don was a great worker in practice. Let's say, for example, that we were going into the hard part of the season. I think we were going 15 by 200, and we were going 5 sets of 3, descend the first 3, and the first 200 in the next 3 had to be as fast as the second 200 in the first set, and then they had to descend that set, and they had to keep going, and they got down to 14.

"Spitz and Schollander were not exactly what I would call we'll-go-out-and-have-a-beer-together-types. Schollander would be in one lane, and Spitz would end up in his lane and drag on him. He was the greatest drag swimmer of all time. Schollander didn't like that one bit. Neither did he cherish the thought that this young swimmer was going to knock his socks off if he hung around long enough."

Schollander was the first swimmer in the world to break 2 minutes for the 200-meter freestyle. He brought the time down to 1:54.3 (Long Beach, August 30, 1968). For 4 years, Schollander remained the only swimmer in the world to break 2 minutes for the 200. Said Haines, "Remember, nobody else was breaking 2 minutes, not in the U.S., not anywhere."

For many years, making the American men's Olympic 800 relay team was the toughest task in the world. Haines said, "To make that team, a swimmer had to shave. Don Schollander made the 1964 team without shaving. He was the last person to make the team without shaving. Don did not shave until his first event in Tokyo.

"Even the great Roy Saari, along with all the other guys, had to shave to make the team, but then you must remember that he had been ill and was hard put to it. He made the relay but he had to shave to do it, and then, with the 400 IM and the 1,500 coming up later, I think it took a little bit of the edge off him.

"In the 400 IM, Saari was swimming a pretty good guy by the name of Dick Roth. Roth had a big attack of appendicitis at the Tokyo Olympics, and he was hospitalized. The hospital said they wouldn't release him. Well, when we got there, he was actually going down the hall, hopping on one leg, getting his pants on to get the hell out of there. He was scared because they had told him that they were going to operate on him. And, when we did get him back home from Japan, the next day his family doctor took him in and took his appendix out right away. That's how bad it was."

Mike Burton

"Back in the '30s Buster Crabbe, Jack Medica, and Ralph Flanagan were unbelievable. George Breen was one of our first real impact swimmers over the distances. This guy didn't start swimming until he was in college, and he broke the world 1,500 record in our Olympic trials in 1956, I think, and then again in the heats of the 1,500 in the Melbourne Olympics with a time of 17:52.9. But then, of course, Australia's Murray Rose bombed everyone over there in the finals."

Haines said, "Brian Goodell in Montreal, 1976 [15:02.40], and George di Carlo in Los Angeles, 1984 [15:01.51] were uncanny in the distances.

But, before them, there was Mike Burton, maybe the toughest guy who ever pulled on a Speedo.

"Burton won the 1,500 in Mexico City, and 3 or 4 days before the 400, he and a couple of other guys became violently ill. When we were riding back and forth from the Olympic Village to the pool, we kept seeing a sign, Chucky's Pizza, or something like that, and the swimmers kept saying, 'Gee, we ought to get off the bus and get a pizza.' I said, 'You guys get off to get a pizza, you're not going to swim in the meet. Don't get off. I don't want to catch you!'"

Haines continued, "So, one day, I wasn't on the bus, and they got off, and on that day the elevators in the Olympic Village weren't working, and we had to carry Mike Burton down four flights of stairs, and take him to the infirmary where they fed him intravenously for about three days. Then he snapped out of it, and he just managed to qualify seventh for the finals. He just barely made it in. Five-tenths of a second more, and he would have been a spectator."

Just before the final of the 400, Burton asked Haines what time he thought it would take to win, and Haines replied, "Ralph Hutton says he's going to go 4:11.0." Burton said, "Well, I'm going 4:09.0 tonight."

Haines said, "Well, that's what Burton did; he went 4:09.0—exactly! And, of course, he won. Not great by today's standards, and of course, it's all relevant, but he won. Then, in the 1,500, Burton won in world and Olympic records."

Talking about the American trials for the 1972 Munich Olympics, Haines said, "Burton was in an outside lane in the heat of the 1,500-meter trial, and when I looked over to where he was swimming, there were about 20 or 30 people, coaches, swimmers, and parents running along the pool deck, yelling for Mike Burton to qualify. Then he made the team and went to Munich. That guy was unbelievable!"

Quick Psych-Up

"The reason I say that Burton was one of the toughest guys in the 1972 Olympics is that he was not swimming well there until we got to the 1,500. In Munich there was the great fiasco of Rick de Mont's disqualification. Just before he walked out on the pool deck to swim the event, Burton found out that de Mont was not going to be swimming the 1,500 that night. Actually, Burton and de Mont heard the news at the same time.

"They had disqualified de Mont because of the fiasco in the 400, and why he got disqualified was that he had asthma and had taken an over-the-counter medicine called marex, and it might have been more of a medicinal thing than a performance-enhancing drug, but it was on the banned list, and so he got knocked out of the 400, and lost his gold medal to the Australian swimmer."

Haines said that Burton had only about two minutes in which to gather himself for his new role as favorite. "I don't think Burton was the favorite to win, but by the time he found out about it in the ready room, and went out on the pool deck, Burton got himself together and swam one of his great races. As a matter of fact, he was in such great possession of that race, that, about halfway through, he allowed the Australian swimmer to go ahead of him, and got on the guy's hip.

"The other swimmer didn't move over, and so Burton stayed right there with the guy until about the last 150, and then he tumbled and got away from him and won the race. Burton was the first 1,500 swimmer in history to win back-to-back 1,500s in the Olympic Games. Of course, Vladimir Salnikov, the great Russian swimmer, has done it three times. I consider these guys to be impact swimmers."

Haines cited more great impact swimmers. "Donna de Varona was one, Claudia Kolb, of course, was another. Claudia was one of the toughest swimmers of all time. And then there was Mark Spitz, a lot of people remember him for his 100 and 200 fly, but he could swim every distance from 100 to 1,500. Many people don't know that, or don't remember that he swam in a meet one day in torrential rain over at San Leandro, a junior college school. At about 300, I stood up and called, 'Am I the only guy here who knows this guy is breaking the world record?' "

Haines said, "Then everybody started to take notice. Nobody was watching because the rain was pouring down on them. Mark broke the world record in the 400. And later that summer, on the way to the mile, he set world records in the 800 and the 1,500. Of course, they didn't stand for long, because later in the nationals, Mike Burton annihilated these times, but, nevertheless, I mention this to show that Spitz was also able to break world records over the longer distances. Spitz's background of aerobic, over-distance training prepared him for the 100 and 200 distances."

Importance of Over-Distance

Haines said that he had always been an advocate of aerobic training, over-distance training. "The reason that Spitz, Clarke, Schollander, and all these guys were able to do what they did, was because they had a background in over-distance training. And, if you go through the history of swimming, and you look at the great 100-meter champions, you'll learn that practically all of them were great 200 and 400 swimmers.

The moment of truth, or was it? In the 1972 Olympics in Munich, USA's Rick de Mont (right) sweeps to a lead over Australia's Brad Cooper to win the 400-meter final only to be later disqualified for taking an over-the-counter medicine for his asthma.

"Johnny Weissmuller was 400-meter American champion, and he was the 100 champion. Wally Ris, who won the 100 in the 1948 London Olympics, was a great 200 swimmer, although you don't read much about him swimming 200—but he trained for the 200. The great Australian swimmers all dropped down from the 400, 200, to the 100, and these guys were impact swimmers. Although Janet Evans's times are plateaued now at a higher level than her world's best, she is undoubtedly one of the great impact swimmers in history."

Haines said that another girl that he had the "good fortune to coach" was Keena Rothammer, one of the few swimmers to have beaten the great Shane Gould of Australia. "Shane won the 400 in Munich, and Keena, I think, was third or fourth, I don't even know if she got a medal. But, when she got through, she came up to me and said, 'George, I'm going to win the 800.' I said, 'I think you can, Keena.' I had my tongue in my cheek, you know, because here she's going to be racing Shane Gould."

Haines related how Keena Rothammer swam "one of the greatest negative-split races, maybe of all time, up to that point, anyway, because her second 400 was about one half a second faster than her first 400, and she won in new world and Olympic record times. Her time was about 8:55, not great compared with today, but it was good then."

Subdued Kicking

Haines said that Keena Rothammer had an unusually powerful kick. He described how he tried to get her to subdue her kick, to make it more relaxed, and to teach her how to use it only when she had to. Don Schollander also had a very powerful kick. "That guy could break a minute for 100 yards on the kickboard. We had to subdue his kick," said Haines. "A lot of six-beat crawl swimmers have a tendency to overkick. When you see swimmers turn blue around the lips and back of their shoulders, the first thing you ask is, 'Are they in condition? Are they overkicking? Are they holding their breath on the way out?' Haines said that swimmers such as Schollander, Keena Rothammer, and Chris von Saltza, all of whom had a powerful kick, had to learn to subdue their kick, and make sure they were breathing properly, and with the right pattern."

Haines pointed to Australia's Kieren Perkins as a great impact swimmer. "He is a perfect example of a guy who can kick, and use his legs throughout the 1,500, as well as in a straight 400 swim. But he subdues his legs and is able to change from a little bit of a four-beat kick into a six-beat. All leg-talented swimmers have to be able to do that. Perkins is one of the great ones, and must be a tremendous trainer.

"The guy is unbelievable," says Haines, as he bestows on Kieren Perkins an accolade he reserves for only the greatest of the great.

❖ ❖ ❖

L. DE B. HANDLEY—THE "GENTLEMAN JIM" OF SWIMMING

Born in Rome in 1874 of American parents, Louis de Breda Handley, athlete, coach, educator, and communicator, was a man of singular accomplishments. He was one of the great figures in the history of swimming.

His father, Francis Montague Handley, American sculptor, residing in Rome, was Private Chamberlain of Sword and Cape to two Popes (Pius X and Leo XII), as well as the first American to be made a Commander of the Order of St. Gregory.

Handley's two sisters were nuns. One of them, Mother Mary Angeliquem, was Superior of several convents in the United States, before becoming Superior of the Convent of the Good Shepherd in Rome.

Handley came to America at the age of 22, where he was to spend a long life as a volunteer dedicated to promoting the new American crawl, as well as the emancipation of women swimmers. When he died of a heart attack in New York on December 28, 1956, at the age of 82, Louis de B. Handley had transformed the sport of swimming.

Handley refined the early Australian crawl-stroke, and, in so doing, developed the American crawl, in effect an entirely new stroke soon adopted all over the world. To this day, the American crawl, albeit in more highly advanced form, remains the stroke of choice in freestyle events.

Handley was a dandy, but he was no weak-kneed fop; he competed against the toughest and the best, and he was swimming's first great coach-educator.

Courtesy Swimnews

Handley's creative thinking, skilled coaching, and lucid writing on all phases of swimming brought him fame and a universal following. He was acknowledged as the foremost authority on swimming, water polo, and watermanship. L. de B., as he was popularly known, was coach-educator to the world, and swimming's first great communicator.

Australia's three pioneer swimmers, Fannie Durack, Mina Wylie, and Annette Kellerman, first "captured public sympathy" for the plight of early women swimmers. But, in America, it was L. de B. Handley's influence that was responsible for the complete emancipation of women swimmers. Annette Kellerman had said, "Not only in matters of swimming but in all forms of activity women's natural development is seriously restricted and impaired by social customs and costumes, and all sorts of prudish and Puritanical ideas. The girl child long before she is conscious of her sex, is continually reminded that she is a girl and therefore must forego many childhood activities.

"As womanhood approaches these restrictions become even more severe and the young woman is corseted and gowned and thoroughly imbued with the idea that it is most unlady-like to be possessed of legs or to know how to use them. All of this pseudo-moral restriction discourages physical activity in woman, and yet she manages fairly well as a land-animal, and accommodates her steps to hampering petticoats with a fair degree of skill" (Kellerman, 1918).

He Put Women's Swimming on the Map

The influence of Handley's work at the Women's Swimming Association of New York, whose membership quickly grew to over 300, eventually put women's swimming on the map worldwide.

Handley developed America's first female Olympic champions. Outstanding WSA swimmers such as Gertrude Ederle, the first woman to swim the English Channel; Charlotte Boyle; Ethelda Bleibtrey; Aileen Riggen; and many others, were household names. They inspired young women everywhere, so much so that the *New York Times* of October 7, 1924, reported: "It is interesting to note the amazing strides made by girl swimmers since the games in Antwerp four years ago.

"Nothing more remarkable has featured athletic activities the world over. Even our watermen have not improved at the same rate as a class. With very few exceptions the present topnotchers are girls with several years improvement before them, while child mermaids are displaying speed never attained by their predecessors. There is every assurance, therefore, of increasingly brilliant exploits as the champions and newcomers grow to maturity."

Role of Women in Developing American Crawl

The Women's Swimming Association was formed in 1917, after the Amateur Athletic Union had undertaken to standardize water sports for women. The founders of the WSA could not afford the expense of a professional coach so they appealed to Handley to oblige them with his help and he consented, and contributed his services gratis. He retained the post of head coach for the best part of 40 years. Under his guidance, WSA women swimmers were chiefly instrumental in developing the American crawl stroke.

At a time when American authorities and leading contestants were unanimous in declaring that it would never be possible to effectively use a leg thrash faster than a four-beat for more than a hundred yards or so, L. de B. Handley's pupils introduced and proved the value of the 6-, 8-, and 10-beat varieties.

As a result WSA stars dominated the national and world pictures for many years. Charlotte Boyle, Helen Wainwright, Gertrude Ederle, Ethelda Bleibtrey, Aileen Riggen, Alice Lord, Helen Meany, Eleanor Holm, Claire Galligan, Ethel McGary, Lisa Lindstrom, and Agnes Garaghety, were among the many champions produced by L. de B. Handley; and he developed from novicehood 6 of the 12 girl stars who represented the United States in the Olympic games of 1920 at Antwerp.

Throughout his career, L. de B. Handley volunteered his services and never took a penny in return. His import business suffered severe losses during the two world wars. He recovered from the first setback, but never completely from the second. He spent his closing years living in reduced circumstances in a small apartment, without a telephone, on lower Manhattan, refusing to accept assistance from his many followers and admirers. Handley gave his services to the WSA for nearly 40 years, and, even in his old age, he came to the club once a week (on Tuesdays) to coach the senior team from 7 to 8 PM.

A Renaissance Man

Louis de B. Handley came to the United States in 1896 where he obtained employment with an importing firm in New York City. An all-round athlete, he was first a member of the old Knickerbocker Athletic Club then, after it disbanded, he joined the New York Athletic Club, where he devoted his efforts mainly to football, rowing, swimming, and water polo.

Handley won renown as a competitor in aquatic sports. He was on the Knickerbocker Athletic Club's 11 from 1898 to 1900, rowed sweeps and sculls for the Atlanta Boat Club and the Knickerbocker and New York Athletic Clubs. Among L. de B. Handley's many hobbies were cross-country horseback riding, training and breeding bird dogs, hunting, and sailboat racing.

Louis de B. Handley was educated by the Christian Brothers in Rome. He studied many languages, including Latin and Greek and was fluent in French, Spanish, and Italian. He mastered the art of writing, acquiring a classic style not unlike that of Macaulay, the great essayist. He used this gift to promote swimming for women, and the use of the American crawl stroke from an early age, and at all distances.

Handley was immaculate in speech, manner, and dress. Early photographs show him as a dapper, handsome, and fair-complexioned young man with the build of an athlete. His hair was neatly parted in the center, and he sported a crisply curled mustache. He wore, according to the occasion, either a homburg hat, or a straw boater. In the city he usually wore tweed suits, with watch chain stretched across his buttoned vest coat. His high, white starched collars reached just below the chin where a WSA pin was proudly displayed in the tie knot.

Although Handley dressed fastidiously, he certainly was no week-kneed fop. He played water polo with and against some of the toughest and roughest who ever played the game. In fact there are those who likened him to the elegant and fashionable world heavyweight boxing champion, "Gentleman Jim" Corbett, the man who beat the great John L. Sullivan in 21 rounds on September 7, 1892. But, back to the point. Not only did Handley play water polo with, and against, the toughest and best, and was a top goal scorer, he was considered the authority on the game.

Handley was captain and participant in both NYAC swimming and water polo teams at the St. Louis Olympic Games in 1904. Both teams won Olympic gold medals. He was captain of the Knickerbocker Athletic Club water polo team. And when the Knickerbocker Athletic Club closed down, he became captain of the NYAC water polo team. These two teams accounted for all the National Amateur Athletic championships from 1898 to 1911, with the exception of one indoor and one outdoor match. At one time, Handley held the American record for 440 yards freestyle.

Handley's Salmon Leap

It was commonly said that there had never been a stronger water polo team than the one that represented the NYAC during the season of 1903–1904. The team was organized in the fall of 1902, just after the breaking up of the Knickerbocker Athletic Club, and was composed of the best men from the two clubs. It was coached and captained by L. de B. Handley, and since its formation it hadn't suffered a single defeat, "although it boasted of never having refused a challenge." During the season 1903–04, seven important match games were played, and the team won every one, averaging a total of 35 points to their opponents' nothing.

In one memorable match, The NYAC water polo team defeated the Columbia University All-Stars by a score of 3 to 0, in one of the fastest and most interesting games ever seen around New York. The three forwards, Goodwin, Handley, and Hesser, gave a fine exhibition of trick scoring. Handley made the first goal with the celebrated salmon leap that he and Goodwin had worked successfully on almost every team in the country; then Hesser tallied on a submerged criss-cross, and Goodwin scored the last point with one of his famous hurdles. Steen, Bratton, Van Cleaf, and Ruddy, the backs, covered the goal so closely that the All-Stars never had a chance to get near it.

On another occasion, that same year, Handley won the NYAC's 100-yard handicap race in 1:09²/₅ seconds, with Olympic champion, Charles M. Daniels, finishing in second place. It should be explained that handicap races were a frequent feature of swim meets in those days, the idea being to extend the faster swimmers while giving slower swimmers a better chance to excel. The slower swimmers started first, and then the starter walked behind each remaining swimmer, calling the time from the moving stopwatch needle. Unfortunately, there is no existing account of how many second's start Daniels gave Handley on this occasion, or of how many second's start Handley, in turn, gave to the swimmers who started ahead of him.

The St. Louis Olympic Games in 1904. The gold medal relay team from the New York Athletic Club. Left to right: L. J. Goodwin, C. M. Daniels, J. A. Ruddy, and L. de B. Handley. Handley was also captain of and player on the NYAC Olympic water polo team. That team also won an Olympic medal. At one time, Handley held the American record for the 440-yard freestyle.

Water Polo Made Swimmers Fit

Nearly all the top male swimmers of the time excelled at water polo, including the great Charles M. Daniels, America's first great champion. It made them very fit and tough. When the English game of water polo, dubbed "soccer" polo in imitation of the English football game, was introduced into America, the NYAC held a remarkable trial of this style of water polo. The first "soccer" team, which won after two lively halves by six goals to two, consisted of Daniels, Handley, Ruddy, Dockrell, Wahle, Ruberl, and Adams. On the second team were Webb, Trubenbach, Mulvey, Naething, Steen, Kress, and Well.

The new game was taken up with considerable interest by all the swimmers, many of whom had never played the American game. They rapidly became skillful players. The game was devoid of many of the rough features of the regular water

polo, and was more exhausting because the players were constantly on the move. The new game had the effect of causing the swimming squad to exercise without really knowing it. In 1906, the *New York Athletic Club Journal* reported that each Sunday afternoon the regular practice attracted the whole squad of swimmers who played the game with great zest.

In 1908, Handley started coaching and lecturing as a volunteer (unpaid coach) at a number of colleges, schools, and clubs, and in several states. He also served as a volunteer coach at Yale, Princeton, and New York University, and the New York Athletic Club.

Typical of Handley's complete interest in every aspect of swimming was his contribution to water safety. When the press charged the New York City authorities with employing incompetent life guards at the public beaches, L. de B. Handley was engaged to organize and conduct qualifying tests for candidates. The examinations proved so successful that L. de B. Handley was retained to establish tests for city swimming instructors as well.

Experiments with the Crawl

When the Australian crawl first arrived in the United States in 1903, American swimming was in its infancy. The new Australian stroke was considered a novelty, and athletes continued swimming the trudgen which was still considered the premier stroke. But Handley's earlier training had taught him the value of keeping an open mind. He made the effort to obtain a detailed description of the new stroke from Australia. This information reached him in the form of newspaper clippings from correspondents in that country.

Handley set to work analyzing the technical information now at his disposal. From all accounts, the Australian crawl was characterized by a very fast arm action with a leg kick timed with the arm stroke. As one arm pulled downward the opposite leg kicked downward. There was a very pronounced deep knee bend, far more than in the modern crawl stroke.

This was the stroke that Handley tried to copy. But he couldn't get it to work. His legs kept sinking. And all the other swimmers at the New York Athletic Club had the same experience. Then it dawned on them; the stroke had been developed in the pools around Sydney Harbour, where saltwater gave the legs better flotation to perform the desired two-beat action.

Then Gus Sundstrom, the NYAC's instructor had an idea. He demonstrated his favorite stunt, the so-called swordfish stroke. He stretched his arms out in front of him with thumbs locked together and sped across the pool with a continuous drive of the legs.

Those who were watching quickly got the point. They practiced Sundstrom's rapid leg action, and soon acquired the knack of it. Then they combined the skill with the double overarm stroke. Thus was born a completely new stroke, the American crawl. The new stroke had a fast leg kick, and the thrash was narrow with the feet opening less than in the Australian crawl. But the stroke was still crude and energy consuming.

Handley, Wahle, and Daniels Refine the American Crawl

Handley and another club member, Otto Wahle, (pronounced Wally) set about refining their crude invention. They were both keen students of the

In his later years, L. de B. Handley still called in at the Women's Swimming Association of New York pool to coach on one or two afternoons a week.

sport who helped the club's swimmers and water polo players, although still active participants themselves. Wahle, an Austrian by birth, was fortunate in that he had the ideal subject on whom to try the ideas that he and Handley were developing—a youngster by the name of Charles M. Daniels. Daniels had newly transferred to the NYAC from the defunct Knickerbocker Club. Wahle was to coach Daniels throughout his long career (from 1903 to 1911).

Both L. de B. Handley and Otto Wahle became a big influence in the career of Charles M. Daniels. Daniels was to spend two more years, 1903–1905, developing his power and expertise as a conventional trudgen swimmer, before taking up the American crawl, and modifying it to suit his own needs, with results that echoed around the world.

International Swimming Hall of Fame

Even at the beach, Handley cut a striking figure. He alternated his activities between swimming, coaching, and journalism. His clear prose sent his innovative ideas around the world.

The American crawl was distinguished from the Australian crawl mainly by a faster leg kick and a more stretched out arm action. There was no conscious timing between arms and legs. For the first time in the history of swimming, a stroke was used in which the legs were independent of the arm stroke, resulting in a more relaxed free-flowing action. But the new American crawl needed refining to make it easier to swim over longer distances. With each succeeding year of his competitive career, Daniels's action became more polished, and other swimmers, particularly those who learned the crawl as their first stroke, were able to swim farther without undue strain.

The combined work by Handley and Wahle, with Daniels as their talented and successful protégé, was the subject of an important book, *Speed Swimming*, written by Daniels with the assistance of his two mentors. The book remains one of the most authoritative books on the early development of the American crawl stroke (Daniels, Handley, & Wahle, 1919).

A Stroke that Lends Itself to Many Variations

At one stage there was great confusion because of the many types of crawl stroke that were being swum.

Writing in "The Swimming Stroke of the Future" for the April 1914, issue of *Outing*, L. de B. Handley said, "American coaches were reluctant to give up the wide scissors kick of the trudgen stroke. Frank Sullivan, one of Chicago's leading instructors, with the idea of making the crawl useful for distances over 100 yards, experimented with a stroke that combined the features of the trudgen and the crawl."

"Symposium of the Crawl Stroke" was held in 1918, and was published in 1922 in the *Intercollegiate Swimming Guide*, and the opinions of L. de B. Handley, Hindman, Kistler, Langner, MacKenzie, Manley, Mann, Nelligan, Sullivan, Whitaker, and White were given on many important details of the crawlstroke technique.

Handley's summing up was that, "The American standard accepted today is the six-beat trudgen crawl. Results in national and international competition have furnished convincing proof of the supremacy of the American crawl, so there can be no question concerning the advisability of adopting it."

The teachings of L. de B. Handley did much to bring about remarkable performances with the crawl stroke. It developed to the stage where it was not only being used over the short sprint distances but also over the longer swims, and even the marathon swims of 10 or more miles. Exponents of the American crawl completely eclipsed all records set with other strokes, and defeated conclusively devotees of the latter over the longer marathons. The greatest feats of combined speed and endurance soon stood to the credit of swimmers using the American crawl.

Swimming's First Great Coach-Educator-Communicator

During this period of his life, Handley commenced a long career as a freelance author and writer on swimming, contributing to such newspapers as the *New York Times*, the *New York*

Herald Tribune, the *New York Globe*, *The World*, and *The American*. In addition, he contributed regular articles to *Outing* magazine.

Although a quiet, shy man, Handley was a captivating public speaker. But it was through the power of the written word, the clear, renowned prose of which he was a master, that he sent his innovative ideas around the world. Handley published five books, all of which became best-sellers. For many years, Handley was invited to write the section on swimming for *Encyclopaedia Britannica*. Handley's famous "Questions and Answers" column, published in *News*, the monthly journal of the Women's Swimming Association of New York, spread the

gospel of the new American crawl. The *News* was read worldwide by swimming enthusiasts, as well as his peers, who freely acknowledged their gratitude for what he taught them.

✧ ✧ ✧

KIPHUTH'S CATHEDRAL OF SWEAT WHERE MR. YALE HELD THE KEY TO GLORY

He converted swimmers worldwide to a new system of training.

Some Examples of Handley's "Questions and Answers"

Here are some examples of questions answered by L. de B. Handley in the *Women's Swimming Association News* (February, 1923). (To the modern reader these questions may seem somewhat quaint, if not self-apparent. But it should be remembered that, at the time, very few were proficient at crawl swimming. Most people preferred to swim breaststroke, trudgen, or sidestroke. Handley was pioneering an entirely new technique. Ask yourself how you would have answered these same questions, with the wisdom of hindsight and today's knowledge!)

Question: If the arm movements of the crawl are alternate, how does one obtain continuous application of arm power? It seems to me that there will be a momentary check when the arms reach full extension simultaneously, one forward, the other back.

Answer: Continuous propulsion is obtained by so timing the movements that each arm will apply power (catch) while the other still retains pressure on the water at the end of its drive. In other words, the right arm should start its drive before the left comes to the surface in recovery, and vice versa.

Question: I am told I breathe on the wrong side. Will it be easier for me to change the breathing or the leg drive?

Answer: It is hard to say which will be easier, but there is little doubt that you will profit more in the long run by changing the breathing, for almost invariably the action of the legs indicates natural inclination concerning roll of the body.

Question: How soon after the entry should one start to bend the arm in the propelling drive of the crawl?

Answer: After about one-fourth of the driving movement (from full reach to thigh) has been made.

Question: What is the best way to acquire the six-beat crawl after one has become accustomed to the four-beat?

Answer: Make the leg movements faster and narrower, occasionally counting one-two-three during the drive of the top arm and four-five-six during the recovery of the same arm. Time the action by counting as each leg starts its downward movement.

Question: Is it advisable to finish the arm drive vigorously in swimming the crawl?

Answer: One should keep pressure on the water to the end of the drive, but any jerk at the finish causes unnecessary waste of energy, for very little benefit is drawn from the power applied as the arm completes its pull.

Whenever I see swimmers doing their land training exercises, I think of my friend, the late Bob Kiphuth of Yale, the acknowledged father of land training for swimmers.

His full name and title was Professor Robert John Herman Kiphuth, director of the Payne Whitney Gymnasium, Yale University. But to us, the great Olympic coach was plain Bob Kiphuth. But any familiarity, during working hours, ended there. Kiphuth ruled Payne Whitney with a rod of iron.

Any man with more than casual contact with him came away with some of the Kiphuth stamp. He was one of those men you don't forget. Last September at the Pan Pacs in Atlanta, I recalled a veritable Kiphuth kaleidoscope of memories with Peter Daland, who was Kiphuth's assistant in the 1950s.

Authoritarian Coach

The essence of charm outside of the gym, Kiphuth's manner changed as soon as he passed through those Gothic portals. Without doubt, Kiphuth was what today's sport psychologists would call an authoritarian coach.

Woe betide anyone who had not completed a Kiphuth assignment, or the person who left the steam room door open, or the swimmer who swam without showering first. On one occasion, a swimmer swam down the pool and sat down in the shallow end. "If you want to take a bath, bring a cake of soap with you!" boomed Kiphuth's big baritone voice.

While Kiphuth made many great technical contributions to swimming, his greatest gift to the sport was an abstract one. Through sheer force of intellect and the example he set, he created a new image of the swimming coach as opposed to the then existing one of a bathrobe-clad swimming bum. Kiphuth always wore a suit, and herringbone tweeds were his favorites. On the Yale campus, his blue fedora hat with its jaunty pheasant feather trimming was his trademark.

The Payne Whitney Gymnasium

The 12-floor Gothic structure was known to generations of Yale students as "Kiphuth's Cathedral of Sweat." He made swimming coaching a well-respected profession. He wrote four books, all of them bestsellers. His books on land exercises, *Swimming* and *How to be Fit*, converted swimmers worldwide to this new system. In the water, Kiphuth introduced a training method, wind sprints, which the Australians developed into interval training, still in use today.

Bob Kiphuth started as a physical training instructor in 1917, and was Professor Emeritus of physical education when he died in 1967. His kingdom was the beautiful 20 million dollar Payne Whitney Gymnasium donated by the New York philanthropist of the same name.

Beneath its towers many of the world's greatest swimmers trained in the third floor, 50-meter practice pool, then shattered world records in the basement Payne Whitney Exhibition Pool before 1,500 spectators in a theater-type arena. More world records were broken in this pool than in any other pool in the world.

Early in his career, Kiphuth noted that many swimmers had excellent technique but lacked the muscular strength and power needed to follow through in the fatigue stage of a race. He also believed that training on land conditioned swimmers much quicker than an equivalent time spent in the water. While today's gymnasiums are equipped with advanced, and often expensive exercise machines, it was Kiphuth's initial concept that was to lay the foundation for the modern development of this important phase of training.

Robert John Herman Kiphuth was the U.S. Olympic coach in 1924, 1928, 1932, 1936, and 1948. At the London Olympics in 1948, his U.S. men's team won first place in every event. Kiphuth was athletics director and physical education professor at Yale, as well as head swimming coach.

Lithe, Lean, and Lasting

Kiphuth maintained that flexibility was "a decided asset for a swimmer, in fact, practically a necessity." Kiphuth's exercises were directed to those muscles mainly involved in the propulsive movements of the arms and legs, and also the muscles involved in providing good body position in the water.

Courtesy of the late R. J. H. Kiphuth

In 1950 the United States team under Coach Bob Kiphuth visits Japan for the first postwar swim meets. Top row from left: Dick Thoman, Dennis O'Connor, Dick Cleveland, Ford Konno, Bob Brawner, Jimmy Thomas, Jimmy McLane, Wayne Moore. In front of McLane with face partially hidden is John Marshall. Bottom row from left: Bowen Stassforth, Allan Stack, Clarke Scholes, Ron Gora with face partially hidden, Coach Bob Kiphuth, John Curran, and Ken Abe.

Courtesy of the late R. J. H. Kiphuth

American and Japanese teams together with leading Japanese officials and dignitaries. Bob Kiphuth, in center wearing bow tie, with members of the Japanese Royal Family.

Kiphuth knew more about the human body in motion than anyone I've met. Unknown to most swimming people, Kiphuth coauthored an authoritative tome on the diagnosis and treatment of postural defects. His coauthor was Winthrop M. Phelps, son of William Lyon Phelps, the great American literary figure, and once voted Yale's most inspiring professor.

"Lithe, lean, and lasting, that's the way I like them," Kiphuth would say as he fine-trained his swimmers in the gym. When I arrived at Yale, early in 1952, to study his methods, I mentioned that I was particularly keen to observe his land training workouts. As he was sometimes apt to do, Kiphuth pretended to be hard of hearing. "So you are keen to sample my land workouts?" he said, his steel-blue eyes boring right through to the back of my skull. My heart sunk. How could I be so base as to refuse my host's hospitality?

Within the hour, there I was, five years retired from swimming and never a workout since, clad in nothing but shorts, duly signed up for one long month of torment under a world-recognized master of torture.

Kiphuth appeared through the doorway. "Good afternoon, gentlemen," he boomed in his rich baritone, sounding for all the world like Mr. Magoo, the famous cartoon character. He had changed into what was known as "Bob's gray workout suit," an outfit that resembled a long fleece-lined night shirt.

Exercises "Diabolically Designed"

He had with him his dual-purpose bamboo pole. In the

gym he used it to tap out the rhythm of the exercises. On the pool deck it became a harpoon that prodded swimmers who drifted into their turns.

"Catch, swing, throw," Kiphuth called as we threw the 16-pound medicine ball back and forth to each other in continuous rhythm. My partner was John Marshall, holder of every freestyle record from 200 to the mile. Catching John's every throw was like trying to stop a cannonball, the momentum each time pushing me back several feet. "Catch, swing, throw," Kiphuth kept intoning mercilessly. "Will the young gentleman from South Af-ricker please pick up the rhythm?" he said.

Each workout lasted one hour. Twenty minutes of almost nonstop free exercises, 20 minutes of medicine ball work, then 20 minutes on the pulley weight machines. These exercises were cleverly designed, or should I say diabolically designed to increase muscular strength and power, endurance, and flexibility.

Kiphuth's methods were highly successful. He coached many famous champions, including Alan Ford who was only 5 feet, 9 inches, and weighed a sparse 150 pounds, yet became the first man to beat 50 seconds for the 100-yard event, thus breaking the great Johnny Weissmuller's 17-year-old record. Other great swimmers such as Olympic champions Jimmy McLane, Alan Stack, multi–world-record holder John Marshall of Australia, Jeff Farrell, and many more, helped Kiphuth's Yale teams to win 200 consecutive dual meets. Kiphuth was the 1924, 1928, 1932, 1936, and 1948 American Olympic coach. At the first postwar Olympics in London, 1948, Kiphuth's U.S. men's team won every event, the only team in history to do so.

Hero-Worshipped in Japan

Kiphuth became well-known in physical education circles. He was the first editor of *Swimming World*, and was in worldwide demand, making no fewer than 33 overseas trips.

He was like a national god in Japan. It has often been said that he was the father of modern Japanese swimming. On one occasion, when Kiphuth and his American team emerged at Osaka station, over 100,000 people thronged the streets to welcome them.

They overwhelmed him with adulation and fine presents. In turn, he became an authority on the Japanese theater, the Bunraku drama, the Kabuki dancers, and the Kno puppets; he could discourse for hours on Japanese culture.

Kiphuth was a pocket battleship of a man. He stood only five feet five inches tall but there was really nothing small about him. At a clinic in South Africa at the age of 70, he gave a vigorous demonstration of his medicine ball exercises. His bullet head, bull shoulders, and booming baritone voice were part of the Yale scene for exactly 50 years. On a campus of world-famous scholars and athletes, he was "Mr. Yale."

Kiphuth's achievements are aptly described in his citation on being inducted into the International Swimming Hall Of Fame:

"As Athletic Director and Physical Education professor at Yale, as a much traveled ambassador of swimming, Kiphuth played a key role in sports administration, coordination and politics helping to break down much of the traditional thinking that a coach is a trainer and should be seen and not heard."

✧ ✧ ✧

FUTURE STAR TRAINED WHERE BARNACLES AND OYSTERS FLOURISHED

John Devitt describes training in a venue where "sudden temperature changes caused shock to the system and severe cramps."

One day last year, at the end of the morning heats of the 1996 Australian Olympic trials in Sydney, I was touring the magnificent new venue for the Sydney 2000 Olympics, when John Devitt asked me if I would like to see the marvelous winter facility where he had trained as a young lad.

We were both leaving to watch a rugby game that afternoon, but John said he would take a detour to show me his old training venue. As we drove, John explained how, following World War II, there were no indoor heated swimming pools in Sydney that were open to the general public but, eager to ensure the success of their swimmers, a number of Sydney coaches had sought to set up some form of year-round swimming.

John told me that his first coach had been an innovative fellow by the name of Tom Penny, who had a hunch that somewhere in Sydney he would find warm water where his swimmers could train.

Penny figured out the problem this way: Australia had abundant coal supplies. Coal was used to drive the country's electrical power stations. The turbines in these power stations tended to overheat. Water from Sydney Harbour was used to cool them. The water was taken through a screening process to extract debris, then pumped through a canal into the turbines with the result that hot water came out the other side. Devitt said, "By now, you'll have guessed where our coach finally found winter swimming facilities for us."

Under the Boardwalk

Devitt said, "At White Bay power station, on Sydney Harbour, there was a stretch of water under the wharf that provided a square swimming course, and this is where Coach Tom decided we would train, under the boardwalk, as you might say, hidden from sight."

To some degree, swimming under the wharf in the mostly heated, swift-flowing water from the White Bay power station helped Devitt and his training partners to swim year-round and obtain good conditioning, at a time when lack of formal facilities would have made such activities impossible. Obviously this wasn't a year-round program in the proper sense of the term, but it taught them to handle very primitive conditions.

"White Bay Clam Bake"

Barnacles and oysters flourished in this warm seawater environment. They grew everywhere, and especially on the rocks and on the piles that supported the wharves. For protection the swimmers wore shoes, even while they swam. Devitt said, "The only suitable shoes available in those days were sand shoes which allowed us to tread safely on the bottom. The shoes filled up with water and became heavy, hence I developed the sort of two-beat Australian kick that stayed with me throughout my career."

When swimming for distance, Devitt and his friends swam along the perimeter of the square course, and each complete circuit totaled about 400 meters. Because the current flowed into the course at right angles to it, they would encounter the current from different directions as they turned each corner of the square. First, they swam head-on into it, then, as they turned, the current battered them from the side, and they had to try hard to keep on a straight course. Then, coming down the third side of the square, they had a free ride, as the current pushed them from behind to the next turn, where the current again swept them sideways, until they turned the corner to start the next circuit, and face yet another tough head-on swim, straight into the full force of the current.

Primitive Conditions

They swam against what was often a substantial rush of water. But, the speed of the water coming through the channel depended upon the tide, and whether the power station was using two, three, or four of its turbines at any particular time of the day.

When the turbine power was reduced, not only did the flow slow down, but there were also sudden changes in water temperature. Without much warning, the swimmers would find themselves in water as much as 15 to 20 degrees colder, causing shock to the system, as well as severe cramps.

Devitt said, "The current enabled us to develop strength and power, and, as we grew older, we took advantage of the speed of the current to learn pace judgment. We knew just how fast the current was moving and how long we could stay in a particular spot while swimming against the current. We continued swimming these 400-meter laps until we were thankful to hear the coach call a halt. This routine provided quite a good workout. Some of us called it square bashing.

"As if square bashing wasn't enough to keep us fit, Tom Penny, always innovative, discovered a canal on the other side of the power station, about 20 meters wide, through which a strong current flowed in one direction. Penny quickly noted that the canal provided the potential for about 120 meters of continuous swimming. We knew our coach well, and so we weren't too surprised when he decided that it would be a good idea for us to swim directly into the current. He didn't call these effort swims, but he would have been considered ahead of his time had he done so.

"After we had swum up against the current in the 120-meters course, we would drift back in its flow to the starting point, all the time practicing tumble-turn somersaults on the barnacled walls of the canal. This routine helped us to develop a fast approach into the turn, when actually turning in a proper swimming pool. In this way, we used our time in the water to best effect."

Team Spirit

"In the winter, we trained at White Bay, 20 minutes from downtown Sydney, on the weekends. Every Saturday and Sunday, we would swim for 2 hours in the mornings from 10 to 12, have lunch, then swim from 2 to 4. From the age of 8 until I was about 16, this routine was a big part of our training program and swimming development."

Devitt said that, in the late 1940s and early 1950s, there were about six or eight swimmers in their group at any given time. It was also an educational experience for them, because they had to overcome numerous other difficulties. "We had to travel 15 miles by train into the city. Then we had to travel by tram for another 8 to 10 miles to get to the 'facility.' All this created a team environment; we learned to work in a squad, and be part of a team. All these factors helped to develop a competitive personality, and a good attitude towards the sport.

"The conditions were tough, and only those who really wanted to succeed, continued to do it. It was hard work and it was difficult, but no one was forced to do it. The experience stood all of us in good stead, because as we got older, we found ourselves able to meet other difficulties without getting ruffled.

"Keep in mind, we didn't always have beautiful heated swimming pools with magnificent lighting, and all the other modern functions, such as we now have at Homebush. In those days, there were many tidal swimming pools with no such thing as a black line to guide you. Neither did we have good lane lines. Swimming straight was a very important part of the race, because it was easy to become fouled in the ropes. As I say, all this helped us to adjust to any difficult situation we were likely to encounter in our racing careers."

Devitt said that today's swimmers would not be able to handle these earlier conditions. Neither would he want them to handle anything similar. "We've made too much progress for that to occur; at least I hope so. But, these early difficulties, tough as they were, did help us to lay a good foundation, and a very good standard, for postwar swimming in Australia.

"The type of environment in which we trained produced some great swimmers, and those guys lifted our standards in the late '40s, especially one swimmer by the name of Barry Darke. Barry was the first great Australian swimmer to emerge after the war. He raised our immediate postwar standards, set new records, and set levels for us to attempt to emulate. In doing so, we were able to help Australian swimming move away from the need to swim in facilities such as those we endured at White Bay."

Deserted Wharf

By this time, John had turned the car off the expressway, and we were driving along the west-

Ruins of the boardwalk under which John Devitt trained in the 1950s.

ern edge of Sydney's dockland, steering between cranes and bumping over old railroad tracks. We got out of the car. Except for a giant tanker at its moorings and a drab old power station in the distance, the place was deserted. The scene could have provided a movie set for some gangster film.

"Well, where did you train?" I asked.

"You're standing on it!" Devitt said. "Come with me, and I'll show you."

We climbed over a barbed wire security fence, and there, between the cracks in the dangerously rotted timber beams in the darkness below, I could just make out the remains of the old swimming enclosure where, long ago, Australia's future champions had trained.

Swimming in the dark cavern below the wharf must have been a claustrophobic experience, and I knew now why John had made a special point of mentioning the magnificent lighting at the Homebush Olympic Pool.

I turned to John and said, "Yes, I don't think many of today's swimmers would jump at the opportunity of getting in some winter training down there."

"No, I don't think so either," said John as we carefully made our way back to the car.

✧ ✧ ✧

PABLO MORALES— LORD OF THE FLOW

From tiny splash to big splash—that's the story of Pablo Morales who was destined to become one of the most consummate manipulators of the flow in the history of butterfly swimming. Yes, the career of this future Olympic champion started with a small splash—in fact, with a series of small splashes. The tall, thin kid, with the Latin good looks, delighted in splashing the others in his beginner class. Pablo wanted them to share in the fun of being in cool water on a hot afternoon.

"I was a terror during those swim lessons," says Pablo. "I didn't really listen. I'd splash the other kids. I failed my first three beginning lessons because I couldn't do what was then called the elementary backstroke, which was an odd sort of a drill, but one you had to master in order to pass. Finally, on my fourth attempt, I succeeded.

"I look back on those days with amusement, but it does show that, when you're starting out, just because you don't have a great feel for it, it doesn't necessarily mean that you can't achieve a certain level in the sport."

"Tadpole" Days

Pablo Morales was born in Chicago, but when he was 18 months old, his family moved to California, the lotus land of swimming. As children, both parents had nearly drowned on the beaches of Cuba, so they made sure that Pablo and his sister learned water safety by enrolling them in a summer club program.

Once both children had become safe in the water, Pablo's parents thought that it "would be healthy, and a good idea" for them to join a year-round swim team, and they joined the nearby Santa Clara swim team.

Pablo, now eight years old, was placed in the tadpole group, and, even there, in the lowest tier of the great Santa Clara hierarchy, the kids were pretty advanced. And, at a time when Pablo wasn't feeling all that secure about himself, it was John Spencer, his first coach at Santa Clara, who made swimming a lot of fun, with the result that Pablo soon began to feel at home among his peers. Spencer wisely allowed Pablo to develop slowly, and to improve at his own rate. This was important to him at a time when he didn't believe that he had any more natural ability than the next person in the group. Young Pablo learned early on that he had to work hard for every ounce of success that came his way.

Pablo's next coach at Santa Clara was the age-group coach, Bill Thompson. "He really taught me how to improve my workout habits, and he was just a really great age group coach for me. Bill Thompson continued along the same lines as John Spencer, making it a lot of fun, but Bill had more of a coach's whip-edge to him. Even though he had a great sense of humor, and made everything fun, he nevertheless taught us how to really apply ourselves in given sets."

By the age of 9, Pablo had learned to swim all 4 strokes. As a 9-year-old, he still hadn't become particularly adept at any one stroke. But, at the age of 10, his butterfly started to show real promise. Says Pablo, "I worked a lot on it. It didn't come to me right away but when I started doing it well, I began to like it. I swam my first double-A time in the 50 fly. As a result, I developed an affinity as well as an affection for butterfly."

Inspired by Mark Spitz

Pablo's first memories of competitive swimming were of Mark Spitz's successes at the Munich Games. Mark Spitz inspired many swimmers of that era, and none more than the young Pablo Morales. "I remember Mark Spitz swimming in Munich before I had really gotten into swimming. Every day, I followed his progress, and the media seemed to highlight his butterfly races because, although he was the world's champion freestyler, his butterfly was considered his real forte. His butterfly made a big impression on me.

"Later I met Mark Spitz at the 1984 Olympic trials, and I spoke to him briefly. I had naturally drifted towards butterfly because of his influence, and because, after a couple of years, my butterfly was improving fairly rapidly."

When Pablo moved up to the senior team at Santa Clara, he came under the tutelage of Mitch Ivey, who by then had become head coach after the departure of George Haines, the man responsible for building the great Santa Clara dynasty.

Mitch Ivey coached Pablo for 4 years until he was 16, when Ivey left to coach at Pleasant Hill Swim Team. But, at the age of 18, during the summer following Pablo's graduation from high school, Pablo rejoined Mitch Ivey at Concord to prepare for the 1983 nationals at Clovis.

Pablo freely acknowledges Mitch Ivey's contribution to his development as an athlete. "He gave me the skills, not only the physical skills to do well, but also the confidence that I could compete at an elite level."

First World Record

Pablo's first world record came in 1984 when he swam the 100 butterfly in 53.38 seconds in Indianapolis.

"I had missed setting the world record the year before by about six hours," quipped Pablo. "This was at the 1983 long course nationals at Clovis, California. Matt Gribble set a world record of 53.34 in the morning, and at night, we were both under the old world record by a couple of tenths of a second, with Matt winning the race by two one-hundredths of a second. So I guess you could say that I missed the record by six hours!

"That year the Nationals at Clovis represented a breakthrough for me. I had made Nationals before, and had qualified for the finals. But that was the meet where I started butting heads with individuals who really were my heroes, people like Craig Beardsley, Matt Gribble, Bill Barrett, and Ricardo Prado in the IM.

"I was stepping up, and starting to compete at close to the same level. This was a big breakthrough for me at that time, and a great motivation to try even harder."

Morales said that winning a gold medal was "a goal that I had since the age of seven, having watched athletes like Mark Spitz."

Seven-League Boots

I told Pablo that I remembered the first time I saw him swim. It was in the early 1980s at Indianapolis, and he was practicing his kick in a side lane. I was walking along the side of the pool, and was amazed at the power of his kick, and how far his body shot forward with each kick. I remember mentioning to someone that "this fellow swims like the legendary giant with seven-league boots."

But Pablo insists that his strong kick did not come naturally to him. "I don't think I really had a great kick. Early on, I just had this single-beat kick, and this sort of hitch in my stroke, this little squirmy hitch, trying to do a two-beat kick. You know that little hitch stroke that kids do, when they're trying to learn a double-beat kick; they kick out in front, and then they pull through, and they kick again, but the hands won't come out of the water (laughs)—you know that kind of thing. Well, I was doing a lot of that."

Pablo said that the development of his kick, getting distance per kick on the downbeat and the upbeat, was the result of a comment made to him by George Eadington, who coached him as a 13-year-old, when he made the senior development team at Santa Clara, and first started doing twice-daily workouts.

"But first let me tell you that, of all my years in swimming, this was a very tough year. The transition from 11–12, now into the 13–14 group was

Photo courtesy of Nick Thierry/Swimnews

Pablos Morales, "The Comeback Kid." After his disappointment at the 1988 Seoul Olympics, Morales came back to win the 100-meter butterfly at the Barcelona Olympics in 1992.

tough. I had grown taller, but not really filled out, and so improvement was very difficult, and really didn't come that quickly as a 13-year-old, plus it was a tough transitional year in terms of double workouts. George was a great coach, but he really was a taskmaster. As I say, it was a difficult season to get through.

"But, back to the point. Just casually, during one workout, when we were doing a kick set, George mentioned how one swimmer he used to coach had such an amazing kick because, not only did he have a remarkable downbeat, but he got so much out of his upbeat as well. I'm sure he intended this comment as a correction for me to follow out, but I just said, 'Hey! I can do that too!'"

Dolphin Kick on the Back

Pablo worked hard to achieve a full and balanced kick. He also started doing dolphin kick while lying on his back. "I don't know if it was Mitch's idea or if it was George's idea, but I started kicking on my back, and, after a while, I did all my kicking on my back. And, don't forget, this was the guy who couldn't pass his elementary backstroke as a beginner!

"For many years, all I knew was that when it was time to kick, I never grabbed a kickboard. I just got into my streamlined position on my back, and just cranked out upside-down kicking sets."

Pablo explained that, when he kicked on the board, he did a strong downbeat, but tended to relax on the upbeat. However, when kicking on his back, he didn't forget about the upbeat which was now actually the downbeat when he was on his back. In fact, he emphasized it more when on his back. "I believe it gave me better balance between my downward beat and my upward kick. Not only that, it was a great workout for the abdominal muscles, and it also helped my streamlining."

Pablo said that a butterfly swimmer definitely gets more thrust out of the downbeat, but kicking on the back helps to get the feet up. "Not only was I getting some propulsion from my upbeat, but it really helped me to get my feet up quickly, and ready for a powerful downbeat, which is the most propulsive part of the kick."

To Undulate or Not?

I asked Pablo whether he agreed that today's fly

swimmers tended to use less body undulation and concentrated on starting the dolphin motion from the hips down. Pablo said that Pankratov stays very low in the water on his breathing cycle. When he is swimming on top of the water, there doesn't seem to be much of a difference between his breathing and nonbreathing cycles. There is very little extraneous undulation from the waist up.

Told that the Australian, Scott Miller, also seems to use less body undulation, Pablo said that he hadn't had the opportunity to study Miller, but that he thought too much hip undulation could induce drag.

"I think that too much undulation, especially for sprint fly, can put you at a disadvantage against somebody whose front end of the body is more in alignment, without too much up-and-down motion."

Asked what he thought were the key points of butterfly, Pablo said, "Looking back over the years, I always thought that a high hip position kept my body in alignment. I guess there's a debate about kicking, and whether one should overkick or not overkick, whether kicking too hard is a bad thing.

"One thing that most people will agree on is having a high hip position. In workouts, I practiced getting a high hip position by emphasizing the entry point of my hands. As my hands ride forward for a while, before the catch phase, my hips were forced up."

Asked if pushing the hips up, as the hands enter, causes the first downward kick to just happen, Pablo said, "Yeah, early on, I always thought about forcing the hips up, but, as an older swimmer, as a 27-year-old, coming back into the sport, and always learning something new, and getting to know Bill Boomer a little bit, I understood from him that a good, high hip position is also attained by pressing the T. By the T, I mean the lateral spread of the arms at the entry, and the line that crosses from chin to belly button, and from shoulder to shoulder. That makes a lot of sense, if you're pressing the T out in front. It's only natural that your hips will stay high in the water."

The Entry and Body Position

We discussed Mary T. Meagher's beautiful stroke, and how, as her arms enter, her hands actually seem to be higher than her elbows, and she looks almost like a giant condor about to launch itself from a cliff to soar out over the ocean. Pablo agreed, and said, "I'll tell you who had the most natural high hip position, without having a lot of leg drive, was Summer Sanders. Her balance forward was amazing. The fulcrum at her hips brought her naturally so high out of the water."

Asked if he allowed his chest to submerge lower than his elbows at the entry, Pablo said, "I can only answer your question by making the motion now, as I talk to you, visualizing what I do in the water. I can only guess without having looked at it on video, nor having specifically concentrated on it, and I feel like it does. I feel my chest does go lower than my hands, maybe slightly, but, mind you, not so much that the elbows drop. I had a tendency to overreach, as a 16- or 17-year-old, because I always thought that length equaled efficiency.

"I did that to such an extreme that I was overextending my arms and slipping at the front end of my stroke, and, at that point, I was getting some elbow drop."

I asked Pablo if he was entering his arms, then waiting out front too long. "Yes, and I would be slipping water and overreaching so much that my elbows would drop slightly. I wasn't getting anything out of the catch that I could grab."

Pablo said that he swam everything in training, "A lot of freestyle, a lot of IM work, even though, as a 13- to 15-year-old, I didn't compete in the 800 and the mile, but I trained different sets using these as multiples, and I tried to enter in a lot of events in some meets, using them as training meets. I would enter the mile, and I would enter the 800, but, as I got older, this became less and less frequent."

Asked what he thought was the difference in arm posture between the crawl arm entry and the butterfly arm entry, Pablo replied that he thought the arm is straighter in the butterfly entry.

"When I recover my arms, and when they enter the water, I tell myself not to extend my arms too much, but to enter as my thumbs slide into the water. Having watched myself swimming on video, it looks as if my arms are as extended as far as they can go without really overreaching. I feel as if my elbows are still up, but not quite as high as when my hands enter the water. In the butterfly entry, my arms probably extend more than they do in the freestyle entry."

Commenting on the feel of the water during the butterfly entry, Pablo said that he felt the water first on his hand, and then on his forearm, as he started to reach forward into the catch. "So, as my arms enter, I feel the water first on my thumbs, then on my forefingers, then wrists and forearms."

Q's and A's on Technique

CC: Do you allow your shoulder girdle to move forward, almost as if you are hunching your shoulders as your arms reach into the stroke?

PM: I've never thought about it, but I think, yes, that does happen.

CC: Tell me about your stroke timing. Many young swimmers seem to have trouble mastering the two-beat timing in the butterfly.

PM: I really don't know what to say about that, or how. I think that in getting the correct timing, with two kicks for each arm stroke, as a youngster growing up, I did a lot of one-arm drills to get the rhythm going a little bit.

CC: What about timing your breathing?

PM: As you start your arm press, at the start of the stroke, right when you're pressing, the head starts lifting forward slightly, and, I guess, later on, I felt that made sense because by timing your breathing with the press of your hand, instead of late in the pull, you can maintain a higher body position. By waiting too long to start raising the head, you can easily lose your high body position.

CC: When do you actually inhale?

PM: (laughs) As soon as my head comes out of the water! You know, I've never really thought about it!

CC: Do you inhale before your hands start their recovery?

PM: Well, let me see, You're asking tough questions, Cec, because I've never really thought about it!

CC: You're lucky, because you're a natural, you don't have to think about it! What do you think about it, anyway?

PM: I think you're right. I think I breathe before my hands exit.

CC: Pankratov has swum a 1:55.22 in the 200 fly, maybe even faster, and he is also the world-record holder in the 100, and so was Gross the holder of the world record in both events. Would you say that these people are exceptions to the rule that most fly swimmers excel either at the 100 or the 200?

PM: I really think that it depends on the individual. Melvin Stewart swam an excellent 100 fly, though I think that, genetically, he is more suited for the 200. This same could be said for Gross, even though he set the world record in the 100 meters at one point. Pankratov does both equally well, even though he seems to have focused more on improving his 100 in the last two years.

Gross did a 53.08 in the 1984 Los Angeles Olympics. I remember that very well! When I set a world record in the 100 at the 1984 trials, I went 1:58 in the 200 and 1:57 at the Games. But Sieben came up with a 1:57.04. There were three 1:57s in that race, and I was fourth. I was very much concentrating on the 200 fly as well. I don't think the two distances are too contradictory.

CC: Are you a race swimmer, in that you produced your best times when racing?

PM: I was a very hard worker, but I think I was a better racer.

"Pablo a Gentleman-Athlete" Says George Haines

When I asked George Haines if he remembered Pablo when he was a young swimmer at Santa Clara, George responded in typical fashion, "Did I know Pablo? I've known him since he was knee-high to a grasshopper!

"When Pablo was going to preschool, my son, Kyle, who is the same age as Pablo, was there with him. It was right off the campus at Santa Clara High School. I could look through the fence of the athletic field at these kids at the nursery school. They couldn't see me. I could watch Pablo and my son playing on the swings together.

"Well, when he was older, he swam for John Spencer at Santa Clara, and then he swam in Bill Thompson's group. I was still there, and then, in 1974, I went down to UCLA, and I think, a year later or so, he went up to Mitch's [Mitch Ivey] group, and Bill Thompson had him for a couple of years before I left. He was some talent. They used to call me over and say, 'Look at this guy.' And I'd say, 'Hey son, what's your name?' And he'd say, 'Pablo.' And I'd say, 'Pablo, you keep at it!' "

"And then I left to go to UCLA. This boy became a gentleman-athlete, and I put him in the same class with Steve Clark and Don Schollander. Pablo Morales never forgot his early coaches. He remembers guys like John Spencer, and he remembers Bill Thompson. He knows who the coaches were who gave him his background. When I went to Stanford, my first year at Stanford, Pablo was a freshman on the men's team. I was coaching the women's team, but Pablo came over to me and started talking all about the Santa Clara Swim Club, and what he did there, and who coached him. He never forgot. He said, 'I owe a lot to all those people, and to the Santa Clara Swim Club.' That guy's unbelievable!"

Goal Setting on the Path to Success
Today, Pablo modestly insists that everything he achieved in competitive swimming involved "only a little bit of ability," but that the main ingredient to success lies in perseverance and realistic goal setting.

Pablo emphasizes that improvement didn't always come right away. For example, improving his butterfly action only came very gradually.

Pablo set his goals at the beginning of each season. He stresses that he didn't just set goals and forget about them. Each workout demanded a specific mind-set.

Over time, Pablo learned how daily workout performance related to the accomplishment of his goals.

"I had to always focus on my goals, on a daily basis, and not only from day to day and from week to week, but also from each training set to the next, and from repeat to repeat."

Pablo says that he thought constantly about his goals, and what he needed to do to achieve them. In time he developed a workout focus that helped him improve and produce the kind of effort that yielded positive results. More than anything, it was this approach that eventually contributed to Pablo Morales's success as an athlete.

"My Three Greatest Races and Why"
1. **100-Meter Butterfly Final, Barcelona:** Winning an individual gold medal at the Olympic Games is a goal that I had since the age of seven, having watched the 1972 Munich Games and the performances of athletes like Mark Spitz and Dave Wottle [800 meters, track and field]. Being able to come back in 1992 and win when most did not give me much of a chance to win—because of my age, the fact that I was out of the sport for three years, and following the disappointment of 1988—was tremendously fulfilling.

2. **200-Yard Butterfly Final, 1987 NCAAs, Austin, Texas:** My final race at NCAAs gave me my 11th individual title, eclipsing the previous record of 10 held by John Naber, a hero of mine from the 1976 Olympics. There had been a great deal of talk about the record and pressure to win the 11th title. In the race I went up against Anthony Mosse, the great 200 butterflier from New Zealand, who was my teammate from Stanford, and who had gone 1:57 low to win the Commonwealth Games the summer before, and who had been swimming great all of the collegiate season, whereas I had been struggling in this event. I felt I needed to execute the perfect race to win. Despite the pressure, I felt I focused and executed about as perfect a race as I was capable.

3. **100-Meter Butterfly, World Championship Trials, 1986, World Record, 52.84:** Because the morning preliminary swim of 53 low felt so effortless, I was going for the world record in the final. In truth, at the time, it was as important to me that the swim was under 53 and a life best time as the fact that it was a world record. However, as the record held up over time, eventually extending to nine years before Pankratov's swim, I appreciated more and more the fact that it was a world record and that it survived those years.

✧ ✧ ✧

THE STAR WHO DIDN'T DREAM
OF OLYMPIC GOLD

"I didn't grow up with a dream about Olympic gold," says Penny Heyns, 1996 Olympic 100- and 200-meter breaststroke champion.

"It's interesting that different people have asked me if I had dreamt about winning at the Olympics. But, the answer is no, because in South Africa we were so isolated all those years, I never thought about the Olympic Games.

"Even in 1992, when I knew there was a chance we would go, I swam that season, thinking, 'Oh, well! I'll just do the best I can, and if South Africa is invited to participate, and I make the team, I'll go—but even Barcelona wasn't the wonderful, overwhelming experience that it should have been."

However, despite Penny's lack of an Olympic dream, her life portents were always connected in a subtle way with gold and water.

For instance, the gold in her two Olympic medals could have been mined in the gold-mining town of Springs, where she was born. (Springs is only a few miles east of Johannesburg, the center of the world's richest gold fields.)

And, when Penny was a year old, her family moved to Amanzimtoti, which, in the Zulu language, means "The Place of Sweet Waters."

"That's quite appropriate," I said to Penny, "The waters have been sweet as far as you are concerned."

"Yes!" said Penny, "Did you know that Dingaan, the Zulu king, gave the site this name, over 150 years ago? Well, this is where the water first called me. I was very, very young, swimming in the sea, and in either our pool or the neighbor's pool, playing on the sands, and in the rock pools, this was my place—I was a water baby I suppose."

A Stupid Idea
"When I was seven years old, I told my mother I wanted to race and swim for the school team. Our neighbor overheard me, and was amused. She told my mother she thought this a stupid idea.

"I was only in Class Two, and the school wouldn't let us start swimming until we were in the next class, Standard One, and about eight years old. Nevertheless, I went up to the teacher and asked if I could swim, and I tried out for the team, and made the team. This was my introduction to competitive swimming.

"I think it was around Standard Three that I made the South Coast and Natal Districts team and then went on to swim in the Natal school trials in order to go to the South African Schools' Championships.

"I was about 10, and until then, I had never swum for a club. I recall always trying to swim a little better in my backyard pool. You know, working on my stroke. My mother's got a good eye for stroke, and she used to help me. She wasn't a swimmer, but I think she just had a talent for teaching."

Early Career
"When I was about 12 or 13, I joined the club at Amanzimtoti High school; it consisted of a bunch of parents and teachers who basically just formed their own club."

Penny said that she had no professional coaching until 1988, when Graham du Toit, a former Transvaal swimmer, came to Toti (as Amanzimtoti was colloquially called), and he coached her until 1992.

"Graham didn't believe in doing a lot of distance work which, in retrospect, was good for me, because I still feel fairly fresh in terms of swimming and competition. We would go 5 workouts a week, each one ranging between 3 and 3½ thousand meters, that's all. But in a lot of it, the emphasis was on quality and not quantity. Most of the stuff was all 100 percent effort work. I think this program served my 100 well, but my 200 suffered. I didn't start seeing results in my 200 breaststroke until after I came to Nebraska.

"In my first nationals in 1989, I came third in the 200, and my second nationals was in Johannesburg in 1990, and I got two silvers in the 100 and the 200, after Lizelle Peacock, the reigning South African champion."

Beneficial Stroke Changes
"Around 1991, a coach by the name of Tubby Lynn came up to me and asked me if I wouldn't

Asked what she thought was the strong point in her swimming, Penny said, "Mainly my stroke, I think. Apart from that, you have to be mentally tough."

give him the chance to look at my stroke and comment on it. He suggested a couple of changes: for instance, using my head more in the forward throw, sort of copying the Barrowman style, but not quite yet, at that stage.

"With just these couple of adjustments, I went on to the nationals in Cape Town in 1991, and broke the South African record in the 100 breaststroke in 1:12.57. This was also where I got my Springbok colors [South African international blazer]. I won the 200, and I think I went a 2:40.

"The following year [1992] was the Olympic trials, and in the prelims I went a 1:12.8, or something, and in the finals, I touched second to Sheila Turner. There was a lot of controversy about my being in the team."

Chase Your Own Dreams
"I always seemed to find somebody I looked up to, or admired a lot, and initially, it was Julia [Russell]. She had been swimming since she was a lot younger. She was my role model. We swam in the same age group.

"And so, all along, even later on in my swimming career, it would have been people like, I suppose, most recently, Samantha Riley, because she had broken the world record. So it was always people that I admired and, initially, I wanted to swim and be like them."

Penny said that she later realized that it was important "not to always chase people, because their performances will fluctuate, so rather chase your own goals and dreams.

"Along the way, I learned many lessons, and I suppose these all started when I came to Nebraska in January '93. I felt my breakthrough, in terms of, let's say, international competition, would have started with the Commonwealth Games in 1994. That's where I got the bronze medal in the 100 breaststroke."

Asked if she had started to put post-apartheid South Africa on the map with that swim, Penny said, "Well, I didn't look at it that way, because I did compete at Barcelona, but I was so young in terms of experience, and I maybe didn't make as much of the opportunity as I should have done.

"But, obviously, when I swam in the Commonwealth Games, I had already had some experience against either international swimmers, or swimmers of a high caliber, through the NCAAs and the American program in general."

More in Control
"When I went to the Commonwealth Games, I was more in control, and had more feasible goals for what I wanted to do, and so, looking at my performances there, I went on to Rome for the World Championships, intending that I possibly could get a medal.

"In the 100 breaststroke, I qualified second going into the final. After that performance, the South African coaches, who were there at the time, said, 'Oh! You're looking great. Maybe you can win!' I started thinking, 'Well, maybe I can,' but, deep down inside, I knew that I wasn't at that point yet.

"That was a good lesson for me, because I went into the race and, because I so badly wanted to win, I didn't have respect for the other two medals, which would have been better for me, at that stage.

"I dived in, and I swam Samantha's race. I didn't swim my own, and I got sixth place, and the girl who got the bronze medal had a time slower than what mine had been in the heats. So, had I swum my own race, I possibly would have had a medal.

"Usually, I would count my strokes, even during a main race, but in Rome, I didn't. I just swam. I went out with Samantha Riley. I tried to stay with her, and then died coming back. Maybe I scrambled through my stroke. I made a lot of mistakes in that race. I didn't swim my own race. I tried to pace it according to everyone else."

At the 1995 Pan Pacs

I told Penny that I had seen her compete against Samantha Riley in the 200 at the 1995 Pan Pacs in Atlanta, and I asked her how she felt about that swim. "Well, I think I knew going into the Pan Pacs that the 200, whatever happened, would be a creditable swim, because in our nationals that year, I had gone 2:29 which ranked me first in the world for the season. Of course, my 100 was a much better swim in comparison. I went 1:08.4."

Penny expressed disappointment that Samantha was disqualified in the 100. "I had prepared for the 100 that season, and so, of course, I thought I stood a chance of beating her in the 100, and then she was DQ'd. But, in the 200, I knew that I just wanted to stay as close to her as I could. So I felt that I learned a lot about myself in that race, as well as how to swim the race.

"That 200 was an important race for me; when I came out of it, I knew how much work I needed to do, and where I was in my planning for 1996."

Self-Analysis and the Perfect Race

Penny said that she does a lot of thinking about her swimming. After a race, she sits back and analyzes it. "Not to the extent of being tied up with too many little details, but to work out in pretty simple terms what happened in that race, what I did that was good, what I did that was bad, and where I could learn and improve. I think, everytime I race, there's always something I can find that I can do better."

I questioned Penny closely on this aspect of her swimming. "Do you think you've ever swum a perfect race?"

"No," she said.

"Do you think anybody ever swims a perfect race?"

Quick as a flash, she replied, "I think people swim close to perfect. I don't think there's such a thing as perfect, because if you are doing yourself justice, you will always manage to find something you can improve."

I said, "That's a good comment. To be a champion or a world-record holder, you've got to know every tile in the pool. Every stroke you make must

have meaning, any stroke that slips the water is a stroke you are not using properly, and it all adds up by the end of the race."

At the Atlanta Olympics

Penny said, "That's true. It's a good thing you asked me about a perfect race, because I've often been asked, how come after my swims at the Olympics, didn't I seem that happy?

"Well the reason was that in the 100, I knew that I'd get the record in the morning, although I also expected Amanda Beard and Samantha [Riley] to probably break it in the fifth heat. They were in the fifth heat, and I was in the sixth heat, I think."

"Did that worry you?" I asked.

"No, I expected it," she said. "I was waiting for it to happen. I had the attitude that I would then have to go quicker. Whatever they did, I had to go quicker. I was really surprised when they didn't improve on the time, and I just went out to still swim my best race, and, when I touched, I was happy with the time, although I had hoped that when I broke the world record, it would be under 67. Because of that, I thought, well OK, I can go faster tonight.

"Also, during that race, I remember diving in, and, for the first three or four strokes I didn't feel great. I wasn't on top of the water and I didn't feel as powerful as I would have liked to have felt. Also, I glided into the turn. So, looking at that record swim, I thought that there was a lot I could still do to improve upon it.

"Unfortunately, in the evening, it wasn't that I was nervous of the other girls; I so badly wanted to go faster, and I just knew that there were things that I could improve to make me swim faster, and it would be ideal if I could do it in the final.

"But, because I was so anxious and eager to break the record again, I rushed my stroke towards the end of my race. Because of this mistake, I came up short at the wall, and that's where that wonderful glide came into it. So there are always mistakes."

Penny said that her 200 race at the Olympics was probably her best ever effort.

"I knew that I could either go out pacing it with Amanda, and then come back and beat her at the end, or I could go out hard, and hang in there.

But, I knew that my speed would count in my favor, and so I decided to go out hard. I had to use my speed to benefit my race, and then just try to hang in there."

Streamlining for Speed

Asked what she thought was the strong point in her swimming, Penny said, "Mainly my stroke, I think. Apart from that, I think, you have to be mentally tough."

Penny Heyns is noted for her unusually straight and streamlined body posture, especially during the underwater phase of her stroke. I asked her to talk about her technique. She said, "I think that, if you break my stroke up, in the sense of a front and back half, then obviously my kick is my strong point.

"My kick is a lot stronger than my pull, although, hopefully, my pull is getting stronger every season. But, recently, I was reading an article; I can't remember who wrote it, but the person was saying that the body position is 70 percent and the arms and legs motion is 30 percent, and, that's true because I believe that to be true, not just watching my stroke, but even watching Julia's [Russell] improvement over the last season."

Penny said that female swimmers naturally tend to kick down. "If you work on it, you can kick more directly backward, which is what guys have in their favor. I think it's something to do with their hips. I know that I've been kicking directly backward for a long time. This helps to balance out your body position. And I know Julia's starting to do this now, and I can definitely see an improvement in her stroke."

Noticing that Penny has very long thighs, I asked her, "If you were to draw your knees up too much, you would get a lot of resistance. Maybe your natural body build makes you want to keep those thighs streamlined in line with your body, and also to use the strength in those quadriceps muscles?"

"Yes, definitely," she said. "I don't think it's so much strength—we do a lot of leg work—but it's the efficiency of catching the water. You've got to hold the water and cut resistance in every way you can."

Mentioning that too many breaststrokers apply too much power in the early part of the kick, I asked Penny to talk about her kick.

"It's difficult to think about it when you're not in the water," she said (demonstrating). "But the way I think about the kick is that, when you bring your feet up, instead of just kicking back, like you would kick start a motorbike, you want to flex your feet outwards, and almost the whole bottom area of your legs should whip around, rather than just go directly down.

"Without bringing the thigh forward, you want to lift your ankles and the lower part of the legs back. The moment you pike at the hips and you draw your legs up, then you alter your body position, and then you create resistance. I know they supposedly modeled this after the Barrowman stroke and the wave technique."

Breaststroke Arm Action

The rest of our conversation on technique went like this:

CC: *Now, your arm action; when you start your stroke, and you go into the lateral phase of the pull, what do you do with your hand on the wrist? Do you flex your wrist, or do you keep your hand in line with your forearm?*

PH: Let's just break it down. To start the stroke, you want to keep the palms out, facing outwards. The reason for that is when you start bending your elbows, your elbows will be higher than your hands. A lot of breaststrokers, when they start pulling like this [demonstrates], this happens—the elbows drop.

CC: *They get into the praying mantis position?*

PH: That's right. So, if you keep the palms of your hands out, that would be the easiest way for one to learn. It's almost like getting your fingers into a crack in the wall, and then you pull yourself through. OK So that's the first motion. After that, you want to try and keep your hand and forearm like a paddle. So this is the theory outside the water. I don't know exactly about when you're in the water. Obviously, you've got to get a feel for it, and I think that's where Julia and I are lucky, we tend to have a good feel for our strokes.

At this point, you start to pitch your hands more downward, and the idea is to then start sculling in, keeping your elbows in front of your chest. And this sculling in motion also lifts your body up, which allows you to breathe, but I have the impression that a lot of swimmers are coming up very high, and then going down, and they're causing a lot of resistance.

What we try to do when we scull in, is to shrug the shoulders and drop the head, almost on the chest. Initially, for breaststrokers, trying this stroke, they will feel that their forward vision is somewhat reduced. They can't see, it's a lot more obscure, but when you get stronger, you'll lift up high enough, and you'll still be able to see in front. The lift happens without your making it. If you try to make it happen by using your kick, it will cause you to kick down, and you'll cause a lot of resistance.

CC: *A good breaststroke style is like a good butterfly stroke—either it's all right or it's all wrong.*

PH: I have the feeling, or the opinion, should I say, sorry, that you're either born with a talent for breaststroke or you're not. I mean it's

"I think people swim *close* to perfect. I don't think there's such a thing as perfect because if you are doing yourself justice, you will always manage to find something you can improve on."

very difficult. You can learn breaststroke, but I don't think you can be a top breaststroker without having a natural talent, a knack for it. It just seems to me that people, who are in the top range, seem to be more purely breaststrokers, and if they're lucky in that their other strokes are good, they can do IM. You find people, who are freestylers or backstrokers, tend to be good in the other strokes except breaststroke. The breaststroke swimmer tends to be purely a breaststroker.

CC: *Do you ever swim the other strokes?*

PH: [Laughs] Very rarely. I did do the 50 free, and I've done the 200 IM, but it's only been for college swimming, because they needed me. It wasn't something I'd do internationally.

Coach "Tubby" Lynn

I asked Penny to tell me more about Tubby Lynn's influence on her swimming.

"I don't know his first name," she said. "Everyone calls him Tubby, but he doesn't look tubby. Well, he's definitely had a big influence, and I still keep contact with him. When I go home, I always go and check my stroke with him. He's been responsible for both my style, and for Julia's [Russell]. A lot of the improvements that we've had over the last three years can be attributed to Tubby."

I said, "You both have beautiful techniques, very fluent, a pleasure to watch."

Penny said, "I think this is due to our background—what we did when we were in South Africa. You know Julia is more accustomed, I think, to the kind of training that we do here, incorporating a lot more, not heavy miles, but distance to the point of doing between 5,000 and 6,000 yards, whereas, before, I used to just do sprints. I never knew what drills were, or anything like that."

Asked her opinion about drills, Penny said, "I like them. I think they are necessary, especially my favorite which is two kick, one pull. However, Tubby doesn't really like it much because he thinks you get into a bad habit of dipping too low under the water and sinking. But I can't do drills slowly. When I do a drill set, I'm just as tired as I would be if I did a normal swimming set. And I think, in order to get the benefit out of the two-kick, one-pull drill, you have to go hard, otherwise you do tend to sink, and that's going to start spoiling your timing."

Coach Jan Bidrman

Asked about the difference in her training since arriving in Nebraska, and whether she did more distance work, Penny said, "It was always a steady increase each season. When I first came to Nebraska, I swam with my coach's wife, Amy Tidball, before they got married. She was a freestyle swimmer. During that season, I got accustomed to swimming a little more distance, but nothing extreme, and just really getting settled in the U.S."

Penny said that when she returned home to South Africa for the summer, she worked out a great deal with Tubby. "I think it was during that period of time, that I really caught on to what I was supposed to be doing with my stroke. That was between May and August 1993.

"So, it was during that summer period that I worked on my stroke and caught on to all Tubby's ideas. When I got back to Nebraska it was still one semester before Julia would join us. At that stage I was the only female breaststroker on the team.

"There were two other male breaststrokers on the team, and they happened to be European, so they gave those swimmers to Jan [Bidrman]. Jan wasn't an official coach at that stage. He was just a grad assistant—in international business, I think—he was studying at the university.

"I had a choice of swimming with Jan, half a season, and the other half with Keith Moore, the sprint coach, and I said to them that I would prefer to swim with one or the other for the whole season. I don't want to chop and change.

"Then I spoke to Jan, and I felt very comfortable with his philosophies about swimming, and I knew that he had a lot of experience as an international swimmer himself. So I felt I had the confidence in him as a coach."

Asked to describe Jan Bidrman's coaching philosophy, Penny said, "Well, I think, first of all, Jan isn't just the kind of coach who stands on deck and dictates to you what to do. He taught me how to get to know myself as a swimmer, basically, to be independent of the coach, although still appreciate advice and whatever, which I think is very important. And he cares about the swimmers. He's not just a coach, he's a friend.

"The first thing he said to me, when we met each other, and we decided he would coach me, is that, if I'm willing to give 100 percent, he'll give a hundred percent. But it's all up to me. The commitment must come from me. He doesn't want me to come to the pool, because he's standing there. I must come because it's from me. And I really appreciated that honesty, and I knew then, if I put in all the effort, then he would be there for me."

"So, in other words, it would not be a one-way trade?" I asked.

"Yes. It's a two-way relationship, and I really appreciated that honesty. So I started swimming with Jan that season, and we were actually fortunate, in the sense that—it's a pity though for the other two swimmers, but the one was injured, and the other went home for a period of time—so I was the only swimmer swimming with Jan at the time, and that allowed him to really just see what I needed, and get to know me as a swimmer.

"At the same time, I got the work done that I needed to get done. We slowly started setting goals each season, and, every season, Jan believed that I needed to do something different to retain my interest, and also to detect scope for improvement. In so doing, one of the things was to increase the distance.

"Also, by the '94–'95 season, I started doing breaststroke pulling with paddles. Up until then, I hadn't [used them]. This last college season, I worked a lot more with stretch cords, swimming against the resistance. Each season, we've thrown in something as an experiment. It also breaks the monotony, and makes it fun.

"We experimented with introducing new items to the program, but not too much, always still maintaining the control. And, you know, I always feel I have the freedom with Jan to say that, at a certain point of my training, 'I'm sorry, maybe I just need a week away from everyone. I'll see you again in a week.' And he trusts me enough to know that I'm only doing it because I believe it's best for me and, if he says to me, 'OK, I agree you should do it,' then I know that I'm on the right track."

(Note: The University of Nebraska's Media and

Recruiting Guide, quotes Jan Bidrman's coaching philosophy as follows: "Athletes, in cooperation with their coaches, need to form their opinions about training and competition. Only when a coach and an athlete work together can an ultimate goal be accomplished.")

A Greater Realization of Self

I suggested to Penny that what Bidrman had helped her to achieve was really a greater realization of self. "This comes out in everything you've said in this interview."

"Yes, that's so," Penny said. "I think it's really something he has imparted to us. You know it's also up to the swimmer, though. I mean, some of us, Julia and I were talking—it seems that the girls in the squad have always performed better than the guys in the last two seasons, but I think it is just because we have taken what he has given us, and used it."

CC: A lot of people think that, because you have a coach, you automatically get better. The coach can only tell you what to do, and how to do it, and, in the final criterion, something has to come from the swimmer.

PH: Definitely, and I think, like you said, sometimes I think that I think too much about my swimming and my stroke and everything.

CC: How so?

PH: Well, I'm inclined to do so, at this period of my training [early season]. It's the worst for me always, because I'm impatient. I want everything to happen now. I know what I need to do in my stroke.

CC: You don't look impatient!

PH: I'm getting more control over it these days [laughs]. But during the last college season, it was like the devil was chasing me.

CC: You're not swimming college any more?

PH: No, I'm not.

Penny Heyns for Calgary?

CC: I hear a rumor you may come to Canada. Is that correct?

PH: I may. Jan's got the head coach position at Calgary.

CC: So, it's been announced, yes.

PH: And, right now, I think the best thing for both

him, and the swimmers in the team at Calgary, and for me, is that he goes ahead, until May, on his own. That gives him the opportunity to develop a relationship with the swimmers there, without me being around. And then, Julia may also, I don't know, go up for a while in the summer, but I'm definitely going to go up in the summer for a while, and swim with Jan.

CC: Will you become affiliated to a Canadian club or am I going ahead of the piece?

PH: I don't know yet. I'll see what it's like in Calgary. I don't want to just jump into a decision and move. I want to first see what it's like, and then I'll decide. There are a lot of pros to moving, and there are a couple of things I'm not sure about. For instance, if I move to Canada, I leave behind a very big support base in Lincoln. Jan's biggest concern is that I would leave behind a lot of friends, because there are a lot of South Africans there.

Meets President Nelson Mandela

I asked Penny how important it was for her to represent South Africa in international competition. She said, "I think, as I'm growing older and realizing the privilege of making these international teams, it's becoming more and more important. It really became important to me, after I had met President Nelson Mandela. I met him in . . . well, actually I met him in May '95, briefly at the Presidential Sports Awards, and then this year [1996], after I had broken the world record, they flew me down, and I met him and spoke to him at a private tea for about half an hour.

"First of all, he shook my hand, and said he'd never wash his hand again. So I said I'd never wash mine! Then he wanted to introduce me to his grandson; that was just a joke, but he indicated that he was very pleased with all the young athletes in the country, and that we were ambassadors, and that it was our responsibility to carry ourselves well in international arenas of sport. And also he told me that he was pleased with the world record and wished me the best of luck for the Olympic Games, and I said, "Well, you know I'm now more inspired to go on and try and win the gold.""

The Aftermath of Victory

Penny commented on the public reaction when she returned to South Africa, having won at the Olympics. "The hype was a bit of a surprise to me. Already, I had got a feel for what it might be like, while I was still in Atlanta, because the media went quite wild, and there was this building they called The Pavilion, just outside the village, it was like 'South Africa House,' and I was forever being asked to be there.

"It was either media, or it was somebody who suddenly decided they would be a great agent for me. That was the most overwhelming thing for me at the time, that people were suddenly talking money, and things that I had never been accustomed to, and people were saying, 'Strike while the iron's hot,' and 'You've got to make these decisions now,' and I didn't know which way to turn, and my parents didn't really know either. But, fortunately, I had some people from Nebraska there, who helped me and advised me, and it wasn't too bad.

"Because of that hype, I really expected it would be bad when I got home. I really expected the worst, I think, and, when I got there, I just dealt with it, one day at a time. It was wonderful when we arrived at the airport, the whole of Johannesburg International Airport was full of people. The response was great. The people, I think more the black people, their response to our achievements was just wonderful, and we had a ticker tape parade through the streets of Johannesburg on the second day we were back. And then the medal winners also had a bit of a banquet. And after that, we were driven to Pretoria where we met President Nelson Mandela.

"It was just amazing. I mean, it was something. I can't explain it, even now, after being in America for a month and going back, I thought it would have died down, and it really was a surprise. When I got back home, people were still talking about the Olympics, and, especially about the swim team. I think they realized that the achievements of the swimmers were remarkable. They said, per capita, we did better than any country in the world."

Ian Thorpe (Australia), the second-fastest ever in the 200-meter and 400-meter freestyle, is already a world champion and relay world-record holder. Born in 1982 in Sydney, Thorpe should dominate middle distance freestyle into the new millenium.

2000 IN SYDNEY: THE MODERN ERA COMES FULL CIRCLE

SWIM-CITY SYDNEY TO HOST 2000 OLYMPICS

Written upon the announcement in 1993. It is a fitting tribute to Sydney's great contribution to world swimming that it should host the first Olympics of the new millennium.

Within minutes of hearing that Sydney had been awarded the Olympic Games of the year 2000, I was on the phone to congratulate my friends there. It was only 5 AM local time, but they didn't seem to mind. Forbes Carlile, doyen of Australian coaches, and his wife, Ursula, had been awake for hours waiting for the IOC's announcement. They were beside themselves with excitement because, at last, their city had been awarded the Olympic Games.

"The whole city is going wild!" shouted Forbes over the noise of local celebrations. "We can see the fireworks over at Homebush, the suburb that will be the site of the Olympic stadium. It's only 10 minutes from where we live." We talked for a while and then he added, "Now we've been awarded the Olympics, we must lobby to ensure that in future the Games are moved from continent to continent in strict rotation."

One can only agree with Carlile's viewpoint because, on a population-to-percentage basis, there are few cities that can rival Sydney's contribution to world sport in general, and to swimming in particular. It is hard to understand why Sydney has not been awarded the Olympic Games before now. The only valid reason could be that Sydney has been a victim of what is known in Australia as "the tyranny of distance," implying that Australia is both too far away and too expensive to reach.

If Sydney is not exactly part of Polynesia, its citizens certainly act like Polynesians. Everyone

Courtesy of NSWASA

Australia's great revival. These three great swimmers grew up along the shores of Sydney Harbour. Left to right: Murray Rose (Olympic champion 400 and 1,500 meters, 1956, and 400 meters, 1960), Jon Hendricks (Olympic champion 100 meters, 1956), and John Devitt (Olympic champion 100 meters, 1960).

Murray Rose, Dawn Fraser, Lorraine Crapp, Karen Moras, Shane Gould, Kevin Berry, Neville Hayes, Terry Gathercole, Jon Konrads, Ilsa Konrads, Robert Windle, Ian O'Brien, Beverly Whitfield, Michael Wenden, Gail O'Neil, Brad Cooper, Graham Windeatt, and so on and on.

People have swum in Sydney Harbour from the time the First Fleet arrived there in 1788. The first pool was a seawater enclosure built in 1879 at Rushcutters Bay in Sydney Harbour by "Professor" Fred Cavill, head of the famous Cavill clan of great swimmers. Later he built another pool at Lavender Bay, close to the present-day site of the North Sydney Pool where so many world records were broken over the years, and where the world's first pace clock, designed by Professor Frank Cotton, of Sydney University, and his then protégé, Forbes Carlile, was installed.

There are many parts of the city which have played an important role in the development of the sport, and I suggest that the International Swimming Hall of Fame seriously consider erecting plaques at these venues in time for the Sydney Olympics. Better still, they should consider establishing an associate Hall of Fame in Sydney, in the same fashion as it has already done in Japan.

For example, Sydney is the original home of continuous swimming, in the sense that this is where "the continuous stroke," namely the crawl, was born—continuous in that this style of swimming has no stop-start phases such as in its predecessors, breaststroke, sidestroke, and trudgen. The crawl was first swum at Bronte seawater pool in Nelson Bay, and later refined by the Cavill family at their pool at Lavender Bay, which was only demolished in the early 1940s.

On a personal note: I well remember an enjoyable evening when the New South Wales Swimming Coaches' Association kindly invited me to dinner at a picturesque restaurant situated close to the north exit of Sydney Harbour bridge and the former site of "Professor" Cavill's Lavender Bay Swimming Academy. The coaches present were obviously very proud of the fact that we were dining close to the spot where so much world swimming history had been written by their countrymen and women.

Sydney has always bred a tough, goal-oriented breed of swimming coach—people such as the

wants to swim or surf because Sydney's warm sun calls them out to the three score beaches which indent its long shoreline. Yes, it's not surprising that Sydney has a history of over 100 years of great swimmers, shrewd coaches, and colorful achievements. Sydney is saturated with swimming history; it has contributed more to competitive swimming, in achievement and development, than any other city in the world.

The world and Olympic swimming record books abound with the names of Sydneysiders who made it to the very top. Again, population-to-percentage wise, they have the greatest record of achievement in the history of the sport. Names such as Dick Cavill, Barney Kieran, Freddy Lane, Cecil Healy, Fanny Durack, Annette Kellerman, Mona Wylie, Andrew "Boy" Charlton, Clare Dennis, John Davies, John Devitt, Jon Henricks,

Cavill family, Frank Guthrie, Sam Herford, Forbes Carlile, Ursula Carlile, Terry Gathercole, Harry Gallagher, Don Talbot, Vic Arneil, and many others—coaches who were enterprising as well as innovative. Many of them built their own indoor pools so that they could operate efficient swim schools that catered to every level of swimmer, from rank beginner to Olympic champion. Furthermore, they never tired of experimenting with stroke mechanics and training methods.

The story of swimming in Sydney rests not entirely on a great tradition but is also the tale of a dynamic, able, and hard-working personnel—enterprising coaches and magnificent swimmers, trained from early age to always fight back and to "rise when the whips are cracking," to use the appropriate Australianism. It is a saga of people steeped in swimming lore who discuss and act out the deeds of their beloved sport with the same finesses displayed in tracking, hunting, and fighting by the old native peoples of North America.

The whole history of swimming in Sydney is an epic of native flair for improvisation, of matching inadequate numbers and facilities through natural ingenuity in competing against the world's large battalions. And now, as their just and well-deserved reward, the Olympic Games will be situated almost in the dead center of the world's greatest swimming city.

Visitors to the Sydney Olympics would be well-advised to set aside a little time to see how Sydney's many entrepreneurial coaches operate, especially the remarkable Forbes Carlile swimming organization which has been a bulwark of Australian swimming for over 40 years. They should find the experience inspirational and, as a result, may want to become somewhat more self-directed in their own coaching efforts when they return home.

In addition to what Olympic visitors may learn from Sydney's leading coaches, they will not fail to notice the high motivation of local swimmers, based, not only on pride of performance, but also as custodians of a long, successful tradition in world swimming. It has been my pleasure to work with many of these swimmers on visits to Sydney, and I can vouch for the fact that I haven't seen tougher swimmers anywhere.

An interesting, and significant, fact: Most Australian swimmers can tell you what the world

International Swimming Hall of Fame

Andrew "Boy" Charlton. He was an Australian national hero because of his modesty and his willingness to continue doing surf lifesaving patrols, despite the fact that he was the 1924 1,500-meter Olympic champion. One commentator of the time said that Charlton had the "shoulders of a lumberjack and the ankles of a ballet dancer."

record is for the events they swim. They tend to focus on achieving top international honors, and the local record is sometimes of little interest to them, unless the local record also happens to be the present world mark!

A final note: The one and only other time the Olympics were staged in Australia was at Melbourne in 1956. On that occasion, Australian swimmers won the major share of medals, largely as a result of their coaches developing improved stroke mechanics and training methods. History has a habit of repeating itself. Be warned—the Australians, without doubt, will probably take a very close look at every phase of current coaching practice, and make a determined attempt to come up with new and more successful methods. They will be very dangerous, and hard to beat—especially on their own turf!

On October 27, 1962, Dawn Fraser became the first woman to break a minute in the 110 yard freestyle. During her career she broke 39 world records, including 12 relay records.

✧ ✧ ✧

AUSSIES PLAN FOR SYDNEY 2000

"This has been a rehearsal for the year 2000," said Don Talbot, Australian head coach, as the 1995 Pan Pacific swim meet ended in Atlanta's new Olympic pool. "We're finding out where we've got to improve. That's putting it simply. It's a matter of consolidating our strengths, and building depth to our program. I think our depth is improving, but we are not yet where we want it to be.

"The '96 Olympics will serve as an important springboard for us into the next four years," said the chipper Aussie leader. "We were second in this meet. We're trying to lift our standing in the world, if we can. We're now fourth in the world picture.

If we can get up a rung or two, we'll be very strong in our own country five years from now. So really we're planning now."

Despite several outstanding performances and one world record, it's likely the major teams present were not showing all they had. Richard Quick, U.S. women's Olympic coach, said, "It would be foolish for leading contenders to reveal their very best form so soon before the start of the 1996 Olympics."

Nevertheless, all countries present will use this meet to assess their progress—or lack of it. Now comes a time for serious stocktaking, and careful final-stage planning. Then will follow 11 critical months before the Atlanta Olympics—and many a swimmer's moment of truth.

Keeping the Program Simple

Two great Australian former Olympic champions were in Atlanta as observers: John Devitt, 100-meter freestyle, Rome, 1960, and Michael Wenden, 100- and 200-meter freestyle, Mexico City, 1968.

Devitt, now vice president of the Australian Olympic Committee, will be assistant chef de mission (athletes' services) to the Australian 1996 Olympic team, and his fellow AOC executive member, Michael Wenden, will assist him. Both men commented on the resurgence of Australian swimming.

Devitt said Australia would continue to keep their program simple, as they had always done, while putting in a lot of hard, hard work. "We have the money now to expand and identify much more new talent. We've never before been in a position where we could identify nearly a thousand swimmers, as we have done now. In 1956, Australia made an almost clean sweep at the Melbourne Olympics, but at that time we didn't need a thousand swimmers. We only needed a hundred as a base. We've got the funding now to do it with a thousand, and so we should get better results."

Devitt said, "Future prospects are identified by several criteria, on times, positions within the peer groups, and age group programs—and by casting the net far and wide. Since they were very young, we've been identifying our boys and girls for the year 2000. We are sure that they will be at about the right ages for the Sydney Olympics."

Devitt thought that "national training centers have their merits" but "they are only an adjunct, only a spoke in the wheel. They are not the complete wheel."

More Australian Elite-Level Coaches

Michael Wenden said Australia is in the midst of "a well-thought-out program that has been in the making for some years." A principle area is the development of an increasing number of elite coaches, as opposed to past years, when many coaches preferred to concentrate mainly on learn-to-swim programs to earn their living.

Wenden said, "We went through a phase when there was no recognition, or financial recompense to enable coaches to set themselves up primarily as elite level coaches. Now this has been slowly changing in Australia."

Wenden said that successful coaches are financially rewarded, based on results achieved, and not on mere promises. "There are now far more elite-level coaches at the core of our development program," he said.

Coaching Development in Australia

Wenden said the educational push in Australian coaching, in progress now for years, had been enhanced by annual conferences staged by the Australian Swimming Coaches' Association (ASCA). He said, "These conferences have become world-class events. We invite people who can contribute significantly, both at the lower end of the program and at elite levels. There have been significant advances in educational facilities and opportunities resulting from these conferences."

Wenden added that the coaches' association was very good at circulating information. The spread of information was also undertaken by the National Institute of Sport, as well as the individual state institutes and academies. These programs help to educate coaches, and bring them up to date with advances in many relevant fields, ensuring that coaches have the knowledge needed to coach swimmers to world standards.

Leadership Comes from the Coaches

But Australian coaches are not spoon-fed. Wenden said, "ASCA is a very strong organization, very professional, well organized, and works hard to develop the individual talents of coaches.

A number of years ago, ASCA invited the then executive director of the Australian Institute of Sport to their annual dinner. The director, who came from an athletics background, asked, 'Who are all these people?' I replied, 'They are coaches.' He was surprised because there were several hundred coaches there! He asked, 'Surely, they don't all earn their living from coaching swimming?' You see, this bloke came from athletics where the coaching depth isn't anywhere near what it is in swimming."

Wenden said, "When the Institute of Sport was founded, it was thought that only a small number of coaches was needed—coaches with the expertise and ability to interface with sport scientists and researchers. They would all be based at the Institute in Canberra. But the coaches realized very early—and very vocally—that this wasn't working."

Wenden added, "The institute system was then set up at state levels, and, furthermore, it wasn't based on residential programs. The emphasis was identify the coach, identify the athlete, and then give all necessary support to already existing programs. This has resulted in the large number of coaches who are now supported at the elite end of the program."

Wenden said Australia had about 50 swimmers in the Pan Pacs. "They came from about 30 different coaches. That's not a reflection of anything except that there were about 30 coaches who consider themselves at the elite end of the program, and there are others at this level, who are being encouraged and supported, but who, at this time did not place swimmers on the team."

Wenden made the point that, in the search for talent, the net should be cast as wide as possible, not just over the potential swimmers, but over potential elite coaches as well.

Positive Interaction Between Coaches

Wenden said that, for years, there had been jealousy between coaches, and a rivalry that "didn't turn into friendly competition at the appropriate time." In fact, it was "characterized by in-fighting and dissent, rather than cooperation." Over the last few years, this has changed, and now the coaches work as a team.

Wenden gave the example of "unofficial and voluntary" visitation programs arranged between coaches to have their swimmers train together for limited periods. Coaches either accompany their swimmers, or send them on their own to train with a coach who has some particular expertise to offer—either that, or certain swimmers just benefit by training with each other.

At a more organized level, swimmers and their coaches come together periodically in event camps. For example, they may have a breaststroke camp, a backstroke camp, or a distance freestyle camp, and they will swap ideas. Said Wenden, "These camps provide positive interaction, and gone are the jealousies and the fights. Certainly, there is rivalry, but it's a very healthy rivalry these days. I'm pleased with the way it is going."

Asked whether these gatherings resulted in coaches attempting to recruit each other's swimmers, Wenden replied that he was "sure that this occurs, but the urge to change often comes from the swimmer rather than a poaching coach. As swimmers mature, and progress to higher levels of the sport, they become able to consider whether a long-term personal coach continues to offer the quality of coaching they need."

Wenden had spoken to a number of coaches whose swimmers had decided to go to another coach. "Without exception, it's been hurtful, and hard to take, but it's accepted in good faith as probably beneficial to the swimmer."

Tribute to Talbot's Leadership

Wenden paid tribute to Don Talbot's leadership. "Talbot is the greatest innovator I've seen. For many years, Don has always been willing to try something new, but he doesn't hesitate to discard it if it doesn't work."

Wenden said, "Don has developed the ability to interact with people. In years gone by, he was a bit prickly, but, through hard work, he has won the trust and confidence of the coaches and the swimmers."

Wenden said, "You may recall, back at the 1990 Commonwealth Games in Auckland, just after Don came back to Australia from Canada, there was a great fuss and conflict between some of the swimmers and Don. I think this was a communications failure based on the unique swimming culture that exists in each country, both at the swimming level and at the coaching level. He now

communicates very well. Not only does he understand the coaches and the swimmers, but the coaches, in particular, understand Don. They know when to keep away from him. They know when to approach him with specific requests. They understand his personality, and I suppose the bottom line is that it's working!"

Talbot on Program Development

Talbot said he was "paying attention" to promising youngsters all over Australia. He said, "They are not lost in just an amorphous mass of swimmers out there. We identify various age groups, and provide opportunities for them, even if it's only in a minimal situation where they can get some experience in camps or specialized selections, just general coaching like that. We may have trouble reaching a thousand swimmers, but that's one of my goals, to reach that figure or a little higher."

Asked to elaborate, Talbot said that there were one-on-one visits to the swimmers' home programs "to let them know that we are interested in where they are going and that we want to watch their development, and contribute to this if we can."

Asked about his personal role in the program, Talbot said that, as chief coach of Australian swimming, his job was to set up a total plan, organize all the various programs, whether it be an identification group of a thousand people, or national camps, national competitions, international competitions. Talbot said, "I'm a team selector. I also sometimes work hands on. But I'm trying to move out of that a bit more, because I feel that this distracts me from the total program, rather than acting as an aid. I guess I do whatever is needed on the technical side of swimming. When you come to think of it, the job is pretty broad. But I want to keep it that way so that I can walk in, or walk out of a situation, or any part of a program when I want to."

Program Strongly Performance Oriented

Talbot stressed that the Australian program is strongly performance oriented. Even the identification of young talent is based on performance. They look at the fastest swimmers in each age group and what events they swim. Said Talbot, "We try to find the top people in these areas, and we start with them. But I try to make it flexible, because when you lay down rules that are too tight, it's possible to omit someone who should be in. So I make it my right to include anybody whom I feel should be in these identification groups—even if it's only a gut feeling that I may have about somebody."

Talbot said that this method had come in for a little criticism but, in the long run, he felt it would pay off. "I don't like to see programs too clearly defined because sometimes a potentially good swimmer can't fit exactly into a particular definition. We're trying to keep it fairly simple if we can. And to do that is a very difficult situation in itself," said Talbot.

Asked whether it was easier to do this in Australia where there is a tradition in swimming and most of the coaching personnel have a good intuitive feel for the sport, Talbot replied, "Yes, that's true in a way. The big difference between Australia and Canada is that the coaches in Australia are much more prepared to work with one another than they are in Canada, and they are not so ego involved. Like John Carew with Kieran Perkins, and Bill Nelson with Daniel Kowalski, and that sort of thing, as long as they are getting their recognition, they're OK about that, and they don't mind—I'll use the word "intruding"—or having input into their programs, and guarding them, because we debate it anyway. But the final decisions in that area rest with me, and, once we've made a decision, they're prepared to cooperate. I didn't find that happening in Canada."

Asked about the attitude towards hard work of the modern Australian swimmer, Talbot said, "We are going through a bit of trauma about that, just the same as with every other part of the world. You know our tradition is distance, and we try to maintain that, particularly with people who have any sprint ability at all. I think people want to look for less, and I do believe, even though everyone fervently denies it, there is a trend to shorter racing, and that bothers me quite a bit. In fact, I've accused the Technical Committee of FINA of having a hidden agenda of trying to get rid of 1,500s at the Olympic level. Now they say that's not true, and I hope it isn't true, and it would certainly strike us very hard if they did. I still think the 1,500 is a great event. It is the event in which we recognize the true guts of a swimmer, if you like."

Questioned about the use of scientific advisors, Talbot said that he had four or five people assist-

ing him in this respect. Said Talbot, "They have swimming in their hearts, or they are ex-swimmers, and they just love the sport. That's a necessary prerequisite. From each of those people, we get something that is concrete. Of course, getting them to agree is a very difficult thing to do! Scientists don't want to do that, but I arbitrate on that, too, and usually give them areas in which to work. I make the sole decisions on whether or not we use their materials. The sport scientists don't decide what we will use. I decide this."

Tri-Series Meets with Japan and New Zealand

Talbot mentioned that the New Zealanders and the Japanese had done a great job in the Pan Pac meet. Talbot said, "We see the Japanese frequently; they come to Australia and run quite a few camps here with the various coaches. Their women are doing well. I knew they were going to be strong here, and I prepared our team to be ready to race them. They look well coached. Their stroke techniques are far superior to what we do in many ways—stroke length, and things like that. When I talk about techniques, I'm talking about their strokes generally, timing and turning and everything else.

"They are doing a very professional job right now," said Talbot. "They've made big progress, and we have to be very conscious of them. We're trying to compete with them more often, and getting them involved in our program, competitive wise, and they're beginning to do that. In fact, we have a tri-series meet each year that includes New Zealand. This year, the Japanese participated in half of the series, but next year they are going to become full-blown members and I'm very happy about that."

✧ ✧ ✧

TERRY GATHERCOLE TALKS ON INTERNATIONAL AND DOMESTIC COMPETITION

An interview in Coolangatta, Queensland, in 1996.

Surviving the Circuit

Terry Gathercole commented on the effects of too much competition on the annual training cycle.

The swimmers arrive home from the international circuit fatigued, and although they need to renew their aerobic base, they are soon competing in state and national championships.

Says Gathercole, "Australia competes in the World Long and Short Course Championships, the Commonwealth Games, the World Cup meets, and numerous other meets around the world. Eventually it may not be the fastest swimmers who succeed at these meets, but rather those who can survive the travel and nonstop competition, almost day after day. They may not necessarily be the fastest, but those who can handle these conditions."

Gathercole said that he was not sure that this was good for swimming. "We in Australia probably suffer more than most other nations, because everywhere we go offshore is a long way, and we have to recover from the large time changes. We have spent a lot of time working in this area to ensure that our competitors get into as good a shape as they can."

Gathercole mentioned that sports, such as tennis, appear able to overcome this problem. "You often read about a world top tennis player who gets off the plane, and, within five hours, is on the court playing. But swimming is somewhat different because it is an individual sport, and you have to be the fastest over specific distances."

Distance Events Affected

A program of constant travel must affect the various phases of cyclic preparation. Gathercole believes that today's swimmers don't have enough time to do the distance work, and, as a result, the 400 and 800 have become very soft events. "Look at today's world standards in these events. We haven't been able to get anywhere near what we were doing in the '80s."

Gathercole said, "Despite these difficulties, Australia has become very experienced in being able to swim well at any point of the year. We have had to handle this for years, as most competitions are held in the Northern Hemisphere. But with our small swimming population, we can only go to the well so many times with any one swimmer.

"You can't keep asking swimmers to come back and swim at a very high elite level, week after week, month after month. Now they can keep up fairly high, but may not be able to produce the really high-quality times specifically when they are needed, especially in events that require endurance."

Constant Competition

When asked how many top Australian swimmers traveled the world and competed almost continuously, Gathercole said, "We take virtually the same people. Since the World Championships in Rome, we've had the Pan Pacific Championships in Atlanta, the World Short Course meet, and just before that, they were at the Commonwealth Games.

"Now they have come back, and only in December, a few months ago, they were in Rio at the World Short Course Championships—the same people virtually. They came straight back from that meet into our midsummer, and competed from January onwards in our domestic program. A coach has to decide what meets the swimmers will use as a swim through, and what meets to take more seriously."

Asked whether the swimmers had to swim in their state championships in order to qualify for the national championships, Gathercole replied, "Not specifically. It's a time thing, but the tradition of Australian swimming has been that competitors swim in their state championships. That's the showpiece of each state. The various state championships are held from January to February."

Improving the Domestic Program

Gathercole said that, previously most Australian states had their championships in January. "It is recognized by coaches and swimmers that good, hard, fast competition is required to reach top performance. Therefore, we lobbied for the state championships to be held at different times so competitors could go from one state to the other to seek the best competition. As a result, we don't have all the state championships on the same weekend.

"Changing the state championship dates has proved successful because many swimmers now enter the different state championships. But this still involves a certain amount of travel, a stay in a motel, and getting back and forth to the pool."

About Terry Gathercole

Terry Gathercole, President of Australian Swimming Inc., was born in West Wyalong (population 3,000), a small country town in New South Wales. He first broke the Australian breaststroke record in 1953, without any previous coaching. Then Forbes Carlile sent him instructions through the mail, before he came to Sydney to train under Carlile in person.

During Gathercole's career, FINA was constantly changing the breaststroke rules, first allowing underwater breaststroke swimming, then finally disallowing it in May 1957. Gathercole was a surface breaststroke swimmer, and, for most of his career was at a disadvantage when competing against expert underwater swimmers, with their double-length pull through to the hips. Nevertheless, in 1958, at the age of 23, he had his revenge when he broke the world breaststroke records six times within a two-month period.

Gathercole won two Commonwealth gold medals at the Cardiff Empire Games in 1954. In 1956, at the Melbourne Olympics, he came in fifth in the 200-meter breaststroke, competing against rivals who spent most of their time completely submerged, surfacing only to take the occasional breath. A few months before the Rome Olympics, Gathercole was involved in a car crash. Nevertheless, he led the field into the final lap of the 200-meter breaststroke, when his lack of conditioning caught up with him, and he finished unplaced after one of the most exciting races of the 1960 Olympics.

As a coach, Gathercole has produced two Olympic breaststroke champions, Ian O'Brien (1964) and Beverley Whitfield (1972). At the 1991 World Championships in Perth, West Australia, Linley Frame, yet another Gathercole breaststroke protégé, won the 100-meter breaststroke title in world-record time.

Gathercole coached in Midland, Texas, for five years, and was president-elect of the American Swimming Coaches' Association, an unusual honor for a non-American to achieve, but decided to return home so that his children could be raised in Australia.

Terry Gathercole, who was inducted into the International Swimming Hall of Fame as an Honor Swimmer in 1985, is highly respected in Australian swimming for his knowledge and experience, not to mention his well-considered opinions on many aspects of the sport.

Commenting on the sequence of state championship dates, Gathercole said, "Queensland is always the first to have their state championships, and these are in January. Then follow Victoria and New South Wales. The swimmers travel mostly to these eastern states to compete in their state championships. A swimmer wanting to go over to the west coast to race against a specific rival, would be looking at a 500-dollar to 1,000-dollar return airfare."

Asked about the potential clash between the World Cup Series in Europe and the dates for the various Australian state championships, Gathercole said, "Well, that's their coach's choice, depending on what they're coming back to. Usually, the World Cup Series competition in Europe is in January and early February, and then they come right back into the thick of the Australian season. I believe that the intelligent coach and swimmer, in the next little while, will select very specifically what they want to do, both in international and national competition.

"This raises the problem of swimmers having to say to their own state, 'Look, I'm not going to swim in our state championships,' and this causes a problem for the state people because of their promotions and their sponsors, and so forth, and of course, the athletes themselves. Many of them are now privately sponsored by various organizations. These people want their exposure, and so swimmers have to appear at high-profile meets."

Australian Olympic Preparation

Gathercole said that, following the trials in Sydney, the selected Australian team members would go into a 12-week cycle of training in preparation for their first Olympic races in Atlanta, starting in mid-July.

Gathercole said that the swimming team will train at altitude in Flagstaff, Arizona. "The Australian plan is that we will go to altitude training on the 6th June. We will leave to go to Athens, Georgia, on the 28th June, and stay there until the 10th July. At this point the Olympic association takes over, and the swimmers will go into the village on the 10th July. The opening ceremony is on the 19th July. They race on the 20th July."

Out-of-the-Country Training Camps

Terry Gathercole, who has been deeply involved in planning altitude training facilities for the Australian swimming team, says that Flagstaff, Arizona, has a number of advantages. "Flagstaff is an extremely nice city. It's at 7,000 feet, or 2,000 meters. The facilities are excellent at the University of Northern Arizona, a beautiful 50-meter indoor pool, and they have set up there a high altitude training complex which encourages people to come there from all the world."

At this point, our conversation went like this:

CC: I believe the Hungarians were there as well.

TG: When we were there, the Japanese team, the Italians, the Irish team were there—people are coming there.

CC: They're not training together, are they? Watching each other train?

TG: Absolutely! Yeah! The Japanese were training in the lanes next to us (laughs) . . .

CC: That's good or bad?

TG: I don't believe that it's harmful at all. We put our training programs up on the board. Whether those training programs are of specific use to another competitor is something else, because they are written for the aims and goals of specific athletes, and, as such, may not suit individual swimmers.

CC: I'm digressing slightly, and I don't want to dwell on it for too long, but I believe that some of the drug-testing teams descended on the Hungarians while they were there. Do you know anything about that?

TG: I do not know anything about that. I have not heard anything, but I would like to think that we are adhering to the policy that, if a nation is sending any of its swimmers to another country, they must notify that country that they are there. That's the first thing I do when I arrive in the United States with the team. I call United States Swimming Inc. and I tell them that we're there, and where we are, and how long we'll be there. Their policy is that you come under our drug-testing policy while you are in our country, and that's why I call them to let them know we have arrived.

CC: Is that the correct protocol? I was speaking to Niels Bouws at the ASCA conference in New Orleans, and he told me that, in Germany, swimmers have to obtain a passport to go out of the country to train, and also report where they will be, and from what dates, so that the testers know where they can go to find them. I think that is very important.

TG: That is extremely important, and I know that international competitors who come to Australia are under Australian Drug Agency rules, and are eligible to be tested. But, if you don't know that they are in the country, that's very difficult. I mean a team can come and be training in Broome in Western Australia, and unless somebody in Broome told us they were there, we would never know. That's why it's important that each national federation tell FINA where they are going, or tell the country they are going to visit, that they will be there.

CC: *I was in South Africa three years ago, and there was a team from another country training there, in the very pool where I was conducting a clinic.*

TG: I know from the 1991 World Championships in Perth that the Hungarian team, which is a small team, as you know, had been in Perth, sometimes, I'm told, up to three months at a time, on a number of occasions before those World Championships, and we Australians had no idea. And what is more to the point, I think, is that they didn't tell anybody, nobody knew, and they knew more about the swimming facility and the Perth environment than most of our Australian kids who come from the East. Not many of them had spent very much time in Perth at all. The Hungarians knew more about it than we did.

Funding and Accountability

CC: *We were talking about swimmers using their funding to swim interstate against main rivals. On what basis are swimmers given funding by the Australian Sports Commission, for this or any other purpose?*

TG: At this point, the Sports Commission gives our national federation a pool of money. Australian swimming, in turn, has a system of awarding dollars to rankings in world swimming. This has taken a couple of forms in the past, such as outright world rankings, two per nation, and we've even used the international points score chart to apportion those funds. But the higher your ranking, the more money you can get, and that ranges from 2,000 dollars to 6,000 dollars.

CC: *Is it correct that swimmers, earning over 50,000 dollars a year, are not eligible for that?*

TG: The Sports Commission has a policy that, if you are earning more than 50,000 dollars a year, you should not apply. Now they don't have a means test, or whatever, and it's more an honor system, but they are asking people in that bracket not to apply so that there are more funds available for people who aren't in that area.

CC: *So, after the Olympics, each national federation is reassessed on the basis of its performance in the Olympics?*

TG: Yes, the Australian Olympic Committee and the Sports Commission, and the government, have said that, following the Olympics, each of our Olympic sports will be assessed on their success, or lack of it. Those that are the most successful at this point will be apportioned more funding. Of course, this is all to do with 2000, and the four-year plan for the Olympics in Sydney.

This is one of the reasons why we want our Atlanta drive to be as successful as possible. Swimming has a very proud tradition in Olympic sports in Australia, because we've virtually won more medals than all of the other sports combined. Now they don't like you saying that, but that's pretty much a fact. All the same, other sports are beginning to make—well, there have been many other sports added, for instance, cycling, women's cycling, all the canoeing and kayaking things, you've got women's events in there. I'm not saying it's bad, but it's now giving other sports more opportunity. We've had women in swimming since 1912, and so our medals have been fairly equally split between men and women in the Olympics.

CC: *That's a good indication. The bottom line is that you get grants from the Australian Sports Commission, based on your performance at the Olympics, and so there is accountability. You have to be accountable, in that sense, for what you have spent. It boils down to accountability. You have to produce results or your funding is reduced.*

TG: That's the indication that we have at this point. One of my concerns, looking at that statement, is that I'm not sure how they are going to measure success, if it is just straight first, second, and third at the Olympic Games. That may be just one measure of success— the depth of your team and what you are achieving in your own country.

CC: *Your age-group program? Your age-group nationals?*

TG: All those sorts of things measure a sport's success. I would think that, with our Olympic Games coming up, that what our people are really looking for are winners.

CC: *Do you think that the third golden era of Australian swimming has arrived, or is it still four years down the road?*

TG: I had made a statement as the head coach of the Australian Olympic swimming team in 1976 that, from 1956 to 1976 it took us 20 years to go downhill that far, and I made a statement that it would probably take us another 20 years to regain our former status.

CC: *That brings you to 1996 . . .*

TG: You said it!

CC: *This could be the start of the new golden era!?*

TG: That could be so.

❖ ❖ ❖

AT THE AUSTRALIAN OLYMPIC TRIALS

More than 2,271,000 viewers tuned in to watch Kieren Perkins battle it out with Daniel Kowalski in the 1,500-meter freestyle for a place in the Olympic team.

Swimming's Big TV Ratings

In Sydney, when the popular program "Hey, Hey It's Saturday" was preempted for the event, ratings jumped from 612,000 to 1,022,000 viewers. All the other channels were affected as viewers switched to watch the 1,500, the last event of the last day of the championships.

All over Australia, the ratings were similarly affected. The Nielsen ratings reported 1,043,800 viewers in Melbourne, 579,000 in Brisbane, 267,000 in Adelaide, and 164,000 in Perth. Not since the 1994 Commonwealth Games, when Perkins broke the world 1,500 record in Victoria, BC, had the number of viewers increased so suddenly in so short a time.

"It was incredible," said Channel Nine director of publicity, Andrea Keir (*The Daily Telegraph*, April 30, 1996). "Australians have always been very swimming minded, and we were expecting it to be a highly watched event because it was critical to Kieren's inclusion in the team, but we didn't expect anything of this magnitude."

The ratings jump was seen as a good omen for the Seven Network, which will be screening the Olympics later this year.

Private Boxes

This was the first time in Australia that domestic swimming received seven consecutive nights of live TV coverage, and the first time that private boxes were sold at a swimming meet. It was also the first time that tickets were sold through Ticketek, the Australian version of Ticketmaster.

A 20,000-dollar screen was mounted at the end of the pool to provide spectators with close-ups of the swimmers as they raced.

The low glass windows of the John Konrads pressroom looked directly on to the pool deck, and housed 100 media representatives from international press agencies and Australian radio, television, and newspapers.

A unique feature of the pressroom, ably managed by Publicity Director Ian Hanson, and his assistant, Alison Roberts, was the on site fully-equipped photo lab which allowed photographs to be processed and scanned around the world within minutes of the end of a race.

Kieren Still Needs to Work

Graham Hannan, vice president of the International Management Group, said that, although Kieren Perkins is far more comfortable than most young men of his age, he certainly is not in the millionaire class, and can't afford to take it easy for the rest of his life.

Thanks to his father's advice, Kieren owns his own home, and a healthy investment portfolio. Kieren is said to earn almost 500,000 dollars (AUS) a year as a result of major sponsorships from Saab, the Swedish car manufacturers; Eyeline Swimwear; National Dairies; and Uncle Toby's breakfast food. With the exception of Uncle Toby's, all these deals will end after the Olympics.

Hannan denied that sponsorship commitments had hindered Kieren's training. He said that Kieren's workload, including the time spent at his part-time job with TV Channel Seven, had been reduced since the end of 1995.

Had Kieren Perkins not made the Australian Olympic team, he would have lost up to 100,000 dollars (AUS) in incentive bonuses for gold medal and world record swims. Furthermore, his corporate value would have been severely reduced.

Scientific Data

Present throughout the trials was a team of 35 sport scientists who analyzed the swimmers' stroke frequency, stroke length, and overall velocity, and made the results available to the coaches.

The amount of space given to swimming by Australian newspapers is little short of amazing. The morning after the Perkins-Kowalski 1,500 duel, a detailed analysis, complete with graphs showing the stroke length, stroke frequency, and velocity, recorded by both swimmers over each of the 30 lengths of the pool, appeared in full in the *Sydney Morning Herald*.

Dr. Bruce Mason, head of biomechanical studies at the Australian Institute of Sport, who prepared the report, said that Perkins had used up too much energy by lengthening his stroke. "Kieren had a game plan worked out but he could not keep to it because people are not robots. They are influenced by one another."

On the other hand, according to Mason, "Daniel Kowalski was able to stick to his game plan and actually increased both stroke length and velocity at the end of the race. It is unusual for a swimmer to be able to do this."

"The Dawn Fraser Room"

The various meeting and committee rooms in the Sydney International Aquatic Centre are named after famous Australian swimmers.

Swimming great Dawn Fraser, who held 39 world records during her career, and won the Olympic 100-meter freestyle title at three Olympics (Melbourne, 1956; Rome, 1960; and Tokyo, 1964), was known not only for her sensational swimming but also for her head-on collisions with Australian officialdom. Now, with typical Aussie whimsy, the officials' room at SIAC has been named "The Dawn Fraser Room." Good on yer, Dawn!

© 1998 Marco Chiesa/Swimnews

Michael Klim (Australia), in a moment of jubilation, acknowledges applause after winning the 100-meter butterfly at the 1998 World Championships.

✧ ✧ ✧

DON TALBOT'S VIEWS ON THE AUSTRALIAN OLYMPIC TRIALS
An interview in Coolangatta, Queensland, in 1996.

CC: *I think you will have a tough team in Atlanta after the high-pressure trials in Homebush last week.*

DT: Well, it was certainly a tense trial, I can agree with you there. I think the team does look pretty good. I tend to agree with you. I'm not altogether convinced at this point that times are significant because each of those swimmers who have qualified now has done much better. I feel we can get back to those times all right. There were a lot of subtleties in this whole meet, people questioning the qualifying times, the first time the meet was run over seven days—that sort of stuff doesn't lend itself to high performance. But the swimmers who made it have been toughened by the whole experience, and as a result they will be able to better handle Atlanta, and they will also get behind each other. It's a good team. There are a few rookies in there. But those rookies are pretty tough kids.

CC: You have about six rookies.

DT: About that, and they're all pretty good. So I feel OK about it. Our women's team is a bit weaker than I wanted it to be. That was a bit of a disappointment to me. I can't quite put a finger on why our women didn't swim well because normally they outswim our men.

CC: Are you referring particularly to the lack of a distance base?

DT: No, I'm looking across the board at the women. They are not nearly as good as they ought to have been, not in any one event. You know we had Sam [Samantha Riley] down a bit, and that probably could have been a bit of a catalyst there that rubbed off on the other swimmers, and Susie O'Neill got sick just before the trials. I mean she still swam a 2:08+ in the 200 fly, which is not bad.

CC: She's a great swimmer.

Susan O'Neill (Australia), wins the 200 butterfly at the Perth 1998 World Championships in a sparkling 2:07.93.

DT: Yeah, a good kid, but I think her 100 was a little disappointing. A 60+ is nothing to get too excited about. She can go better than that. When you get the key people in your team not firing quite as they ought to do, and then the media presentation making such a big thing of it, that's a bit of a wet blanket over everything. But I still feel pretty good about it. I look at those girls, some of them are pretty darned good, and I feel that they will come through. I'm not feeling too bad. I mean you always wish for better than you get. But, at this stage, I don't feel too bad.

CC: It seems to me that there were a lot of stresses acting on those kids, and I don't think that you can pinpoint any one factor, because it was probably an accumulation of factors.

DT: That's what I was trying to say. It's more of a global thing. The couple of factors that I have mentioned are there, but who knows anyway. If you look back, we've had about six or seven great meets, going back to the World Championships. Rome was a good meet for us, and the Pan Pacs was an excellent meet. We toppled the Americans in the men's 4 by 200 meter freestyle, something we haven't done in 45 years.

CC: And that's a hard team to make. A swimmer has to shave down to make that team.

DT: Very hard. Very, very hard, and we stacked up well against them in the Pan Pacs. And then, on top of that, we went to Rio and won the World Short Course Championships, and these are pretty heady sorts of wins, and performances, for us.

The Americans are better on paper than we were here, but I think our team can swim much better. Somewhere along the line you've got to have a bad swim. It hit us here in spades, in some of our performances. But again, if you take the philosophical view, OK, get that out of the way, and let's go. Then, if we can convince the coaches and the swimmers that that's what you've got to do—and I think we have done that already—then I would say that we should perform well in Atlanta. At least, I hope we do. You can never guarantee it, you just do the best you can do.

CC: *Going into a meet of that caliber, it's always an advantage to be somewhat of an underdog, and not as heralded as perhaps you were before, and I think that if you are going to have a bad meet, it's better to have it now, not at the Olympics.*

DT: Yes, I think that this is particularly important about the psyche of Australian athletes. It's not the Australian way—you know they're cocky people. For people who don't know what cocky means, they're up and they get wrapped up in themselves, and they get a little big-headed about it all.

CC: *That was the feeling at the start of the meet. Quite a few swimmers were thinking that they had arrived already.*

DT: Yes, that's right, and I try to warn our swimmers about that. I've seen this happen in other sports too, and then they get a big kick in the backside. I think they got the kick in the backside, and they realize now, "Hey, gosh we had better be very careful," and to me, that's why I'm not so perturbed about the results at the trials. We had enough good swims in there with kids like Scott Miller, Scott Goodman, Susie O'Neill, and a couple of others—nothing wrong with those at all. So we had that glimmer that, OK, if we just keep our feet on the ground, we will be OK So going in as underdogs, as you say, for Australian swimmers is not a bad position. I've seen it many times, if we go in ranked number one, and looking like we can beat the world, we usually get belted, and I'm hoping the reverse happens.

CC: *I noticed that the swimmers waiting to be called to the blocks were exceptionally tense. Some of them looked as if doomsday had come. You could see that they had a lot at stake.*

DT: Yes. I think that's right. Everybody in Australia wants to make the Olympics. There's no question which is the most important event that we go to. In our society an Olympic champion is really hero-worshipped. And so the trialists knew that the standards were tough, but they also knew that they had to race hard because the depth in most of our events was much better than it has been for a long time. Funnily enough, some of our in-

Marcel Wouda wins first gold for the Dutch men in the 200-meter individual medley (2:01.18) at the 1998 World Championships.

dividual performances were not that great but the depth in every event was far, far better than we've ever had. While the rest of the world probably might not notice that, but for us, that was significant. And so, when they get up there now, it could have been any one of three or four swimmers in the final who could have kept them out of the team.

CC: *This alone creates stress.*

DT: But some of them rose to the occasion.

CC: *I made up a little phrase for that. I call it the PAT Triad. First there's Pressure on them to perform. This, in turn, results in Anxiety, and then later, this causes Tension, which shows up in some swimmers as disorganized stroking, false starting, etcetera*

DT: I think that's a good observation because I

could see it too from where I was sitting with the other selectors which was quite a fair way from the start. You could see the tension there, and even on the blocks, we had many more false starts than we've ever had before. And we had one DQ, of one of our boys who had a pretty good 200 freestyle that would have made the team. But, as a result of being DQ'd, he didn't make it.

CC: *I think you have some young male 100-meter freestyle swimmers there who are going to come through one day.*

DT: Yes, I think that our work on sprinting is coming along nicely, but you know it takes a long while to build a sprinter, and, of course, there's the maturity factor involved. I like the look of our youngsters, and I think they're coming through, and, with a bit of luck too, we may just have more than one.

CC: *You take Scott Logan, for example, who came fourth in the 100. He's just like a great, big puppy but, when he hardens up, I think he could be a great sprinter. He has a good temperament.*

DT: Yes, he's with a coach too who has a mature head.

CC: *Bernie Wakefield . . .*

DT: Bernie Wakefield, and he showed up well as a very young boy, and he has continued to improve, is excited now at being on the team. He's got all the characteristics I like in a swimmer.

CC: *He's certainly a good swimmer. Now, talking about mature coaches, I think that not many people, if any, gave him credit for it but John Carew helped Kieren Perkins to handle a weeklong pressure situation at the trials very well, and so did Scott Volkers with Samantha Riley, for that matter. I think they really showed coaching ability in the way that they didn't get uptight in the midst of it all. If they did, they didn't show it.*

DT: Yes, they didn't wear it on their sleeves. I think you're right about that. I think that John Carew is not given enough credit for what he's done, his ability to coach. I mean people recognize him as being good, but he's not demonstrative. You compare him with say Laurie Lawrence, who is a showman, and people like that, and that's good.

CC: *And Laurie is a fine coach.*

DT: And John Carew is a great coach too, and I believe he has brought a new concept, a new dimension actually, to 1,500-meter swimming, and I think it would be wise for people to listen carefully to what he is talking about, because he is not a man who expresses himself that well, and you've got to listen carefully to what he says, and to ask him more searching questions to properly get at the root of what he's getting at. But John Carew is certainly a talented coach, and he is an older head, and he did handle himself very well, and I've got to hand it to him. He was philosophical about the whole thing. He knows that you can have a bad swim, and he was a steadying influence on Kieren.

CC: *He handled that boy very, very well indeed.*

DT: Yeah, he did.

CC: *A lot of people ask, "Is it the singer or the song?" Well, he proved his coaching mettle. It's not when you're doing well and riding on the piggy's back that you need a coach, it's when you're doing badly.*

DT: That's right . . .

CC: *. . . that's when the mettle of a coach shows up . . .*

DT: Yeah, that's when it shows up, and I think John Carew showed that in spades.

CC: *And so did Scott Volkers. He handled Samantha very well.*

DT: Scott Volkers, with the difficulties that he has had, you know, and all his team got involved, in fact, not only Samantha Riley, but Susie O'Neill, Angela Kennedy, Ellie Overton—all those kids have all had a tough time of it with Sam being suspended and then being excused, and then two years for Scott Volkers was reduced to one year— what a shambles. You can understand the pressures that have been on that group, and for those kids to swim as well as they did— they never stopped trying. For example, Ellie Overton went on trying to the last event almost, and got herself selected for the team, which was good.

CC: *They did handle the situation well. Here you've mentioned the accumulation of stresses that the swimmers experienced. Also, I think some of the swimmers who went to altitude training for the first time must have been wondering if it would help them.*

DT: Sure.

CC: *That could have been a question mark for them until the very time they entered the water again at sea level. A lot of that also may have had an effect. All in all though, it looks really good for your team when you consider all the unusual factors. Those kids could probably swim in a meet, say 10 days from now, and wipe those times out, once the stresses are removed.*

DT: Well, I hope you're right. I feel OK about it. I mean I'm not euphoric, but I've been around long enough to know too that one bad swim doesn't mean that's the end of the world. In fact, as I said just a little while ago, I feel this was a little dose of the medicine we needed. But now we've got to get down to the business of getting ready.

CC: *Changing the subject, what do you think of the world picture at the moment?*

DT: Well, it's funny. There's a general depression in world times, and I don't know . . .

CC: *You can't pinpoint the reason?*

DT: Not really, except that I do think that, with the advent of random drug testing which is being done in a more meaningful way, but not comprehensive yet, it may have slowed down the people who do get into that sort of thing. There is a general pall.

CC: *Do you think that there were some people who got off the juice, and now they're not performing?*

DT: Well, maybe someone may want to jump on me for agreeing with that statement.

CC: *It's up to you.*

DT: I think, yes. I think that's true. But I'm just going to say that there is a pall, it seems to me, something heavy hanging over swimming in the world at the present time. The only thing that I can see is that there is a determination by us and other people to try to clean up this whole drug mess if we can,

Jenny Thompson (USA) won 4 gold medals in the 1998 World Championships, was voted 1998 U.S. Swimmer of the Year, and received the Phillips Performance Award.

and get it to be more controlled, if you like. And I think that probably, for the first time, we're getting ahead of the game a little bit, although I don't for one minute think that people still haven't learned how to get around the drug testing.

CC: *Do you think that the newly developed GC-MS [gas chromatography-mass spectrometry] technology is going to help in drug testing?*

DT: It may solve the problem, but technology is made to be beaten, and probably somebody will find a way around it. Certainly, I applaud the fact that now people are beginning to try to do something about drugs in sport. Before, I believe that the leaders of our sport weren't doing that, and I'm hoping that the efforts of the coaches generally around the world, the good guys I call them, will succeed. There is an effect that seems to be working at the moment, and I hope it continues.

CC: *I think that the IOC and FINA don't seem to*

*have the political will to do the job properly.
Either that, or they don't have the ability or
the understanding of the repercussions to our
sport.*

DT: I'm a little more critical than that, and I think
that there has been a distinct reluctance on
their part to do anything about it, and you've
only got to take note of the Chinese situation where people in very high places still
come out and support the Chinese as being
clean and not doing anything wrong, and
they're going to compete. Well, I think that
is pretty much a blind approach, and it bothers me that people leading our sport feel that.
You know, I don't even really know the full
reasons. It could be financial. It could be just
political. It could be just any one of a number of things, but whatever the reason, it
doesn't help our sport.

✧ ✧ ✧

SCOTT VOLKERS ON ATHLETES
UNDER PRESSURE

Scott Volkers had more swimmers on the 1996
Australian Olympic team than any other coach.

His six Olympians, Samantha Riley, Susan
O'Neill, Angela Kennedy, Ellie Overton, Lise
Mackie, and Jade Winter, all swim for the Com-
mercial Swimming Club in Brisbane.

Colloquially known as Commercial, the club has
a successful tradition in Australian swimming.
Founded early in the century for ladies only, Commercial has long been open to both sexes.

The club is unique in that swimmers from anywhere in Australia can join as a social thing, and
club members are not compelled to train with any
one coach. Scott Volkers, and top coaches, John
Carew and Michael Bohl, all have swimmers who
compete for Commercial.

Scott Volkers, over the years, has mainly produced his own swimmers, taking them through
the ranks to the higher levels of competition, but
recently Ellie Overton and Angela Kennedy joined
his group.

Volkers says that changing one's coach is a serious step to make because the patterns used by
individual coaches vary greatly. "It takes 18
months to 3 years to become accustomed to my
program, if you haven't come out of one that's
similar."

Institutionalized and Overanalyzed

"For the coach it's often a no-win situation," says
Volkers. "If they swim well, they were good before
they went there, and if they swim badly, then it's
your fault. It's difficult for someone to completely
change to a different regime overnight. And, if
you're going to the Australian Institute of Sport,
to be institutionalized, as it were, it means a re-
focus to a total swimming life down there."

Volkers said, "There's a life going on outside,
apart from swimming; it's not just swim, swim,
swim. I try to keep a much more relaxed atmosphere. That's what I believe in."

Asked whether a swimmer in a national training center, attended by scientists and other
support staff, could become a swimming guinea
pig, Volkers said, "It depends on whether a
swimmer is being overanalyzed. Overanalysis
can hurt anyone. I've definitely seen it in the
past."

Volkers said that there is a benefit to be derived
when scientists work on the pool deck under a
coach's direction. "It's a matter of the scientists
inquiring, 'What can I do for you?'

"I ask them, in effect, to tell me what I should
do to help my squad now and in the future, and
not to tell me what has happened after it's over. A
sport scientist who can provide the coach with new
ideas in the practical situation can be beneficial
to the program."

For example, in the morning heats of the 100-
meter freestyle, Susie O' Neill couldn't get her
stroke going, so Volkers consulted with sports
scientist, Graeme Maw, who told Volkers that
O'Neill was stroking too fast in the first 50
meters of the race, thus leaving herself with
insufficient energy to finish strongly. As a result, Volkers advised O'Neill to take fewer
strokes and make them longer, and she went
on to win her fifth Australian 100-meter
freestyle championship.

A determined Alex Popov flies from the blocks at the start of the 100-meter freestyle at the 1998 World Championships which he won in 48.93 seconds, a new meet record.

Impressive Communication

Volkers's pool deck demeanor is calm and confident. He has tremendous rapport with his swimmers. They gather around him like a small family. When Samantha Riley didn't swim as well as expected, Volkers handled a potentially tense situation with aplomb. Within a short while, Samantha was all smiles.

Questioned on his impressive communication with his swimmers, Volkers said, "It doesn't happen by accident. Number one is I try to keep them happy. It doesn't matter what else you do, or how hard you train them, an unhappy swimmer won't perform. That's how I work, I guess, and that's what I believe in, and so I just keep doing it."

Volkers added that he believed swimmers should enjoy coming to the pool and doing the hard work, and they should leave the pool feeling happy and with a sense of accomplishment.

Samantha Riley

Samantha Riley started training with Scott Volkers as a 15-year-old with little aerobic capacity. Volkers said, "She was very weak when she came to me 8 years ago. She was a breaststroke swimmer with good legs, and that was about it."

Volkers discussed his reactions to Samantha's performance in the trials: "There's no point in the coach showing panic. That's for sure. We just worked hard enough to get her up for the meet. It didn't really matter what time it was in the end. But, for some reason she hasn't produced the performances that her training indicated she could achieve. Like Kieren, eventually Samantha could have been talking of millions of dollars riding on two swims. This can create a hell of a lot of pressure on one."

Volkers says that tension is the big enemy of the top-flight swimmer. This is particularly true in Australia where the media attention to swim-

Emiliano Brembilla, Italy's great distance swimmer, wins the 1,500-meter freestyle at the 1997 European championships in Sevilla in the excellent time of 14:58.65.

ming is probably unmatched in any other country. While this has its benefits, the enormous focus on swimming creates a great deal of pressure.

Volkers says that different situations create diverse pressures. "Competing in the Olympic Games creates one kind of pressure, the excitement and the need to do well in tough competition. Here, at the trials, it's the desire to make the Olympic team, and, if you don't, the outcome is disaster.

"The pressures acting on leading swimmers are different to those affecting younger swimmers still on the way up. At a meet like this, the younger swimmers don't have to cope with external pressures so much as those they create for themselves.

"In Samantha's case, she has had to come through the whole drug situation, and all those pressures accumulated and added to the pressure of the meet."

Volkers said that he often uses the saying out of adversity comes greatness. "Well, we just wish that the adversities would stop occurring a little bit right now. We've just about had enough of those, and we would like something to go in our favor!"

Gradual Development

Volkers believes in building a swimmer gradually over a long period. "I don't like to see anyone

become great overnight. You see the person who comes up quickly—bang! They do something great, set a world record or whatever, and then, just as quickly, they are back down the ladder again.

"So I believe we should spend time working on them mentally, working on the person mainly, making the person a better person and developing a belief, a positive self-image. Then the swimmer will start to climb the ladder of success. I believe it important to do that."

Volkers stresses the importance of not treating a swimmer as someone you can flog, like a work horse. "Swimmers have emotions, and if they're not having a good day, I certainly don't want to belt the hell out of them. I'd rather say, 'Hop out. Stop work, stop for today. We'll come back tomorrow and do a better job.'"

Training Philosophy

Volkers said, "I believe we have to build swimmers up from a young age, young teenagers, and take them through into their 20s." Volkers said that he had coached at all levels, from 6-year-olds, through to good age-groupers, but now he mainly coaches seniors.

Says Volkers, "The work is fairly intense, but we do it scientifically, and we carefully work out the recovery times we give each swimmer." Volkers says that recovery time is a critical factor in training, and he is giving increasing attention to achieving fast recovery rates in his swimmers.

The maximum distance covered by anyone in Volkers's squad is "about 50 kilometers on a big week." Volkers uses a lot of recovery-type sessions. "We design the weekly cycle scientifically so that it covers all the energy systems. We allow enough recovery time to maximize the amount of work we can do in each energy system. I'm working on ways to perfect this, and I'll probably keep trying different things to come up with a better mixture."

Volkers said that he tries to avoid a lot of wasted kilometers that are not doing any good. "After a major session, we do active recovery swims. We don't try to stress the body in these recovery swims, so that we can come back and do a better job the next afternoon."

Volkers said, "A lot of people tell me, 'We did a hundred kilometers this week.' Well, we did 40, but probably 25 of them were high quality, and the others were warm-ups and swim-downs."

Unusual Admission

"We do heart rate sets twice a week, and we try to do them about three days apart, if possible, to allow full recovery in a particular energy system. So that might mean that on Monday and Thursday, we have quality sessions.

"What I call quality is speed work: 50s within a second of your best time, 100s within 5 seconds of your best time, and 200s at a fast pace as well. Anything that requires maximum effort at almost race speed.

"We do quality swimming with long rests. In these quality sessions, we also include lactate tolerance sets, but with shorter rests and higher lactate. These workouts cover the whole gamut of the lactate system."

Volkers said that he once systematically tested every training item for a whole week. "I wanted to see whether we were actually achieving what we had set out to do. We noted that some sets encroached on another energy system, and this detracted from the ability of that energy system to work in the next session, when we needed it. In the process we discovered some interesting things."

Volkers made an unusual admission: "We found that we were actually trying to push the kids through some workouts that they simply couldn't do, but it was the coach's fault and not theirs. Some coaches too readily jump down the swimmers' throats and accuse them of laziness.

"But, when a coach has done the thing wrong, I think it important to admit it. Most of our workouts seemed to be working, but we did need to change some. I was giving some wrong items in maybe one or two sessions a week. I had to reassess the week and change it around, just the mixture, not so much the content."

Asked about Samantha Riley's maximum heart rate achieved in heart rate sets, Volkers said, "Her maximum used to be 211. I say used to be because it seems to have come down a little bit to maybe 205 to 208. In a heart rate set, we finish with up to 205, and so she's at maximum heart rates—that's in a set covering as much as up to 2,000 kilometers."

Volkers said, "We use heart rate monitors for all those sets, every one of them. The 100s or 200s that we do are timed and monitored and written down.

Greatest Attribute

Asked what he thought was his greatest attribute as a coach, Volkers replied, "Probably my ability to have swimmers perform above their past levels of achievement. I guess it's a motivational thing, but it could be a combination of different factors. Let's just say that I enjoy getting people to believe that they can swim well. This what I've had to do with Samantha here at these trials.

"Samantha's a great girl, and she deserves to do very well, and sensationally so. There's no way she'll take this as the end of the line. That's for sure. She'll get back up. She got swamped at the Commonwealth Games trials, then she got back up, and went on to win every race until this meet. Now she has to turn around again, get her confidence back up, for the Olympics."

❖ ❖ ❖

AUSTRALIA'S EVENT CAMPS AIM TO PRODUCE WINNING COACHES AND SWIMMERS

Pen-and-paper certification tests have given way to developing practical ability.

Dr. Ralph Richards, Coordinator of Australian Coaching Development, says that Australia has moved away from written exams.

Richards believes that coaches should concentrate on developing practical ability, rather than moving from one certification level to the next.

The Australians have done away with such traditional methods as pen-and-paper tests, with the aim of developing more practical values, such as how coaches run their programs and develop professional skills. As a result, their coaches are now assessed according to their ability to take swimmers to higher levels of ability, and to help them make qualifying standards.

While Richards concedes that certification provides coaches with professional status and legal protection as well, he says that academic knowledge is valuable only if it can be put into practice.

Richards says that people learn and progress in different ways, and that accreditation is not the end product but just a piece of paper that tells you where you are along the road. "We know that, between point A and point B, you might take a turn and do a few loops before you get to your destination, or you might go directly.

Practical Emphasis

For example, student coaches might be asked to develop a seasonal training model in which they explain why they have included certain types of training sets, and how they would use sports psychology principles as part of their program.

Richards says, "This can be as simple as having team meetings to discuss specific topics. The coach combines several items of knowledge into something as basic as a seasonal plan, a living, breathing document that the coach can put to practical use."

Richards and his department work in close liaison with the Australian Swimming Coaches' Association in staging regular clinics, where coaches meet to exchange ideas, and perhaps even develop new ones.

Both coaches and swimmers participate in these clinics where many of Australia's top seniors are brought together with some of the country's most promising youngsters.

National Event Camps

Richards says that national event camps are conducted to concentrate on one particular stroke and competitive event. These are more than just training camps, but an important learning experience in which there are as many coaches as swimmers. Members of the national support staff are also present—physiotherapists, nutritionists, sports psychologists, sports scientists, physiologists, and medical people—and they help to provide a practical educational component to the program.

"One of the unique aspects of this program is that we don't just invite the senior national team members. For example, if we have 20 butterfly swimmers at a camp, we might have 12 who are senior elite athletes, but we'll also bring in 8 or 10 developing age-groupers," says Richards.

"Whenever you bring coaches together you are bound to have a stimulating exchange of ideas. We're willing to listen and share and debate these ideas, quite vigorously at times, always with the intent of ensuring a nonthreatening situation."

Richards says that two things take place when swimmers and coaches participate in the national event camps. "First, through discussion with their peers, coaches often find support or confirmation of ideas they had believed to be correct.

"The second fundamental is to identify differences between athletes, and this opens up discussions in which coaches and their athletes are apt to explore different training methods, especially those that seem to work for other people."

Richards says that this process helps coaches to identify the practical elements that most closely fit the requirements of the individual athlete. "The principle we work on is maintain your strengths, but improve your weaknesses. We work at it from both ends.

"This helps them to observe how other people train, and to develop role models and bonding. Sometimes we have senior coaches who still want to coach younger swimmers. So it's not always the case that the young swimmers have young coaches. This provides a good mixture of youth and experience, on the swimmers' side as well as on the coaches' side.

"Part of the interaction in our national event program is that we have a mixture of people who've coached on international teams as well as people who haven't yet reached that level. This exchange of information helps the progress of our coaches into the next generation. We're preparing coaches for periods well beyond 2000."

✧ ✧ ✧

COACHES AND SWIMMERS LEARN TOGETHER IN AUSTRALIA'S AGE-GROUP CAMPS

Bill Sweetenham has designed a plan to guide and monitor young swimmers through all stages of development.

The main emphasis in the Australian National Age-Group Plan, sponsored by Tip Top, Australia's leading bakery, is on the education of both swimmers and coaches.

Bill Sweetenham, national youth coach of Australian Swimming, says, "There is a progression of 5 camps, and we want each swimmer to be exposed to each one of the 5 camps during their years in the program. Ideally, we want to identify promising swimmers—the females at 13, and the males at 14, and then take them through 3 years of progression.

"The overall concept of the Australian age group program is that, when swimmers finally make the national open senior team, they will have developed the competitive skills to cope at the top level, and they will be used to working with different coaches. They will be able to accept the camp environment and know how to make the environment work in their favor."

The program identifies the best swimmers in each age group—13, 14, and 15 for girls; 14, 15, and 16 for boys. Then the progress of each swimmer is monitored until the swimmer reaches the senior ranks.

Development Camps

Each year swimmers and their coaches meet at a seven-day development camp. Data is collected at these camps on both the swimmers and their coaches to provide a career record of each swimmer's mental, physical, and technical development. The professional development of their respective coaches in this practical pool deck setting is also noted.

When the swimmers finally reach the national senior open team, the coaches in charge have a useful, and carefully recorded, history of the swimmers' progression through the ranks.

Sweetenham says, "We run a national-level camp each year, and the best swimmers attend these camps. Three to 5 camps a year are conducted for the individual states, Queensland, NSW, Victoria, Tasmania, Northern Territories, and Western Australia. The camps are of 4 to 6 day's duration. We try to start each camp on a Sunday afternoon and progress through to the following Saturday. Because we run these camps for 13- to 16-year-olds, it is important that they don't interfere with their schooling, and so we confine these camps to school vacation time. Camps are conducted for a wide range of athletes."

A camp is held for the national age-group team immediately following the national age group championships, wherever they are being held. The

---

About Bill Sweetenham

Bill Sweetenham, Australia Medal, has been in his current position as Australian Swimming's National Youth Coach for the past two years.

Prior to this appointment Bill held the following positions:

- Four times Olympic head coach and five times Commonwealth Games coach
- Four years national head coach in Hong Kong and head coach of the Hong Kong Sports Institute (1991–94)
- Ten years at the Australian Institute of Sport
- Eight years as Australia's national coach
- Four years as Queensland's director of coaching

During his career, Bill's credits include Olympic gold medalists, world champions, world-record holders, and Commonwealth Games and Pan Pacific gold medalists in various events.

Two of his former swimmers, Michelle Pearson (Australian 200-meter freestyle national record) and Tracey Wickham (ex-world 400 meter and 800 meter) held the longest standing records in Australia.

Prior to his national coaching appointments, Bill had great success as a club coach in both country and metropolitan areas of Australia.

Bill's vast experience at the international level has never taken him far from the grassroots of Australian swimming. Bill has always worked with junior programs and as a learn-to-swim consultant.

camps are held in all parts of the country. Sweetenham tries to visit each state and national camp, although it is not always possible for him to attend for the full period of time.

Sweetenham says, "We select a head coach for each camp, and we also appoint several assistant coaches. My job at these camps is to assist and advise the head coach."

Educational Skills

The national team has about 50–60 swimmers, and the open team comprises 130 to 140 swimmers, all identified in their respective age groups. Young, and even not so young, developing coaches are invited to work at the camps, where they are exposed to a wide range of educational skills.

At the end of a camp, a competition may either be held at the camp venue, or the swimmers may travel to another venue for this purpose.

Sweetenham says, "Usually we stay at a school facility that has a pool. Sometimes, we stage the competition at the camp, for instance, on the last day, and we structure it so that the swimmers can put into practice the tapering skills learned during the camp.

"We may even go by bus to a venue 45 minutes to 90 minutes away. We travel to heats and finals, and thus provide experience of twice-daily return bus travel. This, in its way, is also an educational experience."

The age-group program for swimmers aged 13 to 16 is based on education, while the national youth program, which is for swimmers aged 16 to 18, focuses almost entirely on training.

Says Sweetenham, "The youth team emphasis is training based, so that when the swimmers arrive in Don Talbot's national open team, they have been exposed to all the different things that can go wrong.

"They've learned how to cope with problems, they've learned self-management skills, they've learned all the skills that are essential to competing successfully in the Olympic Games. Assuming that most swimmers are only going to make one Olympics, hopefully two, they don't want to use the Olympics as a learning experience. They will need to have the skills to capitalize on the opportunity first time out."

Although the 13 to 16 groups do have workout sessions at camp, the basic philosophy is that, because the swimmers receive enough training in their home environment, the emphasis at the age group camps should be mainly on education. But, as mentioned above, the opposite applies at the youth camps.

Adequate Training Background

The swimmers are expected to arrive at camp with an adequate background of training, and to this end, there is a preliminary liaison with the swimmers' home coaches, as well as a short checklist for the swimmers to complete. Says Sweetenham, "There's no point in having swimmers at the camp who haven't accumulated an adequate background of work."

Sweetenham points out, that the coaches who accompany their swimmers to camp, also help to disseminate the knowledge they gain to their other swimmers who were not yet good enough to be invited to camp. In this way, the camp experience has a wider effect on all phases of national swimming development.

Sweetenham says, "We provide an open opportunity for any home coach to come to any of the camps and observe. Over the last 12 months we've had approximately 52 to 60 coaches come through the camp situation. It is important that the coach comes to these camps for younger swimmers, before they go on a national team."

Sweetenham meets once a week with Don Talbot, the Australian national head coach. In these discussions Talbot identifies any area with which he is having trouble at the national open level.

Says Sweetenham, "In other words, if Don has a camp and he finds that certain things are not exactly as he wants them, he will talk to me, and I'll make sure to address these problems during the swimmers' developmental stages at the Tip Top camps.

"So, if Don says that he is having trouble with any aspects of a swimmer's performance, adjustments are made to overcome them. The idea is that when he receives swimmers on the national open team, they will be far more advanced than we have had them in the past, not only in their education, but also in their training."

Specific Testing

As the swimmers progress through the five different camps they are presented with a range of goals. "At the first camp we do a number of measurements. We measure and record everything that is measurable, and an ongoing record is kept at successive camps. This is quite an exercise in logistics, but we have a camp package that covers all these points.

"At the first camp, the training is moderate, not too hard. The second camp is based on developing technique and skills. The third camp provides for specific testing, and this is usually based on early to midseason performance. It is an endurance-based camp, and we certainly look at the basic energy systems, and use the national testing protocols.

"At this age we expose them to the same step tests that Don will use with the senior team. Attendance at the fourth camp is only open to swimmers who have attended the first three camps. Similarly, the fifth camp is open only to swimmers who have attended all the previous four camps. It is basically a training camp where they work hard, but still use all the educational skills received in the first four camps. In this way, they will put together the accumulated experience of all the preceding camps.

"Camp number five is the only camp that has such a great emphasis on training. Of course, all the preceding camps do have a training component, and the swimmers train twice or three times a day at every camp, but the only camp where we will really put the emphasis on training is at the last camp."

Asked whether there were disciplinary problems when youngsters come together from a wide variety of backgrounds, Sweetenham said that there would be small problems, but the coaches are briefed on camp procedures on the day the camp starts.

"We have some skills for the coaches to use. We believe it important that the coach who is going to work at a camp should have the ability to gain the confidence of the swimmer within the first day or two of the camp, so that the swimmer feels comfortable about being at camp."

Integrated Athlete

"Our goal is to build a total integrated athlete, and in this process, we want to build a total inte-grated coach as well. We have found the coaches are very supportive. Making allowance for fast-trackers and slow-trackers, the progression through our system is ideally based on identifying swimmers of 13, and then taking them through the age groups 14 and 15 in the Tip Top program.

"Then we have a national Tri-Series program of meets against New Zealand and Japan, then into a national youth program of 16–18, at which stage, hopefully, we will start to see an emerging team, that will eventually move into Don Talbot's senior national team. And when the swimmers reach the national open team, Don Talbot will have swimmers who have been exposed to every possible contingency that might arise. In other words, Don will have a fully experienced team of both swimmers and coaches."

Sweetenham said that although the camps had only been in existence for 12 months, they had already produced good results. "We are very happy

Americans Lindsay Farella (left) and Amy Van Dyken celebrate their win in the 4 x 100-meter freestyle relay at the 1998 World Championships. They clocked 3:42.11.

with the way it has gone. The situation looks very good for the camps, and there has been very positive feedback from the coaches. Everything seems to be working very well.

"We conduct short camps so that we can keep them punchy and with a lot of impact. We continually evaluate the progress of the camps. As well as the camps, I visit those coaches who have swimmers in the program. I spend one-on-one time on the deck with the coach as well."

The camps are designed to eventually fit into the main body of senior swimming as the swimmers mature.

From 16–18 the emphasis will shift to training, but still using the educational skills the swimmers have developed during the preceding three years. They will form part of the emerging team that travels to Europe every year. By this time, they should be moving into the national senior team.

Sweetenham says that he is very happy at the way the age-groupers are progressing. "We do comparisons all the time with last year's results, Basically, we look for about a three percent improvement over a year for the age-group kids, and if someone is not making that sort of progress, we follow them up to find out why, and how we can help."

Sweetenham says that he also tries to identify weaknesses in the system. For instance, if he finds that he doesn't have enough good backstroke swimmers, he will make it his job to convince coaches that they should run specialist backstroke programs, or camps, to improve the standard in that event.

Coaching Development

Sweetenham said that the best tool for developing coaches in Australian swimming has been Don Talbot's national events camps, where the coaches attend and learn from each other.

"We're trying to extend this to the point where I will identify a pool of about 20 young coaches around the country and encourage them to have a mentor coach, in other words, someone whom, if they feel uncertain about any area, they can call upon to discuss the matter on a one-on-one basis. They can use the services of that experienced coach to help them through."

I told Bill Sweetenham that I had spoken to Dr. Ralph Richards, Coaching and Development Coordinator for Australian Swimming, who had outlined in detail how he liaises with Sweetenham on coaching development within the Tip Top age-group program.

Dr. Richards advises Sweetenham in advance on the accreditation levels of coaches about to attend a camp, so that Sweetenham can provide assistance in any area of training while the coach is there. Sweetenham says, "I will make sure that this happens, and I will encourage the coaches to pursue their education."

Sweetenham makes a point of identifying areas of concern for the coaches as a group. For example, one question that the coaches consistently asked was on ideal tapering methods. As a result, Sweetenham sat down and wrote an article on the topic both to provide information and the opportunity to use it.

"I thought that this would help a lot of coaches who felt that this was an area of concern or weakness. I do the same with other topics, and, if I don't have the time or don't feel adequate to write on the subject, I ask someone else to do it. For instance, one of the things that concerned me was the subject of the aerobic conditioning base, and I didn't have the time, and so I asked Dr. Richards, whom you've just mentioned, to put pen to paper."

Sweetenham said that he had also done an article in the previous month's *Australian Swim Coach* (journal of the Australian Swimming Coaches' Association), on an evaluation of age swimming in Australia. "In this article coaches could compare 1990, when we were five years out of Atlanta, and the end of 1996 when we were five years out of Sydney. So we can compare our age-group results five years out of Atlanta and five years out of Sydney, and we'll continue to do that every year."

Through to the Senior Ranks

I asked what has been the pattern of age group swimming development in Australia over the years, and whether there was a pronounced tendency for many age-groupers not to reach the senior ranks, as happens in several countries, including Canada. Sweetenham replied that his job was to help swimmers to move successfully through to the senior ranks.

He said that his prime points of concern in achieving this aim were to make sure that swimmers limit themselves to three percent improvement a year, not to do too much in one year, and then plateau the following year. Training under coaches, who are skilled in the area of preventing plateaus, will leave room for the swimmer to improve in the following years. Says Sweetenham, "So we avoid the plateau that occurs when a swimmer stops growing. We avoid the plateauing effect that causes a swimmer to fall by the wayside." He added that, in other words, the aim was to achieve gradual progression.

Asked about avoiding parental pressures on the developing swimmer, Sweetenham says that he visits clubs to talk with coaches and parents. "If a coach feels that this is an area of concern, then I'll talk to the club parents on this topic as well."

Rather than discussing such aspects as the danger of pressuring swimmers so that they become tense and disorganized, Sweetenham says that he takes a more positive tack by telling parents how they can do it well, rather than how they can do it wrongly.

Sweetenham agrees that tapering the age group swimmer is a great deal different from tapering the mature swimmer. "With my attitude to tapering, you have to know what's measurable. Then you measure it. You have to look at what's controllable. And, if it's controllable, then you should control it. What two things fit into the one area? If they are measurable and controllable, those are the things that really have an influence—something that's controllable and measurable.

"So if you do that, then you have the areas in which you can really make significant improvement. So, with senior athletes in most cases, these things become very easily identified, what is actually measurable and controllable. But, with age-groupers, you have so many things going on, that it is difficult to do this. With the swimmer who is less muscular, less developed, more aerobic based, of course, the taper can be much shorter. It's a resting, rather than a tapering philosophy. With age-groupers, it's just resting. With senior athletes, it's tapering.

Because a coach is involved with the development of youngsters over several years, one should be aware of the other aspects of their lives. Asked to comment on this phase of development, Sweetenham said that "the whole thing is to be a whole athlete, an integrated total athlete where they have all the other things in their lives in balance.

"Swimming is one part of their lives, and it doesn't become catastrophic, if that happens to be going bad, when there are several other aspects of their lives that are still going well. If they put all their eggs into swimming, and they happen to flounder for a while, then they will feel totally devastated. If they have other things in their lives, then they can say, 'Well, I've got six or seven other things, and swimming's only one of them.'"

DAVID PYNE TALKS ON PREDICTIVE VALUE OF SCIENTIFIC TESTING

This interview took place at the 1996 Australian Swimming Coaches' Conference at Coolangatta, Queensland.

Dr. David Pyne is the sports physiologist at the Australian Institute of Sport (AIS) where he is primarily responsible for swimming. David Pyne has worked on the pool deck with top-flight swimmers for 10 years, and is said to be one of the world's most experienced swimming physiologists. He is also involved in testing swimmers in specialized camps, as well as observing their performances in competition.

Pyne says that swimming in Australia is a coach-driven situation. "The coach is in the middle and so provides the link between coach, swimmer, and the scientist. Our work is really directed through the coach. This has been the hallmark of our success."

Pyne believes that the quality of swimming in a nation is a combination of the system in place, and the quality of the people in that system. In this respect, he says that Australia has developed a good system with its national team and its support structure. "Our coaches work very well with each other, as well as with the scientists. This is something that Don Talbot and Bill Sweetenham have really emphasized. We have really been encouraged by the coaches to come on the deck and work together with them. We've pooled our knowledge and used it very effectively."

In addition to working at the AIS, Pyne is physiologist to the national swimming team. He attends altitude and sea-level training camps, and accompanies the team to national championships and worldwide major meets. His activities include involvement with the national event camp program, started a few years ago under the direction of Don Talbot, Australia's Head Coach.

Predictive Value

Pyne says that one of the first things people want to know is the actual predictive value of scientific testing. From a physiological viewpoint, the normal variations in such biological parameters as heart rate and lactate tend to limit their predictive power.

Pyne says that a number of scientific applications can be used to evaluate responses. While one application can view progress in each training session, and how individual swimmers respond to a particular session, another application can be used to monitor long-term progress, on a month-to-month basis over an entire season. However, he tends to give more emphasis to viewing the long-term effects of training, because this approach is probably the best way to use the actual predictive power of science.

Some studies have shown that most short-term scientific tests don't necessarily fit closely with actual performance. This is obviously an important issue, because many factors contribute to performance, and it is difficult to determine the importance of any one factor in isolation. One needs to look at the holistic model to be able to distinguish the really important factors.

Scientific Testing

The Australian national team is supported by a wide range of sports science expertise. As team physiologist, Pyne leads a two-prong approach. First, the swimmers are given a series of tests known as the national testing protocols, which have been in place since 1993. About once a month, all national team members undergo a set battery of tests, directed by Wayne Goldsmith, Australian swimming's full-time science coordinator.

Pyne says, "This routine testing is one of our more visible roles, but the real value of what we do lies in the cumulative effect of our day-to-day work, looking at the responses of swimmers in actual training, and the consultations we have with the athletes and their coaches. Our real value is something the Australians have done quite well, and that is to work actively with the coaches and swimmers on a continuing basis, from day to day, and week to week."

The tests are divided into a number of basic areas, of which the most specific are those actually done at the pool, using the 5 by 200-meter incremental test steps. Pyne's team of scientists conducts a range of other activities, including blood tests, and the measuring of body composition.

Pyne intends to broaden the range of these activities to include physiotherapy assessments, particularly with reference to postural and musculoskeletal alignments. These assessments will

---

About Dr. David Pyne

- Ph.D. in biochemistry and molecular biology.
- Since 1987, sports physiologist involved with swimming at the Australian Institute of Sport
- Works with both the AIS swimming team and the Australian National Team
- Travels extensively with the AIS and Australian teams to national- and international-level competitions and training camps
- Research interests: applied physiology of swimming; exercise, training, and immune system; environmental physiology
- Secretary to the Australian Swimming Sports Science Advisory Group
- Writes coaching/scientific articles for *The Australian Swim Coach*, other coaching publications, and scientific journals

Lenny Krayzelburg (USA) leaps off the wall in the 200-meter backstroke at the 1998 World Championships. Lenny won in 1:58.84 with Ralf Braun (Germany) and Mark Versveld (Canada), second and third, respectively.

be added periodically through the training year, together with nutritional and psychological assessments. So far, the main thrust to the program has been in the physiological area, particularly in the amount of testing done in the pool.

On the pool deck, Pyne utilizes heart rate monitoring, blood lactate analysis, and more recently, he has been observing biochemical parameters, which previously had been restricted to the laboratory. "We are doing these from capillary samples taken from the fingertip or earlobe, and we are studying measures of muscle breakdown to some protein markers, such as creatine phosphokinase, or CPK, and also markers of protein excretion related to high-intensity work, such as ammonia, uric acid, and some measures of liver function. So what we are viewing are protein metabolism related to protein breakdown of muscle, CPK, also high-intensity work, observing what we call metabolic stress, and then markers of excretion, such as uric acid, as well as markers of liver function."

Pyne is trying to isolate two or three of the more sensitive measures. "One of the things about science is that we can measure so many aspects, but in our work we've tried to refine the tests to just the most basic, sensitive, and specific items. In the pool, there's a range of testing that can be done. We've used the 5 by 200, but this method does have a number of limitations. We've worked on heart rate testing, biomechanical analysis, and, in recent years, we have introduced competition analysis at all our major meets."

Integrated Program

Pyne said that the biomechanical analysis is done by Dr. Bruce Mason and his team. The measures taken in training are then related to competition. "We are trying to integrate the biomechanics and the physiology, and we're trying to integrate the training with the competition analysis."

Pyne said that one of many activities that scientists and coaches do together is to evaluate new technologies coming onto the market. He believes that the Coachmate, an innovation developed in Australia, could prove to be beneficial in studying performance. This computer system records the heart rate and split times of every swimmer in a team, throughout every item of a workout. A feature of the Coachmate is that it has a range of applications in training, including a starting block with a light that flashes until it reaches the optimum time at which the swimmer ought to take off.

Quick Fixes

Pyne believes that the modern generation is looking for the quick fixes. "Those of us who have been in the sport a long time know that success comes through hard work and experience. Australia is rich in swimming tradition. We were quite a successful nation in the '50s and '60s, and I guess that sometimes we should look back at what we've done in the past in order to move forward. It's always nice to find the short, direct route, but if you look at the example of distance swimming, it seems to have played out worldwide."

Pyne says there is a need to look back to where swimming was in the '70s and '80s. "We talked to some of the coaches here at this conference, the Australian coaches as well as the visiting coaches, and many of them believe that the whole environment and culture of distance swimming has been eaten away in the quest for more sprint-oriented events."

Pyne says, "I don't think we are quite doing the right type of training and the right volume of training. One of the trends in world swimming, through the '80s, has been towards a more sprint-oriented, high-intensity, low volume program, particularly coming out of North America. I think this certainly has set distance swimming back."

Distance Background

Pyne admits that a high-intensity program does have its place for some swimmers, particularly the more mature sprint-oriented swimmer. This can be an effective way of training, providing an athlete has already established a background of distance training. However, the majority of swimmers, both the developing youngsters and certainly the middle-distance and distance swimmers, need a more varied traditional program that integrates both endurance and speed.

"We derived great success with this type of program in Australia, and I think we need to go back and revisit this with our distance swimmers." Pyne says that coaches tend to focus on the short term, because obviously that's where their day-by-day responsibility lies, but one of the hallmarks of the more experienced coaches is that they can see the wider picture, and know that a swimmer's progress should be built up over a number of years.

"The better coaches appreciate the longer term implications of training, and this goes back to Doc Counsilman's comments on residual training. This same philosophy is also identified in Eastern Europe. The Russians call this "footprints," and the best coaches worldwide certainly have identified this important aspect of training."

Pyne has worked closely with coaches and swimmers over the last 10 years, applying basic scientific principles in a real-world situation, both in the training pool and in competition. He has tried to identify the more important scientific parameters through specific pool testing, as well as using other basic testing procedures known to be important, including body composition and basic blood testing to make sure an athlete's health is at the correct level.

"The bottom line is that ours has always been a coach-driven exercise, and, as I've said before, I've been really fortunate that I've been able to work with some of the best coaches in the world. Here in Australia, we have coach-driven programs, not athlete-driven programs, or scientist-driven programs. It all comes through the coach."

Chapter 9

INTO THE MILLENNIUM

THE OLYMPICS TURN PRO

Swimmers, and the coaches who train them, will seek their fair share in a multimillion dollar entertainment industry.

The 1996 Atlanta Olympic Games marked the end of the first century of what has come to be called the modern Olympic movement. Unfortunately, the modern Games are now characterized by the same crass commercialism that led to the demise of the ancient games.

The Olympic ideal, manifested by the ancient Greeks in continuous striving toward a goal, was praised in art, music, and literature but gradually gave way to a narrow and greedy snatching for victories. To cap it all, an atmosphere of commercialism and professionalism eroded the early lofty motives for staging the games.

By AD 394, the Olympic Games had changed so much in character, from the fine, clean festivals of the Greeks to the brutal Roman exhibitions, that the Christian Emperor Theodosius decided to end them, and it is said that few people missed them. In one century we have almost reached the same point which marked the end of the road for the Ancients, after almost 12 centuries of unbroken history. Baron de Coubertin's dream has begun to unravel.

Shamamateurism and Sportsmanship

The number of participants at Atlanta (10,700) has more than doubled since the first postwar Olympics in London, 1948 (4,099). But this is not all that has changed.

Fifty years ago, the Olympic authorities were intent on preserving amateurism. They excluded from competition anyone, or anything, with any connection to professionalism. Each national body in every country had to complete a special form certifying that each competitor was an amateur. Officials kept a wary eye for signs of "shamamateurism," then considered the predominant evil of the day. Every athlete had to sign a personal declaration that he or she had never been a professional in this or any other sport, and had never been paid for competing in, or teaching, any game.

Consider the Olympic oath taken on behalf of all participating athletes: "We swear that we will take part in the Olympic Games in loyal competition, respecting the regulations which govern them and desirous of participating in them in the true spirit of sportsmanship for the honor of our country and the glory of sport."

Stop right there at the word, *sportsmanship*. When did you last hear it mentioned? Is sportsmanship becoming a dead concept or is the word merely politically incorrect?

The public persona presented by many top athletes has changed from the quiet hand-shake of congratulations, and perhaps a pat on the back of yesteryear. In those days, athletes were taught to win modestly and lose graciously, or to win as if you're used to it, and lose as if it doesn't matter, but those are far-off days.

Granted, we still see swimmers at the end of a race ducking under the lane ropes to congratulate fellow competitors and hug each other, and other displays of, let's say it, genuine sportsmanship (oops!). But, at the same time, we also witness distasteful examples of histrionic behavior: face-pulling, weird gesticulations, and prancing around, sometimes wrapped in one's national flag. These antics, confused with creating an impression of star quality, are probably staged to impress potential sponsors, but are an embarrassment to those who know the real product.

Not only do we hear winners unabashedly boasting about how good they are, how much they have improved, and how hard they have worked to get there, but it is also commonplace to hear adept excuses presented by coaches and athletes alike, as to why their performances did not come up to expectations. It wouldn't be too difficult to produce and market a computer software program called "The Excuse-o-Matic"—a ready reference

for those who can't cut the mustard, or who suffer from fear of failure (FOF), also known as "choke."

We live in the age of megabucks for those who win by fair means or foul, as long as you're not caught. Come to think of it, staging competition where anything goes, drugs included, wouldn't really catch on because, strangely enough, there would be no unfair advantage to be gained from competition where everyone is a cheater. The game just wouldn't be worth the cost of the candle—or the drugs.

The Olympics Turn Pro

After the 1976 Montreal Olympics had left a debt of close to 1 billion dollars (CAN), the financial future of the Olympics seemed in jeopardy. Then came the 1984 Olympics, the first free-enterprise games in which Los Angeles produced a 225 million dollar revenue surplus. In 1985, the IOC started a world-wide marketing scheme called The Olympic Programme (TOP) in which sponsorships or licensing fees were sold to companies for 5 million dollars (US).

Sponsorship revenues for the Los Angeles Summer Olympic Organizing Committee realized 42 million dollars (US), and by the Seoul Olympics (1988) sponsorship revenues reached 200 million dollars. In Barcelona, 1992, commercial sponsorships zoomed to 420 million dollars, and in Atlanta, 1996, together with income from joint marketing ventures with the US Olympic Committee, the total revenue income is expected to be a whopping 750 million dollars.

The Olympics are no longer solely a competitive arena for athletes. The world's leading companies meet in another type of competition, namely to test brand names, technologies, and marketing strategies. While the IOC remains firm about designating the Olympic sites as commercial-free zones where advertising is not permitted, this provides no solace to those who mourn the loss of the once-prized spirit of the Olympics.

The IOC maintains that their insistence in not permitting advertising within the arena has cost the organizers millions of dollars, but experts believe that not a penny more could have been wrung out of "the 17-day marketing blitz, which is unprecedented in its size and scope."

Advertising Age magazine said that the Atlanta Olympics have become known as the marketing event of the century. In fact, even within the IOC, there are those who now would prefer to see a curtailment of the number of Olympic events, and a return to shared expenses between government and the market place, but such reversion would appear a forlorn hope.

The IOC has chosen a path towards ever-increasing commercialism, not to mention professionalism, from which any turning back seems impossible. Gone are the Olympics of ancient times as well as the spirit of amateurism, and participating for the sheer joy of it, so much cherished by de Coubertin and the protagonists of the early modern movement.

The Olympics may well have become the world's most remarkable and spectacular quadrennial entertainment event, but, despite the continuing display of ritual and panoply, the Olympics are no longer what its founders intended it to be. It has become a sad parody of the old Olympic movement and its altruistic intentions for the youth of the world.

Sponsors Become Partners

In *Ottawa Today*, Richard Pound, Canada's senior member on the IOC and a swimmer in the 1960 Olympic Games, who has led the IOC's marketing schemes, said, "Each time we have an Olympics, we learn something from it. But the big lesson we learn is that when you get into a marketing relationship you move away from philanthropy; you're out of the charitable donation list and into something more akin to a partnership."

So what Mr. Pound is, in effect, saying is that companies around the world, who are falling over themselves to buy a piece of the Olympic action, are no longer sponsors but are now actually active partners in the colossal Olympic entertainment industry. For them it is important to get their brand names before the public, and also to steal a march on their competitors.

Incidently, one can readily appreciate the seeming reluctance by the IOC to come down hard on the Chinese when their athletes are caught cheating en masse. If only to maintain the extremely large potential audience and revenue base, it becomes important for the IOC and its partners to keep China, with a quarter of the world's population, within the Olympics. (This is irrespective of whether or not the IOC deserves to receive the Nobel Peace Prize for keeping China in the Games.)

This is easy to understand when you have global Olympic partners such as Coca-Cola, IBM, Time Inc., Matsushita, Kodak, Visa, Bausch & Lomb, *Sports Illustrated/Time*, Xerox, UPS, and John Hancock Financial Services, whose contributions average 40 million dollars (US) each, including goods and services. (Source: IEG Sponsorship Report, Chicago.)

Profit Sharing

Although champion athletes already receive payments and gifts from their individual Olympic bodies, sports equipment manufacturers, and other sources, the day is coming when more and more athletes, and the coaches who train them, will ask for their just share in this multimillion dollar entertainment industry. One suggestion is that, in swimming, the top athletes in each event should be paid according to scale, and regularly drug tested by an independent agency, appointed and paid for by the sponsors, to ensure the integrity of their athletic performances.

✧ ✧ ✧

WHATEVER HAPPENED TO AMATEURISM ?

FINA, the once fierce guardian of amateurism, now governs a sport in which its leading athletes are full-time professionals.

For most of this century, FINA, the international governing body of amateur swimming, enforced strict rules of amateurism. There were any number of no-no's, infringement of which, would have made you a professional, and, as such, a pariah and a lesser breed without the law.

Now, suddenly, poof! Amateurism has vanished, and we behold the strange spectacle of FINA actually governing a sport in which the leading athletes are almost all full-time professionals. Indeed, FINA now promotes meets for prize money around the globe almost year-round. Avery Brundage, one of the chief antiprofessional inquisitors of all time, must be turning in his grave. After a hundred years, the wheel has turned full circle.

How the times have changed. The other day, Ron Masters, writing in the *Sydney Morning Herald*, said that "a decision by the Australian Tax Office to tax grants from the federal government to Australian Olympians has thrown the entire athlete support system for the 2000 Sydney Games into disarray." Apparently, the Australian Tax Office had redefined the term *professional*, rendering all income accruing to a professional athlete liable to tax.

As a result, the Australian Sports Commission was "at a loss to define a professional as opposed to an amateur." Said executive director, Jim Ferguson, "It may come down to deeming a professional as someone who undertakes sport to earn a living, as opposed to an athlete who might earn some winnings from time to time." Rather like being a little bit pregnant!

A few days later, also in the *Sydney Morning Herald*, Glenda Korporaal described how no less an august organization than the European Union had ruled that athletes "are professionals who have a right to work." The EU said that four-year bans for drug taking are too long. Even if a ban is reduced to two years, the EU suggested that athletes should be given more flexible penalties, such as being allowed to train during their period of disqualification. There you have it: In this enlightened age, we now have restraint of trade laws in the once pristine strongholds of amateurism.

The Myth of Ancient Amateurism

Whence the concept of amateurism in the first place? The restoration of the Olympic Games in Athens in 1896 was said to have brought with it a revival of what was supposed to be "the classical ideal of amateurism." But this was not based on fact because no ancient Greek would even have understood the idea, so foreign was it to antiquity and the ancient Olympics. The money aspect was in fact a red herring. The real distinction was between upper-class English gentlemen, who sometimes dabbled a little in sport on the side, and the professional who was the socially inferior son-of-toil who participated for the money. (Hodge, 1988).

In the ancient Olympic Games, the athletes competed for prizes. These prizes were simple at first, but eventually the winners had all sorts of gifts and privileges showered upon them, both on the spot and even more so when they returned home. And, at Olympia, the scene of the ancient Olympic Games, on the north side of the Altis, there were no fewer than 12 treasure houses (would this number suffice the modern IOC?) which contained the dedicated gifts and thanks—offerings for Olympian victories gained by citizens of the Greek states.

The word *amateur* certainly did not originate in ancient Greece, but was first used in France during the reign of Louis XIV (1643–1715) to denote a connoisseur of the fine arts. The term was first recorded in Britain in 1784, also with reference to appreciation of the polite arts of painting and music.

The earliest use of the term *amateur* in sport referred to gentleman amateurs as ringside spectators at prize fights. The distinction in British sport between an amateur and a professional was not so much financial as social. Example, in 1831, the Oxford and the Leander Clubs rowed at Henley for the sum of 200 pounds a side, yet there was no question of professionalism.

Such sportsmen underlined their amateurism by showing that, unlike artisans, they could well afford to lose. Conversely, a blatant example of class distinction as the basis for amateurism came as late as 1871, when the Henley committee declined a local entry for the Wyfold Cup on the grounds that the crew included people who were, or had been mechanics, artisans, and laborers. This was not a question of their having rowed for money, but merely that they were not gentlemen amateurs.

With the formation of the Football Association (1863) and the Amateur Athletic Club (1866), sport ceased to be a gentleman's preserve. Though mixed games of players and gentlemen had been successfully played in cricket for over a century, the gentleman amateurs, now merely amateurs, reacted against this: Since they could no longer apply social sanctions, they resorted to monetary ones. By 1880 the distinctions between amateurs and professionals had generally become a financial one.

FINA Adopts the English ASA Rules

In the mid-nineteenth century, the future of the newly-formed Amateur Swimming Association of Great Britain was in jeopardy because many good swimmers preferred to compete for money and other prizes. However, the ASA eventually was able to enforce their amateur definition throughout the country.

The success of the ASA in enforcing their new amateur rules resulted in such fine swimmers as T. Cairns, Joey Nuttall, W. Evans, S. W. Greasely, J. H. Tyers, and Dave Billington being declared professionals. These great swimmers had held most of the championships from 100 yards to 1 mile, and Cairns, Nuttall, Tyers, and Billington were world famous. Their banishment was hailed as a victory for amateurism, but perhaps it was also a victory for exclusivism.

At the London Olympics, 1908, George Hearn, the president of the English ASA, was asked to draw up an Olympic swimming code. He was assisted in this by another Englishman, William Henry, and Max Ritter (USA), and Hjalmar Johansen (Sweden). Because the representatives of 10 nations (England, Germany, Denmark, Sweden, France, Ireland, Finland, Hungary, Belgium, and Wales) were participating in the Olympic meeting in London, George Hearn decided to use the opportunity to form an international swimming association with a set body of rules. Thus it was that FINA (Federation Internationale de Natation Amateur) was formed, and its rules were based on the model of the English ASA.

Exclusivism and the Origins of Amateurism

In 1967 Dr. Wildor Hollmann, the prominent German sports physician and longtime president of the International Federation for Sports Medicine (FIMS), visited the International Olympic Academy at Olympia on the day of its annual inauguration "with King Constantine himself in attendance" (Hoberman, 1995).

"Naively assuming that the Academy was an open forum for thinking about the past, present, and future of the Olympic movement, Dr. Hollmann expressed the view that, in the not too distant future, the Olympic idea itself would eventually fall victim to the logic of development inherent in the professionalization and commercialization of elite sport. The words were hardly

out of his mouth before Dr. Hollmann was engulfed in a storm of indignation, during which an Italian member of the IOC declared that merely expressing such thoughts was, in his view, nothing less than a desecration of this holy site" (Hoberman, 1995).

Much has been said and written about de Coubertin's "revival" of the Olympic ideal as being part of the games of antiquity. But, in reality, the ancient Olympics were not revived but reinvented, and then presented to the youth of the world in a version more suitable for modern consumption. There was just enough hoopla about the sacred Olympic ideal of ancient Greece to capture their imagination—the panoply of the opening and closing ceremonies, the furling and unfurling of the Olympic flag, the grand diapason of swelling musical harmony, the release of the doves of peace, the relay of the sacred torch, the lighting of the sacred olympic flame, the taking of the sacred oath of amateurism, the marathon, and so on and so on.

All told, this was harmless stuff, and the Olympic motto, "Citius, Altius, Fortius"—"Faster, Higher, Stronger," nevertheless inspired the youth of the world to better performances. Yes, by and large, bringing the youth of the world together in clean competition, and, in a spirit of what used to be called "sportsmanship," was a wonderful development—if only we can ignore the fact that the so-called "Olympic movement" has never really been a democratic organization.

When de Coubertin formed his International Olympic Committee, the first 15 members included 5 European nobles and two generals; the rest were wealthy bourgeois. "Between 1894 and the turn of the century Coubertin added 10 more princes, counts, and barons. From then until 1914, 35 more toffs graciously accepted invitations to run the people's Games. Among them was Coubertin's successor as president of the committee, the Belgian Henri de Baillet-Latour—a count, of course" (Jennings, 1996).

The IOC elects its members for life, and it is a unique organization, in that its members do not represent their countries, but are delegates from the committee to their countries. Work that one out!

Furthermore, members may not accept from other organizations or from their governments any instructions that may bind them or interfere with the independence of their votes. This means that the president of any affiliated international sports federation may not be invited to be a member of the IOC, unless that person agrees not to accept instructions to the IOC from his or her own international federation! In such an instance, the obvious question here is, Who is binding whom? One's own federation or the IOC?

Gentlemen of Means

Baron de Coubertin was influenced by the English concept of character development through sport which originated in the English public schools. The idea of a few amateur athletes participating in heavy training in a training camp originated more than a 100 years ago when the Oxford and Cambridge rowing crews trained together for as long as six hours daily, in a highly disciplined regimen. They were gentlemen of means, and had the private financial resources to be able to do so.

When intensified training in groups for prolonged periods was extended to the broad masses "hands were raised in horror and the cry of professionalism rent the air. It was only when the butchers and bakers, clerks and bricklayers, the plumbers and engineers—especially those of Eastern Europe—applied the Oxbridge formula for sport that the Cardinals of international sport protested" (Riordan, 1978).

After World War II, came the advent of the state amateur. In the former Soviet Union, and other Eastern European countries, sport was conducted under government political control. Every permitted activity had a political significance, and, in reality, there was no distinction between professional and amateur (Riordan, 1978).

Of course, in the West, as elsewhere, many a top athlete found ways and means to cheat the system. But, despite the hypocrisy of shamamateurism, practiced by many individuals and nations, an amateur Games remained the cornerstone of de Coubertin's Olympism.

The Amateur Rules Were Strict

No one was allowed to compete, coach, or officiate for money. Neither could you demand or receive excessive or improper expenses. Selling or pawning prizes was also against the amateur laws.

No amateur could compete against professionals; participate in radio or television broadcasts that advertised any product; capitalize on athletic fame by endorsing products; or sell or solicit the sale of sporting goods, prizes, trophies, and so on used chiefly in connection with sports.

Reimbursement of out-of-pocket expenses, incurred while traveling, was limited to a few dollars per day. Not long ago, there was a rule that restricted traveling to swim meets outside of one's country, apart from major international games, to 30 days in any one year.

From the beginning of the modern Olympic Games a continuous and well-policed effort tried to stem the tide of professionalism. Prior to the Games, each national body was required to certify on a special form, countersigned by the National Olympic Committee, that each competitor was an amateur. Each athlete had to sign a personal declaration that one had never been a professional in any sport.

The great all-round athlete, Jim Thorpe, lost his amateur status and forfeited the Olympic medal he won in Stockholm in 1912, because he admitted having played professional football. Other great athletes deprived of their amateur status based upon proof of having demanded or accepted payment in the guise of grossly excessive expenses were Paavo Nurmi of Finland, Jules Ladoumege of France, Gunder Hagg and Arne Andersson of Sweden, and Wess Santee of the United States. The latter's attempt, by court action, to enjoin the Amateur Athletic Union from enforcing its rules pertaining to amateurism was emphatically rejected by the Supreme Court of the state of New York, on May 15, 1956.

Professional Coaches Were Ostracized

Although the FINA rules only stipulated who could or couldn't compete as an amateur, in many countries, the amateur rules were used to exclude paid coaches from the governing bodies of swimming, and from official coaching assignments with international teams. This was despite the contribution of paid coaches to most of the sport's technical knowledge, and their development of the great swimmers of this century. Instead, they were often openly criticized for having the audacity to make money out of sport.

In several countries, professional coaches always traveled to national and international meets at their own expense to assist their swimmers. Often their swimmers were handed over to amateur managers on the eve of important international meets, and their coaches weren't allowed near them. When the swimmers did well, some managers were apt to take credit for their success, but when the swimmers performed below expectation, their coaches were blamed. In stark contrast was the progress made in the United States, where career coaches were officially recognized as a welcome and integral part of their swimming organization.

A classic case of discrimination against professional coaches, widely noted in the world media at the time, was the treatment by their national governing body of four of the world's finest coaches, who were chiefly responsible for the dramatic resurgence of Australian swimming at the Melbourne Olympic Games in 1956.

Coaches Sam Herford and Frank Guthrie (both now deceased), and Harry Gallagher and Forbes Carlile, were appointed professional coaches prior to the start of the 1956 Games. In the six months preceding the Games, they trained the Australian team at special camps in Townsville, Brisbane, and Sydney. At these venues, while still in training, their charges continually broke world records. In fact, they practically rewrote a good part of the world-record book. But when these much-heralded swimmers arrived in Melbourne for the start of the Games, their coaches were told that "unfortunately, passes to the pool deck could not be obtained for professionals." Neither were they able to stay in the Olympic Village at Heidelberg, and "much contact with their swimmers was cut off."

From Big Losses to Big Money

The strict rules of Olympic amateurism were abandoned through the sheer expediency of saving the Games. The big losses sustained by the organizers of the 1976 Montreal Olympics, said to be close to one billion dollars, put the future of the Olympics in jeopardy. This wasn't helped by the boycott of the 1980 Moscow Games, protesting the Soviet invasion of Afghanistan, led by the United States and a number of other nations, which, in turn, was followed by a Soviet retaliatory boycott of the 1984 Games in Los Angeles, the only city to have applied for the 1984 Games.

The 1984 Olympics, the first free-enterprise Games, produced a 225 million dollar revenue surplus. In 1985 the IOC started a worldwide marketing system called The Olympic Programme (TOP) in which sponsorships or licensing fees were sold to companies for 5 million dollars (US). In this respect, it is interesting to note that Rule 11 of the Olympic Charter states that "The Olympic Games are the exclusive property of the IOC which owns all rights relating thereto, in particular, and without limitation, the rights relating to their organization, exploitation, broadcasting, and reproduction by any means whatsoever."

Cheapening the Product?

The question arises: Is the commercialization of sport cheapening the product? Take for example the increasing number of activities. The number of Olympic events has doubled in the last 50 years, and, in more recent years, the Olympics have been commercialized to the extent that even ballroom dancing has been added to the 2000 Sydney Olympics, undoubtedly because of its large TV following.

The IOC has turned their Games of ancient Greece into a media event, even to the extent that there is no longer room for such sports as the modern pentathlon. Instead, ballroom dancing, professional basketball, and professional tennis have been admitted, and there has even been a sustained effort on behalf of professional golf. Of course, the criterion is money and value to sponsors.

What are the changes brought about by IOC head Juan Antonio Samaranch's vision? Now there is hardly room at the Olympic Games for other than full-time professional athletes. The amateur sports are being squeezed out. The coach is no longer in sole control of the athletes' activities, but rather their agents, business managers, and public relations persons. The place of sport as part of our culture will suffer because, unless there is nearly full-time dedication to training, there can be no thought of Olympic participation. In large measure, the incentive for many a promising athlete who wishes to strike a balance between academia and sport, and who wishes to prepare for a career after sport, has effectively been removed.

Some questions for the future: Will athletes and their coaches call for a greater share of the gigantic Olympian profits? After all, they are the leading players in what constitutes the greatest sporting extravaganza on the planet. And, on a more somber note: Will the prospect of greater financial rewards increase the temptation to join the ever-growing number of drug cheats? Will there be more unannounced drug testing? Will the testers finally get ahead of the chemists? Will the IOC come right out and acknowledge that doping is far more prevalent than they care to admit? Or would such an admission be bad for their corporate image, as well as that of their commercial partners?

The Demise of Amateurism

The ancient Games had always been connected to some religious event. Some say they started as funeral rites to the gods, and it was not until the fourth century that they were held in honor of a living person. Few human enterprises have lasted as long, and perhaps this was because of the connection with religiosity, of one sort or another. The sacred ancient Games lasted from about 776 BC to AD 394. The love of the athletic body, call it athleticism if you will, which was praised in art, music, and literature, and which was probably an important part of the early Olympics, was eventually adulterated by a narrow and greedy desire for victories, primed by an atmosphere of corruption and commercialism. Thus it was that nobody seemed unduly miffed when the Roman emperor called a halt to the entire affair.

Is it possible that history could be in the midst of its usual process of repeating itself? There are many who feel that many aspects of the modern Olympics are likewise becoming irretrievably corrupted.

❖ ❖ ❖

DENIAL IS THE SUREST AFFIRMATIVE

Widespread suspicion greeted the recent performances recorded at the Chinese Games in Shanghai, particularly as there has been the same sudden and astonishing improvement in the three power sports of track and field, swimming, and weight lifting.

Many observers believe the Chinese provinces have increased their systematized doping of athletes after the Atlanta Olympics in a bid to ensure success at the national games, which determines funding levels.

The times recorded by the, er, ladies in the swimming events at the China Games are incredible. They exceed the laws of probability, and therefore we should listen to the prompting of our intuitions. Training should enhance one's powers by means of the body's normal functioning. But drugs do more than just enhance normal functioning. They cause the body to behave abnormally—not unusually well, but unnaturally well.

Illegal technologies are subverting the integrity of sport when we feel inclined to speak of the body, and not the athlete, performing well. We want sport to reward real courage, not sophisticated science. Many think this is not happening, especially when we study the times recorded in Shanghai at the China National Games, in October of 1997.

A Right to Be Suspicious

People recognized the familiar symptoms, when, out of the blue, the Chinese staged an unbelievable recovery from a dismal showing at the last Olympics, and once again, started sweeping all before them. And the Chinese came up with nearly all the same explanations for sudden success that we had heard many years ago from their original mentors, the cheating East Germans.

For 20 years the East Germans cheated. And for 20 years FINA dithered. FINA failed miserably in not making every effort to catch the East Germans who, like the Soviets, were experts at pretesting their athletes to ensure they were clear before allowing them to compete. This was at a time when steroids were fat soluble and stayed in the body longer, making them more easily detectable.

For two decades, the East German officials lied and lied and lied. They insisted, just as the Chinese do now, that they were winning fairly by dint of a superior system, great coaching, and superb athletes.

Names Still Not Erased

All this time, the world of swimming remained highly suspicious, but, to the detriment of dozens of athletes who didn't cheat, not one East German athlete was caught. Investigations have since proved that thousands of East German athletes and swimmers were involved in a program of systematic, state-sponsored, performance-enhancing drug use between 1973 and the collapse of the Berlin Wall in 1989.

Despite these revelations, the IOC and FINA has still not seen fit to erase the offenders' names from the official lists of records and results, and to retroactively award the medals and other honors to those who were dispossessed of what is rightfully theirs.

We are still extremely resentful that these injustices have been allowed to prevail for so long. And we are determined that it will not be allowed to happen again. Therefore, when FINA contends that it is continuing to make out-of-competition tests on Chinese swimmers, we are loathe to take their word for it that all is A-OK in the world of swimming, especially when we recall that, in 1994, FINA, and the IOC too, swore blind that the Chinese swimmers were clean after they had taken 12 of the 16 titles at the 1994 World Championships in Rome.

But, surprise! surprise! Not long afterwards, just prior to the Asian Games later that year, a Japanese testing team caught the Chinese dead to rights as they left their plane at Hiroshima. Our suspicions proved justified when 7 swimmers were among the 11 Chinese who tested positive, before they could reach for their masking agents.

Now, this time around, when we study the sudden and unbelievable results of the Chinese Games in Shanghai, not only in swimming, but also in track and field, and, get this, in the new Olympic sport of women's weight lifting, everyone, except in the abodes of the guilty, agrees that cheating MUST have occurred.

Will Perth be another tainted World Championships? With only three months to go, swimmers and coaches worldwide fear that Perth may produce yet another tainted world championship meet.

Certainly the sport can rely on little succor from the FINA Bureau. FINA is already adopting the same attitude toward the Chinese as they did at the time of the longtime East German cheating. Unless something is done, and done very soon, our sport will have moved from the pool to the cesspool.

So far, despite the stepped-up testing announced by FINA at the World Short Course Championships in Gothenborg, they do not appear to be catching many drug cheaters. With all the testing being conducted by various labs, one would expect a much higher incidence of people testing positive, especially based on the evidence of abnormal recent performances. Whatever the case, FINA can no longer bury their heads in the sand and revert to the "where is the proof?" response used during the erstwhile East German regime.

At this point, I want to quote John Hoberman who wrote in his excellent book, *Mortal Engines,* "Drug testing is difficult for both bureaucratic and scientific reasons. The collection, custody, and accurate scientific analysis of an athlete's urine sample require the personal integrity and competence of all parties concerned, if the system is to work and inspire the confidence that is vital to upholding the moral reputation of elite sport. In addition, scientific knowledge is easily abused: It is common practice to discontinue steroid use long enough in advance of testing to escape detection. Indeed, the East German scientists developed this method to near perfection" (Hoberman, 1992).

Greater Accountability Needed

There are many now who believe that it is FINA that should be providing the actual proof, and no longer their mere verbal assurances, that all the world's leading swimmers are being regularly tested, especially in the all-important three months before major competitions.

Furthermore, the results should be published regularly on the Internet, specifying who was tested, as well as when and where and by what lab. Information should also be provided on which athletes are never available when the testers call. And, while we are at it, it might be a good idea for the swimming public to know the names of all the certified labs employed in testing swimmers worldwide.

Instead of asking those who doubt the recent Chinese performances to back their accusations with facts instead of intuition, the time has come for FINA itself to become fully accountable for providing testing results right out front, in full view of the swimming public. Such an action would do much to establish some confidence in FINA, and the job it says it is doing.

FINA has a chance to redeem itself by putting officers into China (at the invitation of the China Swim Federation, helping them to save face, if you like) to oversee a massive and regular testing campaign both in their sports schools and the provinces, between now and the World Championships in Perth next January. Furthermore, they now know who to test, and their coaches should know where and when to find them, and, moreover, how to find them quickly.

It is more than likely that FINA will respond negatively to such a suggestion because they cannot risk China spoiling the cash cow by pulling out of the 2000 Olympics. According to the World Bank, China is one of five nations, along with Russia, Indonesia, India, and Brazil, expected to experience the fastest economic growth over the next quarter century, and the IOC certainly would be loathe to let this source of potential funding slip through their hands. If China were to pull out of the Olympic family, a.k.a. the world's largest professional sports conglomerate, it is not inconceivable that China, through her trade and political connections, could influence several other nations, both in Asia and Africa, to do the same.

Hoffmann Confesses: Australians in an Uproar

As far as the Australians are concerned, the new round of obvious cheating by the Chinese could not have come at a worse time. Almost simultaneously with the news from Shanghai came the sensational confession by Jorg Hoffmann, the former East German 1,500 world-record holder, that, way back in 1988, he had started taking oral Turinabol, a banned anabolic substance.

In the 1991 world swimming championships in Perth, Hoffmann had triumphed over the two young Australians, Kieren Perkins and Glen Houseman, breaking the world record with a time of 14:50.36, still ranked fourth fastest of all time. Swimming is a national sport in Australia with a long and honorable tradition, and so it is understandable that the Australian nation was particularly riled to learn that their two young heroes had not only been cheated, but cheated on their own native soil.

Don Talbot, the head Australian swimming coach, was furious, and, suffice it to say, his description of Hoffmann was highly unflattering. Kieren Perkins, for his part, said that he wouldn't request that Hoffmann's gold medal be taken from him.

When I read the caption to this story in the *Sydney Morning Herald*, "I don't want Hoffmann's drug medal, says Perkins," I couldn't help but reflect on how much the sport of swimming has changed in recent years.

Perkins also said that "the latest drug-taking revelations had shown that in-competition testing was useless." Perkins also called for tough penalties for athletes who kept avoiding out-of-competition testing. Perkins said that, technically, people who avoided a drug test in competition, were supposed to be banned for two or four years automatically, and that a no-show is classified as a positive result. Perkins believes that the same rule should also be enforced for out-of-competition testing, and with an iron fist, because at the moment, people are throwing obstacles in the way of the testers. "It gets to the point where after a while they can't find athletes, they can't test them, and at the end of the day, they can't really come down hard on them."

Back to the Old Cat-and-Mouse Game

I wrote two years ago in "We're in for a Long Siege," (*Swimnews*, October 1994) that "attack and retreat will be the order of the day, and that, given the opportunity, China could play a waiting cat-and-mouse game well into the next century. In the end, if long-term suspensions prove completely ineffective, total expulsion may become the only answer."

Whatever happens, as I've said before, it is possible that international swimming could split right down the middle between those who play the game according to the rules and those who don't. As it is, the IOC is seeking uniformity among all the Olympic sports in suggesting that there should be a maximum two-year suspension for testing positive instead of the four-year suspension that exists in swimming, for example. In the light of the recent events in Shanghai and elsewhere, there is little chance now of a large segment of world swimming agreeing to water down the four-year maximum suspension as punishment for contravening the laws governing performance-enhancing substances.

Keeping FINA on Their Toes

Ian Hansen, media representative of Australian Swimming Inc., said that the Australian head coach, Don Talbot had particularly noted "the remarkable improvement of Chen Yan in the 400-meter individual medley and freestyle. She had taken 20 seconds off her best times in both events in the last 12 months.

"She's gone from 22nd in the Olympic freestyle to number one in the world and, in the medley, from 4 minutes 53 seconds in the Olympics to a world record 4:30," Hanson said. "At 15, such an improvement is unheard of. There's no explanation other than drugs."

Hanson added that Australian Swimming had written to FINA "to keep them on their toes and ensure out-of-competition testing is done. We believe it's time for other countries, particularly European, to stand up and be counted and follow Australia's antidrugs stance."

New Drugs?

Don Talbot fears that even if IOC drug testing is stepped up in China, cheats will escape because they are using undetectable growth hormones. "If we are serious about drug testing, then you have to do more than pee in a bottle," said Talbot, who called for blood testing to be introduced to help detect the illegal use of hormones.

How Do the Chinese Explain It? Asks One of the Pioneers of Swimming Science

"They have had a huge improvement in the last 13 months, and how do they explain such dramatic increases in nearly every event in swimming?" asked Forbes Carlile, who is a member of the World Swim Coaches antidoping commission.

"As well as two world records in the pool, including astounding results by medley swimmers, Chen Yan and Wu Yanyan, who slashed nearly two seconds off the 400-meter and 200-meter individual medleys, respectively, Chinese women have set 10 times which were faster than those at the Atlanta Olympics. At the 1996 Games, the Chinese won only one swimming medal—to Le Jingyi—and blamed their poor results on inadequate training methods.

At Shanghai, records have been smashed in weight lifting and track and field. Three world records have been set by male lifters and the females have bettered world standards in all eight weight divisions.

On the Running Track as Well

On the track, Li Xuemei clocked a phenomenal 10.79 seconds for the 100 meter, which bettered that of U.S. world champion, Marion Jones, who clocked 10.83 at the World Championships in Athens. Li also competed in Athens, but clocked 11.2 and was ran out in the second round.

In the heats of the 1,500 meter, there were 12 female athletes who clocked under 4 minutes. In comparison, the previous fastest time in the world this year was 3:58, set by Briton Kelly Holmes.

Carlile said FINA needed to impose regular weekly and unannounced drug tests on the Chinese athletes, to reassure the rest of the world that their performances were not aided in artificial ways.

"What's needed is for FINA to station a drug tester permanently in China, to test swimmers with no notice and with great frequency," Carlile said. "It will be a battleground in Perth if there are positive tests. We can't stand by and watch this happen."

✧ ✧ ✧

DISCUSSION WITH JOE KING

Coolangatta, Queensland, Australia, May 1996. When Joe King started to coach his twin daughters, he soon had a squad of about 30 youngsters under his tutelage. Before he knew it, he had become hooked on the sport.

Joe King, the 86-year-old Australian swimming coach, is probably the world's oldest swim coach. He's not only the oldest, but also one of the sport's feistiest and most successful.

You'll have no problem in spotting Joe King at a swim meet. Just look for a white-haired, suntanned gentleman in a maroon track suit. Yes, always a maroon track suit. Not for Joe King the designer golf shirts worn by fellow coaches, most of whom are about two generations younger. Wearing his familiar track suit is Joe's way of showing that he is there to do a job of work, to be always in the thick of things, just like his swimmers.

And, when warm-up time is over, Joe stands on the deck, radiating enthusiasm and good humor, cheerfully chatting to coaches and swimmers alike. You'll rarely see a coach so obviously enjoying every moment of a swim meet.

I spoke to Joe in 1996 at the Australian Olympic trials at Homebush, Sydney. "If anyone had told me that I would one day coach or manage an Australian Olympic swimming team, I would have said, 'You're stark, staring mad.' In fact, I had been very ill with ulcerative colitis, and I was in a bit of a mess as a result. I was as thin as a whip. Mahatma Gandhi would have looked like 'Jake the Fat Man' compared to me."

Joe took ill in 1949, and was in poor health for a few years, but it was about this time that he became interested in swimming. One of his twin daughters contracted meningitis at the age of seven weeks, and, as a result, she became totally deaf. When she was older, Joe decided to enroll her in a swimming club to broaden her social skills.

An Interfering Age-Group Coach

One Saturday, Joe King was sitting at the pool watching the coach work. "I thought to myself, 'Well, I don't know anything about this sport, but if I can't do better than that, I'll eat my hat.'" The result was that Joe started to coach his daughters. "I started off as an interfering age-group parent, you might say. Then their friends saw what was happening, and they too wanted to come along."

Soon, King had a squad of about 30 youngsters under his tutelage, and, before he knew it, he had become hooked on the sport, so much so that, in 1956, when the Australian Olympic team arrived from their pre-Olympic training in Townsville to train in the Valley Pool in Brisbane, King spent day after day watching them train.

"I was amazed at their freestyle arm action, and the way they got their shoulders well into the stroke. One of the very interesting aspects of that training period at the Valley Pool was that they trained on pure oxygen. They had tanks of oxygen there, and immediately after an effort swim, they would go to the tank, clap the mask on, and then inhale pure oxygen."

King became so absorbed in coaching that he worked about 15 hours a day, coping with his regular job, while at the same time improving his knowledge of coaching.

A Difficult Choice

At this early stage of his coaching career, King was faced with the choice of either retaining his regular highly paid job as circulation director of Queensland newspapers or becoming a full-time coach. It is common knowledge that a coach renting a public pool could never be sure of not being outbid at the end of the rental period.

King thought long and hard about the problem. Finally, the difficulty involved in retaining a long-term tenure of any pool in Queensland deterred him from giving up his existing job. King said, "A swimming pool tenure rarely lasts longer than three years, at which point someone is bound to outbid you eventually, and so you would lose the use of the pool."

King couldn't see the benefit in conducting a full-time coaching school. It would have involved turning in a very good job with a high salary, so he decided to carry on coaching part-time. "I never imagined where I would finish up," he said.

An Impressive Coaching Record

Joe King became an assistant coach at the Leander Club, one of Australia's most famous, and eventually became the head coach. In addition to his full-time job, and his part-time coaching, Joe King astounded everybody by successfully coaching netball and basketball at the same time. "I undertook these extra assignments so that I could involve my daughter with a variety of different people and thus broaden her horizons."

Joe King says that he had no formal training in how to coach swimming, "perhaps only a natural aptitude." It was not until 1965 that he produced his first Australian swimming champion, a girl by the name of Jill Groeger. "She went to the last of the British Empire Games in Kingston, Jamaica, in 1966. She was a very good flyer. She got beaten by a fraction of a second by Lyn McClement who went on to win the Olympic butterfly title in Mexico City two years later. That's the way it works out in sport, I suppose," says King. "You have to be spot on at that particular moment when history is being made."

Another of Joe King's early swimmers, Joanne Marnes, was selected for the Australian team at 12 years of age, when she broke the Australian record for 200 breaststroke. In the other states they could not believe that she had broken the 200 record at this tender age, and even though she didn't participate in the trials she was selected for the team.

Joe King developed a spectacular coaching record over the years, made all the more meritorious by the fact that he remained a part-time coach, while continuing to hold down a demanding full-time job that carried great responsibility. Yes, this amazing, erstwhile, age-group parent went on to produce Australian champions in all strokes, swimmers such as Hayley Lewis, Lisa Curry, Rebecca Brown, Michelle Pearson, Judy Hudson, Paul Moorfoot, Sue Landells, Jill Groeger, Joanne Marnes, Lindsay Spencer, Alison Smith, Glenda Robertson, Joe Dixon, and many, many others. Yet, for 13 years, Joe King was never appointed to coach an Australian team, probably because he was "only a part-time coach, a hobbyist, as it were!"

Appointed to National Teams

"At that time the officials were responsible for appointing the team coaches. It was not until the 1976 Montreal Olympics that I was appointed manager of the swimming team. In 1978 I was a coach for the Edmonton Commonwealth Games team. That was a rare milestone in my coaching career. After that, I was on every Australian team and had some great experiences.

"One tour that stands out in my mind was a six-nation meet in 1983 at Chundo-do, 3,000 kilometers deep into China. It was quite a revelation. I can't remember the point score, because this was some time ago. The meet was efficiently conducted, and they were eager to learn. They invited Coach John Rogers and myself to give an in-depth coaching seminar.

"One of the things that I thought would influence their swimming was that the Chinese people from the countryside were brought up on very basic sustenance foods. They were living very close to the earth, and I felt that they had the physical resources to become great swimmers. At that stage, their team was under the charge of a Chinese coach. East German coaches had yet to visit

China. After that, their women's performances seemed to predominate."

King said that he was coach of an Australian team until 1986 in Edinburgh. He didn't represent Australia again until 1992 at Barcelona. "But, even though I wasn't officially on any team at that time, I traveled at my own expense to meets where my swimmers were competing on the Australian team."

Training to Race Well

King's swimmers produced some outstanding performances at the 1990 Commonwealth Games, where his swimmers won nine gold medals, and Haylie Lewis became the first woman to win five golds.

King said that, although he wasn't on the team, he coached his swimmers to be self-sufficient and capable of performing well on their own.

King coaches on the basis that a swimmer needs two things to win a race: speed and endurance. "In my squad, everything they do has to be oriented towards racing. I want them to do the job absolutely perfectly all the way."

Perhaps the most impressive aspect of Joe King's approach to coaching is that he never loses sight of the fact that he is not only training swimmers to swim fast, but also to be able to race well. He says, "All your training should be devoted to the end goal of racing. A swimmer should develop good habits, not bad habits. Good habits should become engrained in the subconscious mind so that the swimmer will not be able to do it in any other way."

He continued, "It is remarkable to what extent lack of concentration will adversely affect a swimmer's performance. For example, you see a large number of swimmers who swim around the black line, instead of on it, and, as a result, they will swim further than they have to do. Inevitably this sloppiness will add to their racing times."

Asked how he impressed these important aspects of racing upon a swimmer's mind, King said that he achieved this goal by having the swimmer swim a time trial at the start of a training session. This becomes an actual rehearsal of the race, to be done with error-free swimming. This means having the swimmer swim straight down the center of the lane, insisting that the turn be absolutely spot on, and that the finish also be as perfect as possible, with no breathing once the swimmer has passed under the flags, doing everything as absolutely perfect as possible.

King says that when his swimmers enter the water to start a training session, they have to dive off the starting block as if they are actually starting a race for the gold medal.

Genetic Superiority of Champions

King doesn't believe it possible to coach an average, ordinary individual to a championship standard. "They need to have genetic superiority over other individuals in the sport of swimming. The funny thing about it is that the genes are passed down over the years, and all of a sudden, they match up, and a supreme athlete is born. It spreads away again, and it never seems to happen again in the same family. It's amazing. There's only one instance I know of in Australian sport where this has been contradicted, and that was with the two Konrads, and they were different sexes. There was never another boy the same, and never another girl the same."

King believes that, at the present time, Australia's level one coaches are not applying enough attention to stroke correction. "They are tied up with the modern terminology of stroke rate, etcetera. Now, I cannot come to terms with stroke rate unless you have stroke distance at the same time, because, if your stroke length is not relevant, stroke rate is entirely unrelated to speed through the water. I believe that the most important factor is stroke length: the application of force against the water. For instance, if you double your stroke rate and decrease your stroke length by half, all that you are doing is that you're burning yourself out faster, with no gain in speed."

Still talking about stroke rate, Joe King said, "I've developed a reputation for knowing a little bit more about breaststroke. What I find is that, in about 90 percent of young breaststroke swimmers, they don't apply the hand and forearm efficiently against the water. The reason is that they slide the hand across the water without really catching the water, and they turn over too fast. In the case of Rebecca Brown, I changed her arm stroke completely by making her roll her arm right over until her thumbs were pointed down, with the whole of the hand and forearm against the water. Then she squeezes the elbows down and inward, in front of the body. I felt that gave her greater application against the water.

"One question that interests me is: What can we do in the future to make swimming more efficient, and more fish-like? And this leaves me to speculate on what our swimmers will be doing in another 40 or 50 years time."

Asked to take a guess, King replied, "I don't know. If I knew, I would be applying it today, but it makes me wonder what will happen in the search for greater application on the water."

King came back to represent Australia as a coach at Don Talbot's request. "I had four swimmers on the 1992 Barcelona team. Don wanted me on the team and asked me to put my name forward for nomination, and I did, and thoroughly enjoyed it. Barcelona was a great meet, and I enjoyed the experience all over again."

Ernest Joseph ("Joe") King, Australia Medal, Olympic swimming coach, born in Ipswich, Queensland, Australia, January 24, 1911, died in Brisbane on December 21st, 1997. He was 86.

Epilogue

SWIMMING FIGHTS FOR ITS LIFE

Not in their wildest dreams was anyone prepared for the drama that unfolded at the 1998 World Championships in Perth.

All eyes were upon the Chinese team when they arrived to compete in the World Championships in Perth last month. Only a year after their dismal showing at the Atlanta Olympics, they had shown a sudden and unbelievable recovery at the Chinese Games last October in Shanghai. There was worldwide suspicion that, after seven of their number had tested positive in September 1994, at the Asian Games, and six more in January 1996, they were once again using performance-enhancing drugs.

Without a doubt, the scene was set for a conflagration of the first order should anything untoward happen. But not in their wildest dreams was anyone prepared for the drama that was to unfold on January 8, 1998.

Ironically, on this same day, 100 years earlier, Alick Wickham had first swum his overarm crawl at Bronte, only a mile from where Sydney Airport now stands, and where a customs officer was to discover 13 vials of somatropin, a synthetic human growth hormone in the baggage of a 21-year-old Chinese swimmer, Yuan Yuan. They had been placed there by her coach, Zhou Zhewen, who said that he hadn't enough space in his own luggage.

After the contents of the vials had been analyzed and confirmed by the Australian Government Analytical Laboratory, FINA suspended Zhewen from national and international competition for 15 years, and Yuan was banned for 4 years.

On that same day, 2,500 miles to the west in Perth, another story was unfolding. The first contingent of Chinese swimmers had already arrived, and were being tested by officials from the Australian Drug Agency, acting on behalf of FINA, the sport's international governing body. Six days later, another bombshell dropped when it was announced that four swimmers, Luna Wang, Cai Huijue, Zhang Yi, and Wang Wei, had tested positive to the banned drug, Triamterene, a diuretic used to mask steroid use. They were temporarily suspended pending confirmation.

China was most fortunate that the four swimmers had not been caught with actual steroids in their systems rather than the diuretic masking agent. Had this been the case, the entire country automatically would have been banned from international competition. However, FINA had decided at their 1995 congress that penalties for diuretic offenses would apply only to individuals, and carry a maximum two-year ban.

A Cry from the Heart

The resultant media coverage of the drug scandals at the World Championships in Perth was unimaginable. It quickly became a major international news story carried by newspapers worldwide, and viewed on TV by millions.

To the dismay of the organizers who had worked hard for some years to make the event a success, the meet threatened to become a fiasco even before it got started. Never in the history of competitive swimming has the sport received so much publicity, and most of it very distressing.

Every newspaper in Australia, from the most conservative to the tabloids, ran pages and pages on the developing scandals, usually on the front page and back page, and several inside pages as well. In Europe and much of Asia, the news hit the front pages of sports sections of the big metropolitan newspapers.

In China, in the abodes of the guilty, little or nothing was said. In the United States and Canada, where swimming is a minor sport, the reporting was minimal.

The clamor in Australia was not surprising. Many of Australia's top swimming journalists are either knowledgeable former swimmers, or people steeped in the traditions of their country's illustrious swimming history. They had long resented the insult to their intelligence caused by the continued and persistent cheating by Chinese swimmers with their large number of positive tests. Thus enraged, they gleaned the story and dissected it to the very bones, often to the acute embarrassment of FINA's highest officials.

They were astonished that, over the last 4 years, the Chinese had taken such small heed of world opinion as to continue brazenly along the reckless path that now has led to widespread ostracism by their fellow competitors. A total of 28 Chinese swimmers have tested positive for banned substances, and one coach also has been suspended for 15 years. The vast majority of the cases have occurred over the last 8 years. In comparison the record for other countries is USSR 7; Austria 4; USA 3; Canada, Germany, Australia 2; and Britain, Tunisia, Egypt, Argentina, Poland, Indonesia, Brazil, Finland, France, New Zealand, Ukraine 1.

Many of the world's leading coaches and swimmers, including Olympians Mark Spitz, Murray Rose, Shane Gould, Jenny Thompson, Tracy Wickham, and many others, were outraged that the long-recognized drug problem in swimming had been allowed to fester for so long and become an open, bleeding wound. For them, and many like them, this was a cry from the heart for the salvation of the sport. They called for the outright banning of China from all international swimming. "They should be banned for 10 years," said Mark Spitz, who had won a record 7 gold medals at the 1972 Munich Olympics. Even Juan Antonio Samaranch, head of the IOC, felt moved to say that "persistent cases of doping by Chinese athletes hurt that country's hopes of one day holding the Olympics."

No Useful Purpose

No useful purpose is served, at this late date, by delving too deeply into what was said in the midst of the uproar. There has been too much divisiveness in the sport already, largely as a result of the actions of those who persistently sought to flout the rules, and those in high places who likewise continued to ask for proof of wrongdoing when, in their heart of hearts, they must have known that something was badly wrong.

In fairness to FINA, however, it must be said that the amazing course of events, highlighted by the continued impudence of the offending swimmers caught everyone unaware. And, to its credit FINA, at last, has announced the formation of a task force of international experts in medical science, research and forensics, to strengthen its drug-testing procedures. The team will include experienced team doctors and administrators, and will hold its first meeting in Lausanne on March 5–6 where it will examine new testing methods, including random blood testing, in an effort to speed up the detection of hGH and erythropoietin (EPO). FINA also promised to send a delegation to China in February to examine the issues and concerns raised by positive drug tests and to report back with recommendations on various subjects within six months of being appointed.

But, even now, the story still simmers as the media and the swimming public wait for further developments in the midst of threatened boycotts of World Cup meets in China, that well may not come to pass if FINA manages to dissuade the various parties from doing so. (For example, it is reported that Germany has done a backflip, and has now decided to participate.)

Nevertheless, the obvious need to urge the Chinese Swimming Association to establish control over the sport in its country remains even more pressing now than when seven of their swimmers tested positive in 1994. At that time, the Chinese authorities promised the visiting FINA commission to clean their house by "introducing strict punitive measures to discourage drug cheats," but now, four years later, the situation hasn't changed.

In fact, with the first-time discovery of hGH in a swimmer's possession, the situation has worsened and needs to be urgently addressed and rectified. The Chinese Swimming Association needs to rid itself of the perception that they have been unfairly victimized. The serious problems they have are problems that they have brought upon themselves.

For a start, their drug testers should examine a little more carefully the dynamic curves caused by maximum peak performances (such as at their national games), and the necessary subsequent downtime needed to enable target cells to regenerate. Even better, they could discontinue these national games, where reportedly large rewards are made to successful athletes, and where, as a result, they often swim faster than they do in the Olympics.

Demoralizing Effects

The demeaning aspect of the drug problem is the way it tends to drag us all down. A large element of distrust exists in the sport, not only because of drug cheating, but because so many self-seeking politicians and bureaucrats now hold sway.

The drug problem has caused acrimony and divisiveness, accusations and counteraccusations. The persistence of the drug pestilence in competitive swimming is destroying the integrity, the morale, and the very fiber of our sport. Consider the suspicion that often greets an outstanding performance. "Is this swim drug tainted or not?" This tendency is one of the worst side effects of the drug problem. Not too long ago, it would never have entered our minds to think that someone was cheating.

Contrary to what some have said about the media tearing the house down, a great debt of gratitude is owed to those who have focused attention on the fact that something is radically wrong with our sport. Their continued focus on the problem may yet help to turn the tide in swimming's fight for survival. The only ray of light that remains is that so many swimmers, even though there may be a cash reward at the end of the line, continue to develop their skills, strength, and endurance by self-discipline and natural means, rather than by resorting to performance-enhancing drugs. They continue to show the courage, faith, and honor that may yet reclaim the sport for those who still believe in its finer values.

SOURCE LIST IN CHAPTER ORDER

Much of the material reproduced in this book was first published in the journals listed below. The author once more acknowledges with thanks the cooperation and encouragement of the respective publishers and editors.

Swimming World and Junior Swimmer, Swimming Technique, and *Swim Magazine,* published by Sports Publications, Inc., P.O. Box 20337, Sedona, AZ, 86341. Telephone: (520) 284-4005, Fax: (520) 284-2477, E-mail: SwimWorld-@aol.com, website: http://www.swiminfo.com. Publishers: Richard Deal and Gerry Rodrigues, editor-in-chief: Phillip Whitten. *Swimming World*: Long-established (1952) monthly magazine for competitive swimmers of all ages, as well as for coaches and opinion leaders in the sport, covers all major meets in the world, provides profiles of leading swimmers, offers tips on stroke techniques. *SWIM Magazine*: The world's leading authority on adult swimming is written for adult fitness and Masters swimmers. Published bimonthly, it offers advice on training, health and nutrition, technique and training tips, as well as feature articles profiling leading Masters swimmers. *Swimming Technique*: Published quarterly, it is written primarily for coaches (and for self-coached adult swimmers). Each issue focuses on aspects of technique and training being utilized by top swimmers and coaches around the world.

Swimnews (previously published as *Swim Canada* 1974-Oct.1996.) 356 Sumach Street, Toronto, Ontario, Canada, M4X 1V4 Telephone: (416) 963-5599, Fax (416) 963-5545, E-mail: swimnews@ibm.net, website: http://www.swimnews.com. Publisher and editor, Nick J. Thierry. *Swimnews* covers major meets worldwide, provides expert comment and opinion on topical issues, as well as personality profiles on the world's leading swimmers and coaches. A unique feature: regularly updated statistics by International Statistical Support Group.

❖ ❖ ❖

Prologue
Colwin, Cecil M. (1994). Swimming in the little town of Bethlehem. Swim Magazine. 10(2), Mar./Apr., 25–27.

Chapter 1 THE COACH-SWIMMER-TEAM-PROGRAM DYNAMIC
Colwin, Cecil M. (1994). The intuitive coach. *Swim Canada*, 21(6), Jun. 4–5.

Colwin, Cecil M. (1993). Thoughts on the team dynamic. *Swimming Technique*, 20(4), Feb./Apr. 7–8.

Colwin, Cecil M. (1993). Swim pools, clubs, and coaches. *Swim Canada*, 20(4), Apr. 8–9.

Colwin, Cecil M. (1994). Eagles don't fly in formation. *Swimming Technique*, Aug./Oct. 9–11.

Colwin, Cecil M. (1993). Let's put the swimmer first. *Swim Canada*, 20(1), Jan. 4–5.

Colwin, Cecil M. (1995). Gold that doesn't glitter. *Swimming Technique*, 32(2), Aug./Oct., 7.

Colwin, Cecil M. (1993). Should swimmers be lean and mean or just plain happy? *Swim Canada*, 20(2), Feb., 8.

Colwin, Cecil M. (1993). Beware the psych-out artist. *Swim Canada*, 20(3), Mar., 12.

Colwin, Cecil M. (1993). Valid criticism: an essential part of coaching. (Original title: Well intended criticism.) *Swimming Technique*, 30(1), May/Jul., 8–9.

Colwin, Cecil M. (1995). Societal changes and commitment. (Original title: A sport in transition.) *Swimming Technique*, 31(3), Nov./Jan., 34–36.

Colwin, Cecil M. (1996). High school swimming is big in South Africa. *Swimming Technique*, 33(1), Jul./Sept., 7–8.

Colwin, Cecil M. (1993). Program planning: the human factor. *Swim Canada*, 20(5), May, 8.

Colwin, Cecil M. (1974). Taking stock at Concord. *Swimming World*, 15(10), Oct.

Colwin, Cecil M. (1975). East German swimming. *Swimming World*, 16(8), Aug.

Colwin, Cecil M. (1994). Layers not depths. *Swim Canada*, 21(10) Oct., 27–28.

Colwin, Cecil M. (1993). Keeping your cool when anger strikes. *Swimming Technique*, 30(3), Nov./Jan., 7–8.

Colwin, Cecil M. (1995). Mental aspects of the taper. *Swimming Technique*, 31(4), Feb./Apr., 6–8.

Chapter 2 SWIMMING TECHNIQUES

Colwin, Cecil M. (1997). The butterfly. *Swimming Technique*, 34(3), Oct./Dec., 6–9.

Colwin, Cecil M. (1998). The backstroke. *Swimming Technique*, 34(4), Jan./Mar., 5–8.

Colwin, Cecil M. (1998). The crawl stroke. *Swimming Technique*, 35(1), Apr./Jun., 10–13.

Colwin, Cecil M. (1998). The wave action breaststroke. *Swimming Technique*, 35(2), Sept./Nov.

Colwin, Cecil M. (1997). The bandwagon effect. *Swimming Technique*, 34(1), Jul./Sept., 7.

Colwin, Cecil M. (1993). Improve your feel of the water. *Swim Canada*, 20(9), Sept., 11.

Colwin, Cecil M. (1995). We don't swim in dry water. *Swim Canada*, 22(5), May, 4–8.

Colwin, Cecil M. (1996). Stroke technique or stroke production? (Original title: The purpose of stroke drills.) *Swimming Technique*, Winter, 6–10.

Colwin, Cecil M. (1995). "RTR"—Relating training to the pace of the race. *Swimming Technique*, 32(2), May/Jul., 7–8.

Colwin, Cecil M. (1984). Tethered swimming. *Swim Canada*, 11(3), Mar., 20–21.

Chapter 3 FROM THE PACIFIC CAME THE CRAWL

Colwin, Cecil M. (1994). Introduction: Why study swimming history? *Swim Canada*, 21(3), Mar., 5.

Colwin, Cecil M. (1993). English swim coach executed for treason. *Swim Canada*, 20(6), Jun., 25.

Colwin, Cecil M. (1993). Thevenot (1620–1692)—the world's first scientist-coach. *Swim Canada*, 20(7), Jul., 21–22.

Colwin, Cecil M. (1993). How Ben Franklin coaxed his pupils into the Delaware. *Swim Canada*, 20(8), Aug., 19.

Colwin, Cecil M. (1997). From the "Huki" came the crawl. *Swimming Technique*, 33(4), Apr./Jun., 18.

Colwin, Cecil M. (1993). How "Little Alick" crawled to fame. *Swim Canada*, 20(10), Oct., 36.

Colwin, Cecil M. (1994). The "School of Sydney." *Swim Canada*, 21(2), Feb., 5–6.

Colwin, Cecil M. (1995). The crawl becomes a distance stroke. *Swim Canada*, 22(1), Jan., 8.

Colwin, Cecil M. (1994). The Daniels dynasty. *Swim Canada*, 21(5), May, 10–11.

Colwin, Cecil M. (1994). Duke Kahanamoku: the gentleman swimmer. *Swim Canada*, 21(8), Aug., 11.

Colwin, Cecil M. (1995). A Japanese swimmer was one of swimming's great visionaries. *Swim Canada*, 22(3), Mar., 20.

Colwin, Cecil M. (1997). 50-year saga of the breaststroke rules, part 1. *Swimnews*, 24(2), Apr., 22–23.

Colwin, Cecil M. (1997). 50-year saga of the breaststroke rules, part 2. *Swimnews*, 24(5), May, 28–29.

Colwin, Cecil M. (1997). 50-year saga of the breaststroke rules, part 3. *Swimnews*, 24 (6), Jun., 6–7.

Colwin, Cecil M. (1997). When is a stroke not a stroke? When it's a kick. *Swimnews*, 24(6), Jun., 8–9.

Colwin, Cecil M. (1997). Wanted: exhibition events for underwater swimming. *Swimnews*, 24(8), Aug., 30–33.

Chapter 4 SWIMMING THE 1,500 METER: THE BLUE RIBBON OF SWIMMING

Colwin, Cecil M. (1996). Introduction: Whatever happened to the distance base? *Swimming Technique*, 33(2), Summer, 4–6.

Colwin, Cecil M. (1996). Bill Nelson discusses 1,500 meter star, Daniel Kowalski. (Original title: Will the "old swimming factory" produce an Olympic champion?) *Swim Canada*, 23(7) Jul., 22–23.

Colwin, Cecil M. (1996). The author talks with John Carew. (Original title: Swimming the 1,500 out fast: John Carew was looking for a swimmer to prove a pet theory. Then Kieren Perkins, a skinny eight-year-old, came along.) *Swim Canada*, 23(7) Jul., 8–9.

Colwin, Cecil M. (1997). What made Kieren great? *Swimnews*, 24(2), Feb., 28.

Chapter 5 THE PIONEERS OF WOMEN'S SWIMMING

Colwin, Cecil M. (1996). Fifty women started a world-famous swim club. *Swim Canada*, 23(1), Jan., 18.

Colwin, Cecil M. (1995). Amateur coach was the world authority on the crawl stroke. *Swim Canada*, 22(8), Aug., 16–17.

Colwin, Cecil M. (1995). Handley stood for more than winning at any cost. *Swim Canada*, 22(10), Oct., 38–40.

Colwin, Cecil M. (1996). The pioneers of women's swimming. *Swim Canada*, 23(1), Jan., 18.

Colwin, Cecil M. (1996). The progress of women's swimming. *Swim Canada*, 23(2), Feb., 8–9

Colwin, Cecil M. (1993). A vintage year for women at the Hall of Fame. *Swim Canada*, 20(6), Jun., 12–13.

Chapter 6 THIRTY YEARS OF DISCUSSIONS WITH LEADING FIGURES

Colwin, Cecil M. (1983). Discussions with "Doc" Counsilman. *Swim Canada*, 10(2), Feb., 18–20.

Colwin, Cecil (1969). The author talks with James Counsilman 1966. *Cecil Colwin on swimming*, (pp. 151–154). London: Pelham Books. Copyright by Cecil Colwin.

Colwin, Cecil (1969). The author talks with Forbes Carlile 1967. *Cecil Colwin on swimming*, (pp. 200–204). London: Pelham Books. Copyright by Cecil Colwin.

Colwin, Cecil (1969). The author talks with Arthur Cusack 1967. *Cecil Colwin on swimming*, (pp. 205–207). London: Pelham Books. Copyright by Cecil Colwin.

Colwin, Cecil (1969). The author talks with Sherman Chavoor 1966. *Cecil Colwin on swimming*, (pp. 149–150). London: Pelham Books. Copyright by Cecil Colwin.

Colwin, Cecil M. (1984). Discussion with Sherman Chavoor. *Swim Canada*, Mar., 12–13.

Colwin, Cecil (1969). The author talks with Peter Daland 1966. *Cecil Colwin on swimming*, (pp. 155–159). London: Pelham Books. Copyright by Cecil Colwin.

Colwin, Cecil M. (1983). Discussion with Peter Daland. *Swim Canada*, Aug., 18–19.

Colwin, Cecil (1969). The author talks with Donna de Varona 1966. *Cecil Colwin on swimming*, (pp. 182–183). London: Pelham Books. Copyright by Cecil Colwin.

Colwin, Cecil (1969). The author talks with John Devitt 1966. *Cecil Colwin on swimming*, (pp. 208–211). London: Pelham Books. Copyright by Cecil Colwin.

Colwin, Cecil M. (1983). Discussion with Ray Essick. *Swim Canada*, 10(4), Apr., 16–17.

Colwin, Cecil (1969). The author talks with Don Gambril 1966. *Cecil Colwin on swimming*, (pp. 162–167). London: Pelham Books. Copyright by Cecil Colwin.

Colwin, Cecil M. (1983). Discussion with Don Gambril. *Swim Canada*, 10(4), Jul., 14–15.

Colwin, Cecil (1969). The author talks with George Haines 1966. *Cecil Colwin on swimming*, (pp. 168–172). London: Pelham Books. Copyright by Cecil Colwin.

Colwin, Cecil M. (1983). Discussions with George Haines (Original title: Colwin talks to Haines.) *Swim Canada*, 10(6), Jun., 12–13.

Colwin, Cecil M. (1983). Discussion with Jim Montrella. *Swim Canada*, Oct., 34–35.

Colwin, Cecil (1969). The author talks with Walter Schlueter 1966. *Cecil Colwin on swimming*, (pp. 173–175). London: Pelham Books. Copyright by Cecil Colwin.

Colwin, Cecil M. (1983). Discussion with Mark Schubert. *Swim Canada*, Mar., 30.

Colwin, Cecil M. (1984). Discussion with Jonty Skinner. *Swim Canada*, Apr., 30.

Colwin, Cecil (1969). The author talks with Gus Stager 1966. *Cecil Colwin on swimming*, (pp. 176–177). London: Pelham Books. Copyright by Cecil Colwin.

Colwin, Cecil M. (1984). Discussion with Don Talbot. *Swim Canada*, Jun., 32–34.

Colwin, Cecil M. (1984). Discussion with Karen Moe Thornton. *Swim Canada*, May, 14–15.

Colwin, Cecil (1969). The author talks with Stan Tinkham 1966. *Cecil Colwin on swimming*, (pp. 178–180). London: Pelham Books. Copyright by Cecil Colwin.

Colwin, Cecil M. (1996). Discussion with Gennadi Touretski on Alexandre Popov. *Swimnews*, 23 (10), Oct.

Chapter 7 GREAT PERSONALITIES PAST AND PRESENT

Colwin, C. M. (1994). The talent is the call. *Swimming World*, 35(10), Oct., 52–57.

Colwin, C. M. (1994). Finishing what he started. *Swimming World*, 35(11), Nov., 26–31.

Colwin, Cecil M. (1996). The George Haines story. (Original title: Learning from great athletes: George Haines has witnessed more than 50 years of swimming history, and often been an important part of it.) *Swim Canada*, 23(5), May, 8–10.

Colwin, Cecil M. (1995). L. de B. Handley the "Gentleman Jim" of swimming, part 1. *Swim Canada*, 22(7), Jul., 16–19.

Colwin, Cecil M. (1996). Kiphuth's "Cathedral of Sweat" where "Mr.Yale" held the key to glory. *Swimming Technique*, 32(4), Feb./Apr., 7–8.

Colwin, Cecil M. (1997). Future star trained where barnacles and oysters flourished. *Swimnews*, 24(3), Mar., 20–21.

Colwin, Cecil M. (1997). Pablo Morales: Lord of the flow. *Swimnews*, 24(1), Jan., 10–13.

Colwin, Cecil M. (1997). The star who didn't dream of Olympic gold. *Swimnews*, 24(1), Jan., 10–13.

Chapter 8 2000 IN SYDNEY: THE MODERN ERA COMES FULL CIRCLE

Colwin, Cecil M. (1993). Swim-city Sydney to host 2000 Olympics. *Swim Canada*, 20(10), 20–21.

Colwin, Cecil M. (1995). Aussies plan for Sydney 2000. *Swim Canada*, 22(9), Sept., 4–5.

Colwin, Cecil M. (1996). Terry Gathercole talks on international and domestic competition. (Original title: The intelligent coach and swimmer will select what they want to do, both in international and national competition.) *Swim Canada*, 23(6), Jun., 22–23.

Colwin, Cecil M. (1996). At the Australian Olympic trials. *Swim Canada*, 23(7), Jul., 10.

Colwin, Cecil M. (1996). Don Talbot's views on the 1996 Australian trials and the state of swimming. (Original title: Talbot on the Australian trials and the state of swimming.) *Swim Canada*, 23(6), Jun., 12–13.

Colwin, Cecil M. (1996). Scott Volkers on athletes under pressure. (Original title: Scott Volkers on athletes under pressure: Samantha could have millions of dollars riding on two swims.) *Swim Canada*, 23(6), Jul., 12–13.

Colwin, Cecil M. (1997). Australia's event camps aim to produce winning coaches and swimmers. *Swim Canada*, 24(2), Feb., 29.

Colwin, Cecil M. (1996). Coaches and swimmers learn together in Australian age-group camps. *Swim Canada*, 23(9), 12–14.

Colwin, Cecil M. (1997). David Pyne talks on the predictive value of scientific testing. *Swimnews*, 24(3), Mar., 36–37.

Chapter 9 INTO THE MILLENNIUM

Colwin, Cecil M. (1996). The Olympics turn pro. *Swim Canada*, 23(8), Aug., 40–41.

Colwin, Cecil M. (1997). Whatever happened to amateurism? *Swimnews*, 24(9), Sept., 29–31.

Colwin, Cecil M. (1997). Denial is the surest affirmative. *Swimnews*, 24(10), Oct., 14–15.

Colwin, Cecil M. (1998). How an age-group parent became an Olympic coach. *Swimnews*, 25(1), Jan., 14–15.

Epilogue

Colwin, Cecil M. (1998). Swimming fights for its life. *Swimnews*, 25(2), Feb., 30–31.

REFERENCES AND RECOMMENDED READING

Barrowman, Mike. (1989). An athlete's perspective. *Swimming Technique*, 26(2), Aug.-Oct., 13.

Beaurepaire, Frank. (1942). The changes in swimming strokes. In R. J. K. Kiphuth (Ed.), *Swimming* (p. 1–16). New York: Ronald Press.

Borish, Linda J. (1995). Telephone interview with Aileen Riggen Soule. Associate Professor of History, Department of History, Western Michigan University, Kalamazoo, MI, June 16, 1995.

Brown, Janet G., Abraham, Lawrence D., & Bertin, John J. (1984). Descriptive analysis of the rip entry. *Competitive Diving Research Quarterly for Exercise and Sport*, 55(2), 93–102.

Carlile, Forbes. (1963). *Forbes Carlile on swimming*. London: Pelham.

Carlile, Forbes. (1994). Personal correspondence.

Clarkson, Alan (1990). *Lanes of gold: 100 years of the NSW swimming association*. Sydney, Australia: Lester-Townsend.

Colwin, C. M. (1969). *Cecil Colwin on swimming*. London: Pelham.

Colwin, C. M. (1984a). Fluid dynamics: Vortex circulation in swimming propulsion. In T. F. Welch (Ed.), *American Swimming Coaches' Association World Clinic Year Book 1984* (pp. 38–46). Fort Lauderdale, FL: American Swimming Coaches' Association.

Colwin, C. (1984b) Kinetic streamlining and the phenomenon of prolonged momentum in the crawl swimming stroke. *Swim Canada*, 11(1), 12–1.

Colwin, C. M. (1985a). Essential fluid dynamics of swimming propulsion. *American Swimming Coaches' Association Magazine*, July-Aug. 22–27.

Colwin, C. M. (1985b). Practical application of flow analysis as a coaching tool. *American Swimming Coaches' Association Magazine*, Sept.-Oct., 5–8.

Colwin, C. M. (1987). Coaching the feel of the water. In T. F. Welch (Ed.), *American Swimming Coaches' Association World Clinic Yearbook 1987* (pp. 87–98). Fort Lauderdale, FL: American Swimming Coaches' Association.

Colwin, C. M. (1992). *Swimming into the 21st century*. Champaign, IL: Human Kinetics Publishers.

Counsilman, J. E. (1971). The "X" factor in coaching. ASCA world clinic proceedings, Montreal.

Counsilman, J. E., & Wasilak, J. M. (1982). The importance of hand speed and hand acceleration. In R. M. Ousley (Ed.), *1981 ASCA world clinic yearbook* (pp.41-45). Fort Lauderdale, FL: American Swimming Coaches' Association.

Counsilman, James, & Counsilman, Brian. (1994). *The new science of swimming*. Prentice Hall: Englewood Cliffs, NJ.

Cureton, T. K. (1934). *How to teach swimming and diving* (vol. 1–2). New York: Association Press.

Daland, Peter. (1981). Distance base key to every event. *Swimming World Magazine,* 22(10), 13-18.

Daniels, C. M., Handley, L. de B., & Wahle, Otto. (1919). *Speed swimming*. New York: American Sports.

Dawson, Buck (1987). *Weissmuller to Spitz*. Fort Lauderdale, FL: International Swimming Hall of Fame.

Finney, Ben, & Houston, James D. (1996). *Surfing: a history of the ancient Hawaiian sport*. San Francisco: Pomegranite Art Books.

Firby, H. (1975). *Howard Firby on swimming*. London: Pelham.

Gordon, Harry (1994). *Australia at the Olympic Games*. St. Lucia, Queensland: University of Queensland Press.

Haines, George. (1993). Evaluation and opinions on American swimming. *American Swimmer Magazine*. Jan.-Feb., 24-25.

Handley, Louis de B. (1910). Evolution of the latest swimming strokes. *Mind & Body*, June.

Handley, Louis de B. (1912, April). The best swimming stroke. *Outing*, 60, 537–543.

Handley, Louis de B. (1914, April). The swimming

stroke of the future. *Outing*, 60, 99–103.

Handley, Louis de B. (1920). *Swimming and watermanship*. New York: MacMillan.

Handley, Louis de B. (1922–1929). Questions and answers. *Women's Swimming Association News*.

Handley, Louis de B. (1927). *Swimming for women*. New York: American Sports.

Handley, Louis de B, & Howcroft, W. J. (1929). *Crawl-stroke swimming*. London: E. J. Larby.

Hannula, Dick. (1995). *Coaching swimming successfully*. Human Kinetics: Champaign, IL.

Hoberman, John M. (1995). Toward a theory of Olympic internationalism. *Journal of Sport History*, 22(1), Spring, 1–37.

Hoberman, John M. (1992). *Mortal engines: The science of performance and the dehumanization of sport*. Toronto: Free Press.

Hodge, T. (1988, January). The ancient Olympics: a run for the money. *The Ottawa Citizen*, B3.

Howard, S. (1849). *The science of swimming as taught and practiced in civilized and savage countries*. New York: (s.n.)

Howell, R., & Brooks, M. (1988). *Aussie gold: The story of Australia at the Olympics*. Albion, Queensland: Brooks Waterloo.

International Young Women and Children's Society. (1935). *Swimming in Japan*. Tokyo: The Society.

Jennings, Andrew. (1996). *The new lords of the rings*. London: Simon & Schuster.

Jochums, D. (1982). The dissident's view of distance freestyle training. In R. M. Ousley (Ed.), *1982 ASCA world clinic yearbook* (pp. 139–151). Fort Lauderdale, FL: American Swimming Coaches Association.

Kellerman, Annette. (1918). *How to swim*. New York: George H. Doran.

Kiphuth, R. J. H. (1942). *Swimming*. NewYork: Ronald Press.

Kiphuth, R. J. H. (1950). *How to be fit*. London: Nicholas Kaye.

Korporaal, G. (1997, September 2). Drug cheats face new rules. *Sydney Morning Herald*.

Laughlin, Terry. (1996). *Total immerson*. New York: Simon & Schuster.

Lawrence, Laurie. (1993). *Lawrence of Australia: stories of inspiration*. Randwick, N.S.W.: Ironback Press.

Leonard, John. (1992). *Science of coaching swimming*. Champaign, IL: Human Kinetics.

MacDonald, John. (1993). *The first 100 years: a century of swimming in Victoria*. Melbourne, Victoria: Swimming Victoria.

Maglischo, Ernest. (1993). *Swimming even faster*. Mountain View, CA: Mayfield Publishing.

Maltz, Maxwell. (1960). *Psycho-cybernetics: a new way to get more living out of life*. North Hollywood, CA: Wiltshire.

Mann, Matt, & Fries, Charles C. (1940). *Swimming*. New York: Prentice-Hall.

Masters, R. (1997, August 21). Taxman hits Olympians. *Sydney Morning Herald*.

McCutchen, C. W. (1976). Fluid dynamic phenomena can be demonstrated with stereo shadowgraphs of stratified fluid. *American Journal of Physics*, 44, (10), 981–983.

Morehouse, Lawrence E., & Miller, Augustus T. (1948). *Physiology of exercise*. St. Louis: C. V. Mosby.

Muchenfuss, Mark. (1989). Catching the wave. *Swimming Technique*, 26(2), Aug.-Oct., 11–12.

Nagy, Jozsef. (1989). From a technical angle. *Swimming Technique*, 26(2), Aug.-Oct., 16–19.

New York Times. February 20, 1916. (Reference to Duke Kahanamoku in Chapter 3.)

O'Connor, Terrence. (1949). World storm over butterfly stroke. *Swimming Times*, March, p. 70.

Oppenheim, F. (1970). *The history of swimming*. North Hollywood, CA: Swimming World.

Riordan, J. (1978). *Sport under communism*. London: C. Hurst.

Sachs, F. (1912). *The complete swimmer*. London: Methuen.

Schleihauf, R. E. (1979). A hydrodynamic analysis of swimming propulsion. In J. Terauds & E. W. Bedingfield (Eds.), *International Symposium of Biomechanics: Vol.8. Swimming III* (pp.70-109). Baltimore: University Park Press.

Schubert, Mark. (1990). *Competitive swimming:*

techniques for champions. New York: Sports Illustrated.

Shoulberg, R. (1983). Distance freestyle training. In R. M. Ousley (Ed.), *1983 ASCA world clinic yearbook* (pp. 209–213). Fort Lauderdale, FL: American Swimming Coaches' Association.

Sinclair, Archibald, & Henry, William. (1893). *Swimming*. London: Longmans, Green.

Sullivan, Frank. (1927). *The science of swimming*. New York: American Sports.

Thornton, N. (1987). A few thoughts on training or a closer look at the path U.S. Swimming seems to be currently following. *American Swimming Coaches' Association Magazine*. Jan.-Feb., 11–14.

Von Holst, E., & D. Kuchemann. (1942). Biologische und aerodynamische probleme des tierfluges. Luftwissen: abridged translation in the *Journal of the Royal Aeronautical Society*, 46, 39.

Weissmuller, J. (1930). *Swimming the American crawl*. London: Putnam.

Whitten, Phillip. (1994). *The complete book of swimming*. New York: Random House.

Worthington, A. M. (1908). *A study of splashes*. London: Longmans Green.

Yesalis, Charles E., & Cowart, Virginia S. (1998). *The steriods game*. Champaign, IL: Human Kinetics.

INDEX